'Compelling . . . Hennessy describes the new machinery of government – all its levers on the PM's desk – with the clarity and detail that has become his hallmark . . . immensely entertaining . . . *The Prime Minister* ought to be required reading in Downing Street' Roy Hattersley, *Independent*

'It is the sharp tastes of the different premierships . . . that make this book . . . quite simply the best analysis yet of the modern practice of prime ministership' Sarah Hogg, *New Statesman*

'He knows as much as, probably more than, anyone else about how this country has been governed since the Second World War, and conveys his learning with wit, cogency and a fairness that is as rare as it is admirable' Philip Ziegler, *Daily Telegraph*, Books of the Year

'Impressive, authoritative and comprehensive' Andrew Roberts, *Literary Review*

'[Hennessy] paints a remarkable picture of centralization and the withering of the cabinet system . . . The best of the new material comes from recently declassified files and relates to that dark, secret core of the prime ministership: wartime and nuclear planning . . . It is a heart-stopping and yet occasionally comic story' Andrew Marr, *Daily Telegraph*

'It is hard to imagine a more readable or insightful book about the highest elected office in the land being written for a long time' Simon Heffer, *Country Life*

'Highly readable . . . Peter Hennessy has acquired a matchless knowledge of modern British government, and he has a rare ability to write about it clearly, wittily and thoughtfully' John Grigg, *The Times*

'An extremely rich dish, spiced with numerous telling stories – some poignant, others funny – on the often ironic foibles of British government' Peter Catterall, *History Today*

'The book is full of the characteristic Hennessy virtues: wide historical knowledge, an unerring eye for the striking quotation, and, above all, an encyclopedic command of the files at the Public Record Office . . . a wonderfully entertaining book' Vernon Bogdanor, *The Times Higher Education Supplement*

'Professor Hennessy is an unrivalled guide to the secret workings of British government' Michael Cockerell, *Daily Mail*

ABOUT THE AUTHOR

Peter Hennessy, described by the *Independent* as the 'giant of modern constitutional scholarship', is Attlee Professor of Contemporary British History at Queen Mary, University of London. Among many other books, he is the author of *Whitehall* ('Much the best book on the British civil service ever to appear', Anthony King, *Economist*); *Never Again: Britain 1945–1951* ('Written with the combination of scholarship and élan which makes Hennessy's work a joy to read', Roy Hattersley, *Sunday Times*), which in 1993 won the NCR Award for Non-Fiction and the Duff Cooper Prize; and *The Hidden Wiring: Unearthing the British Constitution* ('Peter Hennessy has become the irreplaceable analyst of the inner core of the British system of government', Andrew Marr, *Independent*).

PETER HENNESSY

The Prime Minister

THE OFFICE AND ITS HOLDERS
SINCE 1945

PENGUIN BOOKS

PENGUIN BOOKS

Published by the Penguin Group
Penguin Books Ltd, 80 Strand, London WC2R 0RL, England
Penguin Putnam Inc., 375 Hudson Street, New York, New York 10014, USA
Penguin Books Australia Ltd, 250 Camberwell Road, Camberwell, Victoria 3124, Australia
Penguin Books Canada Ltd, 10 Alcorn Avenue, Toronto, Ontario, Canada M4V 3B2
Penguin Books India (P) Ltd, 11 Community Centre, Panchsheel Park, New Delhi – 110 017, India
Penguin Books (NZ) Ltd, Cnr Rosedale and Airborne Roads, Albany, Auckland, New Zealand
Penguin Books (South Africa) (Pty) Ltd, 24 Sturdee Avenue, Rosebank 2196, South Africa

Penguin Books Ltd, Registered Offices: 80 Strand, London WC2R 0RL, England

www.penguin.com

First published by Allen Lane The Penguin Press 2000
Published with new material in Penguin Books 2001

6

Copyright © Peter Hennessy, 2000
All rights reserved

The moral right of the author has been asserted

Printed in England by Clays Ltd, St Ives plc

*For the staff and the students of the Department of History
at Queen Mary and Westfield College, University of London,
the stimulus of whose companionship since 1992 has made
the preparation of this book such fun.*

Contents

PART FOUR   CODA

List of Illustrations

(Photographic acknowledgements are given in parenthesis)

1. Four premiers in the Members' Lobby of the House of Commons, November 1979 (© Telegraph Group Ltd)

2. Wheels of fire: Mrs Attlee (© Alpha/Sport & General)

3. The Attlees tread the Pilgrims' Way in Surrey, 1946 (© PA News)

4. Attlee returns to No. 10 from Washington, December 1950 (© Times Newspapers Ltd/S. Martin)

5. Attlee in Walthamstow, 25 October 1951 (© Times Newspapers Ltd/ Warhurst)

6. Attlee in old age (© Times Newspapers Ltd/Hermann)

7. Churchill at the start of his 1,000-mile tour, June 1945 (© Times Newspapers Ltd)

8. Churchill at the Cardiff City football ground, February 1950 (© Times Newspapers Ltd/Tonge)

9. Churchill with Rufus the poodle (© Associated Press Ltd)

10. A doubting Churchill with an edgy Eden (© Times Newspapers Ltd/ S. Devon)

11. Churchill arrives at the Palace in January 1957 to advise the Queen (© Times Newspapers Ltd)

12. Churchill with Toby the budgerigar (© Paris Match/VinMag Archive)

13. Sir Anthony with Lady Eden, April 1955 (© Hulton Getty)

14. Eden's one and only meeting with Nasser, Cairo, 1955 (© Times Newspapers Ltd)

15. Eden at RAF Wittering in September 1955 (© Hulton Getty)

Acknowledgements

The idea behind this book sprang from the extraordinarily fertile mind of the incomparable Sean Magee as our families roistered through Epping Forest one Sunday afternoon in 1987. He signed it up for his then employer, Blackwell. How Sean came to be in his present post of Publishing Director at Politico's and this book to rest in the hands of another old friend and ace editor, Stuart Proffitt at Penguin, is not a story to be told here. But to Sean must go my profound gratitude for conception and to Stuart my warmest thanks for gestation. To the midwife, my friend and agent Giles Gordon, goes the thanks of someone who adores gossip and a good publisher's advance in equal measure.

There are a large number of hands and minds apart from my own that have gone into the making of *The Prime Minister*. It will be plain from the text just how much my teaching colleagues and my students at Queen Mary and Westfield College since 1992 have shaped my thoughts and analysis (hence the dedication) as have friends from my previous life in print and broadcast journalism. Peter Riddell and I have been discussing this and related themes since our late adolescence which we spent in Cambridge and the balance of trade is in my favour, for his knowledge is matched only by his generosity.

Buttressing this book is a considerable intellectual infrastructure: the BBC Radio 4 *Analysis* programme, which enabled me to garner a great deal of material for this volume and provided a succession of fine minds with whom I could process it; Rob and Gill Shepherd of Wide Vision Productions and Phillip Whitehead of Brook Productions, who showed that television can still scale the heights of historical documentary; the Twentieth Century British History Seminar at the Institute of Historical Research, which has enlivened my Wednesday evenings for nearly twenty years; the Department of Government at the University of Strathclyde, which I have been visiting for almost as long; the Economic and Social

Research Council/Goldsmith's Civil Service seminar; my own 'Cabinet and Premiership' undergraduate seminars and the 'Hidden Wiring' MA seminar, all at QMW.

Perhaps my greatest dependency culture is that which envelops me at the Public Record Office and the departmental records offices which feed it. The civil servants who staff them have treated me with extraordinary care and friendship. It has a one-person equivalent – my former student Elizabeth Lynch, without whose word-processing skill this volume would not have appeared. In the final stages of preparation, my daughter Polly has proved an acute proofreader and a determined chaser of the last and most elusive footnotes.

Even in these more open times, my own private army of behind-the-lines operators have to remain just that. They know who they are and how much greater the gaps would be in these pages but for their help. To be cited as 'private information' in the footnotes is not much by way of recognition, but it is all that I can safely manage.

Specific gratitude and acknowledgement can go to the Trustees of the Harold Macmillan Book Trust for permission to quote from the Macmillan diaries. The staff at the Bodleian Library at Oxford University made my days consulting the originals very pleasant. I am also indebted to Lord Callaghan of Cardiff for permission to use the photograph from his private collection which adorns the back cover of the book.

Stuart Proffitt's colleagues, first at HarperCollins and later at Penguin, have been unfailingly kind and helpful. Only those who have written books themselves can appreciate fully how much their skill and cheerfulness matters.

Finally I must record my huge debt to the Council, the Provosts and the Registrar of Gresham College, who appointed me Professor of Rhetoric and provided me thereafter with the perfect platform for trying out the early drafts of many of the chapters which follow in a series of public lectures on 'Premiership' during 1995–97. Too few people realize just what a gem of an institution works out of Barnard's Inn Hall in High Holborn.

Peter Hennessy
Walthamstow, Mile End and Holborn
July 2000

PART ONE
PRELUDE

I

The Platonic Idea and the Constitutional Deal

. . . the Prime Minister is the keystone of the cabinet arch.

John Morley, 1889[1]

The office of the Prime Minister is what its holder chooses and is able to make of it. *H. H. Asquith, 1926*[2]

'We do have a system in which very great power is given to people if they have a large parliamentary majority as well . . . The deal is that you give people very considerable power for five years, then they can be thrown out. And, in the meantime, if things get bad enough there are ways of getting rid of them. That is the deal of our constitution.'

Lord Butler of Brockwell, Secretary of the Cabinet 1988–97,
Principal Private Secretary to the Prime Minister, 1982–85,
speaking in 1998[3]

'. . . I am talking for the present about the essential nature, the Platonic idea, of the system . . . We have a system of Cabinet Government, not a system of Presidential or Chief Executive Government. Cabinet Ministers are explicitly collectively responsible for the policies and actions of the Governments of which they are members . . . virtually no powers are formally vested in the office of Prime Minister, and those formal powers the Prime Minister does have are powers of patronage and not of policy. He is the chairman of a collective, which is called the Cabinet; and, once he has chosen his colleagues – and unless and until he fires them – his own strength lies essentially in being the Chairman of the Cabinet.'

Lord Armstrong of Ilminster, Secretary of the Cabinet 1979–87,
Principal Private Secretary to the Prime Minister, 1970–75,
speaking in 1999[4]

3

'The debate about the powers of the Prime Minister is not sterile. It strikes at the heart of the British Constitution.'

Professor George Jones, 1998[5]

Arguments have raged around the powers of the British Prime Minister for nearly 300 years. Sir Robert Walpole, widely agreed to be the first of the line, relished the power but could not abide the job description.[6] The debate has been indissolubly bound up with the powers and the purposes of what Robert Armstrong has called 'the Committee of the Privy Council which is the Cabinet, the apex where politics and administration come together and where differences and conflicts have finally to be reconciled and resolved'.[7]

Lord Armstrong, in describing the 'Platonic idea'[8] underpinning what one might call the classical notion of Cabinet government for my students at Queen Mary and Westfield College in early 1999, was well aware of 'the ways in which the system has been adapted, stretched and distorted at particular times'.[9] As an official who had served as Principal Private Secretary to Ted Heath and Harold Wilson, and as Mrs Thatcher's Cabinet Secretary, he could hardly fail to appreciate how easily the Platonic can give way to the pragmatic in real-life as opposed to textbook government and politics. And it was this ruling reality to which Robin Butler had been referring at another seminar a few weeks earlier.

Butler, too, had an abundance of front-line experience, having worked as one of Armstrong's assistants in the Heath and Wilson Private Offices in the 1970s and having run Mrs Thatcher's for part of the 1980s before replacing his old friend Armstrong as Cabinet Secretary in 1988. Between them their insider knowledge of Whitehall embraces virtually the whole of the second half of the twentieth century.

Robin Butler's public version of his IHR seminar, delivered at the Mansion House two months later as his Attlee Foundation Lecture on 'Cabinet Government',[10] concentrated on charting the decline of the *full* Cabinet (as opposed to Cabinet committees and increasingly informal ministerial groups) as the *decider* of important business. He deployed statistics which embrace the period covered by this book to illuminate his theme:

'During Attlee's Premiership (and excluding the part years of 1945 and 1951) there was an annual average of 87 Cabinet Meetings and of 340 circulated papers. The lowest year for circulated papers was 1949 when there were 252. By the early 1970s, when I first sat in the corner of the Cabinet Room as a Junior Private

Secretary in Mr Heath's Office, there was an average of 60 meetings a year and of 140 Cabinet memoranda per year.

'By the early 1990s, a significantly different pattern had emerged. There were, by then, no more than 40 meetings of the Cabinet per year (and, if statistics were kept of the length of the meetings, much shorter ones). More significantly, there was a very marked reduction in the number of memoranda considered. In only one year of the 1990s were more than 20 memoranda circulated.'[11]

These 1990s Cabinet papers, Butler explained, 'would have mainly covered the annual public expenditure plans, the economic material on which the Chancellor of the Exchequer collected the views of his colleagues four weeks in advance of the Budget and the legislative programme for the coming year'.[12] The remaining business of the Cabinet in the Major years 'was introduced orally under four standard agenda items – Parliamentary Business, Home Affairs, Foreign Affairs and European Affairs'.[13] Under Tony Blair this pattern was maintained, with virtually every item of his historically very terse Cabinets (ministers and officials made much in early 1999 of Cabinets sometimes lasting 'at least an hour, up from the 30 to 45 minutes' of the early Blair years[14]) arising under one or other of the four regular headings.[15]

Robin Butler's conclusion drawn from his study of the changing pattern of Cabinet government over fifty years was quite striking. 'By the 1990s, it could be said that, from being an executive body (at least in a formal sense) in Attlee's time, Cabinet had reverted to something close to what it was in the late eighteenth and early nineteenth centuries – a meeting of political colleagues at which the issues of the moment were informally reported or discussed.'[16]

The differences between the two arch insiders, Robin Butler and Robert Armstrong, should not be exaggerated. But Butler seemed more at ease with and more readily accepting of the reality of power as exercised during the 1990s (including the first twenty months of Tony Blair's premiership) than the man who had taught him much of his craft during their time together in No. 10. I invited him during his IHR seminar to describe and tread the jagged line between prime ministerial power and Cabinet power. The full exchange (from which I have already quoted in part) concluded the seminar and ran like this:

HENNESSY: Can I ask a final question? The subject is this endless debate about prime ministerial versus Cabinet government . . . You have always been rather like the Cabinet system you have presided over – you have always been adaptable, and managed to portray whatever is going on as pretty well consonant with at least one bit or other of the past (which is, as you know, how you have run the constitution for so long with such aplomb applauded by me and others). But do you think there is a degree to which we ought to worry abut excessive prime ministerialism, creeping prime ministerialism? Give us the Butler benchmarks against which we can judge this and when we might have to start making a bit of a fuss on behalf of that beautiful constitution which you so carefully preserved for so long.

BUTLER: I do not think so. I think the instruments are all there for, if a Prime Minister gets off the leash, doing something about it. What could illustrate it better than what happened in the Margaret Thatcher case in 1990 . . . ?[17]

HENNESSY: One of her Cabinet ministers said to me that it took a very long time.[18]

BUTLER: Well, it was not eleven years that a serious number of them seriously wanted to get rid of her. What two, three years maybe? If that situation develops then the instruments are, I think, still there. We do have a system in which very great power is given to people if they have a large parliamentary majority as well. John Major did not have that and so John Major's power was very greatly constrained during the last government. The deal is that you give people very considerable power for five years, then they can be thrown out, and, in the meantime, if things get bad enough there are ways of getting rid of them. That is the deal of our constitution. And I think there are enough means to get rid of them that it is not seriously our concern.

HENNESSY: On that reassuring note, we can all sleep easier in our beds.[19]

In fact, I was not altogether reassured, not least because it took a quite exceptional concatenation of circumstances to eject Mrs Thatcher in November 1990.[20] Like George Jones, I have always believed that this debate lies at the heart of the British Constitution as it involves the necessary restraint of the potentially overmighty powers that have fallen into the hands of the British Prime Minister since Sir Robert Peel's time at least. And I do not see the British system resting on those self-righting characteristics with which Robin Butler sought to calm his listeners. The debate has exhibited an extraordinary durability and vitality not because it has been a job-creation scheme for generations of historians and political scientists but because it matters – and continues to matter to the likes of Robert Armstrong and Robin Butler, too, and those they have left behind in Whitehall.

When Lord Armstrong addressed my MA students in January 1999, he concluded with some observations on the Blair style of decision-taking which he acknowledged was 'far from the Platonic idea of Cabinet government'. Because, he continued,

'it was familiar from the days of opposition, ministers were comfortable with it. It seems to have worked well enough while ministers new to government were learning how to run their departments and manage their policies, and while those policies were for the most part policies already formulated and agreed in opposition. But we have been seeing these last few weeks just how fragile the system is, with little local difficulties becoming serious enough for ministers and commentators alike to talk about a "re-launch" of the New Labour government. [Lord Armstrong was talking shortly after Peter Mandelson's resignation from the Department of Trade and Industry and the departure of Charlie Whelan, Gordon Brown's press aide, from the Treasury – both in the wake of the furore about the home loan to Mandelson in Opposition days from Geoffrey Robinson.] I think that we are seeing that this system is not well suited to the strains and stresses and complexities of responsibility in government.

'We can already hear the commentators predicting – no doubt with the benefit of spin-doctoring guidance – a return to more conventional Cabinet government, as the government encounters unforeseen developments and crises – "events, dear boy, events"[21] – to which they have to respond with policies and decisions, not just with criticisms and comments which are easy enough to make when you do not have responsibility for dealing with them. The further away from the last election we go, the greater the need to develop policies and decisions to deal with events and to look towards the future. And the more important it becomes for the Prime Minister to carry the government wholeheartedly with him and his immediate colleagues, as the next general election begins to loom ever closer. A return to a more collegiate style of government will not surprise me; perhaps it is already overdue.'[22]

Armstrong's analysis accorded more closely with mine than did Butler's. By coincidence, the same day Lord Armstrong spoke at QMW I received a letter from a highly placed official at the heart of central government to whom I had sent the proofs of my latest attempt to photograph the Blair administration in flight. This particular snapshot reflected the position in the autumn of 1998,[23] before the 'events' of December 1998 which saw the spectacular demise of Peter Mandelson on the field of his greatest expertise – crisis-managing the media. This is what the senior official wrote in what I interpreted as a fusion of the Butler notion of the 'constitutional deal' and the Armstrong argument about the collective grain of government reasserting itself in response to time and chance:

... the departures of Peter Mandelson and [Charlie] Whelan have changed the landscape, the former much more than the latter. Your next over-flight should nonetheless find the reins of government still firmly in the hands of No. 10 . . .

There has, however, to my eyes, been another change in recent months. Following the election when the manifesto and the campaign triumph allowed the Prime Minister in effect to set his own agenda, and to assume that his followers would follow him, the role of Cabinet as a consensus-building body has begun to increase since the second half of last year. It is still more a forum in which colleagues inform each other what is going on rather than ask for views, let alone contrary views. But these views are beginning to appear in increasing volume. Which presumably meets some of your criteria for Cabinet Government. And of course the Prime Minister's control of the Cabinet remains as absolute as ever.[24]

From this January 1999 snapshot one can sense the fluidity of the picture and feel the interplay of power and personality that lies at the heart of both real-life government and the scholarly debates which feed off it. It is that interplay and those real-life, real-time overviews, which are the essence of this book.

The early weeks of 1999 proved especially fruitful and intriguing for long-time observers of such interplaying forces and factors. The issue of prime ministerial power intruded (and not for the first time) into the consciousness of Tony Blair who was, perhaps surprisingly, quite sensitive to the ebb and flow of the debate. An insider close to him had told me during the previous autumn that:

'Tony is very good at the wide sky – the big picture – and very good at handling tomorrow. It's the bit in between that's the problem. He is interested in how history regards him as a Prime Minister. He doesn't approach it in an intellectual way, though he is very interested in what intellectuals say about him.'[25]

It was only a few months later, in February 1999, during a debate on Lords reform that the House of Commons became aware of a plan to curb the powers of the Prime Minister when that veteran observer of premiers and the constitution, Tony Benn, told the House that: 'What we really need – and I am drafting it now – is some legislation. I am going to call it the Modernization of the Premiership Bill.'[26]

The genesis of this idea had arisen at a meeting of Tony Benn and my students at Westminster a few days earlier, during which he compared the style of Labour prime ministers.

'Clem [Attlee] was very collective in character ... Clem was the chairman of a committee but also very decisive ... Wilson was very much a committee man ... Jim [Callaghan] was an old trade unionist who believed you ought to discuss ... And now we have the president.'[27]

Mindful of the Government of Britain Bill he had published in 1991,[28] I suggested he might now draft a 'Prime Minister of Britain Bill'. He expressed great enthusiasm for this, announced his intention on the floor of the House five days later and sent me a copy of it in the middle of February.[29] Four clauses long, it reflected Mr Benn's argument, as outlined to my students, that 'We have shifted from a parliamentary system to a presidential one because the British Constitution allows that to happen because the powers of the Crown are at the disposal of the Prime Minister.'[30] The Benn Bill proposed that eleven prerogative powers (two of which – the dissolution of Parliament and the appointment of a premier – are personal to the Monarch, not the Prime Minister) should henceforth 'require the assent of the House of Commons before having effect'. They were, in addition to the Queen's personal prerogatives:

- The declaration of war or the committing of the Armed Forces to conflict, except in self-defence.
- The signing or ratification of treaties.
- The recognition of foreign governments.
- The assenting to legislation or directives issued by the European Union.
- The appointment of bishops, judges, peers, ministers, European commissioners, ambassadors, chairs of public bodies.
- The establishment of royal commissions.
- The issuing of orders in council.
- The exercise of executive powers not conferred by statute.
- The declaration of states of emergency.[31]

Given that the Benn Bill had no chance of a successful passage through Parliament and into law, it no doubt afforded Tony Blair minimal grief.

The question of Mr Blair's style of premiership, however, did cause him a degree of bother at much the same time, thanks to a passing remark in a lecture of mine on exactly this theme (to which I have already referred) which was published on 1 February, the day Mr Benn outlined his plan to curb the premier's powers in the Commons.

In *The Blair Centre: A Question of Command and Control?* I had disclosed that in the spring of 1998, Lady Thatcher 'found herself at a banquet in Buckingham Palace separated from the Queen and Blair only by a vast bowl of flowers. "I'm worried about that young man," confided the warrior queen (as opposed to the real one) to her neighbour, a former colleague, without a trace of irony. "He's getting awfully bossy." '[32]

The Sunday Times picked up the story and ran it on its front page on 31 January, its Political Editor, Michael Prescott, writing that: 'Those who remain close to the former Prime Minister confirmed last night that she is concerned about Blair's "bossiness".'[33]

The unfortunate Mr Blair had to take questions on this the following morning when he appeared with Richard Madeley and Judy Finnegan on ITV's *Good Morning with Richard and Judy* programme as part of what was then a new strategy of by-passing the politicized and sceptical metropolitan media.[34] Questioned about Lady Thatcher's opinion, he said: 'I don't actually think I'm a very bossy person at all. You have to be firm as a leader.'[35] The story ran on-and-off for over a week until Jimmy Young, putting the same point to him on his BBC Radio 2 programme on 9 February, almost trapped the Prime Minister into an uncharacteristic criticism of his predecessor-but-one:

'Yes, I mean, when I heard about this and I was thinking about Margaret Thatcher calling me bossy I was . . . well, anyway. But I don't think I'm bossy but I do like to give a lead and I do think it's important to do so . . .'[36]

It was quite plain in early 1999, as it had been from the outset of Mr Blair's premiership (and indeed from Mrs Thatcher's),[37] that the question of power at the centre would not go away (although the first two months of that year did represent an unusually rich and vivid recrudescence of an old debate).[38]

In fact, premiership and Cabinet will matter as long as Prime Ministers and ministers and meetings called 'Cabinet' exist. This is an issue that has straddled the coming and going of the British Empire; wars total, limited and cold; the extension and completion of the franchise; and the accession to what was then called the European Economic Community. It will surely survive still closer European integration, a rebalancing of the wider British

Constitution and a renegotiation of the relationship between the constituent parts of the United Kingdom. For the debate is a kind of running commentary. It is about a governing state of mind, about process as much as policy, about the nature of political power and its arbitration at the epicentre of British government. It matters to insiders and outsiders, ministers and civil servants, Prime Ministers and electors, professors and students. Sterile it is not. Boring it will never be, any more (I hope) than what appears between these covers. For the tension between Robert Armstrong's 'Platonic idea' and Robin Butler's 'constitutional deal' can never – and should never – be resolved. And each new arrival in No. 10 experiences it and manages it afresh, which is why transitions of governing and prime ministerial power repay especially close study.

2

Continuity and Cottage Pie

'It's never a misfortune to become Prime Minister. It's always the greatest thing in your life. It's absolute heaven – I enjoyed every minute of it until those last few months of the "Winter of Discontent".'

James Callaghan, 1991[1]

I was haunted by tales of embarrassing episodes as one prime minister left and his successor entered the office: Ted Heath's departure from No. 10 was a case in point. I now could not help feeling sorry for James Callaghan, who just a little earlier had conceded victory in a short speech, both dignified and generous. Whatever our past and indeed our future disagreements, I believed him to be a patriot with the interests of Britain at heart, whose tribulations had been inflicted by his own party.

Margaret Thatcher, 1993, recalling Friday 4 May 1979[2]

'It started with my absolute determination that this occasion would be conducted with the dignity that befitted the office of Prime Minister. . . There is no theory [about premiership]. It's just about life and living. It's No. 10, Parliament, party, family connections and all that personal background that a Prime Minister brings with him or her. It can't be left at the front door and it all has to be fitted together.'   *Sir Kenneth Stowe, Principal Private Secretary to the Prime Minister, 1975–79, recalling 4 May 1979 in 1997*[3]

'Ken Stowe', said one of his fellow private secretaries of the transition from Callaghan to Thatcher, 'made sure it was done decently.'[4] He had had talks with Richard Ryder, Mrs Thatcher's Political Secretary, about the procedures if the electorate gave Ryder's boss a crack at the premiership. Appointments were provisionally made at the Palace to meet such a contingency. Jim Callaghan would visit the Queen to resign at 2 p.m. Mrs Thatcher's appointment would be for 3 p.m. 'The Queen was without a Prime Minister for fifty-nine minutes,' Stowe told me many years later.[5] (The Palace and Whitehall have a traditional and powerful bias against gaps in the premiership, as we shall see in the next chapter.) It had become clear in the small hours of the previous morning that the mechanics of transition would be activated once Callaghan had conceded defeat.

'The private secretaries had a final lunch with Audrey and Jim Callaghan and we had cottage pie. It was a very sad occasion,' another member of the Private Office said.[6] The No. 10 staff applauded the Callaghans as they walked down the corridor to the most famous front door in world politics. Jim Callaghan was surprised and very moved.[7]

Ken Stowe accompanied him on the short journey from No. 10 to Buckingham Palace in the special, bomb-proofed, prime ministerial car, a vehicle fitted with the most advanced communications equipment of the day. He was taken upstairs for his meeting with the Queen (*à deux* by long tradition, as are the regular Tuesday evening sessions between the Head of State and the Head of Government) by Sir Philip Moore, Her Majesty's Private Secretary. Moore rejoined Stowe. What passed between the Queen and her outgoing Prime Minister on that occasion is not recorded but, the meeting over, Stowe showed Callaghan to a second car, markedly less hi-tech, which took him away from ministerial life for ever. Moore and Stowe chatted while waiting for Mrs Thatcher to arrive. Back in No. 10 'we had a kind of hush for an hour', recalled a member of the private secretaries' team.[8]

The message formally summoning Mrs Thatcher to the Palace reached her at 2.45 p.m.[9] She went accompanied by her husband, Denis. Moore showed her in to the Queen and, once she had 'kissed hands' (the 'kissing' element has long since stopped; the Monarch simply asks if the politician is able to form an administration), Moore took her down to meet Stowe. Stowe greeted Mrs Thatcher and told her that she should drive to Downing Street in the special, prime ministerial car, suggesting she sit on the right-hand side so that she could alight on the pavement ready to talk to the cameras once the vehicle had moved on.[10] 'As we drove out through the Palace gates,' Mrs Thatcher recalled in her memoirs, 'Denis noticed that this time the Guards saluted me.'[11] At such moments, no doubt, new Prime Ministers begin to appreciate their changed and singular circumstances. Stowe explained that once the car reached Downing Street he would nip out smartly and enter the building through the garden door at the back to be ready to greet her at the front door by the time she had finished delivering her words to the press.[12]

Another Private Secretary takes up the theme: 'The triumphal party arrived. Mrs Thatcher gave her St Francis speech outside. ["Where there is error, may we bring truth. Where there is doubt, may we bring faith. And where there is despair, may we bring hope."][13] They swept in. We shook hands. Then there was this tremendous activity.'[14] The whirlwind rush of appointments and briefings which followed lasted unbroken for five hours until 8.30, when the new No. 10 household took a supper break.[15] 'We all had supper together,' a private secretary remembered. Present were the same group of Private Office people plus Mr Thatcher, Willie Whitelaw (the new Home Secretary and number 2 figure in the Government, though he was never officially given the title of Deputy Prime Minister), Lord Carrington (the new Foreign Secretary), Michael Jopling (new Chief Whip), Richard Ryder and other members of the new PM's personal entourage – Caroline Stephens, her Diary Secretary, had brought in takeaway Chinese food for the extras.[16] 'We had cottage pie,' the Private Secretary added.[17] 'You can guess who cleared up the plates,' said Stowe.[18] Nothing could better illustrate the continuity and the frugality of the British system of government: the same civil servants and the same humble menu linking a day of transition and transformation. It was, as Stowe put it a generation later, a question of 'attention to detail'.[19]

The events and the details of Friday 4 May 1979 illuminate several of the purposes of this volume, which are to examine and explain the continuities and changes, the constraints and the possibilities inherent in the job of being Prime Minister. The book begins with a reminder of the dual nature of the headship of the British political nation by examining the residual personal powers enjoyed by the head of state (the Queen): the dissolution of Parliament (triggering an election) and the appointment of a First Lord of the Treasury (in recent times synonymous with the office of Prime Minister, as we shall see later). It discusses also the largely undesigned accretions of history which shaped the office of Prime Minister in the often broken and indistinct trail that wound from Robert Walpole to Clement Attlee.

The half-century and more between Attlee and Blair represents a transformation in terms of the ecology of the job and some of its instruments that is exceeded only by those mutations which took place over the two and a quarter centuries that divide Walpole's accession to the First Lordship and Attlee's. Such a stretching of the job requires a chapter of its own. The premiership is such a personally shaped instrument that it cannot be understood without an account of how each incumbent operated it. The core of this volume, therefore, is a study of how the postwar first eleven filled out their possession of the office during periods that ranged from just over eleven and a half years (Mrs Thatcher) to a day or two short of one year (Sir Alec Douglas-Home).

In the penultimate chapter I have reluctantly attempted an audit of relative performance – my reluctance stemming from the myriad of circumstances and differences which have attended each and every prime ministerial stewardship. With the incumbencies of No. 10 one is never comparing like with like. As Roy Jenkins aptly put it when writing about the 'nineteen disparate lives' of his Chancellors of the Exchequer from Randolph Churchill to Hugh Dalton, 'the attempt to draw patterns . . . is a tenuous and even sterile exercise. It is like trying to break a cipher from an imperfect text. Perhaps happily, Chancellors do not come as diestampings.'[20] Finally, wearing my political scientist's hat rather than my political historian's cap, I have essayed some thoughts on how the premiership might be conducted as it meets its fourth century.

This is not, however, an essay in political science. It is quite consciously a work of political and administrative history with a large dash of biography running through it. As David Knowles put it in 'The Historian and Character', his celebrated Inaugural Lecture as Regius Professor of Modern History at Cambridge in 1954, the historian 'must not . . . present a character such as never was on sea or land'[21] (a phrase which sometimes comes to mind when contemplating certain social-science approaches which eschew character and suck the sap from political life as it is actually lived). And yet the historian, belonging as he or she does to a rich and settled branch of scholarly endeavour, must not allow the pleasures of the historical craft to smother the utility and validity of other disciplines whose practitioners do not accept the utility or the validity of the historical profession at face value.

As Eric Hobsbawm has written, 'Theoreticians of all kinds circle round the peaceful herds of historians as they graze on the rich pastures of their primary sources or chew the cud of each other's publications.'[22] This is a picture that most historians who love the chase along the archival trail would recognize. It was appreciated too by that innovative sociologist and critical creator of the concept of 'the meritocracy',[23] Michael Young, when he called upon R. H. Tawney in the 1950s in his famously messy Bloomsbury rooms in Mecklenburgh Square, with old tobacco tins stacked in the fireplace and half-eaten, forgotten meals behind the piles of books on the floor.[24] 'There he sat,' Lord Young told me, 'at his table covered with documents on Tudor society and economy – surrounded by the comforts of History.'[25]

Documents, of course, may possess the sanctified status of *primary* sources: the newly mined ore of history which the scholar examines and refines before allotting it a place in the pattern of knowledge and discovery or, if so minded, into a past or a still-developing theory. And some theoretical approaches, including those derived from political science, that stress the need to examine No. 10 in the context of a 'core executive' which includes not just the Cabinet Office but the Treasury and Foreign Office too, have added substantial value to the study of power at the centre.[26] But documents are only part of the story. The personalities of even the most richly flavoured of our recent Prime Ministers – a Churchill, a Macmillan or a Thatcher, for example – are but palely reflected in the documentary spoor they leave behind; yet from these paper shards many an insight and intricacy can be discovered or reconstructed. The lodestones of the Public Record Office (the 10 Downing Street and Cabinet Office files especially) are extraordinarily rich. Here, as Sir Percy Cradock put it with the authority of a 1980s and early 1990s insider in both No. 10 and the Cabinet Office, we are dealing with the 'hard world of shocks and accidents, threats and crises'[27] in the rawest form available to us – unless we were ourselves participants in the events they record.

These documents impart, too, a sense of what Cradock called those factors 'which may be overlooked by the layman or the academic commentator . . . [by which] I mean the almost unsustainable pressure of events and the blizzard of official paper which attempts to record and analyse them.'[28] Familiarity with and fairly deep immersion in that paper 'blizzard' is indispensable for anyone who would understand the requirements and the practices of the modern and contemporary British premiership. And this, after an interval of thirty years, becomes a possibility for those who acquire a reader's ticket for the Public Record Office's reading rooms at Kew.

The philosopher and former politician Bryan Magee is right to warn against those who 'are narrowly provincial in time'.[29] In a deeply traditional political culture such as that of the United Kingdom, a polity whose constitution is historical rather than written, a sense of the historical dimension is a prerequisite of current understanding. As Magee puts it, 'In society as a whole, artistic and intellectual life are both for the most part lived in thrall to fashion. People in each generation tend to believe that what matters most is what is being done by themselves and their contemporaries.' Yet, as Magee concludes, 'Nearly all of what is done in any generation is quickly forgotten. Only a tiny amount, if any, survives to become part of the accumulating treasure of an ever-extending remembered past.'[30]

These pages contain necessarily very tiny amounts of what went on in the Downing Street experiences of the eleven individuals who have occupied No. 10 since VE Day. But I hope that through them to some extent, even the least remembered rise once more and walk. And here the importance of participants' memories – of oral history – comes into its own, though one must always be sensitive to the dangers of the tinting and touching of time on memory. The once-powerful have reputations to enhance or restore which, deep into their anecdotage, they often seek to do. Checking is possible, however, both with other players and with the documents. And the knowledge that this is possible does prevent all but the most shameless from seriously doctoring their pasts.

The same test applies to the contemporary historian, in a slightly different way. What he or she writes must be recognizable to the survivors of the events, episodes and periods depicted. All too often one hears them complaining that they do not recognize themselves as they were, when what they did is forced into a neat but artificial political scientist's configuration such as the 'core executive'. For the thrust of the contemporary historian's approach to political science is inductive rather than deductive. Patterns emerge from a range of instances instead of behaviour being deduced from a spread of assumptions. The historian's craving for evidence – for knowledge of what really happened and why – is the motive force, and this involves more than a stringing together of anecdotes and stories. All modern premiers face a similar though never identical set of problems, even on such prosaic matters within their own domain as the most effective organization of Cabinet or the more efficient deployment of the Civil Service. There are lessons to be drawn and suggestions to be made even by those who eschew the modeller's craft. It would be an exaggeration to adapt wholesale Herbert Morrison on socialism[31] and declaim boldly and baldly that premiership is what the Prime Minister does – but there is a large element of truth in it.

PART TWO
THE PREMIERSHIP

3

The Double-Headed Nation

... as the King should not exercise, or appear to exercise, any political bias, he would normally choose as Prime Minister the leader of the party having the largest number of seats in the House of Commons.

Entry in the Cabinet Office's 'Precedent Book', 1949[1]

'It's all about good chaps. 'Fraid so.'   *Sir Kenneth Stowe, 1997*[2]

There is only one precept which should concern the triangle (the Cabinet Secretary, the Queen's Private Secretary, the Prime Minister's Principal Private Secretary) in the appointment of a Prime Minister ... and that is that it is the Monarch's prime duty to find a Prime Minister who will be able to command a majority in the House of Commons regardless or not of whether the sovereign approves of his politics.   *Lord Charteris of Amisfield, Private Secretary to H.M. the Queen 1972–77, 1997*[3]

The scene is St James's Park on Saturday 2 March 1974 and the setting another prime ministerial transition – the most difficult and fraught in the postwar period. The park is wet and windswept and pretty empty. But if, by some curious chance, you actually had found yourself there that afternoon and noticed two tall, rather military-looking men walking through the rain deep in conversation, you would have seen the British Constitution at work in, as one of them expressed it later, 'very dicey' circumstances. The distinguished pair were the Secretary of the Cabinet, Sir John Hunt, and the Queen's Private Secretary, Sir Martin Charteris. They were, in effect, retilling that patch of the constitutional soil in which are rooted the two powers that make up the remaining 'personal prerogatives', as they are called in Palace circles, of the Monarch: the power to dissolve Parliament and the power to appoint a Prime Minister.

These are the parts of the Constitution that only the Queen can reach. Potentially, she is still a central player in the political life of her realm.

Across Horse Guards Parade in No. 10 Downing Street that afternoon sat a depressed and dispirited Edward Heath, who, to almost everybody's surprise, had seen his majority melt at the general election held two days before on Thursday 28 February. In the teeth of the second miners' strike within two years and buffeted by a global energy crisis of intense ferocity (oil prices were in the process of quadrupling in almost as many months following the Yom Kippur War),[4] Heath had gone to the country on the question of 'Who rules?' Willie Whitelaw said later that it is always a mistake for a government to resort to the polls sooner than it has to and ask 'Who governs?', because the country tends to reply, 'We thought you were'.[5]

In this case the electorate had answered 'nobody', producing the first hung result since 1929. Labour was four ahead in terms of seats (301 to the Conservatives' 297), but the Tories had slightly more of the percentage of votes cast (37.8 to 37.1 per cent for Labour). On the Friday afternoon Heath informed the Queen, just back from opening the Australian Parliament in Canberra, that instead of resigning straight away he intended to try to strike a deal with the Liberals. He would stay on in No. 10 over the weekend.

The Palace was content with this. Until 1868 it was normal practice for a Prime Minister whose party had been defeated at the polls to meet Parliament and take defeat there too on a confidence vote or its equivalent before resigning (thereafter administrations normally resigned before a new parliament assembled).[6] Baldwin reverted to pre-1868 practice in January 1924 after losing the general election of December 1923.[7] As Lord Charteris told me later in a television interview, '. . . the point that has to be remembered . . . is that a Prime Minister remains Prime Minister until he resigns. That's the starting point, anyway. Ted Heath tried quite hard to come to a deal with [the Liberal leader] Jeremy Thorpe. The result of that was, instead of coming round as soon as the Queen had time [to return to the Palace from Heathrow] and resigning, he hung on till the following Monday. So there was this rather agonizing weekend when we weren't quite sure what was going to happen.'[8]

It is at such moments that crown servants like Charteris and Hunt become the 'continuity girls' – no disrespect or sexism intended – of the British system of government. On the basis of precedent, they advise their respective bosses – Her Majesty and the Prime Minister – on whether particular courses of action do or do not cut with the grain of traditional constitutional nostrums, insofar as they can be divined from past practice.

By the time Hunt and Charteris stepped into the park, Labour's Shadow Cabinet were, in effect, in purdah. The previous afternoon, steered very much by the Shadow Foreign Secretary and Party Chairman, Jim Callaghan, they had, in Callaghan's words,

'decided that we would not challenge Mr Heath; we would allow him to carry on and to try to make any arrangement that he could. We did this because we were fairly satisfied that he wouldn't be able to make such an arrangement. But if he had seemed likely to, then I think I would have taken a very different view about the situation because in some ways, Mr Heath was acting in a way I think was rather prejudicial. The country had expressed its lack of confidence in the Conservative government . . . I won't say it was improper of Mr Heath because there are no conventions on this matter, I think it was stretching the thing a bit for him . . . I remember I took the bold step of saying we should allow Ted Heath . . . "to swing slowly in the wind".'[9]

An old pro like Callaghan knew that, even with Liberal support, the electoral arithmetic would not add up for Heath when converted into what counts: MPs on seats in the House of Commons. If Heath had won over the fourteen Liberals, he would still have been short of an overall majority; he had no joy from those 'loyalist' Ulster MPs who were also approached (though not all of them were), during the course of the weekend as many were still outraged by the power-sharing executive in Northern Ireland created by the Sunningdale Agreement the previous December.[10]

By the time Hunt and Charteris took their walk around the Constitution, Heath had seen Thorpe for the opening coalition bid. Thorpe held out for electoral reform, a longstanding Liberal cause and one central to their hopes of future political influence. Thorpe undertook to consult his colleagues and return the next day.[11] Hunt and Charteris rehearsed the possibilities as they paced the park. 'We were quite certain', Lord Charteris told me many years later in a television interview, 'that Ted Heath remained Prime Minister until he resigned, regardless of what the newspapers were saying, regardless of the fact that people were saying the Queen should send for somebody else. Not at all . . . and, if necessary, it would not be improper for him to meet Parliament and produce a Queen's Speech and see if he could get away with it.'[12]

Thus far, the constitutional position was clear. Hunt and Charteris sought refuge from the rain in the Cabinet Secretary's room in the Cabinet Office. Another Cabinet Office resident, Jim Prior, Heath's Lord President of the Council (again as Lord Charteris recalled) 'suddenly put his head round the door and said, "Are we behaving all right?" We said, "Yes, you're all right, you know."'[13] There can be a touch of Ealing Comedy about these things. But, Lord Charteris continued, 'it was all very dicey'.[14] Why? Question number one was: what would happen if Heath failed to strike a deal but faced the new Parliament with fewer seats than Labour anyway, found himself in difficulty (which he would have been) and asked the Queen for another dissolution of Parliament, thereby – should she grant the request – triggering another election?

'I think it's very tricky this,' Charteris explained. 'You see, another sort of rule is that people don't get dissolutions twice. And, after all, Ted Heath had asked for the first dissolution.'[15] At such moments which test the unwritten constitution, the Queen's advisers like to talk the problem through with political historians (Lord Blake filled this role in 1974)[16] and scholars steeped in the constitutional side of the monarchy (in this case Sir John Wheeler-Bennett, George VI's official biographer).[17] Wheeler-Bennett quoted Arthur Balfour to Martin Charteris, to the effect that 'no constitution can subsist on a diet of dissolutions'.[18] Charteris interpreted this as meaning: 'If you have a Parliament that is fresh from the electorate, it should somehow serve its time before you have another election.'[19]

So, Heath would not be the problem. If he failed to strike a deal with Thorpe or went down to defeat on a Queen's Speech, Her Majesty would send for the Leader of the Opposition, Harold Wilson, and ask him to form an administration. And this is precisely what she did on the Monday evening after Heath, having completed two more sessions with Thorpe on the Sunday and Monday mornings[20] and two gloomy Cabinet meetings on his last day in office, called at the Palace to resign.[21]

But Wilson, himself thirty-four seats short of an absolute majority over all parties, might take office only to go under either in the vote on his Queen's Speech or on a confidence motion shortly thereafter. What would the Queen do if the prime-ministerial Rover then swept through the gates of the Palace and Wilson asked for a dissolution? This second was the rather more vexing question. Charteris had already been in touch with Elwyn Jones, Wilson's Lord Chancellor-in-Waiting, over that 'anxious and uncertain week-end', as Elwyn Jones put it in his memoirs, and they 'discussed the constitutional position, which was that until Ted Heath resigned or, if he persevered, he was defeated on the Queen's Speech, his government continued in existence'.[22] Elwyn Jones was to be the Palace's back-channel to Wilson on the delicacies of the Queen's position if Wilson wished to increase the diet of dissolutions.[23]

Lord Charteris remembers saying, 'It isn't automatic [that] the Queen's going to say "Yes" or "No". You know, just watch it . . . that prerogative does still exist.' But, Charteris continued, if Wilson had asked for a swift dissolution, 'the Queen would have been very pushed not to give it to him. But . . . it was much better the way it was – that he carried on until the autumn.'[24] The thinking in the Palace on this issue was that Heath had been granted his dissolution, hence the general election on 28 February. Equity required Wilson to be granted one too if he persisted in such a request.

The reason why the television interview with Martin Charteris is so important, and the reason why I have dwelt at length on the walk in the park, is that the events of early March 1974 demonstrate that, at such precarious moments, the British system of government depends on the Queen and a handful of insider advisers, such as Charteris and Hunt, and informal outside consultants, such as Blake and Wheeler-Bennett, spinning between them what Philip Ziegler has called 'instantly invented precedents'[25] from the warp and woof of constitutional practice and experience.

At such times, rare though they may be, (to borrow Sir Stephen Sedley's marvellous notion) ours is a 'silent constitution',[26] without pieces of paper that bespeak the principles, the conventions or even what Sir Sidney Low called the 'tacit understandings'[27] on which it rests. The advisers have to interrogate ghosts like Balfour and old files in No. 10, the Palace and the Cabinet Office archives as they seek to brief the Monarch, the sitting Prime Minister and, should the need arise, the premier-in-waiting or his potential coalition partners, on how best the overriding requirement that 'the Queen's Government must be carried on'[28] might be met. (This notion is attributed to the Duke of Wellington in the 1830s and has been cited as a nostrum of the British constitution ever since.)[29]

Such a process of interrogating the past took place even in the spring of 1997 under the guise of prudent contingency planning in the pre-election period, in case the electorate, to universal surprise, should put the opinion pollsters on the rack again by producing a hung result, thereby denying both John Major and Tony Blair an overall majority. The problems always arise, as Lord Armstrong of Ilminster has expressed it, when 'none of us has any experience to guide us' (he was speaking in the context of a second hung Parliament in quick succession).[30] Lord Armstrong, like Lord Charteris, has a feel for the tangibles and the intangibles of the Queen's 'personal prerogatives': he was Heath's Principal Private Secretary in 1974 and the only other person in the Prime Minister's study when Thorpe came to call. Armstrong, Hunt and Charteris made up the so-called 'golden triangle' (though their successors in more recent times have tended to be irritated by the phrase; they think it gives the erroneous impression that they are fixers-in-chief as opposed to mere advisers behind this particular patch of the constitutional arras).[31] Armstrong had his own walk in the park with Martin Charteris on 2 March 1974. A passer-by recognized them and said to his companion: 'There go the two most discreet men in England.'[32]

There is a kind of apostolic succession here. For also in No. 10 that anxious weekend was Robin Butler, who served with Armstrong in the Private Office and succeeded him as Secretary of the Cabinet in 1988. A file on the dissolution of Parliament in March 1966 released at the Public Record Office in 1997 revealed an even earlier Butler connection with the finer points of dissolution. As a bright young civil servant and Secretary of the Budget Committee in the Treasury, this same Robin Butler saved Harold Wilson a degree of embarrassment hours before the poll was announced.

There is a tightly choreographed drill for election timing (a procedure to which I shall return in a moment). As the No. 10 'Dissolution' brief for 1966 (the most recent that has been declassified) has it,

Parliament is dissolved by Proclamation by the Queen in Council after having been prorogued to a certain day . . .

The Proclamation dissolving one Parliament calls a new one and fixes the date of its first meeting.

The issue of the Dissolution Proclamation automatically sets in motion the machinery for a General Election.

It has become customary to give the country a period of notice of the date of a General Election (since the war, at least 9 days), unless this occurs unexpectedly, following a defeat in the House of Commons.[33]

The file goes on, in this rather staccato language, to give the timings as the clock ticks towards election day and lists the elements that must be taken into account – which is where the eagle-eyed Butler came in:

Issue of Proclamation dissolving Parliament and calling a new one to meet on a stated date.

Nomination [of candidates] up to *eight* days after the issue of the Dissolution Proclamation.

Polling Day on the *ninth* day after the last day for Nominations.

(Sundays, Bank Holidays and days of Thanksgiving are excluded from these calculations).[34]

What both No. 10 and the Home Office (the department in charge of electoral matters) failed to notice, but which Butler spotted, was that in Northern Ireland St Patrick's Day (17 March) was still a Bank Holiday.[35] The first Parliamentary Counsel and the Home Office's Legal Adviser, prompted by Butler's caveat, discovered that, despite Irish partition, the Bank Holiday (Ireland) Act of 1903 still applied in the province.[36] Almost at the last minute, the date for dissolution had to be brought forward by one day to 10 March to allow for this.[37] An 'emergency' telegram was flashed to the Queen, who was on a royal tour in the Caribbean,[38] and she signalled her approval for the change of date.[39] A rejigging of the timetable at a later stage, assuming anybody had noticed the Northern Irish problem, would have been embarrassing as it would have proved inconvenient.

The rest of this record, for all its prosaic qualities, alerts us to a constitutional and legal dimension which could matter if a future election were hung in a fashion that led either to coalition-brokering or to pact-mongering. We might call this the 'ticking clock' factor. Lord Armstrong has spoken publicly in the past about the 'ticking clock and a deadline, the time when the bomb goes off',[40] implicit in the standard election timetable. But in messily hung circumstances, the clock might have to be stopped, the drill altered and prolonged.

The 1966 material traces a detailed choreography clearly drawn-up on the basis of past practice over many elections. Under the rubric of 'Meeting of Parliament' it explained that

It is necessary to allow 4 working days or about a week for the return of writs to the Crown Office, i.e. between polling day and first sitting day of the new House of Commons.

A new Parliament cannot meet earlier than 20 days after the date of the Proclamation dissolving the old Parliament. But, as Sundays would seem to be included in the calculations, the new Parliament could not meet till the day following polling day. This is an impracticable date because only a few election returns would have reached the Crown Office.[41]

Here we reach the key passages dealing with Lord Armstrong's ticking clock and how to reset it. The key word in what follows is 'prorogue', which reaches back, in its constitutional usage, to 1455. The indispensable *Shorter Oxford English Dictionary*, which proclaims that its compilation rests 'on historical principles', explains its meaning.

Prorogue . . . To discontinue the meeting of (a legislative or other assembly) for a time without dissolving it; to dismiss by authority until the next session. Orig. and chiefly in ref. to the British Parliament. 1455 [of course it was solely the *English* Parliament then].[42]

Here is the passage in the 1966 No. 10 drill:

An interval of a week between polling day and the meeting of a new Parliament allows little time for the reconstruction of a Government or the final preparations for the forthcoming Session [of Parliament].

When the Dissolution is decided upon, it is customary to announce the relevant dates of the General Election, the meeting of the new Parliament and the date of the State Opening. The meeting of Parliament may be deferred, however, by further proclamation proroguing it to a later day, not being less than fourteen days from the date of such proclamation (Prorogation Act, 1867). But it cannot be accelerated.

The date of the State Opening could also be deferred by Motion in the House because the daily Adjournment has to be proposed at the end of each Sitting from the day the new House first sits.[43]

The Prorogation Act 1867. Not the most familiar of statutes, but it reminded me of a conversation I had had with Sir David Steel (as he then was) about the discussions he and his Alliance partner, David Owen, engaged in prior to the 1987 election with the then Cabinet Secretary, Sir Robert Armstrong, about the contingencies which a hung result might throw up (what Tom McNally, Jim Callaghan's former Political Adviser in No. 10, has called a 'Rubik cube' of possibilities).[44] Sir David said,

'There is a set timetable, but – the great glory of the British Constitution being that it is unwritten – there is nothing that says "because you have appointed 3

November as the date for the State Opening, you have to stick to it". There is nothing whatever that prevents the Prime Minister and the Palace agreeing that, in view of the political situation, you can put it off for a week, ten days, two weeks.'[45]

Sir David was talking to me in 1991. His words led me to suspect very strongly that Armstrong had briefed him and Owen on the contents and scope of the obscure Prorogation Act 1867.

A former student of mine, Amy Baker, has excavated the genesis of the tiny, two-clause Bill which became the Act. She explained:[46]

It appears that the Bill was non-contentious and passed through all the stages of Parliament merely as a formality.[47] The purpose of the Bill was to abolish the rather awkward ceremony that used to take place on the Prorogation of Parliament during Recess.

This was deemed by ministers to be 'entirely useless and unmeaning'.[48] Baker continued: 'Abolishing the ceremony did not change the powers of the Sovereign in any way, and the restriction of 14 days is perhaps a little meaningless when a string of Proclamations can be issued.'[49] The Prorogation Act, however, could be seen as a pleasing example of how a statute, intended for entirely another purpose, can, quite legitimately, be adapted to future needs.

How would it operate? The statute makes it plain that the Queen would activate it 'by and with the Advice' of her Privy Council. A Prime Minister would be in being. It would be either the incumbent, if he had not resigned, or his successor if he had accepted Her Majesty's commission to try to form an administration that would command a majority in the House of Commons – as Lord Home did on 18 October 1963 after the outgoing premier, Harold Macmillan, mindful of the precedent of Queen Victoria and Lord Aberdeen in 1852, had suggested this procedure to his Sovereign.[50] Home was not Prime Minister as he sat in No. 10 that afternoon persuading his colleagues to serve under him; only when he returned to the Queen to say he could form an administration did he become her First Lord of the Treasury and Prime Minister.

On the morning of 18 October 1963 Macmillan was giving informal advice (with a little 'a', as the Palace likes to put it);[51] advice which, as it touched her personal prerogatives, the Queen did not have to take (unlike formal capital 'A' Advice from a premier, which she does have to accept).

If the Queen were to receive a request from a Prime Minister to invoke the Prorogation Act 1867, it would be exactly that: a request, a piece of little 'a' advice which she could set aside[52] (though it is hard to envisage the circumstances in which she would).

But we need a touch of realism here. The early 2000s are very different from 1852, or even from 1974. The political weather now changes dramatically, especially when it is driven by those two hurricanes of irrationality – the media and the money markets. The more recent 'golden triangles' have been as aware of this as anybody.[53] Since 1974 we have seen the electronic revolution creating the hyper-sensitive, quick-reaction twenty-four-hour global money markets and the electronic news-gathering system which now means that, unlike the long March weekend in 1974, every player in any future rerun will be followed by a camera team. Someone somewhere will say something silly but plausible enough for the markets to believe that the pound is about to succumb to a build-up of domestic political uncertainty and instability. As Tom McNally put it in 1991, a repeat of March 1974 would 'be a moment of great hysteria, and individuals and organizations will have a spotlight trained on them with an intensity they've never experienced before'.[54]

Sir David Steel may have had a point when, speaking of a possible coalition-building pause, he argued: 'To some extent the fact that we haven't got a written Constitution is an advantage. There are no ground rules here. There are historical precedents but, basically, you make them [the rules] up as you go along.'[55] But, even more powerful in my view, given the media/money market problem, was Robert Armstrong's counterpoint when he spoke of its being 'not a bad thing' that there was normally a clock ticking in the background as it 'sharpens people's minds very considerably'.[56]

There is another factor which bothers the 'triangle'. In no circumstances must the Queen be embarrassed or drawn into or be *suspected* of being drawn into political strife or partisanship. This has always been and remains their joint number one rule (the other being that 'the Queen's government must be carried on'). Lord Armstrong was speaking for all postwar 'triangles' when he told me:

'In . . . the hung Parliament situation, the Sovereign and the Sovereign's advisers – and, one would hope, the politicians concerned – would have as primary objectives to ensure that the government of the country was carried on, and that everything possible was done to avoid the Sovereign being put into a position where action had to be taken which might bring the Crown into the area of political controversy.'[57]

Sir Robin Butler has publicly confirmed that the transcript of the BBC Radio 4 *Analysis* programme, 'The Back of the Envelope', which I made with my producer, Simon Coates, and which preserved Lord Armstrong's words as delivered in 1991, was an encapsulation of the current constitutional thinking on the Queen's personal prerogatives.[58]

Lord Armstrong's point about the avoidance of both embarrassment and apparent politicization have often drifted into my mind when scouring the PRO files for what Mrs Cooper, the No. 10 Archivist, admitted to Derek Mitchell, the Prime Minister's Principal Private Secretary, in 1966, are 'the few papers we have on Dissolution'.[59] In particular, it was on first discovering Mitchell's plan for the 'Deadlock' contingency in October 1964[60] (based on his predecessor Tim Bligh's 1959 version for Harold Macmillan[61]) that I realized how little could be taken for granted.

Just imagine if this memo – prepared by Derek Mitchell in the small hours of 16 October 1964 in case Sir Alec Douglas-Home returned to No. 10 majorityless but still leader of the largest single party in the House of Commons – had leaked in the first edition of that Friday morning's London *Evening Standard* as Harold Wilson travelled to Euston from his Liverpool constituency, still not knowing what to expect in terms of the final result. After considering how Sir Alec might seek succour from the Liberals by offering their leader, Jo Grimond, the post of Lord Privy Seal, Mitchell's 'Deadlock' brief outlined the Queen's choices in the hung contingency. 'She may', he wrote of Her Majesty,

(a) press him [Douglas-Home] to stay on until defeated in the House,
(b) press him to stay on in the hope that he may form a Coalition, or
(c) send for someone who is not the leader of either Major Party in the hope that some sort of compromise Government could be carried on until it were feasible to have another General Election.[62]

If the circumstances were such that contingency (c) had been acted upon, many in the Labour Party and the Labour-sympathizing media would have claimed loud and clear (though erroneously) that the Queen was a Tory and had acted in an unfair and partisan spirit.

The thought occurred to me more than once in the 1990s – given the travails of some members of the royal family and the flammability of much of the media on this issue – that, in the event of a hung result in a future election, Her Majesty might find herself in a degree of danger on this front. Could there be a way round it? In the past, I have suggested that consultations between the party leaders, the Palace, the Cabinet Office and No. 10 conducted on the Privy Counsellors' net (all the leaders of parties of any size are Privy Counsellors) might be used to produce an agreed set of principles (not detailed drills) which could be published as an indication of how the Queen would approach the exercise of her personal prerogatives.[63] This would have the twin advantages of furthering public, political and media enlightenment while increasing the chances that Her Majesty would be protected from extravagant, damaging or erroneous accusations if she had to exercise those prerogatives.

Neil Kinnock was unhappy as Leader of the Opposition in 1992 with some of the 'tacit understandings' (especially the possibility of the Conservatives clinging to office in hung circumstances while they chose a new leader better placed to cinch a deal with the Liberal Democrats)[64] as they were explained to him in the run-up to the 1997 election, and has made a similar suggestion. Addressing a meeting of senior civil servants in December 1994, he called for 'the identity of those advising the Queen in the event of a hung Parliament to be made known with agreements between Government and Opposition on procedures and principles'.[65]

Those in the 'triangle', past and present, have yet to be persuaded of the case. They are, generally, shrewd, careful and decent people and their reasons must be respected. Those reasons embrace the following counter-arguments to my view and to Neil Kinnock's suggestion:

- First, that flexibility is all important; precise contingencies cannot be predicted, no two are alike. Published principles would bring rigidity to a part of the Constitution which works well partly because of its capacity to adapt successfully to the unforeseen.
- Second, why should the Queen be the one person to be tied down? Party leaders might, under the pressure and heat of events, be capable of causing difficulties, but the Monarch could find herself trammelled by principles agreed with a set of departed party leaders while she remained in post being the one figure in public life who can never retire (privately, she has always ruled out the possibility of abdication).[66]
- Finally, there is the doctrine of inappropriate time – that a period of trouble for the royal family is the wrong moment to suggest that the head of

state may not be in a position to carry out this part of her job safely and satisfactorily, if required, without change to past practice.[67]

These views have heavyweight support in political and academic circles. Former Prime Minister Lord Callaghan once turned the question about the prerogatives back on me: 'Well, it works, doesn't it? So I think that's the answer, even if it is on the back of an envelope and not a written Constitution with every comma and every semicolon in place – indeed, sometimes they can make for difficulties that common sense can overcome.'[68]

The constitutional historian Vernon Bogdanor believes that the realities of political life would vitiate the production of such principles and that crude power, rather than refined principles, would determine the outcome in crisis circumstances. 'The Queen', he writes,

... could only publish such principles upon the advice of her ministers. But her ministers are drawn from the ruling party or parties. There is no reason to believe that leaders of the other parties would concur with the government's view of which particular principles were relevant.

Constitutional crises, then, cannot be resolved through a statement of principles; nor, by the very nature of the Constitution, could there be a 'hidden code' with the power of determining how such crises are to be resolved. It is not that the Constitution consists of 'instantly invented precedents', but rather that, when the precedents conflict, as they invariably will, there can be no authoritative guidance as to which are relevant in advance of a political crisis . . . the outcome of the crisis is as likely to be determined by the facts of power as it is on the basis of an appeal to principle.[69]

I expect the Bogdanor–Callaghan–'triangle' view to prevail, probably unless or until the UK moves to a system of proportional representation for its elections to the Westminster Parliament, in which case a royal drill will need to be spelled out and the Prorogation Act would need to be looked at again.

After a trawl of the files and some private conversations, I prepared in the mid-1990s a version of what the resulting one side of A4 paper might look like if an attempt were made to distil the essence of the Queen's personal prerogatives.

- Only the Monarch can dissolve Parliament, thereby causing a general election to be held.

- Only the Monarch can appoint a Prime Minister.
- After an indecisive general election, the Monarch is required to act only if the incumbent Prime Minister resigns before placing a Queen's Speech before Parliament or after failing to win a majority for that legislative programme in the House of Commons.
- The overarching principle at such delicate times is that the Queen's government must be carried on and that the Monarch is not drawn into political controversy by politicians competing to receive her commission to form a government.
- Normally an outgoing Prime Minister is asked to advise the Monarch on the succession, but the Monarch has to ask for it, and, if given, it is informal advice which can be rejected, rather than formal advice which must be acted upon.
- After an inconclusive result, if the incumbent Prime Minister resigns the Monarch will normally offer the first chance to form an administration to the party leader commanding the largest single number of seats in the House of Commons.
- A Prime Minister can 'request', but not 'demand', a dissolution of Parliament. The Monarch can refuse. The circumstances in which this might happen would be, in Lord Armstrong's words, 'improbable'. But the power to withhold consent could be a check, in Lord Armstrong's words, once more, on the 'irresponsible exercise of a Prime Minister's right to make such a request'.[70]
- The circumstances in which a royal refusal could be forthcoming are according to Sir Alan ('Tommy') Lascelles, George VI's Private Secretary, if 'the existing Parliament was still vital, viable and capable of doing its job' or if the Monarch 'could rely on finding another Prime Minister who could carry out [his or her] Government for a reasonable period, with a working majority in the House of Commons'. (Lascelles, writing pseudonymously in The Times in May 1950, included a third ground for refusal: that 'a General Election would be detrimental to the national economy',[71] but that criterion has been quietly dropped during the intervening years.)[72]

These are, to the best of my knowledge, the tacit assumptions that would suffuse the thinking and the advice of the 'triangle' in foreseeable contingencies. It remains my belief that such a principle-establishing exercise could and should be done, with beneficial results all round. And since 1999 a fully working and wholly transparent model of an alternative system has been available north of the Border. Under the Standing Orders of the Scottish Parliament, the Presiding Officer conveys the will of the Parliament (as expressed through a vote) as to who shall be the Queen's First Minister in Scotland to the Sovereign herself. The Queen then sends for the person concerned and appoints him or her. Given this wholly accepted development there can now be no overriding reason for reticence. And a degree of foreknowledge could prevent both misunderstandings and misrepresentations should the personal prerogatives need to be exercised in future. I would certainly prefer Her Majesty to remain the umpire of this particular constitutional pitch. I am asking simply that the pitch be prepared in a more public and transparent fashion.

If the electorate should ever again wobble inconclusively inside the polling booths of a general election Thursday, you will find me on the following Saturday forsaking my customary weekend pleasures at the South Chingford Sainsbury's for a bench in St James's Park. Should they take a stroll in duo or trio formation to think through another reinvention of the Constitution, the 'golden triangle' will find a student from the Department of History at Queen Mary and Westfield College, University of London on every park bench as far as the eye can see, come rain or shine. For who could resist witnessing the British Constitution in motion against such a perfect backdrop?

A final thought in case readers are feeling baffled, as I often am, when faced with the magic and the mystery of the British Constitution. We are in good company. It baffles itself. As the Queen once said when leaving an undergraduate seminar on the subject, 'The British Constitution has always been puzzling, and always will be.'[73] And she, of course, is it. But the best and perhaps the only way to grasp the pieces in 'Her Majesty's Puzzle',[74] or that part of it which relates to the conduct of the premiership, is to retrace the various landmarks in the developing geology and geography of power since the time of Sir Robert Walpole.

4

Organized by History:
The Premiership Before 1945

'The complex forms and balanced spirit of our Constitution were not
the discovery of a single era, still less of a single party or of a single
person. They are the slow accretion of centuries, the outcome of
patience, tradition and experience . . .'

The words of G. M. Trevelyan in the mouth of King George V,
Silver Jubilee Address to Parliament, 1935[1]

'. . . I don't want to bother you with these theoretical possibilities,
because in fact we have evolved by the usual British system of hit and
miss a system which, having been rationalized after the event, is found
to be quite logical and sound.'

Sir Norman Brook, Secretary of the Cabinet, in a private
lecture to the Home Office on 'Cabinet Government', 1959[2]

The person who walks for the first time through the door of Number
10 as prime minister does not create or re-create the prime ministership: the job, to a considerable extent, already exists.

Professor Anthony King, 1991[3]

The paradoxical nature of the premiership is already apparent. How can
Asquith's dictum that the office of Prime Minister is largely what its holder
chooses or is able to make of it, with its implications of choice and individual
flexibility, be squared with Anthony King's description? Can both be accurate? I think they can – and are. For the job, like the wider British Constitution, is a product of history. History deals each new incumbent a certain
hand, the bundle of customs and conventions, practices and expectations
that go with the office and whose steady accrual will be described in this
chapter. The legacy of the past has a definitive *shaping* effect, but not so
powerful a *constraining* impact. Because the Constitution or the law actu-

ally prescribes or requires so little by way of functions, a Prime Minister *can* make of the job a very great deal of what he or she wishes, provided other circumstances (size of majority, state of the economy, passivity of Cabinet colleagues, personal health and energy) allow it.

For all but the most insensitive or deliberately ahistorical new arrival (and it's hard to think of a single one, though Margaret Thatcher and Tony Blair often behaved as if history was chiefly a guide on what *not* to do), the premiership radiates the past as much as any cathedral or cloister. Two things strike one on entering No. 10 Downing Street – its tranquillity, whatever the turmoil in Parliament, the country or the wider world, and the near tangible feeling of a deep and richly accumulated past whose resonance is such that the walls almost speak. Harold Wilson undoubtedly had a powerful sense of this. He was a great connoisseur of the office he held between October 1964 and June 1970, March 1974 and April 1976. So much did he cherish its mechanics and its past that he devoted to them a sizeable chunk of *The Governance of Britain*,[4] which he sat down to write almost the moment he left 10 Downing Street for the second time. It was a much better volume than he was given credit for in the late 1970s, when his stock among both the political and the commentating classes was low – so low that I remember a civil servant who *was* well disposed towards him saying to me that the trouble with Harold was he concentrated too much on immediate events rather than on the issues which were seriously important.[5]

The Governance of Britain was pure Wilson – steeped in the past,[6] dismissive of what he saw as arid academic debates about prime ministerial versus Cabinet government[7] and brimming with statistics about his workload as premier.[8] This was not Wilson mesmerized by the exciting and the immediate, it was Harold the King's Scout, the eternal member of the 3rd Colne Valley Milnsbridge Baptist Scouts.[9] Other Prime Ministers have had an acute sense of their career, even their personal destiny in the making, but with Wilson it was the degree and detail of this near obsession which was special. He had spent his whole life collecting the equivalent of scout badges – at Oxford, in the wartime Civil Service, within the Attlee governments and during the doldrums years in Opposition before he became Leader of the Labour Party in 1963. Finally, in 1964, he had acquired the biggest badge of all to pin to that laden sleeve – the premiership – and, until his last illness, he always enjoyed communicating the pleasures its possession had brought him, not least in his retirement study of the job and its holders, *A Prime Minister on Prime Ministers*.[10]

For Wilson, much of the glory of the premiership lay in its antiquity. Insofar as his study of *The Governance of Britain* concentrated on the prime ministerial role in Cabinet government, Wilson wrote: 'it describes the day-to-day working of a calling that must be one of the most exciting and certainly one of the best organized – organized by history – in the democratic world: Britain's prime ministership'.[11]

And it is true that everyone who steps through that famous Downing Street door for the first time as Prime Minister must to some extent be as thrilled as Churchill was on 10 May 1940 when, after receiving the King's commission to form a wartime coalition government, he 'felt as if I were walking with destiny'.[12]

Yet the emergence of that destiny-laden office which fell into Churchill's hands during the extreme national emergency of the spring of 1940 was anything but pre-destined by history, to adapt Harold Wilson. What E. P. Thompson once called 'the enormous condescension of posterity'[13] places Churchill 43rd in the line of succession from Sir Robert Walpole,[14] yet the man upon whom history had laid the mantle of Britain's first Prime Minister spent his entire career denying he was any such thing.[15]

A 1950s file at the Public Record Office misleadingly titled 'British Constitutional System' reflects the continuing imprecision about the origins of the premiership. The core document in those files, a 'Historical Table of Changes in Government Organisation', contains this following cryptic, almost shorthand entry:

1714   13th October

Post of Lord High Treasurer finally put into commission. The *Board of Treasury* included the First Lord of the Treasury and the Chancellor of the Exchequer.

It was not at that time self-evident that the First Lord of the Treasury would be head of the Government, but since Walpole's appointment as First Lord of the Treasury and Chancellor of the Exchequer in 1721, there has almost always been such a correlation. Origin of Prime Minister.[16]

The 'correlation' has held virtually throughout the twentieth century since A. J. Balfour succeeded his uncle, Lord Salisbury, as Prime Minister in July 1902 (previously Balfour had combined the First Lordship with his Leadership of the House of Commons).[17]

A Whitehall handbook baldly noting 'origin of the Prime Minister' is one thing, but Sir John Plumb, in his celebrated eighteenth-century volume in the Pelican History of England, rightly warned generation after generation of history students from 1950 onwards against any overprecise or schematic interpretations of the waning of royal power at the expense of a 'Cabinet' led by a 'Prime Minister' after Walpole became First Lord of the Treasury in 1721. 'Walpole and George II', Plumb wrote,

encouraged the development of a small inner cabinet, consisting of the [two] secretaries [of state, for the Northern and Southern Departments], the Lord Chancellor, Lord Privy Seal, Lord President of the Council, and the Chancellor of the Exchequer. This body met informally: it had access to all secret papers and it was here that the real decisions on policy were taken.

It was quickly realised that if a minister belonging to this inner circle disagreed with his colleagues on a vital issue he had no alternative but to resign, an attitude which gave rise later to the idea of the collective responsibility of the cabinet. This small inner or efficient cabinet was the true ancestor of the modern cabinet, but still a remote one, and it is extremely misleading to try to impose modern, or nineteenth-century, constitutional ideas on the eighteenth century ...

In this inner ring of ministers there was frequently one who by common consent was the foremost, whose word carried the most weight and who acted as the principal vehicle in their relations with the King. Sometimes he was called the Prime Minister, but usually only by his enemies and as a term of mild abuse. He was still very much the King's servant.[18]

Despite Plumb's strictures, Walpole's portrait continues to hang on the wall behind the Prime Minister's seat in the Cabinet Room[19] as the *de facto* father of the breed. And despite William Rees-Mogg's observation that, 'However skilful the British Prime Minister may be, he cannot have the world impact of a Pitt, a Disraeli, a Gladstone, a Lloyd George or a Churchill,'[20] that seat beneath that portrait in that room remains the ultimate prize for which the politically ambitious strive in Britain.

So how did a notion which started its life during the reign of Queen Anne as a term of abuse hurled at Robert Harley, the leader of the Tories,[21] come to be the ultimate spur to British political fame? Following the upheavals of 1688–89 it is best seen as one among a number of linked elements which sprang out of and enhanced the growth of political stability first in England and Wales, then, after the Act of Union with Scotland of 1707, in Britain as a whole.

The Bill of Rights of 1689 had, without doubt, clipped the prerogatives of the monarchy and forged powerful new weapons for Parliament, both legislative and financial,[22] but it had by no means determined the real power flows in late seventeenth-century England. The new 'system was a fragile thing. It was neither party government nor non-party government; while not royal government it was not cabinet government in any collective sense either. It contained a number of able men . . . but none of them had the full confidence of the King . . .'[23]

For a few brief years at the beginning of the eighteenth century it looked as if the country might consciously separate the powers of the executive and the legislature. The Act of Settlement of 1701 laid down that once Queen Anne was dead, no placeman of the Monarch (a minister in modern parlance) could be an MP and that every piece of advice given to the Monarch by the Privy Council should be made known to the House of Commons.[24] Had this part of the Act not been repealed in 1705 before it could be implemented (the Whigs disliked this restriction on the royal prerogatives and feared it might deter the Hanoverians from taking the crown so they got rid of it as soon as they were able), the tectonic constitutional shift, roughly delineated by the eighteenth century, from a monarchical system of government to one based upon collective Cabinet government, albeit a collective led by a leading 'First' or 'Prime' Minister, would not have occurred. Nor would the fusion of the executive and the legislative branches of government which Bagehot rightly saw in the mid nineteenth century as the singular, 'efficient' secret of the British way of governance.[25]

Walpole's significance is that, buttressed by the stability of more effective departmental structures and fiscal arrangements in Whitehall,[26] his gifts and his personality were such that he became the key figure in whose person these potentially conflicting power flows and practices were combined and, thanks to his immense political skills, moderated. The whole enterprise was lubricated by that potent mixture of money and patronage which passed through Walpole's hands as First Lord of the Treasury. As his biographer, Brian Hill, explains:

British government in Walpole's time, and for most of the eighteenth century, was in a process of transition from the dominant monarchy of the Stuart era to the Cabinet government of the nineteenth century. In Anne's reign there was a Cabinet which at first sight seems recognisably modern . . . Despite appearances, however, there was not yet full collective responsibility, so that ministers often assumed a semi-independent role . . . Yet Walpole's control was never monolithic, being often challenged by parliamentary opposition and finally overthrown by the straightforward and constitutional means of defeat in the House of Commons.

He had to please two masters, Parliament and the King, and the loss of support from either could have destroyed him politically at any time.[27]

A modern Prime Minister would recognize elements of present-day reality in this, for in the Walpole years the enduring, DNA-like strands were spun which continue to determine the strength and scope, as well as the vulnerabilities of the job.

But as in any living organism, there is more than one strand of DNA. And the growth of the office of Prime Minister – its power and its functions – has to be seen in the context of other developments which, sometimes singly, often in combination, have determined the political ecology of that potent little cluster of power at the poky end of Downing Street. Over the grand sweep from Walpole to Blair (which embraces fifty-one Prime Ministers in between), one has to examine at least six sources of power or influence and the contexts in which they have fluctuated: the powers of the Monarch; the Cabinet; the Prime Minister; the electorate (increasingly important after 1832) and, from the late nineteenth century, the powers of public opinion and the media.

Insofar as it is possible to freeze any moment of transition involving such shifting variables – for power is a relative concept – let me cite an example from the early nineteenth century when Peel won a decisive victory at the polls despite Victoria's views being decidedly Whiggish at that time. After 1841, the Monarch was unable to exert any real sway over the choice of ministers following a general election. Once the electorate had roughly doubled in size after 1832, with one in five adult males eligible to vote, it was only a matter of time before monarchical patronage began to seriously decay in the face of electoral power. At the end of her reign, Victoria still badgered her premiers, Gladstone especially, about church or military appointments and occasionally ministerial ones (for example, though she could not persuade Gladstone to keep Sir Charles Dilke out of his Cabinet in the early 1880s, 'she did insist on him sending her what amounted to a written recantation of his [Dilke's] republicanism').[28] But by this time, the personal royal prerogatives were, in real terms, already reduced to dissolving Parliaments and appointing Prime Ministers. The power to make or unmake administrations was moving out of the House of Commons to the electorate. Inside the chamber, ever tougher whipping and tautened parliamentary procedure were reducing the behavioural scope of the individual member, and the power to initiate legislation was moving steadily away from Parliament and into the executive.

Inside the Cabinet Room, the Prime Minister was an increasingly important figure, partly for functional and procedural reasons which I shall come to later, but also because of the increasing importance of party leaders due to the personalization of British politics, which grew with changes in the nature of electoral contests, party organization and the media. These shifting relationships took place against the rise of labour (with a small 'l') at home and of international competition (in terms of both trade and political influence) abroad, and the changed political agenda which resulted.

This, however, is to leap ahead too far and too fast. Let us return to those crucial shaping influences which had determined what Victoria, Peel, Gladstone or Disraeli could do and how. It is best to see the eighteenth century in fluid terms as a series of changes which together altered the nature of government from that of a monarchical chief executive dominating a 'Cabinet Council' to a collective executive led by a sometimes dominant figure, a Prime Minister, who none the less fell short of being a chief executive himself.[29] *The* great debate of recent times is whether or not in the second half of the twentieth century Britain saw a reversal of that process through the supersession of the collective executive of the Cabinet by the 'elected monarch'[30] of the Prime Minister.

By the end of the eighteenth century a consensus was forming among those who had to deal with the stresses of first ministership, that the system could not cope without such a designated figure. The hapless Lord North, for example, begged George III to allow him to resign because 'in critical times, it is necessary that there should be one directing Minister, who should plan the whole of the operation of government and control all the other departments of administration . . .'[31] This, poor North confessed, he could not do (which was not surprising; he was a man of some ability but, 'in the end [he] could not cope with the triple burden of being First Lord of the Treasury, Chancellor of the Exchequer, and Leader of the Commons' at a time of acute crisis in the North American colonies in the 1770s and 1780s).[32] The younger Pitt put it more tersely when he said 'there should be an avowed and real Minister, possessing the chief weight in the [Cabinet] Council, and the principal place in the confidence of the King'.[33]

Pitt has some claim to be the first modern premier, certainly the first real one since Walpole in terms not just of his appetite for power but in his centrality to his administration and his own power relative to that of his Cabinet colleagues. Part of the evidence for this is the folk memory of that most peculiar of trade unions – the Right Honourable Society of Ex-Premiers – of which in retirement Harold Wilson became a kind of house historian. Wilson wrote in *A Prime Minister on Prime Ministers*:

If Walpole was the creator of the office of Prime Minister, Pitt is rightly described by historians as the first to hold the office in a sense in which it could be recognised today. While he could still be summarily dismissed by the King, even though enjoying the confidence of Parliament, he was, in the language of those days, the 'efficient' head of his Cabinet. Subject to some grumbles and queries by the King, its members were chosen by Pitt, and where necessary dismissed at his request. More than that, Pitt's administrations were more coherent than those of any of his predecessors, and the policies he enjoined on them and which they accepted were the policies of them all, and were collectively recommended to Parliament . . .

Peel . . . described himself as a disciple of Pitt, and Peel himself has generally been regarded as the first 'modern' Prime Minister, in the sense that his premiership more closely resembles that of a Prime Minister of the 1930s or 1950s than that of Walpole, whose term of office ended a century before Peel's only real administration began.[34]

Wilson rather overdoes some points. For example, not until Balfour's premiership at the beginning of the last century could a Prime Minister be absolutely certain of his power (by recommending their dismissal to the Monarch) to hire and fire other ministers.[35] Even Gladstone was not.[36]

Wilson's disquisition on the mutations of premiership holds good in the sense that Gladstone modelled himself consciously on Peel,[37] and Rosebery, another member of the Honourable Society of Ex-Premiers, described Peel as 'the model of all Prime Ministers'.[38] We should not be surprised by this. Not only does it stem from the sense of the past that most Prime Ministers possess, it has to do with there being no official job description for the premiership, let alone any statute which delineates the premier's functions or powers.[39] (There is no reason to believe, as we shall see, that any of the eleven Prime Ministers since World War II ever saw the one stab at this which was made in the Cabinet Office, the Treasury and No. 10 between 1947 and 1949.)[40]

There are two ways of depicting the development of this extraordinary creation of British history. The standard way is to trace it in terms of the large-scale changes in the political system: the growth of political stability in the first half of the eighteenth century, the executive exigencies created by wars in North America and with the French in the second half of that same century, the charges whose fuses were lit by the 1832 Reform Act and exploded by its successor in 1867 in terms of the growth of mass parties beyond Parliament which led, in Le May's words, to 'Gladstone . . . more than anyone else . . . creating the conception of the party leader as demagogue'.[41] Allied to these wider factors was the ever tighter discipline exerted on voting patterns inside the Commons. Methods of political communication were changing, too, in response to the growth of a mass electorate. The first half of the twentieth century saw still further changes in the nature of the premiership thanks to the cumulative effect of total war, the growth of the state and the burgeoning technologies of new mass media.

I shall tackle this prime ministerial phenomenon from a different angle, a more microscopic approach which helps illustrate the accumulation of function and relative power over the past 200 years while recognizing that there is nothing either linear or inevitable about it. This, in a way, has been the approach of the more historically minded members of the Honourable Society: 'Can I do this? Doesn't Balfour or Gladstone or Lloyd George provide me with the precedent to stymie those who say I am pushing the boundaries of the premiership beyond the constitutional?' Yet it would be wrong to imagine that, except on rare occasions, First Lords of the Treasury have the time or the inclination to reflect upon the degree to which the topology of the premiership is changing around them. As Gladstone, writing as Prime Minister, noted in his diary on the last day of 1868, 'Swimming for his life, a man does not see much of the country through which the river winds.'[42]

Some modern-day functions were attached to the office from the start in Walpole's day – most notably the disposal of a secret fund, his inheritance from a long line of crown servants beginning with Sir Francis Walsingham in Elizabeth I's time, though the money side only acquired a degree of formal organization in the following century. As Christopher Andrew has explained:

From the Restoration there was a Secret Service Fund and, from 1797, an annual Secret Service vote in parliament which continues to this day. But the pre-Victorian Secret Service Fund did not provide for an established Secret Service. It was used instead to finance British propaganda on the Continent, an assortment of part-time informants, a variety of secret operations by freelance agents, and an elaborate system of political and diplomatic bribery. During Walpole's twenty-one years as Britain's first prime minister . . . the Secret Fund was probably used more for political bribes at home than for diplomatic bribes abroad.[43]

We can identify overseeing the secret world, together with chairing the Cabinet, dealing with the Monarch and managing Parliament, as one of the core functions of the early premiership. Another is responsibility for warfare. It is significant that the 1950s Cabinet Office file on 'The Constitutional System' refers to a body created in either 1620 or 1621 as 'A Standing Council for War'. 'Probably a committee of the Privy Council', it notes, without quite declaring it to be the prototypical 'War Cabinet'.[44]

We need to move on another sixty years from Walpole's appointment as First Lord to find the next rash of historical accretions which begin to develop a kind of doctrine of prime ministerial indispensability. They came in a cluster in the early 1780s and in spurts thereafter. Let me itemize them, starting with the Prime Minister becoming sole chairman of the Cabinet in the 1780s and finishing with Churchill establishing the primacy of the premier over nuclear weapons policy in the 1940s:

- 1781: Last appearance of a Monarch (George III) at the larger Cabinet Council (the 'Nominal Cabinet', so-called to distinguish it from the smaller or 'Efficient Cabinet' where the real business was conducted).[45]
- 1782–83: Reluctant acceptance by the Monarch that virtually all members of the 'Efficient Cabinet' should change with the appointment of a new Prime Minister,[46] a change which added substantially to the collective nature of Cabinet government. The fall of Lord North's ministry in 1782 is also treated as a constitutional landmark because it demonstrated the difficulty of a Monarch sustaining a government which had lost the confidence of the House of Commons.[47]
- Changes in the scope and nature of warfare. Although, as we have seen, war had long been a central concern of the Privy Council, it was the Napoleonic Wars at the turn of the eighteenth and nineteenth centuries which demonstrated that warfare had become an intensely prime ministerial function. Henceforth, war was added to money (it is important not to forget the importance of the Prime Minister as First Lord of the Treasury; Mrs Thatcher did not)[48] as a great enhancer of the relative power of the Prime Minister.[49] George III could not cope with the executive demands of war, though it would probably be an exaggeration even to see the younger Pitt as presiding over the first of a long line of 'War Cabinets'. As late as the Crimean War in the 1850s, Lord John Russell could describe the Cabinet as 'a cumbrous and unwieldy instrument'.[50] It was worse than that. One historian of that war has claimed that a majority of the Cabinet were asleep during the meeting when it was decided to take Sebastopol[51] – a problem that afflicted the Cabinet

frequently when it was standard practice to meet over dinner.[52] Not until the Hartington Commission of 1889 were serious steps taken to plan for a substantial reshaping of government in time of war.[53] Yet so poorly did Whitehall adapt to the demands of the Boer War that the then Prime Minister, the Marquess of Salisbury, was moved to admit to the House of Lords in 1900 that he did 'not believe in the perfection of the British Constitution as an instrument for war'.[54] Only with the creation of the Committee of Imperial Defence by Balfour in 1904 did matters seriously improve.[55]

- During the same period of what one might call both prime ministerial and Cabinet consolidation in the late eighteenth century, Pitt demonstrated the indispensability of collective responsibility by persuading the King to dismiss Thurlow, the Lord Chancellor, after he had criticized Pitt's Sinking Fund (a more rigorous version of a 1717 device for reducing the National Debt)[56] in the House of Lords in 1792.[57] (Though not till 1801, when Addington finally removed another troublesome ex-Lord Chancellor, Lord Loughborough, was it established that former Cabinet ministers could not simply turn up at Cabinet meetings.)[58]

- That great prime ministerial device for managing both issues and ministers – the modern Cabinet committee – probably dates from 1831 when Grey asked Durham to 'take our Reform Bill in hand' by proposing 'the outline of a measure . . . large enough to satisfy public opinion and to afford some ground of resistance to further innovation, yet so based on property, and on existing franchises and territorial divisions, as to run no risk of overthrowing the [existing] form of government'.[59] The committee of ministers which Durham gathered to advance this, the prototype of a hugely important instrument of modern governance, met regularly at Durham's house in Cleveland Row.[60] (Peter Catterall makes the case for an even earlier appearance of the Cabinet committee in the shape of the 1716 ad hoc committee created to consider the fortification of the French port of Mardyck.)[61]

- In 1835, Peel and Wellington in an exchange of correspondence established the convention (it is no more than that) whereby ministers can be recruited only from the House of Commons or the House of Lords, a move which reduced the pool of talent available for service in the Cabinet Room while tautening the bonds of prime ministerial patronage in the Palace of Westminster. Peel wrote in January 1835, 'The holding of a seat in the Cabinet by a responsible adviser of the Crown – that adviser being neither in the House of Lords nor Commons, is, I fear, extremely unusual if not unprecedented in modern times.' (The only recent precedent was Vesey Fitzgerald, who had carried on as President of the Board of Trade until March 1829 after losing the famous Clare by-election in June 1828.)[62]

As with all constitutional conventions, one must take care not to be dogmatic or overly comprehensive in asserting the primacy of this particular one. For example, in relatively recent times there have been breaches of the Peel convention: Richard Casey was appointed by Churchill as the War Cabinet's Minister of State in the Middle East in March 1942. Casey was an Australian politician and there was no intention of finding him a seat in the House of Commons or of asking the King to make him a peer.[63] Similarly, there is a long tradition of appointing some Scottish law officers from outside Parliament (both Lords Advocate and Solicitors General).[64]

Patrick Gordon-Walker was a rather separate case. Though he lost his seat at Smethwick in the West Midlands after a notoriously racist local campaign by the Conservatives against Labour's stance on immigration during the general election of October 1964, Wilson nevertheless appointed him Foreign Secretary. Reg Sorensen, the sitting Labour member, was eased out of the safe Labour seat of Leyton and into the House of Lords to make way for him.[65] After losing the Leyton by-election in January 1965, Gordon-Walker had no alternative but to step down and Wilson acknowledged the same day that 'the events of the past 24 hours make it impossible for you to carry on at the Foreign Office'.[66]

The only absolute requirement for a Cabinet minister is that he or she must be a Privy Counsellor for, as Lord Curzon wrote in 1924, the Cabinet is but a Committee of the Privy Council (the ancient medieval body for providing advice to the Monarch), a view with which, in more recent times, Lord Hailsham (twice a Lord Chancellor) and Robert Armstrong (as we have seen) concur.[67] And as Lord Hankey, the former Secretary of the Cabinet, confirmed in 1946, all the Monarch's 'principal ministers' are Privy Counsellors.[68] This, for example, enabled Lord Poole, Joint Chairman of the Conservative Party, to attend Cabinet meetings in 1963–64 at the invitation of the Prime Minister even though he held no ministerial office.[69]

Constitutional interpretation has moved on since Curzon's time. All Cabinet ministers are still required to be Privy Counsellors, but 1990s Whitehall practice followed Sir William Anson's view, elaborated in the mid-1930s, that 'To describe the Cabinet a Committee of the Privy Council is misleading . . . The Cabinet does not meet as a Committee of the Privy Council, for it is not so constituted . . . The Cabinet considers and determines how the King's government may best be carried on in all its important departments; the Privy Council meets to carry into effect advice given to the King by the Cabinet or a minister, or to discharge duties cast upon it by custom or statute.'[70] This particular piece of insiderdom strikes me as over fussy and over finessed and in no way overrides the fundamental point made by Lords Curzon, Hailsham and Armstrong.

- In 1861 Gladstone, as Chancellor of the Exchequer, began the practice of bundling a whole range of tax and spending issues into a single Finance Bill.[71] By tradition, the Cabinet is given a Budget's details only on the morning of the speech. Until then, only the Chancellor and the PM are fully apprised and, to greater and lesser degrees, work in tandem on its preparation.[72] (Palmerston, the first premier to benefit from this stretched, or enhanced, Finance Bill was, ironically, far from happy with Gladstone's position on the issue which led to it – the controversy over the abolition of duties on paper, the famous 'taxes on knowledge'.)[73]

- Once he became Prime Minister, Gladstone increased enormously the power of the premier by ending in 1870 the right of any Cabinet minister to call a Cabinet meeting if he had an important item of departmental business requiring collective discussion.[74] To this day only the Prime Minister can summon a Cabinet meeting.

- Summitry has become an increasingly frequent prime ministerial activity. Though the word is of relatively recent vintage, having been invented by Churchill during the 1950 general election campaign,[75] I would date its first modern form from the Congress of Berlin in 1878. When Bismarck fixed the time and place in June that year 'there could be no question', Robert Blake wrote, 'who would represent England. When it had been merely a matter of a conference the Cabinet had selected Lord Lyons but at a full-scale congress attended by the imperial chancellors of the Northern Courts Disraeli and Salisbury [the Foreign Secretary] were bound to be the English plenipotentiaries.'[76]

- Prime Minister's Questions in the House of Commons in their twice-weekly bear-garden modern form began only in 1961 and lasted until May 1997 when, in an attempt to restore a tad of reason and an element of genuine debate to the occasion, Tony Blair combined the two fifteen-minute slots into a single one of thirty minutes on Wednesday afternoons. But their earliest appearance as a recognizable phenomenon, though one far removed from our current televised trial-by-soundbite, took place in 1881 when 'Questions to the PM' were grouped at the end of the day's list. In 1904 they were arranged, on the instructions of the Speaker, from Question 51 onwards. This was later amended to number 45, where they remained until 1960–61, when Harold Macmillan acceded to backbenchers' demands that a regular time of 3.15 be established twice weekly for the premier to be held to account.[77]

- Top appointments to the civil, diplomatic and armed services and to the Church of England are very much part of a modern Prime Minister's patronage portfolio (and PMs vary considerably in their propensity to take advice from the professionals concerned with such matters). But not until the final argument over the removal of her cousin, the Duke of Cambridge, as Commander-in-Chief of the Army in 1895 (a highly vexatious matter for Rosebery and his Secretary for War, Campbell-Bannerman) did Queen Victoria's sway in such matters publicly diminish, though she maintained until her dying day in 1901 that her prerogatives remained intact in this area.[78]

- The absolute right of a premier to remove ministers came even later, during A. J. Balfour's autumn crisis in 1903 over tariffs. As John Mackintosh put it: 'The most clear-cut demonstration of self-confidence on the part of a Prime Minister was when Balfour decided it was better to shed the free traders, Balfour of Burleigh, Lord Hamilton and Ritchie, faced them in the Cabinet and accepted their resignations without disclosing that he had Joseph Chamberlain's resignation [over this issue] in his pocket.'[79]

- Another Balfourian innovation, the Committee of Imperial Defence, whose secretariat was created by Treasury minute in May 1904,[80] reaffirmed, as Anthony Eden said later, that 'Defence is very much a Prime Minister's special subject.'[81] As John Ehrman has noted, 'It is . . . no accident that the Committee of Imperial Defence should be peculiarly Balfour's monument. He was himself well aware of its dependence upon him; he took care to be present at every one of the meetings held during his premiership,' and it was the main reason why he stayed in office during the fractious year of 1905, because he and the Committee of Imperial Defence were deeply involved with the Anglo-Japanese Treaty.[82] Planning for the contingency of war is not the same as waging it but, to a large extent, the linkage – like a Prime Minster's overall responsibilities for both – is complete. It was in this sense that Eden wrote as he did.

- A spin-off from war, the hurried circumstances of the first general election after the Great War, gave the British Prime Minister another 'special' function, that of requesting the Monarch for a dissolution of Parliament, thereby triggering a general election on his personal say-so rather than as the bearer of a collective request from the Cabinet. This convention was established in the peculiar and complicated circumstances of the Lloyd George coalition ahead of the 'coupon' election of 1918.[83] Though some premiers still consult the full Cabinet ahead of such a request, as was standard practice pre-Lloyd George,[84] and others confide in an inner group,[85] the final decision to approach the Monarch is the premier's alone.

- At about the same time as LG was siphoning away from the Cabinet the power of decision about the timing of elections, he was extending the Cabinet's collective nature down the decision-taking structure by creating in July 1918 the first *permanent* standing committee of the Cabinet (there had been many examples of temporary ones since Durham's ministerial group of 1831) in the shape of the Home Affairs Committee, which has existed continually to this day in various mutations.[86] (Technically, the first standing group was the Economic Defence and Development Committee created in June 1918, but this did not turn out to be permanent.)[87]

- For all the accretions of functions and powers into what Campbell-Bannerman called 'this rotten old barrack of a house',[88] the apparatus in No. 10 has remained a relatively slim machine, certainly compared with what is available to most heads of government.[89] It was not until 1928, however, when Sir Robert Vansittart became Principal Private Secretary to Baldwin, that the career Civil Service fully captured the Prime Minister's Private Office with the departure of Sir Ronald Waterhouse (who, in fact, as George Jones has pointed out 'was the last of the old style personal and political appointees, and the first of the new style civil servants' as he stayed on during the first ever Labour premiership under Ramsay MacDonald in 1924).[90] The position held – just – after the 1997 general election. Tony Blair considered appointing Jonathan Powell as his Downing Street Chief-of-Staff *and* his Principal Private Secretary on the departure of Alex Allan from the Private Secretary's post. After a fuss in the press and private advice from the Cabinet Secretary, Sir Robin Butler,[91] a compromise was reached whereby Powell remained Chief-of-Staff and John Holmes, the Foreign Affairs Private Secretary, assumed also the title of Principal Private Secretary when Allan left to become the British High Commissioner to Australia.[92]

- In the past, such changes usually took place away from the gaze of a public then as now less than enthralled by the finer points of bureaucratics. But in Baldwin's time a very public development occurred which thrust party leaders, and premiers in particular, into the public eye with a novelty not experienced since Gladstone's Midlothian campaign of 1879–80.[93] The initial instrument of the transformation which continues to this day (and forms the crucial component in what Michael Foley has called 'leadership stretch')[94] was the radio, or the 'wireless', as it was then known. If I had to date the beginnings of the 'mediafication' of the British premiership it would be 16 October 1924, when Baldwin delivered his first broadcast in the general election campaign of that year. To widespread surprise, he proved a natural at the 'fireside chat' approach when, as his biographer G. M. Young puts it, 'his diffidence dropped away . . . a note of authority came into his voice . . .',[95] a capacity Baldwin utilized to great effect during the General Strike of 1926.[96] Baldwin's successor, MacDonald, reformed the internal workings of No. 10 to enable it to cope with new media realities. In 1931 he appointed George Steward as the first Downing Street Press Secretary. Almost immediately Steward arranged fixed times for briefing the Westminster lobby correspondents inside No. 10, thereby converting them, in the disapproving words of James Margach, from 'old style competitive "outsiders" . . . into a fraternity of organised "insiders"'.[97]

● Of all the changes in the powers, responsibilities and reach of the British Prime Minister not illuminated by the arc light of publicity, the development of atomic weapons has been the most awesome and most secret. Churchill kept knowledge of the bomb to the tiniest circle of advisers and colleagues for over five years. He simply did not think it a subject fit for the Service Ministers let alone the full Cabinet. In March 1944, Sir John Anderson, in effect the 'Minister for the bomb', as Martin Gilbert records, 'suggested to Churchill that the time had come to give "full information" about "Tube Alloys" – the atom bomb research programme – to the three Service Ministers and to the War Cabinet. Churchill minuted, however, "I do not agree", asking in a note in the margin of Anderson's request, "What can they do about it?" Anderson, as Lord Cherwell later wrote to Churchill, "was perturbed by your decision", but as a result of it the atomic bomb "was never discussed at Cabinet or in the Defence Committee" at any time before the dropping of the bombs on Hiroshima and Nagasaki a year and a half later.'[98]

Churchill took the decision to give British consent to the use of the weapons on Japan, as required by the Quebec Agreement of 1943, on 1 July 1945 without consulting the War Cabinet.[99] For over fifty years the decision about who should be consulted on nuclear weapons policy and in which forum has been an intensely prime ministerial one.[100]

This extraordinary progression from 1721 to 1945 of developments usually scarcely noticed at the time, represents a huge accumulation of functions, procedures and sheer power waiting to be handed over by Mr Churchill to Mr Attlee on the evening of 26 July 1945, after the electorate had inflicted one of what David Butler calls its 'civilised evictions'[101] on the old warrior. But none of the functions I have described is statutory (or was in 1945, to be more accurate).[102] There was very little a Prime Minister *had* to do.

This is not the kind of speculation one ever hears from insiders. As Lord Salisbury (the 5th Marquess, grandson of the late nineteenth-century premier) wrote in one of the many niggling, resignation-threatening letters he sent his premiers (this one to a flu-stricken Anthony Eden in September 1955), 'No one alas! can take the place of the Prime Minister.'[103] And the next chapter will examine just how many demands have stretched the premiership further in the years which span the gap between two very different arrivals of Labour leaders, Clem Attlee and Tony Blair, at the Palace to be converted into the Monarch's First Lord of the Treasury and Prime Minister.[104]

5

Beyond any Mortal?
The Stretching of the Premiership
Since 1945

'A Tory is someone who thinks institutions are wiser than those who operate them.'   *Enoch Powell, 1986*[1]

The Prime Minister is the person who offers advice to the Sovereign, backed by the prospect of being able to deliver a majority vote in the House of Commons in which he is representing the majority. The loss of the constitutional sense that the Sovereign governs on the advice of Parliament accounts for the tendency to treat the office of Prime Minister as to a certain degree independent. *Enoch Powell, 1997*[2]

'There are three classes which need sanctuary more than others – birds, wild flowers, and Prime Ministers.' *Stanley Baldwin, 1925*[3]

'Ours is a pretty hard and unrewarding life.'
*Harold Macmillan to Selwyn Lloyd on appointing him
Chancellor of the Exchequer, July 1960*[4]

It is now a plausible contention to claim that the pressures and opportunities, the expectations and motivations, and the restraints and problems associated with the business of being and remaining a prime minister are sufficiently analogous to the equivalent conditions faced by an American president to justify the term 'president' being applied to the occupant of Number 10. In fact, it would be no exaggeration to assert that what this country has witnessed over the last generation has been the growing emergence of a British presidency.   *Professor Michael Foley, 1993*[5]

Whenever the 'presidential' epithet is applied to the UK prime ministership I think of the most exaggerated form in which it has ever been expressed.

Paradoxically, the phrasemaker was Winston Churchill, probably the most self-conscious practitioner of genuinely (as opposed to partially) *collective* Cabinet government during his 1951–55 premiership. The occasion was the appointment of Lord Halifax to the Foreign Office in 1938; the place, the House of Commons. Reacting to objections at having so senior a minister in the House of Lords, Churchill, supporting Halifax's appointment, pointed out that the Prime Minister was in the Commons, adding: 'What is the point of crying out for the moon when you have the sun and you have that bright orb of day from whose effulgent beams the lesser luminaries derive their radiance?' This hyperbolic gem was exhumed to comfort Macmillan in July 1960 when accusations of excessive prime ministerialism were hurled at him (as we shall see in a moment) for appointing Lord Home to the Foreign Office, his thoughtful Private Secretary, Tim Bligh, informing him that the relevant volume of the 1938 'Hansard has a piece of paper in the place and is by your chair in the Cabinet Room'.[6]

Once in No. 10, I suspect that most Prime Ministers find themselves in increasing sympathy with the self-pity of Baldwin and Macmillan (though Macmillan was prone to self-contradiction on this point, telling Ludovic Kennedy, for example, that the premiership was 'much the most relaxed of the offices I held').[7] Nearly all would echo Asquith's reply to a lady who remarked upon how nice it must be to enjoy such power. 'Power, power?' he said. 'You may think you are going to get it but you never do.'[8] There are some premiers who sustain a version of the sun/moon image summoned by Churchill, in the early days of their tenure at least. One such was Harold Wilson. In an interview he gave Kenneth Harris of the *Observer* in 1965 to mark the completion of his first year in office, Wilson declared,

'No. 10 is what the Prime Minister of the day makes it. The levers of power are all here in No. 10. In the Cabinet Room [which is where Wilson did his work at that time; during his last premiership he preferred to work in the first-floor study overlooking St James's Park].[9] The ability of the Prime Minister to use them depends on the Prime Minister being in touch with what is going on – and not going on . . . The more things you take an interest in, the more information comes back to you. A Prime Minister governs by curiosity and range of interest.'[10]

There is a great deal to deconstruct in that typically Wilsonian soliloquy. First, does a PM *govern*? Should he (or she)? Isn't the key to the British system, its safety catch, the tradition that the British people are governed by a collective executive (the Cabinet) rather than a single chief executive (the Prime Minister)?[11] Second, isn't an approach such as the early Wilson's a recipe for stress and overload on the premier's part *and* the route to an increasingly resentful Cabinet irritated by the overmighty intrusiveness of a figure who is far from the *primus inter pares*?[12] And, third could one talk so confidently of 'levers of power', let alone claim that all of them reside in No. 10? In his determination to convince Kenneth Harris that he had indeed converted Downing Street from Alec Douglas-Home's alleged 'monastery' into the 'powerhouse' he promised,[13] Harold Wilson raised in a few short paragraphs most of the issues that have fuelled the great postwar debate about the alleged metamorphosis of Cabinet government into a prime ministerial, or even a presidential, mutation away from the traditional British breed.

That debate was already five years old when Wilson crafted those words. It started, interestingly enough, before John Mackintosh's great work, *The British Cabinet*, first appeared in 1962.[14] Macmillan's appointment of a peer, Alec Home, as his Foreign Secretary in 1960 stimulated the vigorous little debate referred to above about alleged overmightiness in No. 10 which drew Lord Boothby, Earl Attlee and Professor Max Beloff into the public prints, their combined contributions carefully preserved in one of the Cabinet Office's constitutional files. Unknown to any of them, Macmillan had toyed with the idea of creating a Prime Minister's Department just before he won the 1959 general election and had come to what Norman Brook called 'the (rather reluctant) conclusion that it would be unwise for him to establish anything of that nature'. Almost exactly a year later Beloff began his mini-debate with Attlee and Boothby in the correspondence columns of the *Daily Telegraph* by claiming of Home's appointment to the Foreign Office that: 'Taken together with the other Cabinet changes, and in the light of the development of the office of Prime Minister over recent decades, it may well be that it marks a further stage in the evolution of British government from a Cabinet system to what is virtually a Presidential system.' Boothby concurred with this analysis and suggested Parliament needed to develop a system of committees comparable to those enjoyed by the United States Congress 'if the legislature is to regain effective control of any kind over the executive'. Attlee disagreed with both Beloff and Boothby profoundly, discerning no 'continuous trend towards a Presidential system in recent years' and arguing that: 'The essential principle of our British system is that of collective responsibility. Ministers are not mere creatures of the Prime Minister . . .'[15]

The 1960s produced a further rash of argument – a rather classic set of exchanges, in retrospect – which enticed Dick Crossman and George Jones on to the field mapped so brilliantly by Mackintosh.

Mackintosh claimed baldly in 1962 that:

> The country is governed by the Prime Minister who leads, co-ordinates and maintains a series of Ministers . . . Some decisions are taken by the Prime Minister alone, some in consultation between him and the Senior Ministers, while others are left to the heads of department, the Cabinet, Cabinet Committees, or the permanent officials . . . There is no single catch phrase that can describe this form of government, but it may be pictured as a cone. The Prime Minister stands at the apex, supported by and giving power to a widening series of rings of senior ministers, the Cabinet, its committees, non-Cabinet Ministers, and departments.

A year later, Crossman, never shy of coining a catch phrase, asserted that: 'The postwar epoch has seen the final transformation of Cabinet Government into Prime Ministerial Government'.

George Jones, writing in 1965, took on both Mackintosh and Crossman, stressing the ministerialism (as opposed to prime ministerialism) of British central government, emphasizing the degree to which laws and the spending that goes with the functions they allocate place real power in the hands of individual secretaries of state before concluding that: 'The Prime Minister is the leading figure in the Cabinet whose voice carries most weight. But he is not the all-powerful individual which many have recently claimed him to be . . . A prime minister who can carry his colleagues with him can be in a very powerful position, but his is only as strong as they let him be.'[16]

Echoes of the original 1960s debate have sounded down the decades ever since. The argument is driven and regularly revived whenever a Prime Minister pushes – or appears to push – his or her own policy in such a way that Cabinet colleagues seem cowed or overridden. The arrivals in Downing Street of Margaret Thatcher and Tony Blair are now the best known but by no means the only examples. (There were outbreaks of the debate, too, during Harold Wilson's early years and for much of Ted Heath's tenure.)

The scholarly disputes, unlike the press treatments which erupt whenever political journalists sniff a whiff of overmightiness in No. 10, go beyond the personality factor, however. The Mackintosh–Crossman school advance changes in the nature and scope of the state, as well as in the internal discipline of party and the extension of a leader's powers of patronage, as almost structural factors which work constantly in the direction of increasing prime ministerial power, largely irrespective of the personality element. Michael Foley has extended the debate into presidentialism using his concept of the 'leadership stretch'[17] (the gap between the premier and all others) that has come with the transformation of the media's reach and increasing personality obsession in the thirty-plus years since Crossman and Mackintosh were writing. Other observers, George Jones in particular, have maintained throughout that statutes assign functions and the public expenditure associated with them to named ministers, not the Prime Minister, and that the grain of central government lies against an overweening chief executive whatever the superficial appearance of overmightiness some premiers display.

I have long thought this classic debate to be lacking in one important respect as it has, to some extent, deteriorated, in Anthony King's apt phrase, to 'the level of a bar room brawl' with competitive anecdote and counter-example flying across the seminar rooms like so many chair legs or broken bottles.[18] A higher level of precision would be possible if we could be clearer about what the job involves – in short, what is a Prime Minister for? In this chapter, therefore, I want to cut a few slices across the accumulated practice of premiership since 1945 in a way that illustrates both the increasing reach of the job and the resultant stresses put upon it – an interesting commentary in itself on the concentration of powers on the Monarch's First Minister at a time when the Sovereign's dominion, precisely defined, has been drawn narrower still and narrower. In doing so I hope to add a little context as well as a dash of data to the great debate about the relative clout of Prime Minister and Cabinet.

There were two sources of immediate inspiration for my first attempt at such measurement. Shortly after the 1992 election, it came to my notice that Mr Major's Downing Street Policy Unit had suggested, in the spirit of the Citizen's Charter, that Cabinet ministers should be subject to a regime of performance-related pay. 'Oh, no,' the cry went up from the Cabinet Room, 'you can't measure what *we* do!'[19] So, an idea occurred to me: if I could construct a set of tasks for the Prime Minister as an exemplar it would be only a short step thereafter to devising a range of performance indicators for him.

And there was a model to hand. This was the Cabinet Office file, to which I have already referred, that was created between 1947 and 1949 to describe the functions of the Prime Minister and his staff.[20] As far as I can see from a close examination of the dossier, it was never shown to Mr Attlee or any of his successors. The original stimulus for its compilation was a cry for help from the Institute of Public Administration, which had to prepare a paper on the job of the UK's political chief executive for a comparative conference in Switzerland. The tidy-minded Cabinet Office took the result over for its own purposes, adding sensitive bits on the very special relationship between monarchs and premiers which they did not divulge to the public administrators.[21]

This late-1940s file reduced the job to about a dozen functions. Top of the list, as always, was managing the relationship between the Monarch and the government as a whole and – *the* great twentieth-century prime ministerial weapon – the power to hire and fire ministers. Chairing the Cabinet and its most important committees and the arrangement of other 'Cabinet business' (the chairmanship of committees over which he did not preside himself, their memberships and agendas) represented another central function and instrument of prime ministerial power. Overall control of the Civil Service lay in the Prime Minister's hands thanks to his status as First Lord of the Treasury, as did top Civil Service appointments. The allocation of functions between departments as well as their creation and abolition left the structures of Whitehall (save those parts which rested on statutes such as the Ministry of Defence Act, 1946) very much a Prime Minister's to change.

The external side to the premiership was recognized by the paper's stress on relationships with other heads of government and a Prime Minister's especially close involvement in foreign policy and defence matters. The external patronage functions were represented, too, with what were called top appointments to many institutions of 'a national character' (a charming phrase when compared with the more modern 'quango'). The Trollopian side of the job was not neglected; 'certain scholastical and ecclesiastical appointments' got their mention. Finally, the document reached the distinctive heart of the British way of government: the unwritten Constitution. For the handling of 'precedent and procedure', as the file puts it, represents largely, though not wholly, oversight of the practical workings of the Constitution itself. No trace of checks and balances or separation of powers here. The most powerful single individual in the land is also *the* effective quality controller and interpreter-in-chief of the rules of the game – a hugely important, though often overlooked, ingredient in the potentially overmighty power of the British premiership.

The late-1940s job description was surprisingly limited if one considers the accumulation of functions outlined in chapter 1. A fully historical awareness of the makings of the mid-twentieth-century premiership would have led to the addition of specific items such as overseeing the preparation of the 'War Book' (including the increasingly important nuclear aspect), the Prime Minister's close involvement with the Chancellor of the Exchequer in budget-making, the co-ordination of the intelligence and security services and oversight of the government's media and publicity arrangements. I would have added, too, private dealings and discussions with Opposition leaders on sensitive matters on the so-called 'Privy Counsellor basis', which, as we shall see, was a continuing feature of the postwar period.

A tabular summary of the late 1940s file would look like this:

1. Managing the relationship between the Monarch and the government as a whole.
2. Hiring and firing ministers.
3. Chairing the Cabinet and its most important committees.
4. Arranging other 'Cabinet business', i.e., the chairmanships of other committees, their memberships and agendas.
5. Overall control of the Civil Service as First Lord of the Treasury.
6. The allocation of functions between departments; their creation and abolition.
7. Relationships with other heads of government.
8. An especially close involvement in foreign policy and defence matters.
9. Top Civil Service appointments.
10. Top appointments to many institutions of 'a national character'.
11. 'Certain scholastical and ecclesiastical appointments.'
12. The handling of 'precedent and procedure'.

But the file, for all its gaps, is of continuing significance as it serves as a hanger over which to drape the fabric of the late-twentieth-century premiership. It led me to draw up my own mid-1990s equivalent, with a little help from my friends in the inner circles of late-twentieth-century government. The result demonstrates a considerable waxing of functions over a fifty-year period. Before examining the changes in detail, certain limitations to the exercise must be underlined.

First, the list embraces only those tasks or duties which fall to a Prime Minister as head of goverment. PMs are also, throughout the years since 1945, leaders of a party. And at times the difficulties which stem from the job of party leader can appear to all but overwhelm the head-of-government aspect of the premiership (one thinks, for example, of Major at the height of the Conservatives' Euro-neurosis 1992–97).

Similarly, it is important to recognize that not all of a premier's functions as head of government are demanding simultaneously. An example of this is the 'War Book'/nuclear element – a necessary and terrible preoccupation in, say, Macmillan's time, but much less so for later premiers. Several of the functions, too, are self-evidently occasional (requesting a dissolution of Parliament) or latent (hiring and firing ministers). It is especially important to remember such variations upon the functional theme when examining specific incumbencies or the individual performances of Prime Ministers. What follows is not a set of management consultants' 'performance indicators' against which each premier must be awarded a mark on a scale of 1 to 10. Rather, it is a description of a growth in reach or, in some cases, expectation.

Yet so abundant are the premier's current functions (potential, latent or activated) that it is best to divide them into seven kinds: procedure and the constitution; appointments; the conduct of Cabinet and parliamentary business; organization and efficiency; budgets and market-sensitive economic decisions (though here the position changed radically in May 1997); and special foreign and defence functions.

CONSTITUTIONAL AND PROCEDURAL

Managing the relationship between government and the Monarch

The Home Office, by tradition, is the department for royal affairs (from royal births to the use of the royal prerogative for declaring war). But, in practical terms, any serious or sensitive matters involving the Monarch or the most immediate members of the royal family (such as the heir to the throne) are dealt with by the Prime Minister. His or her Principal Private Secretary is in regular touch with the Queen's Private Secretary on what is, perhaps, the most delicate of all governing membranes. Its special sensitivity is reflected in Buckingham Palace's unwillingness to release any material from the Royal Archives relating to the present Monarch's relationships with her premiers since 1952.[22] What primary material we have is gleaned almost entirely from Whitehall files, those of 10 Downing Street in particular. The exchanges of advice and comment between the head of state and the head of government fall into a category so sacrosanct that only the rules protecting the operations of the secret services rival them. On exceptional occasions, such as the aftermath of the death of Diana, Princess of Wales in the summer of 1997, the toing and froing between the Palace and No. 10 becomes semi-public even if not wholly transparent.

Special it may be, but the No. 10–Palace relationship has its routines. There is the regular Tuesday evening meeting at the Palace to be prepared for,[23] an occasion taken immensely seriously by both sides. And some one-offs can be both protracted and time-consuming. During John Major's horrendous late summer and autumn of 1992, for example, he had to spend a great deal of time on the separation of the Prince and Princess of Wales and the Queen's decision to pay tax while wrestling with pit closures, the destruction of his currency policy on Black Wednesday and the rolling political and parliamentary woes stimulated by his need to pilot through the House of Commons the Maastricht Treaty provisions to which Britain had signed up.

Managing the relationship between government and Opposition on a Privy Counsellor basis

All new Privy Counsellors are required to swear the Privy Counsellors' Oath of Confidentiality (which requires them to keep all matters entrusted privately to them a secret). Whitehall operates as if it takes the oath seriously, but there is private scepticism ('for what any oath may be worth', as the somewhat sarcastic Parliamentary Counsel, Sir Noel Hutton, put it in 1963).[24] The Leader of the Opposition (who is always a Privy Counsellor) and any of his Opposition colleagues who are former Cabinet ministers can be briefed on Privy Counsellor terms by the PM and other ministers for the purpose of providing background on sensitive matters. Only when the files are declassified at the PRO does one begin to appreciate this hidden flow of information. It usually involves foreign policy or defence matters. In recent times Northern Ireland has been one of the most important questions dealt with on the PC net.[25]

Examples from the postwar years include the Middle East in the mid 1950s,[26] the Cuban missile crisis and Macmillan's conversations with President Kennedy during it,[27] Whitehall security against subversion by the Soviet Union,[28] the reorganization of the Ministry of Defence,[29] the Profumo affair and the creation of the Security Commission in its wake,[30] the future of the nuclear deterrent[31] and the pound sterling (Douglas-Home saw Wilson about the gold and dollar reserves in February 1964, for example, and Callaghan, as Chancellor, briefed Heath on devaluation three hours ahead of the announcement in November 1967).[32] But the most extraordinary example, in procedural terms at least, is the handling of Churchill's six-page memo on British Defence in the light of the Soviet threat in May 1949.[33]

Not only did Attlee establish a special Cabinet committee to examine the concerns of his old World War II chief, he invited Churchill and no fewer than four of his Privy Counsellor colleagues on the Conservative benches to sit on that same Cabinet committee, GEN 293, to discuss defence matters over three meetings in the summer and autumn of 1949[34] – all this at a time of intense party strife over the nationalization of iron and steel and the power of the House of Lords. These talks represent an intriguing piece of evidence in the 'great debate' about the extent (even the existence) of a consensus in the early postwar years: rival sets of historians have stressed either the degree of policy harmony between the parties, nationalization excepted, or the distance and partisanship between them which an artificially created afterglow from the wartime coalition government and the creation of the welfare state has camouflaged.[35] The Liberal Democrat lawyer, Philip Goldenberg, cited these talks as the precedent his leader, Paddy Ashdown, might use in pressing for the joint Government/Liberal Democrat Consultative Cabinet Committee which was created and began meeting in the autumn of 1997.[36]

There were precedents, too, for the 1949 talks. The tradition started on foreign and defence matters in 1908, when A. J. Balfour was called to give evidence to his own creation, the Committee of Imperial Defence. In 1913 Asquith invited Balfour to sit on a CID sub-committee charged with examining the UK's vulnerability to attack from overseas.[37] As we have seen earlier, the basis for all such dealings throughout the twentieth century has been the fact that, as the former premier Lord Rosebery put it in his celebrated 1899 essay on Robert Peel: 'The Prime Minister . . . is technically and practically the chairman of an Executive Committee of the Privy Council, or rather perhaps of Privy Councillors.'[38] (Though we now know that since the 1930s Whitehall has treated it as the latter.) And it must always be remembered that, compared with the premiership, the Privy Council is a truly ancient and established instrument of governance.

(The Cabinet Office's 'Historical Table' traces the first mention of it to 1218, almost 500 years before Walpole assumed the First Lordship of the Treasury. Even then, according to the Cabinet Office's reading, 'probably a distinction between an inner and an outer circle was normal'[39] – traces of an 'inner cabinet' even in the thirteenth century!)

Establishing the order of precedence in Cabinet

This matters more than one thinks in terms of establishing the power of a Prime Minister in relation to his most senior colleagues. In recent years it has been updated at the beginning of each parliamentary session (or after a reshuffle) and released as part of the annual list of ministers. It is published almost invariably in full by the quality newspapers and in the *Civil Service Yearbook*. As the full and detailed files at the Public Record Office show, only a Prime Minister can determine the pecking order. As a briefing for the War Cabinet Secretary, Sir Edward Bridges, put it in December 1939, he 'has a completely free hand'.[40] And where a minister is placed by the premier really matters to him or her.

This is partly because the annual publication of the list can be used to indicate promotion or demotion (the new list released after a reshuffle is especially carefully scrutinized for this purpose) and partly because if Minister A needs to talk to Minister B and B is higher up the order, A has to call on B in what one might call the choreography of power. The files have some choice examples of status anxiety on the part of Cabinet ministers. After Ormsby-Gore complained to Baldwin in 1936 about 'the lowly position he occupies in the list of the Cabinet as Colonial Secretary',[41] as the No. 10 brief for the Prime Minister put it, Baldwin bumped him up a little.[42]

The most neurotic example in recently declassified files is that of Duncan Sandys, Macmillan's tough, demanding and seemingly self-confident Defence Minister. A new order of precedence is naturally published after a general election,[43] and the imminence of a new Parliament being summoned after the 1959 general election produced the following exchanges between Macmillan and Sandys, who was to be moved from Defence to the Ministry of Aviation:

13 October 1959

My dear Prime Minister,

Thank you very much for your nice letter of yesterday.

   It goes without saying that I shall always be happy to serve in whatever capacity you think I can be most useful. It is an honour to have the opportunity to continue as a member of your team.

You kindly said that you would see that the impression was not given that I was being 'demoted', which would weaken my influence in the new job.

I hope that, so as to make this clear, it will be possible for me to keep my present place in the order of Cabinet seniority, when the new list is published.

With every good wish for continued success in your second innings.

Yours ever
Duncan.[44]

14 October 1959

Dear Duncan

Thank you so much for your letter of October 13.

I will certainly make sure that you are not 'demoted' and you will certainly keep your present place in the order of Cabinet seniority. You will, in fact, be one up!

Once again let me say how grateful I am to you for taking on this new department. It is of the greatest importance to this country, and I know you will do all you can to make it a success.

Yours ever,
Harold Macmillan.[45]

As a senior Cabinet minister, Macmillan himself had not been free of the status neurosis. A protracted exchange of notes with Eden about his position relative to Butler accompanied his eventual agreement to be switched from the Foreign Office to the Treasury in December 1955. He was particularly keen that Butler should enjoy neither the title nor the status of 'Deputy Prime Minister' and Eden agreed to this. The initial letter was vintage Macmillan. In a handwritten note accompanying it, he told Eden: 'DO NOT be alarmed. Dorothy typed it for me.' Lady Dorothy tapped out her husband's reluctance to leave the Foreign Secretaryship which was 'the fulfilment of a long ambition'. There was no point in his quitting the FO 'to be an orthodox Chancellor of the Exchequer. I must be, if not a revolutionary, something of a reformer. However, to reform the Treasury is like trying to reform the Kremlin or the Vatican. These institutions are apt to have the last laugh . . . As Chancellor I must be undisputed head of the Home Front under you. If Rab becomes Leader of the House and Lord Privy Seal that will be fine. But I could not agree that he should be Deputy Prime Minister.' If Butler were so appointed, Macmillan concluded, 'my task would be impossible'.[46]

The establishment and interpretation of procedural guidelines for both ministers and civil servants

This may sound flat, almost a routine area of prime ministerial activity, but of its nature it is profoundly revealing of the British Constitution. For, as the constitutional lawyer-turned-Conservative MP Sir Kenneth Pickthorn famously observed in 1960, living in a political nation without formal, written rules of the game means that 'procedure is all the Constitution the poor Briton has'.[47] And if the single most powerful executive figure is also the chief and often the final determinant of procedure, the true extent of the lack of checks and balances in Britain's system of central government becomes dazzlingly apparent. It represents the political equivalent of insider trading.

The important pair of procedural documents over which the Prime Minister has the final say are *Questions of Procedure for Ministers*, which we shall examine in a moment, and the *Civil Service Code*, which is intended to protect the public service from deceitful or politically partisan instructions.[48] There is no statute that governs civil servants or diplomats, though there are statutes for the crown (as distinct from civil) servants who people MI5 and MI6 (the secret servants of the state have never been made part of the civil or diplomatic services) and the 4,500 or so officials working at the Government Communications Headquarters who are civil servants. Though the *Civil Service Code* was framed in 1996, after consultation with the parliamentary select committees which the Major government deemed politic,[49] a Prime Minister could amend or even abolish the code if he or she so chose (and it would be as a courtesy only, rather than as a right that Parliament had a say in any changes). This position could change if the Blair administration finds the parliamentary time to enshrine the *Civil Service Code* in a statutory form.

But the most important set of procedural guidelines of which the Prime Minister is the ultimate quality controller are *Questions of Procedure for Ministers* (renamed *Ministerial Code: A Code of Conduct and Guidance on Procedures for Ministers*, when Blair published his version in July 1997).[50] Since John Major made them public in 1992, these have had an increasing influence on a wide range of governing issues, not least ministerial resignations.[51] The document ranges from high constitutional matters, such as the conduct of Cabinet business and ministerial relationships with Parliament, to personal matters such as arrangements for personal shareholdings or membership of Lloyd's of London during the tenure of ministerial office. *QPM*, as the document is still known in Whitehall, has been essentially a prime ministerial instrument since the rules were drawn together in a newer, more coherent form for Attlee in 1945, enabling premiers to set behavioural expectations as well as to frame precise rules.[52] And, as Amy Baker has shown, they acquired a stronger, more permanent status inside the constellation of the constitution when they successfully made the transfer from a Conservative to a Labour administration in 1964.[53] At that time the Cabinet Secretary, Sir Burke Trend, described *QPM* to Wilson as 'an entirely non-Party document, which codifies the general principles of ministerial conduct as they have evolved over many years. It has the authority of a good many Prime Ministers, of different party complexions.'[54] Longevity gave *QPM* the kind of status it did not appear to have when power moved from Attlee to Churchill in 1951.

Even though a pair of select committees (the Treasury and Civil Service and the Public Services Committees of the Commons) and a duo of inquiries (Nolan on standards in public life and Scott on arms to Iraq) made some contribution to the 1990 revisions of *QPM* (the Blair *Ministerial Code* reflects them too), its application remains very much a prime ministerial matter. With the PM acting as both judge and jury the view from No. 10 is usually the determining factor in whether a minister in trouble goes or stays. As Peter Clarke puts it, 'Politics is the final arbiter under an unwritten constitution.'[55]

Oversight of changes to Civil Service recruitment practices

The bulk of the detailed work here is carried out by the Civil Service Commission, the body invented by Gladstone in the mid nineteenth century to depoliticize the Civil Service by placing responsibility for recruiting officials in the hands of commissioners who answered to the Monarch rather than to ministers. Nowadays the Commission sets the standards required of the Recruitment Services Agency which was privatized in 1996 to widespread condemnation from former permanent secretaries.[56] The

Commission is attached to the office or department which currently houses the minister with day-to-day responsibility for the Civil Service. But, once more, the Prime Minister is the ultimate overseer of the process whereby, as the Civil Service White Paper *Continuity and Change* stated in 1994, 'the key principles on which the British Civil Service is based: integrity, political impartiality, objectivity, *selection and promotion on merit* [emphasis added] and accountability through Ministers to Parliament' are 'sustained'.[57] If the Civil Service orders in council were altered in such a way that the political neutrality of the career Civil and Diplomatic Services was removed,[58] it would, as a matter of the royal prerogative, be a prime ministerial responsibility.

Classification levels and secrecy procedures for official information

Considerable strides have been made away from the closed system of government which had long kept Whitehall the world leader in the degree of administrative secrecy which could be maintained while remaining within a democratic society.[59] The scope of secrecy legislation was narrowed under Mrs Thatcher (criminal sanctions being removed from unauthorized disclosures involving all but an inner ring of activities such as defence, security and intelligence, Cabinet matters and relationships with other nations),[60] but John Major was the first premier in history to seriously try to institute a positive regime of greater openness. His 1993 Code of Practice on Open Government, while falling short of a statutory right-to-know, none the less provided a figure outside the governing circle, in the shape of the Parliamentary Commissioner for Administration (the 'Ombudsman'), to report on disputed cases.[61]

Unless and until a piece of primary legislation establishes freedom of information by statute (which the Blair administration began to do during the 1999–2000 session of Parliament), it will be perfectly possible for future premiers to steer Whitehall back into its covens of confidentiality without troubling the parliamentary draftsmen (though there would be a row in Parliament as various codes and guidelines, including *Questions of Procedure for Ministers*, the *Civil Service Code*, and the 'Osmotherly Rules' governing what civil servants can and cannot say before select committees[62] would need to be rewritten). But without a Freedom of Information Act, the tones of openness and confidentiality are very much set by No. 10. Significantly, Tony Blair reiterated the government's manifesto pledge to introduce a Freedom of Information Act almost at the outset of his administration in the Foreword to his *Ministerial Code*.[63]

But, as we shall see, the FOI Bill, when it was finally published in December 1999, fell short of the full-blooded measure expected in the early days of the New Labour Government.

Requesting the Sovereign to grant a dissolution of Parliament

Until 1918 this was a matter for the full Cabinet when, as we have seen, Lloyd George changed it to a prime ministerial function. Since then thus it has remained, though most premiers usually consult their senior colleagues, if not the whole Cabinet, before asking the Monarch to fire the starting-gun for an election.[64]

APPOINTMENTS

Downing Street distinguishes between crown appointments and public appointments. The distinction is historical if arcane. It rests on those posts which serve the Crown and act directly in its name (such as 'ministers of the crown') or those that are filled by royal patronage (Regius professors are an example). Public appointments cover the remaining areas of Downing Street patronage. The distinction means that the armed forces and the secret services are crown appointees, whereas members of the Civil Service and the Diplomatic Service are not.

CROWN APPOINTMENTS

Appointment and dismissal of ministers

Here lies the true locus of prime ministerial primacy in terms of the relative power of the *primus* over the *pares*. And the instrument of that power is, in Enoch Powell's vivid phrase, the equivalent of Henry VIII's axe, which a Prime Minister always has beside his chair in the Cabinet Room.[65] In terms of firing ministers, it really can be a matter of off-with-their-heads, though political reality does limit the scope of wholesale butchery, at least. Conventional wisdom is right to see Macmillan's 'Night of the Long Knives', when he sacked a third of his Cabinet in a terrible rush (fearful of a leak), as to some extent a self-inflicted wound. As Alec Home told me, Macmillan was never the same premier again.[66] Macmillan himself had a sense of overkill the moment he had swung the axe. As he put it in a personal note to one of the victims, Charles Hill, who had until then handled the government's press relations with considerable aplomb:

Of course, you will realise that I had to do *prematurely* what I knew had to be done some time this or early next year. Even so – although I felt a change at the Treasury vital (not so much in present policy but in approach to the next set of problems) I had hoped to go a little more quietly. But when the situation (and the Press speculation) began to develop, the only way to avoid disaster was to act swiftly. I deeply regret the apparent discourtesy involved, especially to old friends like you and David Kilmuir and Harold Watkinson.[67]

The No. 10 file dealing with the events of 13 July 1962 is wonderfully revealing of the elaborate care with which most Prime Ministers consider their moves on the ministerial chessboard. It is worth lingering over, not merely because of the intrinsic importance of the event to postwar British political history, but also because it offers a very rare insight into the brutal realities of ministerial departure. I have found no other file in the archives which comes as near to recording or capturing the human or the manipulative aspects of such moments.

What is different, however, about the 1962 exercise – compared with, say, Attlee's personally typed permutations before the September 1947 reshuffle (his careful concern for age, trades-union background and regional balance),[68] or Wilson's plans for the autumn reshuffle of 1965 (how intriguing that his first thought for a new Home Secretary to replace Sir Frank Soskice was not Roy Jenkins but Arthur Bottomley)[69] – is the intensely political role played by Macmillan's Principal Private Secretary, Tim Bligh. Though a civil servant, Bligh briefed Macmillan on a 'possible reconstruction' of the government as early as 19 April 1962. 'It is possible', he says in his personal and confidential memo to his boss, 'that you may have been giving some thought to a major Cabinet reconstruction some time in the future. I apologise for these few random thoughts.'[70]

There was nothing 'random' about them. They were a pre-med before a messy piece of surgery. A list of over-55s was drawn up, with Bligh saying, 'of these you would want to keep Mr Butler, Lord Home and Mr Brooke in any new Cabinet'. (What, I wonder, would, for example, Selwyn Lloyd at the Treasury have made of his omission from Bligh's list of the seriously mature to be saved from the abattoir?) The Chancellorship of the Exchequer, Bligh continues, now needs 'the right sort of man, young, tough, imaginative, politically strong and publicly articulate'.[71] There is more in this vein, the whole memo making a mockery of the notion that the Prime Minister's Private Office is free of party political considerations, not least because of the coincidence of Bligh's early thoughts and the reality of the July purge when it took place.

The same Bligh choreographed the executions when the time came, suggesting the wording of the resignation letters[72] and providing the speaking notes for Macmillan's chats with those affected. Ted Heath, for example, was to stay where he was as number 2 to Home at the Foreign Office. 'You wish to tell him', Bligh informed Macmillan, 'about the main reconstruction changes. He must not be worried. One day he will be Foreign Secretary.'[73] He never was, of course. Though they did not reach the PRO in Kew until 1996, the smell of blood still clung to those 'Night of the Long Knives' papers, as did the sense of prime ministerial power in the raw.

Headships of the intelligence and security services

This is an especially important area of prime ministerial patronage. Even in the era of statutory frameworks for the agencies concerned (since 1989 for MI5 and 1994 for MI6 and GCHQ) and with a measure of parliamentary oversight (since 1994) for the whole secret world, prime ministerial choices at the top remain crucial to the restraint as well as the effectiveness with which the state applies its instruments of intelligence and security. Prime Ministers rely here to a considerable extent on the advice of the Cabinet Secretary, who usually chairs the small group of permanent secretaries which interviews the candidates for the top jobs in the secret agencies. The first requirement is to avoid those who will dress up the products of their secret activities to suit ministerial wishes or cherished mind-sets.

Sir Percy Cradock, former Chairman of the Joint Intelligence Committee (the 'high table' of British Intelligence, as he liked to call it,[74] where each week the intelligence yield from all sources, covert and overt, is appraised in the round and an agreed overall assessment is prepared for the Prime Minister and a small group of ministers), made the seriousness of this criterion plain when discussing the need to separate intelligence analysis from policy-making. 'If there is no partition,' Sir Percy declared, 'there is a risk of intelligence being slanted to provide the answers the policy-maker wants. This is a grave sin: the analyst must convey his message, usually unpalatable, without fear or favour.'[75]

The performance indicator here was articulated by Sir Maurice Oldfield as chief of the Secret Intelligence Service, MI6. Asked by his new Foreign Secretary, Jim Callaghan, in March 1974: 'Sir Maurice, what is MI6 for?' Oldfield replied, 'Our job, Secretary of State, is to bring you unwelcome news.'[76] Even the new openness, however, has left us (not surprisingly) largely without the archival means to assess the degree to which the Oldfield test has been met by his fellow intelligence chiefs in the postwar period, though the progressive release since 1995 of the papers and minutes of the postwar Joint Intelligence Committee is helping.

Senior appointments to the armed forces

The degree to which Prime Ministers are *au fait* with senior military officers varies enormously. Some premiers rely heavily on the advice of their Ministers of Defence when making their dispositions. Churchill, of course, had a deep and sustained knowledge of the personalities: he even persuaded two of them to join his last government at full Cabinet level – Field Marshal Lord Alexander going to Defence and General Lord Ismay to the Commonwealth Relations Office. Attlee, a great believer in civilian control of the military, once remarked tartly of Field Marshal Lord Montgomery, who had not been a success as Chief of the Imperial General Staff after the war, that 'the self-confidence that inspired the 8th Army [during World War II] is not always useful in complicated affairs in which many of the factors are outside his ken'.[77] Mrs Thatcher acquired a high level of knowledge about the senior soldiers, sailors and airmen of the 1980s owing to their enforced intimacy during the Falklands campaign, during which high levels of mutual regard were engendered.[78] But whatever their insights into the characters and the prowess of the men concerned, Prime

Ministers have to take a careful interest when the Secretary of State for Defence enters with a list of candidates for top posts, both because of the service chiefs' importance to the size and shape of the Defence budget and also in case military emergencies occur that are likely to project them to the centre of decision-taking.

Senior appointments to the judiciary

This, I suspect, is not an area of patronage in which most premiers feel at ease, so they tend to rely very much on Lord Chancellors for advice. This was apparent, interestingly, when John Major was seeking senior judges to chair both the inquiry into standards of conduct in public life in 1994 and the inquiry into the arms to Iraq affair after the collapse of the Matrix Churchill trial in 1993. He simply did not know anybody suitable. James Mackay, his Lord Chancellor, found in Lord Nolan and Sir Richard Scott two very independent-minded lawyers, both, for different reasons, imbued with a high moral charge.[79]

Unless a premier has been Home Secretary en route to the top (only Churchill and Callaghan have among the postwar eleven, though Tony Blair was Shadow Home Secretary), or is himself a lawyer by professional training (only Attlee and Blair fit the bill), they are unlikely to pick up any real knowledge of the senior judicial figures of their day.

Top ecclesiastical and Regius academic appointments

Not for nothing is the No. 10 Appointments Secretary known as 'Heaven's talent scout' (though his scouting has been powerfully assisted by the Anglican Church's own Crown Appointments Commission since its formation in 1977)[80] and his is the only Civil Service job that has to be filled by a practising Anglican.[81] The Appointments Secretary advises the Prime Minister on a wide range of jobs – potentially everything, in fact, which is not directly political, such as the choice of ministers, or is not covered by the heads of the home and diplomatic services. There is invariably more than one name submitted to the Prime Minister after his 'talent scout' has completed a range of discreet inquiries with the people and the institutions concerned. The Anglican element is a big component of his job.

It is this aspect of No. 10 life that can most amaze foreign visitors. For example, at the London G7 summit in 1977, President Carter's National Security Adviser, Zbigniew Brzezinski, was allocated the Appointments Secretary's room. During one of the early breaks he accosted the Cabinet Secretary, Sir John Hunt, to ask about the map on the wall. 'What is it?' he inquired. 'All those little pins over the country – are they missile sites or oil refineries?' 'They're bishoprics', Hunt replied to the utterly incredulous American.[82]

On more than one occasion Tony Benn has been heard to declare that the only privatization he is in favour of is the established church. On one level, he has a point. Until Tony Blair's arrival, the last practising Anglican in No. 10 had been Ted Heath. It has always struck me as odd that premiers with no personal, let alone spiritual, connection with the Church of England should have the final say in recommending candidates for preferment to the Monarch (who in the case of the Queen is not only the non-spiritual head of the Church, but a believer too).

The same applies to the Regius professorships. Mr Major had many virtues, but a deep scholarly background, to his regret, was not among them. Someone claiming to be his friend remarked unkindly and unfairly in the mid 1990s that: 'The Prime Minister has both Jeffrey Archer and Anthony Trollope by his bedside. The trouble is he can't distinguish between the two!'[83] Heaven's talent scout, however, is also scholarship's.

There are twelve Regius chairs. They embrace two ancient universities (Oxford which has eight; and Cambridge which has four) and nine subjects. The chairs at Oxford are: Civil Law, Divinity, Greek, Hebrew, Medicine, Modern History, Ecclesiastical History and Moral and Pastoral Theology; those at Cambridge: Civil Law, Physic, Modern History and English Literature.[84]

Under John Major there was an important break with tradition. The appointments were still prime ministerial, but the Regius chairs of Ecclesiastical History and Modern History at Oxford in 1997 went to Dr Henry Mayr-Harting and Professor Robert Evans, respectively, after the vacancies had been advertised and the Department of History at Oxford had made its preferences known to Mr Major via his Appointments Secretary, John Holroyd.[85]

Top public sector appointments and appointments to royal commissions and top committees of inquiry

Here a special problem arises for prime ministers: do you treat such preferment as an extension of political patronage (the chairmanship of the BBC is an especially sensitive example) or do you try to rise above the mire of partisanship and strive for balance and merit? Here, I think, was the terrain Mrs Thatcher did politicize (by contrast with the senior Civil Service), and, I believe, she did the same in appointing chairs of committees of inquiry (she eschewed the ponderous magnificence of the traditional royal commission). Since the Nolan Committee began to report, appointments to the 'quangocracy' have come under the scrutiny of an independent commissioner (first Sir Len Peach and, later, Dame Rennie Fritchie), who publishes an annual report on the health of the system as well as enjoying access to the Prime Minister, ministers and Cabinet Secretary and the Head of the home Civil Service about cases that cause concern.

In practice there are variations from premier to premier and era to era. All senior appointments of this kind flow through No. 10 to some degree. Ministers are required to submit their preferred candidates. In an era of incomes policy, for example, a Prime Minister would take great care over the head of a pay or relativities board or an old-style inquiry into a particular industrial dispute, such as Lord Wilberforce's into miners' pay in 1972.[86]

In Tony Blair's first eighteen months in No. 10, considerable and increasing prime ministerial attention was paid to arts appointments in a manner which often appeared to override the Culture Secretary, Chris Smith. Appointments such as Gerry Robinson to the Arts Council were Smith's, but the Prime Minister's direct interest in both arts policy and personnel was vividly demonstrated by the supposedly secret Downing Street 'summit'[87] on 29 June 1998.[88]

Award of peerages and honours

This is the area of greatest magic and mystery. The working of the honours system has never been opened fully to public scrutiny. The Main Honours Committee, which consists largely of Whitehall permanent secretaries and which the Cabinet Secretary chairs, has never had its terms of reference or its membership avowed any more than have its satellite committees which embrace various walks of life. The files of the PRO remain almost barren on honours, partly because of the personal delicacies involved and partly because it impinges on the inner core of royal activity and sensitivity as the Monarch, in name at least, is the fount of all honours. (This, it was explained to me in the early 1990s by a real honours insider, is why the House of Commons Table Office will not accept any parliamentary questions on honours. 'It's the Palace,' he explained confidentially.)[89]

Yet these are, after ministerial appointments, the most potent pieces of patronage in a premier's hands. Apart from honours such as the Order of Merit or the Royal Victorian Order, which remain wholly in the personal gift of the Monarch (and, apart from the close involvement of her Private Secretary, we know very little about how the Queen takes advice on the bestowal of OMs), the Prime Minister can intervene – to add or to strike-out – names at all other levels. The hope of an honour and the sense of obligation once one has been conferred soften the edges of dissent or rivalry.

Those blood-soaked files from the 'Night of the Long Knives' are of special and historical value here, too, as they contain some choice examples of this. Bligh's early trip around the field earmarking ministers for the slaughterhouse considered the possibility of the House of Lords as a form of 'life after death' (as that fine Methodist, Lord Soper, once said of the quality of debate in the Upper House).[90] 'How many', Bligh inquired of Macmillan, 'would be prepared to go into the House of Lords? Messrs Watkinson [Defence Secretary] and Marples [Minister of Transport] probably feel that they have got as far as they are likely to get politically, and might be ready for the Lords . . . Mr Lloyd [Chancellor of the Exchequer] at present feels on top of the job, but might be persuaded to become Lord Chancellor.'[91]

When the moment came for plunging the blade on 13 July 1962, Bligh's speaking notes for Macmillan's interviews with the victims contained several 'life after death' clauses:

Lord Mills – 10.15 a.m.

You are reconstructing your Cabinet and have to make a number of changes. You hope that after his many years of outstanding service to the country he will accept a *Viscountcy*. [Macmillan underlined this].[92]

Mr Maclay – 10.30 a.m.

You are reconstructing your Cabinet and feel sure he will agree that it would be right for you to appoint a new Secretary of State for Scotland (Mr Michael Noble). You would like to recommend him for a *CH* [Companion of Honour] *Now* and a *Viscountcy* later at a suitable time.

['Yes he agrees', Macmillan wrote by the CH. 'It's yours at any time', he scribbled next to the proposed Maclay Viscountcy.][93]

Bligh's briefing note for Harold Watkinson contains the following paragraph:

Would Mr Watkinson like an honour? You would be pleased to recommend him to the Queen for a Baronetcy and he could go to the House of Lords in due course if he so wished.

[Beneath this Macmillan wrote 'For next CH vacancy'.][94]

I am sure Bligh's briefing notes reflected the wishes Macmillan had conveyed to him, but the utility of the honours system and the cynicism with which the preferment weapon was fired are wonderfully apparent in these rare files, which I suspect neither Bligh nor Macmillan thought would ever see the light of day.

Nearly all Prime Ministers spend a great deal of time on shaping the honours lists they submit to the Monarch. Ted Heath was an exception and I have heard it argued that those on his backbenches who had been disappointed were not quite as ready to rally to him as they might have been when Mrs Thatcher challenged him for the Conservative Party leadership in 1975. Harold Wilson, though suspending the award of honours for political services, liked to sprinkle 'stardust'[95] on his lists with a generous (and generally politically astute) eye for a showbiz celebrity or two. His notorious Resignation List in 1976 led to a refreshed membership of the Political Honours Scrutiny Committee (great faith was placed in the appointment to it of the austere and honourable philosopher and public servant, Lord Franks), which was encouraged by Whitehall to watch especially carefully for cases where merit gave place to personal acquaintance with senior politicians.[96] Above all else, the Scrutiny Committee requires the government to show that honours are not being used to reward party funders, and Chief Whips have to certify this. Much greater transparency is required here, which may come when the *modus operandi* of the proposed Appointments Commission for life peerages becomes clearer.

Peerages always have been a special category because, as the political philosopher Michael Oakeshott pointed out, they have an instrumentality about them: they convert the recipient into a legislator.[97] Here again obligations are often involved, particularly if the Whip of the Prime Minister's party is taken by the new peer in preference to the institutionalized independence of the cross-benches. It may be apocryphal, but there is reason to believe that the following exchange took place between Mrs Thatcher and her gloriously funny and outspoken Chief Whip in the Lords, Lord Denham, during her last summer as Prime Minister, when their lordships continued their occasional practice of voting down government measures:

MRS THATCHER: Bertie! I do not create peers to have them vote against me in the House of Lords.

LORD DENHAM: Prime Minister, even you should know better than to expect me to find you a majority during Gold Cup week.[98]

Quite apart from the Wodehousian shades of Bertie Wooster confronted by his Aunt Agatha, this exchange, if true, is a perfect example of the old and the new Tory parties talking right past each other. What *is* certainly true is that Mrs Thatcher was heard to rage during her last year as Prime Minister against the 'landed and the unelected' in the House of Lords who would not do her bidding[99] in an unconscious echo of Lloyd George's legendary Limehouse speech of 1909, when he referred to the peers as 'five hundred men, ordinary men chosen accidentally from among the unemployed'.[100]

PUBLIC APPOINTMENTS

Trustees of national museums and galleries

These have emerged in recent years from the quietly decorous pastures of the Great and the Good. The adoption of charging for entrance, and modern marketing methods, as well as the financial travails of the British Library, have raised the level of media attention and with it, significantly and inevitably, the degree of political sensitivity. This, for example, was another swathe of activity discussed by Tony Blair's arts 'summit' in 1998.[101]

Members of pay review bodies

There has always been intense political delicacy here. Even governments like Mrs Thatcher's or Mr Major's that have eschewed a formal incomes policy as an instrument of counter-inflation, always have one for public sector workers. And when those 'workers' embrace generals, permanent secretaries and judges, not to mention MPs and ministers, the tabloid press (those monuments to perpetual class war) are poised to beat their drums against the financial wellbeing and proper rewarding of those allegedly in a position to enhance and featherbed their own economic interests. As a result, recent premiers have taken great care about top pay awards and the phasing-in of increases.

Top appointments to the Home Civil Service and the Diplomatic Service

Here, in contrast to the judiciary and the military, Prime Ministers do tend to know many of the civil servants and diplomats who aspire to the most glittering prizes the bureaucracy has to offer, unless, of course, they are Tony Blair entering No. 10 with no previous ministerial experience and a slate of top public service appointments awaiting his attention. The other premiers in the postwar first eleven had quite a width of departmental experience before reaching Downing Street, Mrs Thatcher being an exception with only her time at the Ministry of Pensions and National Insurance and the Department of Education and Science as her formative experiences. Churchill, the most experienced of them all, unfortunately by 1951 found it hard to remember the names of those officials who served him unless they had been part of his wartime circle, so the seasoning of decades was of little advantage to him.

Since William Armstrong's headship of the Home Civil Service (which spanned the years 1968–74), there has been a Senior Appointments Selection Committee which, unless a competition involving outsiders is mounted (in which case the First Civil Service Commissioner will preside over a board), provides the PM (and the Secretary of State concerned) with a list of possibles (usually three, one of whom carries a preferred recommendation).[102] We will assess the allegations of politicization during the Thatcher years when we examine her premiership in chapter 16. What was undeniably true was the close attention she paid to such appointments compared to most of her predecessors.

CONDUCT OF CABINET AND PARLIAMENTARY BUSINESS

Calling meetings of Cabinet and its committees

The Prime Minister dominates the processes of Cabinet government. Only he or she can create a Cabinet committee and appoint its personnel. A premier not keen on a genuinely collective approach, such as Mrs Thatcher, can easily be tempted to steer in advance the result of a meeting, keeping particular ministers off a committee and certain issues off its agenda. Some premiers prefer to confine much of their effective decision-taking to groups which do not qualify as Cabinet committees (Tony Blair joins Margaret Thatcher in this category, especially on economic matters).

The calling of 'Political Cabinets'

There have, by tradition, been certain regular occasions where the Cabinet goes purely political and officials are not present. The discussion of the Budget a few hours before its delivery is one such – a strange tradition as Budgets are thoroughly governmental matters as well as political occasions. John Major made 'Political Cabinets' a regular feature of his premiership and used them chiefly to plot Conservative strategy and tactics to counter Labour's advances in the opinion polls after September 1992 and the events associated with the UK's withdrawal from the European exchange rate mechanism on 'Black Wednesday'. Tony Blair revived the practice of 'Political Cabinets' in the autumn of 1999.[103]

Cabinet Secretaries have been very sensitive to such metamorphoses when full Cabinets have changed into 'political' ones. Burke Trend was especially good at this. If he thought the Cabinet had crossed the line he would put down his pen rather noisily as a signal to his fellow minute-takers to leave the Cabinet Room as unobtrusively as possible.[104]

Deciding issues where Cabinet or
Cabinet committees are unable to agree

Naturally, this has been an element of prime ministerial leadership since Pitt. But it was one of Major's ministers, Lord Wakeham, who talked about it in a lecture designed to show that proper collective Cabinet government had been restored once Mrs Thatcher had departed.[105] What was unusual about this was the public candour involved. Most Prime Ministers have preferred to maintain the public fiction of collective responsibility – that all decisions emerge from shared discussions which bind them all. The implication of Wakeham's admission was that Major's colleagues did not resent the occasions when he made an individual decision because genuine collective discussion was his normal and preferred practice.

Granting ministers permission to miss
Cabinet meetings or to leave the country

Only a summons from the Queen takes precedence over a meeting of the Cabinet if a Cabinet Minister is in the country.[106] To be absent from the country requires the Prime Minister's permission, which can be rescinded at any time.[107] The Callaghan government and the last months of the Major administration saw a familiar procession of ministers arriving jet-lagged at Heathrow before being driven off to Westminster for an important vote in the House of Commons.

Ultimate responsibility with the Leaders of
the House for the government's legislative programme
and the use of government time in Parliament

Commanding a reasonable majority in the House of Commons automatically gives a government both the lion's share of parliamentary time and a powerful chance of deploying that time in a way that will deliver the outcomes its leader desires. Awarding a Bill a place on the legislative timetable is an important piece of political rationing as well as policy-making. (The failure rate of Bills brought forward to the Cabinet's legislation committees is high; even in relatively light legislative years, only about one in four finds a place.)[108]

Answering questions twice and (later) once a week in the House of Commons

This piece of political theatre, as we have seen, gained its regular place as a parliamentary fixture in 1961. Only since the late 1970s, however, has it acquired its all-embracing character. Until then, premiers would not take questions on subjects where there was a clear lead department; the questioner would be referred to a particular Secretary of State. Since then, however, the portmanteau question ('Would the Prime Minister list his engagements . . .') has enabled almost anything to be asked unannounced. The inquiring MP is able to say, 'If the Prime Minister *had* found time to visit my constituency he would . . .', thereby introducing any issue which takes his fancy.

This added greatly to the stress and intensity of the preparation required in No. 10 on PMQ days. Yet the process came to be fashioned into an instrument of prime ministerial power. For it gave a Prime Minister a valid (and unanswerable) reason for asking about any aspect of a department's activity in case a question was put on it.[109] It was an irony that an increase in prime ministerial accountability to Parliament after 1961 strengthened the possibility of an overmighty premiership.

One of Tony Blair's first acts, without consulting Parliament, which had still to meet,[110] was to announce that henceforth he would take questions only once a week on Wednesdays for half an hour.

ORGANIZATIONAL AND EFFICIENCY QUESTIONS

Organization and senior staffing of No. 10 and the Cabinet Office

This is the locus of prime ministerial power, the core of the core executive and what a former head of the Central Policy Review Staff, Sir Kenneth Berrill, has called the 'horseshoe of power' that embraces No. 10 and the

Cabinet Office.[111] All debates about what the former Cabinet Secretary, Lord Hunt, called the 'hole in the centre'[112] and the desirability or otherwise of a Prime Minister's Department, have to do with this patch, its configuration and the relationships within it.

The way the horseshoe is fashioned strongly reflects a premier's wishes. There are, however, some fixed points:

(a) The job of Cabinet Secretary has seemed safe from abolition since Sir Warren Fisher of the Treasury (who wanted his department to absorb the Cabinet Office) was seen off by the Cabinet Secretary, Sir Maurice Hankey, after Lloyd George had been replaced by Bonar Law in 1922.[113]

(b) Until May 1997, it similarly seemed unlikely that the job of Principal Private Secretary to the Prime Minister would be prised out of the hands of the career Civil Service after Vansittart had replaced Waterhouse, as we have seen, in 1928.

(c) Though Mrs Thatcher initially thought she could dispense with them,[114] no Prime Minister could operate without a Cabinet committee structure of some kind, unless all pretence at collective responsibility were abandoned.

(d) The No. 10 Policy Unit, created by Harold Wilson in 1974, had by the mid to late 1990s acquired the air of a permanent fixture.

That quartet apart, the 'horseshoe' is to a large extent the plaything of the Prime Minister of the day, who can reshape it quite substantially to meet his or her particular interests and style of working.

Size of the Cabinet; workload on ministers and the Civil Service; the overall efficiency of government

This is a huge area. 'Overload' is a theme deserving a book on its own.[115] And many of the constituent problems which together make a peculiarly malign compound have a perpetual and a repetitive air about them. The size of the Cabinet is a classic example. The files of the postwar Prime Ministers are replete with briefs on how to trim the size of the Cabinet, starting with Churchill's construction of his 'Caretaker Cabinet' in May 1945 (he had the idea of keeping the Lord Chancellor out to get the number down to 16),[116] through to Wilson's wrestling in October 1964 with ministerial numbers. (These burst the limits prescribed by the Ministerial Salaries Act 1957 with eight secretaries of state, seventy ministers in all, and no fewer than twenty other statutes ranging from the Succession to the Crown Act 1707 to the Defence (Transfer of Functions) Act 1964.)[117] Several postwar premiers had a similar stab at the problem of numbers, usually with limited temporary success.[118]

The difficulty with the stress/overload factor is that even if others suggest an attack upon it (as Norman Brook did to Macmillan a few weeks after he became Prime Minister),[119] only a premier can initiate the thinking required and take action on the basis of such inquiries. All too often since 1945 such efforts have run into the Whitehall sand because, ironically, the pressure of events has shoved them off immediate or priority agendas.[120] This is one of those problems of government that only the PM can reach; if he or she is not minded so to do, paralysis results and the status quo creaks on.

The overall efficiency of the secret services; their operations and their oversight

The Prime Minister is the only minister who can lead the entire UK intelligence and security effort. Only he or she is in a position to take a complete overview and, therefore, to provide the oversight since the Joint Intelligence Committee was removed from the Chiefs of Staff in 1957 and brought under the purview of the Cabinet Office, partly to enhance the flow of intelligence to ministers.[121] A small group of ministers have received what became the famous 'Red Book', the 'Weekly Intelligence Summary' provided by the Joint Intelligence Committee. Copy No. 1 goes to the Queen, who is its longest continuous reader, having received her first edition in February 1952 – she is, and always has been, interested in it and asks her intelligence chiefs very astute questions on the basis of what she has read in it.[122]

The full summary, like all intelligence and security material, is kept to the smallest number of readers who 'need to know' in Whitehall parlance, for fear of leaks. But the Prime Minister has, in addition to the 'Red Book', his or her individual feed in the special box known as 'Old Stripey' from the red band in its blue leather carapace.[123] And each intelligence chief has the right of personal access to the premier.[124] Here, too, Prime Ministers have acquired an indispensability; the most delicate special operations have to be cleared with the Prime Minister.[125] Most premiers love this side of their work – so much more exciting than dealing with local government finance.

The creation, abolition and merger of government departments

Some premiers relish this. Harold Wilson in his 1960s premierships was particularly keen on tinkering with departmental boundaries as an accompaniment to his reshuffles. They are mainly achieved by statutory instruments through dissolution orders or transfer of functions orders. But a surprising number of departments enjoy (or have enjoyed) a statutory existence, the most notable of today's crop being the Ministry of Defence (which acquired this status partly because it was given certain executive powers).[126]

Preparation of the 'War Book'

Supervisory though this function may be, it is important both traditionally (Balfour made it part of the Prime Minister's portfolio) and currently. Since the early days of the Committee of Imperial Defence plans have been in existence for the transition to serious and large-scale wars that would require not just a widespread mobilization of the armed forces but also the transformation of the Whitehall machine. They are updated routinely and, very occasionally, they require sudden and substantial rethinking. For example, the sudden demise of the Soviet Union and the military apparatus organized under the old Warsaw Pact left Whitehall's contingency planners at a loss. Far from a 'new world order' materializing, as President Bush had predicted in 1991,[127] a high level of fluidity ensued which meant there would be no return to any kind of steady state for the foreseeable future. So from the fall of the Berlin Wall until the mid 1990s, there was a hiatus in War Book work which began to be put right only in the later Major years.[128] The Central War Plans Secretariat, a joint Ministry of Defence/Cabinet Office enterprise (housed in the Cabinet Office from its creation in 1954), had long since gone as a separate entity with important prime ministerial input.[129] In the 1990s the responsibility belonged to the Overseas and Defence Secretariat in the Cabinet Office.[130] The work has always been immensely sensitive; even with the ending of the Cold War and a new climate of openness for public records, the Ministry of Defence was not able to meet my request in the mid 1990s for the complete declassification of a post 1945 War Book.[131]

Contingency planning of other kinds

Much of this is delegated to the Home Secretary. Important permanent machinery exists in the Cabinet Office to cope with the emergencies that arise from strikes which hit the essentials of life (such as water, heat and light) and intense, individual terrorist incidents (such as the Iranian Embassy siege of 1980). Again, it is a sub-activity of the Cabinet Office's Overseas and Defence Secretariat, the most important body for the sustenance of essential services (whatever the cause of their disruption) being the Civil Contingencies Unit. As the occasion demands, this unit can transform itself instantly into a mixed committee of ministers, officials, the military, the police and the security services with the Home Secretary in the chair[132] (though there were worrying signs of a downgrading of this work in the Cabinet Office following the death of its Secretary, Brigadier Tony Budd, in 1997).[133]

Overall efficiency of the government's media strategy

Usually this is delegated to another minister on a day-to-day basis. Willie Whitelaw took on the task for Mrs Thatcher in the 1980s and Michael Heseltine for John Major after assuming the job of Deputy Prime Minister in 1995. Peter Mandelson's role as Minister without Portfolio in 1997 probably aroused more media attention than any of the new government's jobs during its first 'hundred days' apart from Mr Blair's, and Blair's Press Secretary, Alistair Campbell, achieved the status of a bespoke biography in the autumn 1999.[134] The Prime Minister's Press Secretary, however, is always an influential figure, and in Bernard Ingham's time with Mrs Thatcher the job of Press Secretary was combined with that of Head of the Government Information Service.

It is, of course, utterly misleading to conceive of this as a mechanical or a straightforward function. The 1990s saw a burgeoning of what William Waldegrave rightly called 'the media-political complex . . . by which we are ruled',[135] to a degree that seemed unimaginable – not just in the Attlee–Churchill era but even in the Macmillan–Wilson days (and these two were on their day no mean manipulators of the media).

Richard Eyre, then director of the Royal National Theatre, invited by the *Financial Times* to 'review the acts of the players' during the 1997 general election campaign, concluded that since the days of Churchill and Attlee

all politics has declined to the condition of show business, and all politicians have been obliged to become performers. They choose their costumes carefully, their decor fastidiously; their fellow actors and their agents; they study their scripts, they rehearse, they put on make-up and they give performances; they adapt their acting styles from the would-be intimacy of the small screen to the not-to-be-avoided histrionics of the public platform; and sometimes, often disastrously, they improvise.[136]

Allowing for a slight degree of exaggeration, this fitted the picture of not just electoral politics but of the politics of government, too. By the change of administration in 1997, sensitivity towards the media had infected governmental life so deeply and comprehensively that its contagion affected and distorted virtually every aspect. In many ways, this represented the largest single change in the day-to-day conduct of the premiership. Mr Attlee would not only have found the media life of Mr Blair incredible, he would have recoiled from it absolutely. Indeed, he almost certainly could not have existed within it. No winnable Labour seat would have selected such a modest, unassuming, non-media friendly figure as their prospective parliamentary candidate. The man who, in many ways, set the gold standard against which other postwar premiers have been judged simply would not have been a contender in late-twentieth-century politics. He would not have passed the first hurdle. Even John Major shone by comparison.

BUDGETS AND MARKET-SENSITIVE ECONOMIC DECISIONS

The Budget

Budgets are an overblown ritual. Bundling a ragbag of measures together under a financial wrapping was a clever Gladstonian device for slipping changes through on a crude, take-it-or-leave-it basis – as useful for dragooning ministerial colleagues as for applying the brute force of the whipped vote in Parliament. Given the degree to which ministers (other than the Chancellor of the Exchequer and the Prime Minister) are excluded from the Budget-making process, it has been since the 1850s a kind of institutionalized breach of the collective nature of Cabinet government, which the short-lived combined Budgets of the Major years after 1993 (with a much more collective input into the public expenditure component) only partially filled.

The taking of market-sensitive decisions

Here, more even than nuclear weapons policy or intelligence (which usually have their own Cabinet committees), one used to find the secret garden of the governing system. The post-1992 changes opened the gates to the arguments conducted inside that garden a month after they have been concluded, when the minutes were published of the Chancellor's exchanges with the Governor of the Bank of England. Until May 1997, prime ministers and chancellors together determined the procedures and the outcomes and, to an extraordinary extent, Cabinets put up with it.

All this changed out of the blue on 6 May 1997, five days after the general election which carried Tony Blair into No. 10 and Gordon Brown into the Treasury. With only the other two members of the 'Big Four', Prescott and Cook in the know[137] (and the decision was Blair's and Brown's, not theirs), it was announced that henceforth the Bank of England would be given the power to set interest rates as a matter of 'operational responsibility', subject only to government override at a time of national crisis.[138] As interest rates since 1979 had become government's chief instrument for manipulating the domestic economy, this was a change of the first magnitude and a rare example of power shifting from that tightest of nexi – the PM/Chancellor relationship – to, in this instance, a Bank of England Monetary Policy Committee consisting of the Governor of the Bank plus eight others[139] (who proceeded, once convened, to raise interest rates no fewer than four times during the Blair government's first 'hundred days').[140]

SPECIAL FOREIGN, DEFENCE AND EUROPEAN FUNCTIONS

There are certain matters which can only be managed at the highest political level. Probably the most important continuous or regular example has to do with the special intelligence relationship with the United States (which dates from the secret UKUSA Treaty of 1948) and the special nuclear relationship (which was restored in 1958 after a twelve-year disruption, on most if not quite all atomic matters). These very practical relationships tend to purr on whatever the personal chemistry between the President and Prime Minister of the day, though each President on arrival looks at such relationships anew and any changes to them have to be handled at the top.

As a senior British insider put it when the government changed in 1997: 'There is still no other European country that has the capacity to provide intelligence on a global basis and the nuclear element continues to be very basic to the [US–UK] relationship. It ticks on and the British have been very shrewd in ensuring that the nuclear and intelligence relationships, and all that is associated with them, depend on reaffirmations by Presidents and Prime Ministers.'[141] Just occasionally, rare examples of these highly secret reaffirmations reach the surface at the Public Record Office. In 1997, for example, the exchange of letters between the newly installed President Kennedy and Harold Macmillan on the 'operational control' of the joint decision process governing the launch of US Polaris missiles from submarines in UK territorial waters, turned up in a Cabinet Office file on 'Nuclear deterrent policy'.

'Our understanding', Kennedy told Macmillan, 'on the use of British bases is that the President and the Prime Minister will reach a joint decision by speaking personally with each other before certain forces equipped with US nuclear weapons and operating from bases in the United Kingdom will use nuclear weapons . . . There is a second, more general understanding with the British that we will consult with them before using nuclear weapons anywhere, if possible' (this last pledge was given by Eisenhower first in 1953 and more recently in October 1960 with the proviso that it was 'not intended to be used publicly').[142]

Representing the UK at summits of all kinds

The frequency and importance of such gatherings has added powerfully to the proportion of prime ministerialism within the governing collective, whatever a premier's place on the spectrum of collegiality. For example, deals struck in the small hours at European Councils or Inter-Governmental Conferences require a great deal of discretion, and effective decision-making power to be placed in the hands of a Prime Minister. Of course, he or she is subject to Cabinet discussion once home and must report to Parliament. It was, after all, Mrs Thatcher's failure to carry her Cabinet with her on her hardening line towards further European economic and monetary integration after the Rome summit of November 1990 which began the rapid sequence of events that led to her resignation as Prime Minister. Such European events made much of the more volatile domestic political weather in the UK of the 1990s, and preparing for summits, negotiating a way through them and managing their consequences in many ways set the rhythm of a premier's life.[143]

The use of Her Majesty's armed forces in action

This is such a special, important and revealing activity that it deserves to be dealt with separately, which it is in chapter 6.

Making or annulling of treaties; recognizing or unrecognizing of countries

These activities usually involve the Cabinet or its overseas and defence policy committee. But the Prime Minister and the Foreign Secretary are the ministers most closely concerned. And here, the royal prerogative is all. Unless primary legislation is required, Parliament does not have to be routinely involved at all. There is one exception: the only concession the Union of Democratic Control (a political pressure group which argued that secret diplomacy had been largely responsible for triggering the Great War and that public opinion might curb such excesses if only it knew what was happening) won from the Labour government of 1924, after a long campaign, was the so called 'Ponsonby Rule', whereby treaties must be laid before the House of Commons for twenty-one parliamentary days before they take effect.[144] All this means, in reality, is that the treaty is placed in the House of Commons Library where MPs can read it.

Launching a UK nuclear strike

Only the Prime Minister can activate the codes that do this. It is, as both Alec Home[145] and Jim Callaghan[146] told me and as a late-1960s Chief of Staff file makes plain,[147] a purely prime ministerial function. The launching of a Trident missile, very possibly the last act a British Prime Minister would take, would settle once and for all the great debate about prime ministerial versus Cabinet government. (Sometimes I feel nothing else will.) Since Ted Heath's time, a Prime Minister's wishes would prevail from his or her grave. Should he or she be wiped out by a bolt from the blue, the Royal Navy commander of whichever Trident submarine is then on patrol in the North Atlantic, after some days of scanning the air waves for signs of life back home (the failure to pick up the BBC *Today* programme for a few days is regarded as the ultimate test),[148] will, accompanied by his executive officer, open the sealed instructions which that Prime Minister must make ready within a few days of taking office. (The choice, crudely put by one insider, is 'let them have it' or 'sail to New Zealand if it's still there'.)[149] These instructions are perhaps the greatest secret of all, for on them depends the whole theory of the British version of nuclear deterrence (always assuming that the Trident commander *would* obey prime ministerial instructions from the grave).

Their nuclear briefing in 'PINDAR', the secret operations room deep beneath the Ministry of Defence, marks the moment, I suspect, when new Prime Ministers first fully appreciate the dreadful (in the proper sense of the word) responsibilities which fall upon them. Tony Blair went through his initiation during the middle of his first full week as premier.[150] Three weeks later he told a ceremony in Paris to mark the signing of the Founding Act on Mutual Relations, Co-operation and Security between NATO and Russia that 'ours is the first generation able to contemplate the possibility that we may live our entire lives without going to war or sending our children to war'.[151] Like all his predecessors, Blair must have had a sense of what it might be like if he ever had to tread for real the 'secret' corridor under Whitehall which links No. 10 and the Cabinet Office with PINDAR.

The Prime Ministerial Files

The mid-1990s warehouse of prime ministerial functions is awesomely large. Most involve a high degree of indispensability. It is, too, a warehouse filled with 'kegs of political dynamite', to borrow a phrase of the former Home Office civil servant, Robert Hazell.[152] Yet it strikes me that still more detail is needed on the prime ministerial workload, especially if the qualitative and quantitative changes since Attlee are to be appreciated. Range of activity is one thing; frequency is quite another. What actually passed over prime ministerial desks is the next puzzle to be pondered, and the key lies in the Public Record Office, at least until the Thirty-Year Rule ceases to bite.

Mercifully, the PRO has allocated special classes for Prime Ministers' subject papers in the postwar period – PREM 8 for Attlee; PREM 11 for the four Conservative Prime Ministers between 1951 and 1964; and PREM 13 for Wilson onwards. Culling and categorizing them has proved a revealing and fascinating exercise but, before exposing the results, I must come clean about its crudities. These are of two main kinds: not every file that crossed the PM's desk is to be found within the bounds of these PREM classes. Some of them are scattered across various Cabinet Office categories; the intelligence material, an occasional mistake and JIC assessment apart, has been stripped from the PREM series for the postwar period leaving no trace, for example, of the regular flow of so-called 'CX' reports from the Secret Intelligence Service.[153] (Though a dash of scepticism is needed here. One former Cabinet Secretary has confessed to me that he would sometimes place the magic letters – 'CX' – on a brief he particularly wanted a busy PM to read in the certain knowledge that it would have the desired effect.)[154]

Secondly, my categorizations of files by type are necessarily imperfect. For instance, sometimes material dealing with atomic weapons is best placed under the heading of 'Defence'. At other times it fits more accurately under the caption 'Foreign Policy (USA)'. Others, might have chosen a different variety of label to affix. Some subject headings carry different meanings in different periods: Ireland in the late 1940s, for example, had largely to do with the South's eventual abandonment in 1949 of dominion status within the British Commonwealth for independent republican status. Northern Ireland until 1966–68 usually meant trade and industry policy as opposed to terrorism and security.

With those qualifications in mind, here is the result. Let us take first Mr Attlee's tally for 1948 (table 1).[155] I chose 1948 as the year to measure because the comparisons I wish to make are, relatively speaking, for peacetime years and I wanted to move beyond the immediate shadow of World War II, some of whose unfinished business might have produced an abnormal workload. Distortions there are, of course, in 1948. For example, the leading category by volume, Imperial/Commonwealth, is distended by the transfer of power in the sub-continent. India accounts for 25 of those 54 items.

Apart from the overall total of 215 files (some of which, as with the whole twelve months surveyed, ran on from previous years), what is striking is the preponderance even in peacetime of foreign, defence and imperial concerns as an absorber of prime ministerial attention. Imperial and Commonwealth matters alone outstripped the Economic/Industrial/Regulatory category at a time of considerable shift in the public sector and the continuing transfer of industry to a peacetime footing. The Domestic Policy items, too, are surprisingly low in number during a year when

Table 1
Prime Minister's Office: papers and correspondence (individual files); Clement Attlee, 1948

Rank	Category	No.
1	Imperial/Commonwealth	54
2	Economic/Industrial/Regulatory	42
3	Defence	39
4	Foreign policy (excluding USA and Middle East)	26
5	Whitehall/Ministerial/Constitutional/Parliamentary	18
6	Domestic policy	14
7	Security/Intelligence	5
8=	Foreign policy (USA)	4
8=	Foreign policy (Middle East)	4
8=	Monarchy	4
11=	Trades Unions/Strikes/Pay	2
11=	Ireland (excluding NI)	2
13	Party matters (Lab.)	1
	Total	215

the last big piece of the postwar welfare state – the National Health Service – was put into place.

Let us turn now to the supposedly relatively hands-off premiership of Winston Churchill (table 2).[156] Churchill was re-elected in 1951, partly on a ticket of reducing the waste and bureaucracy of what he liked to depict as a socialist government.[157] (This is not the place to debate just how 'socialist' were the policies of the Attlee government.) I have taken 1952, the first full year of his last premiership, as my test-bed. There are distortions here too, chiefly in the Monarchy category: following George VI's death in February 1952, considerable effort went into preparing for the coronation of Elizabeth II, a matter in which Churchill took an intense personal interest.[158]

But look at that total: 314 items, up 46 per cent on Attlee's tally four years earlier. The primacy of Defence is no surprise; it was Churchill's

Table 2
Prime Minister's Office: papers and correspondence (individual files); Winston Churchill, 1952

			1948	
Rank	Category	No.	No.	Rank
1	Defence	66	39	3
2	Economic/Industrial/Regulatory	65	42	2
3	Foreign policy (excluding USA and Middle East)	53	26	4
4	Whitehall/Ministerial/Constitutional/Parliamentary	38	18	5
5=	Domestic policy	20	14	6
5=	Security/Intelligence	20	5	7
7	Foreign policy (Middle East)	17	4	8=
8	Monarchy	14	4	8=
9	Imperial/Commonwealth	10	54	1
10	Foreign policy (USA)	9	4	8=
11	Trades Unions/Strikes/Pay	2	2	11=
12	Ireland (excluding NI)	0	2	11=
13	Party matters	0	1	13
	Totals	314	215	
	Percentage increase	1948–52 = 46%		

great preoccupation. Foreign Policy (USA) is surprisingly low, given the immense importance he placed on restoring the 'special relationship' which he thought had decayed under Attlee, in nuclear collaboration especially.[159]

Lord Salisbury, the great nineteenth-century Marquess (not 'Bobbety', who resigned ostensibly over the return of Makarios to Cyprus in 1957),[160] would have been fascinated to observe the remorseless rise of prime ministerial activity over the six years from Churchill in 1952 to Macmillan's first full year in 1958 (table 3),[161] given Britain's decreasing influence in the world post-Suez, and given Salisbury's distrust of expert advice in particular[162] and his scepticism about government intervention in general. The Suez shadow is pronounced here, with Foreign Policy

Table 3

Prime Minister's Office: papers and correspondence (individual files); Harold Macmillan, 1958

			1952		1948	
Rank	Category	No.	No.	Rank	No.	Rank
1	Foreign policy (excluding USA and Middle East)	75	53	3	26	4
2	Imperial/Commonwealth	58	10	9	54	1
3	Foreign policy (Middle East)	43	17	7	4	8=
4	Economic/Industrial/Regulatory	42	65	2	42	2
5	Defence	41	66	1	39	3
6	Whitehall/Ministerial/Constitutional/ Parliamentary	40	38	4	18	5
7	Domestic policy	20	20	5=	14	6
8	Foreign policy (USA)	14	9	10	4	8=
9	Monarchy	9	14	8	4	8=
10	Trades Unions/Strikes/Pay	8	2	11	2	11=
11	Security/Intelligence	6	20	5=	5	7
12	Party matters (Con. 1; Lab. 2)	3	0		1	13
13	Ireland (excluding NI)	1	0		2	11=
	Totals	360	314		215	
	Percentage increases	1948–58 = 67%; 1952–58 = 15%				

(Middle East) in third place, though Defence has tailed off from its Churchillian pre-eminence.

It was the release of the 1965 files for Harold Wilson's first full year as Prime Minister which stimulated the idea of this exercise for there had, quite plainly, been an explosion of activity since the late 1950s. The tally of files was up 63 per cent on Macmillan's 1958 figure, 87 per cent on Churchill's 1952 accumulation and a staggering 173 per cent on his Labour predecessor's score seventeen years earlier (table 4).[163] Part of the inflation can be attributed to the Rhodesia crisis (34 of those Imperial/Commonwealth files dealt with it). Wilson's delight in tinkering with the machinery of government and its minders makes the Whitehall/Ministerial/Constitutional/Parliamentary figure understandably, if unusually, high.

Wilson, as we shall see, was an 'almost a natural generator of "overload"'[164] – a very high price to pay for his determination to turn No. 10 from an alleged 'monastery' into a putative 'powerhouse'.[165]

Crude though these file-based comparisons are (not least because Downing Street private secretaries vary in how material is categorized and presented to their Prime Ministers), they do, I think, amount to a new and useful indicator of 'overload'. To the best of my knowledge, they have not been compiled in the UK before, nor does my friend Professor Richard Neustadt think there is anything comparable for the US presidency in the postwar period.[166] Their value is demonstrated by the itch I have for the impossible – access to the files of successive Prime Ministers since yesterday. For the period in which the archival treasure has still to reach the Public Record Office we are very much in the dark in terms of detail. Though from several conversations with retired and serving ministers and officials I have acquired the firm impression that the weight of material passing across a premier's desk continued to expand in the 1970s, 1980s and 1990s, despite periodic attempts to ease it.

Wilson afforded one last beam of insight for the twilight of his final premiership. As befitted a former President of the Royal Statistical Society,[167] he published in *The Governance of Britain* an analysis of his diary for the period 1 October to 31 December 1975 (table 5).[168]

Rather plaintively, Wilson added: 'Christmas apart, I was not able to record a single private or social engagement.'[169]

There is nothing comparable in Mrs Thatcher's *The Downing Street Years*. All we get is the following passage (though it's a quite revealing one):

Table 4

Prime Minister's Office: papers and correspondence (individual files); Harold Wilson, 1965

Rank	Category	No.	1958 No.	1958 Rank	1952 No.	1952 Rank	1948 No.	1948 Rank
1	Imperial/ Commonwealth	117	58	2	10	9	54	1
2	Whitehall/Ministerial/ Constitutional/ Parliamentary	110	40	6	38	4	18	5
3	Economic/Industrial/ Regulatory	102	42	4	65	2	42	2
4	Foreign policy (excluding USA and Middle East)	93	75	1	53	3	26	4
5	Domestic policy	52	20	7	20	5=	14	6
6	Foreign policy (USA)	38	14	8	9	10	4	8=
7	Defence	37	41	5	66	1	39	3
8	Trades Unions/Strikes/ Pay	10	8	10	2	11	2	11=
9	Foreign policy (Middle East)	9	43	3	17	7	4	8=
10	Monarchy	8	9	9	14	8	4	8=
11	Security/Intelligence	6	6	11	20	5=	5	7
12	Party matters (Con. 1; Lab. 2)	3	3	12	0		1	13
13	Ireland (excluding NI)	1	1	13	0		2	11=
	Totals	586	360		314		215	
	Percentage increases 1958–65 = 63%		1948–65 = 173%; 1952–65 = 87%;					

The hours at No. 10 are long. I never minded this. There was an intensity about the job of being Prime Minister which made sleep seem a luxury. In any case, over the years I had trained myself to do with about four hours a night. The Private Office too would often be working till 11 o'clock at night. We were so few that

Table 5

Pattern of prime ministerial business, 1 October to 31 December 1975

Rank	Category	No.
1	Ministerial meetings (excluding Cabinet or Cabinet committees)	43
2	Meetings with industry, prominent industrialists etc.	28
3	Official meetings (unspecified)	27
4	Cabinet committee	24
5	Official lunches and dinners	20
6	Ministerial speeches	17
7	Visits within Britain	13
8=	Cabinet meetings	11
8=	Political meetings (no speech)	11
10	Political speeches	9
11=	Audiences of the Queen	8
11=	Receiving foreign VIPs	8
11=	TV or radio broadcasts (excluding party conference)	8
14	Visits by heads of government	5
15	Visits abroad	2
16=	Visits to Northern Ireland	1
16=	State visits	1
	Total	236

there was no possibility of putting work on someone else's desk. This sort of atmosphere helps to produce a remarkably happy team, as well as a formidably efficient one. People are under great pressure, and there is no time for trivia. All the effort was to go into getting the work done.[170]

'No time for trivia'; a deliciously Thatcherian phrase. It is striking how, over a period of thirteen years (which is the gap between the two most dramatic and highly unusual insights into the most secret processes of 1980s policy-making: the Franks Report of 1982[171] and the Scott Report of 1996[172]) just how *little* (especially in the case of arms and equipment to Iraq; less so the Falklands) reached prime ministerial level in No. 10 at the time for all the attention they demanded and got from Mrs Thatcher (in the case of the Falklands) and Mr Major (on arms to Iraq) at a later stage.

It is worth dwelling on another aspect of Mrs Thatcher's premiership which underscores a central aspect of the job of Prime Minister – the linking of the party political with the administrative in the business of government. Mrs Thatcher would constantly remind her ministerial colleagues that she, as Prime Minister, felt herself 'the guardian of the strategy' – hence her habit of intervening early and often in ministerial discussions.[173] Guarding a government's overall strategy has been a key function of all postwar premiers, whether they were overly intrusive in the Cabinet Room or not. It was – is – a function which falls into every PM's lap. No one else can be expected to do it, even if they are designated 'Deputy Prime Minister' with co-ordination and Cabinet committee functions, as was R. A. Butler in 1962–63[174] and more so Michael Heseltine in 1995–97.[175]

This requires premiers to be kept up to speed on a huge range of matters – some issues which, in the end, only they can handle; many more issues of such magnitude that they invoke questions of collective responsibility at their most intense; and finally the kind of issues that could steal up on government suddenly and, sometimes (for example – again – the Falklands) in a way that can threaten a premier's, even an administration's, survival. The dilemma of the job of Prime Minister is that its holders must be selective in their detailed interventions yet constantly sensitive to virtually the whole range of government activity (a theme to which I shall return in chapter 20).

The federal nature of Whitehall demands a high degree of policy devolution from the centre, but it has to be a knowledgeable and essentially sympathetic form of devolution. As Ferdinand Mount (a man with direct experience of No. 10 life as the head of Mrs Thatcher's Policy Unit in 1982–83) put it in his marvellously sensitive novel based on the life of Lord Aberdeen, 'George [as Prime Minister] encouraged and nudged and approved [Gladstone at the Treasury, Palmerston at the Home Office and Wood at the India Office]. These were not his fields, but he was happy to lean on the gate and watch them grow.'[176] This was as true of Whitehall in the late 1990s as it was in the 1850s.

The PREM files for the post-1945 period show, too, an intriguing and important linkage with the wider analysis of the centre of central government – the so-called 'core executive' approach – developed by British political scientists over the past decade. As one of its leading lights, Rod Rhodes, has written, it is time to get away from 'the textbook Prime Minister'[177] (by which he means an over-concentration upon what happens in No. 10 Downing Street) and into the wider realms of a premiership in the context of that 'core executive' which he describes as 'all those organisations and procedures which co-ordinate central government policies, and act as final arbiters of conflict between different parts of the government machine'.[178] An historian's trawl through the Prime Minister's Office files at any point in the postwar period would illustrate just such linkages and processes in routine abundance though, as the differences between the Franks and Scott reports underline, it would be wrong to think that all powerlines and every delicate issue find their way automatically into No. 10.

What does find its way into No. 10 – constantly and relentlessly – is politics. The analysis of the job of Prime Minister in this chapter has concentrated on the governmental and not the party functions. But get the party politics wrong and the whole apparatus can be removed from your hands at a speed which surprises the rest of the world – as happened to Mrs Thatcher in November 1990 (though the elaborate, all-party ballot required to choose a Labour leader in the age of one member, one vote means the hold on power of a Labour Prime Minister could be much surer than his Conservative counterpart).

Party is a constant factor for all premiers. And, as a retired permanent secretary put it as the premiership was about to change hands in 1997, leverage of your party is a resource that premiers must husband carefully. Prime Ministers, he explained, 'possess a limited amount of credit with their parties. If they are really determined they can usually whip their MPs through the division lobbies on a particular issue. But if, as Major did on the Maastricht vote in 1993, they use up their capital beyond a certain point, they are never quite the same again.'[179]

The way premiers manage the party factor is very revealing of them and their style of politics and, naturally, it fluctuates according to circumstances. I shall examine it as part of the treatment of individual tenures which follows. It cannot be isolated from the governing functions or administrative processes upon which I have concentrated in this chapter. This was illustrated neatly by another experienced former permanent secretary at a private seminar just before Easter 1997 which, among other things, examined the perils that awaited Tony Blair if, as the signs strongly indicated, he adopted a command rather than a collective approach to the premiership. 'Cabinet government,' he said, 'has been failing over the past eighteen years because Mrs Thatcher didn't want it and John Major has not had a chance to run it.'[180]

It is the last part of this judgement – 'not had a chance to run it' – which is both interesting and significant, because John Major was firmly at the collegial end of the spectrum as a chairman of Cabinet. Yet the fissiparous tendencies within his Cabinet Room, especially on European matters, which (to borrow Lord Denning's famous metaphor on the Treaty of Rome) was a constantly 'incoming tide' flowing up nearly every estuary of policy,[181] prevented him from leading successfully through a collective approach. The preconditions of collegiality simply were not present. His 'put up, or shut-up' self-inflicted leadership challenge in 1995 was designed to engineer these preconditions but that, too, failed. In Norman Lamont's bitter words (echoing A. J. P. Taylor on MacDonald's first Labour government)[182] he all too often gave the impression of being 'in office but not in power'.[183]

Yet Major demonstrated a powerful grip on the office of Prime Minister despite the appearance of external weakness to which Lamont alluded. He defied for over four and a half years (from Black Wednesday, 16 September 1992 to his loss of office on 2 May 1997) Churchill's iron law of premiership and party leadership: 'The loyalties which centre upon number one are enormous. If he trips he must be sustained. If he makes mistakes they must be covered. If he sleeps he must not be wantonly disturbed. If he is no good he must be pole-axed.'[184]

'If he is no good' – a phrase as imprecise as it is haunting for any individual taking on the premiership. Can anyone be expected to be 'good' at it in modern circumstances? Do those relentless demands – the great bundle of tasks that now fall into a premier's lap, the constant and often excruciating attention of the media, the demands of party management, the intermingling of the domestic, the European and the international, not to mention Macmillan's 'events' – mean, as one of the most seasoned of postwar Cabinet Office hands put it, that the job of Prime Minister is now 'beyond any mortal'?[185] The pole-axe in Churchill's metaphor seems perpetually to hover. Churchill, of course, was referring to premiership in conditions of war.

No strand of the warp and woof of the modern British premiership I have just described has been as taut or as important as every other during successive phases of the past fifty and more years. But the individual tapestries spun by each incumbent can only be appreciated and understood in the context of a wider backcloth. For like the England of George Orwell's *The Lion and the Unicorn*, 'There is something distinctive and recognisable'[186] about the job of Prime Minister, however much the personalities and the externalities pummel and pound it.

Even during the most intense pounding imaginable, nuclear war, the Whitehall planners' assumption was 'that some political control must be maintained for as long as possible in the days preceding the outbreak ... and must be revived as soon as possible after the initial period of devastation ...' Political control in such a context meant 'supreme control' by an effective Prime-Minister-as-war-leader, backed up by a small 'War Cabinet'.[187] Armed conflicts, even those well short of total war, can be the makers or the breakers of a Prime Minister. Aberrational rarities though war or limited war premierships might be, they are great revealers of individual Prime Ministers and of the powers and constraints latent in the job.

6

Where the Buck Stops: Premiers, 'War Cabinets' and Nuclear War Planning Since 1945

'Everybody knows that the system won't produce by itself effective executive control, and what is required is the right kind of personal leadership.'
> *Sir Norman Brook, Secretary of the Cabinet, on War Cabinets, 1959*[1]

'Distant, yes; but none the less an obligation.'
> *Clement Attlee on the UK's response to the United Nations' call for assistance following the North Korean invasion of the South, 1950*[2]

'We are in an armed conflict; that is the phrase I have used. There has been no declaration of war.'
> *Sir Anthony Eden on the Suez Crisis, 1956*[3]

From the moment I heard of the invasion [of the Falkland Islands], deep anxiety was ever present.
> *Margaret Thatcher recalling the events of March–June 1982 in 1993*[4]

'It may be very nice to have the capacity [to mount an invasion of the Suez kind], but all the thinking was moving towards a major war with Russia. That was the trouble. And that meant a NATO war, and it meant that if we had the things we wanted for NATO we would inevitably not have the things we wanted for these little operations all round the world.'
> *Marshal of the Royal Air Force Sir Dermot Boyle, recalling the mid-1950s in 1987*[5]

'Grandfather [Harold Macmillan] told me that as an old man he only had nightmares about two things: the trenches in the Great War and

what would have happened if the Cuban missile crisis had gone
wrong.'   *Lord Stockton, 1998*[6]

War is an intensely prime ministerial activity. Nothing defines, or can
offer so much historical insight into, the unique role of the PM as his or
her responsibilities and powers during war or the preparations for it.
'The nuclear', as Harold Macmillan liked to call it,[7] has underlined this
powerfully since November 1953, when the first British atomic weapon,
the Blue Danube bomb, was delivered to Bomber Command's Armament
School at RAF Wittering alongside the A1 near Peterborough.[8] As a top
secret internal RAF paper on the 'initiation and control of nuclear strikes'
put it during the Macmillan premiership in 1962: 'The decision to use
nuclear weapons is reserved to the Prime Minister or his designated deputy.
Adequate arrangements have been made for the Prime Minister or his
designated deputy to be continuously available in a period of tension to
receive information . . . and to give decisions.'[9] And, as we saw in the
previous chapter, arrangements have been in place since Ted Heath's time
for a Prime Minister's wishes to be available to Royal Navy commanders
on Polaris and later Trident submarines in the event of a pre-emptive
strike eliminating the premier before instructions could be transmitted.

But it is not just the contingency of World War III (or any conflict that
might involve an exchange of nuclear weapons) which sees the buck
stopping with the Prime Minister, to adapt the famous motto inscribed
on the wooden plaque which rested on President Harry Truman's desk in
the White House between 1945 and 1953.[10] So-called 'limited' wars such
as in Korea, Suez, the Falklands and the Gulf have tested prime ministerial
mettle and revealed much about their styles of government under duress.
'Near War' committees, like the one which Attlee used during the Berlin
crisis of 1948 or the plethora of groups Wilson spawned in the early days
of the Southern Rhodesian unilateral declaration of independence after
November 1965, also need to feature in any treatment of a premier's
stewardship, and will do so in the chapters on individual Prime Ministers
which follow.

The special nature of this aspect of the job and the importance of past
practice to it was vividly, if privately, illustrated in Mrs Thatcher's flat in
No. 10 Downing Street on Sunday 4 April 1982 and in her room at the
House of Commons the following Tuesday afternoon during the early
phase of the Falklands crisis. Her visitor on what might be called 'Falklands
Sunday' was Sir Frank Cooper, Permanent Secretary to the Ministry of

Defence, who had been among the small group of officials and military men who briefed her the previous Wednesday evening when it became clear that a sizeable invasion force was on its way from Argentina to the Falkland Islands. The briefing left her, in Cooper's words, 'very shaken ... [and] ... deeply angry that this had come and there had been no warning'.[11] By the time of Cooper's Sunday meeting, the Cabinet had already agreed that a task force would be sent to the South Atlantic (they did so at a meeting on the Friday evening) and Parliament had been informed of this during the Falklands debate on the Saturday.[12]

Frank Cooper, a Spitfire pilot in World War II who joined the Air Ministry in 1948,[13] had had direct personal experience not just of nuclear planning but of virtually all the variations of War or Near War Cabinets in the post-war period. His special role in transmitting the fruits of Whitehall's folk memory of 'War Cabinets' and premiers as war leaders only came to light in a conversation in 1996 when I asked him if he knew whether, how and by whom Mrs Thatcher had been briefed on past practice. 'What nobody knows,' he said, 'is that I told her at a private lunch on the Sunday. I was ushered up to her little flat on the top floor. Carol [Thatcher] took lunch out of the fridge – a bit of ham and salad. We had a gin and she [Mrs Thatcher] asked me "How do you actually run a war?" '[14]

I asked if he had written anything down.

'No, I didn't write it down. I knew it and I said, "First, you need a small War Cabinet; second, it's got to have regular meetings come hell or high water; thirdly, you don't want a lot of bureaucrats hanging around." Then we talked about its composition.'[15]

I wondered in what sense did Sir Frank 'know it'?

'One had seen it so often in a funny sort of way ... I knew about Berlin, Korea, Malaya. We'd had Suez, which was a monumental cock-up. Cuba was different – very much a No. 10/Kennedy thing. And we'd long had this Transition to War Committee [In 1956 it was called the Defence (Transition) Committee. It became TWC in 1961.][16] which actually met at the time of Suez and was the biggest shambles of all time. The one thing I was quite clear about was that you couldn't have this bloody thing where people weren't going to take decisions.'[17]

In a later interview, Cooper elaborated still further upon his conversation with Mrs Thatcher on 'Falklands Sunday'. He stressed to her that 'the chain of command should be kept as simple as possible'.[18]

In return Mrs Thatcher 'raised some ideas of her own ... she didn't, for example, want to have too many ministers on the core group and she didn't want the Chancellor [of the Exchequer] ... She thought that the money could be too much of a distraction.'[19] Sir Frank's evidence is significant here as the idea of keeping the Treasury out of the Falklands 'War Cabinet' is usually attributed to Harold Macmillan who, as is well known, called on Mrs Thatcher just after Prime Minister's Questions the following Tuesday (6 April 1982) to be asked the same question she had asked Cooper: 'Harold, how do you run a war?'[20]

It is interesting to compare the versions of the two participants in the Macmillan–Thatcher exchange. First 'Uncle Harold', as older Tories like to call him, in conversation with Ludovic Kennedy in 1983:

MACMILLAN: I did try to help her about how to run a war because it's such a long time since anybody's run a war – I mean the technical methods of running a war – which she did very well.

KENNEDY: What were you able to draw on there in your own experience?

MACMILLAN: Well, I mean that you have to have a War Cabinet, you have to have a Committee of Chiefs of Staff, that the Secretary of the Committee of Chiefs mustn't be the Secretary of the War Cabinet. It must be the nearest thing you could get to Lord Ismay ... [Military Secretary to the War Cabinet 1939–45 and, in effect, Churchill's personal Chief of Staff] ... it was just the tip how to run it ... All of which I'd learnt from Churchill, of course.[21]

Now Mrs Thatcher's account in her memoirs of her Overseas and Defence (South Atlantic) Committee, commonly known as the Falklands 'War Cabinet':

Its exact membership and procedure were influenced by a meeting I had with Harold Macmillan who came to see me ... to offer his support and advice as the country's and the Conservative Party's senior ex-prime minister. [Reliable inside knowledge suggests that Macmillan asked to see her rather than the other way round.][22] His main recommendation was to keep the Treasury – that is Geoffrey Howe – off the main committee in charge of the campaign, the diplomacy and the aftermath. This was a wise course, but understandably Geoffrey was upset. Even so I never regretted following Harold Macmillan's advice. We were never tempted to compromise the security of our forces for financial reasons.[23]

There was, as always with Uncle Harold, slightly more to the occasion than met the eye. Macmillan did not care for Mrs Thatcher or her style of government. Seven years earlier, shortly after she had become Leader of the Opposition, he told me, 'You couldn't imagine a woman as Prime Minister if we were a first-class power . . .'[24]

On that April day in 1982 he shuffled in 'doing his old man act',[25] and gazed around the room he had come to know so well between 1957 and 1963. It was unusually empty. Mrs Thatcher was due to see a group of her backbenchers that evening and space had been made ready. 'Where's all the furniture?' said the old statesman to the new. 'You've sold it all off, I suppose.'[26]

The first question he asked her was 'Have they got the Bomb?'[27] On being told the Argentinians had not, he imparted his wisdom about keeping the Treasury out and bringing in a 'Pug' [Lord Ismay's nickname]. In fact, Whitehall could not produce an Ismay. Some figures with real fighting experience were considered, such as the former Chief of the Defence Staff, Lord Carver. But he was not a sympathetic colleague for Mrs Thatcher, being in her view 'unsound' on Trident and other defence matters.[28] So Sir Michael Palliser, the outgoing Head of the Diplomatic Service, was kept on to do the job.[29]

Privately Macmillan later expressed his ambivalence towards Mrs Thatcher on that occasion. As one of his friends said, 'His attitude towards her was a mixture of admiration and disdain: admiration because she obviously had the backbone; disdain because she should have had more background knowledge – at least 150 years, perhaps 500 years, of the history of the country concerned.'[30]

Background knowledge. That is an important theme in this context, because in April 1982, as it had for the previous fifty-four years, the Cabinet Office archive contained a rich and accruing seam of distilled wisdom about the adaptation of the United Kingdom's system of Cabinet government for the purpose of fighting wars. The first key initial document is a paper the then Secretary of the Cabinet, Sir Maurice Hankey, prepared in 1928 for the Prime Minister and the Committee of Imperial Defence (of which he was also secretary) entitled 'Supreme Control in War'.[31] In a sub-section of his draft on 'Alternative Systems for the Exercise of Supreme Control', Hankey examined the variations of 'War Cabinet' or 'War Committee' that might be used in conflicts of varying scope and severity. (Sir Frank Cooper told me he was aware when briefing Mrs Thatcher that Hankey had produced a study of war cabinets, though not of the 'limited' version of the breed.)[32]

Hankey's paper, though drafted long before the nuclear age, remains a seminal document for any treatment of the adaptation of the British

Cabinet system for warlike purposes and for the place of the Prime Minister within it. Thanks to the work of Colin Seymour-Ure in the mid 1980s[33] and more recently of some of my own students who have been plundering the riches of the Public Record Office,[34] we are moving towards a position where a respectable brief on post-1945 practice could be written for a future British Prime Minister confronted with a crisis that might lead to a serious spell of military activity of the hostile kind.

But, even now, such a briefing would have to start by going back to Hankey in 1928, drawing up the lessons of the 1914–18 Great War for future use. This review came rather late, one might think, for, as he noted in his paper, since the Armistice of 1918 the full Cabinet had been advised by a smaller group of ministers during successive crises in the Near East, Egypt, Iraq and China 'all of which involved questions affecting the fighting services; questions of high policy were reserved for the decision of the Cabinet advised by a Special Cabinet Committee, which was some-times empowered to take decisions on questions within the order of ministerial competence, without prior reference to the Cabinet'.[35]

It must be remembered that Hankey, with Lloyd George, had been instrumental in transforming the Whitehall war machinery on the demise of Asquith's premiership in December 1916.[36] By 1928 he was, by any standards, the Civil Service's supreme technician of state.[37] On such mat-ters as War Cabinets he was, quite simply, the oracle. 'Although the War Cabinet proved by far the most efficient method for the exercise of the supreme control of our war effort in the Great War', Hankey reflected ten years after its end,

it does not follow that this plan should be adopted in all wars. For example, to take an extreme case, it would be absurd to unsettle the ordinary constitutional machinery of Government by setting up a War Cabinet in order to conduct a war with Ibn Saud or the Imam! Each case must be considered on its merits by the Prime Minister of the day. It must be remembered that the appointment of a War Cabinet involves a very considerable dislocation of the ordinary machine of Government. Moreover, the exclusion of Ministers who in normal times are members of the Cabinet from the conduct of the vital affairs of the nation could never be popular among the excluded Ministers, and would only be tolerated in case of a national emergency of the very gravest kind.[38]

Hankey described four models for the supreme control of war (for the interwar Committee of Imperial Defence read, in today's circumstances, the Cabinet Committee on Overseas and Defence Policy which, like the CID of old, the Prime Minister chairs):

(A) The normal peace system, the Cabinet, advised by the Committee of Imperial Defence.

(B) The Cabinet, assisted by a Special Cabinet Committee, with powers of decision on questions within the order of ministerial competence [i.e., those ministers actually sitting on the Special Cabinet Committee], but not necessarily designated 'The War Committee'.

(C) The Cabinet, assisted by a 'War Committee' with fuller executive powers than the Cabinet Committee referred to in (B) above.

(D) A War Cabinet, which absorbs the functions of both the Cabinet and the Committee of Imperial Defence.[39]

'Whichever of the above systems is adopted,' Hankey continued, 'the Supreme Control must be provided with: (a) co-ordinated advice on questions of detail; and (b) adequate secretarial staff.'[40]

The Hankey-like wisdom which Frank Cooper conveyed to Mrs Thatcher over lunch on 'Falklands Sunday', the Lloyd George–Hankey experiences as adapted by Churchill during World War II and refined still further during a series of emergencies post-1945, represented the latest mutation in Whitehall's thinking. For example, in a highly unusual fashion for the British way of government, the law became – and remains – involved. Since the Ministry of Defence Act 1946, not just that department but the Cabinet's Defence Committee, through its various labellings and rejiggings, has been a creature of statute – the only Cabinet committee with that singular status.[41] This is an important factor as many, though not all, of the limited wars in which Britain has been engaged since 1945 have been 'run' by either the Defence Committee [Attlee and Korea] or offshoots of it, OD (SA) [Overseas and Defence (South Atlantic)] for Mrs Thatcher and the Falklands, and OPD (G) [Overseas Policy and Defence (Gulf)] for the Gulf War under Major. The one big exception is the Egypt Committee, the inner group on Suez, which did not create a happy precedent, though the disasters associated with that episode can hardly be attributed entirely to inadequacies in Eden's approach to the machinery of government at a time of intense stress. (Yet these mechanical inadequacies did undoubtedly add to the malign shambles of Whitehall in the late summer and early autumn of 1956, as we shall see in chapter 9.)

Increasing tension between East and West after 1945 also stimulated significant rethinking. As the Cold War chilled and Attlee began in 1948 to consider the outlines of a World War III War Cabinet, the new legal status of the Defence Committee presented a problem. Would it be possible to exclude regular members in the event of major war requiring a different ministerial configuration?[42] By the spring of 1951, with the Korean War raging in the Far East, Whitehall's collective mind turned once more to the possibility of total war. It was decided by Attlee that in such circumstances he would assume the job of Minister of Defence as well as Prime Minister, as Churchill had done during World War II. The then Minister of Defence, Manny Shinwell, was informed accordingly.[43] In the event of World War III erupting, Attlee would have presided over a War Cabinet of nine: Foreign Secretary, Chancellor of the Exchequer, Minister for the Co-ordination of Economic Affairs, Minister of Labour and the Home Secretary, plus up to four non-departmental ministers who would chair the War Cabinet's Committees.

All this contingency planning was very much the work of Hankey's successor-but-one, Sir Norman Brook. It was Brook, too, who advised Attlee on the creation of a fistful of War or Near War Cabinets between 1948 and 1951, the most important of which, apart from the 'doomsday' one we have just examined, were

- GEN 241, the Cabinet Committee on Germany which met between June and September 1948 to run the British end of the Berlin airlift. (This was the group chaired by Attlee but dominated by Bevin that permitted the stationing of US B-29s on East Anglian airfields, leading to an American Cold War military presence in the UK and, eventually, a nuclear one too,[44] which came to an end only in October 1996 when the F1-11 bombers of the USAAF flew out of East Anglia for the last time.)[45]
- GEN 363, the Persia Committee, again chaired by Attlee, in May 1951, to handle the crisis created by Dr Mossadegh's nationalization of the Anglo-Iranian Oil Company.[46]
- The Malaya Committee, established in March 1950, which Shinwell chaired for the purposes of closer co-ordination of the various Whitehall interests involved in the Malayan emergency.[47]
- The Defence Committee itself, which was Attlee's chief instrument for handling the Korean War from its outset until Labour lost office in October 1951.[48]

It would take another book to examine fully the details of these committees: their memberships, terms of reference and relationship to other

Cabinet committees and, above all, to the full Cabinet itself. It is, however, worth mentioning that the picture is mixed in terms of full Cabinet involvement even under a usually strong advocate of Cabinet collegiality such as Mr Attlee (especially on Berlin, as we shall see in chapter 7). Churchill, another great Cabinet government man, more so even than Attlee when it came to consulting the full Cabinet about nuclear weapons policy during his peacetime premiership (in sharp contrast to his World War II practice, as we shall see), ran Korea after October 1951 with a personal mix of government-by-committee, government-by-small-group and personal diplomacy.[49] As Paul Addison has remarked, 'One tends to forget that Churchill ran another war.'[50]

As can be seen from the Attlee and Churchill years, it is somewhat artificial to demarcate too rigidly between Near, Limited and possible Nuclear War Cabinets. The same ministers, civil servants and planners are involved in all three. But from the last months of Churchill's postwar premiership, a distinction has to be made between the World War III contingency and the rest. This became plain when Whitehall confronted the dreadful realities of thermonuclear warfare in the mid 1950s, as hydrogen bombs were at least a thousand times more powerful than atomic weapons. Their development by the United States and the Soviet Union in the early 1950s and the Churchill Cabinet's decision in the summer of 1954[51] to manufacture a British thermonuclear weapon stimulated a revolution in the scope and nature of war planning and the Prime Minister's role in it.

So I shall treat the post-1954 World War III element of the premiership separately from the limited conflicts (or near conflicts) in which Prime Ministers found themselves thereafter (which will be examined in the chapters dealing with individual premierships). There are three reasons for concentrating on 'the nuclear' in this fashion: the magnitude of the contingency; the secrecy of the planning associated with it which, until the declassifications of the 1990s, left the Public Record Office – let alone the public's perception of this side of a Prime Minister's life – virtually bereft of any substantial or reliable information; and finally because, mercifully, none of the eleven postwar premiers found themselves their country's World War III war leader (though during the Cuban missile crisis of October 1962, as we shall see, Harold Macmillan's closest advisers thought he might be a day or so away from becoming it).

As we have already seen, Attlee began thinking about the rudiments of a World War III War Cabinet in 1948. The following year the Chiefs of

Staff Joint Planning Staff began to design a military command structure to underpin it and the chiefs themselves agreed the following year that 'a joint command organization should be established in war'.[52] But these early efforts were swiftly overtaken by technological events.

As Whitehall's scientists and military planners caught up with the implications of the US thermonuclear test at Eniwetok in 1952[53] and the Soviet Union's comparable explosion in Kazakhstan the following year,[54] it became apparent, as Norman Brook put it to Harold Macmillan (then Minister of Defence) in December 1954, that a combination 'of "fall-out", added to the destructive power of the thermonuclear weapon' meant that in a future war, 'the United Kingdom – the nerve centre of European resistance – would be extremely vulnerable to nuclear attack [and] there is not in sight any air defence system which could protect us effectively'.[55] Not only, Brook argued, did this mean that 'to maintain the strength of the [nuclear] deterrent must be the heart of our defence policy . . . The latest scientific appreciation of the nuclear weapon demands a fresh reappraisal of our defence plans, both military and civil . . . The implications of this need profound study.' Existing plans required 'a radical reshaping'.[56]

Five days later, Macmillan, with Churchill's approval, appointed a six-person committee of three senior civil servants, two military men and the Scientific Adviser to the Ministry of Defence to study 'the effect of "fall-out" on our war plans'. William Strath of the Cabinet Office took the chair[57] and the group reported to the Cabinet's Defence Committee, which the Prime Minister chaired, some four months later.[58] Churchill, for his part, was good at keeping the Queen informed on matters thermonuclear. In July 1954 he told her the Cabinet was on the verge of authorizing the manufacture of a British H-bomb[59] and in December 1954 he sent her a copy of his Cabinet Paper on Atomic Warfare, which is still classified.[60]

The Strath Report remains secret, too. It has been removed from the Defence Committee's papers for 1955 under section 3(4) of the Public Records Act 1958 (which allows for the retention of specially sensitive items beyond thirty years).[61] We know, however, that it exerted a profound and continuing influence over the machinery of government under conditions of nuclear war. From Brook's brief on Strath to Eden (who had just replaced Churchill) we can reconstruct its essentials including the 'broad conclusion . . . that, although a determined hydrogen bomb attack against this country would cause human and material destruction on an appalling scale, it would be possible to contain its effects and enable the nation to survive if adequate preparations had been made in advance'.[62]

In general terms, Strath had an air of unreality about it from the start. Brook's memo to Churchill made plain the huge cost of large-scale civil defence and the difficulty of evacuating substantial sections of the population.[63] Philip Allen, the Home Office's man on Strath, underlined this for me many years later when he said:

'I can remember sitting on a committee working out the horrors of the H-bomb as distinct from the much more modest A-bomb. And, although it seemed like Never-Never Land at the time, we did work out these theoretical methods of keeping on the government – setting up organizations. One had a feeling that, if it came to it, nothing would work quite in the way one was planning. But, nevertheless, one simply had to plan.'[64]

And plan they did, in immense detail – at least for the sustenance of government during and after a thermonuclear attack on the UK.

From other documents influenced by Strath it is possible to piece together most of its assumptions about a Britain close to or under thermonuclear attack. There would be:

- A 'Precautionary Stage'[65] of about seven days between a period of international tension reaching a point which indicated it was likely to crash into 'global war'.[66]
- A 'Destructive Phase' in which 'the devastation caused by the nuclear attack on the United Kingdom would be very great' during a 'period which might last from 48 hours to 7 days'.[67]
- A 'Survival Phase'.[68] Planning for this would be aimed 'solely at tackling the problems of *survival*' with a high degree of devolution, initially at least, to Civil Defence Regions, each with its own complement of ministers, officials and military.[69]

But for students of the British premiership, it is the central element of immediately pre- and post-attack Britain – what Norman Brook called 'a very small nucleus at the centre'[70] – that is of especial interest. For, post-Strath, 'Ministers . . . accept[ed] the view that it would be extremely unlikely that central control would continue to operate from London after attack and that the government of the United Kingdom would be conducted by a central nucleus in protected accommodation in the country.'[71]

Only in 1998, when previously immensely secret Chiefs of Staff papers reached the PRO, in a file that contained information too sensitive to be placed amongst their normal material, did it became possible to map the transformation of Cabinet government to what would, in effect, have been virtually prime ministerial government (one hundred per cent so if the use of British nuclear weapons was authorized). The plan, part of an update of both the Government War Book and a 'Top Secret Supplement to the Ministry of Defence War Book', was circulated to the Chiefs of Staff on New Year's Day 1959.[72]

But before tracing what might have been the last ever mutation of British Cabinet government, it is important to depict the magnitude of the decision-taking involved. Harold Macmillan, the Prime Minister of the day, was the first UK premier to have a finger on the thermonuclear trigger. The earliest British hydrogen bombs, the Yellow Sun Mark IIs, were fitted to the RAF's V bomber forces from 1961 onwards after the successful Operation Grapple tests on Christmas Island nearly four years earlier.[73]

In 1957–58 Macmillan had distilled the purposes of the UK's 'independent nuclear capability' in specific terms:

(a) To retain our special relation with the United States and, through it, our influence in world affairs, and, especially, our right to have a voice in the final issue of peace or war.

(b) To make a definite, though limited, contribution to the total nuclear strength of the West – while recognising that the United States must continue to play the major part in maintaining the balance of nuclear power.

(c) To enable us, by threatening to use our independent nuclear power, to secure United States co-operation in a situation in which their interests were less immediately threatened than our own.

(d) To make sure that, in a nuclear war, sufficient attention is given to certain Soviet targets which are of greater importance to us than to the United States.[74]

RAF Bomber Command, then the sole carrier of the British nuclear weapon, was highly integrated with its US equivalent, the Strategic Air Command. Bomber Command was, however, carefully prepared for its own 'strategic target policy' should 'purely national, *unilateral*, action' be authorized by the Prime Minister.[75] It was known in the trade as a 'cities policy': 'If the UK should be forced to take unilateral retaliation against the USSR, the target policy of Bomber Command should be to attack the

Soviet centres of administration and population. This is the most effective target system for our limited forces.'[76]

In 1958–59 the RAF converted their planned nuclear strike capacity into a '30–40 cities' policy[77] (though before Macmillan left office in 1963 this had been scaled down to sixteen cities because of improvements in Soviet air defences).[78] Once up to strength, the '30–40 cities' targeting was estimated to break down as follows:

(a) 35 bombs on 15 cities with populations in excess of 600,000;
(b) 25 bombs on 25 cities mostly with a population in excess of 400,000.

It was estimated that when the force is armed with megaton [hydrogen] bombs the casualties per bomb dropped would be of the order of:

(a) killed about 135,000 – total about 8,000,000;
(b) injured about 135,000 – total about 8,000,000.[79]

So the 'button' designed for Macmillan's use, once the V force reached its peak in the early 1960s, would within a few hours have enabled him if he pressed it to kill eight million Russians and injure a further eight million. That, at least, was the plan, though technical developments on the Soviet side swiftly reduced those estimates. But the body counts remained horrifying by any standards.

By late 1959, 'structural work for [the government's World War III] headquarters [was] almost complete, and the installation of communications [had] begun'.[80] This was the huge underground capability known as 'Turnstile' (though it went under a variety of codenames including 'Burlington') deep beneath the limestone of the Cotswolds between Bath and Corsham in Wiltshire.[81] So, how would Macmillan and his ministerial colleagues have taken their decisions if the plans for the transition to World War III had been activated and adhered to?

On receiving a 'strategic warning' from the Joint Intelligence Committee based on 'intelligence constituting a positive indication that an enemy attack is to be expected',[82] the Cabinet would meet and, on advice from the Chiefs of Staff, it would decide whether or not to declare that Britain was in a 'precautionary stage'. If it did so decide, various 'emergency measures' would be triggered, including the placing of UK 'air defence systems on a war footing [and] bringing assigned and earmarked forces to a war footing' as well as activating 'home [i.e., civil] defence measures'.[83]

Throughout this stage, the plan assumed that the full Cabinet would, when 'necessary', receive recommendations from the Minister of Defence and the Chiefs of Staff.[84]

On receipt of a 'tactical warning, i.e., when attack is imminent and the Allies have received definite information of an enemy attack having been launched, probably by the identification of enemy aircraft or missiles on the radar screens',[85] the Chiefs of Staff would proceed to a meeting with the Prime Minister and '(a) the Home Secretary, (b) the Foreign Secretary, (c) the Minister of Defence, (d) the Secretary of the Cabinet.'[86]

Here we find the post-hydrogen bomb World War III War Cabinet – the PM, plus three ministers and the Cabinet Secretary. It is one-third the size of the World War III 'War Cabinet' designed for Attlee in the atomic bomb era – no sign here of a Minister of Labour or a Minister for the Co-ordination of Economic Affairs. As Norman Brook had predicted to Eden at the time the Strath Committee reported, there would no longer be any point in having the kind of 'skeleton organization of wartime industrial controls' previously planned for.[87] This 1959 version, had it materialized, would have been the tiniest War Cabinet ever. Though, as the files make plain, only the Prime Minister or his designated deputy could authorize the RAF to retaliate.

There is an intriguing curiosity here. We know that Macmillan's designated deputy at this time was Derick Heathcoat Amory and, when he retired in 1960, the mantle fell on Selwyn Lloyd.[88] Both were Chancellors of the Exchequer. Neither had a seat on the attack-imminent War Cabinet.

From the 1962 file of an intensely secret Working Group on Nuclear Retaliation Procedures chaired by Bill Geraghty of the Cabinet Office we know that, since the Soviet Union had been judged to have acquired the capacity to attack all its UK targets with missiles the previous year, 'Deputies to the Prime Minister would be appointed in peacetime'.[89] The same file when it was released in 1998 solved a mystery which had baffled me for years and which Alec Home, privately, asked me not to draw attention to – why, unlike any other nuclear-tipped leader, the British Prime Minister is not accompanied everywhere by a military officer carrying the launch codes. The Geraghty report, bafflingly, declared that 'when the Prime Minister is travelling by car or rail . . . it should be possible to intercept him [and recall him to Whitehall] through police or rail channels, but the Working Group recommend that consideration should be given to providing a radio link in the Prime Minister's car'.[90]

Other questions arise which the files still do not answer. Where would the decisions be taken? In the Cabinet Room, presumably, before and for much of the 'Precautionary Stage'. With a few minutes to go, one assumes the PM and the designated four would be a hundred feet or more below the Cotswolds in 'Turnstile'. As the former Permanent Secretary at the Home Office, Lord Allen of Abbeydale, told me, he was earmarked to go underground with the Home Secretary and was issued with, he thought, a ticket of a particular colour for this purpose.[91] It was the Cuban missile crisis of October 1962 which brought Britain to the verge of having to activate these immensely secret plans when, as Philip Allen recalled, 'for a time we did think those coloured tickets might be used for real'[92] as the inner government headed down the A4 (the M4 had still to be built) to 'Turnstile'.

Before examining that crisis and the question of whether Allen's Law – that 'nothing would quite work out in the way one was planning'[93] – came into operation, it is necessary to determine the degree to which the military controllers of the British nuclear force, the Chief of RAF Bomber Command in particular, possessed powers delegated by the Prime Minister to launch the V force during an emergency and, in extreme circumstances, to order the bombers to deploy their nuclear weapons on Soviet cities. This contingency is jocularly known in Whitehall either as the 'bolt-from-the-blue', the 'decapitation' or the 'headless chickens' scenario.[94]

The first time an official mention of this possibility came to light was in a PRO file unearthed by Dr Stephen Twigge. It was contained in the penultimate paragraph – it appears almost as an afterthought when read in full – of a letter from the Vice-Chief of the Air Staff, Air Chief Marshal Sir Edmund Hudleston, in August 1959 to the newly appointed Chief of RAF Bomber Command, Sir Kenneth Cross, on the state of readiness of his force. 'It is also appreciated', Hudleston told Cross, 'that circumstances could exist, such as a total breakdown in communications, under which you would have to assume responsibility for launching the attack.'[95]

Such scraps of archive can lead to important breakthroughs in knowledge. This one certainly did. Hudleston's letter had a circulation list of six people. Number five was 'Mr Cooper', who as Sir Frank Cooper later headed the Ministry of Defence as its Permanent Secretary. While interviewing him for the television programme *What Has Become of Us?* I drew his attention to the paragraph and asked him to comment. He replied,

If the country was attacked and if you couldn't get any political clearance, and it was clear beyond peradventure, then I think the C-in-C [Commander-in-Chief of] Bomber Command and later the submarine captain [of a Royal Navy Polaris or

Trident vessel, though, as we have seen, since the early 1970s instructions from the Prime Minister on whether or not to retaliate have been kept in a safe on these boats] would have said it was his decision whether to do it or not to do it.

'The decision to launch that strike going to a man in uniform seemed to me a very unlikely thing ever to have happened. But supposing everybody was dead – all the politicians were dead. The country had got to have some kind of leader. Where else are you going to get a leader from?'

Sir Frank added that 'You would probably have had to have had a military government anyway.'[96] There is no detailed plan for this in the 'War Book' material declassified so far, though Norman Brook told Home Office officials in 1959 that 'We plan to maintain central direction ... even in the most rudimentary form, for as long as possible in the intensive period of nuclear attack and ... the capacity to re-assert civil control, and, as soon as possible, central political control, for the period of recovery after the initial nuclear phase.'[97]

Seven months before Hudleston informed Cross of the circumstances in which the launch decision would fall to him, the planners had drawn up the 'positive control' scenario whereby the Chief of the Air Staff could order the bombers into the air 'to avoid loss on the ground by enemy action. In this sense "positive control" means the aircraft will fly on pre-arranged routes toward targets, but will not pass beyond a specified line pending the receipt of further definite instructions. The time at which aircraft are scheduled to reach this specified line will be made known to the Prime Minister ... and the Chiefs of Staff.'[98]

In September 1962, a few weeks before the Cuban missile crisis, Cross was given revised detailed instructions from the Chief of the Air Staff, Marshal of the Royal Air Force Sir Thomas Pike, on what to do if:

(a) From all sources of information available to you, you judge that your force in this country is about to be attacked with nuclear weapons and there has been no preceding period of strategic warning that a nuclear attack is imminent, or
(b) nuclear bombs from an enemy attack have burst on this country before you have been authorised to retaliate, you are authorised

    (i) to order all bomber aircraft within your Command to be airborne under positive control in accordance with the agreed plans covering this procedure;

    (ii) to seek contact by any means of communication open to you with the Prime Minister or his Deputy in London or at the alternative

Government Headquarters (Burlington) and act in accordance with his instructions.[99]

If enemy nuclear weapons had fallen on the UK and attempts to contact the Prime Minister had 'proved abortive, you are authorized in the last resort to order on your own responsibility nuclear retaliation by all means at your disposal'.[100] (This later archival discovery by Stephen Twigge and Len Scott fleshed out that sparse paragraph from Hudleston to Cross discovered over three years earlier and confirmed what Sir Frank Cooper had told me on the basis of it.)

A mere twenty days after Cross received that directive, a United States U2 spy plane on a reconnaissance mission over Cuba found evidence that the Soviet Union was in the process of placing intermediate-range ballistic rockets on Cuba capable, once operational, of striking American cities with their nuclear warheads within minutes of being launched. President Kennedy was informed of this two days later, on 16 October, and the Cuban missile crisis began.[101] On 19 October two members of the British intelligence community were briefed on the Cuban missiles by the CIA while on a visit to Washington.[102] The British Ambassador in Washington, Sir David Ormsby-Gore, an exceptionally well-informed intimate of President Kennedy's, cabled the Foreign Office on Saturday 20 October about 'reports which suggest that the types of arms introduced [into Cuba] may not be entirely defensive'.[103] Ormsby-Gore was personally briefed by Kennedy about the developing crisis on Sunday 21 October[104] and Kennedy sent Macmillan a personal message about it that evening.[105] For the next seven days the world, in Macmillan's own words, stood 'on the brink'[106] while Khrushchev and Kennedy conducted the most alarming and intensely studied of the Cold War's stand-offs. Macmillan, who returned to Admiralty House (No. 10 was undergoing renovation) from Chequers on Monday 22 October in time to receive David Bruce, the US Ambassador to London, and a CIA officer bearing intelligence at noon, dubbed it in the notes he made at the time the 'first day of the World Crisis!'[107]

There was much debate at the time (and since) about whether Britain, far from being the most 'special relation' of the USA (the fundamental premise of Macmillan's case for the UK being a nuclear power four years earlier),[108] was, as the Labour front-bencher, Dick Crossman, swiftly alleged, a powerless observer, and that as for British nuclear weapons giving the UK a place in the 'councils of the nations' and making sure 'that the Americans will listen to us more than to any other ally . . . that little myth is exploded'.[109] British scholars have subsequently probed the degree to which Macmillan fully commanded and controlled the UK nuclear strike force during those seven days which he later described as 'the week of most strain I can ever remember in my life',[110] claiming that 'neither Sir Alec Home [the Foreign Secretary] nor I ever slept at all during the whole seven days'[111] (though his diary suggests he did – albeit fitfully). But the crisis, until recently, had remained curiously under-examined as a case-study of the British Cabinet system under stress and the true testing time for what was by this stage an elaborate set of contingency plans for central government action during a period of international tension which might culminate in an exchange of nuclear weapons. As a very senior defence and intelligence figure put it many years later: 'Cuba was the big one – *the* defining moment.'[112]

Neither Macmillan nor his war planners had worked on the assumption that Cuba might be the world's nuclear flashpoint in the Cold War. Berlin was always treated as the most likely locus and there had been a series of Berlin crises since the 1948–49 airlift (1958 and 1961 being the most recent). The British and the Americans from the outset in October 1962 saw a direct linkage between Cuba and Berlin. As Macmillan put it to Hugh Gaitskell, when he and Home briefed the Opposition leader and his senior colleagues, George Brown and Harold Wilson, on a Privy Counsellor basis at Admiralty House on the evening of Tuesday 23 October:

It seemed to him [Macmillan] very likely that Khrushchev wished to force an international conference which he would then face with two cards in his hand – Cuba and Berlin. He might then hope that he would secure an advance on Berlin by appearing to make a concession on Cuba.

This, Macmillan added, 'might be a brilliant coup on the part of the Russians'.[113] Just over a year earlier, the ever meticulous Sir Norman Brook had drawn up a plan to deal with just such 'a crisis in Berlin'.[114] In June 1961 Macmillan thought, as he confided in his diary, that the Russians' latest attempt to prise the Western Allies out of their zones in Berlin might produce a 'drift to disaster . . . a terrible diplomatic defeat or (out of sheer incompetence) a nuclear war'.[115] The following month Macmillan and Brook exchanged notes on the preparations to be taken in case the position worsened.[116]

In August Brook consulted senior officials and the intelligence community on a rejigging of the Whitehall machine to enable it 'to deal promptly with the issues which may arise over Berlin in the months ahead'.[117] In September he produced his plan.[118] The following month, almost exactly a year before the Cuban crisis erupted, Macmillan reached the point of designating which of his ministerial colleagues would, in the event of war, join him below ground at 'Turnstile' and which ministers would be dispersed to the bunkers that comprised the regional seats of government (sadly, the file does not tell us who would have gone where or which ministers would be left to do as best they could above ground).[119]

Brook's plan, one might have thought, would have proved almost ideally crafted for the crisis of October 1962. He wrote in September 1961,

We must be prepared for a lengthy period of fluctuating political tension with the possibility that, either suddenly or in the course of negotiations if they begin, a critical politico-military situation may develop. If such a situation arises urgent consideration will have to be given to the possibility of action – diplomatic, economic or military.

The Whitehall machine, therefore, would need to be arranged in such a way as to 'allow vital decisions to be taken in an orderly and speedy way'.[120]

Brook, in essence, designed a halfway-house system to bridge the gap between the normal peacetime mechanics of government and the 'strategic warning stage . . . [at which] point we might have to consider the possibility of a small War Cabinet'.[121] During such a halfway contingency, in Brook's words, 'we shall not go underground or have executive decisions taken by "map rooms". But the normal methods must be accelerated.'[122]

At this point, Brook continued,

the Prime Minister would appoint a Ministerial Committee on Berlin. It is likely that this Committee would consist of:

 Prime Minister (in the Chair)
 Home Secretary
 Chancellor of the Exchequer
 Foreign Secretary
 Commonwealth Secretary
 Minister of Defence.[123]

This committee would be serviced by the 'Cabinet Office Berlin Room' into which the departments affected, the Chiefs of Staff and the Joint Intelligence Committee would feed on a twenty-four-hour basis. The 'Berlin Room' would be linked by scrambler telephone and teleprinter 'to all the major points of the central government concerned with the emergency'.[124]

Needless to say, RAF Bomber Command would have been plugged into this central centre of decision-taking. In July 1961, the V-bomber airfields had received the latest version of their 'alert and readiness procedures' which were the ones that were operational during the Cuban missile crisis – the so-called 'alert conditions 5–1':

5. *Normal.* Bomber Force in normal peace time condition.
4. *Precautionary Alert.* Instituted during periods of political tension . . .[125]

Bomber Command, or one of its sub-groups, could order action on 4.[126]

The next alert condition – 3 – was designed to enable the Commander-in-Chief of Bomber Command 'during a period of political tension, to take certain precautionary measures short of the full and specific measures involved in the calling of higher alert conditions'.[127] It is important to consider this carefully as this is the condition to which Air Marshal Cross ordered the V force at 1.00 p.m. on Saturday 27 October as the Cuban crisis approached its peak.[128] It read as follows:

3. *Aircraft Generation.* The maximum number of aircraft are to be made Combat Ready. At Main Bases, aircraft planned to operate from those bases are to be prepared for operational take-off; the remainder are to be armed and prepared for dispersal.[129]

Alert condition 2 would have seen much of the V force dispatched to around twenty-six airfields in the UK under the 'Dispersal Plan' to reduce the risk of aircraft being destroyed on the ground.[130] Alert condition 1 involved placing 25 per cent of the nuclear strike force 'at 5 minutes readiness'.[131] All five alert conditions, as we have seen, remained subject throughout the Cuban missile crisis to the Commander-in-Chief of Bomber Command's 'last resort' power to launch a retaliatory strike if Soviet bombs had burst over the UK and the Prime Minister or his designated deputy was beyond reach.[132]

So, how did Macmillan react to Kennedy's messages, to Ambassador

Bruce's noontime briefing on Monday 22 October and the U2 photographs of the missile sites on Cuba which the CIA's Chester Cooper (who was accompanying Bruce) brought with him to Admiralty House?[133] Did he consult Brook's careful 1961 plan and order Whitehall to its halfway-house condition? Did he press the Chiefs of Staff to bring the armed forces to a state of readiness? Did he ask for 'Turnstile' to be made ready? Did he decide which ministers would go to what bunkers?

He did none of these things. I have often wondered what Brook, the supreme organizer, would have advised had he not been ill and off work.[134] Despite the likelihood, as Macmillan told the full Cabinet the following day, that if Kennedy took steps to remove the Cuban missiles and Khrushchev retaliated by blockading Berlin it 'would lead either to an escalation to world war or to the holding of a conference',[135] the Prime Minister took no steps to create a Berlin-style committee or operations room, let alone a War Cabinet. The nearest he came to establishing any formal machinery was on Thursday 25 October when he told the Cabinet: 'The situation was still developing rapidly and it might be necessary for him to call a meeting of Ministers at short notice.'[136]

In fact, it seems as if Macmillan quite deliberately decided to do the reverse (though there is evidence that he had doubts about this during his post-Cuba rethink, as we shall see in a moment). Why did he take such a line? We know from his official biographer, Alistair Horne, that Macmillan, like Kennedy, had been 'profoundly affected'[137] by the recently published *The Guns of August*, in which Barbara Tuchman made an eloquent case for the great powers tumbling into a world war through miscalculation and inadvertence in 1914.[138]

On the evening of Monday 22 October Macmillan struck a very Tuchmanesque note in conversation with General Lauris Norstad at a long-planned dinner in Admiralty House to mark the American's farewell as NATO's Supreme Allied Commander, Europe.[139] This, Macmillan recorded in his diary that night,

lasted from 8–11. But it gave me a chance of a private talk with General Norstad. Washington, in a rather panicky way, have been urging a Nato 'alert', with all that this implies (in our case Royal Proclamation and call-up of Reservists). I told him that we wd *not* repeat *not* agree at this stage. N. agreed with this and said he thought NATO powers wd take the same view. I said that 'mobilisation' had sometimes caused war. Here it was absurd since the additional forces made available by 'Alert' had *no* military significance.[140]

In his memoirs Macmillan quoted most of this diary entry omitting the reference to 'a rather panicky' Washington and adding: 'Indeed, apart from certain precautions affecting the Royal Air Force, we maintained this position throughout the crisis'[141] (we shall examine those 'certain precautions' in a moment). In his reflective and retrospective diary entry when the crisis was past, Macmillan recorded that his first post-Cuba week had 'seemed rather unreal, compared to the week before – with all those messages and telephone calls, and the frightful desire to *do* something, with the knowledge that *not* to do anything (except to talk to the President and keep Europe and the Commonwealth calm and firm) was prob. the right answer'.[142]

The Kennedy–Macmillan conversations have become a very well-known piece of history. There was a high degree of consultation between Kennedy and Macmillan which the President accorded to no other head of state or head of government. So close were the contacts that Ernest May and Philip Zelicow (whose moment-by-moment reconstruction of the Washington end of the decision-taking process became possible when they gained access to presidential tapes for October 1962) concluded thirty-five years later that 'It is . . . obvious from these records that Macmillan and Ormsby-Gore became *de facto* members of Kennedy's Executive Committee [the President's equivalent of a war cabinet]'[143] thanks to the frequent use of the transatlantic scrambler telephone which Macmillan had had installed in Admiralty House. (His lack of dexterity meant that Macmillan could never master the buttons on this machine and Philip de Zulueta, his private secretary for foreign affairs, had to work it for him.[144] As another of his private secretaries put it, 'Harold Macmillan could never handle the 'hot-line'. He would always talk to the air.')[145]

What has still to be reconstructed in any detail is the way in which he did make use of the Cabinet and Whitehall machinery, having failed to activate Brook's contingency plan. It is possible to go some way towards this thanks to Macmillan's memoirs, his own diaries, the diary of his Press Secretary, Harold Evans, and various public records.

It is quite plain that the management of the British end of the Cuban missile crisis was very largely a Prime Minister–Foreign Secretary affair conducted throughout from Admiralty House, to which the full Cabinet were admitted for three quite long discussions on the morning of Tuesday 23 October, the afternoon of Thursday 25 October and the morning of Monday 29 October.[146] (And on 26 October, Macmillan allowed the Acting Cabinet Secretary, Michael Cary, to circulate a Joint Intelligence

Committee paper on 'The Threat Posed by Soviet Missiles in Cuba' to all Cabinet members.)[147] As soon as Bruce and Cooper had left on the Monday afternoon, Macmillan summoned Lord Home and his 'chief advisers' from the Foreign Office to discuss the Air Staff's analysis of the U2 photographs and to draft a reply to Kennedy's first long telegram.[148] Thereafter, as Macmillan recorded in his diary after the Thursday Cabinet meeting, 'I told the Cabinet about Cuba (which they seem quite happy to leave to me and Alec Home)'.[149]

Confirmation of the centrality of the Macmillan–Home axis came in the post-crisis thankyou note penned on behalf of the Queen by her Private Secretary, Sir Michael Adeane. 'As I mentioned to you last night', Adeane wrote to Macmillan on 31 October,

I made a rough note of the various contacts which took place during the last weekend between the Queen on the one hand, and yourself and the Foreign Secretary on the other. These were numerous and as a result Her Majesty was fully and continuously informed of what was going on in the relations between this country, the United States and the USSR.

The Queen knows very well what a heavy strain both you and Lord Home and your staff were working under during these days and she wishes you to know how much she appreciates the trouble which was taken in your own office and the Foreign Office to see that she was kept up to date with the rapidly changing news.[150]

Intriguingly, the PRO material gives no indication of which place of safety was set aside for the royal family when the missiles looked likely to fly. The Royal Yacht *Britannia* was a fully fledged command and control centre with washdown facilities to tackle nuclear fall-out. I have always suspected the argument that it would have served as a hospital ship in time of war was a particularly feeble cover story. But the Queen, like her Minister, stayed above ground during the Cuban missile crisis.

In his retrospective diary entry of 4 November, Macmillan gives pride of place on the UK side to himself, Home and Ormsby-Gore, a primacy which the public records corroborate: '. . . the President and [Dean] Rusk [US Secretary of State] (and, above all, the President's 'chef de cabinet', McGeorge Bundy) were in continuous touch with Alec Home and me. David Gore was all the time in and out of the White House. The whole episode was like a battle; and we in Admiralty House felt as if we were in the battle HQ.'[151]

Once it was all over, on Sunday 26 October 1962, when Khrushchev agreed to withdraw his missiles from Cuba in return for the USA withdrawing its Jupiter rockets from Turkey, Harold Evans, in an atmospheric entry in his diary, described Macmillan's Cuba inner group (if, indeed, the ministers involved deserved such a precise designation):

'It's like a wedding', said the PM, 'when there is nothing left to do but drink champagne and go to sleep.' He had flopped down in the chair by the tape machine, with Tim [Bligh, Principal Private Secretary], Philip de Zulueta and myself as audience. The captains and the kings had departed and this was the No. 10 family.

The captains and the kings – Rab [Butler] and Alec Home in particular, plus Ted Heath [Home's number 2 at the Foreign Office] plus Harold Caccia [Permanent Secretary at the Foreign Office], plus (this morning) Thorneycroft [Minister of Defence] – had spent most of the last twenty-four hours in and out of Admiralty House.[152]

To Evans's list I would have added (for the first days of the crisis at least) the Chancellor of the Exchequer, Reginald Maudling. For example, as soon as Home had left Admiralty House on the afternoon of Monday 22 October, Macmillan sent for Maudling 'and put him in the picture. His advice was sensible. He wd see the Governor of the Bank. There wd be heavy buying of gold and a general fall of all stocks and shares – but no panic.'[153]

By the time of the Cuban missile crisis, Butler was not only the number 2 in the government, he carried the title of Deputy Prime Minister as well. Macmillan saw him privately at 3.15 on the afternoon of Tuesday 23 October (just before Gaitskell, Brown and Wilson came in to be briefed by the Prime Minister and Foreign Secretary). Macmillan wrote in his diary: 'Butler. I had not been able to keep him fully informed, so I thought it wise to have a good talk.'[154]

Butler's number 2 position in the administration in October 1962 did not imply, any more than it had before he acquired the title of Deputy Prime Minister, that he would be Macmillan's 'designated deputy' when it came to authorizing the use of nuclear weapons should the PM be dead or beyond reach. Selwyn Lloyd had been the most notable victim of the July 1962 'Night of the Long Knives' reshuffle. We have no knowledge of who Macmillan chose to replace him in the nuclear role. My own guess would be that it was Home, and not merely because of his responsibility for and knowledge of foreign affairs. Macmillan had a very high regard for Home's judgement and decisiveness. Though Butler was part of the Admiralty House group during the Cuban crisis, the surviving records suggest that he was there because of what he was rather than who he was. Macmillan's diary confirms Evans's – noting Butler's presence 'for a short time'[155] in Admiralty House on the especially tense Saturday evening, 27 October. (It was on this evening that Philip de Zulueta, arriving home late for a dinner party, told his wife and friends sombrely that 'we may be at war tomorrow'.)[156]

The Prime Minister's Cuba files contain no minutes of ministerial meetings. It appears to have been a remarkably fluid example of crisis management, with ministers mingling not just with officials but with younger members of the Macmillan extended family too. The Prime Minister's grandson Alexander (then aged nineteen) was living in Admiralty House at the time. 'I could tell from people's body language that it was serious,' he recalled. 'I remember Dennis Greenhill [a senior Foreign Office diplomat] coming in to brief Grandfather and looking at me. "It's all right," Grandfather said. "You can speak in front of Alexander. If we get this wrong it is his generation that will suffer." '[157] Evans's account adds further touches of domesticity, describing his (Evans) arriving in the dining room with 'chairs pulled back from the table and Ted [Heath] still eating before discussion shifts to the drawing room'.[158]

The Cabinet minutes for the three Cuban crisis meetings (which, naturally, do form a traditional recorded part of the processes in Admiralty House) give the impression of fairly full briefings by Macmillan and Home and fairly wide general discussions resulting on the wider implications of the crisis. (The Lord Chancellor, Lord Dilhorne, for example, had at the Cabinet's request prepared for its Thursday meeting a paper on the legal justification for Kennedy's naval blockade of Cuba.)[159]

On the Tuesday, Macmillan gave the first Cuba full Cabinet of the crisis what from the minutes appears to be a substantial picture of his dealings with Kennedy (and he used his colleagues as a sounding-board for the way he proposed to handle Parliament).[160] As he put it in his diary that night,

'Cabinet 10.30 – 1. I explained the whole Cuba situation, and *read* out aloud (but did *not* circulate) the vital documents – viz, (a) The President's confidential message to me, (b) The Ambassador's démarche and the summary of the evidence about the missiles in Cuba, (c) my replies, (d) summary of our telephone talk. Ministers seemed rather shaken, but satisfied.[161]

That evening, before completing his diary entry while feeling 'exhausted' (he was sixty-eight by this time), Macmillan had briefed the Queen at 6.30 and had supper with his close friend, Ava Waverley, the widow of John Anderson, Lord Waverley, the former Chancellor of the Exchequer and member of Churchill's World War II War Cabinet.[162] Just as the absence of a Cuba War Cabinet is surprising given all the prior contingency planning, Macmillan's use of the full Cabinet as a forum for discussion – if not decision – is quite striking. There was no attempt to use the Cabinet's Defence Committee as a halfway house between the full Cabinet and a War Cabinet. The Defence Committee did meet under Macmillan's chairmanship in Admiralty House on the afternoon of Wednesday 24 October (its last meeting in 1962). The first item under discussion is still secret (the others were the export of guided missiles and air defence and air traffic control). But it is most unlikely that the missing section was about Cuba, as it was devoted to the discussion of a prepared paper (which also remains classified), which suggests that it was a long-planned piece of business.[163]

There is evidence that had the Cuban missile crisis developed into a very strong likelihood of armed conflict, it was the full Cabinet to which Macmillan would have turned for authorization of a 'precautionary stage', as the War Book prescribed. Had this happened, the state whereby during the Cuban crisis 'We ... were involved but detached', as Sir Frank Cooper described it,[164] would have been overtaken by rather more intrusive events.

From Ministry of Defence and Chiefs of Staff files it is clear that the warlike possibilities became substantially more alarming after Kennedy made it plain on Friday 26 October that, as Peter Thorneycroft, the Minister of Defence, put it to the Chiefs of Staff two days later,

unless he [Kennedy] received assurances regarding the disarming of Russian missiles in Cuba, the cessation of further construction work, and a halt to the shipping of further offensive weapons, he would have to consider what action should be taken to meet these ends.[165]

'In the light of this,' Thorneycroft continued, 'it would have been prudent to consider what precautionary measures the United Kingdom should take; dispersal of the V force [i.e., alert condition 2] and possibly even mobilisation represented possible options.'[166] Sunday 28 October was clearly to have been a key day of decision for Macmillan, his ministers and his military advisers had word not come through that Khrushchev was backing down. (Macmillan was finishing eating lunch with Butler, Home, Thorneycroft and Heath when 'the news came (by radio) that the Russians had given in'.)[167]

The previous day Macmillan had told Pike, the Chief of the Air Staff, that 'if the situation deteriorated further [he] intended calling a Cabinet meeting on the next afternoon [Sunday]' with the Chiefs of Staff in attendance.[168] Thorneycroft's meeting with the chiefs just after his Sunday lunch with Macmillan had plainly been intended to co-ordinate military advice ahead of the Sunday afternoon Cabinet meeting had it convened. Given Khrushchev's climbdown, Thorneycroft told the chiefs, he 'did not ... consider that any immediate precautionary measures were necessary'.[169]

To what extent *had* certain precautionary measures been taken already, despite Macmillan's insistence that Tuchmanism prevail? As we have seen from the contingency plans, the Cabinet was to be invited to consider declaring a 'precautionary stage' on receipt of a strategic warning from the Joint Intelligence Committee that the intelligence community had 'a positive indication that an enemy attack is to be expected'.[170]

We now know that the Soviet military intelligence officer, Colonel Oleg Penkovsky (an agent-in-place recruited by the British Secret Intelligence Service who since April 1961 had been passing high-grade information on nuclear capability to Whitehall and Washington), was arrested by the KGB on Monday 22 October 1962 (the day Macmillan received the U2 photographs) at the moment, probably, of the West's greatest need of him (he had a system for warning the Secret Intelligence Service, SIS, and the CIA of sudden dangerous developments).[171] We know from his official biographer that Macmillan believed Penkovsky's information about the capacity of Soviet missiles, including the SS-4s installed on Cuba, had an important bearing on the 1962 crisis.[172] Two messages indicating imminent danger were received by the SIS and the CIA from 'Penkovsky' (i.e., his captors and controllers) on 2 November 1962, nearly a week after the crisis had dissipated and eleven days after Penkovsky's arrest.[173] His SIS controller in the British Embassy in Moscow was convinced they were not genuine and, mercifully, made his advice to this effect plain to his superiors.[174]

In the absence of Macmillan's daily Cuban crisis intelligence feed, from SIS especially, we can only conclude that up to Sunday 28 October, he had received nothing to trigger a move to the 'precautionary stage'. Had

Kennedy 'taken out' the missiles on Cuba or invaded the island on 29 October or thereafter, a Soviet move against Berlin was widely expected which would have swung the War Book into action. (And Macmillan expected Khrushchev to make just such a 'counter-move' on Berlin even after his climbdown on Cuba.)[175]

Following the publication in 1980 of the memoirs of Air Vice Marshal Sir Stewart Menaul, Senior Air Staff Officer at Bomber Command's Head-quarters in High Wycombe in October 1962, it became widely believed that on his own initiative, Menaul's chief, Air Marshal Cross, had 'increased the readiness' of the V bombers to fifteen minutes away from take-off.[176] This, rightly or wrongly, created the impression that the country's leading nuclear airman had extended a routine readiness exer-cise, thereby exceeding his powers in contravention of the wishes Mac-millan expressed to General Norstad on 22 October and to the Chief of the Air Staff on 27 October (when an 'adamant' Prime Minister told Pike at the Saturday morning meeting in Admiralty House that even now 'he did not consider the time was right for any overt preparatory steps to be taken such as mobilisation'[177]). Macmillan, it should be remembered, had been *au fait* with War Book matters since his spell at the Ministry of Defence in 1954–55. As Prime Minister he had also observed a V-bomber 'scramble' exercise at RAF Cottesmore some years earlier. (There exists some marvellous newsreel footage of him standing on the tarmac bowler-hatted, erect as the Guardsman he once was, umbrella by his side as the Klaxon sounds and the airmen race to their bombers).[178] In short, he was neither naïve nor a novice when it came to the transition to war.

It is slightly surprising, however, that Macmillan waited until the morning of Saturday 27 October before summoning the Chief of the Air Staff, Sir Thomas Pike, to discover what was 'the current alert posture of our forces' (as Pike put it when reporting to his fellow chiefs on the Saturday afternoon).[179] Pike told Macmillan 'that at the moment the three Service Ministers had warned their senior officers to be available, if required, at approximately one hour's notice'.[180]

Macmillan briefed Pike on what Kennedy had told him over the 'hot-line' the previous evening – that if the Russians did not stop the shipment of missiles to Cuba or the work on the missile sites and did not 'defuse' the weapons already there within forty-eight hours, 'he [Kennedy] would take action to destroy the rocket sites either by bombing, by invasion or by both'.[181] The US invasion force, Macmillan continued, would not be ready until Monday 29 October but, once it was, Kennedy might take 'definite action' informing his allies of this rather than consulting them in advance.[182]

Despite the possibility that within two days Kennedy might take direct steps against Cuba, thereby triggering a response from Khrushchev against Berlin, Macmillan none the less, as Pike told his fellow chiefs, 'had been adamant that he did not consider the time was appropriate for any overt preparatory steps to be taken such as mobilization. Moreover, he did not wish Bomber Command to be alerted, although he wished the force to be ready to take the appropriate steps should this become necessary.'[183] In other words, Macmillan asserted firm political control over his nuclear war machinery that Saturday morning. It is plain from the records that Pike passed on the Prime Minister's instructions to the Chief of Bomber Command, Cross.[184] At one o'clock on the afternoon of Saturday 27 October, Cross placed the V force on alert condition 3 in line with Macmillan's wish that they be made ready. And this condition was maintained until Guy Fawkes Day, 5 November 1962.[185]

When the Chiefs of Staff met an hour and a half after alert condition 3 had been declared to hear Pike's account of his conversation with Macmillan in Admiralty House that morning, they considered what action to recommend to the Cabinet (if, as Macmillan warned Pike might happen, a meeting was called on the Sunday afternoon). The Chiefs believed that 'Bomber Command should be alerted and dispersed [i.e., moved up to alert condition 2] in the event of positive indications that the United States propose to operate against the Cuban mainland'.[186]

Like Macmillan, the Chiefs thought: 'One of the most likely Russian reactions to the United States action over Cuba would be to occupy West Berlin.'[187] This, quite plainly, would have activated all the elaborate nuclear War Book planning developed piece by piece since the Strath Report over seven years earlier. And, from the way the Chiefs put it, there would have been more than a touch of *The Guns of August* had the Russians moved against West Berlin:

In view of the overwhelming force that they [the Russians] had available, this could be conducted with little warning. Moreover, Berlin was indefensive [sic] militarily and the [Western] forces there were in token strength only . . .

It would be essential for Bomber Command to be alerted and dispersed as soon as the situation so warranted in order that its deterrent effect should be seen to remain credible. This measure would be the most effective that could be carried out short of general mobilisation . . .[188]

1. A quartet of premiers pay their respects to Clem Attlee in the Members' Lobby of the House of Commons, November 1979: (*left to right*) Jim Callaghan, Harold Wilson, Margaret Thatcher and Ted Heath.

2. Wheels of fire: At election time Mrs Attlee drove up to 400 miles a day often at high speed. Mr Attlee would do the crossword, pausing occasionally to feed her a peppermint.

3. A step-by-step approach to socialism: The Attlees tread the Pilgrims' Way in Surrey, 1946.

4. War as a very prime-ministerial business: Attlee returns to No. 10 from Washington after talks with President Truman on Korea and the Bomb, December 1950.

5. Clem Attlee in Walthamstow on the last full day of his premiership, 25 October 1951.

6. Attlee in old age: As English as a cup of tea and much given to warnings of excessive prime-ministerialsim.

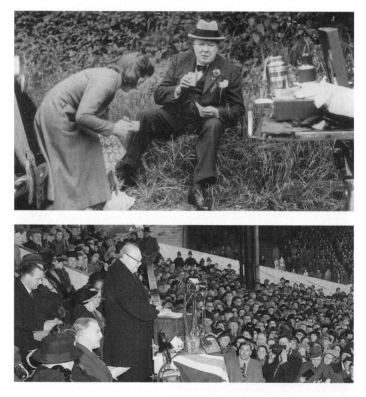

7. A trencherman takes to the road: Electioneering Churchill-style at the start of his 1,000-mile tour, June 1945.

8. The last days of the great open-air election meeting: Churchill at the Cardiff City football ground, February 1950.

9. Churchill with his beloved Rufus: the poodle with the flame-thrower breath.

10. 'I don't think Anthony can do it': A doubting Churchill with an edgy Eden.

11. Ancient influence: Churchill arrives at the Palace in January 1957 to advise the Queen to send for Macmillan rather than Butler.

12. Winston and Toby: beloved if incontinent bird.

13. Sir Anthony with Lady Eden after being confirmed as Conservative Party leader in April 1955: Soon the Suez Canal would start to flow through her drawing-room.

14. Eden's one and only meeting with Nasser, Cairo, 1955: Behind the civility there lay a deep unease.

15. Eden inspecting the new Valiant bomber at RAF Wittering in September 1955: Just over a year later he would unleash them on Egyptian targets.

16. Broken in policy and in health, Eden leaves Downing Street for the Palace to resign, 9 January 1957.

It is quite plain from the secret British archive on Cuba that the UK 'brink', to which Macmillan referred in his memoirs, would have been reached on Monday 29 October 1962 had Khrushchev not backed down the previous day.

So, as Macmillan finished his Sunday lunch in Admiralty House and the news of the Soviet climbdown came over the radio, what nuclear capacity had the Royal Air Force prepared ready to move to alert condition 2 should the political authorization have been given so to do? It is worth pondering, as Saturday–Sunday 27–28 October 1962 is the closest, so far as is known, that any British Prime Minister has come to activating the UK's nuclear forces. (Hence that senior Whitehall figure describing it even in the 1990s as '*the* defining moment' of the postwar period in nuclear terms.)

From the exercise codenamed 'Micky Finn II' undertaken the previous month (it was confined to September 20–22 and did not run on into the Cuban crisis) we can gauge the nuclear strike capacity of Bomber Command in the autumn of 1962. 'It was', as the post-exercise report put it, 'designed to exercise fully the Alert and Readiness Plan, including the dispersal of the MBF [Medium Bomber Force], under conditions of "No Notice" [i.e., the bolt from the blue].'[189] On 20 September, 112 V bombers went to alert condition 2 at 6.00 a.m., moving to alert condition 1 at 8.11 on the same morning – a position they held until 5.30 on 22 September.[190]

From the review conference Cross and his commanders held at RAF North Luffenham on 15 November 1962, we know that under 50 per cent of the V force 'was at readiness' during the Cuban crisis, though all but one of the sixty Thor missiles (operated jointly under a dual-key system with the Americans) were 'made serviceable and ready' at the same time.[191] Exercise Micky Finn, however, suggests that had Macmillan authorized the next stage of alert procedure during Cuba, Cross could have mobilized a substantial number of nuclear-armed aircraft on the simple transmission of the codeword 'Framework'.[192] Indeed, he told the Vice Chief of the Air Staff on 31 October that he had had 'everything ready to bring 75 per cent of the aircraft in the Command to readiness', but he 'could not give the order for fear of the effect it might have (if it became known) on the very tense negotiations being carried on by Mr Kruschev [sic] and Mr Kennedy'.[193]

There is an antiseptic quality about occasions such as Cross's Cuba debriefing with his commanders, as there is about the sparse record of '*the* defining moment' in, for example, the files of No. 1 Group Headquarters (to which the orders were transmitted alerting the bases in Lincolnshire, Britain's 'Bomber County').[194] This is how it reads in No. 1 Group's 'Operations Record Book' for October 1962:

II. *Alert Condition 3, 27ᵗʰ October, 1962*

(a) As a result of the Cuban crisis and the political situation BCOC [Bomber Command Operations Centre] initiated Alert Condition 3 (precautionary alert) at 1300 Z on 27 October 1962. All key personnel were required to remain on stations and Operations Room staff to be available at short notice. Although no generation of aircraft was ordered, some preparations were made to ensure rapid generation if necessary. All measures were to be unobtrusive.[195]

Plainly, Macmillan's Tuchmanesque instructions to Pike had been fully conveyed to the nuclear bases. Two more paragraphs complete the operational record of the crisis:

(c) An increase in the number of aircraft from 6 to 12 on QRA [Quick Reaction Alert] was ordered by Bomber Command at 1547 Z on 28ᵗʰ October 1962, to be effective as soon as possible after 0800 Z on 29ᵗʰ October 1962.

(d) Alert Condition 3 was cancelled at 0900 Z on 5ᵗʰ November 1962. QRA states returned to normal.[196]

But what did this actually mean on the ground in Lincolnshire?

Len Scott discovered it directly from Air Vice-Marshal Arthur Griffiths who, in October 1962, was a Vulcan squadron commander at RAF Waddington near Lincoln. He told Scott in 1993,

'I spent most of that period on Quick Reaction Alert in a flight hut on "B" Dispersal at RAF Waddington. My Vulcan was parked about 20 yards away, fully fuelled, and loaded with a nuclear weapon. All the switches in the aircraft were set for a rapid start on the four engines, the aircraft was locked, and I carried the key to the door on a string around my neck. My crew and I were not permitted to leave the dispersal, so food was brought out to us, and we slept fully-clothed on camp beds. Although we were nominally at 15 minutes' readiness, we could have been airborne day or night within half that time.'[197]

Griffiths' testimony is significant. Under the QRA procedure implemented at V bomber airfields in February 1962,[198] between three and nine aircraft could be placed on pads at the end of the runway and prepared for take-off, complete with H-bombs, in fifteen minutes. This was a state of readiness which did not depend on dispersal and a shift from alert condition 3 to alert condition 2.

While Arthur Griffiths sat in his hut just north of Lincoln that morning, why didn't the Chiefs of Staff prepare to forsake their suite in the Ministry of Defence in Whitehall and race down the A4 to Corsham, taking the Prime Minister and his War Cabinet with them once the full Cabinet authorized a 'Precautionary Stage' when they had met on the Sunday afternoon? As far as we know, neither Macmillan – nor any other Prime Minister since – has ever set foot in 'Turnstile'.[199]

Sir Frank Cooper is of the belief that nobody has 'been there apart from the Ministry of Works and possibly the Cabinet Office'. He recalls that the Chiefs 'never liked the idea of rushing to a bloody quarry . . . people disappearing to the West Country. And nobody really believed that, if the worst came to the worst, this thing was going to work from there in any event. They just didn't see that they could operate efficiently.'[200]

The files support Sir Frank's recollection and add another twist. Six months post-Cuba, the Chiefs of Staff Committee pondered the problem of exactly when to go 'underground'. They had commissioned a briefing on it from their commanders-in-chief. The commanders reminded them in March 1963 that Macmillan's directive the previous year had laid down that 'Turnstile' was

(a) To act as the seat of Government in the period of survival and reconstruction.
(b) To be an alternative centre to London for authorising nuclear retaliation.

But

It is fundamental to all TURNSTILE planning that if its location and purpose were known to the Russians it would almost certainly be destroyed. If its communications were used for operational purposes it is considered that both the location and function of TURNSTILE would be known within a day or so at the outside. It seems essential, therefore, that no plans should be made for the exercise of operational control from TURNSTILE in the pre-attack period . . . A conflict . . . arises because the Commanders-in-Chief can only exercise their post-attack responsibilities from TURNSTILE, and cannot be expected to move there at the moment of attack.[201]

It is not known how (if ever) this dilemma was resolved, though the commanders-in-chief recommended that the already agreed principle 'that control should remain in Whitehall for as long as possible' should mean that everyone should stay in Whitehall 'throughout the Precautionary Stage'.[202] It is difficult to reconcile this with the central nucleus of government running for the cars to Corsham only once a tactical warning had been received with missiles and aircraft already detectable on the radar screens.

Significantly, the Chiefs and their commanders confronting the 'Turnstile' dilemma is but one element of a post-Cuba rethink of 'War Book planning' ordered by Macmillan.[203] Within an hour or two of Khrushchev's climbdown on Sunday 28 October 1962 the chiefs at their meeting with Thorneycroft recognized that the missile crisis had exposed a significant gap in UK planning. They acknowledged that 'Detailed contingency plans existed for the action to be taken in the event of a NATO alert or Berlin crisis. Plans had also been made to meet many other situations in which the United Kingdom was likely to be directly involved.'[204]

But

Little consideration had . . . so far been given to the precautionary measures which it would be prudent for the United Kingdom to take in circumstances such as these when there was a confrontation between the United States and Russia, in which the United Kingdom was not directly involved.[205]

There it is in a nutshell – a demonstration that Allen's Law operated at the British end of the Cuban missile crisis. It also explains why Macmillan and Home treated it very largely as a diplomatic crisis from Monday 22 October to lunchtime on Sunday 28 October (hence their almost joint-management of it in Cabinet and Whitehall). Though by the following day, had Kennedy made a move against Cuba, the crisis could well have turned into a transition-to-war question as foreseen by the War Book. It is, as we have seen in earlier chapters, quite often useful and valid to see the conduct of the premiership as a variant of 'structured busking' (to borrow a phrase of George Bain's).[206] But had the Cuban crisis persisted for another twenty-four hours, the response of the inner core of British government could well have become rather more structured than improvised.

It is plain from records which only reached the PRO in 1998 that Macmillan, in the aftermath of Cuba, brooded on the planning gap identified by the Chiefs of Staff during their Sunday afternoon meeting with Thorneycroft. As the Cabinet Secretary, Sir Burke Trend, put it in a minute to Thorneycroft:

After the Cuba Crisis the Prime Minister directed that the [Cabinet's] Home Defence Committee should review the state of Government War Book planning in order ensure that it was sufficiently flexible to enable us to react quickly and appropriately to a sudden emergency, in which we might have no more than two or three days' warning of the outbreak of war.[207]

A major concern was the need to have World War III emergency powers in place if a crisis should, Cuba-style, come out of the blue and take the UK swiftly to the nuclear brink.

As a result of the review a fierce Emergency Powers (Defence) Bill, 'more drastic than the Regulations in the Second World War', as its framers put it,[208] gave the state the power to break itself up into ten bits or 'Regional Seats of Government', each under the charge of a minister acting as a 'Regional Commissioner' possessing 'such wide powers, particularly financial powers, as to amount to a voluntary abdication by Parliament of the whole of their functions for the period of the emergency'.[209] (Other matters than the financial catch the eye when reading the draft Bill, such as those giving the regional commissioners vast powers over property and 'any class of person so specified' under the proposed defence regulations. Sanctions against malefactors under the regulations could include a sentence of death by the courts, with appeals to 'not less than three persons who hold or have held high judicial office'.)[210]

Not surprisingly, ministers decided it would be unwise to put this Bill to Parliament in peacetime as it 'has always been a politically unattractive proposal'[211] and because the 'political unity which Parliament would display in emergency would be lacking in peace; and the Bill would provoke highly critical debate', as the post-Cuba review put it in the briefing papers prepared for the ministerial group.[212]

A change was made, however, to the ability of the Prime Minister to act alone in a sudden emergency as described by the review. 'The Government War Book', its compilers noted,

at present assumes that the Precautionary Stage will be instituted by decision of the Cabinet. It seems possible however that, if news were received at night or over the weekend of a sudden deterioration in the international situation which seemed likely to call for urgent Government War Book action, the Prime Minister might wish to institute the Precautionary Stage on his personal authority without waiting for the Cabinet to come together.[213]

Macmillan decided to take this power unto himself through a process of self-authorization without even waiting for the ministerial group on the 'Post-Cuba Review of War Book Planning' to meet[214] – another example of a premier simply adding to the reach of his office on his own authority without wider ministerial, let alone Cabinet, approval. When the post-Cuba ministerial group under the Home Secretary, Henry Brooke, finally met on 30 July 1963, they simply 'took note' that Macmillan had already 'authorised' this accretion of prime ministerial power.[215]

In examining the Cuban crisis I have concentrated on high policy-makers, their decision-taking processes and the nuclear weapon. But the World War III plan contained much more than this, including an 'evacuation policy' which involved dispersing 9.5 million people from 'priority classes' (largely women and children) away from nineteen population centres (the big cities, naturally) in the pre-attack phase.[216] It is not clear from the record if this was considered – let alone prepared – as the missile crisis approached its peak.

Cuba is rightly seen as *the* moment since 1945 when the UK came closest to a nuclear brink. But the records show there was one other occasion when British intelligence suggested that the Soviet Union might be about to take imminent and substantial military action against British forces – a warning given with a level of urgency not matched at any stage of the Cuban missile crisis.

This was at the climax of the Suez affair on 6 November 1956. The warning is preserved in the papers of General Sir Charles Keightley, Commander-in-Chief of the combined Anglo-French Forces. It was flashed to all his commanders on land, on sea and in the air, to Whitehall, and to RAF Bomber Command's Headquarters. It read as follows:

ONE. INFORMATION HAS BEEN RECEIVED THAT RUSSIA MAY INTERVENE IN THE MIDDLE EAST WITH FORCE.

TWO. ACTION WILL BE TAKEN FORTHWITH SO THAT ALL AIRFIELDS ARE AT THE MAXIMUM STATE OF PREPAREDNESS FOR AN ATTACK AGAINST THEM. IN PARTICULAR THE GREATEST POSSIBLE DISPERSION OF AIRCRAFT WILL BE ACHIEVED AND MAINTAINED.

THREE. NAVAL AND ARMY FORCE WILL ALSO TAKE APPROPRIATE ACTION TO
MEET THIS THREAT.[217]

We know from intelligence material passed to the Queen that on 6
November 1956 it had been 'reported that jet aircraft have been overflying
Turkish territory. These aircraft are assumed to be Russian reinforcements
for Syria and Egypt.'[218] Two days later Her Majesty was informed that 'it
now appears from the evidence available that there is no truth in recent
rumours of Russian air movements over Turkey and Syria'.[219]

From JIC records it seems that Keightley's alert was based on an
'unconfirmed report' emanating from the Joint Intelligence Committee
(Middle East) based in Cyprus that eighty MiGs 'were to arrive at Damas-
cus and Aleppo' in Syria.[220] It is plain from the Queen's Suez intelligence
briefings that scouring the airwaves for evidence of 'large scale Soviet
preparations to intervene by force in the Middle East' remained a priority
for British signals and other forms of intelligence for at least ten days after
the invasion had been halted.[221]

By an intriguing and faintly alarming coincidence (if you consider
Eden's health and state of mind during the Suez crisis, which we shall
examine in detail in chapter 9) the V force became fully operational only
in October 1956,[222] just weeks before Keightley flashed his 'maximum
state of preparedness' message back to London.[223] As Scott and Twigge
put it: 'Ironically, Britain's nuclear ascendancy accompanied her political
decline: October 1956 not only witnessed the attainment of Britain's
atomic ambition but the diplomatic disaster that was Suez.'[224]

The Suez crisis was the central element in the Eden premiership and its
eventual destroyer. It will be discussed in detail in the chapter devoted to
his stewardship. It produced a spate of inquests that ran on deep into the
Macmillan premiership, some of which had to do with the likelihood of
future limited wars, the UK's readiness to fight them[225] and Whitehall's
capacity to manage them.[226] The capabilities of individual premiers as war
or near-war leaders will be considered in the next part of the book. But it
is necessary here, in analysing the job of Prime Minister itself, to draw up
a set of performance indicators for premiers as limited-war leaders against
which those individuals can be judged.

I think the essential requirements can be reduced to six:

1. The 'War Cabinet' should have as close and constant a relationship with the
   full Cabinet as possible. As Hankey put it when designing the breed, 'All

decisions of a "War Committee" should be communicated as soon as possible to the full Cabinet, those of a more secret character, on which the success of operation or the lives of men may depend, being communicated verbally. The experience of the [Great] War showed that for the smooth working of Cabinet Government it was essential that the general results of the War Committee's deliberations should be known to the Cabinet. Otherwise suspicion and friction are apt to be engendered.'[227]

2. The War Cabinet should consist of no more than six constant ministerial attenders. For the efficient conduct of affairs, diplomatic or military, it needs to meet regularly and have a bias towards the taking of decisions rather than deferring them. The War Cabinet needs to have adequate military, Civil Service and Diplomatic Service back-up, an efficient advice system and a constant flow of high-quality intelligence assessments from the Joint Intelligence Committee.

3. The War Cabinet should take pains to avoid the 'tunnel vision'[228] and technical 'overload' that can afflict small groups directed towards a single overriding purpose under conditions of great stress.

4. There needs to be a constant awareness of the needs, priorities and attitudes of allies (or potential allies) and the politics of those international organizations in which, to whatever extent, the conflict is being monitored or played out.

5. Full, accurate and timely disclosure on matters affecting the conflict or near-conflict should be made to Parliament, the media and the public.

6. Ministers in the War Cabinet should remember at all times, as a thoughtful airman put it over twenty years ago, that the essential nature of armed conflict is 'to destroy things and kill people',[229] and that the highest duty on politicians in authority is, therefore, to ensure that all steps that can be taken to avoid war – whether through early preventive action, quality diplomacy or high-grade intelligence – are taken.

There is a gap in those half-dozen criteria (and in my treatment of the transition to World War III) – declarations of war, or rather, the lack of them. This was an absence which struck me in the aftermath of the Falklands War when I discovered what had transpired in the Home Office (which deals with matters of the royal prerogative) on Falklands Saturday, 3 April 1982, a few hours before the House of Commons debated the crisis.

There was a flurry of anxiety in Queen Anne's Gate that morning because Home Office officials, thinking ahead as their profession required them to do, thought ministers might wish to declare war on Argentina; the invasion of the Falklands could only be seen (from London, at least) as a piece of straightforward aggression by one state against the territory of another. The civil servants did what the British official does best: they looked for the file to see how to do it. But they could not find it.[230]

Britain, after all, had not declared war on anyone since doing so against Siam in January 1942.[231] Ever since, British forces, when engaged in operations outside the UK's jurisdiction, have operated under that mystical but mighty entity, the royal prerogative.[232] But the declaration the officials were seeking, naturally, was not that of 1942 but that of 3 September 1939, when Britain declared war on Germany.

Home Office people do not give in easily. The Cabinet had decided the previous evening that a task force would be sent to the South Atlantic. The civil servants really needed that bit of paper. An official of the Public Record Office was reached at home. The official repaired to Kew. The shelves were searched. Still nothing.[233] The file was eventually found a dozen years later (I had been inquiring after it for years) in time to be shown to my students on one of our regular familiarization trips from Queen Mary and Westfield College in the Mile End Road to the PRO in December 1994.[234]

I have not seen it published in a book before. Here it is. Just two sides. Drawn up by the Foreign Office Legal Adviser, Sir Gerald Fitzmaurice, at the request of the Foreign Secretary, Lord Halifax, on the day of the Molotov–Ribbentrop Pact, 23 August 1939:

Mr Harvey [Halifax's Private Secretary to whom Fitzmaurice's reply was sent].

The Secretary of State's enquiry about how we declare war. The method of procedure is to deliver a declaration of war to the diplomatic representative in London of the enemy Power or Powers at such hour as may be decided upon by the Cabinet and to obtain a receipt recording the time of delivery. The declaration is delivered by a special messenger who should take with him the special passports covering the enemy representative, his family and personal staff and his diplomatic staff and their families. These are now being drafted on the assumption that war would in the first place be only declared on Germany and the Secretary of State would have to sign them.

It is not possible to state definitely at present what the terms of the declaration of war itself would be as these must depend upon circumstances. It is quite likely that our declaration of war might be preceded by an ultimatum which would be delivered in Berlin. This might e.g. take the form that if by a certain time the German Government had not given an assurance that they would proceed no further with their violation of Polish territory the Ambassador had been instructed to ask for his passports and that His Majesty's Government would have to take such steps as might seem good to them. In such a case our actual declaration of war on the expiry of the time limit would take the form of notifying the German Embassy that no satisfactory reply having been received from the German Government, His Majesty's Government considered that a state of war between the two countries existed as from a certain time.

I understand that the declaration would be drafted in consultation with the Dominions Office.

Once the declaration has been delivered a lot of consequential results follow, such as informing the other Government Departments that war has been declared and giving the same information to the diplomatic representatives in London of non-enemy Powers and so forth. Standing drafts for all these purposes exist.[235]

This, by any standards, is a collector's item, and not just because of its awesome significance when the time came eleven days later for war to be declared on Germany. Savour the understatement and the Pooterish attention to procedural detail. Fitzmaurice added an afterthought: 'Cabinet has to approve draft Dec[superscript n] [Declaration].' Halifax, for his part, penned on the document an almost casual note to his Permanent Secretary, Sir Alexander Cadogan: 'You might see this. I presume that if and when the case should arise we shd have to concert with the French.'[236]

Why was this extraordinary historical artefact mislaid for over fifty-five years? Because, as the outer cover of the file and the top right-hand corner of the document make plain, on 12 September 1939 it was consigned to an FO category known as 'General and Miscellaneous' and not copied to the Home Office.[237] Mercifully, neither Mrs Thatcher nor her Cabinet thought of declaring war over that tense weekend in the spring of 1982, partly because they were advised by the Department of Trade and Industry that the Trading with the Enemy Act would come into force if they did, which would cause chaos in the UK's economic relations with Argentina long after what was certain to be a short war.[238] I have since ensured that the file will be to hand in any future contingencies which may require it, for I sent a copy, at his request, to the then Secretary of the Cabinet, Sir Robin Butler. He, in turn, forwarded copies to the permanent secretaries of the Whitehall departments concerned with war-making.

It was intriguing to discover in a No. 10 file from July 1951, re-reviewed and released once the Cold War was over, the complicated briefing which underlay the decision *not* to declare war as part of the United Nations' action against North Korea (and China after November 1950, when Chinese troops arrived in force on the Korean peninsula). After two discussions in Cabinet, the problem was remitted to a committee of officials. In essence, the difficulty arose because conflicts such as Korea, as Brook put it in his brief to Attlee, could 'be considered as police actions or war'.[239]

Brook explained:

[the] problem is of practical importance and urgency because, if the Government decided that all such conflicts should be regarded as international police actions rather than war, important parts of our domestic law would need to be amended if the Government were to be able to exercise on such an occasion all the powers which would be available to them in a state of war.[240]

In a draft Cabinet paper attached to this minute, Brook, summarizing the work of the official committee, declared it was 'arguable that under the United Nations Charter war is outlawed and that any conflict in which we may be involved in pursuance of our obligations under the Charter should, strictly, be considered as an international police operation rather than as war'.[241]

The same paper made it plain just how convenient it was to be able to declare war under the royal prerogative without the formal sanction of the legislature (unlike, as Brook pointed out, the United States): 'Much of the Prerogative and common law, as well as some statutory provisions which would have to apply in a major conflict, have as their fundamental basis the defence of the Realm; and to endeavour to change this fundamental basis to a conception related in the main, not to the defence of the Realm, but to some supra-national idea of universal peace, might well raise legal doubts and complications the extent of which it is difficult to foresee,' the draft paper explained.[242]

A human, and somewhat alarming, question arises from the prerogative powers a Prime Minister possesses, not least because of a premier's capacity to authorize a nuclear strike or a government's capacity to deploy troops in action without consulting Parliament. The question is, what if a Prime Minister goes bananas (as the Chief of the Air Staff said of Eden in July 1956)?[243] This is particularly alarming in the nuclear contingency where time and other pressures would be at their most intense.

Sir Frank Cooper has described this as an area beset by 'lovely constitutional problems'.

'You've got to be quite clear about this,' he said. 'No minister can give an order to the Armed Forces. The Prime Minister can't give an order, nor can the Secretary of State for Defence. They can give a direction saying X should be done. They can approve a recommendation, but it's not an order. The only people who can legally give orders are the military.'[244]

Sir Frank's attention to 'these important constitutional niceties', as he called them,[245] arose in the context of a long interview with Tom Dibble and myself about the Falklands War. The conversation continued like this:

HENNESSY: The only exception, and we're on a different area now, is the launching of the nuclear weapons. Only the Prime Minister can do that.

COOPER: Well, he can give authority to launch.

DIBBLE: That, in effect, must be the same thing.

COOPER: But it's not. It's terribly important. An order given by a politician . . . to a military commander is not a legal order.

HENNESSY: So, if the Prime Minister said 'Let the Trident off' and the CDS [Chief of the Defence Staff] thought that this was crackers . . . and they're in PINDAR [the Ministry of Defence's bunker] and the Prime Minister's got the [launch] codes, can the CDS say 'Right, no'?

COOPER: I believe that would be the giving of authority [by the Prime Minister]. And if the CDS said, 'I'm not going to do it,' he [the CDS] would have to go.[246]

At this point we reverted to the Falklands:

HENNESSY: If Margaret [Thatcher] had said to Terry Lewin [Chief of the Defence Staff] 'I want a V-bomber with a WE 177 [hydrogen] bomb on it and go and drop it on Argentina, and I'm authorizing that', Terry Lewin could have said privately to himself, 'She's out of her mind and I do not transmit the signal to [RAF] Strike Command.'

COOPER: I think anybody would say: 'I'm not prepared to do that . . . there is no military justification.' And then they'd have to sit down and work out whether you would do it or maintain a position that there's no military ground for it and it would mean killing hundreds of people.

HENNESSY: Thousands.[247]

There it is. Only the Prime Minister can authorize the use of nuclear weapons; only a figure in military command can give the order to do so. The Chief of Defence Staff, the nation's top officer, could refuse to convert prime ministerial authority into such an order. Though Sir Frank Cooper made it plain that during the Cold War the military had pondered not so much on the need to restrain a premier but 'whether, however dire the circumstances, the Prime Minister would be willing to give the political authority. It has always been seen more by the military in that light . . .'[248] I have put that question directly only to two British Prime Ministers – Alec Home and Jim Callaghan. Home said: 'Terrible, isn't it, the thought; but reason, cold reason doesn't operate in those circumstances quite often. And I'm not sure what cold reason would tell you either if they [the Russians] were on the march.'[249]

I asked Jim Callaghan would he – could he – in the direst of circumstances have fired a Polaris missile? 'If that had become necessary and vital,' he replied, 'it would have meant that the deterrent had failed, because the value of the nuclear weapon is, frankly, only as a deterrent. But if we had got to that point, where I felt it was necessary to do it, then I would have done it. I've had terrible doubts, of course, about this. And if I had lived after pressing that button, I could never have forgiven myself.'[250]

Unknown to Callaghan, or any of the UK's 'nuclear premiers', there was one moment during the Cold War when, had the Soviet Union failed to be deterred, the British war planners at least would have failed to notice. It was in June 1963 during, ironically enough, the post-Cuba review of readiness procedures. The Russians' 'window of opportunity', as it was described to me by a long-serving civil servant on deterrent matters, had to do with a hot (as opposed to a cold) war. During that last over of the Lord's Test Match against the West Indies, when Colin Cowdrey came in with a broken arm and he and David Allen had to hold out against Wes Hall in full cry if the match was to be saved, every single screen of the Ballistic Missile Early Warning System was displaying the live broadcast on BBC Television.[251] When I was told this awesome official secret (of which I am sure there will be no trace in the records) some ten years after the end of the Cold War, I found the humanity of it – and the sense of priority shown – comforting and reassuring.

We must now turn from the awesome question of what British Prime Ministers might have done (once they became nuclear armed, and cricket permitting) to the rather more prosaic matter of what all eleven of them actually did across a wide range of activity when holding the highest executive office in the land at various times since 1945.

PART THREE
THE PRIME MINISTERS

7

A Sense of Architectonics:
Clement Attlee, 1945–51

'A monologue is not a decision.'   *Attlee to Churchill, undated*[1]

'Often the "experts" make the worst possible ministers in their own fields. In this country we prefer rule by amateurs.'
Clement Attlee, 1957[2]

'Britain is being run by a senior executive officer.'
Top Treasury official, 1947[3]

'A lot of clever people have got everything except judgement.'
Clement Attlee, 1961[4]

In the thirties he [Ernest Bevin] thought of Attlee as a second-rate leader. But that was what he wanted. He had had enough of those who thought they were first-rate with MacDonald. During the war, when for the first time he got to know Attlee well, his attitude changed. He could still make the occasional patronizing remark. 'We must look after little Clem', he told a colleague in 1946. But this was superficial. By then he believed that Attlee was not merely the best leader the Labour Party had got, but the best it was ever likely to get. He made it clear that he would serve under no one else.   *Roy Jenkins on Bevin and Attlee, 1974*[5]

Clement Attlee – top deity in the modern Labour Party's pantheon.
Professor Ben Pimlott, 1997[6]

'He [a PM] must remember he's only the first among equals . . . His voice will carry the greatest weight. But you can't ride rough-shod over a Cabinet unless you're something very extraordinary.'
Clement Attlee, 1961[7]

Unlike some politicians who find themselves at the very apex of public and political life, Clem Attlee did not think he was extraordinary. He neither created a myth about himself nor did he start to believe in it. He reckoned privately that 'If Britain had been a republic and we had had a presidential election [in 1945], Churchill would have been elected as the man in the limelight, but in fact he had to go to election burdened with a discredited party, and that caused his defeat.'[8]

Nobody, least of all the man himself, would have coined the word 'Attleeism' except in the context of his celebrated one-liners (such as the immortal 'a period of silence on your part would be welcome' put-down of Professor Harold Laski, Labour Party Chairman in 1945 – and just the kind of 'intellectual' Attlee disdained). As for the notion of an 'Attlee Project' he would have treated that as an example of political vanity and the personalization of government and politics he abhorred. Shortly after retirement, though, he did pen a faintly self-ironic verse for his brother Tom to mark his enrolment as a Knight of the Garter:

> Few thought he was even a starter
> There were many who thought themselves smarter
> But he ended PM
> CH and OM
> An earl and a knight of the garter.[9]

For all its recognition of his less than overwhelming public image, there is here a genuine (and justified) sense of his own worth.

But by the standards of any British political generation of modern times, Clem Attlee was decidedly diminuendo. On the Richter scale of charismatic leadership, the needle scarcely flickered. He had all the presence of a gerbil. That clever man of biting tongue but limited judgement, Hugh Dalton, declared on the day Clem Attlee beat Herbert Morrison for the Labour leadership in 1935, 'it is a wretched disheartening result!' adding, 'And a little mouse shall lead them.'[10] Some mouse. Dalton was not the last sophisticate to underestimate 'little Clem', and Attlee's reputation has been rising almost ever since, as the stop-gap leader who headed his party for twenty years, the mouse that stayed to become wartime Deputy Prime Minister and then Prime Minister in his own right for six years, 'the little indiarubber man' as that shrewd political journalist, James Margach, described him.[11] Margach, after years of watching Attlee from the House of Commons press gallery and sitting through his rare and profoundly unrevealing briefings of the Westminster lobby correspondents,[12] acquired a crucial insight into the strange effectiveness of this most unlikely of premiers. 'Style', he wrote, is normally 'seen in terms of the sweeping gesture, the dramatic entrance, the flair for histrionic glamour in the spotlight. But style can be equally powerful when it exploits non-style.'[13] This Attlee did to perfection, not just in puncturing the grandiloquent rhetoric of Churchill in their parliamentary exchanges after 1945 or in driving the political correspondents to distraction with his staccato replies to their questions, but in the brusque memorability of his exchanges with ministerial colleagues and top officials. He knew his limitations, made a virtue of them and turned them into collectors' items. As his economic assistant in No. 10 in 1945–46, Douglas Jay, put it: 'He would never use one syllable where none would do.'[14] Denis Healey recalls his colleague in the postwar Labour Party headquarters, Wilfred Fienburgh, as saying 'that a conversation with an ordinary man was like a game of tennis; a conversation with Attlee was like throwing biscuits to a dog – all you could get out of him was yup, yup, yup.'[15]

Anyone could be on the receiving end of such treatment, from the Monarch to a windy Labour backbencher. Legend has it, for example, that at 7.30 on the evening of 26 July 1945 when Attlee came to Buckingham Palace to 'kiss hands' as Prime Minister, a long silence was broken by the new premier finally saying:

'I've won the election.'

To which his equally self-effacing Sovereign replied:

'I know. I heard it on the six o'clock news.'[16]

'I gather they call the Prime Minister "Clem",' the King said to his Private Secretary after this brief encounter. ' "Clam" would be more appropriate.'[17]

My own favourite dates from his final year as Leader of the Opposition in 1954, when the menace of the hydrogen bomb was opening up that intra-party fissure on nuclear weapons that has vexed Labour virtually ever since. The scene is a room along the committee corridor at Westminster. The occasion a meeting of the Parliamentary Labour Party. That eloquent Welshman, Harold Davies, is delivering himself of a long and passionate warning about the dangers of thermonuclear horrors to come. Clem doodles (he was the greatest doodler ever to occupy No. 10 and at least one member of the Cabinet Secretariat used to collect his output after Cabinet meetings)[18] and smokes his pipe impassively as Davies goes into orbit. When he finally subsides, Attlee removes his pipe, lays down his pen and says: 'We'll watch it; meeting adjourned.'[19]

But Attlee's reputation extends way beyond his parsimony with language. It has risen steadily since his death in 1967, so much so that he has become a kind of lodestar for the efficient and successful conduct of peacetime Cabinet government and premiership in the postwar years, and not just on the Labour side. His views on welfare, economic planning or the ownership and organization of industry may well have a very dated air half a century on, but he still provides a kind of gold standard against which future practitioners of the premiership will be judged. Many of those who have succeeded him since 1951 have been subjected to the Clem test.

For example, that connoisseur of the governing profession, Rab Butler, said of Harold Macmillan: 'He was very good, only exceeded by little Attlee, who had a habit of biting people in the pants.'[20] Macmillan himself said of Attlee that he was 'much underrated' and 'one of the best chairmen I have ever sat under'.[21] And I shall never forget Christopher Soames a few years after Mrs Thatcher sacked him from her Cabinet telling me with great brio, despite confinement to his bed with flu, that Mrs Thatcher 'was not really running a team. Every time you have a Prime Minister who wants to take all the decisions, it mainly leads to bad results. Attlee didn't. That's why he was so damn good . . .'[22]

Jim Callaghan learned 'from Attlee the advantage of keeping your mouth shut, and of not really exposing your point of view if you wanted to get your business through rather quickly in the Cabinet'.[23] And he never forgot the brevity or the wisdom of Attlee's advice when appointing him to his first junior ministerial post in 1947: 'Remember you are playing for the first eleven now, not the second eleven. And if you are going to negotiate with someone tomorrow, don't insult him today.' Lord Callaghan was in and out of the Cabinet Room in two minutes.[24]

Harold Wilson spoke of his 'filial devotion'[25] to Attlee, who sent him to the Board of Trade in 1947 at the tender age of thirty-one, and George Thomas (Viscount Tonypandy) attested to Wilson's habit of referring back to 'Clem' throughout his periods in No. 10;[26] though it has to be said that Wilson's prolixity from the chair, especially during the Cabinets of his first premierships after 1964,[27] shows that he had not fully imbibed Attlee's deliciously paradoxical line on the key to successful Cabinet government – 'Democracy means government by discussion, but it is only effective if you can stop people talking.'[28] In Jo Grimond's view, for these and other reasons, Attlee was simply 'the best Prime Minister since the war'.[29] (Attlee presided over the Shadow Cabinet Room at Westminster when Labour was in opposition between 1979 and 1997 in the form of a statuette on the mantelpiece. And once Labour was restored to power in May 1997, his portrait appeared on the wall of the anteroom in No. 10 where ministers gather before their Cabinet meetings.)[30]

Clem Attlee's Downing Street years between 1945 and 1951 have become a benchmark in another important sense, too, which continues to shape how we think about politics, government and the uses of the state power. For example, Nigel Lawson was right to treat what he called the 'Attleeite settlement'[31] and Mrs Thatcher's stewardship as the two great political weather systems that have dominated the ecology of postwar British government.

In a 1988 a lecture to the Centre for Policy Studies, subtitled 'The Tide of Ideas from Attlee to Thatcher', Lawson claimed the Thatcher governments had

'transformed the politics of Britain – indeed Britain itself – to an extent no other government has achieved since the Attlee government of 1945 to 1951 . . . [which] . . . set the political agenda for the next quarter of a century. The two key principles which informed its actions and for which it stood, big government and the drive towards equality, remained effectively unchallenged for more than a generation, the very heart of the postwar consensus.'[32]

For all Lawson's disapproval of the essentials of that postwar settlement, it is no bad epitaph for the pair of Attleean governments charged with reconstructing a nation a third of whose wealth had melted in the heat of war, which still carried huge and, at that time, largely inescapable overseas commitments and with a mandate to foster both social justice and industrial modernization at home, all drawing on what the diplomat Paul Gore-Booth called a 'thinly lined Exchequer'.[33]

Quite apart from the creation of a comprehensive system of state-run social insurance,[34] the fusion of a myriad of hospitals and private practices into a single National Health Service (becoming thereby at the time the world's third largest employer after the Red Army of the Soviet Union and Indian State Railways),[35] the transfer of a workforce of 2.3 million people from private industry to public corporations under the nationalization programme,[36] the Attlee government took the first steps towards changing an empire sustained by territory into a commonwealth based on influence.[37] Attlee also presided over the growth and development of a huge, new secret state apparatus constructed for the purpose of fighting the Cold War at home and abroad, the detailed ramifications of which became apparent only after that confrontation had ended and highly sensitive files began to reach the Public Record Office from the mid 1990s on. It was a matter of huge transformations across a range of fronts in an era when, thanks to the experience of World War II, expectations of the state and those who ran it were high.

For several reasons, therefore, the early postwar years still deserve our current attention and it could well be that future premiers, whatever their political coloration, might benefit from studying the statecraft of the brisk little man in his sixties who presided over such a demanding agenda from within a cloud of pipe smoke as, Cabinet meetings over and his colleagues departed, he sat down to work in the Cabinet Room, red crayon poised to scribble 'Yes', 'No', or, if feeling especially effusive, 'Agreed, CRA' on the papers placed before him.[38]

He could be as much a nightmare to brief as he was to engage in conversation. Twenty years later, Whitehall still reverberated with Attlee stories. Alec Cairncross, Head of the Government Economic Service, noted in his diary for 12 September 1965 that 'Lionel [Robbins] very amusing on Attlee. If one went in the war to brief him he either listened enigmatically without saying a word or could break in with great eloquence and insight. Frank Lee [former Permanent Secretary to the Treasury] used to say that if someone explained circumstantially that hemlock had been added to Lady A's tea he would no doubt have given an abstracted "Quite, quite" as he did to most expositions.'[39]

I remember the far from loquacious Oliver Franks recalling Attlee's visit to Washington for his 'summit' with President Truman on Korea and the bomb in December 1950. Lord Franks, as ambassador to Washington, had developed the practice of briefing the ambassadors to the United States from the Commonwealth dominions over a drink every Friday evening in the British embassy. He asked Attlee if, after his talks with Truman, he could take the session on the Friday at the end of his visit. The Prime Minister readily agreed. Franks, knowing at first hand of Attlee's passion for brevity, attempted to warm him up by opening with an overview on Korea, sharing the burden of rearmament and so on. Attlee puffed his pipe appreciatively as the silky Franks mind ranged over the scene. The ambassador finished and turned expectantly to Attlee. 'Prime Minister,' he said. Attlee removed his pipe from his mouth. 'Quite,' he replied and replaced his pipe, leaving the now near-desperate Franks to pick up the threads once more.[40]

His terseness could cause problems even with the King, for whom Attlee had the highest regard (he wept when news of George VI's death was brought to him in 1952).[41] Ever since that embarrassed exchange at the start of his premiership, so-called 'Audience Notes' have been prepared by both the Palace and Downing Street private secretaries to prevent any more drying-up at the weekly meetings between Monarch and premier.[42] The King, however, continued to fret that his Prime Minister did not tell him more about what was going on[43] but both the Palace and the No. 10 archives show that the moment the King requested more background, Attlee would provide it.[44]

Attlee's brusqueness could frighten people, both ministers and officials. Ronald Fraser, Private Secretary to the Cabinet Secretary, Sir Norman Brook, and a member of that formidable breed of Scottish public servant which enriched postwar Whitehall, has told me how Attlee would send cross memos through the newly installed pneumatic tube linking No. 10 and the Cabinet Office upbraiding him for using Scottish archaisms in covering notes on Sir Norman's influential steering briefs for Cabinet and Cabinet committee meetings.[45]

It was in the Cabinet Room above all, that Attlee, in the words of Sir George Mallaby, a Cabinet minute-taker, 'buzzed . . . [like a wasp] in your face and stung you hard'[46] if you were ill-briefed or long-winded (unless, of course, you were his great friend and much admired protector, Ernest Bevin, who was indulged like no other, except perhaps, for the veteran and greatly respected Lord Addison).[47] Harold Wilson, the youngest Cabinet minister since Pitt (as he enjoyed reminding people)[48] could do a particularly good impression of Attlee-the-wasp:

'Attlee was in complete charge of his Cabinet. He would start, "Minutes of the last meeting," and if anyone dared to raise anything God help 'em. There was one from Scotland, can't remember his name now, and he would say, "Well, Prime Minister, I don't disagree but I do remember a similar occasion three years ago . . ." Attlee said, "Do you disagree with the Minutes?" "No." "All right. Agreed. Next item." '[49]

George Strauss, Attlee's Minister of Supply, was honest about how bruising those stings could be. 'If a minister did something a bit wrong and made a mess of it,' he told Roy Hattersley many years later, 'Attlee would tell him off. And if that minister did something well . . . Attlee would say nothing about it. And sometimes we ministers used to say to ourselves, "It's a pity he's so ready to tell us off and he might sometimes say 'well done'."[50]

And they all feared the summons to No. 10 that might project them once more on to the back benches. Unlike most of his predecessors and successors, Attlee didn't wrap his dismissals up. These encounters were as brief as the moment of appointment. 'He was the best butcher since the war,' said Harold Wilson (who was one of the worst). 'He'd send for a man and say: "Well, you've had a good innings; time to put your bat up in the pavilion." And that was it.'[51] 'This is a most unpleasant task,' Attlee once explained, after outlining the importance of being ruthless. 'But, in my experience 99 per cent of the people I had to sack took it very well and remained loyal.'

Some had to 'take it very well' without even tasting the fruits of office. One was Arthur Palmer, the Labour MP for Wimbledon. 'Mr Attlee once sent for my husband,' his widow Dr Marion Palmer told me many years later. 'He went thinking he might be about to be asked to take on an important job. "You're an engineer who understands mechanical things," the Prime Minister said. "Could you advise me on our Hoover which we can't get to work properly?"'[52] One of the few who took it less well and asked 'Why?' was, according to Harold Wilson, simply told 'Not up to the job'.[53]

Attlee had, in modern parlance, zero tolerance of sleaze. John Belcher, a junior minister at the Board of Trade, who had accepted hospitality from a celebrated 'spiv', Sidney Stanley,[54] left the government in December 1948 without hesitation, though maintaining that 'decisions made by me have never been influenced in any way by any of gift or by any promise'.[55] (Attlee replied with characteristic brevity: 'I am certain that you have taken the right course in offering to resign your Office.')[56]

I have concentrated initially on the tart flavour of Attlee because personality is such a powerful shaper of the premiership. So, of course, is the wider political climate in which those personality traits are displayed. Attlee was perched atop what is still the second largest postwar majority (146) until the general election of February 1950, when it shrivelled to six. However, he had to be protected by that brilliant bruiser, Ernie Bevin (the crucial figure in seeing off the two embryonic challenges to Attlee's leadership of the party on election-victory day itself in 1945 and during the aftermath of the sterling crisis of 1947).[57] His parliamentary party was, by Labour standards, relatively quiescent (with occasional dissenting outbursts, as over foreign policy in 1947[58] or Ireland in 1949[59]) while the labour movement at large was firmly in the grip of trade union loyalists such as Arthur Deakin of the Transport and General and Sam Watson of the mineworkers.[60] The rest of this chapter will concentrate on how Attlee used that accumulated inheritance from past premierships (which I examined in chapter 4) and adapted it to the needs of his present.

Though genuinely surprised to find himself in Downing Street as a result of the 1945 general election,[61] Attlee had thought a great deal about the mechanics of No. 10 and its relationship with the rest of Whitehall, as well as the efficiency of Cabinet government in general, both as Leader of the Opposition between 1935 and 1940 and as a leading figure within the War Cabinet thereafter. (In this he was probably only equalled by Ted Heath among postwar premiers.) Some of his thinking was quite radical. In the early 1930s, on the basis of his experience as Chancellor of the Duchy of Lancaster and later Postmaster-General in the second Labour government (both posts just below full Cabinet rank), Attlee concluded in a memoradum written for his own purposes that: 'The Cabinet today is a gathering of some twenty people who with a few exceptions are immersed in detailed administration. It is quite unable to take a broad view on the strategy of the campaign . . .', a position made all the more parlous by 'the fact that the Prime Minister [MacDonald] was constitutionally averse from taking decisions and entirely incapable of understanding the proper use of committees and experts'.[62] Attlee's recommendation for 'a radical change in the nature and composition of the Cabinet' embraced the idea of what later became known as 'overlords' – a 'Cabinet of ten' senior ministers with light departmental duties and charged with the oversight of bundles of activities to be carried out by ministers below Cabinet rank.[63]

He outlined his thinking publicly in a Left Book Club volume, *The Labour Party in Perspective*, in 1937, turning his attention to the back-up available to the Prime Minister in this new, streamlined scheme of things. 'The Prime Minister', he wrote, 'has no department. He has only private secretaries and the very small Cabinet Secretariat. In order to carry through a co-ordinated plan of reconstruction, there will be required a well-equipped and diversified staff at the centre to work out the main lines of the plan which is to be implemented in the departments.'[64]

At the very least this suggested Attlee had a kind of undeclared Prime Minister's Department in mind, an inclination strengthened by his experience as Deputy PM under Churchill. For example, on New Year's Eve

1942, he circulated a paper to the War Cabinet's Committee on Machinery of Government with the suggestion that the Chancellor of the Exchequer, as Finance Minister, should have his own Permanent Secretary in the Treasury. A separate figure, presumably the Head of the Civil Service, should continue to manage establishments and personnel policy in the Treasury while working 'directly under the Prime Minister, as First Lord of the Treasury'.[65] 'While I should not wish to establish a Prime's Department,' Attlee informed the Cabinet committee,

I think that the development of the Cabinet Secretariat is already tending to give a greater cohesion to the machine of government. The Prime Minister can of course look to all departments for advice and assistance, but in my view requires something more than Private Secretaries for carrying out his functions. In my view this second Permanent Secretary to the Treasury, while being head of the Establishments Branch, should also be something equivalent to a chef de cabinet to the Prime Minster.[66]

Attlee would have been aware of Lloyd George's experiment with his Prime Minister's Secretariat, the famous Downing Street 'Garden Suburb', but, revealingly, Attlee was seeking a Civil Service regular to run his new capacity for him rather than the strange mixture of outsiders LG recruited in early 1917.[67]

Though Attlee never sought to create such a position once Prime Minister, he did, in one sense, acquire a *de facto* chef de cabinet in the person of Norman Brook, who succeeded Sir Edward Bridges as Secretary of the Cabinet in 1947 (though he had been Cabinet Secretary in all but name since Bridges combined the Permanent Secretaryship of the Treasury with his old job in 1945).[68] Brook went on to be the *de facto* chef to Churchill, Eden and Macmillan, becoming the indispensable Whitehall figure par excellence of his generation, and a continuous and influential factor at the heart of any study of the British premiership for the first eighteen years after the war; he deserves a brief treatment here in his own right as, certainly after Bridges' retirement in 1956, but probably from Churchill's return to No. 10 in 1951, he was the *primus inter pares* among the Whitehall permanent secretaries. In short, he was the Civil Service equivalent of a Prime Minister.

A grammar-school boy from Wolverhampton, Brook had risen by that earliest of meritocratic ladders, the old administrative class of the Civil Service, via the Home Office (which he joined in 1925)[69] and the great forcing-house of World War II Whitehall (which propelled him relentlessly up the hierarchy). In 1942 he became Deputy Secretary of the War Cabinet, a post which first brought him into close contact with three of the premiers he would serve so intimately after the war (Churchill, Attlee and Eden). In 1943, at the young age of forty-one, he became Permanent Secretary to the Minister of Reconstruction, Lord Woolton,[70] another fine observation post in terms of the expanded panoply of the state, especially in terms of economic management and welfare services, planned for the postwar period.

By the time he rejoined Bridges as additional Secretary of the Cabinet in 1945, Brook was extraordinarily well primed on both the mechanics of state and the swathe of issues which would confront it at home and abroad. And it was this range of activities and influence which only became apparent to outsiders (and then but a few among the ranks of the contemporary historians and administrative history specialists) once the postwar files were released progressively from 1976, nine years after Brook's death.

Almost everywhere you look in the Cabinet and premiership files of the period, including the most sensitive intelligence, nuclear and war-planning areas, you see not just Brook's spoor but his powerful presence. Nobody carried more secrets of state in his great dome of a head than Norman Brook. He was the insider's insider. Brook's *Times* obituarist, quite plainly an insider himself, was well placed to observe him in action during the years of his maximum influence between 1945 and his retirement from the Cabinet Office in January 1963:

Norman Brook was a man of immense authority. The first impression was of size, with a head that was large even for such a heavy frame, and a calm gaze from heavy-lidded eyes. Then came the quiet, rather slow voice. At the start it might seem casual, even lethargic. But this illusion was dispelled as his voice took on a cutting edge and he shaped the words on which he wished to pivot this thought. And whether he was giving information, or advice, or instructions, his thinking was dominated by the need for good order in public affairs.[71]

He could strike some as funny, almost pernickety, about the formal side of life such as proper dress. He would frown on anyone wearing tweeds to the office, unless it were a weekend.[72] And I suspect he was embarrassed (not least because ministers cheered his arrival) when in December 1950 he rushed from a dinner, bedecked in full white-tie fig, to a sudden late-night Cabinet meeting in the PM's room at the House of Commons to take the minutes while the Cabinet deliberated upon what Attlee would discuss with Truman at their rather improvised 'summit' on the Korean War.[73]

His *Times* obituarist clearly sensed this and hinted at the tension within this faintly obsessional figure:

Good order was also the characteristic of his personal work – the written word pared down to the minimum; the elegant, even hand; the clear desk; scrupulously punctual; responsive to the call of urgency, but never confused, never hurried.

Without imposing such good order on himself he could hardly have become the outstanding exponent of public administration in his time. And it was an imposition for there was much of the artist in the man, and his natural disposition was sensitive, warm, and even impulsive.[74]

The files, of course, tend not to reflect this. But the strength of his own views do occasionally come through. For example, he pressed the reasons for not abolishing capital punishment on Attlee during the preparation of the Criminal Justice Bill in 1948[75] and almost alone he steered the Cabinet away from a draconian and unnecessary counter-subversive statute at the height of the Korean War.[76]

Attlee inherited Norman Brook along with the World War II Whitehall machine with which they were both so familiar. Given Labour's possession of its first-ever absolute majority and Attlee's considerable interest in the administrative mechanics of government, a substantial rejigging might have been anticipated in the summer of 1945. For one of the undoubted powers, almost an absolute one, which falls into the lap of a new PM on 'kissing hands' is the ability to remake, almost to reinvent, his personal machine in No. 10. Premiers, as we have seen, also have a pretty free hand over much of Whitehall, the size and scope of the Cabinet and the nature of the committees and the support systems that sustain it. Such powers were Attlee's from 26 July 1945.

The paper trail he had laid down since 1932 suggested a revolution in the offing comparable to Lloyd George's in 1916–17. And the width and duration of that paper trail, in and out of government, indicates it was not a quick-dash, back-of-the-envelope approach based on passing hunches. Attlee's feeling for governance was genuine. He had that 'architectonic sense', that capacity to 'see the whole building, not only the bricks', a capacity he thought indispensable in a premier after experiencing Mac-

Donald's lack of it.[77] And he knew, too, that the servants of the state needed attention as well as its mechanics. His paper to the War Cabinet's Machinery of Government Committee in 1942 recognized that 'The problem of the relationship of state and private enterprise will be very pressing after the war, and a knowledge of routine Civil Service methods will not be enough.' He suggested the creation of a Civil Service staff college, mixing officials and 'employees of big corporations' as a way of improving matters.[78]

So Attlee entered Downing Street with an impressive storehouse of prior thought about what Ian Bancroft, an early recruit to postwar Whitehall, would later call both the 'hardware' and the 'software' of state.[79] To what use did he put this thinking? In one area he excelled and, I think, remains unsurpassed. In his early 1930s 'Memorandum', just before his disquisition on what he called 'architectonics', Attlee had written: 'The essential quality in a PM is that he should be a good Chairman able to get others to work. He must be able in the last resort to decide between competing policies.'[80] This is not to say that at certain times and on certain issues, especially economic ones (as during the sterling crises of 1947 and 1949), something less than swift sure-footedness was observable beneath the PM's chair in the Cabinet Room.[81]

But, in the main, though 'he had a terribly difficult team to drive . . . he dominated them'.[82] He did this partly by recognizing the special position of Labour's 'Big Four' after 1945 at the heart of his Cabinet (himself plus three others – Bevin, Herbert Morrison and Hugh Dalton until Dalton's resignation from the Chancellorship in 1947, with Cripps replacing Dalton thereafter).[83] This inner quartet was never an acknowledged 'Inner Cabinet' but the chemistry of the Cabinet Room reflected it, as did the weight Attlee placed on their views in summing up discussions. Morrison, Lord President of the Council and Attlee's deputy, usually had his views sought first and Ernie Bevin would be the last to speak before Attlee pulled the threads together.[84]

Attlee generally followed his own line on the importance of being collective in Cabinet and, as the Minister of National Insurance, Jim Griffiths, put it, he would allow ministers their say, doodling in seeming boredom, and would sum up on the basis of consensus without imposing his personal views (if he had any).[85] What volatility there was came not from the little man in the chair but from what the Minister of Labour George Isaacs called the 'triangle of fireworks' between Morrison, Bevin and Nye Bevan, the fiery Health Minister[86] (a prickly trio with little love lost between them). Much of Attlee's strength came from his indispensability as he was probably the only one of the 'Big Four' who at any one time could work effectively with all the others.

Attlee did have developed views on some crucial areas of policy, Indian independence particularly, and here he would take the lead in Cabinet and Cabinet committee, even slapping down (albeit privately) his closest and most important colleague, Bevin, who recoiled from the rush to independence.[87] Attlee's problem lay in his lack of a feel for economics, and his initial staffing of No. 10 reflected his awareness of this weakness.

Here there was a partial implementation of some of his pre-No. 10 thinking, but no more. Instead of that Treasury Permanent Secretary as chef de cabinet in Downing Street, Attlee had Douglas Jay, a wartime temporary civil servant, as his economic assistant until Jay was selected to fight the Battersea North by-election for Labour in 1946.[88] Thereafter he had the services of a career civil servant, William Gorell Barnes, as his 'personal assistant'.[89] But, as George Jones noted, 'there was no political capacity in No. 10 Downing Street to support the Prime Minister on a full-time basis . . .'[90] and Gorell Barnes was not replaced when he was posted to the Colonial Office in February 1948.

Jay described Attlee's problem thus: 'Clem treated economics very much like medicine – a subject on which there were experts and on which it was wise to find a second opinion.'[91] Attlee was quite open about this, telling a meeting of the Cambridge University Labour Club in the 1950s, in reply to a question about the economy, 'Why should I bother? I have got Gaitskell and Wilson.'[92] Wilson himself said: 'Attlee was tone deaf as far as all economic questions were concerned, unless they involved the kind of people he knew – trade unionists, miners, dockers.'[93]

This was a serious weakness, especially in a premier who presided over a government immensely vulnerable on the external economic front. He needed, but did not possess, an imaginative and confident sense both of the domestic UK economy and of economic diplomacy, particularly in terms of the United States, the provider of a dollar lifeline in the American loan and later in the form of Marshall Aid. The mechanics of the Cabinet's economic decision-taking machinery were inadequate, too, until the Economic Policy Committee (EPC) was formed in the wake of the 1947 convertibility crisis (when, under the terms of the American loan, sterling briefly became convertible into dollars, precipitating thereby a disastrous run on the UK's gold and dollar reserves until convertibility was suspended after just over a month).[94] Matters did improve, though no one reviewing the performance of EPC during the protracted sterling crisis of 1949 (with an overvalued pound punishing Britain's exports and placing immense pressure once more on the reserves),[95] which led to the devaluation of September of that year, could believe that the quality of policy-making rose substantially as the government's experience deepened.

On machinery of government matters generally, Attlee did not lack confidence. Yet, when it came to trimming the full Cabinet he came nowhere near his ideal number of ten. He started out with twenty and never culled it below sixteen,[96] despite a partial implementation of his 'overlords' plan during the first two years of his administration in the persons of Herbert Morrison on the economic front and Arthur Greenwood across the social services. Even though Morrison's and Greenwood's co-ordinating functions were largely channelled through Cabinet committees (they chaired the Lord President's Committee and the Social Services Committee, respectively), there is no evidence that they added significantly to the efficiency of the Cabinet process; in Morrison's case quite the reverse, as the Lord President's Committee was the leading casualty of the 1947 currency crisis, being replaced as the leading economic committee by EPC which was chaired by Attlee himself.[97] Greenwood, a victim of drink and overwork, went into retirement altogether when Attlee's 'architectonics' were reshaped in September 1947.[98]

Attlee always claimed that in his time the workload of the Prime Minister was 'heavy but not insupportable' (he told one of his early biographers, Roy Jenkins, 'that he found being Prime Minister rather easy – that the avoidance of those long tube journeys to Stanmore [the family home in the north-west suburbs of London during his period as wartime Deputy Prime Minister] more than made up for the additional responsibilities of being Prime Minister') and on one famous occasion fetched his own tea on the grounds that the No. 10 messenger was 'probably busy'.[99] He made it his practice not to go up to bed from the Cabinet Room until all his red boxes were cleared[100] and he slept the sleep of the just, telling his ministers and officials not to take their problems to bed with them.[101] He probably ranks with Peel and Gladstone as one of the tidiest-minded men to have filled the office of Prime Minister. He was physically robust, though he did succumb to ulcers twice during his years in No. 10: once in 1948[102] and again in the spring of 1951, when his absence from Downing Street in St Mary's Hospital, Paddington may well have exacerbated the Cabinet crisis over defence expenditure, social services and the Budget which led to the resignations of Nye Bevan, Harold Wilson and John Freeman.[103]

The reason why Attlee ranks with Alec Douglas-Home as probably the most tranquil occupant of No. 10 since 1945 in terms of personal peace has to do with more than his orderly working habits or his happy marriage (though Violet Attlee could become upset about 'that part of life in Downing Street which excluded her from her husband').[104] It stemmed, too, from his lack of anguish or complication about his political beliefs. He could almost have said about theoretical socialism what he once declared of Christianity – 'Believe in the ethics ... Can't believe the mumbo-jumbo.'[105]

Attlee's experience in the East End of London as well as the formative experience of shared hardships and comradeship in a string of Great War front-lines, gave him a heartfelt yet almost prosaically practical view of the alleviation of want and the diminution of injustice which lay at the core of his democratic socialist beliefs. Like Denis Healey, Attlee, I suspect, would have approved of Lesjek Kolakowski's acknowledgement that: 'The trouble with the social democratic idea is that it does not stock and does not sell any of the exciting ideological commodities which various totalitarian movements ... offer dream-hungry youth ... Democratic Socialism requires, in addition to commitment to a number of basic values, hard knowledge and rational calculation ... It is an obstinate will to erode by inches the conditions which produce avoidable suffering, oppression, hunger, wars, racial and national hatred, insatiable greed and vindictive envy.'[106]

Attlee's best definition of his creed was reserved for a campaign speech in Sheffield during the 1950 election. 'Communism', he said, 'denies the dignity of the individual, Conservatism ranges the individual in classes.'[107] In Falkirk during the same campaign he declared: 'I get rather tired when I hear that you must only appeal to the incentives of profit. What got us through [the war] was unselfishness and an appeal to the higher instincts of mankind. What is getting us through in these difficult days is a far greater sense of responsibility due to the fact that men and women feel they have a far greater stake in the country than they ever had before.'[108]

Attlee was a believer in step-by-step social reform, through the careful accumulation of improvement and benefits for the least fortunate. It was very revealing of the man when he asked Griffiths, his social security minister, if he, as Prime Minister, could introduce the death-grant clause as the National Insurance Bill passed through the House of Commons, because his East End experience (as a social worker, local politician and MP for Limehouse) of how the poor die had seared him.[109] At a meeting of the University College, London, Labour Club in 1963, Tom McNally asked him 'What led you to the Labour Party, Lord Attlee?' 'Limehouse,' he replied simply.[110]

The orderliness of Attlee's Downing Street and the simplicities of his political philosophy were one thing, but the workings of Whitehall in general were quite another, and here the overall picture was not so pleasingly orderly. That equally high- and tidy-minded figure, Stafford Cripps, whom one might dub God's management consultant, was horrified on his return from the Cabinet mission to India in 1946 to find an ever-more sprawling Cabinet committee system overburdened by ever-increasing trivia.[111] He persuaded Attlee to commission a review supervised by Norman Brook and Edward Bridges.[112] As a result, Attlee circulated a tart Cabinet paper in September 1946 calling for 'a marked reduction in the number of problems put forward for discussion in Ministerial Committees'.[113]

Yet over a year later his Minister of Fuel and Power, Hugh Gaitskell, could complain in his diary: 'Sometimes Cabinet meetings horrify me because of the amount of rubbish talked by some Ministers who come there after reading briefs which they do not understand. I do not know how this can be avoided except perhaps by getting more things settled at official level, and when they cannot be settled there having the issues presented plainly to Ministers. Also, I believe the Cabinet is too large. A smaller Cabinet, mostly of non-Departmental Ministers, would really be able to listen and understand more easily and hear the others arguing the matter out.'[114]

Despite the strictures of Cripps and Gaitskell, and his own architectonic sense, Attlee failed to tackle what Correlli Barnett rightly called the 'administrative elephantiasis' of early postwar government.[115] It really was what Kenneth Wheare called 'government by committee'[116] taken to extremes. Of course World War II had led to a huge explosion of committees despite Churchill's best efforts to curb them.[117] Chamberlain's rather tight little system of five standing ministerial committees and eight ad hoc ministerial committees in the last days of peace gave way to no fewer than 400 War Cabinet committees and sub-committees, for which the Cabinet Office provided a secretariat at no fewer than 8,000 meetings (though, of course, the 400 were not all in existence at the same time and not all of them were chaired by ministers).[118]

Within days of the war in Europe ending, the War Cabinet's Machinery of Government Committee, under the chairmanship of Sir John Anderson, submitted a report to Churchill on postwar 'Cabinet Organisation' which was very much the distilled wisdom of the wartime coalition on the subject. The Anderson Committee broke the subject down into three parts: the possible appointment of 'supervising ministers' (i.e., 'overlords'); the Cabinet committee system; and 'the optimum size of the post war Cabinet'.[119]

It found strongly against 'overlords' as: 'A system of Supervising Ministers in normal times would seriously interfere with the traditional responsibility of departmental Ministers to Parliament, and with the doctrine of collective responsibility, and it would almost inevitably lead to duplication of staff and work at the official level.' Co-ordination would be best achieved 'by adapting to peacetime needs the system of Standing Cabinet Committees which has been developed during the war.'[120]

The report went on to give an outline plan for such a system, arguing that its 'essential feature' would be its flexibility, not least as it would co-exist 'with the appointment of ad hoc Cabinet committees for special subjects as and when required.' Elasticity and effectiveness were the aims and, for illustrative purposes, Anderson sketched a scheme of six Standing Cabinet Committees for a postwar government (Defence, National Development, Economic Relations, External Affairs, Social Services and Legislation). As for the size of the full Cabinet, 'the ideal would be below rather than above twenty'.[121]

The Anderson *structure* was apparent in Attlee's engine room as it was constructed with its mix of standing and ad hoc committees designed to carry a hugely increased peacetime workload at levels beneath the full Cabinet. But the *size* of it plainly got out of hand, partly no doubt because of the range of responsibilities the state kept or extended on the economic and social policy fronts. On the face of it, Attlee's combined total over 6½ years of 148 standing committees (both ministerial and official) and 313 ad hoc[122] reveals an uncharacteristic absence of architectonics even though, in the case of the ad hocs, no fewer than 175 of them met on no more than three occasions.[123]

Chris Brady's work on the committee structure of the Attlee years shows quite graphically the problems of definition and measurement involved.[124] And during the early days of the first Wilson government, Whitehall veterans such as the economists Alec Cairncross and Bryan Hopkin would refer back to the 1945–51 period, not as an example of how to make policy and reach decisions effectively, but as a *comparable* experience in terms of 'indecision and overload all round'.[125] My own tendency in earlier years, especially in my joint study of *Mr Attlee's Engine Room* with Andrew Arends,[126] to depict the Attleean processes of government as the acme of efficiency has had to be modified somewhat.

For even when it came to economic planning, Labour's 'big idea' in 1945,[127] it was more a case of improvise-as-you-go than architectonics-from-on-high. Though planning was supposed to be the superglue of the 1945 Labour Government, it got lost in the structural morass of economic decision-taking. As late as December 1949, the Cabinet Office's Economic Section was still trying somehow to attach wires from Whitehall to the real economy which would provide impetus in such crucial areas of concern as machine-tool production.[128] And from recently discovered files, we find officials as late as April 1951, 5¾ years after Labour's victory, admitting how embarrassing it was to have to refer back in answers to parliamentary questions on planning to Attlee's speech setting up the Central Economic Planning Staff in March 1947.[129]

On the face of it, here *was* an example of a rejigged state tooled-up for the new economic responsibilities of a government committed to full employment and greater economic efficiency. A Central Economic Planning Staff made up of a mixture of insiders and outsiders with a strong bias towards professional economists would service an Economic Planning Board that brought together Whitehall, employers and trade unions for the purposes of advising ministers more effectively. Public documents, a series of *Economic Surveys*, embracing past performance and future aspirations, would convey the required aspirations and signals to the workforce, to Parliament, to the press and to the public generally.

The Economic Planning Board never impinged seriously on either the high policy-making processes of Whitehall or upon what was happening in the real economy (to the relief of the Federation of British Industry, who concluded privately in 1950 that 'the fact that these ambitious hopes have not been realized is regarded by many of those who have been concerned with the Board as one of its most significant achievements').[130] The *Economic Surveys*, the chief visible expression of postwar planning, never became a genuine instrument of change. They veered between the descriptive and the exhortatory. Cripps apart, ministers had a surprisingly small impact on the purposes or processes of these exercises.[131] Here was an area where prime ministerial direction might have made a difference, but the premier's economic 'tone-deafness' simply added to the drift. At root, the problem arose from unwillingness on the part of Attlee and his ministers to recognize the impossibility of serious state direction of the economy without the full-blooded application of physical controls over labour and material of the kind exercised in wartime.

There was, however, one area of crucial engine-room activity where the wartime experience had brought a degree of clarity – the creation of War or Near-War Cabinets. Attlee was adept at adapting the World War II model to fit particular contingencies and the Cold War generally led to a, so far, permanent peacetime extension in the job of Prime Minister that goes much further than the occasional need for a War Cabinet.

Here I would single out three factors – though the first one, nuclear weapons, pre-dates Attlee's incumbency and would, in terms of developing a separate British weapons-making capacity, have almost certainly occurred anyway, Cold War or no Cold War.

However, after US collaboration was largely cut off when Congress passed the 1946 McMahon Act (which prohibited the sharing of American nuclear knowledge with any other nation), this new need to go it alone led Attlee to bring atomic policy-making within the Cabinet system, or certainly its committee sub-structure, even if he kept it away from the full Cabinet itself.[132] (As he said over a decade later, 'I thought that some of them were not fit to be trusted with secrets of this kind.')[133] From the Prime Minister's own 'bomb' file, which did not reach the Public Record Office until the mid 1990s, we can see how Attlee was pivotal to the initial decision to confine the question of making a British atomic bomb to a special Cabinet committee, GEN 163, in January 1947 and to go for a policy of maximum secrecy thereafter.[134] The file shows Attlee was central, too, to the decision to ease secrecy a little and allow the Minister of Defence to announce in the Commons in May 1948 that research on atomic weapons was under way because (as his briefing paper put it), 'the extreme degree of secrecy imposed in January 1947 on research activities on atomic weapons is now becoming increasingly ineffective, as well as being an impediment to progress and a possible source of embarrassment'.[135]

Attlee, however, was not a natural cold warrior. He had that capacity for detached and independent thought which can come to those (now very rare in political or public life) who have seen real military action themselves, as Attlee had with the South Lancashire Regiment at Gallipoli and in France.[136] Though he retained definite traces of 'Major Attlee' all his life, he was not prone to take professional military advice at face value and took a great deal of persuading in 1946 that the Soviet Union really was a power in a position to pursue a policy of world domination even if that were its long-term aim. (All three Chiefs of Staff threatened to resign unless the Prime Minister dropped his opposition to a Mediterranean and Middle East defence posture that would enable the Royal Air Force to strike Russia from bases there. Attlee backed down in the face of this threat only in January 1947.)[137]

He remained far from alarmist about Russia, seeing nothing inevitable about war with the Soviet Union even in the fraught early weeks of the Berlin airlift in the summer of 1948. He told the chiefs at a Defence Committee meeting at the end of July 1948 that 'though there was, of course, a risk that the Berlin situation would lead to war, he did not consider that risk as essentially different from those in Trieste or in Italy'. The minute-taker drily recorded Attlee's reminder to the military of civilian supremacy in the UK system of government. 'He fully appreciated the anxieties of the Chiefs of Staff and was grateful to them for their advice, but the responsibility for deciding whether to accept that advice must be taken by ministers, in the light of the general political situation.' (Attlee consistently backed the British intelligence community's judgement that the Soviet Union would not be in a position to risk major war against the Western Allies until at least the mid 1950s against the more alarmist views of the senior military.)[138]

Attlee's cool approach to the dangers of a hot war with the Soviet Union, however, did not distract him from the post-1945 reality that, as he reminded the Cabinet's Defence Committee during the Berlin crisis, 'in any major conflict the United States must be the predominant partner from the outset'.[139] As early as March 1946 he had concluded a still operational and still secret agreement with the United States on signals intelligence collaboration.[140] In June 1948 this was supplemented by the equally secret and continuing UKUSA agreement on communications intelligence pooling in general.[141]

Cold War sceptic though Attlee may have been in office (and to some extent, remained afterwards), he none the less was the begetter of a kind of Cold War infrastructure at home as well as in terms of the Anglo-American global intelligence reach. Not the least of these responsibilities was the need to bring the contingency planning of the War Book into line with the fearsome new atomic reality. This he did by creating a special official sub-committee, the Defence (Transition) Committee, to work to his main ministerial Defence Committee, with a brief to co-ordinate 'the planning of all necessary measures required to bring the country and its resources into a state of readiness up to the point at which war would be declared'.[142]

It was the Berlin crisis of early summer 1948 which led Attlee and his inner group of ministers on Cold War matters to agree, 'that paper plans for war should be brought to a high state of readiness' while insisting 'that any steps taken should be kept within official circles since any overt action' might 'aggravate international tension'.[143] By the end of 1948, Attlee had lifted this 'publicity ban' as it was hindering effective war planning.[144] By early 1949 an elaborate set of plans were in place for a World War III British state including censorship, internment camps on the Isle of Man and civil defence.[145] By the time the Korean War broke out in June 1950, detailed procedures were in readiness for the transition to an atomic World War III.[146]

On civil defence, Attlee authorized not only the preparation of what became the Civil Defence Act of 1948, but an elaborate network of plans which were augmented by all his successors until, under the first Wilson premiership, home defence was downgraded and trimmed to save money.[147] He was at pains, however, to ensure (as the minutes of his own Civil Defence Committee, GEN 253, expressed it) that the government avoided devoting national resources to civil defence on 'a scale which would cripple the national economy, detract from our power of offence and alienate our allies in Western Europe'.[148] Chuter Ede, Attlee's Home Secretary, took a similar view, admitting that civil defence plans 'contain a large element of improvisation' and that there were limits to what any government could do to protect its civilians in a future atomic war.[149]

Attlee was the first premier who had to plan for the continuation of state when much of his beloved 'green and pleasant land' (he was a great one for 'Jerusalem', which he arranged to have sung at his funeral)[150] would, if the worst happened, be reduced to an irradiated and blackened ruin. Recently released files show him in the last days of his 1950–51 government preparing to respond to intelligence warnings that the Russians might well now be in a position to smuggle an atomic device into the UK. British intelligence painted a nightmarish picture of the bomb entering the UK in fifty small pieces via the Soviet embassy's diplomatic bags. The Russians would assemble the weapon with the aid of skilled fitters in a garage somewhere in London with the result that the whole human apparatus of the British state might go sky high with no warning.[151]

The other Cold War-related area that was to absorb a good deal of the time of early postwar premiers, and which came to impinge seriously in Attlee's time, was the whole question of protecting the UK, especially its public and secret services and weapons research establishments, from espionage. One of the few full sets of Cabinet committee minutes and papers that had to await the ending of the Cold War before they could see the light of day were those of the Committee on Subversive Activities, GEN 183, which Attlee himself occasionally chaired between 1947 and 1951 (A. V. Alexander, the Minister of Defence, was its regular chairman) to examine both the threat from domestic communists and fellow travellers as well as the damage which might be done by KGB agents operating in the country under cover.[152]

Though a good deal of Mr Attlee's counter-intelligence machine can be pieced together from declassified files, we still know relatively little about Cold War intelligence operations conducted abroad against the Soviet Union and its satellites. From his own file on the nature of the Cold War, however, we do know that by late 1949 Attlee had in place a highly secret inner group of ministers whose function was to approve 'in each case' 'subversive activities behind the Iron Curtain' put forward by the Official Committee on Communism (Overseas). This ministerial group consisted of Attlee, Bevin (Foreign Secretary), Morrison (Lord President), Cripps (Chancellor of the Exchequer) and Alexander (Minister of Defence). We know, too, that in the summer of 1950 Attlee approved the reactivation of the old World War II deception organization, the London Controlling Section, under a new cover-name, the Directorate of Forward Plans.[153] As the twentieth century ended there remained almost no sign of detailed documents on such Attlee-authorized subversive operations against the Soviet bloc reaching the Public Record Office. But the considerable accumulation of files released since the collapse of the Soviet Union has demonstrated that cold war, like hot war, was a very prime ministerial matter and, at least until the 1990s, it represented an apparently permanent accretion to a peacetime premier's functions.

There were other areas, too, where the scope of existing prime ministerial functions waxed under Attlee (in fact it is hard to think of anything that waned, for all his distaste for excessively prime ministerial government). He tightened up prime ministerial control over Cabinet procedure by consolidating and regularly updating the key document *Questions of Procedure for Ministers* from August 1945 and after,[154] adopting wholesale as he did so the Anderson Report's argument 'that the internal arrangements which may be made by ministers for discussion among themselves are essentially a domestic matter and no concern of Parliament or the public'.[155] And the extending reach of the state through the nationalized industries and the expanded welfare apparatus meant a considerable growth in the flow of appointments and patronage that passed through No. 10 (though measurement is very difficult here as this remains an unresearched area).[156]

But overall, the Attlee premiership turned out to be in its methods and its instruments a reflection of his profound conservatism with a small 'c', about the British way of government – his conviction, as he put it in the House of Commons in 1950, that 'the British have the distinction above all other nations of being able to put new wine into old bottles without bursting them'.[157] In his approach to the media he was, if anything, *pre*-modern – he was far less adept or PR-minded than Baldwin. He was almost self-parodic on television or the newsreels. Just savour this exchange with an interviewer shortly after the start of the 1951 election campaign:

INT: Tell us something or how you view the election prospects.
ATTLEE: Oh, we shall go in with a good fight. Very good. Very good chance of winning if we go in competently. We always do.
INT: On what will Labour take its stand?
ATTLEE: Well, that's what we shall be announcing shortly.
INT: What are your immediate plans Mr Attlee?
ATTLEE: My immediate plans are to go down to a committee to decide on just that thing as soon as I can get away from here.
INT: Is there anything else you'd like to say about the coming election?
ATTLEE: No.[158]

An extraordinarily unrevealing, almost mesmerizing, exchange that was entirely typical.

Attlee had no interest either in Machiavelli's black political arts or the technology of the media. His press secretary, Francis Williams, only got a news agency tape into No. 10 by selling it to his boss as a 'cricket machine' on which Attlee could read the scores should he need a break from his papers, and a stroll down the corridor.[159] (It remained in place in the Downing Street corridor until the 1990s.)[160] As for reading the newspapers, he gave the impression of not bothering at all, though he did read the Labour movement's trade paper, the *Daily Herald*, 'to see what the chaps are doing, y'know') and *The Times* for the births, marriages, and deaths and the cricket results. His press conferences with the lobby correspondents were as legendary as they were rare. He had a gift for the put-down: 'Nothing in that'; 'You're off beam again.'[161]

But it was not just a question of Attlee being unwilling to modernize the public relations machinery available to the Prime Minister. Even in those areas he did consider essential to the successful conduct of government, cautious conservatism was usually his hallmark. It could be, of course, that the sheer pressure of events, 'with crisis piled on crisis and no sign of letting up either at home or abroad', distracted Attlee from carrying through his plans for a streamlined Cabinet system, a more commercially and managerially minded public service or even a Civil Service College, though the PM 'was able to call on reserves of strength which were not obvious on the surface', as Nye Bevan recalled.[162] Apart from attempts to curb Whitehall numbers,[163] ministers including Attlee left virtually all these matters to Bridges and his permanent secretary colleagues, some of whom made progressive noises but no more.[164]

His wartime writings had shown a profound devotion to 'the Westminster model' and the peculiar historical soil (Britain's 'long history' of 'constitutionalism' was how he put it) that enabled the singular British way of governance to flourish.[165] Attlee believed in increased efficiency but within traditional procedures. Unlike Churchill, he did not step into No. 10 feeling he was walking with destiny ('I had not much idea about destiny', he said over twenty years later).[166] Jim Callaghan said of him on the fiftieth anniversary of the formation of his 1945 administration that: 'The secret of Attlee's success is that he never pretended to be anything other than himself . . . So he won the confidence of them all without ever becoming a faction fighter.'[167]

Herein lies the key to Attlee's effectiveness as Prime Minister. His acceptance of the evolutionary, incremental Cabinet government model as fleshed out in the Anderson Report, rather than his own 1930s thinking on overlord ministers within a tighter strategic Cabinet, did not prevent the growth of the over-large and often overlapping committee structure over which he presided. It was his personal dispatch in handling the business that flowed through No. 10, his brisk chairing of ministerial groups and his concentration on what would in modern parlance be called 'big picture' questions (construction of the post-Beveridge welfare apparatus, the more important nationalizations, withdrawal from India, the formation of NATO) on which his subsequent reputation rests. In that sense, he did have a feeling for the 'architectonics' of state as they related to the condition of the people and the defence of the realm, to use rather old-fashioned phrases with which he would have empathized. The lack of flashiness with which he pursued these essentials added to the decent understatedness with which his premiership is still associated and overwhelms any management consultant-like horror that might accompany a close inspection of his governing apparatus.

Much of this specialness reflected Attlee's wider formation rather than his previous ministerial experience in peace and war. He was, as he put it himself, the scion of 'a typical family of the professional class brought up in the atmosphere of Victorian England'.[168] He bore the imprint of his school (Haileybury, the Imperial Service College) all his life. In a way, during his years in No. 10 he was a kind of colonial district officer charged with ensuring a fair and decent administrative system for all and the UK as a whole was his district. This partly explains his Euro-aversion. He had come to his intellectual formation as the nineteenth and twentieth centuries turned and, for all his sense of the injustices within British society, he never seems to have questioned the UK's natural place as one of the great powers of the world or the benefits to the world of this being the case. A European association for him – as for many in his generation – would not, could not, have been a driving preoccupation, let alone a dominant one.

Attlee was the first Prime Minister to preside over a Cabinet that wrestled with the pros and cons of whether an integrating Europe might include the UK. When, almost out of the blue, Jean Monnet appeared in London in May 1950 with the Schuman Plan for a European Coal and Steel Community, Attlee ran the possibility of joining through a clutch of ministerial and official Cabinet committees as well as the Chiefs of Staff Committee[169] (GEN 322, which he chaired, being the most important ministerial group)[170] before the full Cabinet on 2 June rejected the French demand (delivered on 1 June) that all countries intending to join the ECSC should declare their intentions to do so by 8 p.m. the following day.[171]

Attlee was a believer in the long-term possibility of a kind of world government based on a United Nations *not* dominated by a single group of countries, with a proper 'international police force' at its disposal, without national contingents and without individual sovereign interests, as he told American audiences on a 1958 lecture tour of the United States.[172] But he never modified his views on Europe. The last speech he ever made, in 1967 – the year of his death – was at the behest of his old No. 10 assistant Douglas Jay, recently sacked from Wilson's Cabinet for his vigorous opposition to the Labour government's application to join the European Economic Community.[173] Jay asked Attlee to address a group of anti-Common Market Labour backbenchers. The tiny, frail ex-premier was helped to the platform:

'The Common Market. The so-called Common Market of six nations. Know them all well. Very recently this country spent a great deal of blood and treasure rescuing four of 'em from attacks by the other two.'

And he sat down.[174]

Yet it was this intense sense of national identity which was so much a part of Attlee's decency – a decency that partly accounted for his appeal to all sorts of people from all sorts of backgrounds, young as well as old. He was, though shy, very good with the young. His daughter-in-law Anne, Countess Attlee, showed her father-in-law's most recent biographer, Francis Beckett, a marvellous exchange had in the last months of his premiership with Ann Glossop, a fifteen-year-old schoolgirl in Colwyn Bay, who wrote a poem complaining about a rule requiring her to resit her School Certificate because she was too young when she first sat the papers.

The PM replied in kind, marking his 'Secret'. The poetic conversation went like this:

ANNE GLOSSOP

Would you please explain, dear Clement
Just why it has to be
That Certificates of Education
Are barred to such as me? . . .

I've worked through thirteen papers
But my swot is all in vain
Because at this time next year
I must do them all again . . .

Please have pity, Clement,
And tell the others too.
Remove the silly age-limit
It wasn't there for you.

CLEM ATTLEE:

I received with real pleasure
Your verses my dear Ann
Although I've not much leisure
I'll reply as best I can.

I've not the least idea why
They have this curious rule
Condemning you to sit and sigh
Another year at school
You'll understand that my excuse
For lack of detailed knowledge
Is that school certs were not in use
When I attended college.
George Tomlinson[175] is ill, but I
Have asked him to explain
And when I get the reason why
I'll write to you again.[176]

Not only was he almost certainly the only postwar premier to pen a verse for a schoolgirl, Attlee was a living refutation of Gwilym Lloyd George's law that: 'Politicians are like monkeys; the higher they climb up the tree, the more revolting are the parts they expose.'[177]

This made him a deeply reassuring figure, and not just to his own side. A Conservative MP said of him at the height of his powers as Prime Minister that if Mr Attlee had got up in the House of Commons and announced 'The Revolution' it would have sounded like a change in a regional railway timetable.[178] The point about Clem Attlee is that he had no intention of doing anything about either a socialist revolution or the scheduling of trains by the newly created British Railways. He treated Britain's constitutional practice as if it were his beloved game of cricket. From his Haileybury days onwards he always aspired to play with a straight bat, which is exactly what he did from the moment at his own count at the People's Palace in the Mile End Road on 26 July 1945[179] – the nation had voted on 5 July, but three weeks were needed to garner and count the overseas forces' vote – when he realized Labour might win, until the afternoon of 26 October 1951, when he called on George VI with his resignation.[180] He was certainly the most understated and, perhaps the most deeply, almost narrowly, English figure ever to have occupied No. 10. And therein lay much of his strength.

Clem Attlee was almost the incarnation of that practical pragmatism which the British political class of his generation liked to think was their special contribution to world statecraft (his retirement, as we have seen, was punctuated by disquisitions on the proper nature of Cabinet government). His list of the requirements of a premier, given to his former press secretary, Francis Williams, in 1961, was steeped in this:

'He ought to have a reasonable historical background and a reasonable degree of toleration. He need not necessarily have a charming personality, but it helps. And he should remember that you don't necessarily think the other fellow's a dirty dog.'[181]

Attlee despised Neville Chamberlain, for example, because 'he always treated us like dirt'.[182] And, in a prescient warning to some of his successors-to-be in No. 10, Attlee added 'a fairly egocentric Cabinet minister can get along, but an egocentric Prime Minister can't'.[183]

Yet he was capable of that romantic self-delusion which can occasionally overlie practical common-sense. In the 1960s he genuinely seemed to believe that Labour had ceased to be a class party. 'It has gradually expanded and it is not in the least a class party today', he told a television interviewer in 1965. 'In fact, the Party in '45 was more representative of every part of the nation than any other party before it.'[184]

That may have been true on polling day – 5 July 1945. But as early as the local elections of 1947 Labour Party strategists were aware of the softness of the middle-class vote Labour had attracted two years before.[185] Attlee may well have shared the analysis of both Herbert Morrison and Labour's General Secretary, Morgan Phillips (as early as 1945 in the latter's case) that, in Phillips's words: 'The Party will either become largely unassailable as the first choice of a progressive and competent democracy, or it will forfeit for many years its claim on the electorate's good will.'[186]

Certainly Attlee does not appear to have been 'too surprised' by the drop to a six-seat majority in February 1950, as 1945 had seen Labour take 'a whole mass of seats, really old Tory seats' and subsequent boundary changes to the constituencies had 'seemed very heavy against us'.[187] In October 1951 he sensed, rightly, that the outcome would turn on 'the way the Liberal electors cast their vote in constituencies where there was a straight fight between Labour and Tory'.[188] Labour polled a popular vote not exceeded by any party until 1992.[189] But the Conservatives took a sixteen-seat majority. In any contest the conduct of the premiership, the management of the state apparatus and personality (sleaze factors apart) always take an infinitely lower place than bread-and-butter issues such as rationing and housing (in the 1950 and 1951 cases).

Almost fifty years after the event, the Public Record Office produced confirmation of the ailing King's close involvement in the timing of the election which ejected Labour from power in 1951. One must not overdo the Monarch's influence on Attlee. Unlike Buckingham Palace legend or the late Sir Robert Rhodes James, I do not believe George VI was the decisive factor in persuading Attlee in July 1945 that Bevin, rather than Dalton, should go to the Foreign Office.[190] In September 1951, however, Attlee took very seriously the King's point that political circumstances at home would make it 'very difficult indeed for me to go away for five to six months [on a planned Commonwealth tour] unless it was reasonably certain that political stability would prevail during my absence'.[191] Attlee, sensitive to the needs of both the Monarch and his Commonwealth,[192] gave the King the 'assurance that would set my mind at rest' (as the letter from Balmoral to No. 10 put it),[193] drawing a second communication in George VI's own hand declaring that 'it is a great relief to me that you have come to a decision on this important matter' and looking forward to seeing Attlee on 21 September with his request for a dissolution of Parliament.[194]

Attlee conducted his 1951 campaign in his very personal way, his wife driving up to 400 miles a day at high speed taking him from meeting to meeting.[195] (Legend has it that she was one of the most alarming drivers in the Kingdom – to all, that is, except her husband who sat contentedly beside her doing the crossword and occasionally popping a mint into his wife's mouth;[196] her family continue to insist that their mother *had* to drive at that speed during elections to keep up with their father's Special Branch police escort).[197]

Right at the end of his premiership, two observers in his West Walthamstow constituency captured Attlee's flavour to perfection. Patrick O'Donovan turned up at the peculiar little municipal theatre on the island in Walthamstow's Lloyd Park where there was

No sign that a Prime Minister of Britain was making his first public speech in a fight to retain power . . . the Prime Minister rose to the noise of swift, determined applause, and the lights twinkled in his spectacles. He stood quite still, smiling. The tiredness left his face and he looked affectionately at his loyal electors . . . He did not have that air of being more than life-size that surrounds many British politicians, nor did he display that spurious cheerfulness that suggests that every thing is fine, just fine. He looked like a great headmaster, controlled, efficient, and above all, good.[198]

A very similar impression 'mesmerized' (not a word one associates with Attlee) his young Conservative opponent, Edward du Cann, as they waited together for the result at the count in Walthamstow Town Hall.

In his very last hours in office, Attlee, du Cann recalled,

spoke to me like an old friend and ally and we talked together of literature and politics for a full half-hour without interruption. He spoke of his experiences in Government in peace and war ... I later learned that his kindness to me had been made the subject of some criticism among his supporters. He smoked his pipe and was quite relaxed. You would not have thought he had a care in the world, certainly not that he had been fighting in the general election for his political life and that in the next hour the fate of the government he led was to be decided.[199]

As they talked, Attlee's unsuccessful challenger noticed that

there were fifty or sixty spoiled papers, some mutilated, some with crosses in the wrong place, one or two with obscene messages and a dozen with the word 'socialism' written across them.

'What does that mean?' I asked Mr Attlee.

'They think I'm not socialist enough,' he replied. 'I know them of old.'[200]

What 'they' did not know was that they were witnessing the demise of almost certainly the most left-wing Prime Minister Britain will produce in policy matters and the most socially conformist in personal ones. He went out as he had arrived – shyly, stage left.

8

In History Lie All the Secrets:
Winston Churchill, 1951–55

'I never shared the optimistic views of some of our friends that the old gentleman would be willing to retire gracefully into the background.'

> *Lord Cranborne (soon to be Salisbury and known to*
> *Churchill at moments of irritation as 'Sarum'), 1946*[1]

'I live most of the day in bed; dictating directives would be just like writing a book ... We don't want detail. We propose to give the people a lighthouse, not a shop window ... It's a big job to take on at my age, but there's no alternative. It's my duty.'

> *Winston Churchill to his doctor, Charles Moran,*
> *September 1951*[2]

'I am a great believer in bringing things before the Cabinet. If a Minister has got anything on his mind and he has the sense to get it argued by the Cabinet he will have the machine behind him.'

> *Winston Churchill, April 1953*[3]

'I hate to be disloyal, but the PM is not doing his work. A document of five sheets has to be submitted to him as one paragraph, so that many of the points of the argument are lost.'

> *Jock Colville to Lord Salisbury, February 1953*[4]

'I think it's very easy to exaggerate his decline. He was, I thought, a very considerable figure right up to the end.'

> *Lord Boyd-Carpenter, 1989*[5]

'I always believed in staying in the pub till closing time.'

> *Winston Churchill, undated*[6]

Of all the postwar Prime Ministers Winston Churchill was the patron of my craft. He was a natural contemporary historian. For him past, present and future were in constant and vibrant symbiosis one with another. He lived, acted, thought and dreamt historically. As Paul Addison put it: 'To Churchill the past was alive and Whig history was true.'[7] And Churchill was convinced that the great mass of the British people thought and breathed history as he did, drawing their sense of both probity and progress from its rich insights.

A vivid illustration of this can be found in one of the most colourful and over-egged minutes of his final, 'recidivist',[8] 'Indian summer'[9] premiership, which was stimulated by a letter from Sir Vincent Tewson, the General Secretary of the TUC, complaining about a cut of £25,000 in the Ministry of Education's grant to the Workers' Educational Association and university extra-mural departments.

Churchill had a fondness for trade union leaders of the non-communist, social patriot variety,[10] the clones (if such a thing is conceivable) of the protean Ernest Bevin, his cherished companion in the War Cabinet of 1940–45. Tewson's concerns were taken very seriously and a furious philippic was dispatched from No. 10 to the hapless Education Minister, Florence Horsbrugh.

There is perhaps no branch of our vast educational system which should more attract within its particular sphere the aid and encouragement of the State than adult education. How many must there be in Britain, after the disturbance of two destructive wars, who thirst in later life to learn about the humanities, the history of their country, the philosophies of the human race, and the arts and letters which sustain and are borne forward by the ever-conquering English language? This ranks in my opinion far above science and technical instruction, which are well sustained and not without their rewards in our present system. The mental and moral outlook of free men studying the past with free minds in order to discern the future demands the highest measures which our hard-pressed finances can sustain. I have no doubt myself that a man or woman earnestly seeking in grown-up life to be guided to wide and suggestive knowledge in its largest and most uplifted sphere will make the best of all the pupils in this age of clatter and buzz, of gape and gloat. The appetite of adults to be shown the foundation and processes of thought will never be denied by a British Administration cherishing the continuity of our Island life.[11]

And what did this florid outburst produce? A trimming of the proposed cut from £25,000 to £15,000![12]

Churchill gloried in a constitution sculpted by the singular history of his country and rejoiced in leading a people, as he put it, 'content with their system of government . . . [and] . . . proud as they have a right to be of their race and name'.[13] He was convinced, too, as he told a young American schoolboy in 1953, that 'In history lie all the secrets of statecraft.'[14]

His sense of history and his appetite for adventure were always too great to make him a monogamist in party terms. He 'was a politician without a permanent address'.[15] And in his final, deep, political maturity in mid-twentieth century Britain, he tried to create in both party terms and in his governing style a special, highly personal approach to national and international politics that transcended the sectional and the trivial.

Roy Jenkins captured this in all its grandeur and its absurdity when he revisited the grand old man's final phase in Downing Street some forty years on. 'It is impossible', Jenkins wrote,

to re-read the story of Churchill's life as Prime Minister of that second govern-ment without feeling that he was gloriously unfit for office. The oxymoron is appropriate to the contradiction in his performance. The splendour of his personal-ity, which infused everything he did with style and interest, was not in doubt. He put on a great show. Indeed, there is a constant feeling that he was asking all his interlocutors, the new Queen, President Eisenhower, his ageing crown prince Anthony Eden, the members of the House of Commons, and various insecure Prime Ministers of the Fourth French Republic to live up to a role which they thought was a little over the top for the beginning of the second half of the twentieth century.[16]

With the exception, Jenkins continued, of saving the world from nuclear catastrophe (both superpowers acquired the hydrogen bomb during his last premiership and Churchill set Britain's own thermonuclear pro-gramme in motion in response), too much of Churchill's

attention, in Jean Monnet's distinction, was concentrated as 'being someone' rather than 'doing something'. The struggle to prolong active life became dominant over any policy issue except for the nuclear one. The most important milestones in his political year were the occasions when he would endeavour to show the Cabinet or the Americans, the Conservative Conference or the House of Commons, that he was fit to carry on. It was not so much what he said on these occasions, although he maintained his habit of meticulous preparation, as the fact that he was able to keep on his feet for sufficiently long to say it at all. There was even an element of play-acting about it.[17]

One has to be careful not to overdo the depiction of the old warrior in his final premiership as a kind of walking off-licence-cum-pharmacy, though his stroke in June 1953 left him severely diminished in terms of energy, concentration and grip. From the diary of his doctor, Lord Moran, we now know some detail of the amphetamines – or 'Morans' as Churchill called them – that he took to give himself a boost before key speeches.[18] But the key insight into his last term of office is contained in the final section of Roy Jenkins' description of it.

The most vivid moments of the second premiership were in the bustle of his returning to office: putting together the government, summoning officials, re-creating his staff, sending or acknowledging greetings all over the world. It was as least as much a pageant to commemorate the great days of the first government as it was a realistic preparation for a new period of office.[19]

And this pageant of a premiership, with another nineteenth-century figure, Clem Attlee, bristling Captain Mainwaring-like across the dispatch box, must also be seen in the context of the last flowering of a style of government and politics which began with Mr Gladstone's Midlothian campaign and finished when what Harold Macmillan called the 'hot, pitiless, probing eye'[20] of television, from the 1955 general election onwards, began to usher in the electronic age, usurping the great set speech and the elaborate unfolding of political argument.

The rich flavours of Churchill's peacetime premiership came out very strongly in the hours that followed his acceptance of the King's commission to form a government on 26 October 1951, a few days before his seventy-seventh birthday. Jock Colville, one of the first of the wartime entourage to be called back to the colours as Joint Principal Private Secretary in No. 10 alongside David Pitblado, who the old man inherited from Attlee ('I must have somebody I know', Churchill insisted when Colville attempted to decline),[21] sensed that '"Auld Lang Syne" was ringing out along the Whitehall corridors'.[22]

Indeed it was. Churchill wanted as many of his old wartime team with him as possible. He could not get Lord Portal, the former Chief of the Air Staff, to accept the Ministry of Defence so he persuaded the King and the Canadians to release Field Marshal Lord Alexander from the Governor-

Generalship in Ottawa in order, as Churchill put it in a telegram to Alexander, that 'you can give us your help which we need on national grounds'.[23] 'Pug' Ismay, his indispensable link-man with the Chiefs of Staff throughout the wartime premiership, was summoned from his bed at night and offered the Commonwealth Relations Office.[24] Lord Cherwell, 'the Prof', returned to head his private think-tank, the Statistical Section, and to run atomic energy policy with the sinecure title of Paymaster-General.[25] And Churchill was determined to re-create a version of the War Cabinet by placing a layer of 'co-ordinating' or 'supervising' ministers between him and various clusters of departmental ministers in the teeth of detailed and reasoned argument from Sir Norman Brook that this was undesirable, unnecessary and inefficient in peacetime conditions.[26] (This is a question we shall return to later, not least because of John Prescott's 'overlordship' of Environment, Transport and the Regions which he combined with the deputy prime ministership and second place in Tony Blair's first list of ministers in May 1997.)[27]

Churchill's passion for re-creating his glory days was due partly to an old man's craving for the familiar and partly to being too tired to contemplate new faces (especially when he could rarely put names to them).[28] Partly, too, it stemmed from a misguided sense that the senior Civil Service had become Attlee's possession. As Colville wrote later:

When Churchill returned as Prime Minister in 1951, he had long since reached the age at which new faces are palatable. He inherited Mr Attlee's Private Secretaries. Arriving at 10 Downing Street with Sir Norman Brook he flung open the door connecting the Cabinet Room to the Private Secretaries' Offices . . . He gazed at them, closed the door without saying a word, shook his head and proclaimed to Norman Brook: 'Drenched in Socialism'.[29]

Sensibly none of them was purged. But, given the impossibility of getting Leslie Rowan, Principal Private Secretary in No. 10 when Churchill lost office in 1945, back from the Treasury, Colville, as we have seen, was commandeered from the Foreign Office.[30] In another strong echo of 1940, Churchill assumed the title of Minister of Defence until Alexander returned from Canada, despite the warning from his doctor that the load would be too great for him[31] and his own recognition, in his telegram to Alexander, that: 'There is now a complete Ministry of Defence with elaborate staff and offices and not the "handling machine" which I used in the war.'[32] In a ludicrous rerun of 1940, the Home Guard was also reconstituted in case Stalin's paratroops succeeded where Hitler had failed.[33] And Churchill's bizarre wartime administrative habits returned, too.

He would work deep into the night reading the first editions of the national newspapers and firing off biting minutes to unbriefed ministers on whatever claims the *Daily Express* and the other papers might be making about the people's diet or housing. ('I get far more out of them than the official muck,' he said when reproached for this.) He refrained, however, from attaching his famous red 'Action This Day' labels to these broadsides, even though the No. 10 messengers had carefully put them back on the Cabinet table on the day of his restoration.[34]

For all his obsession with the nation's alimentary canal, Churchill had not the faintest idea about the rationing regime under which the King's subjects still lived in the autumn of 1951. Harold Macmillan, who was put in charge of the economically and industrially foolish drive to build 300,000 houses a year, had the wonderful story of the Minister of Food, Gwilym Lloyd George, being summoned to brief the great trencherman on rationing as the PM found the figures confusing. Lloyd George arranged a mock-up. 'This exhibit duly appeared', wrote Macmillan,

on a large tin dish – a painted piece of meat, a little heap of sugar and the rest. The Prime Minister looked at it with some satisfaction.

'Not a bad meal,' he said. 'Not a bad meal.'

'But these,' cried the Minister, 'are not rations for a meal or for a day. They are for a week.'

'A week!' was the outraged reply. 'Then the people are starving. It must be remedied.'[35]

Often the minister at the receiving end of a furious minute would be summoned to the bedside of the PM the following morning to explain himself.

There, unless the Cabinet or a Cabinet committee he chaired was due to meet, Churchill would lie until shortly before lunch, an unlit cigar in his mouth, his bed covered in papers, a 'Garden Girl' beside it to take dictation. At his feet would be Rufus the poodle, whose breath was likened to a flame-thrower by one of his private secretaries. On his head sat Toby, the constantly twittering budgerigar.[36] Toby, for some reason, was particularly excited by the presence of Rab Butler, the Chancellor of the Exchequer. If Rab was briefing Churchill on the latest strains on the economy, Toby would fly round the room, occasionally opening his bowels on Rab's head. According to one of the private secretaries, Anthony Montague Browne, Toby found the Chancellor's bald head an irresistible target as well as a perch. On one occasion Butler was seen to mop his head 'with a spotless silk handkerchief' and was heard to sigh resignedly, 'The things I do for England . . .'[37]

Toby plainly fascinated the Prime Minister's colleagues. In January 1955, Harold Macmillan, Churchill's last Minister of Defence, was summoned to the bedside to discuss the horrors of thermonuclear war. That night he recorded the scene in a way that defies parody as Toby somehow managed to upstage even the hydrogen bomb. Toby began the meeting sitting on Churchill's head, swooping occasionally to take sips from the whisky and soda beside the Prime Minister's bed:

Really, he is unique dear man with all his qualities and faults . . . The bird flew about the room; perched on my shoulder and pecked (or kissed my neck) . . . while all the sonorous 'Gibbonesque' sentences were rolling out of the maestro's mouth on the most terrible and destructive engine of mass warfare yet known to mankind. The bird says a few words in a husky voice like an American actress . . .[38]

'A bizarre scene', Macmillan concluded.[39]

These working sessions with Toby, Rufus and a rolling *galère* of ministers were sandwiched between a nine-o'clock English breakfast in bed with cold grouse (or partridge if in season) and a whisky and soda.[40] Lunch at 1.30 would be laced with 'enough champagne and brandy . . . to incapacitate any lesser man', as Colville put it.[41] In the late afternoon Churchill would take a nap, often in his room at the House of Commons. Lord Plowden remembers briefing him there one afternoon in the spring of 1954 to the effect that Britain did have the resources to make its own hydrogen bomb. 'We must do it,' he said. 'It's the price we pay for sitting at the top table.' 'And', Plowden continued, 'having said that, he got up and tied a little black ribbon round his eyes, and lay down on his bed in his room and went to sleep.'[42]

Quite often Churchill would return to No. 10 for the nap which was the fulcrum of his day-and-night work routine. 'Undressed fully apart from a long silk vest, he would take a very small sleeping pill and go to bed for one or two hours, awaking refreshed and ready for dinner or work.'[43] When he went to bed properly he rarely had a sleepless night (he could remember only two from the war – when the *Repulse* and the *Prince of Wales* went down and when Crete fell).[44] 'I just turn out the light, say "bugger everyone", and go to sleep,' he once explained to an inquisitive private secretary.[45] All in all, it was a rich, eccentric, selfish (in terms of its demands on the time of ministers and officials) and shamelessly personal way of heading a government, and it was matched by an equally idiosyncratic attitude towards party politics – a very 'broad gauge' approach, to borrow a phrase of Clive Priestley's.[46]

It is well known both that Churchill wished the wartime coalition to continue into the peace[47] in 1945 and that he tried very hard to place the Liberal leader, Clement Davies, in his October 1951 Cabinet as Minister of Education.[48] He also wanted Asquith's son, Cyril, in as his Lord Chancellor[49] and he had spoken personally for his old friend the Liberal candidate for Colne Valley, Asquith's daughter, the magnetic and forceful Lady Violet Bonham-Carter, at a meeting in Huddersfield during the 1951 election, where he shared the platform with her.[50] In March 1950 he had proposed a select committee on electoral reform to the consternation of Conservative Central Office and in September that year he suggested to the Conservative backbench 1922 Committee that the Conservatives make way for the Liberals in between twenty and forty constituencies, a proposal that 'was greeted with silence'.[51]

Such forbearance, naturally, was not forthcoming towards Labour. But, despite some of his platform rhetoric, he was relatively benign in his attitude towards early postwar Labour and he could be funny about their dull respectability. In 1947 he had invented an intriguing way of conveying his reflections on the changes experienced over his already long political life. In a short story entitled 'The Dream' he imagined that, while painting his father's portrait at Chartwell, Lord Randolph appeared in the armchair beside his easel. After an exchange on the Monarchy and the Church, Randolph asks

'What party is in power now? Liberals or Tories?'

'Neither, Papa. We have a Socialist Government, with a very large majority . . .'

'Socialist!' he exclaimed. 'But I thought you said we still have a Monarchy.'

'The Socialists are quite in favour of the Monarchy, and make generous provisions for it.'

'You mean in regard to Royal grants, the Civil list, and so forth? How can they get those through the Commons?'

'Of course they have a few rebels, but the old Republicanism of Dilke and Labby [Labouchère] is dead as mutton. The Labour men and the trade unions look upon the Monarchy not only as a natural but a nationalized institution. They even go to the parties at Buckingham Palace. Those who have very extreme principles wear sweaters . . .'

'What have they done?'

'Not much. They have nationalised the mines and railways and a few other services, paying full compensation. You know, Papa, though stupid, they are quite respectable, and increasingly bourgeois. They are not nearly so fierce as the old Radicals, though of course they are wedded to economic fallacies.'[52]

During his last premiership Churchill's relationship with Attlee was respectful rather than close, its cordiality punctured by occasional eruptions sometimes occasioned by Churchill's appetite for fashioning defence secrets into a weapon and hurling them across the chamber of the House of Commons, as in April 1954 when he claimed that Labour had abandoned the 1943 Quebec Agreement on atomic collaboration.[53]

On one issue – an intriguing and important (if understudied) one for students of the British premiership – Churchill eventually admitted that Attlee's criticism, which the Leader of the Opposition had sustained over nearly two years, had a point. This was on the matter of those 'overlord' ministers. Attlee, like the Anderson Committee in 1945, had come firmly to the view as Prime Minister that co-ordination was best achieved through Cabinet committees and he made this plain in the House of Commons once in opposition.

Churchill, though he had developed in wartime the kind of Cabinet committee structure Anderson had urged him in May 1945 to carry over, in an adapted form, into the peace,[54] returned to office with an animus against superfluous Cabinet committees which he believed were 'luxuriating' and too numerous,[55] especially 'a great number of second- and third-grade committees which, I am assured,' he informed Norman Brook, 'cumber the ground'. These he wished 'to lead to the slaughter'.[56] From the moment the Conservatives returned to office, Brook and Churchill were engaged in a kind of skirmish about the utility of Cabinet committees in which the 'overlords' became entwined.

On 12 November 1951, just over two weeks after his return to No. 10, Churchill asked Brook to let him have 'a list of the Committees, Sub-Committees and Working Parties at present sitting in Whitehall, both Ministerial and Official'.[57] Brook replied to Churchill three days later, carefully outlining only those ministerial Cabinet committees Churchill himself had created since assuming power ('Legislation', 'Persia', 'Steel',

'Financial and Economic Situation'), pointing out that of these only 'Legislation' had 'been formally set up as a *standing* committee of the Cabinet' and suggesting three more – 'Home Affairs', 'Financial and Economic Affairs' and 'Defence'.[58] These Churchill duly created, though 'Financial and Economic Affairs' assumed the title of Attlee's post-1947 group, the Economic Policy Committee. Churchill also accepted Brook's suggestions as to who should chair them, he himself presiding over Defence, Woolton (Lord President) over Home Affairs and, interestingly, Butler (Chancellor of the Exchequer) rather than the Prime Minister (as under Attlee), over the EPC.[59]

'I will', Brook added significantly, 'make a separate submission shortly about the official committees which are now in being.'[60] These, the Cabinet Secretary plainly judged, were part of the permanent government and could, therefore, be disclosed to the new premier without breaking the convention that the secrets of the outgoing administration are not divulged to their successors. Churchill was very funny about this. He had ordered a slaughter, he reminded Brook, and 'In reply you present me with a new crop on the highest level. However there is no difference between us on this point. It is a necessary step in Cabinet organization . . . But now I want you to get on with the real work.'[61] Brook did, and four days later Churchill was presented with a list of 'all the official committees controlled by the Cabinet Office and the Ministry of Defence' which gave 'particulars of the 60 Committees, 47 Sub-Committees and 17 Working Parties which formed part of the Cabinet Committee system at the date of the election'.[62]

Brook's map gave a fascinating overview, not least because it illustrated the vast Cold War state which had been created since 1945. Churchill would have appreciated the sensitivity of this quite naturally but Brook felt it necessary to warn him that the existence of the Official Committee on Communism (Home) 'has been kept specially secret'.[63] He earmarked with an asterisk the nine committees which could be abolished or merged. (One merger, that of the European Economic Co-operation Committee with the Mutual Aid Committee, led to a degree of mockery years later by those who saw significance in a group called the Mutual Aid Committee being the chief Whitehall policy-processor of the Eden government's reaction to the Messina talks of 1955, the discussions from which the Common Market was to emerge.)[64]

Churchill was far from satisfied. 'You seem to have got very few birds out of this enormous covey,' he minuted Brook. 'Pray let me have a list of the ones you say could now be dispensed with so that at least we can make a beginning.'[65] Within a few days Brook had found five more to add to the cull.[66] Churchill, plainly possessed by one of his anti-bureaucratic enthusiasms against a Cabinet system he probably also saw as 'drenched in socialism', persisted. He warned Brook to 'be careful we do not spawn too many of these Cabinet committees' and asked for 'a list of what we have already appointed'.[67]

Brook sent back a tally of five standing and four ad hoc committees, but he attached to it a firm pitch in favour of Cabinet committees (a point he had been consistently making in his attempts to wean Churchill off the idea of 'overlords').

'May I take this opportunity', he inquired of the Prime Minister, 'of putting to you one consideration in favour of having a number (though not too large a number) of Cabinet Committees, viz. That they provide, for Ministers of Cabinet rank who are not members of the Cabinet, an opportunity to join in the collective discussion of policy.'[68]

This was important on both constitutional grounds, as it made it possible 'to operate a small Cabinet . . . without infringing the principle of collective responsibility' and 'on practical grounds' as it enhanced the 'sense of solidarity in the Government . . . [hence] . . . it is desirable that as many as possible of the members of Cabinet Committees should be Ministers who are not members of the Cabinet'.[69] The Cabinet Office's own log book of Cabinet committees suggests that by Churchill's last year in office, his engine room consisted of no fewer than fifteen ministerial committees, two of which (the Defence and Colonial Policy committees) he chaired himself.[70]

In effect, Brook – a wartime protégé of Anderson's – was pressing the philosophy of the Anderson Committee on the very Prime Minister to whom it had reported in May 1945, though Churchill had plainly not absorbed its philosophy or its detail.[71] The difficulty Brook experienced with Churchill over Cabinet committees in the first two months of the new government's life may have contributed to his decision to cull *Questions of Procedure for Ministers* and, in Amy Baker's phrase, 'to remove most of what might be described as Attlee's conspicuous "fingerprints".' It was trimmed by a third: 'The final proof was not circulated until six months after the Conservative government had been appointed. Although this was partly due to the preparation of the document by officials *before* submission to the Prime Minister, there was further delay by the Prime Minister after it had been submitted. It may have been one of those matters that [the Private Office] found impossible to turn Churchill's attention towards.'[72]

Yet the delicacy of easing QPM across the prime ministerial transition and the difficulties Brook experienced with Churchill over Cabinet committees were overshadowed by the vexed issue of the 'overlords', which, as we have seen, the Anderson Committee had no time for in peacetime.[73] Churchill was warned off the idea the moment he returned to No. 10 in the briefing notes on the 'structure of government' which the Cabinet Secretary had prepared ready for a Conservative restoration. Sir Norman Brook was much better primed on Churchill's intentions than some of the intended 'supervising ministers', as Brook called them.[74]

John Anderson himself was both shocked by and, when summoned to Chartwell, Churchill's country home in Kent, unsurprisingly dismissive of the idea that he become Chancellor of the Duchy and, in the words of his biographer, 'surprising "Overlord" of the Treasury, the Board of Trade and the Ministry of Supply'.[75]

John was both shocked and amazed. The concept of 'overlords' in Government was entirely contrary to his beliefs and principles, both as a former Minister and as a former Civil Servant. Though, in a sense, he had occupied an analogous position when Lord President of the Council, this had been a wartime emergency and, in any case, he had been concerned with co-ordinating rather than supervising the activities of the various agencies placed within his aegis. Such a position, he felt, could have no place in the peacetime organization of government.[76]

Those words 'supervising' and 'co-ordinating' are critical and I will return to them in a moment. Continuing his summary of Anderson's objections, Wheeler-Bennett added: 'There were Government Departments which were responsible to Ministers, and there were Ministers who answered for their Departments to the House of Commons. This was the established order of things. It was inconceivable to him to have another Minister, floating around, as it were, above these Departments and Ministers with no fixed responsibility for either. To John the proposed arrangement would prove intolerable, nor did he think it could possibly work, and he said as much to the Prime Minister.'[77] It is a measure of Churchill's determination, as Anthony Montague Browne put it, 'to have his "Overlords" and the people he knew well and trusted, such as Lord Cherwell, to advise him',[78] that he overrode the advice both of the highly respected Anderson (whom he likened to the 'automatic pilot')[79] and of

Norman Brook, on whom he came to rely very heavily in his last spell in No. 10.

Brook's objections to the 'supervising ministers' concept were not surprisingly very similar to Anderson's. It was, he warned Churchill in the brief that was waiting for him on 26 October 1951, 'fraught with serious difficulties both constitutional and practical' because it was difficult to reconcile with individual ministerial responsibility, it was inconsistent with the principle that policy should be formulated by those with the responsibility for carrying it out, it rested on the assumption that policy could be divorced from administration, it was contrary to the traditions of Cabinet government that one Cabinet minister should be subordinate to another, supervising ministers would be served by civil servants whose knowledge was less than that possessed by officials working to subordinate ministers, and, finally, all outside bodies would seek to influence the overlord rather than the overlorded. It would be much better to strive for co-ordination through standing Cabinet committees of the kind Churchill had developed in the war and which Mr Attlee had maintained in the peace.[80]

What Attlee called this 'very ill-starred experiment'[81] of the 'overlords' cries out for detailed, scholarly treatment. What is of practical, retrospective interest as the century turns, particularly in the context of John Prescott's late 1990s 'overlordship', is to draw lessons from the two-year period between Churchill's return to power and the autumn of 1953, when the 'experiment' ended and Churchill grudgingly accepted Attlee's criticisms, explaining to the House of Commons that

'I had no experience of being Prime Minister in time of peace and I attached more importance to the grouping of Departments so that the responsible head of the Government would be able to deal with a comparatively smaller number of heads than actually exists in peacetime. I think we had great advantage ... from the services of the three noble Lords, who did their very utmost to help forward the public service.'[82]

The first problem is who were the noble Lords? Two are beyond dispute, the two 'Freds' – Lord Woolton (who as Lord President was responsible for co-ordinating the then separate ministries of agriculture and food, logical in its own way, given Woolton's fame as Minister for Food during World War II) and Lord Leathers (who was dubbed the Secretary of State for the Co-ordination of Transport, Fuel and Power).

In an article written over forty years ago, R. S. Milne concentrated on these two when examining what he described as 'The experiment with "co-ordinating ministers"' between 1951 and 1953.[83] There are several candidates for third or fourth or fifth or sixth slots, Cherwell (Paymaster-General), Swinton (Chancellor of the Duchy and Minister of Materials), Salisbury (Lord Privy Seal) and Alexander at Defence.[84]

I shall concentrate here on the pair that are included in everybody's list – Woolton and Leathers. And they were the duo on whom Churchill focused in his House of Commons statement on 'Co-ordinating Ministers' in May 1952, when, heavily reliant on Norman Brook's brief,[85] he tried to portray their appointment as a refinement-cum-extension of the co-ordinating powers exercised by the Lord Presidents during World War II (chiefly Anderson and Attlee) and by Herbert Morrison in Attlee's own administration. 'The responsibilities assigned under the present Government to Lord Woolton and Lord Leathers', Churchill explained,

'carry this development a stage further in one respect, and in one respect only, viz. that the specific area of co-ordination assigned to each of them was publicly announced on his appointment. Indeed, so far as concerns . . . Lord Leathers, it was explicit in his title. Coal, gas, electricity, oil and transport represent a homogeneous group of subjects which call for co-ordination . . .'[86]

partly because they embraced a swathe of activities nationalized by the Attlee government.

On the constitutional side, Churchill insisted there was no difference between the functions of Leathers and Woolton, as he launched into a fine piece of circle-squaring. 'The co-ordinating ministers have no statutory powers', he declared.

'They have, in particular, no power to give orders or directions to a Departmental Minister. A Departmental Minister who is invited by a co-ordinating Minister to adjust a Departmental policy to accord with the wider interests of the Government as a whole [some glorious weasel wording there] always has access to the Cabinet and, if he then finds that he cannot win the support of his Ministerial colleagues he should accept their decision. No Departmental Minister can, of course, be expected to remain in a Government and carry out policies with which he disagrees.

'Thus, the existence and activities of these co-ordinating Ministers do not impair or diminish the responsibility to Parliament of the Departmental Ministers whose policies they co-ordinate . . .'[87]

This was Churchill at his most disingenuous. He never grasped the detail of how his peacetime 'overlords' actually performed within the realities of early-1950s Whitehall.

As late as August 1953, fifteen months after delivering his statement in the House of Commons, he minuted Bridges, Head of the Civil Service, and Brook, the Cabinet Secretary, in the following terms:

SECRET AND PERSONAL
(Not to be shown to anyone else)

SIR EDWARD BRIDGES
SIR NORMAN BROOK

1. Please find out the exact relations of the functions of the Secretary of State for the Co-ordination of Transport, Fuel and Power with the work of the respective Ministries concerned. Let me have if possible a diagram.
2. Let me have a short report, one page, on how in practice these are working and what would be the consequences of abolishing, as is my intention, the new office we created when the Government was formed. What arrangements for the co-ordination of business of these Departments are needed as part of the ordinary mechanism of the Cabinet and its Committees.[88]

The minute is rounded off by a deliciously self-ironic touch: 'A statement should also be prepared showing how wise and necessary this was and how what has been achieved justifies me (a) in having created, and (b) in now abolishing the post in question. This might extend to 500 words.'[89]

Brook replied on his own as Bridges was on leave (but Bridges later associated himself fully with Brook's analysis in a minute to Colville in No. 10).[90] Though the memo for the Prime Minister lacked a diagram, its contents pleased Churchill, who scrawled 'excellent, WSC' beneath them.[91] 'There is in practice', the Cabinet Secretary informed the Prime Minister,

very little interconnection between the day-to-day work of the Ministry of Fuel and Power and that of the Minister of Transport – and little scope, therefore, for co-ordination. Lord Leathers has in fact been a supervising Minister rather than a co-ordinator. The two Ministers have come to him with their major problems, e.g. Persian oil, coal prices, railway charges; and he has handled those problems in consultation with the Ministers and their senior officials. In all this, however, he has assisted and directed the two Ministers separately and not jointly.[92]

Brook went on to inform his plainly unknowing boss that: 'Lord Leathers' functions and methods of work have thus been personal to a high degree. He established no special staff or machinery for the purpose. No large adjustments would be needed if his post were abolished.'[93]

Despite the declassification in the mid 1990s of further files dealing with the practicalities of the 'overlords', still more detailed research needs to be directed towards what Leathers and Woolton actually did and how effective they were. This would be far more useful to any future Prime Minister tempted to resurrect the idea of overlords than any constitutional theocratics. In his PhD thesis on Woolton, Michael Kandiah thought him 'arguably the most successful of the Overlords, but this was probably because the Ministers he was to co-ordinate [Food and Agriculture] were related, and because he attempted to maintain only light control – he told the House of Lords [in April 1952] his task was "indeed a very minor one".'[94] In other words, Woolton, too, *was* a supervising minister rather than a co-ordinating one – to sustain Brook's distinction.

Leathers, however, was much more interventionist than Woolton, despite the Cabinet Secretary's observations. And an intervener, almost certainly to no good effect, during the preparation of what became the Transport Act 1953 which broke up, among other things, the British Transport Commission's monopoly on long-distance public road haulage. Paradoxically, the Cabinet committee Churchill set up to prepare the White Paper on transport was chaired for reasons that are not made plain by Woolton, nor Leathers.[95]

Norman Brook, ever sensitive to the harmful effect of blurring chains of command, attempted to persuade Churchill in April 1952 that responsibility for supervising the progress of the Bill foreshadowed in the Conservatives' 1951 election campaign 'should be squarely placed on a Minister of Transport who has strong powers of decision and liberty to go ahead with the minimum amount of consultation with his colleagues . . . the preparation of a complicated Bill in a hurry is really a matter for one man.'[96] Churchill ignored this advice and Leathers was put in the chair of the Cabinet committee commissioned to oversee the Bill's preparation. Chaos resulted. The minister, Alan Lennox-Boyd, and the 'overlord', Leathers, put forward opposing positions and the Cabinet eventually and hurriedly had to decide between two competing draft Bills. To make matters worse, Leathers' position seemed to be closer to the thinking of Lennox-Boyd's Ministry of Transport officials than Lennox-Boyd's own.[97]

So, far from relieving the burden of detail weighing down full Cabinet, the Leathers v. Lennox-Boyd spat actually added to it. Leathers was not a career politician and he was a details rather than a broad-picture person.[98] He always felt an outsider in Churchill's last Cabinet and was glad to go when Churchill ended his 'overlord' experiment in September 1953. Churchill told Moran shortly before the announcement: 'The Overlords are going. Leathers has wanted to resign for a long time. I only kept him by calling him a deserter.'[99] Leathers had, indeed, been itching to go since the autumn of 1952.[100] At that stage, Churchill had told him 'there could be no question of you going now at a moment when the Transport issue is almost paramount at home, and when other matters of which you have special knowledge press for solution. Pray dismiss these ideas from your mind. I hope you have not been paying any attention to all the trash the Opposition newspapers print.'[101]

At about the same time, the other Fred – Woolton – was struck down by illness at the Party Conference and underwent four operations in quick succession which required a prolonged convalescence.[102] By the time the two of them were stood down as 'overlords' in September 1953, Woolton, as Churchill acknowledged in a letter asking him to take over as Minister of Materials, had

. . . already made it pretty clear that your supervisory control of Food and Agriculture has largely fallen into desuetude. I am myself convinced that the system which the Opposition describes as 'the rule of Overlords' is not necessary now that the war emergency has receded and the Armament programme is spread.[103]

Here is another intriguing justification for creating the overlordships in October 1951. Churchill, in his own mind at least, believed that to some degree Britain was once more in warlike circumstances, thanks to Korea, the associated fear of more general war and the huge rearmament programme the Conservatives had inherited from Labour.

But there was a mixture of motives at work here beyond Cold War-related matters. Churchill genuinely believed that both Leathers and Woolton had shone as *de facto* 'overlords' during World War II. As he told Leathers when accepting his resignation (though one must always allow for the element of gush that usually lubricates such occasions):

When this Government took office nearly two years ago, coal and transport were among the most formidable of the problems which faced us. No-one was better qualified than you to help in finding a solution of these problems and I shall always be grateful to you for the loyalty and public spirit which you showed in setting aside your private interests and assuming once more the burdens of Ministerial office. You have brought to bear on these problems an unrivalled knowledge of the coal industry and of transport by land and sea, founded on long years of private experience both in private business and as Minister of War Transport in the National Government of 1940-45.[104]

In a letter to Eden, who was on holiday in Greece recovering from a serious operation in the United States, Churchill claimed to 'have given a great deal of thought' to the winding-up of the peacetime overlords.

'Of course', he told Eden, 'whatever is done will be carped at; none the less some points will probably be welcome. The "Overlords" system for which I was responsible, which is not as necessary in peace as it was in war, disappears.'[105]

Eden replied via the British embassy in Athens that he 'thought, like you, that the "Overlords" system would work. Perhaps we were both unduly influenced by success under Woolton in wartime.'[106] (Woolton, transferring from the Ministry of Food to become Minister of Reconstruction for the last eighteen months of World War II, had had the job of 'political mediator', to use his own description, trying 'to formulate and define the reconstruction policies on which a Coalition Government could agree . . . mainly in the field of "social reform"'.)[107]

Plainly, there were a range of reasons which explain why Churchill was so keen on keeping his overlords until he reluctantly admitted the validity of Attlee's criticism that they were unsuited to peacetime Cabinet government.[108] The 'Auld Lang Syne' factor was certainly part of it as was his desire to deal with fewer ministers than usually make up peacetime Cabinets.[109] Paul Addison reckons that 'The "Overlords" were an interesting experiment in trying to co-ordinate areas of policy in which he perhaps didn't feel entirely confident himself.'[110]

I suspect there is something in this. Even before his stroke in the summer of 1953 Churchill showed a marked reluctance to take solo decisions. His natural romanticism about the Cabinet in the governing scheme of things was reinforced by his desire to ease his own burden by sharing it. Sir David Hunt, who spanned the change of government in No. 10 in the autumn of 1951, was revealing about this when I interviewed him for the

Wide Vision/Channel 4 *What Has Become of Us?* television series.

'Plenty of people', Hunt recalled, 'would come to me and say: "Oh, you must see a great change between the two Prime Ministers that you've been serving." And I would say: "Oh, a tremendous change. You simply can't imagine the difference between them. On the one hand, a man decisive, quick, looks at a question, says 'yes' or 'no' and passes on to the next question. And on the other hand, there's a man who will say: 'Oh, I'm not going to decide that at the moment. That's an important question. It must come to Cabinet.' Or sometimes he'll say: 'I won't look at that now. Bring it down to Chartwell at the weekend.'"'

Not until David Hunt mentioned Chartwell would his listeners appreciate this tale of the unexpected. 'All of a sudden they would discover that Attlee was a man who was good at decisions and Churchill much preferred putting them off.'[111] And on one extraordinary occasion within a few weeks of returning to power, Churchill agreed to alter the planned time of a rare afternoon Cabinet meeting both to ensure a full house of ministers and to enable six of them to lunch with Bertram Mills *and* attend a performance of his circus as, in the Cabinet Secretary's words, 'The Mills brothers will be disappointed if all now decline'[112] – an accommodating approach one would not quite have expected from Clem Attlee, let alone Margaret Thatcher.

Yet for those who stress the virtues of full and frequent collective discussion, Churchill during what Macmillan called the 'sunset scene'[113] of his last premiership is not the perfect example, only partly because of his fading physical and mental powers. As we have seen, his preference for a monologue rather than a decision was a characteristic of his glory days during World War II. This propensity escalated to distracting proportions after his return to power in October 1951.

Macmillan's diaries provide what is almost an obbligato for Churchill's slow slide into senescence. He draws a tragic portrait, albeit a picture punctuated by occasional outbursts of 'vivid and splendid colours'.[114] Even before the stroke of June 1953, the lack of grip in the Cabinet Room was often palpable. To the irritation of some of his ministers, for example, Churchill caused them to interrupt their Christmas holiday at the end of 1952 to hear 'a long and painful soliloquy by the PM about Egypt and the decay of Britain's power – Anthony [Eden] and Rab [Butler] were very patient. Harry Crookshank [Leader of the House of Commons] sent me peevish notes. "We have had half an hour of this and we are getting nowhere." What fun do we have!'[115] Just over a year after the stroke,

Macmillan was painting a diary picture of near senility in the Prime Minister's chair:

Churchill is now often speechless in Cabinet; alternatively, he rambles about nothing. Sometimes he looks as if he is going to have another stroke ... He was always an egoist, but a magnanimous one. Now he has become almost a monomaniac.[116]

This 'monomania' is a reference to Churchill's obsessional desire to cudgel his failing powers into one last great enterprise – the ending of the Cold War before thermonuclear disaster engulfed the world – which, as we shall see, led him to treat the requirements of Cabinet government in a truly cavalier fashion.

Did Churchill's decline matter that much to a Cabinet of seasoned veterans? It did. Lack of a lead from the chair can be as harmful to effective government as an excess of what Lloyd George would have called 'push and go'[117] from the government's number 1. Churchill, I am sure, had a sense of this himself. As his son-in-law and Parliamentary Private Secretary, Christopher Soames, reported, Churchill felt in the days after his stroke that he had to continue unless he found himself 'unable to serve the Queen effectively in the essential works of the First Minister'.[118]

Less than a year after the Conservatives' return to office, Macmillan sensed a lack in the Cabinet as a collectivity. 'Altogether a strange Cabinet,' he ruminated in his diary in December 1952. 'It is a team of, on the whole, very able and in some cases brilliant men, of charming character, all good friends, and led by one of the greatest figures in the long history of this country. But somehow, it doesn't produce an output in any way commensurate with the moral and intellectual horse-power at its command.'[119] Macmillan must be treated an astute observer of the processes of government even before he became Prime Minister himself (and not just because he finally achieved the highest of offices later – a factor which can lead historians to an excessive attention to the jobs which went before in the 'making' of a Prime Minister). It is evident from the Cabinet Office's own files that his reflections in December 1952 were not the product of transient irritation or passing malaise.

At the end of December 1953, for example, Macmillan shared his unease at the shortcomings of Cabinet government under Churchill with George Mallaby, one of the Cabinet notetakers. After teasing Mallaby about the orderliness and precision of the minutes ('future historians would be astonished to find how logically Cabinet ministers had dealt with their business and how easily and wisely they arrived at precise conclusions'),[120] Macmillan

went on to wonder ... if the Cabinet was not perhaps becoming too formal an instrument and whether there would not be advantage in having perhaps one Cabinet a week without Agenda, so that Ministers could really talk freely about the political problems which gave them the deepest immediate concern.[121]

This was a fascinating pre-echo of John Major's habit of calling 'Political Cabinets' forty years later. Nothing came of it at the time (or even during Macmillan's tenure in No. 10). Nor did Macmillan elaborate on his theme to Mallaby as 'We were on the point of discussing this in greater detail when Mr Eden swept him away in the middle of a sentence which I was uttering.'[122] (Eden took Macmillan off for a moan about how difficult he was finding life as Churchill's perpetual heir apparent with the old man vacillating about the timing of his resignation.)[123]

Churchill may have been a genuine Cabinet government man, for all the timewasting and 'Auld Lang Syne' that afflicted Cabinet meetings, but his colleagues could be very direct with him when they felt less than fully consulted, or consulted in less than plenty of time. Rab Butler's hastily compiled and swiftly abandoned plan, codenamed 'Robot', to partially float the pound in the run-up to the 1952 Budget,[124] led to very brisk exchanges at the meeting of 19 February 1952 when this particular method of dashing for currency freedom as a way of easing the pressure on sterling and the country's balance of payments difficulties was sprung on a largely unsuspecting Cabinet.[125]

The summer of 1954 was a protracted season of Cabinet recrimination over Churchill's lack of consultation even in one policy area – nuclear weapons – where, rightly, he has been seen as a more fully collegial premier than his predecessor, Attlee, or any of his successors, Macmillan excepted.[126] This was unfair. Unlike Attlee who, as we have seen, did not lift the original atomic bomb decision up from his Cabinet committee, GEN 163, to the full Cabinet, Churchill told the second of his hydrogen bomb Cabinet committees, GEN 464 on 13 April 1954, that he would 'like to invite the Cabinet at an early date to decide in principle that hydrogen bombs should be made in the United Kingdom'. The decision was also processed through a specially constituted Defence Policy Committee which at its third meeting on 16 June 1954 outlined the production of a British H-Bomb.[127]

This intention was in stark contrast to his atomic practices during World War II, when Churchill declined to consult even the service ministers, let alone the War Cabinet, about the development of the atomic bomb.[128] Yet when the question did reach the full Cabinet on 7 July 1954, Crookshank, the Leader of the House of Commons, recoiling from the surprise announcement from Churchill, as Macmillan recorded in his diary, 'that the decision had been taken to make the hydrogen bomb in England', and the preliminaries were in hand,

> at once made a most vigorous protest at such a momentous decision being communicated to the Cabinet in so cavalier a way, and started to walk out of the room. We all did the same and the Cabinet broke up – if not in disorder – in a somewhat ragged fashion. Walter Monckton [Minister of Labour and National Service] and Woolton seemed especially shocked; not, I think, at the decision (which is probably right) but at the odd way in which things are being done.[129]

The H-bomb question returned to Cabinet the following day before being finally resolved on 26 July 1954,[130] leaving Churchill bruised by what he called 'the constitutional aspect' of the thermonuclear decision and the 'considerable feeling in the Cabinet about the H-bomb decision not having been formally imparted to our colleagues earlier'.[131] He was particularly cross about 'Sarum's' threat to resign. 'Bobbety [Salisbury],' Churchill told Eden, 'this stickler for precise etiquette, obtained [as Lord President and minister for the bomb after Cherwell's retirement] my permission and yours to carry on with active preparations [for the H-bomb] without ever suggesting that the Cabinet should be informed of what had been settled in his presence at the Defence Committee and was actually in progress under his own direct authority.'[132]

The nuclear weapons strand was a very powerful element in both of Churchill's premierships. He was the first and – mercifully – the only British Prime Minister to authorize the use, as opposed to the testing, of a nuclear weapon. Under the terms of the secret 1943 Quebec Agreement, the dropping of the bombs on Hiroshima and Nagasaki in August 1945 was a decision to be taken jointly by the US President and the British Prime Minister. For reasons that are unclear, Churchill asked Cherwell in January 1953 to outline for him 'the principal events leading up to the dropping of the atomic bombs at Hiroshima and Nagasaki'. This Cherwell did and the resulting brief was flown out to Churchill who was in New York.[133]

Cherwell began, interestingly enough, with the 1944–45 version of that constitutional question:

On March 21, 1944, Sir John Anderson [Churchill's Minister for 'Tube Alloys', i.e., the bomb, project] suggested that the Tube Alloys programme should be mentioned to the Service Ministers and to the other ministers concerned but you minuted 'I do not agree'. Sir John Anderson was perturbed by your decision and I am fairly certain that in the Spring of 1945 he made another attempt to persuade you to bring the matter to Cabinet and that I supported him. No papers bearing on this can however be found. In the event, it seems, the question was never discussed at Cabinet or in the Defence Committee.[134]

Cherwell then traces progress reports on the Manhattan Project until

In April 1945 Lord Wilson [Whitehall's man on the Combined Policy Committee which dealt with atomic matters in Washington] telegraphed to Sir John Anderson that the Americans proposed to make a full-scale test in the desert in July and to drop a bomb on the Japanese in August and I told you about this.[135]

At the end of May, after discussion, 'it was agreed that in order to fulfil the Quebec Agreement the concurrence of HMG should be recorded at a meeting of the Combined Policy Committee'. On 29 June 1945 Anderson reminded Churchill of the agreed drill. 'In this minute', Cherwell recalled for Churchill, 'he requested authority to instruct our representatives to give the concurrence of HMG in the decision to use the bomb against the Japanese. You initialled this minute on July 1.'[136] Three days later, Wilson 'formally gave the concurrence' at a meeting of the Combined Policy Committee.[137]

The first British bomb can be seen as Attlee's and Bevin's rather than Churchill's, Anderson's or Cherwell's. But Churchill was Prime Minister once more by the time it was tested in the Monte Bello Islands off the north-west coast of Australia ('Operation Hurricane') in October 1952 and Churchill was party to a deception plan about the test which, strangely, came to bother him. One of the oddest Prime Minister's personal minutes of Churchill's that I have encountered was dictated by Churchill on Saturday 16 August 1952 when news was brought to him that the following morning's *Sunday Express* would carry an article designed to mislead the Russians and, therefore, all its readers about the forthcoming British atomic test.

'Please find out', he instructed the Cabinet Secretary, 'whether the Minister of Defence or the Minister of Supply have been consulted upon this business.' Churchill was cross that he had not been consulted until this last stage as 'It is impossible now to prevent or postpone publication, as the Sunday papers are already largely in print.'[138]

Surprisingly perhaps, given the nature of the Cold War and the special sensitivity of nuclear weapons, Churchill rather recoiled from

The idea of stimulating, through an inspired article, information both true and false, so mixed up as to be deceptive, to any particular newspaper, [as it] is not one hitherto entertained in time of peace. Certainly no departure from the principle that the government tells the truth or nothing should be made except upon direct ministerial responsibility as an exception in the public interest.[139]

The article duly appeared on the front page of the *Sunday Express* the following day under the by-line of the paper's features editor, John L. Garbutt, and carrying the misleading headline 'Tactical atom bomb exercise planned'. The gist of Garbutt's piece was that 'Britain's first atom bomb arrived in Australia' (it hadn't; the plutonium core did not arrive for another month) and that in addition to the bomb proper 'It is believed that a "tactical" atomic weapon will be tested as well.' (It wasn't; this was probably cover for a less than successful explosion which, if it occurred, could be passed off as a smaller device.)[140]

The day after the newspaper article appeared, Brook replied to the Prime Minister in a manner which underscores Churchill's fading powers. Churchill had given clearance for such a deception on two occasions earlier that summer. 'The Minister of Defence', Brook explained,

made two submissions to you in May and June, recommending that deception techniques should be used in order to mislead the Russians about the date and the nature of this trial. You approved these submissions; and the Minister of Defence told Mr Menzies [the Australian Prime Minister], while he was in London, that these attempts to confuse the Russians would be made. The officials in the Ministry of Defence who handle deception work regarded the publication of this particular article as covered by this decision of principle, and did not seek specific approval for this part of their plan from either the Minister of Defence or the Minister of

Supply [who was responsible for the test]. They thought it right, however, to let you know that the article was to be published, because they knew that you would see it in the newspaper and wished you to know that this was not an instance of irregular leakage of official information.[141]

Brook went on to explain that Garbutt and 'to a lesser extent' his editor, were party to the deception, knowing that 'we wished this information to be published for our own purposes and that it was not in all respects accurate'.[142]

At Brook's suggestion, Churchill minuted the Defence Minister, Alexander, asking him about the directorate inside his ministry 'concerned with the techniques which we evolved during the war for misleading the enemy about our future plans and intentions'.[143] He was quite plainly unaware that the wartime body, the London Controlling Section, had been kept going, as Alexander explained, on 'a care and maintenance' basis between 1945 and the middle of 1950 when, after a review by the Chiefs of Staff, as we have seen, it was re-created as an active if small body, under a new cover-name, the Directorate of Forward Plans.[144]

Churchill was genuinely ambivalent about peacetime deception. 'The experience of these Stratagems which we gained in the war', he told Alexander, 'should not, of course, be thrown away: knowledge of the old techniques should be kept alive, and it may be that new methods may usefully be evolved. But it is a nice question how far this weapon should actually be used in time of peace – at any rate for peacetime purposes. It may be a different matter to use these methods for concealing our military plans in operational theatres like Korea and Malaya.'[145] Alexander believed that provided the deception directorate 'sticks, as it does, to military matters, its existence is well justified. We are under continuous and vigorous attack by a hostile Intelligence Organisation [the Soviet Union's KGB and GRU], and it is most important to confuse and mislead that Organisation and to put ourselves in a position to continue to do this if war comes.'[146]

Thanks to the success of the 'Hurricane' test, Churchill became the first British Prime Minister to have his hands on a droppable nuclear weapon when the first Blue Danube atomic bomb was delivered to RAF Wittering in November 1953[147] (an extraordinary thing for a man who had fought at Omdurman in 1898).[148] Almost instantly, however, Churchill had to grapple with the next leap in nuclear technology – the hydrogen bomb. And the horrors of what that instrument could do were vividly apparent to him long before he received the Strath Report on what it might do to his beloved island people.[149]

It was Churchill's misfortune that the arrival of the H-bomb decision in the Cabinet Room in the summer of 1954 coincided with the issue on which he really did short-circuit collective consideration – his last great push to end the Cold War. This stemmed in part from his fear of the consequences of a thermonuclear exchange with the Soviet Union and partly from his sense of new possibilities after the death of Stalin in 1953. He was conscious, too, that he was now the sole survivor of the 'Big Three' who had met at Yalta in early 1945 in an attempt to sustain wartime co-operation into the peace. Here Churchill disdained his heir apparent, Anthony Eden, as having become 'Foreign Officeissmus', of having gone native on a department he (Churchill) denounced as a 'cowardly lot of shuffling scuttlers'.[150]

Here, too, his fastidiousness about the niceties of Cabinet government deserted him. His pursuit of personal diplomacy by telegram with the post-Stalin Russian leadership while aboard the *Queen Elizabeth* returning from discussions with Eisenhower about Cold War tensions and the British H-bomb, among other matters, led to a series of acrimonious Cabinet meetings in July 1954. As we have seen, hints of resignation were made from a number of figures (not just that habitual resigner 'Bobbety' Salisbury) if the old man did not defer to the Cabinet's collective scepticism about the wisdom of his desire for an imminent summit.[151]

Apart from his mishandling of his Cabinet, it is hard to fault Churchill's attempt to halt the Cold War some thirty-five years before it came to its close. The most vivid way into his thinking is to read his draft of the long minute of 'general reservations' he prepared for his Cabinet colleagues on the proposed summit (which he wanted to take place in London) in August 1954 in the wake of those difficult Cabinet meetings. He was plainly worried by 'the argument which must be present in many American minds', namely:

We alone have for the next two or perhaps three years sure and overwhelming superiority in attack, and a substantive measure of immunity in defence. Merely to dawdle means potential equality of ruin. Ought we not for the immediate safety of our own American people and the incidental rescue of the Free World to bring matters to a head by a 'show-down' leading up to an ultimatum accompanied by an Alert?[152]

This prospect horrified Churchill. Instead he sought what he saw as a genuine possibility whereby a twenty-year period of '"peaceful co-existence" although not setting things precisely on paper, might well create a new era in human thought and temper favourable to the survival of individual liberty and the healthy evolution of human society. This hope should not be based on illusions about Communist or Russian good-faith, but only on a correct estimate of Russian self-interest.'[153]

And what was Churchill's own estimate of this that gave him such a powerful sense of opportunity in those early, post-Stalin days?

First, that they [the Soviets] are still far weaker in the thermonuclear sphere, including especially power of hostile delivery.

Secondly, that it is their interest and their wish to have an era of greatly increased material comfort and prosperity, even though it may be attended by a relaxation of Communist theory enforced by police control, and military discipline resting on normal patriotism.

The inter-play of these two forces is at present intricate. Combined as they would be in war or under threat of war, they of course give absolute domination throughout Russia and her satellites to the Kremlin government. They are, however, fundamentally diverse, and even opposed, in character, tradition and mood. Given a prolonged period of peace, or at least of 'non-war confidence' and easement, one force might correct the other or even become antagonistic. This process would not be harmful to the Free World.[154]

It was not to be. Eventually, from Moscow, Malenkov ended the triangular debate between Ike, Winston and the Churchill Cabinet by proposing a conference of all European governments instead of a summit of the great powers. As Martin Gilbert commented, 'Churchill's last great foreign policy initiative was at an end.'[155] He had pursued it relentlessly from the spring of 1953 to his last days in office two years later. Anthony Montague Browne told me of the poignant footnote to the greatest setback of the last Churchill premiership. 'He wanted to be seen as the peacemaker. When he got the Nobel Prize for Literature [in 1953 for his war memoirs] I told him that he'd been awarded the Nobel Prize and he was frightfully excited. Sat up. And I added "for literature". And his face fell. He'd wanted the Nobel Peace Prize.'[156]

The episode of the summit that never was did nothing to raise Eden's standing in Churchill's eyes and his final burst of vacillation in the spring of 1955 over vacating the premiership for him used the possibility of 'some exceptional invitation or prospect of a summit' to postpone what his daughter, Mary Soames, called his 'first death'[157] (even though Conservative Party managers were itching to complete the succession, as Churchill well knew, in time for an early election).[158]

What is one to make of the pageant premiership? Some aspects of it still have the capacity to amaze. The ability as late as the summer of 1953 of a small group of Churchill courtiers to keep the seriousness of his stroke out of the press and to run a kind of surrogate government for him ('a state crisis ... conducted in camera', in Edward Pearce's brilliant phrase)[159] while he recovered during the summer recess and the willingness of the Cabinet, the acting PM 'Rab' Butler particularly, to put up with it is quite extraordinary to modern eyes.[160] And had Churchill died within days of their doctoring the medical bulletin,[161] this same inner circle (especially Colville, Brook and Soames) were party to a scheme whereby the Palace would have invited Lord Salisbury to form a caretaker administration for six months until Eden had recovered from his operation in America. (Several months after the stroke a secret drill was agreed between Buckingham Palace and the Home Office on how the Queen would handle the succession should Churchill die or resign through ill health while she was out of the country.)[162] After dining with Churchill at Chartwell on 2 July 1953 and starting to appreciate the elaborate nature of the public deception as to Churchill's true condition, Macmillan wrote in his diary: 'It was a kind of conspiracy we were all in – and it was rather fun to have such respectable people as Salisbury, Butler and Co. as fellow conspirators.'[163]

On non-Cold War aspects of his country's geopolitical position Churchill was less far-sighted. He could not bear the idea of disposing of parts of the British Empire, not even the base in the Suez Canal Zone.[164] (Though he did not relish at all the British Empire when, as it were, it began to come home in the form of 'coloured immigration' in the 1950s; 'Keep England White' was a good slogan, he told the Cabinet three months before leaving office.)[165] European integration, his great late-1940s theme, was something he meant for them, not for us.[166] In fact, the European question in its *economic* form – the putative creation of a European army was another matter – preoccupied his Cabinet to a remarkably limited degree: relationships with the fledgling European Coal and Steel Community were discussed largely at the level of official committees.[167]

As for the *British* economy, it baffled him in the early 1950s even more than it had when he was Chancellor of the Exchequer twenty years earlier.

On appointing John Boyd-Carpenter Financial Secretary to the Treasury in 1951 he said, 'I was Chancellor of the Exchequer . . . for five years and . . . I never understood it.'[168] Often it seemed as if the scope and pace of peacetime government as a whole was quite beyond him. In an interesting aside to Harold Macmillan which reflected the growing demands on Cabinet government as he had first experienced it in Asquith's time, Churchill said 'at every Cabinet today there are discussed at least two or three problems which would have filled a whole session before the first war'.[169]

His glorious presence in No. 10 distracted his fellow countrymen and women from the realities of their nation's position, too. He was still providing for them what Tom Harrisson so marvellously described as 'a sort of intellectual deep shelter' of the kind he had constructed during the war.[170] This effect was powerfully enhanced in coronation year by what Ben Pimlott calls 'the most visible . . . contrast of all, between youth and innocence and age and experience. The juxtaposition of the angelic Sovereign and the cherubic premier delighted the public . . . [as] . . . It also seemed to delight the incorrigibly – and, as he got older – increasingly sentimental Winston Churchill, who took a very personal pleasure in his weekly audience with a young Queen who knew so little, and had so much to learn.'[171]

Churchill clung on to the premiership for too long, possibly because he thought he might die if he relinquished it and, without doubt, because he grew more and more worried about Eden's lack of prime ministerial fibre. On his very last night in No. 10 he told Colville: 'I don't believe Anthony can do it.'[172] Was he deluded about his country's predicament as a fast-fading great power? Churchill used to remark during his last premiership: 'You cannot ignore the facts for they glare upon you.'[173] Those hard facts may have glared upon him but he was too old, too tired and too bereft of new ideas to begin to reflect the consequences of their unforgiving dazzle. And yet there was a glow about that last premiership, a generosity of spirit that was Churchill's version of consensus. The Cabinet Room seemed a smaller place the day after he left it and it has remained so ever since. That is a measure of his singularity and his enduring status.

9

The Colonel and the Drawing Room:
Anthony Eden, 1955–57

'I think it's important to remember how overpowering Anthony's position was. He was not only Prime Minister but he was considered to be the greatest Prime Minister that we'd had for a long time and the greatest foreign policy expert that we'd had for a long time. It's very difficult to challenge a Prime Minister, but to challenge a Prime Minister on foreign policy if that's his real strength is very difficult indeed.'

Lord Thorneycroft, 1993[1]

'. . . the Suez débâcle'.   *Harold Macmillan, privately, 1962*[2]

'Harold Macmillan was very active on the withdrawing side. He had been very active on the aggressive side.'

Lord Thorneycroft, 1993, recalling the
Cabinet meeting of 6 November 1956[3]

'I got more excited as a human being and as a politician during the Suez business than at any other time before or since in my political career . . . I asked Eden, I think it was his last appearance in the House of Commons,[4] whether we had any foreknowledge of the Israeli attack and he told a straight lie. He said "No" . . . And the interesting thing about the whole affair, which is often forgotten in Britain, is that the only successful use of sanctions in history was the Americans over Suez.'   *Denis Healey, 1994*[5]

'He was already a sick man . . . and he was a great fusser . . . Eden . . . was rather like an Arab horse. He used to get terribly het up and excited and he had to be sort of kept down.'

Sir Frank Roberts, 1994[6]

> The Prime Minister's health gives cause for anxiety ... This gives us
> much concern because of the serious operations in 1953 and some
> subsequent attacks of fever. In our opinion his health will no longer
> enable him to sustain the heavy burdens inseparable from the office
> of Prime Minister.
>
> *Horace Evans, Gordon Gordon-Taylor, Thomas Hunt,*
> *Ralph Southward, 8 January 1957*[7]

Anthony Eden is the most tragic figure to have occupied 10 Downing
Street in the postwar period. A politician of charm, intelligence and
bravery, with a powerful desire to ease the antagonisms of his class-
deformed country, he was the only clear-cut heir apparent to succeed to
the premiership in the period since 1945 – albeit after too many enervating
years as Churchill's number 2. He reached the top in April 1955 only to
see his possession of the greatest prize of political and public life sink
beneath the waters of the Suez Canal less than two years after he won it,
leaving his reputation tarnished to this day. As Robert Rhodes James,
his official biographer, put it (borrowing the phrase used of Curzon by
Churchill): 'The morning had been golden; the noontide was bronze; and
the evening lead.'[8]

Suez stained the otherwise perfect elegance he maintained in the twenty
years of life left to him after he resigned in 1957. As David Dutton's
biographical study shows, he could not leave the subject alone even in his
very last days despite the determination of friends and guests to steer
their conversation clear of that notorious waterway and the man who
nationalized it, Colonel Gamal Abdel Nasser.[9] As the veteran *Sunday
Times* Washington correspondent Henry Brandon put it after encounter-
ing the Avons, as they had become, at the Harrimans' in 1976:

It soon became clear ... that Eden was using my presence to plead ... for justice
before history, presenting his case as he saw it, offering new and dispassionate
after-thoughts ... The ghost of Suez was still stalking Eden as he was getting ready
for the end and wondering about the verdict of history.[10]

'In his mind his whole proud career', Brandon observed, 'had been
scarred by a decision which misfired for lack of American co-operation.'[11]

A measure of his tragedy is Eden's place in the accumulated folklore
which surrounds the job of Prime Minister. The lesson of his premiership
is quite simple – how not to do it; largely, though not wholly, because of

his conduct of the crisis precipitated by Colonel Nasser's nationalization of the Suez Canal Company on 26 July 1956. Lady Eden told a meeting of Conservative women shortly afterwards that throughout those crisis months in No. 10, she felt as if 'the Suez Canal was flowing throughout the drawing-room'.[12] In one sense it has flowed through Downing Street each time a resident premier has sensed a possibility of Britain's armed forces having to resume active service in response to a crisis likely to involve an exchange of fire (as we saw in chapter 6 from that Sunday-lunchtime conversation between Mrs Thatcher and Sir Frank Cooper following the Argentinian invasion of the Falkland Islands).

But first we need to roll the newsreel back *pre*-26 July 1956. Eden had been Prime Minister for fifteen months before the fuse was lit beneath his premiership. It is important to examine initially the forgotten first phase of his Downing Street years from his succeeding Churchill at the beginning of April 1955 to the end of July 1956, when the Canal began to flow in No. 10. On the surface, the start of the fifty-seven-year-old premier's stewardship appeared immensely promising. Apparently recovered from a series of serious bile-duct operations in 1953, Eden made a quick, decisive appeal to the electorate. During the campaign he shone both on the stump and on the television screen[13] *en route* to raising the Conservative majority in May 1955 from sixteen to fifty-eight, the first time an incumbent Prime Minister had increased his majority since Palmerston.[14]

Behind the veneer of success, however, Eden's nerves and other people's doubts were concealed. That great Conservative Party fixer, Lord Swinton, told Churchill early in 1955 that 'anybody would be better than Anthony . . . [who] would make the worst Prime Minister since Lord North . . . But . . . you announced him as your successor more than ten years ago.' 'I think it was a great mistake,' Churchill replied.[15] Lord Moran, Churchill's doctor, had confided to Harold Macmillan that, as Macmillan recorded in his diary, he 'thought Eden would have great difficulty standing the strain [of the premiership]. The state of his inside is not good, and he ought to be careful. If the artificial bile channel (or whatever it is) "silts up again" . . . it will be very serious.' In an interesting aside, Moran reckoned (in Macmillan's words again) that 'one of Eden's weaknesses . . . is that he really has no interests except politics. His mind is never off them . . .'[16]

Despite his absorption in matters political, Eden on becoming Prime Minister dithered privately over a swift appeal to the country, to the consternation of the Party chairman, Lord Woolton,[17] and showed a good deal of his propensity to tantrums to his immediate entourage during the campaign,[18] even though a split Labour Party, riven by Bevanite dissent and led by an ageing Attlee, never had a prayer at the polls. For all the apparent truce between right and left, Labour never succeeded in presenting a united face to the electorate.

Some ministerial doubters among the Conservatives, such as John Boyd-Carpenter, consoled themselves by 'saying it's a pity he knows nothing about economics or social security or finance, but at least we shall be all right with foreign affairs'. 'That', Lord Boyd-Carpenter told me over thirty years later, 'was rather ironic.'[19] Others such as Lord Hailsham saw in Eden both 'the most cultivated [and] civilized of all modern Prime Ministers'[20] (a view which militates somewhat against Moran's accusation of narrowness) and, after the 'one-off job' premiership of Churchill, welcomed what Hailsham foresaw as being 'a real peacetime Prime Minister and a real postwar government ... [led by] a Prime Minister who represented contemporary manhood, rather than the pre-First World War generation.'[21] And Eden's political instincts were progressive – the creation of a 'property-owning democracy' was at the core of his domestic agenda[22] and he was positively evangelical about industrial partnership as the banisher of class divisions between capital and labour.[23]

Yet all of Eden's ministerial experience had been on the foreign and defence side. His lack of confidence in domestic matters was publicly apparent from the start of his premiership, when at the opening press conference of the 1955 election campaign Butler, rather than the PM, fielded questions which required a detailed knowledge of home affairs.[24] And such tentativeness on the domestic and economic fronts remained a feature of Eden's style even after the election was won and Eden had played himself in as Prime Minister.

Over a year later, at the end of May 1956, Harold Macmillan (by this time Chancellor of the Exchequer) was keen to reconstitute the Cabinet's Economic Policy Committee, which he chaired, as a smaller, less formal group, able when it wished to meet without a fixed agenda, and to be more closely involved with the early formulation of policy.[25] Eden agreed to this, scribbling rather plaintively on the Cabinet Secretary's submission: 'But I should like to be kept in touch with main economic questions. How could this most easily be done?'[26] Brook replied that as a result of the streamlining of the EPC, 'more economic problems will come to the Cabinet itself. This will be all to the good, and will go far towards meeting your point. For the rest, I will make it my business to see that you are kept informed of what goes on in the smaller group which is to meet under the chairmanship of the Chancellor of the Exchequer.'[27] It simply did not occur to Eden how *he* might ensure that arrangements which suited *him* were put in place, let alone to chair such an important, strategic ministerial group himself as Attlee (though not Churchill) had done

Yet as premier, Eden sensed the need to consider a whole range of questions on economic, social and industrial relations and would establish Cabinet committees to examine them (wildcat strikes, the possibility of pre-strike secret ballots and the possible need to control Commonwealth immigration are good examples).[28] However, he rarely got to grips with such difficult issues, let alone initiated any action upon them. Some of the most security-sensitive files, releasable only after the end of the Cold War, have filled in the background here. For example, we now know that MI5 briefed Eden that industrial unrest was not a Communist *Party* inspired activity, for it was the view of the Communist Party of Great Britain that, as Norman Brook's summary of the MI5 report put it, 'the advocacy of strike action would more often hinder than help it in its primary objective of penetrating and eventually controlling the trade union movement . . . While its members account for less than one in 500 of the national trade union membership, the Party now controls the Executive Committees of three trade unions; and thirteen General Secretaries and at least one in eight of all full-time officials are Communists.'[29]

To be fair to Eden, he *did* set in train long-term reviews on both social services spending and Britain's place in the world with its associated military expenditure, the latter laying much of the groundwork for the Macmillan/Sandys Defence White Paper of 1957. He was aware pre-Suez of the increasing difficulty of sustaining a world role based on a less than world-class domestic economy. Despite this growing appreciation of the realities of the UK's position, historians generally (and justifiably) have been critical of Eden for failing to see the potential significance of the Messina talks of 1955 on closer economic integration in Europe and the subsequent negotiations in 1956 which led to the transformation of the European Coal and Steel Community (under the terms of the 1957 Treaty of Rome) into the 'Common Market' of the European Economic Community. Eden's Cabinet Committee on Relations with the Coal and Steel Community, for example, met just twice in 1955, once in June at the outset of the Spaak Committee deliberations which flowed from Messina and in November on the withdrawal of the UK's representative, Board of Trade civil servant Russell Bretherton, from the negotiations. Full Cabinet involvement quickened in 1956 as a free trade area plan was developed as an alternative to a common market,[30] but it was a great disadvantage that close Cabinet attention to Europe when it was most needed in early October 1956 was distracted by the Suez crisis.

Yet long before secret Whitehall worries about Nasser, the future of the Suez Canal and the geopolitics of the Middle East, let alone what to do about troublesome Continental integrationists, had emerged from the most obscure of official Cabinet committees,[31] Eden's inadequacies as Prime Minister were the talk of both the private government and the public prints. Not until John Major's post-election traumas of 1992 has a prime ministerial honeymoon been so brief. As Eden's chum, Noël Coward, put it in February 1956, 'Anthony Eden's popularity had spluttered away like a blob of fat in a frying pan,'[32] and his opinion poll approval rating fell from 70 per cent in the autumn of 1955 to around 40 per cent the following spring.[33] Eden was, perhaps, the first conspicuous victim of what Jean Seaton has called 'the politics of appearances'[34] – the vulnerability of telegenic electoral charmers whose surface image cannot for long hold at bay the cumulative exposure, once in No. 10, to Churchill's (as opposed to Macmillan's) notion of 'events' and actions whose 'proportions alter in an ever-changing scene'.[35]

Part of this slump, of course, had to do with the shadow of the great manipulator of events Eden had replaced (something else John Major would understand). Attlee, who knew both Churchill and Eden extremely well, captured this with one of his cricketing metaphors in January 1956 when Gaitskell asked him who would have supposed that Churchill's departure would have made such a difference? 'Yep', observed Attlee. 'It's the heavy roller, you know. Doesn't let the grass grow under it.'[36] Macmillan put it even more graphically when he wrote in his diary for 6 April 1955: 'It is a pretty tough assignment to follow the greatest Englishman of history.'[37]

But Eden compounded mightily the inevitably unfavourable comparisons with his predecessor about which he was immensely sensitive (he had wounded Churchill by virtually excluding him from the Conservatives' 1955 election campaign).[38] Eden famously overreacted to newspaper criticism, uttering 'a pained and pungent oath', according to Rab Butler, when Donald McLachlan penned his famous leading article in the *Daily Telegraph* on 'The firm smack of government', or lack of, it in January 1956 and foolishly let his Downing Street Press Secretary, William Clark, deny rumours that he was contemplating resignation.[39] (What the *Daily*

Telegraph actually printed was: 'There is a favourite gesture with the Prime Minister. To emphasize a point he will clench one fist to smash the open palm of the other hand but the smash is seldom heard.')[40] Rab Butler, characteristically, did not help matters when, leaving for a holiday, he allowed reporters to trap him into agreeing that Eden was 'the best Prime Minister we have got'.[41] On the wider economic and political fronts, inflation moved against the government and so did by-elections.[42]

Above all, it was within his own Cabinet Room and the Whitehall machine over which he presided that Eden aroused serious doubts about his temperament, his judgement and his poor health long before Suez. For Eden was the greatest fusser to have filled the premiership probably of the last century; certainly since 1945. Though, surprisingly, he made no detectable use of that great prime ministerial licence to fuss, *Questions of Procedure for Ministers*. As Amy Baker has noted: 'Anthony Eden was the only postwar Prime Minister who did not issue an updated version of *QPM* during his premiership.'[43] Yet Eden's nerves set other ministers' nerves on edge and civil servants, including those in his own private offices, found him very trying.

As William Clark recalled, 'the private secretaries sometimes refused to take things up with him because they knew it would worry him and cause an explosion. Always at the back of everything was the fear that he would lose his temper and we should be sworn at.'[44] A diary entry made by his Foreign Office Private Secretary, Evelyn Shuckburgh, after a Cabinet Office cocktail party in March 1954 records the mixed opinions of Eden (and Rab Butler too) sculling around the Whitehall private office network at that time. 'Talked to Norman Brook [Cabinet Secretary], George Mallaby [member of the Cabinet Secretariat] and [Tim] Bligh, Bridges' Private Secretary', wrote Shuckburgh,

and they all complained about the Chancellor [Butler]. He is moody and impossible to deal with, having his Budget shortly ahead. Norman attributes his character to the fact that Mrs Butler [the formidable Sydney Courtauld] ought to have been a man – is a man – so that Rab has become a woman. I said pity both the Chancellor and Foreign Secretary [Eden] should be women.[45]

However one reads that, the irritation with Eden is apparent.

Yet as Prime Minister, Eden meant well. He tried to accommodate and reassure his ministers. He imitated Baldwin, under whom he came to his political maturity, by inviting colleagues to Downing Street to chat *à deux* about their departments. But unlike those of his model, Baldwin, or Labour's latter-day Baldwin, Jim Callaghan, who revived the practice twenty years later,[46] Eden's sessions were occasions to be endured rather than enjoyed.[47] As Robert Rhodes James put it, 'it is fair to say that British Prime Ministers tend to fall into one of two categories – the Olympian and the interferer. From almost the day he entered Downing Street, Eden was the latter.'[48]

The telephone call from the Prime Minister was the most dreaded manifestation of this passion for meddling. Even that most amiable of men, Alec Home, the Commonwealth Secretary, found such conversations profoundly exasperating.[49] David Dutton has compiled a kind of lexicon of examples of such irritation in his Eden biography, starting with Harold Macmillan:

'He kept on sending me little notes, sometimes twenty a day, ringing up all the time. He really should have been both PM and Foreign Secretary,' Macmillan recalled.[50]

Initially, this counterproductive impulse might have been seen as a consequence of Eden's not creating the Cabinet he wanted until the reshuffle of December 1955 (a delay in stamping his own mark on Whitehall which he came to regret).[51] But this was not so. It was almost congenital and continued long after the reshuffle and right through to his last days in No. 10. And in Selwyn Lloyd he had from December 1955 the kind of cipher at the Foreign Office that Macmillan never could have been. But, to continue the Dutton lexicon:

Selwyn Lloyd fared no better – thirty telephone calls from Chequers over the Christmas weekend of 1955. 'He *cannot* leave people alone to do their job,' judged Shuckburgh.[52]

And then there were the temper tantrums. The list of those on the receiving end was truly comprehensive, ranging from Lloyd to the 'communists' in the BBC, Foster Dulles in Washington to Randolph Churchill writing in the *Evening Standard*. Of course, it was not just a question of nerves. He was ill. The fevers associated with his botched operation were recurring before the strain of Suez was imposed upon that tired and stressed frame and oh so brittle temperament. As his Parliamentary Private Secretary, Robert Carr, told me many years later:

'He was never the same man after the gall bladder operation that went wrong in 1953. He appeared to be getting very much better, but then within the first six months of his premiership he started getting the fevers again . . . When he actually appointed me to be a junior minister I had to go and see him in his bedroom, where he had a temperature of 102°. That was ten months before the crisis of Suez.'[53]

Eden himself explained his post-1953 condition to the Cabinet on 9 January 1957, the last time he presided over it. 'As you know', he told them a few hours before he went to the Palace to resign,

'It is now nearly four years since I had a series of bad abdominal operations which left me with a largely artificial inside. It was not thought that I would lead an active life again. However, with the aid of drugs and stimulants, I have been able to do so.

'During these last five months, since Nasser seized the Canal in July, I have been obliged to increase the drugs considerably and also increase the stimulants necessary to counteract the drugs. This has finally had an adverse effect on my rather precarious inside.'[54]

According to Dr Hugh L'Etang, (who was until his death the leading British scholar of the pathology of leadership), Eden was suffering from 'the toxic effects of bile-duct infection, and the chemical effects of stimulant and possibly other medication': benzedrine was almost certainly a factor here.[55] Add to the effect of the benzedrine poor sleep and the desperate need for a holiday as the 1955–56 session of Parliament drew to a close, and you have a cocktail of mania-inducing qualities. These were ready-mixed at the precise moment, if Lloyd's Minister of State at the Foreign Office, Anthony Nutting, is to be believed, when Colonel Nasser took his dramatic action in Alexandria on the night of 26 July 1956.

Nutting had experienced a kind of tantrum-dry-run for Suez in the spring of 1956, when Eden reckoned Nasser was behind King Hussein's removal of General Glubb from command of the Arab Legion in Jordan.[56] Thirty years later Sir Anthony Nutting recalled for me the rage of Eden that night of 1 March 1956 as if it were yesterday:

'The telephone rang and a voice down the other end said: "It's me." I didn't quite realize who "me" was for a moment. However, he gave the show away very quickly by starting to scream at me. "What is all this poppycock you've sent me about isolating Nasser and neutralizing Nasser? Why can't you get it into your head I want the man destroyed?" I said, "OK. You get rid of Nasser, what are you going to put in his place?" "I don't want anybody," he said. I said, "Well, there'll be anarchy and chaos in Egypt." "I don't care if there's anarchy and chaos in Egypt. Let there be anarchy and chaos in Egypt. I just want to get rid of Nasser." '[57]

Not the frame of mind one would expect in the most polished political diplomat of his generation whose expertise on the Middle East especially, had waxed mightily since he took his First in Persian at Oxford in 1921.[58]

Though one cannot be sure, I suspect Eden really did want Nasser destroyed. Peter Wright's *Spycatcher*,[59] a notoriously unreliable volume in parts, is not my source for this. Rather it is a somewhat guarded conversation I had with Sir Dick White, Chief of the Secret Intelligence Service ('C') at the time of Suez, almost thirty years later in the early summer of 1986. Sir Dick indicated that even if a Prime Minister ordered an assassination of a foreign leader, there were ways of ensuring it was not carried out.[60] Later White spelt this out more fully for his biographer, Tom Bower, claiming to Bower that in the run-up to the invasion of Egypt he had told Eden directly that he would sanction no further SIS involvement in plans to kill Nasser.[61]

This is not the place to reprise the lengthy and tangled genesis and course of the Suez imbroglio of 1956. It has to be remembered, however, in any treatment of the greatest crisis of Eden's political life that his government was not in good shape when it broke. Macmillan's diary has that boon to historians – a private, unvarnished summing-up of the wider position penned a few days before the nationalization of the Suez Canal Company. On 21 July 1956, Eden's Chancellor of the Exchequer wrote:

The Government's position is very bad at present. Nothing has gone well. In the M. East we are still teased by Nasser and Co.; the Colonial Empire is breaking up, and many people view with anxiety the attempt to introduce Parliamentary Democracy in such places as Nigeria and the Gold Coast; Cyprus is a running sore. The situation regarding Russia is better but the Defence burden goes on. At home, Taxation is very high; the inflation has *not* been mastered; no-one knows whether the new Chancellor will be a great success or a crashing failure (least of all does the Chancellor know!) Meanwhile we see Germany – free of debt, and making little contribution to defence – seizing the trade of the world from under our noses. The people are puzzled; the party is distracted; Eden gives no real leadership in the House (for he is *not* a House of Commons man – he *never* enters the Smoking Room) although he is *popular* and respected in the country as a whole.[62]

Had Eden's health broken in the pre-Suez section of the 1956 summer and had he made way (for Butler, it would almost certainly have been), his premiership would already have been set for a 'promise unfulfilled' epitaph. Disappointing though that would have been, it would have been infinitely preferable to 'premiership destroyed'.

For the purpose of this volume, I want to examine the Suez crisis through the prism of the debate over prime ministerial versus Cabinet government, in the context of how – or how not to – create and use a War Cabinet for a so-called limited war, and in terms of the premier's role as risk assessor and manager, especially for those enterprises (of which the Suez affair was one) where the British government is in a relatively dominant position as the driver or shaper of events, possibilities or reactions. Eden and several of his colleagues, once the Suez Canal Company was nationalized, felt that this was where the British government would have to take its stand or, in Home's words to Eden, 'I am convinced that we are finished if the Middle East goes and Russia and India and China rule from Africa to the Pacific.'[63] Alan Lennox-Boyd, the Colonial Secretary, put it even more graphically when he told his PM that if 'Nasser wins or even appears to win we might as well as a government (and indeed as a country) go out of business'.[64] Eden needed little prompting, and added a fierce personal animosity towards Nasser, whom he felt had personally betrayed him after his efforts as Foreign Secretary to negotiate Britain's withdrawal from the base in the Canal Zone in the teeth of Churchill's initial doubts.[65]

Eden's object was to retake the canal, to 'topple' Nasser in the process and, with both French and American assistance, construct a new regime for the Middle East in defence, oil and international relations terms which would preserve British influence in the region and proof the area against Soviet influence and penetration. He was, in today's argot, going to draw a line in the sand that would end Britain's slow retreat as a great power. Just over three months later he had succeeded in alienating not just the Arab world, but President Eisenhower, the bulk of the Commonwealth and most of the major players at the United Nations. He had also succeeded in splitting his country, dividing his Cabinet and party and causing the near collapse of the pound while leaving Soviet influence uncurbed and an untoppled Nasser's prestige in the Arab world hugely enhanced.

In achieving this singularly malign combination, which included as a cruel bonus the wrecking of his own health and the ruination of his career, Eden managed simultaneously to worry those two great icons of mid-1950s Britain – the old warrior, Sir Winston Churchill and the young Queen, Elizabeth II (though I suspect neither was able to make their reservations plain to him at the time).[66] Intriguingly, Eden briefly considered inviting Churchill to return to office. Near the end of October, Churchill's Private Secretary, Anthony Montague Browne, was invited to call on the Prime Minister in the Cabinet Room. After briefing him on the plans for the Anglo-French invasion and enjoining him to tell no one but Churchill, Eden said: 'I want to ask you this. If I offered Winston a seat in the Cabinet without portfolio, would he accept?'[67] The astounded Montague Browne replied that he thought Churchill would not relish responsibility without power. 'I must say', said Churchill when informed of this, 'you do take a lot on yourself. Turning down the offer of a seat in the Cabinet without even asking me!'[68]

This bizarre offer was not disclosed until nearly forty years after it was made. What did seep out very quickly after the collapse of Eden's policy, however, was Churchill's famous observation on Suez, also to Montague Browne, that 'I would never have done it without squaring the Americans, and once I'd started I would never have dared stop.'[69] For a detailed appreciation of the Queen's views we had to wait until 1994 when Lord Charteris, one of her private secretaries at the time, told me: 'Suez was a matter which gave the Queen a great deal of concern . . . I think the basic dishonesty of the whole thing was a trouble.' She was also alarmed at the effect the operation was having on both the Commonwealth and American opinion.[70] We now know too from a declassified No. 10 file just how well informed the Queen was on both the operational and intelligence aspects of the invasion of Egypt once the attack was under way.[71]

Interestingly, the Queen and Churchill collaborated in the aftermath. She summoned him (after her Private Secretary, Sir Michael Adeane, had been prompted by Montague Browne)[72] to give advice on Eden's successor. On his way up to the Audience Room in Buckingham Palace Churchill asked to be informed of the relative ages of Butler and Macmillan.[73] He advised Her Majesty to send for Macmillan.[74] (Eden, by contrast, informed the Queen of his preference for Butler, which was entirely proper in constitutional terms as the Queen gave him the opportunity 'to signify' his appreciation of Butler's performance as acting Prime Minister during Eden's post-Suez recuperation in the Caribbean – though he did not press his views upon her, which would have been improper.)[75]

Generally, however, Eden has been treated by history as playing fast and loose with the British Constitution, not only by lying to the House of Commons on 20 December 1956 when, as we have seen, he denied there had been any foreknowledge of the Israeli attack on Egypt of 29 October,[76] but by practising a malign and self-defeating version of prime ministerial government to the detriment of the collective pattern of decision-taking which is supposed to lie at the heart of the British system. The case for the prosecution here was put at its most eloquent in the years to come by Rab Butler, Lord Privy Seal and constant Suez doubter and, even later, by Butler's Civil Service Private Secretary at the time, Ian Bancroft.

For Lord Butler, the Suez affair saw Eden acting as a 'one-man band' and moving 'much nearer to being a dictator than Churchill at the height of the war'.[77] For Lord Bancroft the state was turned into a travesty of proper government:

'There was a little committee [the Egypt Committee] . . . everything seemed to be conducted in a hurried, reactive almost furtive way . . . it seemed to me to typify the dangers of trying to run something as if it were a private laundry and not, as we then were, a major country on the world stage engaged in a singularly difficult adventure.'[78]

Butler's and Bancroft's views found a powerful echo on the innermost circle of the permanent government.

Sir Norman Brook was seriously worried by the fraying of proper procedure during the Suez Crisis. Lord Hunt of Tanworth, his Private Secretary at the time, recalls Brook's concern

'about the extent to which there wasn't adequate co-ordination, adequate planning – the extent to which the Prime Minister had a very dominant position [and] would brook no opposition at all where things were being conducted in very small groups within No. 10 without the sort of close, searching examination and thought which I think he felt was necessary'.[79]

Sir Frank Cooper, then an assistant secretary in the Air Ministry, has described how Brook used the Defence (Transition) Committee, diverted, as it were, from Cold War planning to Suez, to inject an element of order, calm and reality to the affair, at Civil Service level at least.[80] It was the wider Cabinet involvement, however, which worried him. Brook, John Hunt explained, 'was a very tidy man in every sense. He believed in proper Cabinet government and I think he regretted the fact that ordinary Cabinet government had, to some extent, been suspended for the duration.'[81]

The Civil and Diplomatic services generally were deeply scarred by Suez – they had been kept in the dark to a very high degree about the secret, collusive diplomacy in mid to late October between France, Israel and the UK – and the scars remained livid to the end of their days. Frank Cooper explained (to a group of my students) in 1999 that 'the shame of Suez was in the way it was handled politically by people like Eden and Selwyn Lloyd and the French who did it in such a hole-in-the-corner way'.[82] The officials loathed it as did many in the military. As Air Chief Marshal Sir Denis Smallwood put it, the public reasons given by Eden for the invasion were 'utterly phoney'.[83] Brook reminded Eden two years later that 'there [were] very few officials' who could tell inquiring journalists anything about Suez.[84] Official advice was spurned in some crucial instances, especially that furnished by Sir Gerald Fitzmaurice, the Foreign Office's top lawyer, that there was no legal case for armed intervention to reverse an act of company nationalization.[85]

Some ministers, most notably Anthony Nutting, shared the horror of the Whitehall advisers. Nutting was present at Chequers on 14 October 1956 when French emissaries presented Eden with the first outline of what became the Sèvres collusion which, in the words of his Foreign Affairs Private Secretary, Sir Guy Millard, 'intrigued' Eden, who clutched it as if it were 'a straw' as he was 'looking for a pretext'.[86] Nutting knew he was on the road to resignation when the Prime Minister told Millard there was no need to take a note of the meeting.[87]

Yet the opening of the archives has softened the view that Eden virtually hijacked proper Cabinet government for the duration. John Hunt's use of the qualifying phrase 'to some extent' is significant. At a full Cabinet meeting the day after Nasser's initial move, the 'fundamental question' before ministers, as the minutes put it, 'was whether they were prepared in the last resort to pursue their objective by the threat or even the use of force, and whether they were ready, in default of assistance from the United States and France, to take military action alone'. The Cabinet in the first flush of outrage against Nasser agreed 'that our essential interest in the area must, if necessary, be safeguarded by military action and that the necessary preparations to this end must be made'.[88]

The Egypt Committee was set up to run both the military preparations and the diplomatic efforts to tackle the crisis.[89] It was an unhappy and scrappy body, far removed from the desirable principles of command and control. John Hunt recalls a day of revealing chaos:

'I always remember one extraordinary happening . . . something occurred and a meeting of the Egypt Committee was called at very short notice indeed – something like twenty minutes (this was happening quite often; the Prime Minister would suddenly say, "I want a meeting of the Egypt Committee"). There was a three-line whip on in the House of Commons. Most ministers were down there and they very naturally assumed that the meeting was going to be in the Prime Minister's Room in the House of Commons. They assembled there: no Prime Minister. The Prime Minister had been working at No. 10. Both sides then realized what had happened. The ministers from the House of Commons got into a car [and] drove to No. 10. On their way up Whitehall they met the Prime Minister, who'd also realized what had happened, driving to the House of Commons.'

It's 'a silly story', John Hunt told me, 'but it gives you something of the atmosphere of unplanned chaos that was going on'.[90]

As time passed, those whom Eden called the 'weaker sisters' in the Cabinet expressed growing doubts and reservations. Some to this day (Ted Heath, then the Chief Whip, for example)[91] maintain that the full Cabinet did not know of the secret arrangements made with the Israelis and the French (Israel would invade Egypt; France and Britain would then go in as peacemakers and protectors of the canal). This was the plan with which the French tempted Eden during the secret meeting at Chequers on 14 October while Selwyn Lloyd, many believe, was within touching distance of negotiating a settlement at the UN in New York.[92] (Lloyd himself told his French and Israeli co-conspirators in Paris on 22 October that he reckoned he could reach a settlement with his Egyptian opposite number, Mahmoud Fawzi, within a week.)[93]

Ted Heath's memoirs, published in the autumn of 1998, shed new light on the pivotal days between the temptation of Eden at Chequers on 14 October and the full Cabinet meeting of 25 October which set the British part of the collusive bargain in the stone of a Cabinet minute. Heath was brought into the loop on 21 October. 'I was alarmed, but far from surprised, that a plan was being hatched to circumvent the negotiations in New York,' he wrote.

Four days later, I went into the Cabinet Room as usual shortly before Cabinet was due to start, and I found the Prime Minister standing by his chair holding a piece of paper. He was bright-eyed and full of life. The tiredness seemed suddenly to have disappeared. 'We've got an agreement!' he exclaimed. 'Israel has agreed to invade Egypt. We shall then send in our own forces, backed up by the French, to separate the contestants and regain the Canal.' The Americans would not be told about the plan. He concluded, somewhat unnervingly, that 'this is the highest form of statesmanship'.[94]

Eden explained to his Chief Whip that the agreement, the Protocol, had been signed in Sèvres, a Paris suburb, the day before and that only he, Lloyd, Macmillan and Butler 'were to know about it'.[95] 'I did my utmost to change Eden's mind,' Heath recalled in his memoirs, 'warning him that it was unlikely that people would believe him – and that, even if the Protocol remained a secret and people accepted the official reason for going in, the very act of doing so was likely to split the country. Eden did not dispute any of this advice, but simply reiterated that he could not let Nasser get away with it.'[96]

But the Cabinet minutes tell, I think, a different story from the all too convenient 'not me, guv' line that some ministers took subsequently. On 23 October the full Cabinet was told that 'from secret conversations which had been held in Paris with representatives of the Israeli government, it now appeared that the Israelis would not alone launch a full-scale attack against Egypt'.[97] (I shall never forget the moment at the Public Record Office when my BBC producer, Mark Laity, found those words in an about-to-be-released Confidential Annex to the sanitized Cabinet con- clusions. It struck us both as a 'smoking minute'.)[98] At the full Cabinet on 25 October, ministers were informed that the Israelis were 'after all, advancing their military preparations with a view to making an attack on Egypt'. Eden went on to tell them that, if British forces went in, 'We must face the risk that we should be accused of collusion with Israel.'[99] He himself was the first to use the 'c' word that dogged him until his last breath.

Some scholars, including David Dutton and Iain Macleod's biographer, Robert Shepherd, reckon there is (in Dutton's words) uncertainty still about what ministers outside the innermost circle understood (the unwieldy Egypt Committee ceased to meet from mid-October until two days before Mac- millan, fearful of American-engineered oil sanctions and the collapse of sterling, led the retreat from invasion in the teeth of Eden's wishes on 6

November).[100] For Shepherd, Eden at the Cabinet meetings on 23, 24 and 25 October 'sought to mislead the Cabinet. He kept the Sèvres Protocol secret and spoke as though the scheme that had in fact been agreed with the French and the Israelis was merely a contingency plan.'[101]

My own view is that this, rather than 6 November (a week after the RAF had started bombing Egyptian airfields, and the day when the Cabinet finally reined the PM in), was the moment for proper Cabinet government to come off ice. Ministers should have subjected those reports and hypothetical speculations of Eden's to the heat of questioning and, ultimately, to decision by the whole Cabinet collectively. They did not need a background at GCHQ to decode the import of those messages given in the Cabinet Room. If ministers remained deceived about collusion, it involved a high degree of self-deception.

My 'smoking gun' reaction to the fuller version of the Cabinet minutes of 23 October was reinforced ten years after it was declassified by the release of another piece of evidence from the Cabinet Office. As late as March 1958, Brook realized that Buckingham Palace had not sent back the Queen's 'Copy No. 1' of the confidential annexes for the Cabinet meetings of 18, 23 and 24 October 1956. Brook wrote to her Private Secretary, Sir Michael Adeane, asking for their return as 'some of the points dealt with ... were of a particularly sensitive nature'.[102] (This request is a trifle baffling as the Royal Archives at Windsor Castle are as leakproof as the Cabinet Office's own records section.)

The Sèvres Protocol laid out a precise sequence of events. It was, as Avi Shlaim put it, 'the most famous war plot in modern history'.[103] In the words of the English translation of the Protocol itself (a copy in French of the original is now available at the Public Record Office courtesy of the Israelis; Eden ordered the British copy to be burned shortly after the event),[104] events were to take the following course:

1. The Israeli forces launch in the evening of 29 October 1956 a large-scale attack on the Egyptian forces with the aim of reaching the Canal Zone the following day.
2. On being apprised of these events, the British and French governments during the day of 30 October 1956 respectively and simultaneously make two appeals to the Egyptian government and the Israeli government on the following lines:
   A. *To the Egyptian government*
      (a) halt all acts of war
      (b) withdraw all its troops ten miles from the Canal

    (c) accept temporary occupation of key positions on the Canal by the
        Anglo-French forces to guarantee freedom of passage through the ves-
        sels of all nations until a final settlement

B. *To the Israeli government*
    (a) halt all acts of war
    (b) withdraw all its troops ten miles to the east of the Canal

In addition, the Israeli Government will be notified that the French and British
Government[s] have demanded of the Egyptian Government to accept temporary
occupation of key positions along the Canal by the Anglo-French forces.

It is agreed that if one of the Governments refused, or did not give its consent,
within twelve hours the Anglo-French forces would intervene with the means
necessary to ensure that their demands are accepted.

    C. The representatives of the three governments agree that the Israeli Govern-
       ment will not be required to meet the conditions in the appeal addressed to
       it, in the event that the Egyptian Government does not accept those in the
       appeal addressed to it for their part.

3. In the event that the Egyptian Government should fail to agree within the
    stipulated time to the conditions of the appeal addressed to it, the Anglo-French
    forces will launch military operations against the Egyptian forces in the early
    hours of the morning of 31 October.

[. . .]

6. The arrangements of the present protocol must remain strictly secret.

7. They will enter into force after the agreement of the three governments.[105]

The full British Cabinet, though without the benefit of the words of the
Sèvres Protocol before them, duly took such contingent decisions.

The Cabinet conclusions are quite specific. On 25 October, as Brook's
minutes put it, the Cabinet

Agreed in principle that, in the event of an Israeli attack on Egypt, the Government
should join with the French Government in calling on the two belligerents to stop
hostilities and withdraw their forces to a distance of ten miles from the Canal; and
should warn both belligerents that, if either or both of them failed to undertake
within twelve hours to comply with these requirements, British and French forces
would intervene to enforce compliance.[106]

On 30 October, the full Cabinet authorized direct military action by
British forces as anticipated and planned for at Sèvres. 'The Cabinet',
Brook recorded,

(1) Took note of the outbreak of hostilities between Israel and Egypt.

(2) Approved, subject to the forthcoming consultation with the Prime Minister and the Foreign Minister of France, the terms of notes to be addressed to the Governments of Israel and Egypt, calling on them to stop hostilities, to withdraw their forces to a distance of ten miles from the Suez Canal and to allow Anglo-French forces to occupy temporarily key positions on the Canal.[107]

Eden now had his Cabinet minutes to wave at those Cabinet ministers who pretended not to know. He did not wave them, in public at any rate. In retirement, however, he complained to Selwyn Lloyd and others that ministers in the Macmillan government were allowing 'our cause to go by default . . . our colleagues under-estimated the degree of popular support for our action and the extent to which the public now realised that we had been right'.[108]

'We had been right.' Eden based much of his later assertions of correctitude on the general lawlessness in international affairs which followed from Nasser's 'getting away with it'.[109] At the time of the crisis much of his rectitude rested on his conviction that Nasser was increasingly the instrument of the Soviet Union's wider geopolitical strategy of replacing Western influence in the Middle East with its own. Such appraisals, of course, themselves rested on secret intelligence assessments whose contents historians were unable to read in any abundance until the late 1990s when the papers of the Joint Intelligence Committee for 1956 were declassified.

In an earlier draft of this chapter, penned before the 1956 JIC material reached Kew in the summer of 1998, I had acknowledged this gap and reached some interim conclusions on the intelligence aspects of Suez based on material which was available. The following italicized passage is what I had written prior to the JIC release.

It is difficult even now to reach a judgement on the intelligence input on Suez which, were we ever to gain access to its secret flow, might require the desperate premier of the autumn of 1956 to be seen in a different light. We know from the briefings the Queen received, which were, to my amazement, declassified in 1994, that British intelligence was seriously worried that the Soviet Air Force could move in the direction of the Middle East.[110]

Allied to this was Marshal Bulganin's threat from Moscow, issued on 4-5 November 1956, that the Soviet Union might use 'rocket weapons' against Britain and France if they did not desist from attacking Egypt.[111]

Daphne Park, one of the SIS officers in place under diplomatic cover in the British embassy in Moscow, confirmed to me many years later that MI6 was sufficiently worried about Soviet capabilities for herself and one of the defence attachés to be dispatched to get as close to 'particular sites' as possible.[112] *And Dick White's conversations with his biographer Tom Bower, made it plain that there was high anxiety in London about Soviet capabilities and intentions at the height of the crisis.*

Bower also disclosed on the basis of his briefing by the former 'C' that Chester Cooper, the CIA chief in London, provided White with the key US intelligence estimate (now declassified by the CIA) which concluded that the Soviet Union would 'almost certainly not attack metropolitan UK or France – primarily because such an attack would make general war practically certain' and that they would not 'employ Soviet forces on a large scale in the Eastern Mediterranean', both because their capabilities were inadequate and 'because the risk of general war arising from such action would be very great'.[113] *Eden, like White, would have been avid for this intelligence and the Bower biography confirms another of White's disclosures to me – that the most sensitive part of the special intelligence relationship was never ruptured in the autumn of 1956, despite Eisenhower's calls on Eden to desist and the disruptive efforts of the US Sixth Fleet in the Mediterranean as the Anglo-French 'task force' made its slow progress ways from Malta to Port Said.*[114]

I suspect we shall never know the identity or the reliability of the source codenamed 'Lucky Break' which the Secret Intelligence Service was thought to have very close to Nasser (some say inside his Cabinet)[115] *who convinced Eden that the Soviets were using him as a pawn in their intended drive across the Middle East and into Africa.*[116] *MI6 is not required by the public records legislation to release its key 'CX' material – its detailed reports – without which anything approaching a full reconstruction of the secret intelligence feed is impossible (though Scott Lucas in his* Divided We Stand *has worked wonders with what is available at the Public Record Office).*[117] *What is known is that Nasser's own secret service rounded up a sizeable MI6 network in Egypt, consisting of thirty plus people, in the period between the nationalization of the canal and the invasion.*[118]

In 1997, however, the release of the Macmillan Diary at the Bodleian Library in Oxford did throw extra light on this necessarily opaque side of the Suez crisis. As early as November 1955, Macmillan, still Foreign Secretary and in Paris for a Foreign Ministers' meeting, records that the late Alan Hare (an MI6 officer, though the diary does not identify him as such),

(who has excellent contacts here) believes that the Israelis are now seriously considering an attack on Egypt, to destroy the Egyptian Army and bring down Nasser. Everyone seems to think this wd be a great disaster – because of the other Arabs. But there wd certainly be compensations.[119]

A few days later, Macmillan traces what I suspect is the first appearance of Lucky Break's intelligence and records its powerful impact on Eden when he convened a very small meeting in No. 10 (which included Rab Butler) to consider it:

We have got hold of very secret but quite reliable information that Nasser has already agreed (more or less) to allow 'Popular Socialism' (in other words, Communism) in Egypt, as part of the Czech arms deal. This is to be finally clinched by the Soviet understanding to build the High Assouan Dam, & take payment over a period of 50 years . . . The Prime Minister was very excited, & wanted us both to go to the USA at the end of next week.[120]

In the spring of 1956 Macmillan records the arrival of 'rather alarming' information that Nasser 'seems to be aiming at some sort of League of Arab Republics'.[121] *Such tantalizing fragments of intelligence only serve to underline the importance of this secret feed as a shaper of minds already disposed to see the worst in Nasser and his designs.*

Between the opening of the Macmillan Diary and the declassification of the JIC files I received a very private piece of information which suggested two things: that 'Lucky Break' was not an SIS codename; and that the British Secret Intelligence Service's key provider of insight into Nasser's world in 1955–56 was somewhere inside the Soviet bloc, rather than in Egypt. In other words, the best information on Cairo's capabilities and intentions came from behind the Iron Curtain on the back of intelligence efforts to acquire information on the substantial Czech arms deal with Egypt concluded in 1955.[122] The phrase 'as part of the Czech arms deal' in Macmillan's note of the Downing Street intelligence meeting on Nasser's political plans in November 1955 perhaps gives a retrospective clue as to its provenance.

Once the JIC files for 1956 were released it was possible to trace a running preoccupation in both its 'Weekly Summary of Current Intelligence' and its larger, bespoke assessments with the arms deal, the growth of Soviet influence in the Middle East in general and Egypt in particular and the likelihood of an Arab–Israeli war in the months *before* Nasser's nationalization of the Suez Canal Company. In February the JIC began to note 'increased military preparedness' on the part of both the Israelis and the Egyptians.[123] And by April it was warning of 'the danger of war from miscalculation' between the two countries.[124] At the end of February the JIC produced a detailed assessment of 'Egyptian Effectiveness in the Use of Soviet Aircraft' (MiG-15 fighters had been in the process of delivery since October 1955 and 'Soviet bloc instructors' began training Egyptian pilots the following month).[125]

Eden, as we have seen, would have been highly attuned to the JIC's intelligence feed on the Middle East. In another file declassified in 1998 there is the record of an exchange between Eden and Millard on the contents of a CIA 'Analysis of Soviet Policy' prepared in the autumn of 1955 and dispatched in summary to Whitehall by the British ambassador to Washington, Sir Roger Makins (later Lord Sherfield), on 14 October. It was fairly optimistic, though far from starry-eyed, about a less confrontational global posture on the part of the USSR in the wake of the Geneva summit on East–West tensions.[126] Eden has scrawled on it, for Millard's attention, 'This is good? AE'.[127]

Millard replies in a handwritten note penned on 18 October which has a certain clairvoyance about it in the light of subsequent events:

Prime Minister

Yes, but it doesn't take full account of the possibility that the Geneva spirit is intended primarily to mask an offensive against the ME [Middle East].

Communism has failed, temporarily, in Europe. In the ME the prize is almost as great – w. [Western] oil supplies, a vast uncommitted area ripe for communism, the possibility of separating us from India, Pakistan and SE Asia.

Our weakness is correspondingly great. British and American policies are notoriously divergent, and even our hands are tied because we cannot abandon Israel.

If this is the Soviet policy, we might have to defend our ME position much more vigorously – with men, money.

[There is a passage deleted here which suggests Millard was dealing at this point with clandestine operations]

+if necessary bring the Americans along in our wake. But we should also have to try to work with Arab nationalism, + not, as so often in the past, against it. GEM [Guy Millard] 18/10.

Beneath the note Eden has written: 'Thank you. No easy task. AE. Oct 18.'[128]

The JIC and Millard thought as one. In an assessment of 'Probable Soviet Attitude to an Arab/Israeli War' prepared in March 1956, Whitehall's intelligence analysts concluded starkly that Soviet Cold War aims in the Middle East were:

(a) to destroy the Baghdad Pact [the Western-sponsored anti-Communist alliance in the Near and Middle East between Turkey and Iraq] or render it ineffective;
(b) to deny the Western powers their Middle East bases;
(c) to deny them their oil supplies, and
(d) to undermine Western, particularly British, influence in the area, replacing it by Communist influence.[129]

A few weeks later the JIC assessors sought to place Nasser in a global, regional and national context. It was an intriguingly balanced appraisal and has the feel of a careful drawing together from all sources (Soviet bloc and the MI6 network in Egypt itself – though, of course, no hints as to provenance are given) in the classical JIC style of so-called 'all-source analysis'.[130]

The portrait painted of Nasser is by no means demonized. He is depicted as a 'successful revolutionary' who wishes to keep in tune with the nationalist forces which put him in power in Egypt as well as with Arab nationalism generally. The views of the British ambassador in Cairo, Sir Humphrey Trevelyan, are given weight – that Nasser's inclination is 'still to seek . . . inspiration and aid from the West; and that his present flirtation with Russia is largely his reaction to the Baghdad Pact, the need for arms against Israel, and the apparently very favourable economic terms offered the Communist bloc'.[131]

The JIC's conclusion, though it strikes a note of urgency, suggests that in terms of Cold War rivalry, there is still all to play for in terms of Nasser's inclinations:

Egypt is already in a position of increasing dependence on Russia; particularly for the arms Nasser regards as essential, but also in economic matters. Moreover, the Egyptians are developing habits of collaboration with Russia; and by way of keeping their benefactors happy, have begun to use their influence to facilitate Soviet penetration into Libya and perhaps also Syria, Yemen, Saudi Arabia and the Sudan, and to market Communist arms in the Middle East.

This does not mean that Nasser has consciously resigned himself to becoming an instrument of Soviet policy. He probably still believes he can steer a middle course, not beholden to either side. He has tried to resist some of the Russian conditions for arms supplies, and seems to want the West to finance the Aswan High Dam if he can get firm assurances and satisfactory terms.

The question is how long this balancing act can last.

The JIC reckoned that 'Nasser will probably soon reach the point of no return.'[132]

Such assessments were *agreed* by all the big players in British intelligence (including the Chief of the Secret Intelligence Service).[133] Contrast their attitude to Nasser in the spring of 1956 with that of their ultimate ministerial boss, Eden, who, as we have seen, was telling Nutting over an open telephone line that he wanted the Egyptian leader 'destroyed'. It has to be said that the British intelligence apparatus was not feeding Eden's anti-Nasser demons prior to the nationalization of the Suez Canal Company.

The JIC, however, did not foresee the trigger for Nasser's reaching his 'point of no return'. In an assessment, completed a few weeks before Nasser's Alexandria speech, on 'The Likelihood of War Between Israel and the Arab States', it foresaw neither the United States and Britain pulling out of the financing of the Aswan High Dam on the Upper Nile (Nasser's prestige project central to his plans for Egyptian economic development) nor the consequences of such an action. It foresaw instead a possibility that 'full scale hostilities' might arise from 'reprisal raids' carried out along Israel's borders with Egypt and Syria.[134]

As part of its substantial exercise in stocktaking and forecasting in the days immediately following the nationalization of the Suez Canal Company, the JIC prepared what can only be deemed one of its most important assessments in the postwar period. It began with an appraisal of Nasser's motives for his dramatic action and an analysis of his character, which did not disguise or downplay Nasser's gifts or the extraordinary boost the move had brought to his own and Egypt's position. The JIC detected 'a considerable element of emotion in Nasser's actions. As a demagogue he is liable to be carried away by the violence of the passions he himself has whipped up.'[135] But the analysts appreciated that the

UK was dealing with a rational and formidable operator beneath the anti-Western and pan-Arabic rhetoric:

As a dictator, his actions over the past three years show subtlety and calculation and have so far all resulted in gain to Egypt. We should be prepared for any action that may enhance his prestige and maintain him in power.[136]

How did they read his dramatic action in Alexandria on 26 July which 'followed promptly upon the withdrawal of the United Kingdom, United States and World Bank offers to help finance the Aswan High Dam'?

Nasser's declared motive was to obtain from the operation of the Canal the funds he needed to build the Dam. We doubt however whether this is the real reason for his action. There have been a number of indications that he himself has recently had doubts whether the High Dam is the best way of solving his power and irrigation problems, and he must have realised that the net annual profit likely to be derived from the Canal is only a fraction of the Dam's cost.

The building of the Dam had, however, come to be seen in the popular mind as the cure for all Egypt's ills and Nasser's own position and prestige were staked upon its accomplishment. When the Western offer of financial aid was withdrawn, therefore, he urgently needed to distract public attention and at the same time find a new method to arouse their enthusiasm and to repair any damage his stock might have suffered in other Arab countries. As a means to this end his nationalisation of the Canal has been a triumph; it has also served the subsidiary purpose of retaliation against the West for the withdrawal of the High Dam offer.[137]

Unfortunately, we do not have Eden's own copies of JIC assessments on which his comments would have been scribbled. The archive preserved is the JIC's own rather than that of the Prime Minister's Office. It is Eden's reactions to the later sections of the big, post-nationalization assessment (which was completed on 3 August and circulated on 10 August, the day after the Chiefs of Staff had approved it) dealing with the likely impact of armed intervention in Egypt which historians crave. For British intelligence warned its customers (Eden, a small group of ministers who received JIC assessments on a need-to-know-basis as well as an inner core of the senior military, Civil Service and Diplomatic Service) that: 'We do not believe that threats of armed intervention or preliminary build up of forces would bring about the downfall of the Nasser regime or cause it to cancel the nationalisation of the canal.'[138]

What about the use of force itself?

Armed intervention by the West to secure control of the Canal Zone would lead to a state of war with Egypt. Although most, if not all, the Arab states would sympathise with Egypt we do not think that in the event they would come to her aid . . .

We also doubt whether the Soviet Union would take any action. She has no treaty of alliance with Egypt and as far as we know, no secret agreement. The support of Egypt in peacetime as a thorn in the side of the West accords with the policy of competitive co-existence, but we do not believe she would embark on global war on behalf of Egypt. The Soviet Government might send technicians and further arms to Egypt but we doubt whether, in the event of hostilities, these would greatly affect the issue.[139]

The JIC rounded off its section on the effects of armed intervention with a sombre and terse warning:

Should Western military action be insufficient to ensure early and decisive victory, the international consequences both in the Arab States and elsewhere might give rise to extreme embarrassment and cannot be forecast.[140]

The JIC may not have foreseen Nasser's *coup de main* on the Canal, but within days it had produced an analysis which proved remarkably prescient. Eden's intelligence watchdog had barked. British intelligence had fulfilled its primary duty of, when, necessary, bringing Prime Ministers 'unwelcome news'.[141] He had been warned.

British intelligence, in the form of its folk memory, has been hard on the Anthony Eden of 1956. They like to see themselves as a force for multiplying British power, not diminishing it. As John Hunt, himself a former Secretary to the JIC, put it, 'Suez was the most terrible trauma.'[142] There is another little-known reason for their retrospective resentment. Over the years I have heard on several occasions how new ministers, when indoctrinated into the secret world, are told a number of past horror stories to make them aware of the damage that can occur if they breathe a word about the UK's signals and electronic capabilities. One of them relates to the warnings relayed to the French in the 1950s about the vulnerability of their ciphers to attack. In 1998 a late-arriving file at the PRO showed that this, too, can be traced to Eden.

The JIC, as the preparations for Operation Musketeer (the invasion of

Egypt) proceeded, were much exercised about security – cipher security in particular.[143] In early August, the Chairman of the JIC, Sir Patrick Dean, was sent to Paris to persuade the French to keep full knowledge of assault locations, objectives, timings and cover plans to their Prime Minister, Defence Minister, the Chairman of their Chiefs of Staff and a small group of military commanders to match British practice and to warn them that 'there is great danger in the use of wireless communications especially between London, Paris and North Africa'.[144] The French insisted on telling a rather wider circle than this.[145] On the note from Selwyn Lloyd's Private Secretary to the Prime Minister's Private Secretary dated 29 August 1956, Eden has written: 'I agree, reluctantly. They have I think been now told about their ciphers.'[146] Quite plainly GCHQ were reading French material. If GCHQ could break their codes, there was a good chance that both the Russians and the Americans could do so, too, learning thereby the details of the planned assault on Egypt.

For, by this stage, Eden knew from direct communications received from the American President, that the United States would not support the use of force to resolve the Canal crisis. Eisenhower reinforced this message to Eden in the plainest language in a personal message on 3 September 1956. 'As to the use of force or the threat of force at this juncture', he wrote,

I continue to feel as I expressed myself in the letter Foster [Dulles, US Secretary of State] carried to you some weeks ago. Even now military preparations and civilian evacuation exposed to public view seem to be solidifying support for Nasser which has been shaky in many important quarters. I regard it as indispensable that if we are to proceed solidly together to the solution of this problem, public opinion in our several countries must be overwhelming in its support. I must tell you frankly that American public opinion flatly rejects the thought of using force, particularly when it does not seem that every possible peaceful means of protecting our vital interests has been exhausted without result.[147]

Eisenhower's view simply could not have been misread by Eden. 'I really do not see', the President told the Prime Minister, 'how a successful result could be achieved by forcible means.'[148]

Just over a week earlier, Norman Brook had written a 'personal and confidential' handwritten note to the Prime Minister, dated 25 August 1956, strangely pre-echoing Eisenhower's strictures to Eden on the need to carry public opinion with him. Brook began by giving Eden his assessment of Cabinet opinion at the conclusion of the conference which met in London to try and fashion an international solution to the crisis. 'As I see it', Brook told Eden,

the position is this. All the members of the Cabinet, without exception, are solidly in agreement that we cannot afford to let Nasser get away with this – for if he succeeds, we lose our oil and with it our standard of life in this country, not to mention our position in the Middle East and our influence as a World Power. The Cabinet are therefore agreed that we must stop this at all costs and that, in the last resort, if all other methods fail, we must be ready to use force . . . But some, in varying degrees, think that, before we resort to force, we must be able to show that we have made an honest effort to reach a settlement by peaceful means and have exhausted all the 'other methods'.[149]

Brook outlines what these might be, the 'first need' being to 'mobilize a good measure of international support'. The United Nations was important in this context.[150] (Three days later the Cabinet agreed to refer the dispute to the UN.)[151] It may be that there would need to 'be some further provocative act by Nasser before we take the final step', Brook continued. 'Some ministers', he explained, 'are less certain than others about the extent to which "middle" opinion in this country would support forceful action at this stage, i.e. before there had been some clearer *occasion* for the use of force. All this leads me to the view that it would be a mistake to put the Cabinet at the final fence too soon.'[152]

'Since I started this letter', Brook concludes, 'we have spoken on the telephone and I have said much of it in our conversation. But you may like to have it all the same. I do hope you are having some rest.'[153]

Of respite came there none. The opinion polls, which Eden was fed regularly by Conservative Central Office from early August, underscored the importance of what Brook called 'middle opinion'. The No. 10 file which preserves these has the Conservative Party chairman, Lord Poole, on the very day the invasion was halted, 6 November, warning Eden 'that the "liberal" element in the country is against the Government and feels extremely strongly. Many of these have supported the Conservative Party by their votes since 1950 and it may be some time, if ever, before we regain their confidence.'[154]

Place the JIC assessments, Eisenhower's personal letters and Brook's letter alongside regular warnings from the Treasury to the Chancellor, Macmillan, from early August onwards, about sterling's vulnerability,[155] and it is hard to appreciate how Eden could rationally have pursued the policy he did. It is possible that some of the warnings, the Treasury ones in particular, did not reach him. I asked Guy Millard, who was at Eden's side in No. 10 throughout the Suez crisis, about this – the 7 September one in particular. Sir Edward Bridges, in his last days as Permanent Secretary to the Treasury, had put the position to Macmillan in the starkest terms. 'Very broadly', he told the Chancellor,

it seems to us that unless we can secure at least US support and a fairly unified Commonwealth, then it is not possible to predict either the exact timing or the magnitude of the strains which are likely to come upon our currency. At the worst, however, the strains might be so great that, whatever precautionary measures were taken we should be unable to maintain the value of the currency . . . On the other hand if we do get overt US support, and support from elsewhere, including the Commonwealth, our general feeling is that our action would be regarded by world opinion as something likely to strengthen sterling . . . What this points to therefore, is the vital necessity from the point of view of our currency and our economy of ensuring that we do not go it alone, and that we have the maximum US support.[156]

Macmillan scrawled beside Bridges' last point: 'Yes: This is just the trouble. US are being very difficult.'[157]

Again, the warning – and its implications – could scarcely have been plainer. But we cannot be sure that they reached Eden in such a stark form. Guy Millard said, 'I'm not sure Eden saw the Treasury warnings. I didn't see them. Macmillan saw them, but he was a hawk.'[158] Sir Roger Makins, who returned to London from Washington in mid-October to replace Bridges as head of the Treasury, found nobody wanted to see him or tell him anything about the inner plans on Egypt. He did not see his boss, the Chancellor, for two weeks.[159] He found out from his own Whitehall sources[160] and 'when I discovered, I was horrified'.[161] Makins believed at the time, and for the rest of his life, that Eden and his ministers on the inner circle were 'running in blinkers'.[162]

Historians are still in difficulty when trying to reconstruct the deliberations of this inner group in the crucial, collusive phase of the Suez crisis because the Egypt Committee ceased to meet for most of it. It met thirty-five times between 27 July and 17 October. The thirty-sixth meeting had to wait until 1 November,[163] the day after the RAF had started bombing Egyptian airfields.

Sadly, I never had a chance to put the 'warnings ignored' or 'running in blinkers' points to a member of the innermost circle. The nearest I came to this was at the Hirsel, Lord Home's home in the Scottish Borders, in January 1987 when my BBC producer Mark Laity and I carried a heap of newly declassified documents to Coldstream to show Alec Home, who had been in the Cabinet as Commonwealth Secretary throughout the Suez affair. After he had examined files he had not seen since 1956, including his own letter of support to Eden of 24 August already quoted, I specifically asked him 'Why did ministers ignore those precise warnings?'

'A warning is a different thing from it happening, isn't it?' Alec Home replied. 'You often get warnings of this sort and then the results are different.' For Home, reality (my word, not his) only prevailed on 6 November, the day of the ceasefire:

'I think what really turned the scale and made the Chancellor of the Exchequer that day so terribly anxious was the American action in really putting the Sixth Fleet alongside us in the Mediterranean, for all the world to see, and therefore announcing in effect that America was totally against us. And the effect on sterling as a result of that was catastrophic. It was the actual effect on sterling rather than the warnings, I think. Perhaps we ought to have taken the warnings more seriously.'[164]

This was the trigger for Cabinet government to reassert itself. On 30 October, the JIC had warned the Chiefs of Staff that 'the United States will adopt a strictly neutral attitude towards the Operations',[165] which itself turned out to be a considerable understatement. There is no evidence that the JIC as a whole was admitted to the Sèvres secret. Its chairman, Patrick Dean, knew, having signed the Protocol on behalf of the British government. But as Dr Alex Craig has demonstrated, there is no indication at all in the JIC archive released so far that the Committee was invited to produce an assessment of the likely impact of the Anglo-French-Israeli war plan.[166]

On 1 November one of the JIC's chief customers, the First Sea Lord, Lord Mountbatten, wrote to Eden expressing his 'great unhappiness about the prospect of launching military operations against Egypt' and offering his resignation. Mountbatten was ordered to stay at his post by his minister the First Lord of the Admiralty, Lord Hailsham.[167]

It was United States action, rather than any event or piece of advice in Whitehall, that caused the complete reversal of policy against Eden's wishes. On 6 November, the Chancellor of the Exchequer, Harold Macmillan, led the about-turn[168] with the US Sixth Fleet having harassed the Anglo-French task force as it approached Port Said, the authorities in Washington blocking British access to its IMF standby credit as the holders of sterling began to evacuate the currency, and the United Nations, with American encouragement, threatening oil sanctions.[169] Eden's authority was gone. Broken, he repaired to 'Goldeneye', Ian Fleming's remote house in Jamaica, to recover.

The Cabinet even insisted on doctoring the statement he proposed to make on his return to Heathrow, removing its defiantly bellicose and anti-American passages.[170] Cabinet government has a habit of reasserting itself eventually when usurped to any serious degree by a prime ministerial variant. The Suez affair, in Kipling's phrase which Anthony Nutting adopted as the title of his book published over ten years after his resignation, was 'no end of a lesson'[171] – not just in terms of foreign policy or in the wider context of the proper conduct of Cabinet government generally, but also in the historiography of War Cabinets.

In chapter 6 (pp. 137–8), I outlined half a dozen criteria for the successful operation of a War Cabinet in limited (that is, non-total war) circumstances and, earlier in this chapter, I intimated that Eden's conduct of the Suez crisis was, quite simply, an object lesson in how not to do it. The first requirement was that the War Cabinet should have as close and constant a relationship with the full Cabinet as possible. Even when allowances are made for what we can now appreciate the full Cabinet knew of the 'secret conversations' in Paris, it is still the case that the full import of the collusive planning (quite apart from operational details which, naturally, are normally confined to the War Cabinet), was kept from the Eden Cabinet as a whole (though this does not absolve their failure to probe, question and, if necessary, dissent during the last days of October 1956). When Eden's Minister of Housing, the forceful Duncan Sandys, had complained about the lack of full Cabinet involvement at the end of August,[172] Eden saw him off firmly. 'I feel I should explain to you', he wrote, '. . . the limits within which the Cabinet can discuss the possibility of a military operation in the Eastern Mediterranean.'[173]

The Cabinet, Eden reminded Sandys, had only so far considered the use of force as a hypothetical question – as a 'last resort'. If necessary, 'the Cabinet as a whole will of course be able to take the final decision, in the light of all the circumstances at the time'. Following a draft reply prepared by Norman Brook, Eden asserted that:

It would not . . . be possible for the Cabinet as a whole to discuss the plans for any military operations that might have to be undertaken. Knowledge of these details must, for obvious reasons of security, be confined within the narrowest possible circle.[174]

In Brook's original draft a truly disingenuous extra sentence had been included in square brackets here which was removed in the final version sent to Sandys: '[I could not widen that circle, even if I wished to do so, without breach of the security plan which we have agreed with the French government.]'[175] 'Such political guidance as the military authorities may need in the preparation of their plans must continue to be given by me, in consultation with a small number of my most senior Cabinet colleagues and, as necessary, such departmental ministers as may be directly concerned.'[176]

One has to distinguish the significance of a 'narrowest possible circle' approach on military details (which is standard and justifiable in operational circumstances) and one which extends to the wider diplomatic backdrop. The Sèvres war plan was a truly transforming factor. Should Eden have taken the full Cabinet into his confidence on 25 October? I think he should – but the implications of this are considerable. Even though the full Cabinet, as we have seen, approved in advance the UK's actions as agreed at Sèvres, it did so in ignorance of the full nature of the conspiracy. If it had known its true scope, would it have agreed those plans? If it did, would there have been some ministerial resignations? Even if not, could Eden have lied to the House of Commons about collusion after the event? If he had, and the whole Cabinet had been in on the secret, they, too, would have been parties to the deception.

If the full Cabinet had balked at the conspiracy, had it been unveiled in full on 25 October, what would have been the consequences? Would it have halted the whole operation? Very likely so, because even without the British air assault on 30 October, let alone the abandonment of the subsequent landings at Port Said, the whole invasion plan would have become unviable. In short, the full Cabinet *had* to be deceived if the Canal was to be retaken along the lines agreed at Sèvres. Eden's temptation had trapped him into a course of less than full disclosure to his Cabinet colleagues as a whole – which, to my mind, is far from 'the highest form of statesmanship'.

Criterion two I adduced as the need to sub-contract detailed work to a War Cabinet of no more than six constant ministerial attenders, which should meet regularly and have a bias towards decision-taking based on adequate military, Civil Service, diplomatic and intelligence back-up. It is hard to fault John Hunt's insider strictures about the inadequacy of the Egypt Committee in this respect for several reasons. First, it was by no means the only conduit for Suez related matters. Chris Brady's researches have shown that no fewer than eleven Cabinet committees were charged specifically with handling some aspect of the crisis and its aftermath.[177]

The original intention was to confine the Egypt Committee's membership to Eden and five colleagues – Salisbury (Lord President), Macmillan (Chancellor of the Exchequer), Lloyd (Foreign Secretary), Home (Commonwealth Secretary) and Monckton (Minister of Defence), with other ministers to be invited to attend 'when matters directly affecting their departmental interests are required'.[178] Butler, as we learned from Hugh Thomas's study ten years after the event, was omitted from the original membership but simply acquired the habit of attending and was allowed to stay (indeed, he took the chair on more than one occasion).[179] The Secretary of State for War, Antony Head, Brook noted in a memo to Eden on 13 September, 'has, by historical accident become a constant attender at the Committee's meetings. It would be difficult to dislodge him now . . .'[180]

Mark Brown discovered that far more ministers than the sixteen Hugh Thomas identified as attenders at various stages[181] had, in fact, done so. Brown, once the Egypt Committee's papers were open for inspection, raised that figure to twenty-two.[182] Chris Brady has calculated the supporting staff which served the committee at various times to be eight military figures, ten civil servants and eight secretaries.[183]

The Cabinet Secretary himself noticed by mid-September that the Egypt Committee had come to perform two different functions:

(a) In relation to the political handling of the Suez question, it acts as a sort of Inner Cabinet . . .

(b) It supervises the military preparations and plans . . .[184]

'A sort of Inner Cabinet' has a vague air, but in bringing together these two functions, the Egypt Committee was, albeit in its unwieldy way, meeting the need for War Cabinets to blend the political and the military aspects of an emergency as well as fulfilling its original terms of reference which were 'to keep in touch, on the Cabinet's behalf, with the situation arising from the recent action of the Egyptian government in respect of the Suez Canal, and to formulate plans for meeting that situation.'[185]

How well did the Egypt Committee perform as a blender of politico-military considerations and as a shaper of strategy and political direction? Atrociously, according to the professionals in their most secret post-Suez inquests. Even allowing for the tendency of professional military people to beef about the inadequacies of the professional political class, their verdicts sear the page. Lieutenant-General Sir Dudley Ward, Deputy Chief of the Imperial General Staff, complained in his 'Lessons from Operation Musketeer' prepared for the Army Council in the early months of 1957 that: 'The lack of a clear political aim and of consistent political direction, bedevilled the mounting and execution of the operation. A further effect was that the soldiers taking part had no clear understanding of the reasons for the operation and thus were deprived of any defence against hostile comment aimed at the operation from home and overseas.'[186]

Were these retrospective criticisms justified? I think so. A paper prepared for the Chiefs of Staff by their joint planners as late as 24 October 1956 established 'H. M. Government's Political Aims' as '(a) The securing of international administration and control of the Suez Canal, (b) The establishment of the authority of a co-operative Egyptian government throughout the country, including the Canal Zone . . .'[187] The problem was, as the planners indicated, that 'Musketeer plans do not extend beyond the occupation of the Canal Area. No consideration has yet been given to the military commitments which might arise after this phase.'[188]

This was a fundamental – almost a breathtaking – lacuna. The Chiefs' files when declassified confirmed the worst suspicions of the Foreign Office's leading Arabist, Harold Beeley, who was kept out of the Suez policy-making loop along with other Middle Eastern experts on Eden's instructions.[189] As Beeley put it thirty years after the event, 'one question that didn't seem to have been asked was what we were going to do in Egypt after we'd occupied the Canal. As far as I'm aware, to this day there is no evidence that the sequence of events after the immediate attack on the Canal had been properly thought out.'[190]

The Chiefs' planners did their best to fill the gap, judging that any occupation force had to be prepared

(a) To maintain the security of the Canal area against considerable guerrilla activity and labour unrest.

(b) To occupy Cairo in order to depose a hostile Government and to render possible the immediate installation of an acceptable successor, with possible commitment of maintaining it in power indefinitely.

(c) To assist in the rehabilitation of Egypt.

(d) To assist the Egyptian Government in the administration of the country.[191]

Yet the military had been given no political directions on this and there was no plan to do so – which speaks volumes about the performance of the Egypt Committee. To make matters worse for the forces sailing towards Port Said, the lack of political intelligence which was coming out of Egypt made 'the assessment of Egyptian intentions very much more difficult during this operation', as Ward made plain in his inquest.[192]

How did the Egypt Committee fare as an overseer of operations once the military assault had begun? It started to meet again, after a gap of thirteen days, on 1 November, when it gathered in Butler's room at the House of Commons to agree a 10 per cent cut in UK oil consumption.[193] It reconvened at 10.45 that evening at No. 10 with Eden in the chair. Eden reported that Radio Cairo was to be bombed but plans to attack Egyptian oil facilities had been abandoned to reduce civilian casualties.[194]

On 3 November the Committee met in Eden's room at the House of Commons at 2.00 to receive reports of a change of tactics in the assault on the Canal in the light of 'the improvement of the Egyptian defences at Port Said' which meant that a bombardment of defensive positions along the sea front would be necessary before the assault forces landed. Eden was concerned, too, to limit casualties in Port Said because of world opinion.[195]

On Sunday 4 November the Committee met twice in what turned out to be its last meetings before the ceasefire. The first meeting at 12.30 heard the Minister of Defence, Antony Head (who had replaced the deeply unhappy Monckton on 18 October),[196] arguing that if the assault force commanders were required to refrain entirely from unleashing a naval bombardment of Port Said before the assault forces attacked, the landing might have to be delayed and the risk of casualties increased.[197]

The Egypt Committee reconvened at 3.30 to hear a report from Lloyd that the Egyptians had agreed to a ceasefire, throwing the collusive time-table into confusion as it made further military operations by the Anglo-French force difficult to justify. As Britain's stated objective was to separate the combatant Egyptians and Israelis, to carry on would cause difficulties in Parliament and with public opinion, particularly if civilian casualties in Port Said were heavy. Yet the Egyptians had still to agree to withdraw behind the designated armistice line. Eden summed up by saying agreement with the French on how to proceed was necessary and the issue should be discussed in the full Cabinet.[198]

It is plain from the records that the Egypt Committee was not functioning as the daily overseer of military operations once the war had started. It was certainly working under great stress, led by a sick Prime Minister who had been exhibiting symptoms of both 'tunnel vision' and personal overload from the outset of the crisis three months earlier. Obsession exacerbated by stress was, perhaps, inevitable given his overwhelming view of Nasser as a deceitful menace who in his eyes, as Alec Home put it, was someone 'who cheated in public affairs' and who was 'a real danger to British interests'.[199] Home, well-placed as a member of the Egypt Committee to make such distinctions, differentiates between Eden and most of his colleagues whose priority was 'to take the Canal, believing that if that was done Nasser's authority in Egypt would go . . . Eden's priority [by contrast] was to topple Nasser.'[200] This was 'tunnel vision' of the most acute, searing and malign kind, the avoidance of which is criterion three for an effective War Cabinet (though perhaps the most difficult of all to stave off, especially in a protracted crisis such as Suez).

Criterion four is the constant need to take account of the attitudes and priorities of allies, potential allies and the international organizations in which, to whatever extent, the conflict is being monitored or played out. On this front, Eden's failure was total, in the last days of the crisis especially. As Sir Guy Millard's secret internal history (an edited version of which has been declassified) put it a year later, when the news of the Israeli attack on Egypt reached New York on the afternoon of 29 October, a meeting of the UN Security Council had already been fixed for the following day.

At the meeting of the Council on 30th October Mr Lodge [Henry Cabot Lodge, US Ambassador to the UN] tabled a resolution calling for a cease-fire and an Israeli withdrawal, and urging member States of the United Nations to refrain from financial, economic or military aid to Israel.

Sir Pierson Dixon ['Bob' Dixon, UK Ambassador to the UN] made a statement to the effect that there was no action which the Security Council could constructively take which would contribute to the objectives of stopping the fighting and safeguarding the free passage of the Suez Canal. The United States resolution was vetoed by Britain and France . . .[201]

Though Millard's memorandum was labelled 'UK Eyes Only', it fails to quote Dixon's desperate telegram of 5 November (a copy of which is preserved in the No. 10 files) sent from the UN, with the landing at Port Said but one day away and the Russians ruthlessly engaged in suppressing the Hungarian Rising in Budapest. Dixon, who was seriously considering resignation from the Diplomatic Service over the government's Suez policy,[202] reminded Lloyd and Eden that:

Two days ago I felt constrained to warn you that if there was any bombing of open cities with resulting loss of civilian life it would make our purposes completely cynical and entirely undermine our position here. Again . . . I urged that unless we could announce that Anglo-French forces were suspending all further military activities until we know that the United Nations were prepared to deal with the situation effectively, there would be no chance of our being able to move towards our objectives without alienating the whole world.

I must again repeat this warning with renewed emphasis . . . we are inevitably being placed in the same low category as the Russians in their bombing of Budapest. I do not see how we can carry much conviction in our protests against the Russian bombing of Budapest . . . if we are ourselves bombing Cairo.[203]

I have never read a diplomatic telegram in the Public Record Office that matches Dixon's for passion and directness.

Dixon drafted his words in the heat of the most torrid hours the United Kingdom has ever experienced at the United Nations. But his point was central and valid. It was reinforced powerfully by the Commander of the Anglo-French Forces, General Keightley, while reflecting in relative tranquillity when compiling his inquest on Suez for the Chiefs of Staff. 'The one overriding lesson of the Suez operations', he wrote in 1957, 'is that world opinion is now an absolute principle of war and must be treated as such. However successful the pure military operations may be they will fail in their object unless national, Commonwealth and Western world opinion is sufficiently on our side.'[204]

Keightley emphasized the degree to which 'this factor' had been 'categorically stated in appreciations to Her Majesty's Government' throughout the 'planning period' prior to the invasion of Egypt 'and the intervention of the United Nations and the ultimate result of the whole operation confirmed its truth'.[205] This entirely justifiable verdict would of itself be enough to damn Eden's performance under the fourth criterion.

Keightley was even more brutally damning in his assessment of the

American factor. 'But it was the action of the UNITED STATES', he wrote, 'which really defeated us in attaining our object.' Keightley's supporting detail for this again entirely apt judgement underscored Alec Home's point about the actions of the US Navy as the Anglo-French Task Force steamed towards Port Said:

Her action in the United Nations is well known, but her move of the 6th Fleet, which is not so generally known, was a move which endangered the whole of our relations with that country. It is not difficult to appreciate the effect of the shooting down of a United States aircraft or the sinking of a United States submarine, but both these might easily have happened if EGYPT had obtained certain practical support from outside which she tried to get [presumably a reference to possible Soviet assistance] or our Commanders had not shown patience and care of the highest order.[206]

Keightley concluded the 'World Opinion' section of his report with a piece of pure political judgement which, in effect, became the leitmotif of British foreign policy for the remainder of the century. 'This situation with the UNITED STATES', said Keightely baldly, 'must at all costs be prevented from arising again.' Returning to the management of the Suez crisis he wrote, 'Conversely a united Anglo-American position would have assured a complete success of all our political objects with the minimum military effort. The achievement of this is a political matter but the effects on military operations are vital.'[207]

Criterion five embraces Parliament, public and media and keeping them as fully informed as possible. The Sèvres deception I have already covered in detail. The JIC agonized a good deal about press censorship on military operations. They concluded, sensibly, on 10 August that 'speculation by the press is more likely to be reduced than increased if information which will inevitably reach them is officially released as much in advance as possible'.[208] The JIC ruled out, too, the possibility of 'an overall cover plan' having any measure of success, though it recommended that 'cover and deception plans' for tactical operations should be considered by the Directorate of Forward Plans (the secret Whitehall deception organization in which, as we have seen, Churchill took an interest in 1952).[209]

Suez dominated the parliamentary weather from the moment of Nasser's nationalization. The first House of Commons debate took place on 2 August and revealed a high degree of shared animosity towards Nasser's action; the Labour leader Hugh Gaitskell observing famously that: 'It is all very familiar. It is exactly the same as we encountered from Mussolini and Hitler in those years before the war.'[210] But this early accord was short-lived. Gaitskell asked Eden to recall Parliament in mid August. Eden refused, and when the House next discussed the crisis, deep divisions were revealed between the government and the Labour Opposition about the likely use of force, with Gaitskell accusing Eden of failing to disclose the full picture.[211]

By mid September the atmosphere in the chamber was poisonous. The government won a vote on its conduct of the crisis quite comfortably (319 to 248) at the end of a two-day debate on 12–13 September.[212] But an unmistakable impression of deep division was created which was reflected too in the opinion polls. (For example, two polls conducted for the *Daily Express* and published on 16 August and 10 September demonstrated a falling off of satisfaction with the government's handling of the crisis from 58 per cent to 40 per cent.)[213] Once the conflict had started, the atmosphere in the House of Commons reached its most feverish level of any time in the postwar years. On 1 November, the Speaker suspended the House for half an hour to allow passions to cool.[214] The clash of opinion between Eden and Gaitskell was further underscored by their television broadcasts on successive evenings on 3 and 4 November.[215] As Keightley put it acidly and succinctly: 'Her Majesty's Opposition "rocked the landing craft" . . .'[216]

Finally, criterion six, we need to examine the all-steps-to-avoid-war requirement emphasized by Brook in his personal note to Eden at the end of August. Can this truly be said to have been met by 30 October when the RAF began to bomb Egypt? No. Selwyn Lloyd was inching towards a peaceful resolution of the Canal crisis at the UN when the French emissaries, Gazier and Challe, arrived at Chequers with the outline of a collusive plan to break the deadlock *and* defeat Nasser. The UN solution in embryo rested on the so-called 'six principles', the most important of which were free international transit through the Canal and its insulation from the politics of any country.[217]

Donald Logan, Lloyd's Private Secretary, who was with him in New York and who accompanied him to the first of the Sèvres meetings, was eloquent on this point once the Suez archive was declassified. Lloyd, he said:

'attached a great deal of importance to the work that he was doing in New York to try and work out, under United Nations auspices, the basis for a peaceful solution to the problem ... He returned to London in the hope that there was something that could be developed ... It was that development over the weekend of 14–16 October [the French mission] that, as it were, foreclosed the peaceful approach. Selwyn Lloyd and the delegation with him were recalled from New York a day or two early in order to come back and deal with that situation.'[218]

Of Lloyd and the French war plan, Logan said, 'I don't think he ever liked it from the start.'[219] As Sir Harold Beeley put it, 'Selwyn Lloyd was a modest man and was not very confident of his own judgement ... and I think Selwyn felt that he ought not to challenge Eden's judgement.'[220] Eden paid a high price for his desire to have a cipher in the Foreign Office.

Suez represents the greatest single failure of premiership in the postwar period. All six criteria were broken. The result was ruinous in both personal and policy terms for Eden. As the JIC put it starkly, five days after the invasion was halted with British troops stopped at El Cap, twenty-three miles down the Canal from Port Said,

(a) the circumstances surrounding the Anglo-French and Israeli operations against Egypt have severely shaken the faith of the Arab States in the United Kingdom. American stock has also fallen.

(b) the Soviet Union will probably seek to win Arab sympathies by anti-Israel propaganda, economic assistance, strong diplomatic support in the United Nations and elsewhere and by offers of military intervention within the framework of the United Nations.

(c) Nasser will remain the principal instrument of Soviet policy in the Middle East.[221]

The Prime Minister's very personal policy had had exactly the opposite effect to that intended.

Less than two weeks before stepping down, Eden penned a kind of political last will and testament, shown only to the Foreign Secretary, Selwyn Lloyd, the Defence Minister, Antony Head, and Eden's old friend, Lord Salisbury. The file was declassified several years after the core archive was opened. It demonstrated that, at last, reality of a kind had broken through; so much so that Eden questioned the value of British bases in Tripoli and Libya (which could not be used during the Suez crisis for fear of inflaming Arab opinion still further),[222] the sustainability of the British Army of the Rhine at its current level and the cost of the welfare state. And, extraordinarily for the man who disdained the notion of a Common

Market and virtually ignored the post-Messina talks which led to its formation so distracted was he by Suez, even Eden in his desperation wondered if Britain's future might not lie in working 'more closely with Europe'.[223]

And yet, it is difficult not to feel some sympathy for Eden. The strain on that overstretched physique and overwrought mind must have been intolerable by the end. Bulganin's threat to use rockets on London on 4–5 November,[224] the flash signal from the Middle East the following day suggesting that Russia might be about to intervene in the Middle East with force,[225] with the USA adamant in its opposition, its Sixth Fleet interfering with the task force, the UN in uproar in New York, the House of Commons in a frenzy in London and, on top of all this, the collusion plan unravelling before his eyes thanks to the Egyptian acceptance of a ceasefire – taken together this is as great a stress as any Prime Minister has been under in a seven-day period. It would have broken a much fitter, more poised man than Anthony Eden.

Eden, too, was utterly sincere in his views of Nasser as a man, the unacceptability of his action in July 1956 and the geopolitical threat to Western interests represented by Egypt's growing closeness to the Soviet bloc. Every time I see his prime ministerial broadcast of 3 November, I am struck by the sincerity of Eden's exhausted self-belief.

'All my life I've been a man of peace, working for peace, striving for peace, negotiating for peace. I've been a League of Nations man and a United Nations man and I'm still the same man with the same convictions, the same devotion to peace. I couldn't be other if I wished.'[226]

As Douglas Hurd put it: 'Very few politicians are hypocrites, because the first people whom they persuade with their arguments are themselves. But in describing the world, its anxieties and its possibilities, they fall too easily into the temptation of the preacher.'[227] The hard truth about Eden, however, was captured by his friend Noël Coward once Eden had called on the Queen on 9 January 1957. 'Poor Anthony has resigned,' he wrote in his diary, 'given up, and is on his way to New Zealand, a tragic figure who had been cast in a star part well above his capabilities.'[228]

10

Quiet, Calm Deliberation:
Harold Macmillan, 1957–63

Since Anthony's illness I have had quite a job to keep the government going and the strength of the Party in the House and in the country maintained. We have been through some pretty rough weather together . . . but we have held on . . . At home we have fully restored the economy. We have a fine situation. A stable cost of living, full employment, booming exports, reduced taxation. This is a good record.

Harold Macmillan to the Colonial Secretary Alan Lennox-Boyd
(persuading him not to resign over the deaths of Mau Mau
detainees in Kenya), June 1959[1]

Of course it will never be the same fun again. And what fun it has been! . . . Obviously, it must be a reasonable time before the end . . . Events seem to me to make the end much nearer (anyway for me and perhaps for the Govt.) than I thought (say), six months ago. I feel sure you understand.

Harold Macmillan to Viscount Kilmuir after
sacking him as Lord Chancellor, July 1962[2]

It was absolute nonsense, he [Macmillan] said, to argue that we were moving towards a presidential system . . . In the British system the Cabinet had collective responsibility. You could not ignore it. Even Winston had made sure he could carry the Cabinet with him in major decisions. As for himself, had it escaped notice that before completing the agreement about Polaris with President Kennedy he had thought it necessary to put the agreement to the Cabinet?

Harold Evans, Prime Minister's Press
Secretary, diary entry 20 January 1963[3]

The Whips want the safe men, as they always have done in every party. But they don't make the future leaders of the party. I reminded Winston again that it took Hitler to make him PM and me an under-secretary. The Tory Party would do neither.

Harold Macmillan, diary entry, 13 October 1954[4]

When it comes to weighing and measuring Prime Ministers, Harold Macmillan causes me particular difficulty. Part of it has to do with my age. I was a few months short of ten when he succeeded Anthony Eden in January 1957 and in my *Daily Express*-infused household in North London I was, for reasons I now suspect had something to do with the advocacy of the Beaverbrook press, convinced that he rather than Rab Butler would carry off the prize (a track record in political forecasting which, I regret to say, has sadly deteriorated with the passing years).

The real problem is this: Macmillan was the first British Prime Minister with whom I was in any way familiar. Though I did not meet him face-to-face until August 1975, it was as if I grew up with him politically and stylistically. He became – and has remained – the human benchmark against which I measure his successors. I expect them all to be witty, stylishly self-ironic; both steeped in the classics and marinated in a very personal sense of their country's history and its place in the world. Generally speaking I have been disappointed ever since. I wasn't surprised to learn that his last known words on Mrs Thatcher, at the height of her powers in the mid 1980s, were: 'I do wish she would read a book.'[5]

Anthony Sampson, in his excellent short life of Macmillan published in 1967, saw him as 'a study in ambiguity'[6] partly because 'like Disraeli, he seemed to see himself as part of a fashionable play'.[7] His capacity to dazzle through this carefully constructed camouflage was a formidable political instrument for getting his way while leaving doubters not only unbruised but purring with pleasure at the sense of occasion Macmillan could create. When I interviewed them in the mid 1980s, both Lord Hailsham and Lord Home retained a powerful sense of the Macmillan effect over the twenty years that had elapsed since his last distressing Cabinet meeting on 8 October 1963 when he sat, crippled by the pain of his prostate trouble, and asked his colleagues if he should carry on to lead them into the next election.[8] (They all concurred with the exception of Enoch Powell;[9] Lord Hailsham wept;[10] Rab Butler offered him a Valium.[11]) The gloom and the anguish of that day was exceptional because, in Home's words, normally 'Harold Macmillan enjoyed the company of Cabinet. He was a very amusing man ... Apart from the business altogether, it was fun.'[12]

This in itself is evidence that at least one aim of his premiership was achieved. As his official biographer, Alistair Horne, put it: 'Perhaps the two most hard-worked words in Macmillan's extensive vocabulary of jocularity were "fun" and a "bore". Being Prime Minister was, whatever the pressures and problems, always "fun" – and he determined from the very first day that working for him should be, too.'[13] Of all our postwar PMs, the laughter rang loudest and longest through the Cabinet Room doors when 'Uncle Harold' was in the chair.

Macmillan's wit could be far from ambiguous when deployed for the purpose of a put-down. As Archbishop of Canterbury, Michael Ramsey loved telling the story of the day in January 1961 in No. 10 when his retiring predecessor, Geoffrey Fisher, had tried to wreck Ramsey's chance of leading the Church of England. The conversation went like this:

FISHER: I have come to give you some advice about my successor. Whoever you choose, under no account must it be Michael Ramsey, the Archbishop of York. Dr Ramsey is a theologian, a scholar and a man of prayer. Therefore, he is entirely unsuitable as Archbishop of Canterbury. I have known him all my life. I was his Headmaster at Repton.

MACMILLAN: Thank you, Your Grace, for your kind advice. You may have been Dr Ramsey's headmaster, but you were not mine.[14]

Shortly after, Macmillan, himself a scholar and a man of prayer, picked up the phone for Bishopsthorpe, the Palace of the Archbishop of York, and read Ramsey the letter he proposed sending the Queen advising her on the Fisher succession at Canterbury.[15]

Macmillan's diary entry describing 'the great archi-Episcopal problem'[16] is partly whited-out in the copy released for public inspection. It reads as follows: '. . . [the] problem is resolved, not without drama, even melodrama [4½ lines missing] now a profound teacher, scholar we need xtian [Christian] apologist.'[17]

It is plain from the diary that Fisher had urged that Dr Donald Coggan, the Bishop of Bradford, be appointed to Canterbury.[18]

Lord Hailsham probably caught the governing flavour of the Macmillan Downing Street best of all when he told me 'there was an element of the dining club or the country house party about his conduct of Cabinets and Cabinet committees. There would be quotations from Homer, there would be vague historical analogies; the trade union leaders would be described as medieval barons in the period of the Wars of the Roses. And some of them would be relevant and some of them would be mildly misleading. But they would all be amusing and detached and very carefully thought out when one had to watch what he was doing as well as what he was saying.'[19]

This, of course, was a product of what Hailsham himself called 'the beautiful acting of Harold Macmillan'.[20] It also had to do with Macmillan's great gifts, not just as a manipulator of mood, but as a deployer of what his political opponent, Hugh Gaitskell, once called in another context 'the subtle terrorism of words'.[21] The whole effect was made possible partly by that constant tension within Macmillan between the 'gownsman' and the 'swordsman'; the scholar and the warrior, a juxtaposition he liked to illustrate by describing 'how he lay in no-man's land [on the Somme in 1916] with a shattered pelvis for a whole day, surrounded by the dead, and distracting himself by reading Aeschylus between the shelling, and feigning dead when the German soldiers passed'.[22] There was an element of contrivance and acting in this, as with much else that Macmillan did, but in essence the tension was genuine and provides a kind of recitative in his diaries. Macmillan could be rather contemptuous of those he regarded as pure 'gownsmen'. This came out in an acid aside in his diary in 1954 about 'officialdom, especially our Treasury Officials, with their narrow and jealous minds. The Civil Servants are really more dangerous when they are good (as at the Treasury). They are all "gown-men" – none "sword and cloak men" [this was unfair, the Treasury's Permanent Secretary, Sir Edward Bridges, had won an MC in the Great War].[23] They are against the aristocracy; the successful businessman; and the adventurer (in its widest sense). They are like the clergy in the pre-Reformation times. It was against them, rather than against any theological doctrine, that our ancestors revolted.'[24]

It was upon 'this duality',[25] as he called it, that Macmillan brooded towards the end of his first hectic week as Prime Minister which had begun with him telling the Queen 'half in joke, half in earnest, that I could not answer for the new government lasting more than six weeks'[26] with the party still in turmoil after Suez.

He wrote, of his new station in life,

There was ... a certain atmosphere of unreality and even absurdity. Perhaps because I had spent so many of my hours of my life in reading, and since my whole education had been based on the old learning, I was at any rate on one side of my nature and training what has been called 'a gown man': a product of a system which was intended to supply in the Middle Ages 'clerks' as priests and administrators . . . Even my family business [publishing] had close connections with this quiet world of literature and art. The First World War turned me unexpectedly into a 'sword man'. Action – harsh, brutal, compelling – ousted learning.[27]

My own personal encounter with him – an 'entirely off-the-record' chat, as he put it – about another gown-and-sword-man, Lord Hailsham (whose profile I was preparing for *The Times*),[28] brimmed with the fluencies and the brutalities which this 'duality' stimulated.

'The English', Mr Macmillan told me, 'they don't like clever people. The whole Tory Party spent 1868–74 trying to get rid of Dizzy. They were distrustful of Churchill . . . If any of my colleagues go to heaven it will be Quintin [Hailsham].'[29] Then came the brutalities (this is August 1975 with Mrs Thatcher still finding her feet as Conservative Leader): 'You couldn't imagine a woman as Prime Minister if we were a first-class power . . . You can't make a foreign policy when you're in the debtors' court.'[30]

'The old Conservative Party at its best it was a national party with many mansions,' he went on before ruminating on what might have been in 1963 when the Party fought over his succession:

'Hailsham had the essential qualities of heart and brain . . . I thought they would probably support Rab. I was surprised when they didn't. Rab is a backroom-boy by nature; a marvellous chief of staff. Macleod and Hailsham had the qualities of a commander. I think the present system of education tends to produce staff officers rather than commanders . . . [But Hailsham] did himself great injury with his weakness and lack of self-control. He's curiously un-English in some ways [with] some of the characteristics of Shelley.'[31]

This was heady stuff for a young twenty-eight-year-old journalist in solo session with an old statesman fifty-two years his senior – almost a command performance, with gown and sword jostling in nearly every line, for somebody he had not met before. But, as Hailsham said, it required care on the part of the listener (especially that bit about his surprise when Butler failed to make it to No. 10 in October 1963).

Yet, on reflection, this old man in his deeply bookish room in the Little Essex Street offices of the family firm was more Gladstone than Disraeli, in the sense that the 'beautiful actor' was to the fore enjoying his undoubted effect on the young man from *The Times*. For Colin Matthew, editor of the Gladstone Diaries (as reported in Roy Jenkins' superb life of the Grand Old Man), reckons that, even by the time of his second premiership, 'there was becoming something contrived about Gladstone's conversational performances, and that "performances" was indeed the right word for them [because] . . . in this period, it was almost certain that one of the guests would note his conversation or mood in a letter or a diary'.[32]

Macmillan had a considerable sense of his own place in the pantheon of Prime Ministers. George Walden, then a young diplomat, captured this flavourfully when recalling a lunchtime of interpreting in Admiralty House to which Macmillan and his staff had repaired while No. 10 Downing Street was being renovated in the early 1960s.

Macmillan was giving lunch for Mme Furtseva, the po-faced apparatchik who was Soviet Minister of Culture at the time . . . Between bites of food and snatches of interpretation I watched Macmillan with awe and fascination. Though in late middle age he was already at his game of playing the old man. As we came down the stairs of Admiralty House after lunch . . . Macmillan, his hand waving laconically from side to side, passed under review the portraits of prime ministers lining the stairs – Pitt, Gladstone, Campbell-Bannerman . . . – as if to remind the Russian provincial that he was the latest in a long line of British brilliance and that after 300 years of it, he was exhausted by his own distinction.

He struck Walden as 'a walrus descending a staircase in slow motion, flippers flapping nonchalantly from side to side as he indicated his illustrious forebears'.[33]

I have concentrated to begin with on the Macmillan style because, as Alistair Horne has expressed it, the style was very much the man.[34] 'It's very important not to have a rigid distinction between what's flippant and what is serious', as Macmillan himself put it to his biographer when deep into his ripest anecdotage[35] (pre-echoing by a decade Roy Jenkins' apt distinction between the 'earnest' and the 'frivolous' in political life).[36] And just such a combination did impinge directly on the conduct of Cabinet government almost from the moment he replaced the brittle Eden.

He had the Klaxon removed from the prime ministerial car[37] and he soothed the nerves of the Private Office, still jagged from the Eden experience, as his Principal Private Secretary, Sir Freddie Bishop, recalled, by writing 'out in his own hand this quotation – which I didn't immediately spot, but I believe it comes from Gilbert and Sullivan[38] – "Quiet, calm deliberation disentangles every knot". And that stayed pinned up on the Cabinet door for quite a long time until he thought that we'd got over our little tremors, and then he took it down and gave it to me.'[39] On a later occasion, when the abrasive Duncan Sandys was expected to give a particular Cabinet committee an especially hard time, Macmillan sent Bishop to the chemist in Whitehall ahead of the meeting to buy enough tranquillizers for every minister. When they sat down, there was a packet of 'Relaxatabs' on every blotter. The meeting went like a charm![40]

Of course, a great deal of this was camouflage at which Macmillan, of all our postwar premiers, was the past master (to use a phrase he liked to apply to others).[41] Before speeches and great occasions generally, he would almost be physically sick with nervous apprehension.[42] And he *was* genuinely excited about assuming the job of Prime Minister. He dined with Sir Oliver Franks within a couple of days of replacing Eden and told him it was like owning a new car – 'One turned the key and the engine started smoothly, one tried the brakes and the steering and found that they were reliable, the seats were comfortable, one could control everything.'[43]

Of all the premiers the long-serving political correspondent James Margach knew well, he ranked Macmillan with Lloyd George, Baldwin and MacDonald as 'extraordinarily difficult men to understand, for they loved to withdraw themselves introspectively into their Celtic mists'.[44] Exhilaration could swiftly be followed by exhaustion as we saw, classically, in chapter 6 once the Cuban missile crisis reached its sudden end in October 1962. Reading Macmillan's diaries is like listening to a treatise on the strain and anxiety of it all punctuated by arias of excitement and satisfaction.

Macmillan's political impulses were similarly mercurial. As Prime Minister, Attlee revealed in private how close Macmillan had come to joining the Labour Party in the 1930s, claiming that Macmillan, not he, would then have led Labour.[45] 'By far the most radical man I've known in politics ... He was a real left-wing radical in his social, human and economic thinking' was how Attlee described the interwar Macmillan during a private conversation in 1951.[46] Macmillan himself had claimed in 1936 that 'Toryism has always been a form of paternal socialism', and reading his loving essay on the Whig tradition, again penned late in life, confirmed my own view that Macmillan was as much a Whig as a Tory.[47] Certainly he was not a 'good Tory', and admitted as much to his biographer, Alistair Horne.[48] Put all this together with his profound admiration for David Lloyd George[49] (who coached him as a young MP on how to make effective speeches)[50] and his admission that he learned his economics from John Maynard Keynes (whose *General Theory* the family firm published in 1936)[51] and it is easy to see why the more narrowly formed of modern Conservatives view 'Uncle Harold' (as they most certainly do *not* like to call him) with such suspicion.

No modern premier, Churchill apart, ever brought such an eclectic experience to No. 10 along with his Sovereign's commission. Macmillan really did have a sense of how his forebears had tackled the job. The ghosts in the Cabinet Room were almost flesh and blood to him, as were the wraiths he saw in the galleries in the House of Commons after his parliamentary triumphs – the spectres of the really brilliant figures who, unlike him, had not survived the Great War. It was, as a friend of his put it to me, almost as if he could hear the Raymond Asquiths and the Patrick Shaw-Stewarts saying, 'What *you*, Harold – *you* Prime Minister?'[52]

How did this complicated, elusive man tackle the job? For all the touch of the country house about his No. 10, Cabinets were run tightly. He was very much in charge. He removed the racks containing writing paper from the Cabinet table on which he and others had scribbled abusive notes to each other as poor Eden underwhelmed them from the chair.[53] Though, oddly for a premier who had not only served as Chancellor of the Exchequer but who had strong views on the management of the economy throughout his time in No. 10, Macmillan followed Churchill and Eden (rather than Attlee) in putting the Chancellor, rather than himself, in the chair of the Cabinet's Economic Policy Committee.

To a recent analyst of his premiership, Richard Lamb, 'The archives show that even more than generally believed Macmillan ran his government on the lines of an American President rather than a traditional British Prime Minister . . . Intellectually Macmillan towered head and shoulders above his Cabinet colleagues and, often mistrustful of their judgement, he insisted on full control . . . [he] interfered continuously with his colleagues' conduct of their departmental affairs.'[54]

This overstates Macmillan's overmighty tendencies. Christopher Soames, who sat in the Cabinet Room under both Macmillan and Mrs Thatcher, had no doubts about their relative position on the spectrum of overmightiness and he put Ted Heath in the frame as 'the nearest parallel to Maggie'.[55] Yet there is something to Lamb's case. Macmillan had strong tendencies towards being his own Foreign Secretary and Chancellor of the Exchequer (especially when Selwyn Lloyd was filling those seats), and not just because he had held both posts himself on the way to the top job.

Though not an Eden-style fusser, Macmillan was a shameless intervener in the business of his ministers, especially those he suspected of lacking dash or grip. In April 1963 he recorded in his diary a very revealing exchange with Ernest Marples, the energetic businessman he had brought in as his junior at Housing in the early 1950s and who, by the early 1960s, in his capacity as Transport Minister, was a key Macmillan ally when it came to 'modernizing' not just the railways but the country as a whole.

Ernest observed to me how queer it was that I spent my time *urging* Ministers forward. He would have thought I would be *restraining* them. So it would be – if they were 'sword' men and not 'gown' men. He discussed how the Beeching principle [for streamlining the railways] might be applied to Government as a whole! It is, of course, true that we have not adapted the Ministry [i.e., central government], Parliament – where any Government – Socialist or Conservative – is forced to take a hand in almost every aspect of commercial and industrial life.[56]

Macmillan, I think, could be a touch ungenerous to some of the alleged 'gown' men in his Cabinets. Another favourite dismissive epithet was to call someone a 'good chief of staff'. When brigaded with the accusation of dullness it could make a truly damning condemnation. A classic example of this was when he was talking in the early 1980s to his official biographer, Alistair Horne, about Ted Heath: '. . . Hengist and Horsa were very dull people. Now, as you know, they colonized Kent; consequently the people of Kent have ever since been very slightly – well, you know . . . Ted was an excellent Chief Whip . . . a first-class staff officer, but no army commander . . .'[57]

A defence can be mounted for the view of Macmillan-as-intervener of a kind that can be made for any Prime Minister. The premier has to be keeper of the government's overall strategy and Macmillan possessed a powerful sense of the strategic – the wholeness, the interlocking nature of government policy – and of his position as perhaps the sole guardian of it. And what was notable about his stewardship of the machinery of state was, I think, his desire to streamline it in order to enable its operators, both ministerial and official, more easily to contemplate the deeper problems afflicting Britain – its economy, its society, its place in the world – and to set changes in train.

From rummaging among his files at the Public Record Office, I would divide his efforts into two parts:

1. The post-Suez rethinks of 1957–60.
2. His avowed pursuit of 'modernization' across the board between 1961 and 1963.

Linking both periods was an intense sense of 'overload' – of the burden on his ministers and the central mechanics of state – and upon himself. Around mid 1961, he seems to have suffered a genuine loss of vitality. His doctor, Sir John Richardson, had examined him. 'I have no more "élan vital"!' he wrote. 'I am finished! In other words, I ought to have a month's holiday. As it is, I am to have four days, starting tomorrow evening.'[58] His wife, Lady Dorothy, could become enraged by his workload. She roared into the Private Office around this stage of the premiership, told the Private Secretaries: 'If it's your intention to kill him, you are going about it the right way!' and stormed out.[59] On top of all this, of course, lay an immense, constant and intensely personal new responsibility for him. As we have seen, he was the first British Prime Minister with a fully fledged strategic nuclear force launchable in a matter of minutes on his own say so (as opposed to that of the Minister of Defence, the Foreign Secretary or the Cabinet as a whole).

Let us look now at those post-Suez rethinks. It is not known if Macmillan saw Eden's own inquest on the significance of Suez[60] (though, as we have seen, Selwyn Lloyd did),[61] but he set in train a series of initiatives and inquiries very similar in their tone and pitch to those thoughts that afflicted this predecessor in the last bleak hours of his premiership. They ranged from the more determined pursuit of science and technology as a national priority[62] to the first ever cost–benefit analysis of the Empire, undertaken in 1957[63] (the Indian Mutiny of 1857, you might think, would have been a more appropriate moment for this rather than the period when the Gold Coast was moving towards independence as the newly constituted Ghana), and to no fewer than two wide-ranging studies of Britain's place in the world. The first of these was undertaken by a committee of permanent secretaries in 1957–58 under the leadership of his friend and constant source of solace and support, the Cabinet Secretary, Sir Norman Brook.[64] The second was carried out very secretly in 1959–60 by what was in effect an expanded Joint Intelligence Committee under the leadership of the Foreign Office's Sir Patrick Dean.[65]

Macmillan drew some very personal lessons from Suez. He took immense pains not to act diplomatically or militarily in any serious way without consulting the Americans first. He may not have seen the Suez inquest prepared for the Chiefs of Staff by Sir Charles Keightley, Commander-in-Chief of the Anglo-French forces in October–November 1956, but he would have agreed with its thrust, especially Keightley's view already quoted that: 'The overriding lesson of the Suez operations is that world opinion is now an absolute principle of war and must be treated as such . . . It was the action of the United States which really defeated us in attaining our object . . . This situation with the United States must at all costs be prevented from arising again.'[66]

In Cabinet, too, Macmillan was determined to be anybody-but-Anthony if the UK's armed forces seemed likely to become engaged in substantial action as during the threatened Iraqi invasion of Kuwait in 1961. 'The Cabinet', he recorded in his diary, 'left the whole management of this affair to me. I got the Foreign Secretary [Home] and the Minister of Defence [Watkinson] to work side by side with me, which they did with admirable loyalty and skill. But, remembering Suez, I was careful throughout to have meetings of Ministers (including Chancellor of Exchequer [Lloyd]; Lord Chancellor [Kilmuir] and Home Secretary [Butler]) and also – before the final decision to launch the forces – of the whole Cabinet.'[67] Overlapping with these policy reviews and procedural and attitudinal changes was an examination of the thousand-and-one inefficiencies that poisoned (and still do) everyday ministerial life. For in 1957 (once more on the initiative of the seasoned Norman Brook)[68] Macmillan commissioned a Committee of Privy Counsellors, under the chairmanship of Lord Attlee, to examine 'The Burden on Ministers'.[69]

What were the results of these attempts to 'rub ministers' noses in the future' (to borrow a phrase Douglas Hurd would later use of Ted Heath's Central Policy Review Staff)?[70] On two levels a great deal. For that great shift in the country's geopolitics – the withdrawal from the tropical empire and the first tilt towards Europe – were powerfully influenced by a combination of what Macmillan liked to call 'events',[71] and those studies, even though the starkly realistic conclusions of the 1959–60 'Study of Future Policy' about the weakness of a once-great power squeezed between a pair of superpowers and certain, should the new Common Market cohere and develop, to be facing increasing economic and political competition from an integrating Europe, were thought to be too bleak to be put before the full Cabinet in February 1960 and the Cabinet Paper summarizing the study's outcome was pulled at the last minute.[72] Interestingly, however, Macmillan in his gloomier moments could even outdo his briefers in his more pessimistic forecasts of the waning of British power –

musing some six months after receiving their report, 'Shall we be caught between a hostile (or at least a less and less friendly) America and a boastful, powerful "Empire of Charlemagne" – now under French but later bound to come under German control. Is this the real reason for "joining" the Common Market . . . ?'[73]

Very little resulted from the examination of 'overload' – with one important exception – apart from a feeble exhortation of ministers to attend fewer dinners and to get their juniors to meet the less important foreign dignitaries flying into Heathrow or Gatwick.[74] The substantial exception was the creation, four years after Attlee had reported, of a second Cabinet minister in the Treasury to ease what the Committee of Privy Counsellors regarded as the 'exceptionally heavy and continuing strain' on the Chancellor of the Exchequer.[75] As Macmillan informed the Cabinet on creating the new position of Chief Secretary to the Treasury (the public expenditure job which survives to this day and whose holder has usually, though not invariably, sat in the full Cabinet): 'The Chancellor of the Exchequer has asked to have the assistance in the Treasury of a senior Cabinet minister; and as my colleagues are aware, Mr [Henry] Brooke has been appointed Chief Secretary to the Treasury . . . to meet this need. I am sure that with the difficult problems which lie ahead of us both at home and abroad, in the financial and economic field, this sharing of the increasing burdens which have fallen on the Chancellor is a timely step.'[76]

As for science, Macmillan in the end did not create a separate Ministry of Science. He opted instead for adding the title of 'Minister for Science' to Lord Hailsham's existing title of Lord Privy Seal[77] (partly in response to fears conveyed to the ever influential Norman Brook by the big names of the scientific community, that a Ministry of Science would interfere 'with the freedom and independence of scientific and medical research').[78] This, too, is the era in which Macmillan (even with a thumping majority of 100 after the October 1959 election) declined to contemplate rigorously the problem of trade union power in the form of unofficial strikes,[79] though he did eventually tread where Attlee, Churchill and Eden had shrunk from going in placing some curbs on unrestricted Commonwealth immigration in 1962 after his Commonwealth Migrants Cabinet Committee had prepared the ground in policy terms.[80]

Macmillan's second phase, his overtly modernizing one, stretched across virtually the whole fabric of government. At one end was the 'grand design' he put to the about to be inaugurated President Kennedy in early

1960 (after a characteristically broody Christmas at Birch Grove)[81] with its emphasis on Britain as the special interlocutor between an integrating Europe it would probably soon seek to join and a pivotal United States on whose strength all of Western Europe depended in the Cold War. 'I will have to base myself now on trying to win him by *ideas*', Macmillan wrote of the newly elected Kennedy in November 1960;[82] 'It is curious', he reflected almost a year later, 'how all American statesmen begin by trying to treat Britain as just one of many foreign or NATO countries. They soon find themselves relying on our advice and experience.'[83]

At the other end of the spectrum lay a more modern Britain with a revitalized infrastructure (a Beeching-modernized railway system,[84] new motorways[85] and relatively traffic-free towns[86]), overseen by a streamlined, less-burdened Cabinet structure[87] with its eye on the future trends of population and employment in late-twentieth-century Britain.[88] All this was to be underpinned by a new accommodation between government, capital and labour through a new National Economic Development Council[89] to replace the old Economic Planning Board, which had survived since Attlee's time, and a new settlement between the classes thanks to a National Incomes Commission.[90]

Macmillan was a great one for bringing these broad themes to Cabinet and for thinking aloud on them before his assembled colleagues. For him the full Cabinet was a sounding-board, especially on his modernization of Britain theme. (Despite the Edwardian pose, he had always striven also to create a forward-looking image for himself – even to the extent of cramming himself awkwardly into one of the new Minis in 1959.) He would prepare very carefully for such sessions in the Cabinet Room and on one occasion arranged for a rare (possibly unique) tape-recording to be made of his remarks.

This took place at the Cabinet meeting on 28 May 1962, which, since its declassification in 1993, has acquired a degree of fame as Macmillan's disquisition on the middle classes – 'the Orpingtonians' (the Conservatives had recently lost this London suburban seat to the Liberals at a famous by-election).[91] And 'the working classes, as we are apt in this room to call them, but I suppose there's some new name for them now'. (Macmillan wanted the working classes to 'feel that they play as full members of the team' and urged on the Cabinet an end to the 'medieval remnant' whereby significant status differences persisted between wage earners and salaried staff.)[92] The whole speech to the Cabinet was a very left-wing soliloquy by late-1990s standards (New Labour, not to mention Conservative), pressing as it did the case for incomes policy as a way of increasing public expenditure. 'If', Macmillan told his colleagues, 'we got the stability out of the general acceptance of the incomes policy ... some increase in government expenditure on the things we know are necessary – the housing, the slums, the universities, the schools would follow.'[93]

By the end of the year Macmillan was converting such thinking into an overall modernization strategy which, with entry into the EEC, was plainly intended as the basis of the Conservatives' next appeal to the electorate – 'a blue print for modernising Britain against which the Government's actions can be judged and to which people will respond', as his notes for a series of Cabinet meetings in late October 1962 put it.[94]

The thrust was to be consciously interventionist, as the notes made plain:

What should be the elements in such a blue print? Have some ideas of my own, but hope colleagues will contribute. Firstly, basic principles. Do we, or do we not, set out to control the pattern of events, to direct development, to plan growth, to use the instruments of Government to influence or determine private decisions? Believe that this is inevitable. Forces at work now too complicated, risks of setback too great to leave to market forces and laisser faire. Dirigisme. But it must be creative dirigisme. This is the thread which should run through our policy and by which new proposals should be judged.[95]

The following month Macmillan created a hybrid system for furthering his modernization programme. He would chair a 'steering group' to oversee the process consisting of Reggie Maudling, the Chancellor of the Exchequer, and Henry Brooke, the Home Secretary, as its regular members.[96] The industrial/economic side of the programme would be run by the existing Economic Policy Committee (which Maudling chaired) and the social/urban side by Brooke's Cabinet Committee on Employment and Population.[97]

A minor burst of domestic Cabinet modernization accompanied these changes. Henceforth, the Cabinet would meet only once a week as 'a deliberate attempt to relieve the burden on ministers', as Burke Trend put it, with more business 'thrust ... downwards' to Cabinet committees.[98] The full Cabinet was informed of this on 6 December 1962 when it took a paper on 'Modernisation of Britain' outlining a 'more radical attack ... upon the weakness of our economy, both productive and structural'. 'Whatever the result of the Brussels negotiations,' Macmillan told his colleagues, 'this need is urgent. In or out of Europe, Britain needs to be brought up to date in almost every sphere of life.'[99] There is something timeless to present-day eyes about the twin themes of modernization and an end to class divisions.

The meetings of Macmillan's modernization steering group ran on into the spring of 1963. The flavour of the discussion was both detailed and interventionist – the one result that lives on in political folk memory being the dispatch of Lord Hailsham, the Lord President, to the North East of England, complete with cloth cap, to 'rehabilitate'[100] the region and eventually to help cover it with some rather good roads.

Macmillan was a nuclear modernizer, too. In civil nuclear terms his administration carried forward the first 'Magnox' generation of power stations[101] and, as we have seen, he made a great point of stressing his involvement of the full Cabinet in proceeding from the V-bomber force to the Polaris submarine squadron as the carrier of the British nuclear deterrent. In bringing the Polaris purchase to the full Cabinet twice, in December 1962 and January 1963,[102] Macmillan was closer to the later Churchill than to Attlee in his management of nuclear weapons policy, though he kept his doubts about the robustness of the Nassau Agreement with President Kennedy (under the terms of which the missiles were procured) to a small group of ministers and officials about whose deliberations the full Cabinet was not informed.[103]

Macmillan's interventionism deeply impressed the Chief Whip he inherited from Eden, Ted Heath, who turned out to be no mean intervener himself when he entered No. 10 as Prime Minister nearly seven years after Macmillan's departure. Of his old chief and mentor he wrote: 'Harold Macmillan had by far the most constructive mind I have encountered in a lifetime of politics . . . Working with him gave great pleasure as well as broadening one's whole life.'[104] (Significantly, Heath asked Macmillan to accompany him to Brussels for the signing of the Treaty of Accession to the European Communities on 22 January 1972 to share the crowning moment of *his* career,[105] and after the ceremony they were photographed together rather oddly listening to the speeches which followed like a pair of choirboys in their stalls.[106])

To help him in his interventions, Macmillan reorganized his Private Office. Freddie Bishop recalled that he converted it into something approaching a miniature think-tank to help him initiate policy.[107] Bishop under Macmillan began the regular practice whereby the Prime Minister's Principal Private Secretary attends Cabinet meetings.[108] As Nicola Bliss has put it in her study of Downing Street support systems for postwar premiers: 'Macmillan had a close relationship with his Private Secretaries and went much further than Attlee, but not as far as Churchill, in turning his Private Office into his private court.'[109]

Macmillan's 'court' also embraced non-civil servants, one of whom, his wartime assistant, confidant and drinking chum John Wyndham, actually worked in the Private Office as an 'unofficial and unpaid' political aide, 'source of constant light entertainment'[110] and provider of 'familiarity, friendship and reassurance'.[111] Roy Harrod, the economist and biographer of Keynes,[112] supplied Macmillan with a steady stream of letters from Oxford which the Prime Minister used to worry and harry those he regarded as arch deflationists in the Treasury. Harrod was a constant reinforcer of Macmillan's own expansionist instincts,[113] although by the end of his premiership, Macmillan's 'greater belief in Roy Harrod'[114] (as opposed to the Treasury) had become a little less pronounced.[115]

Perhaps surprisingly for a Prime Minister who wished to tighten his grip on departments and streamline Cabinet procedure, Macmillan did not make use of *Questions of Procedure for Ministers* as an instrument.[116] He did incorporate a section on greater delegation to junior ministers in 1963, but this did not arise from Attlee's recommendations about greater use of them as part of his 'Burden on Ministers' inquiry in 1957; it had to do with later squabbles between ministers and officials.[117]

Macmillan the would-be modernizer has scarcely been appreciated by posterity. Thanks to the troubles which arrived in battalions after the loss of the Orpington by-election to the Liberals in May 1962,[118] the panic sacking of a third of his Cabinet the following July,[119] General de Gaulle's veto of the British application for EEC membership in January 1963,[120] the Profumo scandal of the summer of 1963[121] and Macmillan's sad, prostate-afflicted demise amidst a rabble of a Party Conference the following autumn,[122] his machinery-of-state (the one bailiwick where his personal writ really ran) remained largely unmodernized.[123] This grim accumulation of misfortunes was crowned – some would say – by his last disastrous act of fixing the succession for the wrong man, Alec Home, usurping those royal prerogatives by which he set such store into the bargain.[124]

What, in the spectrum of postwar premierships, is one to make of this catalogue of hopes and promise unfulfilled? Can one, apart from the perhaps overfast but relatively bloodless dash from territorial Empire between 1960 and 1963, say more than another recent chronicler of the Macmillan years, John Turner, that Macmillan had a broader vision than most leaders of the 1950s and 1960s, and greater courage in facing change. [That] in his time he avoided many of the obvious pitfalls and rescued a little dignity from the wreckage. One man alone can do little more.[125]

For me the key sentence is the last one.

For the immediate post-Suez years illustrate with a vengeance just how reduced were the circumstances of the country of which Macmillan was the Queen's First Minister and how his scope was diminished accordingly. Of course he was the prisoner of atavisms. He was determined that Britain should play its great power role to the maximum for as long as possible. One of the most desperate entries in his premiership diary was penned in July 1959, when it seemed as if the two superpowers would cut Britain out of their serious diplomatic dealings, reducing the Big Three to the Super Two. 'My own position here', he wrote,

will be greatly weakened. Everyone will assume that the 2 Great Powers – Russia and the USA – are going to fix up a deal over our heads and behind our backs. My whole policy – pursued for many years and especially during my Premiership – of close alliance and co-operation with America will be undermined. People will ask 'Why should UK try to stay in the big game?'

[They will ask] 'Why should she be a nuclear power? You told us that this would give you power and authority in the world. But you and me have been made fools of. This shows that Gaitskell and Crossman & Co. are right. UK had better give up the struggle and accept, as gracefully as possible, the position of a second-rate power.'[126]

The UK did attend the 1960 summit in Paris, wrecked as it was by the shooting down of the US U2 spy plane (Macmillan took rueful pride in the fact that the RAF's U2 overflights of the Soviet Union, codenamed 'Oldster', had passed off successfully).[127] But thereafter it was a matter of the 'Big Two', from Kennedy's meeting with Khrushchev in Vienna in 1961 to the end of the Cold War.

Atavism was present, too, even in his avowed quest for modernity on the domestic front. Edmund Dell was right to see huge, public expenditure-guzzling enterprises such as aerospace (Concorde in particular) and nuclear energy as technological surrogates for the imperial impulse.[128] Macmillan was the epitome of this syndrome and he used all his fabled skills of persuasion in its cause. For example, the Cabinet meeting at which final approval was given for Concorde to be developed in November 1962 lives on in Whitehall legend and has been beautifully enshrined by Nigel Lawson and the late Jock Bruce-Gardyne. They described how Macmillan told his colleagues about his great aunt's Daimler,

which had travelled at the 'sensible speed of thirty miles an hour', and was sufficiently spacious to enable one to descend from it without removing one's top hat. Nowadays, alas! people had a mania for dashing around. But that being so Britain ought to 'cater for this profitable modern eccentricity'! He thought they all really agreed. No one seriously dissented. It was all over in a few minutes.[129]

A classic example of sentiment triumphing over cost–benefit analysis.

Yet Macmillan regarded himself as a practical person, a businessman as well as a swordsman and a gownsman. Macmillan, like Mrs Thatcher, had a penchant for scribbling derogatory remarks on papers from colleagues whose views he did not care for (it is said that Mrs Thatcher's habit of inscribing the word 'wet' in such marginalia led to its modern political usage).[130] Such 'heckling' can be very revealing. It was in Macmillan's case.

My favourite example is the savaging that Derick Heathcoat Amory's paper on Treasury control received in October 1958.

AMORY: I would not deprecate [investment], for in the last fifty years we have been not nearly investment-minded enough. But at a time of great shortage of savings, the aggregate of ministers' desires will always outrun the constable. We then need a system of presenting the whole picture so that Ministers can take rational choices on which is the more and which the less important.

MACMILLAN (*in the margin in his spidery hand, the product of the bullet that went through it at the Battle of Loos*):[131] Rot.

AMORY: I am bound to say that these periodic attempts to cut or to increase short-term capital expenditure are likely to frustrate the whole objective of exercising effective control over the long-term programmes and keeping them in line with our long-term resources to carry them out.

MACMILLAN: Have you ever been in (a) war, (b) business, (c) active politics?

AMORY: . . . if we are forced to keep on chopping and changing our control will undoubtedly collapse altogether.

MACMILLAN: Hurrah!

The Prime Minister rounded off his running commentary, gownsman style, as if he were marking an essay: 'Chancellor of Exch. This is a *very bad paper*. Indeed, a disgraceful paper. It might have been written by Mr Neville Chamberlain's ghost.'[132]

It was Heathcoat Amory's predecessor, of course, Peter Thorneycroft (who had left the Treasury the previous January when Macmillan and what Rodney Lowe has called the Cabinet 'paternalists' saw off the 'anti-collectivists')[133] who wished to see public expenditure pegged at 1957 levels and who was prepared to cut planned spending on both defence and welfare to achieve it.[134] (This led to Macmillan's famous dismissal of the resignation of his entire Treasury team as 'a little local difficulty' as he flew away from Heathrow for a six-week tour of the Commonwealth.)[135] Years later, Lord Thorneycroft was lionized by the newer Conservatives for what they saw as his premature Thatcherism, not least by the lady herself who concluded 'wrongly', as Nigel Lawson put it, that this would make him a 'dry' during her own economic battles insider her Cabinet in the early 1980s.[136] And the affable Thorneycroft, with affection in his voice, none the less gained posthumous revenge in his verbal exchanges with Macmillan when he told me in 1993:

'Dear Harold, he was a great spender. He'd been brought up in areas of great unemployment and he thought that writing cheques was the best way of dealing with it. This wasn't my view or the view of the junior ministers [Enoch Powell and Nigel Birch].'[137]

It would be wrong, however, to see Macmillan as careless with the public finances. His most famous remark – 'Never had it so good' (which he lifted from the US Democratic Party's 1952 presidential election campaign slogan)[138] – was coupled when first used in July 1957 with a warning that it might not last thanks to the perils of inflation.[139]

In many ways that famous speech delivered in the Bedford football ground seven months after his arrival at No. 10 pre-echoed his entire premiership – a premiership in which optimism and pessimism, caution and the desire to break free vied constantly. Nearly four years later, a year and a bit before he sacked Selwyn Lloyd from the Exchequer as part of the 'Night of the Long Knives', Macmillan (prompted by his grandson's complaint about Treasury restrictions on racing-cars of all things) minuted his Chancellor thus:

Whenever Britain seems to excel or have the chance to excel in anything, H.M.G. clamps down. We have the drivers; not the cars. Drab; second-rate; without zest or pride. That's what we risk Britain and the British people becoming.[140]

Macmillan was not alone among postwar Prime Ministers in feeling what Harold Nicolson called 'the gigantic pressures of history'[141] when confronted by examples, big or small, of their country's relative economic decline.

Nowhere did the pull of the past and the needs of the future exert their conflicting forces during the Macmillan premierships more powerfully than along the ever-widening political fault line of Europe. As the Cabinet cautiously and, in some cases, reluctantly, moved under his guidance from the European Free Trade Area alternative to the Common Market to an application to join the European Economic Community itself, increasing amounts of both political capital and Cabinet time were absorbed by what can fairly be described as the central question of British politics in the second half of the twentieth century. Under Macmillan's stewardship that question moved centre-stage, where it has remained, with rare and occasional lulls, ever since.

From the moment Macmillan first called GEN 580, his Committee on the Common Market and the Free Trade Area, to order on 7 March 1957, the issue slogged its way through an ever denser network of ministerial and official Cabinet committees. The Common Market Negotiations Committee (CMN) (which, under Butler's chairmanship, handled the London end of the negotiations in Brussels between the autumn of 1961 and the first days of January 1963),[142] mutated, after de Gaulle's veto, into the Post-Brussels Committee, which was also chaired by Butler.[143] On the advice of his new Cabinet Secretary, Burke Trend, Macmillan also established a kind of short-lived 'Inner Cabinet' – a 'steering group' consisting of himself, Butler, Home and Maudling – to oversee the work of the existing Economic Policy Committee and the new Post-Brussels Committee. The steering group reflected the need to pick up the pieces generally after the European setback which led Macmillan to confide in his diary, in a fit of deep gloom, that 'all our policies at home and abroad are in ruins' and Trend to note the need for it to fill the 'vacuum' now that the collapse of the Brussels negotiations had removed the 'one clear and overriding objective' to which all elements of policy had been directed.[144]

This was not the first time that the European question had reduced Macmillan to acute melancholy. Probably the most bizarre manifestation of this tendency occurred in the summer of 1958 when the UK's alternative to a tariff-walled Common Market – a Free Trade Area in Europe – was plainly not going to fly, fuelling Macmillan's animus against both de Gaulle in Paris and Adenauer in Bonn.

Fashioned into a minute for the eyes only of Amory in the Treasury and Lloyd in the Foreign Office, Macmillan's thoughts are so strange and so deeply resentful of the UK's relative decline that they are worth quoting at some length. 'I think sometimes our difficulties with our friends abroad result from our natural good manners and reticence', the Prime Minister began.

We are apt not to press our points too strongly in the early stages of a negotiation, and then when a crisis arises and we have to take a definite position we are accused of perfidy. I feel we ought to make it quite clear to our European friends that if Little Europe is formed without a parallel development of a Free Trade Area we shall have to reconsider the whole of our political and economic attitude towards Europe.[145]

At this point, frustration takes off into mania:

I doubt if we could remain in NATO. We should certainly put on highly protective tariffs and quotas to counteract what Little Europe was doing to us. In other words, we should not allow ourselves to be destroyed little by little. We would fight back with every weapon in our armoury. We would take our troops out of Europe. We would withdraw from NATO. We would adopt a policy of isolationism. We would surround ourselves with rockets and we would say to the Germans, the French and all the rest of them: 'Look after yourselves with your own forces. Look after yourselves when the Russians overrun your countries.'[146]

Macmillan told his two colleagues that he 'would be inclined to make this position quite clear both to de Gaulle and to Adenauer, so that they may be under no illusion'.[147] Quite plainly it was Macmillan who was suffering from illusions. Amory was not. He minuted his Permanent Secretary, Sir Roger Makins, telling him 'I doubt whether this isolationist policy is practicable.'[148] Macmillan obviously subsided, for nothing came of it as, in real life, nothing really could.

Macmillan, it has to be said, was aware not just of the distress the European issue could cause him but also of the party-wrecking capacity of a successful EEC bid once he had accepted that the Free Trade Area alternative was not a long-term runner. He thought he might be 'cast for the role of Peel',[149] splitting the Tories over European tariffs as Peel had rent them over free trade more than a century before. His number 2, Rab Butler, never concealed from Macmillan or the Cabinet his doubts about the Common Market, especially its effects on British agriculture of which Rab liked to pose as the guardian (he once rang No. 10 during the Douglas-Home premiership asking the Private Office to inform the Prime Minister that he had to miss a particular Cabinet meeting 'as it's market day in Saffron Walden [his North Essex constituency] you see').[150]

Butler's coming on side over Europe in the summer of 1962 was a vintage occasion, enhanced by Macmillan's private account of it:

Dined with Butler. This was at Buck's, to which he invited me to come as his guest. The engagement was made in July. It was clearly to be an occasion. And it was. He told me that in spite of (a) the farmers; (b) the Commonwealth; (c) the probable break-up of the Conservative Party he had decided to support our joining the Common Market. It was too late to turn back now. It was too big a chance to miss, for Britain's wealth and strength. But we must face the fact that we might share the fate of Sir Robert Peel and his supporters.[151]

Butler's face, captured by a photographer through the window of Macmillan's car as the pair of them motored (a favourite Macmillan verb) to the House of Commons for the EEC Application statement in July 1961, is eloquent both of his Euro-distaste and, perhaps, his reservations about Macmillan, too.[152]

Macmillan was shattered by de Gaulle's veto. He wrote to his confidante Ava Waverley that he could 'not remember going through a worse time since Suez'.[153] Heath told Hugo Young many years later that in the aftermath of the veto Macmillan 'wouldn't concentrate on anything. This was the end of the world.'[154] Despite much evidence to the contrary,[155] Macmillan and Heath, his chief negotiator in Brussels, had thought until the blow fell that success was imminent, not least because de Gaulle's foreign minister, Couve de Murville, had told Heath over lunch three days earlier that: 'No power on earth can now prevent these negotiations from being successful.'[156]

Too much may have been riding on Common Market membership as the reviver of the fortunes of both the British economy and of the Conservative government, but it was more than a streak of fatalism that held Macmillan back from applying truly ruthless methods to shake his

Britain, its economy and its institutions into the modernity he sought. (He subscribed, after all, to Baldwin's famous dictum that, in Macmillan's version of it: 'There are three bodies that no sensible man directly challenges: the Roman Catholic Church, the Brigade of Guards and the National Union of Mineworkers.')[157] And as his official biographer, Alistair Horne, put it, '. . . how can you actually force regeneration on a country that doesn't want to be regenerated?'[158]

Macmillan certainly had a sense of the difficulty of sounding a warning tocsin in a country muffled by affluence. Over another of his broody Christmas breaks (1961 this time), he wrote: 'The problems which now confront Britain, internally and externally, are really terrifying. No one seems to realize their complexity, although the public are dimly aware of the dangers and *resent* being the victims, when in so many ways life could be so agreeable.'[159]

It may have been the case that, even if the nation had been thirsting for ruthless, across-the-board shake-ups, Macmillan would have lacked Mrs Thatcher's sharklike appetite for the trace of blood in the water – though he did not regard himself as deficient in the nastiness some thought essential to a top-rank political career. At the funeral of his son Maurice (who rose to Cabinet rank under Heath) Macmillan confided in Maurice's old Oxford friend, Woodrow Wyatt, that his son Maurice 'was much nicer than me. I was always a shit. Maurice wouldn't be one so that's why he didn't get on in politics like me.'[160]

Certainly even within the boundaries of his own modernizing inclinations, something held Macmillan back. It was, after all, his sense of political institutions past and present that infused his rebuttal of the prime ministerial-cum-presidential government thesis which shot to prominence during his premiership. A presidential system, he told Harold Evans, 'was about the point of evolution we had reached at the time of Charles II'.[161] Perhaps it was, in part, his Whiggish/Old-Tory respect for traditional institutions which prevailed over his impulse to modernize and, like the great late-nineteenth-century Marquess of Salisbury, Macmillan retained his scepticism about technocrats. ('We have not', he once declared, 'overthrown the divine right of Kings to fall down before the divine right of experts.')[162] The chief areas where Macmillan recoiled from a tough approach were, I think, the UK's internal labour market, which needed a dual dose of reform (greater competition plus some curbing of trade union power), and the resource-hungry efforts to sustain the remnants of great powerdom. A far-reaching review of defence and overseas policy should have emerged from the 'Study of Future Policy'. Instead, Macmillan was prone to take comfort in vague notions of what would now be called 'soft power'. As he told the Cabinet committee which convened to ponder that report: 'Even though the material strength of the United Kingdom would decline relatively, we should still have other assets, which would enable us to play a significant part in world affairs. The best periods of our history had by no means been those, such as the nineteenth century, when we had a preponderance of wealth or power, and for the future we must be ready to consider how we could continue to exercise influence in the world other than through material means alone.'[163]

Yet no postwar premier saw the problems more acutely than Harold Macmillan. And no postwar premier saw the gap between perception and remedy more pronounced. I suspect that as his prime ministership lengthened Macmillan sensed that his attempts to keep airborne the 'four balls', as he called them, of full employment, stable prices, a strong pound and a balance of payments in surplus,[164] were doomed to failure. His Celtic melancholy led him to conclude that his fellow classical scholar and gownsman, H. H. Asquith, was right when he said of the premiership: 'Power, power? You may think you are going to get it but you never do.'[165] Macmillan's own version was 'Power? It's like a Dead Sea fruit.'[166] No wonder he sought solace in literature – *Pride and Prejudice*[167] by day, and as he once so unfortunately put it, by 'going to bed with a Trollope'[168] by night. As a young MP, a certain 'eager' Margaret Thatcher heard Macmillan explain 'that Prime Ministers (not having a department of their own) have plenty of spare time for reading. He recommended Disraeli and Trollope.'[169] She 'sometimes wondered if he was joking'[170] – which says something about both of them.

11

Country Values:
Alec Douglas-Home, 1963–64

'Oh, they must find someone else, once they get away from this Blackpool hot-house. Even if they can't agree on Rab or Quintin there must be someone else. But please, please, not me!'

Lord Home to James Margach during the
Conservative Party Conference, October 1963[1]

In the eighteenth century, he [Douglas-Home] would have become Prime Minister before he was twenty.   *Cyril Connolly, 1938*[2]

In Macmillan's successor, Lord Home, the most authentically genteel Prime Minister took office since the time of Lords Rosebery and Salisbury . . . in many ways, Home was the very end of the thin purple line.   *David Cannadine, 1990*[3]

Alec Home may have been a little uneasy with the particular consensus in which he found himself slightly unexpectedly Prime Minister, but he accepted it. You needed . . . to challenge it a degree of bloody-mindedness, which wasn't a particular characteristic of his, and you also needed a freedom from guilt to challenge the ever-greater power of the state . . . And therefore people with privileged backgrounds – and Alec Home *par excellence* had an extremely gilded background – would have felt a bit awkward in challenging it . . .

Lord Lawson, speech writer and assistant
to Sir Alec Douglas-Home 1963–64, 1995[4]

'. . . we weren't in trouble on the philosophical, ideological side in the Conservative Party in those days, no.'   *Lord Home, 1985*[5]

'The great thing about Alec Home is that he was not media driven. He would have had some difficulty in spelling the word "image".'

Lord Peyton, 1997[6]

'Had a letter from your father [Sir Roy Harrod, the economist] today about inflation . . . or deflation – or something.'

Sir Alec-Douglas-Home to Dominic Harrod, 1964[7]

It was Alec Home's fellow Etonian and great rival for the premiership in 1963, Quintin Hogg, who best captured the man in a book he wrote just after the war when, given their then inevitable ultimate destinations in the House of Lords, neither could have imagined he would be a contender for the premiership. In his celebrated 1947 book, *The Case for Conservatism*, the still-to-be ennobled Mr Hogg declared:

. . . Conservatives do not believe that political struggle is the most important thing in life . . . The simplest among them prefer fox-hunting – the wisest religion.[8]

I have long thought that Alec Home preferred both – that in Quintin Hogg's terms, he was the essence of natural-born Conservative Man, and therefore a kind of talismanic figure as well as a transitional one in Toryism's long march from the third Marquess of Salisbury to John Major, from the aristocratical to the democratical.

His colleague and friend, Lord Boyd-Carpenter, recalled a Scottish peer once telling him 'that in his heart of hearts, Alec believed that the work of government should ideally be carried on by the members of twelve upper-class families, and that nine of these were Scottish!'[9] But not only did Home adjust to the social and political transformation that gave his party to Ted Heath, Margaret Thatcher, John Major and William Hague, he was of direct and regular assistance to the first two at least, by adding his special blue-blooded seal of approval to them during their tenures through his conspicuous loyalty and by his readiness, most autumns, to be wheeled on to the conference platform just ahead of some tricky debate (on Rhodesia perhaps). His immense popularity and his personal dignity would raise both the cheers and the tone while lowering the temperature to the great advantage of the party managers. Friends say he resented being used in this way but concealed his irritation from those who were not close to him.[10]

There is a problem in dealing with Alec Home's premiership, which lasted a mere 363 days. If Bonar Law, in Asquith's phrase, was 'The Unknown Prime Minister',[11] Home is probably the unremembered Prime Minister. That most affable of Labour left-wingers, Ian Mikardo, said as much, when I went to see him in 1992 while preparing Alec Home's obituary for BBC Radio 4.

'I think,' Mikardo said, 'if you stopped, not the first hundred people you met in the street but the first ten thousand people you met in any street in any city in Britain and asked them, "Who was Alec Douglas-Home?" it would surprise me if you got an answer from even two or three of them.' 'Isn't this a rather cruel verdict on a very decent man?' I suggested. 'I wonder if he might be rather proud of it in a funny old way,' Mikardo replied.[12] Strangely enough, I think he might. Certainly, when I once put it to him that he could be described as the most reluctant Prime Minister of the twentieth century, he let out one of his chuckling laughs and said: 'I'd be inclined to plead guilty to that. Yes, I think so. I was the most unexpected one, not only for myself but for other people.'[13]

Even for the *cognoscenti* Home remained an enigmatic figure. Five years after talking to Ian Mikardo, while preparing a lecture on the Douglas-Home premiership for Gresham College, I market-tested once more his trace on the template of memory. The focus group, to use the jargon of today's political marketing, gathered in the autumn of 1996 and consisted of two professors of modern history, two professorial wives plus a Frenchman who had been very high in the intelligence services of his country.

The conversation went like this:

HENNESSY: What flashes across your mind when I mention the name 'Alec Douglas-Home'?

PROFESSOR NO. 1: The only Prime Minister in the postwar period for whom, if he stopped me in the street and asked me to lend him a fiver as he'd left his money at home, I would have opened my wallet without hesitation.

PROFESSOR'S WIFE NO. 1: The teacher in the Giles cartoons. What was he called? Chalky!

PROFESSOR NO. 2: Matchsticks.

PROFESSOR'S WIFE NO. 2: His being heckled at a political meeting in Bedford by a man offering to lend him his box of matches.

FRENCH INTELLIGENCE OFFICER: Who?

PROFESSOR NO. 1: The one who came between Macmillan and Wilson.

FRENCH INTELLIGENCE OFFICER: Ah yes.[14]

17. Harold Macmillan, bibliophile in No. 10: *The Husband of Delilah* by day and 'to bed with a Trollope' by night.

18. Having it so cramped: Mac and Mini in an uneasy moderniser's pose, 1959.

19. A very nuclear premier: Macmillan inspects the V-force at RAF Cottesmore, 1959 (the deterrent was intended to give him the power to destroy 50 per cent of forty Russian cities at the press of a button).

20. Macmillan with his official family, Tim Bligh (*front*) and Philip de Zulueta (*rear*), leaving Admiralty House: Off to Nassau to persuade President Kennedy to part with Polaris at a bargain price, December 1962.

21. Sir Norman Brook: The great technician of state under four premiers.

22. Macmillan with Archbishop Geoffrey Fisher: 'You may have been Dr Ramsey's Headmaster but you were not mine.'

23. Macmillan arriving at Westminster with a sceptical Rab Butler to tell the Commons that the Government would be applying for membership of the European Economic Community, July 19

24. 'I have no more élan vital': Macmillan conceals the strain as he leaves Victoria Station for Brighton and the Conservative Party Conference, October 1961.

25. Macmillan, Sir Norman Brook and President Kennedy outside the White House, April 1961 have to win him ... by ideas.'

26. The agile Earl Home with Henry Brooke at the Imperial Hotel, Blackpool in October 1963: Preparing to sprint for the Leadership finishing-line.

27. The new Prime Minister and his wife, Elizabeth, take the sleeper from Kings Cross to Berwick-upon-Tweed, 24 October 1963: 'A suitcase lay open but unpacked.'

28. 'The most famous flower-arranger in British political history.'

29. The Douglas-Homes at the Hirsel: Premiership as 'a terrible intrusion into one's private life'.

30. Labour in by a whisker: Transport House, 16 October 1964 (*left to right*) Harold Wilson, John Harris, Keith McDowall, Clem Attlee, Ian Aitken.

31. Wilson the miracle worker, Harold with halo: The pipe as political weapon.

32. Wilson at his zenith: Confirmed as Party Leader after his 1966 general election triumph (*left to right*) Bessie Braddock MP, Wilson, George Wigg.

33. The troublesome deputy: George Brown, Mary Wilson and Harold Wilson returning from talks with General de Gaulle, January 1967.

34. Television performer par excellence: Wilson prepares to go on Panorama, September 1967.

35. In place of a policy: Barbara Castle and Harold Wilson leave for Portsmouth to face the TUC Congress after the *In Place of Strife* crisis, September 1969.

But let us deconstruct that private conversational flow among the scholars twenty years after the appearance of Home's best-selling memoir. It may be that both Ian Mikardo, the professors and the French intelligence officer are wide of the mark. Home's *The Way the Wind Blows* sold no fewer than 36,000 copies in hardback after its appearance in 1976 and another 21,000 in paper,[15] very considerable quantities for that period. This could mean that affectionate Conservatives are both moneyed and prone to nostalgia. But there must be more to it than that.

Yet that sequence of exchanges is quite laden with meaning. First, it conveys an exceptional straightness in a politician and its reflection in a high level of trust. (This very much confirmed the view of that most sage of postwar political journalists, James Margach, that: 'At a time when so few public figures enjoyed respect or trust he stood out as a leader of probity. In the standards of conduct which he set for himself and others I have no hesitation in saying that he excelled all the Prime Ministers I know.')[16] Second, the extraordinary appearance which did him no favours in an increasingly televisual political society in the early to mid 1960s. He really did look a bit like the cadaverous Chalky, and in his memoirs he recorded a conversation with the young lady making him up before one of his early appearances on television as Prime Minister:

HOME: Can you not make me look better than I do on television?
MAKEUP LADY: No.
HOME: Why not?
MAKEUP LADY: Because you have a head like a skull.
HOME: Does not everyone have a head like a skull?
MAKEUP LADY: No.[17]

'So that was that,' Home mused philosophically. 'The best I could do for the cartoonist was my half-moon spectacles. Elizabeth [Lady Home] always said that they lost the 1964 election. So one cannot win.'[18]

What about the matchsticks? This is code for Home's lack of grounding in economics which contrasted strongly with Harold Wilson's familiarity with both the slide-rule (then an indispensable piece of technology for the numerate) and the techniques of economic management, a prowess which the Leader of the Opposition took every opportunity to flaunt. As Home told me nearly a quarter of a century after leaving No. 10, the matchstick phenomenon arose from a session with an *Observer* journalist whose speciality was long and charming but candid conversations with politicians:

'It was a purely chance remark at lunch because Kenneth Harris said to me "Do you think you could be Prime Minister?" And I said, "I really don't think so because I have to do my economics with matchsticks." But it stuck, of course ... Harold Wilson wasn't going to miss something like that [another chuckle].'[19]

This was the early autumn of 1962, three months before press speculation began to suggest that the likely constitutional legislation, stimulated by Tony Benn's desire to disclaim his Stansgate Viscountcy,[20] might enable Home to renounce his peerage and emerge as Harold Macmillan's successor – speculation which, according to Richard Thorpe, his official biographer, concentrated Home's mind.[21]

What about that political meeting in Bedford? Home suffered badly from hecklers in the 1964 election campaign. His Joint Party Chairman, Lord Blakenham, reckoned his rough handling in the Birmingham Rag Market on 8 October, a week before polling (which was beamed nationwide on television), was the moment 'that support began to slide away from us'.[22] (The Bedford speech, where the 'matchsticks' remark haunted him, was the occasion when he spoke for the sitting member in a marginal seat, Christopher Soames, with whom he intended to replace the increasingly lethargic Rab Butler[23] at the Foreign Office if the Conservatives won.)[24]

The need round the lunch table to explain to the former French intelligence officer exactly who Home had been bears witness to his limited impact overseas, as PM at least (his twin spells at the Foreign Office 1960–63 and 1970–74 by contrast built up a considerable reputation in diplomatic circles abroad). But what should he be remembered for as Prime Minister apart from being the 'amiable Lord',[25] as Clem Attlee called him, who briefly shot across the political landscape as a kind of tweedy blur?

In real life a cricketer of skill and passion, Home took over his ministerial team in highly unpromising circumstances. There was blood all over the dressing-room walls after the messy fight for the succession to Harold Macmillan. Two members of the First XI, Enoch Powell and Iain Macleod, had taken their bats home and refused to play under the new captain. The wicket was very sticky and in Harold Wilson he faced a strike bowler whose effectiveness and hostility outstripped that of any postwar Opposition leader. And since becoming the fourteenth Earl of Home when his father died in 1951, the new premier had been playing on the benign wicket of the House of Lords. Not until he won the Kinross and West

Perthshire by-election in late October 1963 and returned to the House of Commons did he realize how the intervening twenty-two years had coarsened its ways in what was already fast becoming the age of the professional politician rather than of the gentlemanly amateur. Alan Watkins has long observed that Prime Minister's Question Time began its long decline into parliamentary rough house during the twelve months when Wilson enjoyed such sport at the expense of the noble stag at bay in the person of the former earl across the dispatch box.[26]

This is not the place to reprise the mountain of detail and analysis we now have on the fight for the Conservative succession in 1963 when Macmillan, afflicted by his prostate trouble, announced his intention of shuffling finally from the stage just in time to inspire a feeding frenzy at the Party Conference in Blackpool when Home, by chance that year chairman of the National Union, was required to read out the Prime Minister's letter of intent to the party representatives assembled by the sea. But I do not think Macmillan usurped the Queen's prerogative of appointment in summing-up the party soundings in favour of Home when, having resigned from his sickbed on 18 October 1963, he offered a memorandum to Her Majesty on whom she might send for.

Some of the canvassing results produced by the Lord Chancellor, Lord Dilhorne, strike me as odd (Macleod could hardly be deemed a supporter of Home's, for example).[27] But Macmillan, having ceased to be her First Minister, was not giving the Queen formal 'Advice' with a capital 'A' which had to be acted upon; rather it was informal 'advice', with a lower case 'a', which the Queen could either have refused to hear or declined to act upon.[28] I do not believe, with Ben Pimlott, that this was 'the biggest political misjudgment of her reign'.[29] The canvas of Cabinet and party opinion authorized by Macmillan may have left a good deal to be desired, but not to have accepted his resultant advice, once given, would have been tantamount to saying her premier of six years was misleading his Monarch. And, after hearing of the meeting of possible recusants at Enoch Powell's house in South Eaton Place the night before, Macmillan suggested the Queen follow the precedent of 1852 (when Aberdeen accepted Victoria's commission to form an administration a day after it had been offered as he needed to ensure the services of Russell as Foreign Secretary if the coalition was to cohere)[30] by giving Home time to see if he could construct a Cabinet able to carry on the Queen's government.[31]

As Home well knew, and as he made plain to Reggie Maudling, Maudling, Butler and Hailsham were the key Cabinet recruits he needed. And, as Maudling put it in his memoirs: 'Alec formed an administration and as it was both the will of the Party and, on the whole, the logic of events that he should do so, the other three of us accepted his invitation to join him.'[32] It is significant, however, that Home believed that Macleod lost the Conservatives the election a year later, having penned his legendarily biting 'magic circle' account of the events of October 1963 in *The Spectator* in January 1964. (The afternoon Home ceased to be PM, Richard Thorpe recounts, 'he was seen to be pacing the drawing-room floor of Selwyn Lloyd's flat at Buckingham Gate, blaming the defeat on Macleod in language those who were present had not heard him use before'.)[33]

Home also tacitly recognized the 'never again' feeling about the 'emergence' of Tory leaders after the 'customary processes of consultation', whether fixed by an alleged 'magic circle' of Etonians and anti-Butlerites or not. After the Conservatives lost office, he set in train the review which led to what was for the Tories the novel practice of electing a leader, with the Parliamentary Conservative Party alone comprising the electoral college[34] thereby diminishing, though not removing altogether, the Monarch's personal prerogative of appointing her First Minister.[35]

Where one has to be careful in dealing even with a politician as transparently honest and honourable as Alec Home is in underestimating his ambition and his mettle. Macmillan had caught the man when he told the Queen after returning from the Nassau Conference in December 1962 that 'Alec Home is steel painted as wood.'[36] For it was about this time, as we discover from Richard Thorpe's official life, that Home, stimulated by Anthony Howard's perceptively predictive article in the *New Statesman* speculating on a Home or a Hailsham succession to Macmillan, sat down and contemplated the possibility seriously.[37] (Though it is possible to reconcile this with the sincerity of his anybody-but-me outburst to Margach in the early days of the Blackpool Conference. Part of Home, I suspect, never wanted the demands of the premiership to disrupt his contented and measured life.)

But, to this day, one can only sympathize with Rab Butler when he felt the cold steel as he prepared to lunch with Home before standing up in front of the Conservative Party Conference as acting leader to make what needed to be the speech of his life (which, of course, it wasn't)[38] only to hear, as Butler recalled later, 'that he [Home] was going to see his doctor, which I took to mean he was a possible candidate for the leadership'.[39] Home's timing was perfect. It was as if he had waited for his chief rivals to eliminate themselves – Hailsham by seeming to succumb to a combination of hucksterism and overexuberance from the moment he announced to an overheated fringe meeting at Blackpool that he was renouncing his peerage,[40] to Rab's underwhelming performance in the Winter Gardens which cannot have been helped by the very recent knowledge of the reluctant yet calculating Earl's intentions as he prepared, in effect, to sprint past his rivals to the finishing line of the Queen's commission.

For a long time I subscribed fully to the accidental premier theory. I was taken in by what I might call the Peter Thorneycroft view. Thorneycroft, rightly, I think, reckoned that in October 1963 the Tories, in choosing Home, took 'the decision to be the Conservative Party'.[41] Maudling made the same point when he wrote of the 'extraordinary affection' for Home among the rank-and-file of the party 'who regarded him as the sort of man they would like to be themselves: a good athlete; not brilliant but intelligent, a man of charm, integrity and balance'.[42]

'It's certainly true to say he had no enemies,' Lord Thorneycroft told me many years later.

'He was, therefore, the natural compromise candidate. Anybody there, if they were asked "Would it be a disaster if Alec was Prime Minister?" would answer "No. It would not be a disaster." He wasn't a runner in the real sense of the term and he wasn't taking the trouble to make various announcements or pledges . . . He was just Alec, available as the Duke of Omnium and others have always been available, as aristocrats: perfectly happy to serve his country but equally happy to hunt a pack of hounds.'[43]

There is more than a trace of Hailsham's hunting-and-holy-communion characterization of the Tory Party in Thorneycroft's assessment.

I suspect the Queen felt this way about him too. As one of her Private Secretaries, Lord Charteris, put it to Ben Pimlott, ' "Rab" wasn't her cup of tea. When she got the advice to call Alec she thought "Thank God". She loved Alec – he was an old friend. They talked about dogs and shooting together. They were both Scottish landowners, the same sort of people, like old school friends.'[44] Charteris properly went on to point out to Pimlott that the Palace fully appreciated that the constitution prevails over personal preference: 'We all understood that Alec could not form a government unless "Rab" agreed to serve, and, if not, the Queen would have had to call for "Rab".'[45]

I suppose I succumbed finally to the Thorneycroft/HM Queen view in the spring of 1989. I was waiting with my BBC producer for the taxi to take us from his Borders home, the Hirsel, back to Berwick-upon-Tweed and the London train when Lord Home, then eighty-five, drew my attention to an exquisite magnolia flowering in the Hirsel gardens for the first time in twenty-five years. The conversation went like this:

HENNESSY: You love it here don't you?
HOME: Yes.
HENNESSY: You don't like being away from here do you?
HOME: No.
HENNESSY: You never really wanted to be Prime Minister did you?
HOME: Terrible intrusion in one's private life.[46]

I suspect it was a mixture of duty and ambition that caused him to throw his coronet in the ring in 1963 and, as he once said to me, of course you want to win a general election when you've been devoting everything to it. In his last years, however, Home believed it would probably have been better if Butler had succeeded Macmillan, as to most of the public he appeared the natural heir apparent,[47] though Home gave me the impression when I talked to him in his last decade of life that he believed Butler too might well have lost the 1964 election, owing to his chronic indecision.

It is significant that, like many political observers, I have spent a good deal of time on the frantic days which led to Sir Alec Douglas-Home (as he became known on renouncing his earldom) entering No. 10 as I think he was both the nicest (equalled only by John Major) and the most surprising of the postwar incumbents. Yet the Douglas-Home premiership deserves attention for several other reasons, even though the long election campaign was already upon him when he finally kissed hands on 19 October 1963 and 'all our policies had been put into place and . . . there was nothing to do', as he put it to me in 1985.[48]

For a start there was, as it turned out, one big thing to do – to abolish retail price maintenance (RPM) when, in the face of powerful Cabinet doubts, he backed Ted Heath in his determination to introduce real competition to the nation's shelves. In doing so, a retail revolution was triggered that changed the shopping habits of the country dramatically and irreversibly. This episode was very revealing of his Cabinet Room style – brisk, decisive and consistent once his mind was made up.

Heath, that most presidential of Presidents of the Board of Trade (only Cripps and Heseltine rival him in postwar incarnations of that office), was determined that market efficiency must prevail, whatever its impact on the naturally Conservative, open-all-hours corner shop vote. And, as Home told me many years later in the hypermarket era (though himself still a stranger to the supermarket trolley, I suspect): 'I happened to think that Ted Heath was right on that occasion so I backed him.'[49] On another occasion, while reiterating the correctness of Heath's *economic* analysis, Home admitted that it 'probably cost us seats at the general election'.[50] Though the Nuffield anatomizers of the 1964 contest, David Butler and Anthony King, found RPM 'figured hardly at all at the election',[51] Home's own assessment of its impact is interesting.

Politically, of course, it was a different question and one that even Heath, at his most grocer-like, would not, I think, have raised in the run-up to a general election but for the coincidence of two private members' Bills, one on RPM itself and the other on that backdoor anti-RPM device the Green Shield Stamp (how this little sticky number brings back that particular stage in the consumer history of what Macmillan described as 'this strange people, tortured by material success and affluence' when brooding on Home's qualities as a representative of 'the old, governing class at its best').[52]

Lord Hailsham especially has been critical of Home over the abolition of RPM as 'Alec allowed it to be forced through by tiny majorities [in the House of Commons] in advance of the election without mandate and without adequate consultation, in the false belief, engendered by one Cabinet minister but against the advice of more senior colleagues, that it was an election vote-winner instead of a certain loser.'[53] It may be that Douglas-Home believed he would have lost Heath if he (Home) had listened to doubters such as Hailsham, Martin Redmayne, the Chief Whip, and Selwyn Lloyd, the Leader of the House.[54] And, with Powell and Macleod having refused to serve in October, he could not risk losing another big-hitter from his Cabinet in an election year.

A senior member of the Douglas-Home Cabinet told me that he was sure Heath had threatened to resign if the Prime Minister's backing was not forthcoming.[55] Margach claimed in 1978 to possess what had, until he revealed it in his memoir, *The Abuse of Power*, 'remained a tightly guarded secret within the "magic circle"' – that Douglas-Home 'had no option' but to back his President of the Board of Trade over RPM: 'Heath had put a pistol to his head. He threatened that if he did not get his Bill through intact he would resign from the Government.'[56] Heath's own version is softer than this, but only slightly. He told Douglas-Home on 15

April 1964 that the government could not carry on conceding points of principle to its rebellious backbenchers: 'Although I did not threaten to do so, I was close to resigning at this point, and I believe Alec and the Party recognized that.'[57]

When I put this to Home in 1989 he did not answer the question directly, though he did concede that the measure 'wasn't popular, particularly because . . . a majority of the Cabinet would rather it hadn't been pressed and certainly our majority in Parliament didn't like the Retail Price Maintenance Bill. But I happened to think it was right. And it wasn't far off an election and I thought we'd better settle it one way or the other and go for it.'[58] Lord Hailsham is certainly right, however, to contrast Home's sureness of touch on foreign affairs with his uncertainty on economic or domestic policy,[59] for all his grooming as Churchill's 'Minister for Drains' while working on the local government brief in the Scottish Office of the early 1950s.[60]

Quite apart from the Retail Price Maintenance case study, the fleeting premiership of Alec Home has other elements which repay attention from students of the top job. He could well lay claim to being, in terms of personal organization, the most effective postwar premier since Attlee at combating personal overload in the lack of fuss with which he dispatched his paperwork and his exhortations to his colleagues to curb the wordiness of their submissions. It is no coincidence that Home and Attlee were the least media-conscious of the occupants of No. 10 since 1945. For both of them cricket reports ranked above the political columns in the scale of newspaper importance and they got on very well personally.[61] Harold Wilson thought Home 'was idle'.[62] I think he was sensible and, unlike Wilson and his great contemporary, Sir Alf Ramsey the manager of the England soccer team, Alec Home did not confuse 'work-rate' with effectiveness. And in his quiet way, he was an efficient dispatcher of business (Douglas Hurd noticed his 'great gift for absorbing the essentials out of things – he only wrote four or five words often, a couple of sentences at the top in that spidery red hand, but the thing ran well').[63]

Home did not believe in overwork. He would take time out for the pleasures of the vase. He is, without question, the most famous flower-arranger in British political history and there is a charming picture of him at work on the tulips and the daffodils on the back cover of Kenneth Young's 1970 biography.[64] He was careful with food and drink and developed the interesting habit of taking his meals at London times wherever he was in the world.[65]

No. 10 was a courteous, stress-free place when the Douglas-Homes lived there, even though their hearts lay in the Hirsel rather than in the famous little backstreet off Whitehall. As his Principal Private Secretary, Sir Derek Mitchell, put it:

'He was extraordinarily kind and courteous. He had ... a sort of aristocrat's genuine ease in sizing people up, making them comfortable and generally inspiring affection. People also liked the high degree of informality. The girls in the Garden Room liked the fact that there'd be a grandchild parked outside in a pram ... And in the flat where he and Elizabeth almost camped out during the week, one saw the flowers that had been brought down from Scotland, the suitcase that lay on the floor, opened but not unpacked, ready for the lid to be closed again on Friday evening when they retired, with some obvious relief, back to the country where they liked to be.'[66]

Alec Douglas-Home really was the first thoroughbred countryman in Downing Street since Stanley Baldwin.

Yet there was a modernizer lurking beneath the hacking jacket. As he wrote in his memoirs, *The Way the Wind Blows* ('this book on fishing', as Rab Butler rather wickedly put it):[67]

I confess that I would like to have been given a bit longer at No. 10 so as to get more grip on the machinery of government.

The keys to this are: short and precise paper-work; a chain of government committees each charged to take decisions, resulting in a Cabinet agenda which is cleared of all but the absolute essentials; Ministers who can be relied upon to insist on these rules ...; and lastly a programme of legislation for Parliament which is not overloaded.[68]

He told me that had he won in 1964, he would have invited Enoch Powell to rejoin the Cabinet with a brief to reform Whitehall.[69] What a battle of the titans that would have been – two great national institutions locked in combat.

Douglas-Home showed his pruning instinct to good effect when, newly arrived as Prime Minister, he trimmed the Cabinet committees he had inherited from Macmillan, guided by Sir Burke Trend[70] (who, very privately, found the courteous and decisive Douglas-Home to be the best of the four premiers he worked with as Cabinet Secretary).[71] Very sensibly, too, Home reacted to various hints of Wilson's plans for Whitehall reform by permitting the Leader of the Opposition to discuss such matters with Permanent Secretaries ahead of the election. To this day, the arrangements under which such pre-election meetings take place are known as the 'Douglas-Home Rules' discussions[72] (though Douglas-Home did not approve of what he called Wilson's 'abracadabra' idea for creating new ministries).[73]

In terms of the folk-memory of the Home premiership, Harold Wilson was and remains the problem. As Peter Clarke puts it simply and baldly in *Hope and Glory*, his fine study of twentieth-century Britain: 'The twelve-month premiership of Sir Alec Douglas-Home in 1963–4 was dominated by Harold Wilson. No previous Leader of the Opposition, without the authority of being an ex-Prime Minister himself, had enjoyed such an ascendancy.'[74] The BBC's greatest ever satirical programme, *That Was the Week that Was* (which hurt Douglas-Home, as he admitted in his memoirs)[75] summed up the election contest as 'Dull Alec' versus 'Smart Alec'[76] with some justification. Bill Deedes, Douglas-Home's media minister, meant much the same thing in a minute written for the Conservative Party Chairman in February 1964 when he said of the Prime Minister: 'He is in reality much more comparable to Attlee than Wilson. He is not a presidential candidate but a traditional parliamentary leader.'[77]

Alec Douglas-Home just missed blocking Wilson's allegedly presidential path to No. 10 at the last moment. He lost by a whisker – the result was still in doubt on the Friday lunchtime and Derek Mitchell, his Downing Street Principal Private Secretary, as we have seen in chapter 3, had had to draw up a game plan for 'Deadlock' in the middle of the night between the polls closing and the final result becoming known.[78] But Douglas-Home's near miss, perhaps inevitably, was seen as failure and, ever since, parties have looked for alleged telegenic qualities in their leaders – no more aristocrats, skulls or half-moon glasses.

How should Alec Douglas-Home be remembered as Prime Minister? Above all for a very revealing memorandum about his personal political philosophy which he wrote over his one Christmas break as PM at the request of Sir Michael Fraser, *éminence grise* of the postwar Conservative Research Department. It was, quite simply, a paean to country values – a warning about the future but also a kind of lament for a governing culture, a political landscape already almost gone.

The memorandum was suffused, too, with Macmillan-style melancholy of great powerdom diminished: 'We have shed a terrible lot of power but it is useless to cry over spilt milk,' he wrote. Though this did not dissuade him from asserting an already delusory claim to continuing international influence ('. . . to carry weight we must be in the First XI and not only that but one of the four opening [sic] batsmen').[79]

But perhaps the passages that resonate most are the sections on old values: 'I went into politics', Douglas-Home told Fraser, 'because I felt that it was a form of public service and that as nearly a generation of politicians had been cut down in the first war those who had anything to give in the way of leadership ought to do so.'[80]

He wondered if democracy would last ('touch and go', he thought). The problem of the 'British people' was that they 'decide by instinct rather than reason'. And it was the 'industrial masses' who presented the difficulty:

People who live close to nature act by instinct reinforced by deduction. They are natural conservatives [small 'c' here] – slow thinkers but sound. They get pretty close to true values. It is the townspeople with few roots as yet who need constant leadership. It is, however, they, who have the votes which will sway the election decision.

I took on the job of Prime Minister because throughout my political career I have done what I have been asked to do when I thought it was my duty. But a large part in my decision was the feeling that only by simple straightforward talk to the industrial masses could we hope to defeat the Socialists.[81]

In *That Was the Week that Was* terms, this was almost beyond their parody of their favourite target. Yet it was an utterly authentic evocation of deep, traditional, landed Toryism. He was the most decent and (Willie Whitelaw possibly excepted) the final flowering of an admirable breed. He was like the very last of the steam locomotives which were on their twilight journeys at exactly this time. Perhaps he was a kind of human Coronation Scot. Or more likely, given his country pursuits, he was *Mallard*, pulling one last express from King's Cross to Edinburgh and sounding its distinctive whistle in a plaintive farewell as it crossed the Royal Border Bridge above the River Tweed at Berwick.

12

Centre Forward:
Harold Wilson, 1964–70

In Britain, particularly, the influence of a premier on the character, and hence the activities, of a government is pervasive.

Professor Ben Pimlott on the first two Wilson administrations,
1992[1]

The PM did most of the talking and it trod the familiar path from gimmicks to autobiography and then hot foot to the failings of statistics, this government's favourite alibi.

Sir Alec Cairncross, Chief Economic Adviser to
HM Government, May 1965[2]

'He set up MISCs at the drop of a hat. There was a MISC on this and a MISC on that.'   *Lord Houghton, Cabinet minister*
1964–68, recalling Harold Wilson's creation of Cabinet
committees during the 1960s in the early 1990s[3]

Ian says that if a dozen of the most brilliant men in the country had been charged with planning the worst possible mess they couldn't have done better. 'I can't remember a government discrediting itself so completely and quickly.'

Ian Bancroft, Principal Private Secretary to the
Chancellor of the Exchequer, to Sir Alec Cairncross, July 1966[4]

At lunch Derek Mitchell told me of George's [George Brown's] lunch with EFTA Ministers which went on far too long. D, sent to bring him back, was welcomed in with a roar, 'Derek, get me a girl!' And when the PM, looking like thunder, advances in person to collect George he exclaimed: 'Christ! I ask for a girl and what do I get but the bloody Prime Minister!'   *Cairncross Diary, 2 February 1967*[5]

Constitutional rationalists fail to recognize that Cabinets, and Prime
Ministers too, are essentially human and, being human, are essentially
different ... Some have claimed to notice significant differences
between Douglas-Home and Wilson and between Wilson (Mark I)
and Wilson (Mark II). Let the debate ... continue.

Harold Wilson, 1976[6]

Harold Wilson couldn't wait to be Prime Minister. In October 1964 he
plainly felt that, like Churchill, his life 'had been but a preparation for
this hour and for this trial'.[7] In many ways it had, though the electorate
almost deprived him of it. The poll gave him a majority of four. But the
rich accumulation of his prior experience – superb performer in the Oxford
Schools, bright young research assistant to William Beveridge, sparkling
temporary civil servant in wartime Whitehall, Cabinet minister in an
important economic department at the age of thirty-one, seemingly prin-
cipled resignation with Nye Bevan not quite four years later; Shadow
Chancellor, Shadow Foreign Secretary and Chairman of the Public
Accounts Committee in Opposition[8] – all this meant that no one was
better prepared on paper for No. 10 than Harold Wilson.

His brief spell as Opposition leader between Hugh Gaitskell's death
and Alec Douglas-Home's loss of office was verging on the brilliant. Quite
simply, he made the political running.[9] He was literate, numerate, witty
and possessed of what we would now call a 'big idea' – that through
planning and by the harnessing of science and technology for national
purposes, the remaking of Britain[10] was possible provided the transformation was overseen by people 'with fire in their belly and humanity in their
hearts', as he told a Labour Rally at the Empire Pool, Wembley at the
start of the 1964 election campaign.[11]

In those first hundred days of dynamic action, which, Kennedy-style,
he promised the electorate,[12] he behaved accordingly, even though he had
underestimated quite what a 'trial' his inheritance would prove, on the
balance of payments front especially.[13] The documents we can now inspect
at the Public Record Office still rustle with that special mood in an
extraordinarily evocative way.

The sheer relish at being what seemed both to him and to many political
correspondents in the Westminster Lobby (with whom he was then
enjoying a honeymoon)[14] a polymath premier is very plain with a run of
dinners and suppers for technologists, exporters and vice-chancellors at
which he could display his intellectual and technocratic prowess.[15] He

prided himself on being 'house-trained'[16] (someone who 'knew how it worked from the inside', as he once put it to me)[17] in his dealings with the Civil Service and he was disdainful of those ministers who were not.[18]

In those early days of his premiership he was a genuinely shining figure. The dazzle of his political lustre was extraordinary from the first weeks of his party leadership following Gaitskell's death in January 1963 to the desperate weeks of July 1966 when the unsentimental reality of the money markets, quite unmoved by the ninety-seven-seat majority he had accumulated less than four months earlier and surprisingly unimpressed by his determination to withstand a seamen's strike in the weeks between, forced him into what was meant to be a substantial deflation and a virtual abandonment of the big idea of growth-through-planning. The tarnish which resulted never left him or his reputation. Despite the best efforts of his biographer Ben Pimlott, it still has not.

This is a moment for a declaration of interest. As a young man I was one of those who forsook the traditional Toryism of his home and household largely, though not wholly, because of the promise the early Wilson embodied. The fire-in-the-belly and compassion-in-the-heart side of him enhanced by the technocratic overlay at which he also excelled convinced me and many others in my generation ('Harold's children', David Marquand would call us a generation later)[19] that competence and decency were not incompatibles in government. Wilson seemed to refute the instinctive suspicion of a substantial portion of the British electorate which, as characterized by that influential servant of postwar Conservatism, Michael Fraser, argued that Tories had hard heads but hard hearts while Labour had soft heads and soft hearts.[20]

I was taken in by this and, once taken out, became a lifelong sceptic (though not a cynic, which is a very different condition) about those who aspire to political power and the use to which they put it once they have acquired it. As a result I have never since been susceptible to the apparent promise of new political dawns, whether they be Margaret Thatcher's in May 1979 or Tony Blair's in May 1997. This inability to fall in love politically ever again can spill over into a professional deformation in a contemporary historian and must be acknowledged by an author deformed thereby. In my case, though, I never ceased to warm to Wilson's absolutely genuine generosity of spirit (except when it took the form of recommending certain unsuitable people to the Queen for an honour).

Casting such personal considerations aside, what is one to make of the Wilson style during his first two governments of 1964–66 and 1966–70? To some extent all occupants of No. 10 have to be variable-geometry premiers, altering their operational patterns to suit particular circumstances, but Wilson was so to an unusual degree, which makes him especially difficult to place on the command-collegial spectrum in phase one, his self-styled 'centre-forward' period when, owing to the relative inexperience of his ministerial colleagues, he had had to try and score all the goals himself.[21]

As a political leader who put party unity on a very high pedestal (it was, perhaps, the single consistent aspect of his thirteen years as Labour leader), Wilson had a penchant for letting the Cabinet ramble, encouraging all who wished to speak, doodling as they did so (Ted Short, his Chief Whip, called it the 'doodling Cabinet')[22] and interjecting a little commentary when they finished before catching the eye of the next contributor. Despite his obeisance to the memory and style of Attlee, Wilson used prolixity as a weapon, allowing the Cabinet to talk itself out.

This would infuriate the likes of Barbara Castle, no mean wordspinner herself, who recalled in her diary for 1 March 1965 that the Cabinet had spent 'three-quarters of an hour discussing the creation of new premises at Chelsea for the National Army Museum'. 'I doodled through the endless discussion,' she wrote. 'Crosland complained to me "There are twenty Ministers debating this. If only there had been as much heat generated by Vietnam." I retorted acidly, "The Parkinson's Law of words operated in this Cabinet. Words expand to fill the time available for them." '[23]

Yet the most critical of strategic decisions would often be effectively removed from the purview of the full Cabinet. The very first and most crucial decision, not to devalue the pound, was taken by the economic triumvirate of Wilson, his First Secretary of State and Minister for Economic Affairs, George Brown, and Chancellor of the Exchequer Jim Callaghan *before* the first meeting of the Economic Affairs ad hoc Cabinet Committee, MISC 1, began its formal opening discussion on the morning of Saturday 17 October 1964. 'We three have decided that the exchange rate should stay where it is,' he told the gathering of other ministers and officials once the committee had assembled.[24]

Thereafter, until the rate finally went three years and one month later, the Wilson governments were locked in a titanic and near continuous struggle to reconcile the three incompatible aims of economic growth, a balance of payments surplus and a currency worth $2.80 to the pound. Every member of the full Cabinet, effectively unconsulted on 'The Unmentionable',[25] as Whitehall came to dub devaluation, until the crisis of July 1966 forced the issue on to its agenda, had to live with the political and financial consequences of that decision taken by the inner trio during the first hours of the first Wilson administration.

A second strategic issue of considerable magnitude was the decision to carry on constructing the Polaris nuclear force despite a manifesto pledge to renegotiate the Nassau Agreement concluded between Macmillan and Kennedy in 1962[26] and frequent claims from Wilson during the election period that 'it will not be independent and it will not be British and it will not deter'.[27] (He knew full well, as he told Dick Neustadt privately, that he had little to lose by this stance as he could not compete with Douglas-Home for the 'jingo vote').[28]

There is good reason to believe from conversations which Peter Thorneycroft, Douglas-Home's Defence Secretary, had with Denis Healey, his Labour shadow on a Privy Counsellor basis early in 1964, that Wilson always intended to keep Polaris going under the cover of pooling it with the Americans inside a NATO Atlantic force[29] (Home once told me privately that he always believed the patriotic Wilson would keep it).[30] Yet the skill with which he steered it through his Cabinet system was early, but classic Wilson.

Polaris went first to the smallest ever Cabinet committee on nuclear weapons policy, MISC 16, which consisted of Wilson, Defence Secretary Denis Healey and the Foreign Secretary, Patrick Gordon Walker. It met on 11 November 1964 and decided to proceed with the construction of at least three Polaris submarines which 'would represent the minimum force which would be acceptable to us in the event of the dissolution of the NATO Alliance'.[31] Wilson then took the missiles question to a larger group of himself and ten other ministers, MISC 17, which gathered at Chequers on 22 November 1964 to ponder the continuation of Polaris within the context of wider defence discussions.[32]

The full Cabinet convened on 26 November 1964 to discuss the minimum number of boats needed to sustain the Polaris force.[33] Finally, the standing Defence and Overseas Policy Committee of the Cabinet met on 29 January 1965 to decide that it would be four submarines.[34] Wilson, like Ernie Bevin, was determined, it seemed, that there should be 'a bloody Union Jack' on it (as Bevin put it)[35] partly, as Wilson explained to me twenty years later, because it gave him a window into US nuclear thinking and because 'we might need to restrain the Americans',[36] (which, despite the fact that by the time he spoke to me he was already suffering the mental effects of his last illness, Wilson plainly thought that possession of the bomb had somehow put him in a position to do).

All of this, I suspect, was so much camouflage for the understandable reluctance of any British premier, as one nuclear insider from the Wilson years put it, to risk history judging him to be the one who left the United Kingdom without its ultimate weapon should a nuclear-free home base ever find itself threatened subsequently by a nuclear-tipped and menacing nation.[37] And yet, there was something to Wilson's seeming hubris. As another defence official put it to me shortly after Mrs Thatcher's first administration had decided to replace Polaris with Trident: 'The key to this is for us to possess a small amount of the latest American kit. If it comes to it, the Russian radars won't be able to tell if the Trident missile which emerges from the sea off Norway has a Stars and Stripes or the White Ensign [of the Royal Navy] on it. All they'll know is that it's a Trident and that it's coming at them. . . . This is one of the ways we keep the United States locked into the defence of Europe,'[38] he explained. Wilson could well have received this kind of analysis with his initial nuclear briefing in 1964.

Intriguingly, this precise point was made by Lord Rothschild nearly four years later in a minority report attached to an inquiry into the future of the British deterrent by a committee of outside assessors under the chairmanship of Lord Kings Norton.[39] 'The Committee', Rothschild wrote, 'has been told that Polaris or Polaris-type missiles do not have Union Jacks or Stars and Stripes on them. How, then, would Russia react if such a missile were fired by the USA, for example, at Moscow? *Inter alia* she might well take retaliatory action against the United Kingdom . . .'[40]

By this stage Wilson had convened a special Cabinet committee on nuclear weapons policy (when created in September 1966 it was initially five-strong – himself; George Brown, by this stage Foreign Secretary; Denis Healey, Defence Secretary; Michael Stewart, First Secretary; and Tony Benn, Minister of Technology).[41] Known as PN, its remit included a consideration of 'hardening' the UK-manufactured warheads atop the Polaris missiles to increase their chances of penetrating the anti-ballistic missile screen the Russians were thought to be constructing around Moscow. During the Heath years, these early plans were converted into the 'Chevaline' improvement to the Royal Navy's Polaris arsenal.[42]

As we have seen in chapter 6, the nuclear and intelligence aspects of the job are both highly prime ministerial and intensely secret. Wilson, unlike Tony Blair (who had lunched with both the Director General of MI5 and 'C', the Chief of the Secret Intelligence Service while still Leader of the Opposition)[43] was ignorant of both the practices and the personnel of the clandestine agencies until he actually became Prime Minister. In July 1963, the Philby case had come to public attention once more (the former MI6 officer defected from Beirut to the Soviet Union earlier in the year) and Macmillan summoned Wilson for a briefing on a Privy Counsellor basis 'to explain how the so-called "Security" services really work . . . and he took it quite well'. To Macmillan's surprise, I suspect, Wilson 'had never heard of C', as Macmillan put it in his diary.[44]

In the early days of his premiership, Wilson was briefed by the Cabinet Secretary, Sir Burke Trend, on how the Joint Intelligence Committee worked.[45] Wilson's interest in the secret world was not as obsessive during his first two premierships as it was to become during his last. He showed a 'variation of interest', as one of his Private Secretaries, Michael Palliser put it, in the JIC's 'Red Book', the weekly survey of intelligence, when Palliser was canvassed in October 1966 by the JIC to see whether Wilson was a satisfied customer of its assessments.[46]

Palliser replied: 'I do not always show them to the Prime Minister, sometimes because for one reason or another the situation they are dealing with is not of concern to him at that point . . . To be blunt, some weeks it [the "Red Book"] seems extremely long and boring; on other occasions there are several items which I find well worth showing to the Prime Minster, and as you may have noticed he often sparks on them and throws up comments which produce useful further information for me.'[47] As his premiership lengthened, Wilson seems to have taken a deeper interest in the JIC's product. For example, in August 1968, Palliser bundled together for what he called the PM's 'holiday reading' special JIC assessments of Soviet interests in Middle Eastern oil and Russia's intentions in the Mediterranean.[48]

On the nuclear side, the launch system changed in 1969 during Wilson's second premiership as the main deterrent role shifted from the V bombers of the Royal Air Force to the Royal Navy's Polaris submarines. With the change, the launch facility at the disposal of the PM moved from the Air Force Operations Room in the Ministry of Defence to No. 10 itself. It took the form of a link to the bunker of the Commander-in-Chief, Home Fleet deep under Northwood in Middlesex to enable Wilson and his successors, during a 'period of tension' to 'remain in direct touch with the firing headquarters and . . . [if necessary, to] . . . give political authority for release'. Elaborate arrangements were put in place to ensure that only the Prime Minister, or his two designated deputies (it is not known when or why PMs were advised to nominate more than one deputy), could authorize the launch of Polaris missiles and the installation of a television link between No. 10 and Northwood was designed to prevent anyone impersonating Wilson.[49]

Wilson's political magic, of course, depended scarcely at all on what did or did not transpire in MISC 16, MISC 17 or his PN Committee or in the deeply concealed world of British intelligence. It rested on two separate yet interrelated apparent supremacies – his mastery of immediate, tactical politics as he continued to make what Churchill described as the political 'weather'[50] in both the House of Commons and the country; and the long-term promise of an economic and industrial transformation forging a 'New Britain' tempered in the furnace of what Wilson had pledged (in one of the most memorable Party Conference speeches of the postwar years at Scarborough in 1963) would be the 'white heat' of a technological revolution.[51]

This was the centrepiece of the 1964 election manifesto[52] and here was the terrain on which Wilson and his party would be judged. Should their economic and technological competence prove a sham, it would be Wilson's reputation and Labour's electoral fortunes that would melt in the fabled furnace he fuelled in the autumn of 1963. For Wilson's competitive advantage in political terms rested on his proclaimed or imagined prowess as a manager of the economy who would succeed where past Conservative premiers had failed. Part of this transformation would be achieved by converting No. 10 from 'a failed monastery' into 'a powerhouse',[53] by bringing a 'purposive' (a favourite 1963–64 word, as befitted the author of *Purpose in Politics*)[54] style of policy-making to the Cabinet Room.

The Wilson effect would not stop there. The technological revolution would be furthered by refashioning Whitehall into an instrument for stimulating economic growth based on applied science (a new Department of Economic Affairs buttressed by a new Ministry of Technology), all staffed by a new breed of gritty, better-trained production- and management-minded officials that could rise in a Civil Service open to all the talents, which would be created once his wartime Whitehall chum, Lord Fulton, had finished his inquiry into the personnel and management practices of the central state.[55]

A premier's intrinsic mettle as a modernizer can be swiftly tested without having to wait for the longer-term inquiries or changes they set in train after acquiring power. As we have seen, No. 10 is, to some extent, a piece of clay susceptible to a quick burst of prime ministerial remodelling. PMs can interfere smartly, too, with the constitutional DNA of the wider system of central government when the Cabinet Secretary presents them with a copy of *Questions of Procedure for Ministers* to tweak, amend or approve. 'As the new ministers were almost all without Cabinet experience,' Wilson recalled in *The Governance of Britain*, 'it was a good time for reform.'[56]

Amy Baker has noted that *QPM* 'was of particular importance to the new and largely inexperienced Cabinet team'.[57] Trend presented Wilson with a draft on his first day as PM under a covering note of considerable significance which rather belied his remark, deep in retirement, that the document was a thing of 'tips for beginners – a book of etiquette'.[58] For Wilson, Trend located *QPM* in a definitely higher order which showed how much it had grown in the constitutional firmament since Attlee's early editions. Now, in the Cabinet Office's view, it was a document which transcended personalities, parties and administrations.

Trend, as we shall see later when we examine the D-notice affair of 1967, was an official who saw his duty as being the servant of the Cabinet, not just of the Prime Minister. *QPM*, he told Wilson on day one, was 'an entirely non-party document, which codifies the general principles of ministerial conduct as they have evolved over many years'. Trend explained that 'it has the authority of a good many Prime Ministers, of different party complexions; and it is revised, in the light of changes in practice, at regular intervals'.[59]

Wilson approved Trend's draft (little altered from the Macmillan/Douglas-Home version apart from a new section covering the travelling expenses of ministerial wives) and added a requirement that if a department's estimate of the cost of a proposal differed from that of the Treasury, both were to be cited in the paper which went to the Cabinet.[60] In the version of *QPM* Wilson circulated after the 1966 general election, his fixation about controlling his colleagues' relationships with the press led to a provision that henceforth all ministerial speeches and broadcasts were to be cleared with No. 10 in advance and that future plans were also to be cleared with Downing Street 'in order to co-ordinate the presentation of the Government's policies'.[61]

What the press did pick up, however, was the existence of a group of political familiars around the Prime Minister quite separate from his Cabinet colleagues or his No. 10 or Cabinet Office advisers which has echoed through history as his 'Kitchen Cabinet'. Very close to the top of Wilson's list of journalist pet hates was Nora Beloff of the *Observer* who, as Wilson's official biographer, Philip Ziegler, put it, 'outraged the Prime

Minister by speculating in her column about the political role of the Kitchen Cabinet and in particular of Marcia Williams',[62] who moved from being his longstanding secretary in Opposition to a position of controversial influence as his Personal and Political Secretary virtually as soon as she was established in the converted waiting room at the far end of the Cabinet Room which became her office.[63]

Throughout all his years as Prime Minister, the gregarious Wilson liked a group of cheerful, gossipy intimates whose company late at night he could enjoy and with whom he could mix tittle-tattle and policy. The 'Kitchen Cabinet', however, is very much a phrase associated with his first years in Downing Street and a floating population which fluctuated around the person of Mrs Williams. Perhaps the one factor which linked them apart from their congeniality to Wilson was their position towards the centre left of the Labour Party (this was certainly true of Peter Shore, Thomas Balogh, Dick Crossman, Judith Hart, Barbara Castle, Tony Benn and Gerald Kaufman). This was part, as one insider put it to Ben Pimlott, of Marcia Williams 'keeping the link back to the Left' for her boss.[64] But apart from acting as a collective keeper of Wilson's 1950s leftish conscience, it is hard to winnow out any policies where, as a group (their individual influence as ministers or advisers is another matter) they exerted a decisive influence on policy outcomes (though there was a strong anti-Common Market flavour about them).

As Pimlott puts it: 'Within this group, whose composition was shifting, there was one fixture and undisputed *chef de cuisine* mistress according to the best private evidence available,'[65] Marcia Williams.[66] Throughout her decades-long relationship with Wilson (which did not, despite constant innuendo from his opponents to the contrary, involve her becoming his mistress), Marcia Williams (or Lady Falkender as she became) expressed her views to him with a candour and a directness that took the breath away of those who witnessed it (and often appeared to frighten Wilson),[67] not least when it tipped into what they regarded as a tantrum. She suffered as strong-minded women in politics often do from being deemed shrewish and shrill in a way that does not afflict comparably insistent men. And, swiftly, the friction inside the Prime Minister's household (widely defined) that this engendered, became the talk of Whitehall.

As so often with wider tensions, the gossip centred on an example of the problem expressed in a particular head-to-head way. And in the Principal Private Secretary awaiting both her and Wilson, Derek Mitchell,

Mrs Williams found the kind of elegant, sardonic, Treasury-groomed figure who, if so minded, she could convert into the incarnation of Civil Service (and probably Tory-tinged) superiority that would inflame her every prejudice. Mitchell's wit is not to everyone's taste (though it is to mine) and elegance of manner does not in any way guarantee private Tory opinions. But the Mitchell–Williams clashes soon began to enliven that most efficient and fastidious membrane – the Whitehall net. (An early example was the story of Mitchell telling Mrs Williams that she could indeed travel to Washington at public expense when Wilson visited President Johnson provided she went as Mrs Wilson's maid; 'the trouble with Marcia and Derek', said a close observer of their relationship, 'is that they are both feline'.)[68]

The difficulty of their early relationship is captured in Mitchell's note of a conversation he had with Mrs Williams during the first weeks of their attempts to work together. In what was plainly intended to be an air-clearing session on the afternoon of 6 November 1964, Mitchell noted that he 'called on Mrs Williams in her room at No. 10. I asked how things were going. She replied by saying that she gathered I had complained to the Prime Minister that she was not doing any work. I explained that what I had said to the Prime Minister was that if we were to help her settle down at No. 10 we would have to make sure that she had enough work to do; which was rather different.'[69]

Mitchell's note suggests he used this unpromising start as 'an opening to say that what was needed if we were jointly to give the Prime Minister the kind of service he wanted was the kind of mutual trust and sharing of information that would ensure that the things which concerned the Prime Minister did not fall between two stools'.[70] Mitchell sought her help in sorting out the truth of a rumour spreading round Downing Street that one of the 'Garden Girls' had made offensive remarks about the new PM to the secretary of a Conservative MP:

Mrs Williams then said that what was intolerable was that anyone in No. 10 should be speaking to a Conservative MP's secretary. But it was obvious where the political leanings of the No. 10 staff were and this was something that would have to be dealt with. It explained why Mrs Williams and her colleagues had been treated so frostily from the outset. It was in line also with the fact that the civil service as a whole were doing all they could to obstruct the Labour Government. Pressed to explain this Mrs Williams said she was hearing the same story from all over Whitehall.[71]

Mitchell repudiated these claims

particularly as they affected my own staff. Taking no notice but continuing in a strained and even fanatical way, Mrs Williams said that the only solution would be to 'purge' No. 10 and so make sure that only people sympathetic to the Government worked there; nothing else would do.[72]

Mitchell countered by explaining the position of career officials working in Downing Street:

of course there had been personal loyalty to Sir Alec Douglas-Home. It was not so skin deep that it would be thrown off in an hour but in very little longer than that the staff of No. 10 had moved smoothly into loyal and unquestioning support of Mr Wilson. Their personal politics were beside the point . . . What was important was that we were permanent civil servants with a duty to the present Government. That applied to virtually every one in No. 10.[73]

Mrs Williams, according to Mitchell's record, seemed surprised by this – thinking that most of the staff were temporary. Mitchell's note concluded that '. . . Mrs Williams continued to speak of a purge as something that was urgently necessary. As it was clear that she did not understand the practical difficulties of conducting one, let alone the fundamental objections of principle, I thought it prudent to bring the conversation to an end.'[74]

The No. 10 terrain – where the political meets the administrative all the time – is especially perilous and needs delicate touches all round if it is to be traversed easily and routinely. If such a condition is not present, re-eruption of tension in different forms is a constant possibility. Over six months after that afternoon spat in No. 10, Mitchell had the difficult task of implementing Wilson's instruction that Mrs Williams should see 'all' Cabinet papers flowing to him.[75]

Treading on eggs, Mitchell minuted the Prime Minister on 28 June 1965:

You said that you would like Marcia to see in future all the Cabinet and Cabinet Committee papers which you now see. I looked through the particular ones in the [current] folder and have found that they include two J.I.C. Papers, one Top Secret and one Secret. I imagine that you did not want the arrangement to extend to these or others like them [i.e., those 'with a defence or foreign policy flavour]'.[76]

Wilson scribbled on Mitchell's minute: 'I did not mean her to see Defence (inc JIC) Foreign – or Cabinet conclusions'.[77] The machine won that one.

A note sent under an indecipherable set of initials to the No. 10 paper-keepers on 30 June 1965 told them: 'As you know Mrs Williams is to be shown Cabinet Papers but only certain ones + I attach a list of these. Ordinary C [i.e., standing committee] + Misc [ad hoc committee] papers can be sent to her provided they only cover Home Affairs or any other innocuous subjects. She is not to see anything Top Secret or relating to Defence or Foreign Policy. Neither is she to see all Cabinet Conclusions. If in doubt please refer to Mr Mitchell . . . I fear that a note must be kept of the papers she takes away + they must be checked back.'[78] One gets the feeling that somebody took considerable pleasure in writing those instructions.

Marcia Williams did not get her 'purge' either, though shortly before the 1966 election Wilson was able to move Mitchell to the Department of Economic Affairs after the standard two-year spell of the Principal Private Secretaryship. As Philip Ziegler put it, Mitchell's departure meant a great deal to Wilson 'if only because it promised to end the turmoil which the battles between Marcia Williams and Derek Mitchell had caused in Downing Street'.[79] This time Wilson wanted to appoint Michael Halls, who had served him at the Board of Trade in the 1940s and with whom both he and probably Mrs Williams would find it easy to work.

Senior figures in Whitehall felt that Halls was not up to the job.[80] It fell to Sir Lawrence Helsby, the Head of the Home Civil Service, to tell Wilson that such an appointment would be an improper use of prime ministerial patronage.[81] Helsby asked Wilson to see five other candidates. Wilson saw them, but stuck to Halls and wrote Helsby a minute revealing his own political partisanship, his chippiness towards the mandarinate and the fact that he shared at least some of Mrs Williams's suspicions about Tories in No. 10:

If I am told that this is a question of patronage and challenged to choose between Prime Ministerial patronage and patronage exercised by a small, self-perpetuating oligarchy of Permanent Secretaries, I have no alternative but to say that patronage, if patronage it be, must be exercised by me.

I certainly cannot accept the implied suggestion that such an appointment would imply a deterioration of standards since the arrival of the present administration. I do not know whether the system you extol was responsible, or whether there was at work a system not merely of Prime Ministerial patronage, but Prime Ministerial *Political* patronage, but the fact remains that of four secretaries in post up to October 1963, the two most senior are now on the list for adoption as candidates in safe Conservative seats [presumably Wilson, rightly or wrongly, had Bligh and de Zulueta in mind], a third [Wyndham?] recruited direct from Central Office, now takes the Conservative Whip in the Upper House. My suggested appointment had no political implications. I have not the slightest idea of the political views, if any, of the five I saw.[82]

Wilson would not accept Helbsy's point either about Halls's intellectual calibre. Fitting in was more important:

. . . I do not regard the appointment as patronage, reward for past services, or as a promise for the future, still less as an intellectual accolade comparable to a Fellowship of All Souls. I regard it as the means of ensuring that my office will work . . . as efficiently, smoothly and agreeably as possible. What I want is a Private Secretary, not either a Presidential Assistant nor a Permanent Secretary, actual or in embryo. No. 10 is an office, not a Government Department; it is also a small and necessarily intimate community – it is also a home.[83]

Sadly, as Ziegler noted, 'Helsby was right and Wilson was wrong. Halls was not big enough for the job. He struggled with the work, read papers slowly, was befuddled by complex issues, overworked ferociously, became tired, fretful and demoralized, grew jealous of colleagues who picked up parts of the burden he could not bear himself. A kind and generous man, for whom Wilson had good reason to feel affection, he was made to feel inferior, cracked under the stress, and died, after a heart attack, early in 1970.'[84]

Wilson's minute to Helsby is immensely revealing of the degree to which his use of the No. 10 machine was personal and familial in a genuinely homely way. Marcia Williams was central to that household as treated in the round, just as the Private Office of civil servants was crucial to No. 10's links with the whole official machine beyond. Derek Mitchell himself came to realize this. As he told me many years later when interviewed for the BBC Radio 4 obituary of Harold Wilson: 'He needed desperately to be able to rely on the loyalty of one or two people and Marcia was pre-eminently the one whose loyalty was never in question in any way whatsoever. He told me on one occasion that he knew she was difficult, but the fact was when he was no longer Prime Minister she was the one who would still be there, backing him and helping him.'[85] The 'Kitchen Cabinet' must, I think, be largely treated in the household context, too, for all its importance in helping Wilson keep his feel for the Labour Party. It was more a gathering of politically sympathetic friends – aglow with the warm heat of drink rather than the white heat of ruthless modernity.

Harold Wilson was the kind of premier who needed the company and consolation of personal and political friends in good times and bad. The value of such a grouping was especially acute when troubles arrived in battalions – especially the long-term intractables. These included the Rhodesian rebellion, which absorbed much time and energy from the first days in October 1964, especially so after the unilateral declaration of independence in November 1965 right through to 1970; Northern Ireland from Easter 1966 but ever more intensely from 1968; the protracted economic and currency crises, and the collapse of public support as evidenced in opinion polls and a run of dreadful by-election results from 1967.

Another important and personal distraction which afflicted Wilson from the first days of government until George Brown (not an intimate or a 'kitchen cabineteer') finally left the real Cabinet in March 1968, was the quixotic and erratic behaviour of his number 2, whose political gifts never outweighed the problems which arose from a volatile and often drink-inflamed temperament which, to this day, has left Brown holding the record for the greatest number of threatened resignations on the Labour side (seventeen by some reckonings), probably surpassed (though a precise tally is difficult to compile) on the Conservative side only by 'Sarum', the Marquess of Salisbury, in the postwar period.

The arrival of the 1967 papers at the PRO saw the release of Brown's personal minutes to Wilson dispatched during his DEA years. The most vividly expressed of the 'resignation' exchanges dates from the reshuffle of December 1965 which saw the ineffective Tom Fraser (a friend and ally of Brown's) removed from the Ministry of Transport to the backbenches to make way for Barbara Castle (who was neither a chum nor a political soulmate of the First Secretary's).

It runs as follows:

PRIME MINISTER

I learned tonight from my wife in her kitchen of the changes you have made in what is supposed to be our Government.

There is a theory that I am your deputy – a theory which you use to the utmost when it is a matter of an oil embargo and you are in Washington and I am in London.

This clearly does not apply when you are in London and arranging the affairs of our colleagues and friends.

I know I have threatened several times before to go, but this I think is a very important moment. I am quite prepared to tell the Party that this is the way you run the show; that I am not consulted about what in practice really happens; and that you obviously do not want a deputy in a presidential form of government.

I simply am not prepared to be a Hubert Humphrey [US Vice President at the time]. I understand that Tom Fraser has said he is going to the backbenches: I am going with him.[86]

Wearily Wilson replied the same night that as Brown had not been able to make the Cabinet committee meeting on time at 5.00 that evening, when he intended to brief him on the changes, his tight time-table (needed to avoid leaks) for informing first the Queen and then the lobby correspondents had prevented them from having a discussion. Fraser had been offered a non-Cabinet job but had asked instead 'to be released'. 'It was not my responsibility, and I fully recognize that it was not yours, that we did not meet at 5.00 p.m. as had been arranged. In these circum-stances I do not propose to take action on the last paragraph of your minute.'[87]

But perhaps the most extraordinary of the resignation near-misses in procedural terms turned up in Wilson's files rather than Brown's. In December 1967 Wilson took a Christmas holiday in Australia, leaving Brown (by this time Foreign Secretary) as acting Prime Minister. Brown was in a state over the sale of arms to South Africa (the Cabinet was split over this at a time when, just after devaluation, the need for exports was paramount). Wilson plainly feared not that Brown would resign outright, but that he might be involved in the 'release of secret documents' dealing with the issue in breach of both the Official Secrets Act and the Privy Counsellors' Oath of Confidentiality.

Wilson was so alarmed by this possibility that he asked Michael Stewart, as First Secretary of State and 'number 3 in the Cabinet', 'to take any action in my name you consider right' if Brown behaved in any way 'which would make it impossible for him to be in control of the Government in my absence'. 'A copy of this minute', Wilson concluded, 'is being lodged with the Secretary of the Cabinet, and I am authorising him in circumstances he deems appropriate to show it to the Leader of the House and the Chief Whip.'[88]

On this occasion Brown behaved, though he lasted less than another four months in the government. Brown, his defeated rival and candidate of the Labour right in the race to succeed Gaitskell in 1963, had been essential to Wilson's effort to present the appearance of a united party leadership to the electorate in 1964 and 1966. By the end of 1967 he had turned into a tiresome liability. The tension between Wilson and Brown tended to tug around the question of Wilson's approach to economic policy and his style of government; it was over the handling of yet another sterling-related crisis in the spring of 1968 that they finally parted. And it was from Wilson's economic vicissitudes that the great personal, political and Cabinet crises of his premierships developed – the July measures of 1966, the devaluation of November 1967, the battles over cuts and defence policy in 1968 and the fierce divide within the Labour movement over trade union reform (which Wilson had come to regard as crucial to improved economic performance) during the *In Place of Strife* spring and summer of 1969 which could have cost him his job.

Had he fallen in June 1969, Wilson would have been seen, like Eden before him and Callaghan after him, as a Prime Minister broken by failure in his special area of personal expertise. Not for nothing did he tell Dick Crossman when, in September 1967, a few weeks before devaluation, he took personal control of the government's economic policy (with Peter Shore at the Department of Economic Affairs as his agent): 'If I can't run the economy well from the DEA I'm no good. I was trained for this job and now I've taken the powers to run the economy.'[89] This hubristic extension of the premiership left the country's top economic civil servant, Sir William Armstrong, with the impression that Wilson 'meant to re-organise British industry single handed'.[90]

Wilson had decided at a meeting with civil servants (no ministers were present) at Chequers on 27 August 1967 'to take over responsibility for the Department of Economic Affairs'. Peter Shore would replace Michael Stewart who 'would continue to be First Secretary and would become responsible for co-ordination in the field of home affairs and social services which might include housing and education'.[91] (Wilson had a penchant for vague 'overlordships', as we shall see.) Three days later, Peter Shore rang Wilson 'for guidance on the role of the Prime Minister and himself'. It was Wilson at his most Walter Mittyish, with traces of Churchilliana intruding. 'Defence in wartime', Wilson told Shore, 'was the best precedent for a Prime Minister assuming strategic control of a department, assisted by a Secretary of State.'[92]

The wider question, of course, is whether the UK economy *could* be planned in the economic conditions of the mid-1960s which, as Eric Roll, first Permanent Secretary of the new DEA, has acknowledged were substantially different from those which prevailed in France in the 1940s when the Commissariat du Plan,[93] very much the model for both the Macmillan and Wilson experiments with indicative planning (i.e., setting targets for growth), had begun to operate after World War II. Lord Roll also stressed the structural and philosophical differences between the two countries' approaches to government and political economy as well as the types of Civil Service they possessed. Wilson had seen from the inside a British planning past that had worked in the shape of the thoroughly mobilized wartime UK of 1940-45. Equally he had also seen a postwar attempt at planning under Attlee which, despite the considerable apparatus of a Central Economic Planning Staff, an Economic Planning Board and a myriad of ministerial and official Cabinet committees, had not produced either analytical or instrumental transformations, let alone serious beneficial improvements to the real economy.

Wilson placed great faith in boosting the productive capacity of the UK economy as both a corrector of the balance of payments problem *and* as the alternative to devaluing the currency. Surprisingly, like Churchill, Eden, Macmillan and Douglas-Home, Wilson did not at first chair his government's main standing Cabinet committee on economic matters. Between 1964 and 1966, the Cabinet's Economic Development Committee, ED, was chaired by Brown rather than Callaghan (the Conservative premiers between 1951 and 1964 had invariably placed their Chancellors in the chair of the Economic Policy Committee).[94]

The Prime Minister, however, did chair, as we have seen, the ad hoc group on Economic Affairs, MISC 1 (which attempted to keep a focus on the bigger picture while handling crises as they arose; it also took a look at the still embryonic National Plan in February 1965).[95] But the degree to which Wilson was generally *un*involved in the preparation of the National Plan, the flagship of the enterprise if not quite the catechism for the 'New Britain', was one of the surprises when the papers for 1964, and especially, 1965, reached the Public Record Office.

The 1965 documents show Wilson persisting with unamended wishful thinking within the confines of the spatchcocked National Plan despite advice from such economically literate Cabinet ministers as Tony Crosland,[96] officials such as the Cabinet Secretary, Sir Burke Trend (who reminded him of the problems associated with targets published in the *Economic Surveys* of the late 1940s),[97] and government economists such as Dudley Seers, that the Plan's essential premise – 4 per cent annual growth over a quarter of a century – not to mention its export targets, were wildly optimistic. And that a country burdened by a sluggish economy, required to deflate at the first whiff of pressure on its currency and without any real apparatus for converting 'parochial' wish-lists masquerading as plans into economic, industrial and social reality could not expect a serious and sustained improvement in economic performance to flow from such an exercise.[98]

None of this measured, argued and well-founded criticism deflected Wilson from authorizing the publication of the National Plan in September 1965 or from making it the showpiece of a triumphalist party conference later that month. (This saw a classic brio Wilsonian performance full of absurd juxtapositions – 'We are more interested in the monthly trade returns than in Debrett, more preoccupied with what is said by the industrial correspondents and economic editors than what is said by William Hickey; more concerned with modernizing the machinery of government and the action that will need to follow the report of the Estimates Committee [on the Civil Service, which led to Fulton][99] than in altering the layout of Burke's Landed Gentry.')[100]

For Douglas Croham, who as Douglas Allen was a leading Whitehall player in the DEA during its early days and later became its permanent secretary, the attempt by ministers to pick a growth rate substantially higher than the 2½ to 3 per cent usually achieved by the UK economy without understanding what underlay such levels of performance was 'farcical'. He came to believe that attempts to raise them artificially had the reverse effect in the 1960s.[101]

Another experienced figure from Whitehall's economic departments, Alan Lord, later exposed the minimal chances of success possessed by a top-down plan which converted a 4 per cent target into growth rates for separate industries that carried the commitment of neither the management nor the unions in those industries. Lord also pointed out that the 1965 Plan lacked the built-in flexibility that might have enabled it to be adapted to new circumstances once the government was forced into serious deflation by the money markets less than a year after this talisman of the 'New Britain' had been launched.[102]

In the Commons debate which followed the 1966 measures – the rise in Bank Rate, the wage freeze and the planned cuts in public expenditure and public investment – Brown declared: 'For almost two years now we have tried to manage the economy in a way that no economy has been managed before.'[103] 'The whole House', recalled Edmund Dell, who was present, 'dissolved in laughter.'[104] As Alec Cairncross noted many years later, the July measures of 1966 were not quite the deflationary watershed they appeared at the time. The fiscal year of 1967 did not exactly see draconian cuts, quite the reverse, with public investment nearly £500m up on 1966 and public spending on services and consumables up by £700m, though unemployment did rise as expected to 2.4 per cent in September 1967.[105] But the all-important impression of cutback and setback remained.

The shine was off Wilson and his administration thereafter. As Ken Morgan put it, the run-up to the 1966 general election 'was probably the one, fleeting period since 1945–46 that the British left felt itself to be in control',[106] and the National Plan is very much a part of the memory of that promising hour. The July 1966 measures effectively wrecked it, though its parent ministry, the DEA, lingered on until October 1969 when Wilson finally killed it off. Though it may have been a mirage, a kind of institutionalized aspiration between October 1964 and July 1966, the growth-through-planning department was little but a shadow during the last three years of its life, as were the growth rates for the economy – scarcely more than 2 per cent in 1966 and 1967, half the rate proclaimed by the National Plan.[107]

But it was not merely the analysis that was lacking in Wilson's chosen area of political competition and seeming supremacy: the processes of policy development were seriously deficient, too. From almost the first days of his government, his in-house gadfly, the abrasive and trying Oxford economist Tommy Balogh (who had developed the idea of DEA for Wilson during his leadership of the Opposition[108] and who was now resident in the Cabinet Office) peppered him with memoranda on what Balogh called the lack of 'institutional provision' for bringing 'decisions before well-briefed ministers on the basic problem of how to establish a harmonious balance between the overriding aim of expansion and cautious creation of the necessary safeguards to assure its continuity'.[109]

Balogh's critical thrust was directed against an amateur senior Civil Service brilliant at smooth presentations of policy but unschooled in the problems of modern government and strangers to the practical, intellectual disciplines which might aid their solution.[110] One of Wilson's ministerial critics, Tony Crosland, was urging as early as the first months of 1965 that a 'Labour policy-making body be formed'.[111] Surveying the wreckage of a disastrous year for the government, Dick Crossman merged both the Balogh and the Crosland themes when he observed in his diary entry for New Year's Eve 1967 that 'it is bad luck for us that with all his brilliant powers of opportunism and resilience Harold Wilson has failed at the Prime Minister's essential task of creating a centre of power which imposes a central strategy on the government. That is what we shall need if we are to reassert over our civil servants the authority we have lost as a result of our catastrophes . . . and I agree with Tommy Balogh about the rigidity and cocksureness of the Whitehall machine.'[112]

Shortly afterwards, Wilson was to succumb to the notion of an 'Inner Cabinet' even though before assuming the premiership he had dismissed it, saying publicly 'I don't think this is a very good idea' in a BBC radio discussion in 1964.[113] Once the files were opened it became easier to trace his thinking on how to fill the famous 'hole in the centre', as Sir John Hunt was to put it in later years.[114] The Wilson 'Inner Cabinets' of 1968–70 are significant as he was the first and last of the postwar premiers to avow his creation of such a group though, as Macmillan observed, most Prime Ministers have recourse to periodic meetings of 'a small inner group of Ministers' while leaving the full Cabinet 'collectively responsible for all great decisions'.[115] Tracking their genesis is, therefore, an important element in the taxonomy of the postwar premiership.

As early as July 1965 Wilson toyed with a bizarre idea for injecting greater coherence into the apparatus of Cabinet government by suggesting that Brown, Callaghan, Bowden (Lord President of the Council) and Stewart (Foreign Secretary)

might form a permanent nucleus of the MISC [Cabinet committee] meetings, on the basis that you [the original minute was addressed to Brown] would be free to attend any particular meeting or not, as you saw fit, but that you would be present in a personal, rather than a departmental capacity . . . To this permanent nucleus, other Ministers and officials would be added as the nature of the meeting required; but the nucleus would ensure continuity of general Government policy, and, from time to time, might well meet on its own to discuss major problems or general issues, to take stock of the way our affairs are going, to act as a kind of clearing-house and progress chaser of our business as a whole.[116]

This absurd idea, guaranteed only to dissipate still further the time and thought of intensely hard-pressed senior ministers, is hardly evidence of a second Lloyd George, a great technocrat-of-state, at work. The declassified files show that the inner economic triumvirate of the original MISC 1[117] (which soon accumulated extra ministers) had dissolved by the summer of 1965, with the Treasury seeking to keep Brown from joining the traditional Budget-making duumvirate of the PM and Chancellor in the run-on to the 1965 Budget[118] and succeeding, thereafter, in keeping this turbulent high priest of economic expansion out of intimate No. 10/ No. 11 discussions on such crucial matters as international liquidity.[119]

Did the idea of inviting Brown, Callaghan, Stewart and Bowden to attend any MISC meeting they wished fly? Although, as Robert Armstrong noted in correspondence between the Cabinet Office and the Treasury on the matter, 'The present Prime Minister is making much more use of the MISC technique than his predecessors, and more often than in the past his MISC meetings include officials as well as Ministers', there is no evidence that what Armstrong called such 'proMISCuity' led to the creation of an 'Inner Cabinet' by such peculiar means.[120]

The reason why could be Sir Burke Trend's lack of appetite for a more narrowly based form of Cabinet government or 'small Cabinets' (a rather different concept from the 'Inner Cabinet') as he called them in the internal Whitehall exchanges which followed Wilson's suggestion.

We have tried small Cabinets before in our history; and they have never worked particularly well – mainly, in my view, because what matters most to a Prime Minister in a moment of crisis is to have around him at the Cabinet table a sufficiently representative body of colleagues to make him feel confident that he has the support of his Party in whatever it is he wishes to do.[121]

Trend had a great influence on Wilson, who once told me he admired Trend's 'feline' qualities.[122] The Cabinet Secretary admitted in this memo (which Wilson did not see) that he did 'not know how many men are required for this purpose; but I would not put it much below, say, sixteen or eighteen – unless a Prime Minister is prepared to take the very considerable political risk of operating in detachment from his Party political base in the House of Commons'.[123]

Wilson's MISC idea lacked even the coherence of the 'small Cabinet' notion. MISC committees are, by their very nature, subject-specific. The purpose of an 'Inner Cabinet' is, or should be, to rise above the particles of policy and to achieve the advantages of a 'small Cabinet' while preserving the larger entity as the overarching decision-taking body. Wilson's passion for 'proMISCuity' was a fierce contributor to the problem as the explosion of MISC committees, on Rhodesia especially, graphically illustrated when the Cabinet Office's inner working papers were released in the mid 1990s.[124]

It was a combination of Trend's sense of the higher mechanics of state and the brutal 'opposition of events' experienced by Wilson and his colleagues during the July crisis of 1966, however, which gave the Cabinet Secretary his chance. Though the shock did not lead to an 'Inner Cabinet' in one leap (that had to await the departure of George Brown in the spring of 1968, as we shall see), it did produce another variation in the variable geometry of Wilson's approach to Cabinet government.

Trend's steering brief for Wilson ahead of the crucial Cabinet meeting on the afternoon 19 July 1966 is worth recounting at some length as it is a classic of its kind. That Cabinet was so sensitive that its discussion was recorded in immense detail in a confidential annex (of which only two copies were made initially; the first sent to the Queen, the second kept by Wilson),[125] partly because Brown reserved his position on the question of 'an immediate devaluation' as a better alternative to deflation.

Trend's Top Secret prime ministerial brief for one of the most important single Cabinet meetings of both Wilson Mark 1 and Mark 2, was plainly for Wilson's eyes only. 'PRIME MINISTER', it began, '*Why are we in this suddenly critical position?*' Trend was a veteran of all the postwar sterling crises since the convertibility summer of 1947 when he had been Private Secretary to the Chancellor of the Exchequer, Hugh Dalton. This reply to his own question is as succinct a summary of the background to Wilson's and his Cabinet's defining moment as one can find.

The present crisis (? give figures for the exchange losses in the last few days) is the most recent symptom of the continuing weakness of our balance of payments. This is also illustrated by the fact that, contrary to our earlier expectations, this year's deficit [on the balance of payments] at £350 million, looks like being no less than last year's deficit; and even next year we now foresee a deficit of £250 million. Despite all the measures which we have taken so far, we have not succeeded in relieving the strain on the balance of payments; the inflationary pressure (which appears in the balance of payments context as an excess of imports) persists at too high a level; and the world is aware of this. As a result we have not yet restored international confidence in our ability to maintain the value of the Pound. When there is a basic unsoundness of this sort, anything (however irrational) can touch off a run on a currency without notice – as we know since we are now experiencing it for the third or fourth time.[126]

All new Prime Ministers should be presented with a sheaf of such briefs on taking office by the Records Officer in No. 10 (a) to remind them of the ever-present possibility of Macmillan's 'events', (b) to prepare them for the worst and (c) to remind them that they are not alone – that we (broadly defined) have been here before.

Next, Trend demonstrated his subtlety and his opportunism (in the best sense of that word). 'It is no use looking back and asking how we might have acted differently', he told Wilson.

What we have got to do now is to overcome the present crisis and to overcome it permanently – for good and all. (? But add something here about our intention, once we have got through our present troubles, to bring Ministers more fully into consultation on economic and financial policy, in order that the Cabinet shall not again be asked to deal with a crisis at intolerably short notice.)[127]

Trend then went on to show his non-party political skills by making a powerful case for deflation as: '*Devaluation* is not the right remedy *at this moment* . . .'[128] These were, I have no doubt, Trend's own views and he knew they went with the Wilsonian grain (as the account Trend himself penned of the Prime Minister's remarks in the confidential annex shows plainly enough).

Those minutes make no specific mention of that very Trend-like piece of lobbying on the need to involve more ministers earlier and more fully. But Wilson *did* come round to the idea inside a month when he told the Cabinet on 10 August that he was creating a new ministerial committee on economic strategy, SEP (Steering Committee and Economic Policy), which he would chair.[129] (It coincided with a reshuffle which saw Brown, who decided not to resign over the failure to devalue, moving from DEA to the Foreign Office.) Every Prime Minister thereafter chaired his or her main Cabinet committee on economic policy until Tony Blair left that function to Gordon Brown in May 1997.[130]

The establishment of SEP was, on the face of it, an uncanny repetition of 1947 when Attlee created his Economic Policy Committee in the back-wash of the convertibility crisis. Yet it was surrounded by a miasma of very un-Attleean deviousness. Barbara Castle was taken aback when Wilson refused to divulge the membership of SEP because, as she learned later in the day, it depended upon the reshuffle whose details had yet to be disclosed. 'He kept his secret well,' she noted, 'that is what delighted him. He adores foxing the press.'[131] Unlike Attlee's post-convertibility equivalent, on which Wilson sat for over three years as President of the Board of Trade, SEP retained some highly unusual characteristics for over a year. It was not allowed to see the Treasury's economic forecasts for apparently inexplicable and certainly unexplained reasons (which led Callaghan to believe it was pointless).[132] And not until September 1967 did it become 'a regular Cab.comm', as Alec Cairncross put it in his diary shorthand, 'with the usual procedures in circulating papers and allowing attendance by Ministers involved in issues raised'.[133]

Wilson bids fair to be the untidiest of all the postwar premiers in administrative terms despite his pride in his housetraining. This really was quite extraordinary for someone who had sat at the feet of Edward Bridges in the War Cabinet Office and it sustains the justice of that still vivid political folk-memory, observed by Peter Riddell even in the mid 1990s, 'of the confusion and incoherence which so undermined Harold Wilson's Government'.[134] It was as if he were the bureaucratic equivalent of an experiment-crazed boffin. He reckoned 'overlords' were 'a system which I believe, in general, to be unworkable under our administrative parliamentary system'.[135] Yet he made Douglas Houghton an 'overlord' in all but name for both Health and Social Security in July 1965 as Chancellor of the Duchy[136] and, in effect, that is what he made himself when he 'took control' of the DEA in particular and the economy in general in September 1967. And in 1968 Wilson privately described Crossman as ' "overlord" for the social services' when he began the process of merging Health and Social Security into a single DHSS.[137]

As for reshuffles, he made the practice so frequent that Roy Jenkins later referred to them as Wilson's 'annual gymkhana'.[138] The fun-filled pains he took over these exercises is evident from the files of his earliest ones, which have reached the Public Record Office. The September 1965 reshuffle is especially interesting. His first idea was to send Arthur Bottomley rather than Roy Jenkins to the Home Office to replace Sir Frank Soskice. Jenkins was originally earmarked to preside over a fused Ministry of Civil Aviation and Ministry of Technology. Cecil King, the proprietor of the *Daily Mirror*, who later tried to inspire a coup against Wilson,[139] was down as a possible Minister of State at the Board of Trade, though a line was quickly drawn through his name.[140]

The period from the spring of 1967 to the spring of 1968 offers an intriguing test-bed for an examination of Wilson's Cabinet and governing style. Harold the centre-forward had, by this time, given way to Wilson the crisis-manager as setback after setback accumulated and his senior ministerial colleagues grew in both experience and assertiveness. As we have seen, the senior civil servant who exerted the greatest influence over him, Burke Trend, had made a serious attempt on the back of the 1966 economic crisis to steer the Prime Minister towards a tidier, more deliberate and more effective form of decision-taking at Cabinet and Cabinet committee level in the brief he wrote for Wilson ahead of the 19 July Cabinet meeting.

Early mature Wilson, as one might call this phase of his prime ministerial life, is a thing of contrasts. The matter of Europe – the great stress creator of late-twentieth-century Cabinets – is a prime example of this. It could be argued that Wilson was the first premier to experience serious Cabinet trouble over the issue, though it had taken all of Macmillan's considerable skills to get and then keep his Cabinet in line between 1960 and 1963 on the question of prospective UK membership of the European Economic Community. Douglas Jay, Wilson's first President of the Board of Trade, might be seen as the first senior Cabinet figure to lose his place because of Euroscepticism[141] (though the word did not enter the British political vocabulary until the 1980s).

The possibility of a revived application moved from Foreign Office circles[142] to the collective ministerial loop between the March election and the July economic crisis in 1966 during two Cabinet committee sessions in May. The first of these examined the changing scene since de Gaulle's 1963 veto, the Foreign Office's paper stressing significantly that 'a substantial improvement in the health of the British economy' would be a precondition of UK entry.[143] After the summer sterling crisis, Wilson reconvened an enlarged version of his E (for Europe) Cabinet committee for a special session at Chequers in October.[144] After examining a range of alternatives to EEC membership, the committee paved the way for Wilson and Brown to tour the European capitals of the six common market countries, out of which came the second British application in 1967.

Wilson was not a natural European. He was a classic representative of that special kind of English insularity which kept his domestic emotions bounded by the Scilly Isles at its extremity (where Wilson had a holiday bungalow) and his global emotions confined to the Commonwealth, the 'Old Dominions' especially and Australia in particular (where he had relations whom he had visited as a ten-year-old in 1926).[145] His tilt towards Europe, like so much else in his first premiership, was the result of economic setback and the need to find alternative, external sources of dynamism-by-association. And in Michael Palliser, his Foreign Affairs

Private Secretary in No. 10 during this crucial transitional period in Wilson's thinking, he had a deeply committed and persuasive pro-European.[146]

Wilson's mind became increasingly convinced by the intellectual case for Britain inside the community. Emotionally, his heart was never in it, but he did not negotiate to fail. Entry would have represented a personal and political success and a compensation for the setbacks of the July 1966 economic crisis and after. Europe muddled the sterling question harmfully in 1966–67 as, for the anti-marketeers in the Cabinet (who included Wilson allies-cum-critics such as Crossman and Castle), altering the exchange rate tended to be seen as part of the pro-Europeanists' strategy for creating the conditions of a successful bid to join.

Given this mesh of political and personal sensitivities, Wilson the collegial came to the fore as he used the full Cabinet in the spring of 1967 to handle the detail and the politics of the second UK application to join the EEC. There took place a series of no fewer than seven Cabinets (including two on a marathon Sunday – 30 April) between 18 April and 2 May 1967 when it was decided to go ahead.[147]

Such a sustained use of the full Cabinet on Europe, one might have thought, would have placed Wilson very firmly at the collegial end of the prime ministerial spectrum. Yet at almost exactly the same time, an episode was taking place which represented one of the most pronounced – and foolish – examples of excessive prime ministerialism in the postwar years. It spun around Wilson's handling of the so-called D-notice affair of 1967 when he single-handedly and determinedly set out to rubbish the findings of Lord Radcliffe's committee of inquiry into whether or not the journalist Harry Chapman Pincher and the *Daily Express* had broken the voluntary system of press self-censorship on defence security and intelligence matters (the D-notice arrangement) when they published on 21 February 1967 details of the longstanding government practice of intercepting overseas telegram cables and checking them for security breaches.

Once the bulk of the Prime Minister's file on this affair was declassified in 1998, my student Matthew Creevy established the veracity of Dick Crossman's contemporary claim in his diary that Wilson bounced his Cabinet into agreeing to a White Paper being published.[148] The thrust of the government line would rubbish Radcliffe's report and its finding that a pair of D-notices were not breached by Pincher and his newspaper[149] amounted to 'the first occasion when I can remember him [Wilson] taking the strictly presidential line'.[150]

Wilson was so inflamed by an accumulated loathing of the *Daily Express* (and its great scoop-gatherer, Pincher, in particular) and Colonel Sammy Lohan, Secretary of the D-Notice Committee and suspected by Wilson as being both a Tory sympathizer and in Chapman Pincher's pocket, that it appears he and his security adviser, George Wigg, were determined to nail all three whatever the evidence suggested[151] – a mania so powerful that it led Barbara Castle to conclude that Wilson was 'going off his rocker'.[152] Even Burke Trend failed to move Wilson when the Cabinet Secretary invoked the rare but traditional prerogative of his office of, as one of his successors put it, 'drawing oneself up to one's full height and saying certain things to the Prime Minister',[153] when he told Wilson on 30 May 1967 that it was 'his duty to remind the Prime Minister of his responsibilities to other ministers' in advising on the need for colleagues to be consulted over the handling of the pending Radcliffe Report.[154]

Wilson's management of the D-notice affair was hugely counter-productive. Not only was Cyril Radcliffe greatly respected, in effect the number 1 on the 'List of the Great and the Good' as it was then perceived,[155] it produced great hostility towards Wilson not just from the media members of the D-Notice Committee, but on the part of the press in general[156] which blended its animosity with the picture it was already portraying of a premier whose reputation for economic competence was in shreds. As Ben Pimlott concluded: 'A reading of the newspapers of the mid 1960s makes it easy to understand why Wilson's warmth towards the media turned to coldness. Until 1966–67 he appears in the press to be in control of events . . . After the July [1966] crisis and especially after the D-Notice affair, he is presented, with equal consistency, as rudderless in a stormy sea.'[157]

The great weather-maker, of course, was not an esoteric matter like the D-notices, but the economy. The 'Unmentionable' – devaluation, or the desirability of it – had forced its way on to the Cabinet table in July 1966,[158] and did so once more in the context of the EEC application during the first of the full Cabinet discussions on Sunday 30 April 1967. Such was the continuing sensitivity of exchange rate policy that Wilson kept this part of the discussion away from the standard Cabinet minutes and stored it securely as a top secret 'No Circulation Record'.[159]

Wilson's handling of the sterling question over the next twelve months is intriguing in terms of the spectrum of collegiality as it covers it completely – from full Cabinet to a group so small, so secretive and so sensitive as to rank with the handling of nuclear and intelligence matters on the innermost loops, and forming an interesting contrast with his use of a formal 'Inner Cabinet' from April 1968 until the fall of the government in June 1970.

Trend's 'no circulation' minute, almost a verbatim record as such things usually are, is both full and pivotal in the sense that it reprises the difficulty with and lack of both previous devaluation-related discussions, and those that were to come when the parity was altered the following November and beyond. The Cabinet Secretary's preamble covered the need for a stronger British economy if Britain was to enter Europe, the likely extra pressure that this would bring on the balance of payments, which could not be handled by further deflation and would therefore require serious policy changes either in foreign policy (deeper cuts in overseas defence expenditure) or in exchange rate policy (devaluation). 'But', his note continued,

a decision to devalue sterling could be discussed only by a very small number of Ministers; and both the discussion and the decision would have not only to remain secret but, if necessary, to be denied until the decision had been announced. It was therefore right that there should be some discussion of devaluation before any decision was taken which might, as a consequence, lead to circumstances in which devaluation could not be ruled out.[160]

Wilson concurred with the desirability of discussion in carefully controlled circumstances while stressing that: 'Nevertheless the Cabinet would appreciate that there were great dangers in any discussion of a change in the parity, as was shown by the experiences of last July when a grave run on sterling had resulted from a popular belief that the Government had an adjustment of the parity under consideration. It must always be open to any Chancellor of the Exchequer to consider devaluation at the proper time and in full secrecy.'[161] Wilson quickly expressed his familiar view that while devaluation was an option which they could discuss at *this* meeting, 'it was not a one-way option; it could have economic consequences no less unpleasant than those of deflation' and it was imperative that their discussion 'should remain strictly secret and should not be imparted to any other individual, whether Ministerial official or advisory'.[162]

When the Chancellor, Jim Callaghan, did indeed decide 'in full secrecy' that 'the proper time' for devaluation was imminent (greatly influenced by a personal note and an individual briefing from Alec Cairncross, his

Chief Economic Adviser, to this effect on 3 November 1967),[163] Callaghan saw Wilson in private the following day in No. 10 and 'reported on his conversation with Cairncross and on the accelerating flight from sterling ... A note in Callaghan's hand comments, "He does not demur",' wrote the Chancellor's official biographer, Kenneth O. Morgan.[164] Nine days later, after the Lord Mayor's annual banquet, where the political class meets the moneyed class, Tony Crosland, President of the Board of Trade, was brought into the secret – a devaluation from $2.80 to the pound to $2.40 'was likely on 18 November', probably to be 'bolstered' by serious defence cuts and a withdrawal from East of Suez[165] – in other words, a combination of the two major options discussed hypothetically by the full Cabinet at its immensely secret session the previous April.

The full Cabinet had its own devaluation hour on the morning of Thursday 16 November 1967, when Wilson and Callaghan invited the Cabinet to decide 'in principle to devalue the pound', which they did unanimously.[166] That afternoon, Callaghan's answer to a private notice question in the House of Commons from Robert Sheldon about the possibility of a billion-dollar loan being negotiated with foreign banks led to Callaghan 'stonewalling desperately',[167] thereby precipitating a run on the country's gold and dollar reserves of almost £1.5bn in twenty-four hours (Sheldon has never understood why he was not asked to withdraw his question, which he would have been willing to do)[168] leaving the new Chancellor, Roy Jenkins, believing throughout the remainder of 1967 and much of 1968 that 'we had no more borrowing capacity and ... [that] ... our reserves were down almost to the minimum level, having been almost totally cleared out in the mad thirty-six hours before devaluation'.[169] (Callaghan, unlike Norman Lamont after 'Black Wednesday' in September 1992, took the view that Chancellors of the Exchequer who have seen the monetary scaffolding of their policy crash around them should vacate the Treasury building.)

Jenkins plainly regretted in later life the two-day gap between the Cabinet's approval of devaluation and its announcement in a Saturday-evening broadcast on 18 November by Wilson (which has entered into folklore because of his technically accurate but politically ruinous remark designed to reassure 'the British housewife at her shopping' that: 'It does not mean that the pound in the pocket is worth 14 per cent less to us now than it was').[170] Such a delay, said Jenkins, gave the Americans 'time to put on their funeral crêpe for devaluation'.[171]

Jenkins also came to regret the cuts Cabinets which followed (those 'unpleasant' economic consequences of the protracted nature of devaluation of which Wilson had warned the Cabinet the previous spring) as part of the 'very rambling, long public expenditure exercise in January 1968'[172] (eight full Cabinet meetings lasting thirty-two hours in total between 4 and 15 January)[173] at a time when the new Chancellor felt he was in a truly perilous position.[174] 'Wilson was thoroughly loyal. He supported me on everything. But, God, he let the Cabinet talk about it. It was loyalty not leadership. It went on and on ... It was extremely exhausting,' Jenkins recalled.[175]

It was back to the classic Wilsonian practice of letting the Cabinet talk itself out; though, in this instance, there was a palpable and justifiable purpose. Like Callaghan with his IMF Cabinets in 1976, Wilson had to bind all his ministers, including the heads of big-spending departments, through hard won but necessary collective decision-taking. Wilson described this operation 'of getting it through Cabinet without sensational resignations' as 'the most formidable task in over three years of government'.[176] And the wider significance of those decisions were huge – a phased military withdrawal from East of Suez; an emphatic punctuation mark in the long retreat from empire and the global reach that went with it.

Yet few ministers realized, as Jenkins did throughout the first three months of 1968, that despite devaluation, the pound (and the government, to whom a second devaluation would have been politically ruinous) was 'staring over the precipice into the abyss'.[177] Only with the release of the 1968 archive for the Cabinet Office and No. 10 (the Treasury files have been delayed) did historians come to appreciate what Alec Cairncross meant when he described the world gold crisis of March 1968 as the moment when he was 'far more scared by the situation ... than I have been for nearly twenty years', as he confided to Trend in mid March 1968[178] (a judgement with which Jenkins concurred).[179]

Desperate, dramatic contingency planning for a meltdown of the pound – 'Operation Brutus' – as a consequence of what Jon Davis rightly described as 'the gold-dollar-sterling crisis' of March 1968 'which, though narrowly averted, very nearly caused the arbitrary breakdown of the global trading system as it has operated since the Second World War',[180] is not only the most underappreciated sterling crisis since 1945, but needs to figure in any treatment of the first Wilson governments or the Wilson style of premiership. Such was the extreme sensitivity of 'Brutus' that Peter Shore, one of the members of the tiny group of ministers on MISC 205, the Cabinet committee Wilson eventually convened to oversee it, simply had not 'talked to anyone' about it until my student, Jon Davis, showed him the 'Brutus' files in 1999.[181]

Understandably, Wilson's handling of what he would later call the 'international currency storm'[182] was a complete contrast to the cuts Cabinets of two months before. Its public eruption is best remembered as the moment when the volcanic George Brown erupted too, and quit the Foreign Office and the government in a fury,[183] claiming that the Prime Minister had deliberately excluded him from the late-night Privy Council Meeting on Thursday 14 March (wrongly – he could not be found) which was necessary to meet the US request (with which Wilson and Jenkins powerfully agreed, given the outflow of the UK's reserves that day) for a Bank Holiday and closure of the financial markets the following day.[184] But economic history, as opposed to purely political history, will have to treat the following few days as the battle of Jenkins' 'brink'.[185]

For as the Privy Council met the Queen at the Palace for her approval of the first order in council proclaiming a Bank Holiday since the death of her father in 1952,[186] internal estimates of the state of Britain's gold and dollar reserves varied from a surplus of $1,500m (Jenkins, the Chancellor), through $1,200m (Sir Leslie O'Brien, Governor of the Bank of England) to a *deficit* of $200m (Maurice Allen, an Executive Director of the Bank)[187] – hence the precipice and the abyss in Jenkins' recollection.

The gold crisis was not of Britain's making. The postwar Bretton Woods system of fixed exchange rates was gold-backed. The US pledge, which underpinned it, to exchange dollars into gold at a rate of $35 an ounce, was falling apart under the stress of the financial costs of the Vietnam War. Speculators wishing to cash in on an informal rate above this in the first months of 1968 increasingly moved out of dollars into gold and began to convert their sterling into dollars as a preliminary to shifting to metal. Yet the side winds from this international currency storm were what threatened the pound, as Roy Jenkins explained:

'You see, sterling had got into the position which, when you have a history of weakness in a currency, is that almost any event, put it under pressure ... once you're been knocked down into a ditch several times, it's very difficult to get up without another car coming along and knocking you into another ditch.'[188]

This sums up the cumulative problem of the Wilson administration and sterling after 1964. Devaluation, the intended rebalancer of the UK's currency and trading position, did not ameliorate this, at least initially.

Indeed, the flight of reserves in the days before the rate changed made the position even more precarious.

The weekend of 16–17 March, which straddled the Brown resignation on the 14th, the closure of the financial markets on the 15th and Jenkins' first full-dress Budget as Chancellor on the 19th, left Wilson's gold crisis ministerial group, MISC 205, confronting the possibility of a collapse of the sterling exchange rate when it met for the first and second times on Sunday 17 March. What Barbara Castle would later call 'this most secret and powerful of the Cabinet groups',[189] consisted initially of Wilson and four ministers (Jenkins, Crosland from the Board of Trade, Shore from the DEA and Michael Stewart, Brown's replacement at the Foreign Office).

At the first of its meetings that Sunday afternoon, the Treasury warned of the danger of floating sterling as the pound could fall, so weak were the reserves, to $1.50.[190] But the 'Sword of Damocles' of the sterling balances, as Sir William Armstrong used to describe them to me[191] (the credits accumulated during World War II by sterling area and associated countries supplying goods and services to a beleaguered UK not in the position to pay), hung at its sharpest. If the pound collapsed when the markets reopened on the Monday, Britain would have to default on these debts which totalled just under £4bn and were treated by several countries (including some large ones like India) as, in effect, their own reserves. The so-called blocking of the balances, 'Operation Brutus', was what the innermost group of ministers had to contemplate that Sunday.[192]

Had 'Brutus' been implemented it would have instantly been the finish of the pound as the world's second reserve currency after the dollar. The Bretton Woods system, too, would have been at an end; enormous strain would have fallen upon the dollar; and the UK would have acquired, at least temporarily, the status of a pariah state and would have been plunged into a siege economy and domestic austerity of a kind that would have wrecked the Wilson administration ('. . . the government would have fallen, no doubt', said Peter Shore).[193]

Later versions of 'Brutus' spelled out the resource implications of its implementation – troops withdrawn from overseas and embassies closed to save money,[194] a cutback of 15 per cent on imports, and 'inessentials' such as vintage wine, avocados and imported strawberries prohibited.[195] Such restrictions in a society already largely accustomed to what J. K. Galbraith would later call a 'culture of contentment',[196] would almost certainly have kept Labour out of power for a generation. It is hard to believe that not a word of this leaked until the files were open in January 1999.

Wilson, not just calm but cocky under intense pressure over that March weekend, sought to portray these desperate contingency plans for blocking the sterling balances 'as some measure of blackmail with the Americans so that we could point out to them the horrors of the alternative before us'.[197] This was not a view shared by all his advisers[198] but, by the time MISC 205 met for the second time that Sunday evening, it was plain that William Armstrong in Washington had secured massive backing of over $4bn for the pound in Washington as part of a wider solution to the gold crisis involving a two-tier gold market.[199] Wilson kept MISC 205 in being to oversee further refinements to 'Brutus' in case the currency storm revived. In June 1968, on the advice of Burke Trend, who feared that the circle of those in the know was widening too much,[200] he convened an even tighter group, MISC 209, to review 'Brutus' planning.

Historians have known for years about Wilson's two-year experiment with an avowed 'Inner Cabinet', which also emerged out of the spring crisis of 1968 (though I suspect the possibility of its creation had more to do with the departure of Brown than the gold storm). Flying under two names (the Parliamentary Committee for its first year and the Management Committee for its last) it endured right up to the 1970 general election and, briefly, even beyond it. It met for the last time at 4.00 on the afternoon of Friday 19 June (when it had been plain since the small hours that Labour had lost) as the Queen was at Ascot and Wilson had to wait till 6.00 to resign. Tony Benn took pictures of Wilson leaving his last ever 'Inner Cabinet' with his family movie camera (a rarity in those days);[201] the 'Inner Cabinet' idea was not revived when the electorate put Wilson back in No. 10 in 1974.

Wilson's 'Inner Cabinets' deserve careful attention in case a future Prime Minister is minded to run a marque of his or her own. Conventional wisdom treats them – as it does the 'overlords' – as having been more trouble than they were worth. I am not convinced conventional opinion is right. But as seasoned a figure as Lord Armstrong of Ilminster (who as Robert Armstrong was No. 10 Principal Private Secretary to both Ted Heath and *fin-de-siècle* Wilson in 1974–75, and as Sir Robert was Cabinet Secretary to Mrs Thatcher) tends to echo Burke Trend on 'small Cabinets'. When asked about Wilson's 1968–70 models, whose operations he witnessed from the Chancellor of the Exchequer's Private Office, he replied: 'It started off well, but the trouble was if you have a formal "Inner Cabinet" like that, it became a matter of disgrace to a minister who is not on it and, therefore, a matter of intense manoeuvring to get on to it. And, successively, Mr Wilson conceded membership of [it] to people to whom it ought never to have been conceded.'[202]

Jim Callaghan, who had an in–out existence in terms of Wilson's 'Inner Cabinets', was not a believer in them and made no attempt to create one on his own assumption of the premiership in 1976. Of the 1968–70 marques he wrote: 'I suspect that they were established more to satisfy some ministerial egos than for practical purposes . . .'[203]

How *did* the Wilsonian 'Inner Cabinets' work? Barbara Castle was a constant attender as a minister and, as a diarist, was an accomplished shorthand recorder of what transpired there. The Crossman and Benn diaries feed the story, too. It is important to distinguish between the first version, the Parliamentary Committee, and its successor, the Management Committee, as to which has the greater claim to be treated as an 'Inner Cabinet' in the policy sense.

Wilson created his Parliamentary Committee in early April 1968 on the back of a ministerial reshuffle built around the substantial promotion of Barbara Castle from the Ministry of Transport to a newly refashioned Department of Employment and Productivity as First Secretary of State. Wilson explained the purpose of the new committee to the full Cabinet on 9 April 1968. It was to co-ordinate the political (as opposed to the policy) strategy of the government with a special emphasis on the presentation of policy. In future, the full Cabinet would do rather less. More work would fall on the Cabinet committees, where detailed decisions would be taken conclusively.[204]

Mrs Castle, Roy Jenkins and Dick Crossman (all members of the Parliamentary Committee) did not believe it would work effectively as it would acquire too many members. Jim Callaghan, whom Wilson originally did not want included as he 'had been corrupted by the trade unions',[205] inevitably became a member. Though Castle expected it to prove 'as illusory' as previous attempts at co-ordination, she did recognize that it stood with the Steering Committee on Economic Policy and the Overseas Policy and Defence Committee as one of the three key Cabinet committees.[206]

Did it prove illusory? Largely, yes. It acted chiefly as a clearing-house for problems in Parliament such as House of Lords reform and prices and incomes policy[207] or the government's difficulties with the party's National Executive Committee.[208] Truly sensitive matters, such as sterling, had to be kept away from the Parliamentary Committee because of Dick Crossman's 'incurable propensity to chatter',[209] hence the continuation of MISC 205 even after the 'Inner Cabinet' was created.

Stephen Bailey was the first scholar to analyse the workload of the Parliamentary Committee in 1968 once its papers were declassified. His portrait showed just how haphazard and permeable (in terms of ministers) it was:

What is striking, looking through the Parliamentary Committee's minutes of meetings for 1968[210] ... is the number of people who were invited to attend at various times. It was hardly an exclusive committee when well over 50% of ministers from the full Cabinet attended any one of the 16 meetings in that year.

The issues it discussed, while still of great importance – Race Relations (discussed at 5 separate meetings in 1968);[211] Prices and Incomes (discussed at 3 separate meetings);[212] Industrial Relations (discussed twice);[213] and House of Lords Reform (discussed at 3 separate meetings)[214] – were not kept away from the Cabinet because they were felt to be too sensitive. Indeed, Cabinet was informed as soon as anything had been decided in the Parliamentary Committee ... These are all typical issues which might be discussed in a specialist Cabinet Committee and then refined for a decision in Cabinet.[215]

Wilson appears to have been fairly punctilious about informing his full Cabinet on what the Parliamentary Committee was up to.[216] But the body lacked both the policy focus and the procedural tautness required of a proper 'Inner Cabinet'. Wilson would interrupt his colleagues' contributions with comments and gossipy asides, leading Barbara Castle to conclude in early 1969 that 'these discussions are more like *conversaziones* than Cabinet meetings'.[217] Not surprisingly, some civil servants came to regard the Parliamentary Committee as 'a joke'.[218]

As Barbara Castle feared, the Parliamentary Committee soon lost its specialness, another requirement for a genuine 'Inner Cabinet'. By the end of October 1968, Dick Crossman was recording in his diary that both 'SEP and the Parliamentary Committee were attempts at an Inner Cabinet that, because they were official Committees [not to be confused with 'official', i.e., Civil Service, committees], rapidly extended themselves to include more than half the Cabinet. So we moved back to the old situation where there are small groups of Ministers close to Harold, groups that are not even given names.'[219]

Wilson himself came to realize the shortcomings of the Parliamentary Committee even as a tool of political management when the party and Cabinet crisis over Barbara Castle's *In Place of Strife* proposals to curb trade union powers approached its climactic weeks in the spring and early summer of 1969. Castle, Crossman and Jenkins had met on 8 April to agree to impress upon their Prime Minister 'the urgent need for setting-up an inner cabinet' given 'the crisis in the Party'.[220]

By the end of the month Wilson had succumbed to their pressure, having resisted for three weeks their request for a meeting. 'He greeted us in his study', Mrs Castle recorded in her diary for 29 April,

and, almost before Dick could start on what we wanted to say, he chipped in to tell us he had some news that might make some of what we had to say unnecessary: he had decided to wind up the Parliamentary Committee and have an inner Cabinet instead, probably of seven people. We were taken aback. Never have the walls of Jericho fallen so easily! We explained why we wanted it: Dick said bilateral talks were not good enough, while I urged the need for a body that could give us both coherence and continuity of strategy, linking together all the key issues from Northern Ireland to the state of sterling.[221]

That same day Wilson briefed the Westminster lobby correspondents on the new arrangement. According to his Private Secretary's minute, 'the Prime Minister said that he had found the Parliamentary Committee very valuable since it had been set up. He had now decided to constitute a smaller group of "political heavyweights" who would be concerned with the general political and strategic direction of the Government's work. No doubt it would become known as the "Inner Cabinet". Although he himself was not calling it this. He would let them know when he thought of a better name!'[222] Crossman's verdict was, 'Well, we have got the inner group, something I have been struggling for for five years . . .'[223]

Would an earlier inner cabinet have made a difference on, say, the Wilson governments' sensitivity to the tautening of stress in Northern Ireland *before* 'the Troubles' re-erupted with a vengeance in 1968? It is an intriguing question. One must always be careful about overdoing the mechanics or the processes of Cabinet government as a solver or avoider of problems. But we know from both the work of Dr Peter Rose[224] and No. 10 files for 1965–66 that Wilson did have early and explicit warnings about the danger of a recrudescence of violence in Northern Ireland, especially as the fiftieth anniversary of the 1916 Easter Rising approached.

After intelligence warnings had been received from the Royal Ulster Constabulary[225] and Chiefs of Staff Committee had pondered the IRA threat,[226] Burke Trend suggested to Wilson's Principal Private Secretary, Derek Mitchell, that the Prime Minister send a minute to the Home

Secretary, Roy Jenkins, asking him, as minister responsible for Northern Ireland, 'to explain the preparations which have been made to deal with any trouble that may arise . . .'[227] This, Trend continued, 'would also protect the Prime Minister's own position if serious trouble developed and he were subsequently criticized for not having anticipated it'.[228] This Wilson duly did.[229]

If an 'Inner Cabinet' had been in being in the spring of 1966, Wilson might have raised the issue there, arousing a wider sensitivity to the question, instead of confining it to bilaterals with the Home Secretary (the Defence Secretary, Denis Healey, naturally being involved as well). The matter did not even reach the Cabinet's Overseas Policy and Defence Committee, though Jenkins suggested he could prepare a memorandum for its members on potential IRA violence if the Prime Minister wished.[230]

I doubt myself if a different machinery of government would have prevented the Wilson administration from losing sight of the Northern Ireland question until 'events' rammed it into a high place on their agenda. When it finally reached that position at the end of February 1969, Wilson did not use the Parliamentary Committee as his instrument for crisis management. Instead he set up an eight-strong ad hoc ministerial group, MISC 238,[231] which met five times before troops were sent into the province to patrol the streets in aid of the civil power in August 1969.[232] MISC 238, under Wilson's chairmanship, tried to improve the quantity and reliability of intelligence coming out of Northern Ireland.[233] The JIC set up a special Ulster Working Group in April 1969.[234] MISC 238 also considered a wide range of options ranging from direct rule to British withdrawal.[235]

Quite apart from the handling of Northern Ireland, another reason for my scepticism is the general inadequacy of the real 'Inner Cabinet' when it came to foresight and contingency planning after its creation in May 1969. Tony Benn, who joined it in October 1969,[236] raised exactly this question with Trend early in 1970. He recorded in his diary,

I talked to Burke Trend about the difficulty of getting papers actually written by Ministers themselves discussed at the informal Cabinet Management Committee. Burke, who is a very charming public-school headmaster type with absolutely no experience of real life, said that Ministers must make an effort to devote more time to long-term thinking. But of course we don't because we don't want to, not because there isn't time. There is time for anything you have to do and want to do, and Harold Wilson simply doesn't like forward thinking.[237]

That last sentence is alas truly convincing about Wilson as Prime Minister in each and every phase of his premiership because it fits the accumulation of evidence in document, diary and memoir (including Wilson's own).

Was the 'Inner Cabinet' mark II intended to be a strategy body as opposed to a refashioned instrument of political and party management? It appeared so briefly even to a sceptic such as Barbara Castle. Like Jenkins and Crossman, she was miffed to find at its first meeting that Callaghan, deeply into his rogue-minister phase over *In Place of Strife*, was included on the Management Committee despite their urging Wilson that he should not be, thus making it, initially, an eight-strong body – Wilson plus Jenkins, Chancellor of the Exchequer; Michael Stewart, Foreign and Commonwealth Secretary; Callaghan; Castle; Crossman, Secretary of State for the Social Services; Healey and Fred Peart, Leader of the House of Commons. (Wilson had told the lobby correspondents that: 'Members of the new Committee would be on the Committee in a personal capacity rather than representing Ministerial Offices,'[238] an intention which it is hard to reconcile with the inclusion of the affable yet ineffectual Peart.)

'At last the first meeting of the inner Cabinet!' Mrs Castle almost exulted in her diary entry for 5 May 1969.

And, of course, Jim is in. I asked Harold after lunch whether he had had his talk with Jim and, as I anticipated, he said no. He was going to give him a stern warning in front of the rest of us (of course that didn't happen either) ... We ... had a preliminary discussion as to how we should plan our work on what Harold said he was going to call the Management Committee. We agreed the meetings should be informal, frank and forward looking; that Burke [Trend] should attend; there should be no Minutes [in fact minutes were taken from the second meeting onwards][239] but (as Dick wisely suggested) our decisions should be recorded. These would not be reported to Cabinet as they would be purely private ones, but we hoped that we would as far as possible agree on a united line on key issues.[240]

So far it was all atmospheric and procedural. What thinking did Wilson contribute beyond this? Mrs Castle continued,

Harold said everyone should come 'without any external interest or *arrière pensée*' so that we could meet on a basis of trust – the nearest he got to a warning to Jim. Denis wanted us to identify certain major issues, such as the currency, budgetary strategy, the IR [Industrial Relations] Bill [based on Mrs Castle's *In Place of Strife* White Paper proposals], and not least the organisation of Government.[241]

This represented exactly the kind of agenda a genuine 'Inner Cabinet' would address. Castle, knowingly or not – probably not – revived at this point the old 1965 Wilson idea on MISCs.

I urged that we should between us cover every Cabinet committee and MISC committee so that our group had a direct link with each of them. Harold said we would get all papers, though we wouldn't have time to read them all . . .[242]

Mrs Castle's assessment of the moment of initiation? 'Altogether not a bad start.'[243] But did Wilson ever intend the 'Inner Cabinet' to operate as Castle, Jenkins, Healey and Crossman, in their different ways, wished it to? I suspect not. A *Management* Committee is what Wilson called it, and I think his language was revealing. And when Tony Crosland, as the new Secretary of State for Local Government and Regional Planning (the prototype Secretary of State for the Environment), was about to join it, Wilson tossed him a highly revealing note down the Cabinet table about the nature of the Management Committee. 'In case I omit to mention it when we meet', Wilson had written, 'I'm re-forming the Management Cttee, *so-called Inner Cabinet*. I hope you will join it. Our job is *of course* much more *political strategy, including Parlty strategy*, than day to day Govt business. HW'[244] [my emphasis]. Not a trace there of long-term, strategic *policy* formation.

By then, of course, the Management Committee had endured its first and greatest *management* test – the steering of the industrial relations proposals through a legendary and brutal series of full Cabinet meetings in June 1969. And it had failed that test, even though Callaghan had been removed from it on 13 May[245] as a public punishment for his outspoken dissent (which he took to the Party's National Executive Committee)[246] on the whole thrust of *In Place of Strife* and what followed. Perhaps if the Management Committee's line had prevailed at full Cabinet level, it might have developed into the inner policy-making forum some of its backers wished it to be, though it would be inaccurate to think the Management Committee held firm on the plan to bring the law more firmly into industrial disputes (with conciliation pauses and financial sanctions against unions which did not comply – penal legal sanctions being the sticking point for large swathes of the Labour movement and the Parliamentary Labour Party).

An hour before the crisis meeting of the full Cabinet on 17 June 1969, two key figures on the Management Committee,[247] Crossman and the hitherto firm Chancellor, Jenkins, began to wobble on the tough Wilson–Castle line. ('I didn't think I covered myself in glory,' Jenkins told me many years later.)[248] Only Stewart, the Foreign Secretary, was firm for them.[249] 'By this time', Mrs Castle noted in her diary, 'it was 11 a.m. and we had to go into Cabinet disunited and unprepared.'[250] So much for the 'Inner Cabinet' as the bringer of drive and cohesion to policy-making.

The full Cabinet undid Castle and Wilson then and on the following day[251] – itself, as Ken Morgan has noted, 'a remarkable demolition of Crossman's thesis . . . to the effect that Cabinet government had been replaced by prime ministerial government'.[252] A feeble and meaningless 'solemn and binding'[253] undertaking with the unions to bring *their* best efforts to curb strikes was all the government came away with.[254] For a moment it looked as if Wilson might go or be pushed. The existence of the Management Committee had nothing to do with his survival. It was the rivalry of two heavyweights for the succession – Jenkins and Callaghan – that kept Wilson secure. He may have been prone to varying degrees of political and personal paranoia, but his conviction that if two or more crown princes existed his own crown was safe[255] had an air of gritty rather than gilded reality about it.

Much of the Management Committee's work thereafter mirrored that of the Parliamentary Committee – discussion of issues, bills and statements that might cause trouble in the House of Commons such as Mrs Castle's equal pay legislation[256] and a treatment of anticipated difficulties in the 1969 public expenditure round.[257] As the general election approached, an increasing amount of its time went on political timing and strategy in which Callaghan, re-admitted to the inner group in October 1969 though quite unrepentant,[258] was a major player.[259] (Callaghan in his long retirement did not rate the significance of the Management Committee at all highly. His official biographer, Ken Morgan, reflected the view of his subject when he wrote: 'it met only occasionally and its deliberations were never in the public eye'.)[260]

On 14 May 1970 the 'Inner Cabinet' gathered with no civil servants present to agree upon 18 June as election day. The following day Wilson was to use the words that later came to haunt him at a Management Committee session: 'We're really asking for a doctor's mandate', he said, in an unfortunate echo of Ramsay MacDonald in 1931,[261] 'We're the best doctors the country has got.'[262]

Occasionally, the Management Committee would repair to Chequers and briefly act like an 'Inner Cabinet' with a longer-term focus. On 5 September 1969, for example, apart from electoral strategy, they discussed the 1970 Budget, the re-opening of negotiations to join the EEC, prices and incomes and policy on mergers and machinery of government changes as well as raw personality politics (the coming reshuffle and Callaghan's restoration to the inner group).[263] Such occasions, however, were rarities. It is safe to say that despite the Wilson experiences of the Parliamentary Committee April 1968–April 1969 and the Management Committee May 1969–June 1970, postwar Britain still awaits a genuine experiment with the notion of an 'Inner Cabinet'.

By the late 1960s the white coat of Harold-the-technologist had given way to the white coat of Dr Wilson, as Tony Benn has often characterized the Wilson of the 1970 election.[264] It was as if the object of transforming the industrial fortunes of his country had given way to turning Labour into the natural party of government. Wilson really thought he had succeeded in this by the time of the run-up to the general election. In February 1970, he told Jimmy Margach that already he had achieved it – 'the biggest job I've had to do so far'.[265] He hadn't. In the aftermath of Wilson's shock defeat in 1970, it was a Conservative competitor, Reggie Maudling, who declared both retrospectively and prophetically that 'Britain is a Conservative country that sometimes votes Labour'.[266] Until May 1997, at least, that was a statement which held good.

What did endure from these premierships of promise blighted? Very little in the way of the mechanics of state, apart from the Welsh Office, which Wilson founded in 1964 (though the Department of the Environment might be said to be his creation in all but name). He began the experiment – which others have repeated – of a Cabinet public expenditure committee not dominated by big spenders.[267] He enhanced Attlee's requirement that any proposal going to Cabinet that had a spending implication should be costed by the Treasury by insisting that public service manpower questions be similarly addressed.[268] He changed Cabinet procedure in one other way by instructing that Barbara Castle's chair in the Cabinet Room be covered in cretonne to avoid the laddering of her tights.[269] More seriously, with his economic advisers, Tommy Balogh and Andrew Graham, it could be said that Wilson was operating a kind of Prime Minister's Policy Unit in embryo between 1964 and 1970.[270]

The bulk of his efforts at parliamentary reform were expended on the aborted attempt to change the powers and composition of the House of

Lords between 1967 and 1969. But he did permit an early experiment with select committees which focused on government departments (though when the House of Commons Agriculture Committee began to take a close interest in policy as opposed to administration, ministers began to recoil from the idea).[271]

The Fulton Report urged more Whitehall openness in general.[272] Wilson took this seriously and began consideration of the kind of specific inquiry that would be needed[273] (one which eventually had to wait until 1971 when Ted Heath commissioned the Franks review of section 2 of the Official Secrets Act, 1911).[274] For all his paranoia about the press, Wilson was an opener by temperament. But for his personal insistence, it is unlikely that the fifty-year rule for public records release would have been lowered to thirty by the Public Records Act 1967.[275] In this sense, he can be described as the political patron of the burst of new document-infused writing on contemporary British history over the last thirty years.

Wilson may have some claim to being the first premier to have been made and then unmade by the press (though there was more than a trace of this in the Macmillan years with his media treatment in the dog year of 1963 a far cry from the 'Supermac' of the late 1950s). Wilson courted the press and used the Westminster lobby system, which he ludicrously described as a 'golden thread' running through our parliamentary democracy,[276] with a flair and a care which made the inevitable and mutual disillusionment all the harder to bear once it set in.

It was in the late 1960s that a small number of the more susceptible and conspiracy-minded journalists came to believe that Wilson might be a long-term Soviet agent (a fantasy fed by the speculations of the Russian defector, Anatoly Golistsyn, which began to filter across the Atlantic from the United States[277] – this malign confection grew quite powerfully after Wilson's return to No. 10 in 1974). With the publication of parts of the archive brought out by the KGB defector, Vasili Mitrokhin, we learned in 1999 that Wilson did have the unique distinction of being the only British Prime Minister to have been given a codename – OLDING – by the KGB in 1956 and assessed as a long-term asset[278] (and that they passed on to the Politburo his gossipy tittle-tattle about British politics when on trips to Moscow).[279] Mitrokhin's notes from the KGB files also show, however, that this 'development did not come to fruition'[280] (a view shared by non-fantasists in the British intelligence community, as we shall see in chapter 14). That Wilson's policy impulses were KGB-influenced has to be confined to the garbage of conspiracy theory – a particularly crowded dustbin of history.

In fact, Wilson oversaw improvements to the UK's Cold War intelligence efforts. He approved Trend's 1967 plan to sharpen the Joint Intelligence Committee's all-source analysis capacity, which found institutional expression in the Cabinet Office's assessments staff in 1968.[281] He also approved a reform of Whitehall's counter-subversive apparatus when the highly secret Official Committee on Communism (Home), created by Attlee in 1951,[282] was remodelled in early 1969 into the Official Committee on Subversion at Home.[283]

In assessment of policy more generally, Wilson's defenders tend to make obeisance to the turn-round on the balance of payments deficit after the 1967 devaluation. They also place in the positive scale the necessary adjustments of military aspirations to economic reality with the decision to withdraw from east of Suez in 1968. They concentrate especially on the liberalization of the laws on capital punishment, abortion and homosexuality which the Wilson governments fostered by ensuring sufficient parliamentary time was found for them to be carried through.[284]

Wilson's detractors, while acknowledging his great gifts as a media communicator ('He's the only really competent political TV performer this country has produced,' admitted Lord Poole, Joint Chairman of the Conservative Party, after the 1964 election),[285] point to his debasement of political style and language (the devaluation speech being the exemplar here when, as we have seen, Wilson appeared to imply that the pound's value 'in the pocket' had not declined). Others follow Ted Heath and denounce Wilson's sullying of the job of Prime Minister with his gimmicks: his endless, time-wasting royal commissions, his beer-and-sandwich sessions at No. 10 in misguided attempts to fix industrial disputes and what Wilson himself called the 'stardust' sprinkled in his honours lists.[286]

The 'hard' left take a still different line. They came to develop a long litany of betrayal, to accompany the first Wilson governments from maintaining the British 'bomb'; sticking slavishly to President Johnson's Vietnam policy (though to LBJ's fury Wilson would never commit British troops to the war – 'All we needed was one regiment. The Black Watch would have done', a slightly drunken Dean Rusk, Johnson's Secretary of State, told Louis Heren, *The Times*' Washington editor in 1969. 'Well, don't expect us to save you again. They [the Russians] can invade Sussex, and we wouldn't do a damn thing about it');[287] creating unemployment by deflating instead of devaluing; and for helping to prop up capitalism generally by merely moderating its harsher features and succumbing to City pressure.[288]

The 'betrayal' school exuded at the time (and still does) an air of puritan unreality about the freedom of scope and manoeuvre available to the Wilson administrations. The 'liberal society' apologists have a good and a convincing case. But when it comes to facing up to geopolitical realities in terms of the second EEC application or the withdrawal from east of Suez, Wilson and his senior ministers only confronted serious change when harsh economic vicissitudes obliged them to. As postwar administrations go, they were not alone in this. But they cannot claim any special bravery or foresight for such developments or adjustments.

The early and middle Wilson premierships, now less of an ideological battleground than they were, are in their own way as evocative as the decade with which they are still associated in popular memory – Harold's MBEs for the Beatles in 1965 being, perhaps, the key linking episode here.[289] It is not the smell of marijuana that brings back the Wilson era, however. It is the faint trace of pipesmoke in old BBC studios long since converted into nicotine-free zones. Never again will a premier be able to blot out his interrogator, buy time for thought *and* distract the viewer while appearing human, folksy and reassuring as Wilson could while lighting-up. Not for nothing did Enoch Powell dismiss the 1970 general election as a contest between 'a man with a pipe and a man with a boat'.[290]

13

The Somersaulting Modernizer:
Edward Heath, 1970–74

'I think it's much worse than wartime. In wartime you're operating on one front . . . most people regard winning the war as their main objective and they're prepared to commit themselves to it . . . In peacetime . . . you had a wide variety of problems and the people who were concerned with them didn't have any common interests in solving those particular problems. They each regarded their own as crucial. From that point of view I think the strain on the Prime Minister and the Cabinet is very much greater.'

Sir Edward Heath, 1989[1]

Before he became leader I knew him for twenty years, often on a day-to-day basis, and even when under considerable pressure as a Cabinet Minister he was in the main friendly, outgoing and understanding of the problems of newspapermen. More importantly, during his days in Opposition a pledge of open administration and frank Press relations lay at the heart of his proposed 'New Style Government' . . . After the tantrums, bitter arguments and high tensions of Wilson's Mark-I government there was therefore a sense of optimism as Heath moved into No. 10 . . . Alas, power, which has the ability to mellow some of those who achieve it . . . in Heath's case changed his personality overnight. When Prime Minister he became authoritarian and intolerant.

James Margach, 1978[2]

I do not mean . . . that Mr Heath is a 'dictator', any more than Mr Wilson was, but . . . the fact is that the potentialities of the office have already been considerably extended by Mr Heath and they will almost certainly be expanded still further before he is done with it.

David Watt, 1972[3]

'Beneath that extraordinary exterior there is a little pink, quivering Ted trying to get out.'

Senior Cabinet colleague, 1970–74, speaking in 1993[4]

'Music means everything to me when I'm here alone. And it's the best way of getting that bloody man Wilson out of my hair.'

*Edward Heath, after playing Chopin and Liszt for
a visiting journalist on his piano at his Albany flat, late 1960s*[5]

Come with me to exactly that choicest of London addresses – Albany, just off Piccadilly – one evening in 1969. The Leader of the Opposition, Ted Heath, has invited five top trade unionists to dinner, to get to know them and their movement a little better. He had, in fact, known one of them, Jack Jones of the Transport and General Workers, for thirty years, ever since the days when they both supported the cause of the Spanish Republic against General Franco. They had actually met in Spain in 1938. 'When we stood around chatting that day', Jack Jones recalled in his memoir, *Union Man*, 'we little thought that our paths would cross in later years in Downing Street and other prestigious places, very different to the Ebro front.'[6]

With Jack Jones that evening in Albany were the TUC General Secretary, Vic Feather, Alf Allen of the Shopworkers, Sid Greene of the Railwaymen and Jack Cooper of the General and Municipal Workers. Jack Jones takes up the tale:

The others were pillars of the TUC establishment, who set out to impress our host with their responsible attitude on all matters industrial. I tried to bend Ted's ear to the need for better pensions for the elderly, and industrial training for our young people. There is no doubting Ted Heath's sympathy for people and we quickly established a feeling of camaraderie.

It was a pleasant evening, with Heath talking of his yacht and musical interests. At one stage he showed us a new piano he had bought and at our invitation played one or two short pieces. Then Vic Feather called out, 'Play the "Red Flag" for Jack' and the leader of the Tory Party cheerfully played Labour's national anthem.[7]

I start with this glorious episode because Ted Heath is seen by too many people, and not just his political critics, as a rigid, humourless Easter-Island-statue of a politician who first confronted the trade union movement, and then succumbed to its might before plunging the country into an unnecessary election and a whirlpool of seeming ungovernability.

Apart from Anthony Eden, Heath is the postwar premier most in need of rescue and repair. He is also, I think, the easiest to be so rescued, despite the disdain of those within his own party who continue to see him as the incarnation of a failed 'corporatist' past. Interestingly enough, during his more difficult moments in the House of Commons during the early Thatcher years, Heath would turn not to the sometimes jeering Conservative backbenchers for support when outlining his alternative to the there-*is*-no-alternative economic line pushed from his own front bench, but to the Labour benches and to the former premier, Jim Callaghan, in particular, who would often nod to him in a reassuring manner.[8] And it was the leader of a rival party, David Owen in his Social Democratic Party incarnation, who had the warmest things to say about the Heath approach to the practice of government. 'Ted Heath', he told me, 'had some of the best ideas of any postwar Prime Minister. He ... was a rather radical person.'[9]

It is that side of Ted Heath which perhaps provides the chief enduring interest from his period as premier between the Conservatives' surprising victory at the polls in June 1970 (legend has it his triumph was not a surprise to him, though his biographer, John Campbell, reckons 'that is almost certainly part of the mythology of victory')[10] to their equally surprising (to him as well this time)[11] loss of their majority on the last day of February 1974. I tend to disagree with Campbell, and to think that Heath alone did expect to win in 1970. He certainly thinks that. As he told Michael Cockerell many years later, 'It's said that I was the only one who expected to win the election ... I was quite certain we were going to win it.'[12] Heath is a man of immense self-belief, which often appears to manifest itself as stubbornness or rigidity. He was, and remains, a politician of great consistency in his ideas and philosophy. This may strike some as a very odd judgement of a Prime Minister whose name is almost synonymous with the U-turn. But should it? Any analysis of Heath's Downing Street years has to start with this paradox, for unless it can be resolved to some degree, it is very hard to make sense of his stress-laden incumbency of No. 10.

The old curmudgeon himself does not help much here. He refused to assist John Campbell with his fine and fair biography[13] or to read the book when it appeared.[14] The thesis of Campbell's book is central to the U-turn question. It is this – that both the press coverage and Harold Wilson's

'Selsdon Man'[15] gloss on the pre-election Selsdon Park Shadow Cabinet planning conference at the end of January 1970 was fundamentally misleading about the man, his beliefs and his intentions.

'The philosophy of "Selsdon Man",' Campbell writes,

as formulated in certain phrases of the 1970 manifesto *A Better Tomorrow* and in a number of other dogmatic-sounding statements by Heath himself and others during and after the election, was widely perceived as signalling a decisive break with the post war 'Butskellite' consensus and the 'One Nation' Toryism in which Heath's career had started. From the perspective of the 1980s it could be represented as proto-Thatcherite. It was claimed by Mrs Thatcher's admirers that he had fought the 1970 election on essentially the same prospectus that she offered in 1979, with the difference that she had the courage to stick to her convictions whereas he, a decade earlier, had not.[16]

For Campbell there is a degree of truth in this analysis to the extent that it embraces Heath's planned trade union reforms designed to curb their wildcat power by bringing reason to the processes of collective bargaining and his desire to create a freer and more enterprising economy. 'But', Campbell continues,

to a much greater degree it reflects the misunderstanding which Heath allowed to arise – indeed positively encouraged – by going along with an aggressively free market rhetoric which he did not accept.[17]

Campbell's evidence for this is partly to be found in that very 1970 manifesto with, for example, its advocacy of regional policy.

I share Campbell's overall conclusion that Heath 'never intended to break the postwar settlement accepted by Churchill, Eden, Macmillan and Home. His proposed "revolution" was all about trying to change attitudes and remove obstacles to growth within the existing economic and social structure.'[18] He believed in the mixed-economy/welfare-state model, which was at the heart of that settlement, and had no time for the idea of widespread privatization which a party group under Nicholas Ridley had pressed as an element of the policy rethink in opposition.[19]

While filming Sir Edward for Rob Shepherd's Channel 4 television series *What Has Become of Us?* in the summer of 1994, I had a chance to put the Campbell thesis to Heath himself. This is how the conversation went:

HENNESSY: . . . a debate about you when you became Prime Minister has happened in recent years, about whether you were a prototypical free marketeer, with Selsdon and so on. But others have argued that your premiership was designed to make Britain more efficient so that the virtues of that consensus could be sustained throughout the rest of the century . . . Am I right in thinking you always were a consensus man and all the modernization plans for Britain you put in place in 1970 – no more 'lame ducks' and so on – were designed actually to get an economy to sustain that rather than changing . . . towards something that we might now call 'Thatcherism'?

HEATH: Yes, I've always said that what I wanted was a balance and it's very important to achieve that otherwise you get into difficulties in all sorts of ways – technically and with people. What we wanted to do was to modernize. We'd done tremendous work as a shadow government planning all of this . . . so we had all of this on which to base our attitudes and our work when we took over. And you're quite right, we wanted to increase the efficiency of this country enormously . . . and if you can do it jointly with everybody else, so much the better. It avoids all the rows and you also avoid the dogma which has been the curse of recent years – that we know this and we're going to do this because it's our dogma and let's get on with it; all those who aren't with us are against us. That's not the way to run a country. You can't run a business like that either (can't run anything like it) and you certainly can't run a government like it. So yes, I wanted to modernize, I wanted to do it as far as possible on a consensus. But one always recognizes there are some issues on which it might not be possible to get a consensus. Well, then you have to take your own line in the best possible way.[20]

This peroration, coming as it did at the end of a long interview in which Heath stressed the virtues of the 'one nation' postwar approach to Toryism as the banisher of interwar policies and high unemployment, I took as an endorsement of the Campbell interpretation, even though Sir Edward, in some ways, answered my question tangentially rather than directly. If I was being unkind I would depict this as Heath's version of what Ralf Dahrendorf later accused the SDP of trying to do – to achieve 'a better yesterday'.[21]

That shrewdest of political observers, David Watt, sensed this at the moment Mrs Thatcher usurped Heath's leadership of the Conservative Party in February 1975. Watt saw her accession as probably signalling the 'eclipse' of the old Tory political tradition. 'In a way', he judged,

this should have happened ten years ago when Mr Heath became leader. It was thought then by many who voted for him and by many in the country, that he represented precisely the repudiation of the old ways that they desired – he was self-made, he was classless, he talked the language of managerial efficiency and to some extent even the language of the free market. But it turned out that he was no repudiation at all. He had acquired all the preconceptions he was supposed to be rejecting. He was a liberal in social matters, he felt great responsibility for the unemployed, the low-paid and the immigrant. Moreover he turned out to believe in 'leadership', a dialogue with the workers and economic intervention on a large scale.[22]

Economic success, Watt concluded, would have given 'the old tradition' a new lease of life, 'but the tools broke in his hands'[23] despite his considerable efforts, as we shall see, to modernize them.

Without this feel for the man and his purposes, the Heath premiership is inexplicable. If you accept the 'better consensus' interpretation, he appears not so much a compulsive U-turner but more of a somersaulting modernizer – a premier prepared to execute great leaps of policy for the purpose of continuing to move more effectively in the same direction with its trio of interlocked signposts: full employment and a modernized economy well placed to take full advantage of that other great Heath ambition, UK membership of the European Economic Community. Heath believed that Community membership and the enhanced competition that came with it would invigorate the British economy still further (he was a subscriber to the 'cold douche' theory) enabling the essentials of the postwar settlement (full employment, social peace and as high a degree of consensus as possible between the 'social partners') to be preserved and built upon.

What makes Heath unusual is the degree to which a streamlined system of Cabinet government and public administration was a central, crucial component in his wider scheme of modernization and reform. The Conservatives, stimulated by Heath, had spent a great deal of time on this theme in opposition and Iain Macleod, the Chancellor of the Exchequer cruelly lost to the government in its early weeks, was justified in claiming they were the best prepared administration to have taken office in peacetime.[24] This helped explain in part 'the overwhelming personal dominance' Heath exerted over his ministerial colleagues for virtually all of his premiership. For as David Watt wrote in 1972 of pre-1970 work on both policy and process: 'The key factor has been Mr Heath's decision to take an enormous risk while he was in Opposition and first of all work out a very detailed programme and second to entrust this work only to people who are more or less of his way of thinking. This might have had a disastrous result if the public had been scared off the policies or the party had split because too many people had been excluded from its councils. But the gamble came off . . .'[25]

In fact, no Prime Minister since Lloyd George in 1916–17 had made such a deliberate and determined effort to remodel the whole machinery of state.[26] Like Lloyd George, Heath saw such matters as first-order problems to be tackled as a priority and not as optional extras. They were integral to what he saw as a more focused form of Cabinet government – the traditional collective approach but a sharpened version – another example, perhaps, of the 'better yesterday' impulse (though Lloyd George's brand was much more a tilt towards prime ministerial government than was Heath's: Keynes was right to fear for the Constitution under LG).[27] Both LG and Ted Heath saw change as a symbiosis of improving process and outcome, or management and policy-making. Mrs Thatcher, a more Lloyd Georgian premier than Heath, concentrated almost solely on management reforms.[28] Conviction politicians tend not to be overly fascinated by the quality of policy analysis.

Heath's memoirs, *The Course of My Life*, are eloquent on the 'firm conviction' with which he entered No. 10 'that we needed to change the structure of government . . . a subject which engrossed me . . . because I was concerned that Ministers spent too much time on day-to-day matters, instead of on strategic thinking'.[29] At his first Tuesday evening audience with the Queen he placed 'at the top of the list, the formation of the government, civil service matters and the place of businessmen in the work of government . . .'[30]

Not all of Heath's pre-election thinking, however, survived the attentions of the senior Civil Service when the plans were passed round the Cabinet Office and the Civil Service Department. For example, Mark Schreiber, David Howell and others involved during the opposition years in the party's Public Sector Research Unit[31] had been keen on Heath building a personal 'think-tank' around him in No. 10. Such Americanisms did not appeal to Sir Burke Trend, nor did any seeming increase of prime ministerialism in what was supposed to be a collective executive. Trend persuaded Heath to call the new body 'the Central Policy Review Staff' and to place it in the Cabinet Office where it would service the Cabinet as a whole.[32] Contemporary commentators argued that though there was 'some evidence' that the CPRS in its first months 'encouraged individual Cabinet members to intervene more often in subjects outside their narrow departmental briefs', they also saw it, rightly, as an innovation which strengthened the hand of Heath against individual Whitehall departments.[33]

It is worth lingering over both the thrust and the detail of the White Paper, *The Reorganisation of Central Government*,[34] which Heath presented to Parliament four months after assuming the premiership, as it represented the first serious, across-the-board look at the quality of Cabinet government since the 1918 Haldane Report on the machinery of government,[35] itself a powerful shaper of Trend's thinking.[36]

Heath had sat on the Cabinet committee which Macmillan established in 1957 to examine the Attlee Report dealing with the burden on ministers.[37] He had seen how little of substance came of that (the creation of the Treasury Chief Secretaryship apart) or of Macmillan's revisiting the 'overload' theme in Cabinet as part of his own modernization plans in 1962.[38] I have never asked Heath about these formative experiences but I suspect they were part of his determination to make real improvements in this area (if he got the chance) from the moment Alec Douglas-Home put him in charge of the policy reviews which followed the 1964 defeat. Douglas Hurd has disclosed that Heath 'thought that Harold Macmillan had taken things far too easily so he was wanting to be up and at them . . . he [Heath] was out for the slaying of dragons'.[39]

Once in office, Heath told a pair of *Evening Standard* journalists how he found machinery of government questions 'of extraordinary interest'[40] and railed against the lack of strategic focus of the Cabinets in which he had sat as Chief Whip or as a minister under Eden, Macmillan and Douglas-Home: 'I had seen Cabinets which all the time seemed to be dealing with the day-to-day problems and there was never a real opportunity to deal with strategy, either from the point of view of the Government or the country. What I wanted to do was so to change things that the Cabinet could do that.'[41]

The 'overload' problem was central to the analysis behind the 1970 White Paper. Its second paragraph declared:

This administration believes that government has been attempting to do too much. This has placed an excessive burden on industry, and on the people of the country as a whole, and has also overloaded the government machine itself. Public administration and management in central government has stood up to these strains, but the weakness has shown itself in the apparatus of policy formulation and in the quality of many government decisions over the last 25 years.[42]

Here again is that key Heath linkage between overload, process and the calibre of policy outcomes and his desire, as he put it many years later in a Granada Television interview, 'to get a rational government structure' based on his experience 'at the centre of politics for twenty years'.[43]

It is worth examining in some detail the ingredients of the 1970 White Paper because it remains the starting point for any future Prime Minister or Prime-Minister-in-waiting with a serious intention of streamlining the central instruments of state, even given the substantial changes in the ecology of government over the past thirty years. What were its essentials?

- Fewer and bigger ministries including a new Department of the Environment and another for Trade and Industry.
- This reform would have the double advantage of slimming the Cabinet down from over twenty to eighteen, thereby creating a body better placed for serious discussion and with fewer decisions cluttering its agenda as more could be resolved within the ambit of the new super-ministries (not the same thing at all as the Churchillian 'supervising ministers' who lacked departments of their own).
- Departments themselves would be less burdened thanks to the hiving-off of certain executive functions, for example, by the management of the government estate moving into a new Property Services Agency and weaponry passing to an equally novel Procurement Executive. (These were the areas in which Heath sought the advice of the businessmen he brought into Whitehall, of whom Derek Rayner of Marks and Spencer was the most important and the most successful.)[44]
- The slimmed-down Cabinet would be a better briefed Cabinet as, in the words of the White Paper, 'the necessary basis for good government is a radical improvement in the information system available to ministers'.[45]
- Information flow would be improved by the creation of 'a small multi-disciplinary central policy review staff in the Cabinet Office' which was 'to be at the disposal of the Government as a whole' and though 'under the supervision of the Prime Minister, it will work for Ministers collectively; and its task will be to enable them to take better policy decisions by assisting them to work out the implications of their basic strategy in terms of policies in specific areas, to establish the relative priorities to be given to the different sectors of their programme as a whole, to identify those areas of policy in which new choices can be exercised and to ensure that the underlying implications of alternative courses of action are fully analysed and considered'.[46]
- The new CPRS would become a player in the annual public expenditure

cycle and the quality of that process would be made more thoughtful and rational by a system called Programme Analysis and Review (or PAR) for examining chunks of existing programmes to test their utility and efficiency, an idea developed by Heath's people in opposition after they had experienced the then novel techniques of zero-based budgeting practised in parts of the Washington bureaucracy.[47]

Heath was keen, too, on the Cabinet and its committees working from agreed sets of data, the preparation of which was another task for the CPRS.[48]

Surprisingly, Heath did not reshape the Prime Minister's Office. He just got on with what he found. He did recoil, however, from what he regarded as the media obsession that had developed in No. 10 under Wilson. He quickly stripped out the presentation sections in *Questions of Procedure for Ministers*, though when he circulated his own version of *QPM* in 1971 they had virtually been restored (albeit minus Wilson's section on the use of the journalists' Westminster Lobby).[49]

Asked by Michael Cockerell if he felt a sense of history or a sense of destiny when he crossed the threshold of No. 10 Heath replied, characteristically: 'No, no, really. No. I mean you've got to get on with the job.'[50] Though the new premier did change the personnel in the Private Office. Trend and the Head of the Home Civil Service, Sir William Armstrong, decided that Robert Armstrong (no relation to William) should be the PM's Principal Private Secretary once Heath had quickly decided Sandy Isserlis, whom he had inherited from Wilson, had to go. Heath devotes several sentences of his memoir to the reluctance of Isserlis to provide food for himself and his party managers on that first night in government as they sat down to construct the Cabinet. Isserlis finally produced sandwiches, shouting 'Grub's up!' through the half-open door, sending Willie Whitelaw into 'paroxysms of fury' and a demand that Isserlis had to go – one of the more bizarre sackings in the history of No. 10.[51]

Trend and Armstrong reasoned that the rather solitary bachelor for whom music was such an important, humanizing passion, would take to the charming and polished conductor of the Treasury Singers. ('Grub's up!' is not a phrase one tends to hear on the lips of Robert Armstrong.) They were right.[52] Though Armstrong's description of his first day in the job is a moment of vintage Heath: 'The door opened and Mr Heath came out and saw me and said "Oh. You're here. It's going to be very hard work, you know," and went back into the Cabinet Room.'[53]

Howell and the other planners had originally intended the 'think-tank' to be a part of No. 10,[54] which would have been a step change four years ahead of Wilson creating the No. 10 Policy Unit. But once that intention was modified, there was little else on the drawing-board by way of proposed changes in Downing Street itself. Heath did, however, make use of his experience of the Foreign Office News Department during his days as Lord Privy Seal negotiating with Europe by heading his press office with career officials rather than specialist government information officers. The diplomat, Sir Donald Maitland, who had worked with Heath during the 1961–63 EEC negotiations, was a considerable influence as Press Secretary in No. 10.[55] The ex-diplomat, Douglas Hurd, in Heath's Political Office was 'responsible for liaison with the Party and for those parts of the Prime Minister's life which were mainly political'.[56]

Heath relied greatly on his No. 10 staff. I used to think that it would probably be going too far to suggest that they became a surrogate family for him, but he himself described them in his memoirs as 'a kind of extended family'.[57] They were required to spend a great deal of their weekends at Chequers keeping him company as well as briefing him. At one time thought was given to creating a Private Secretary's flat within the building to make weekend life easier for his Private Office aides.[58] Heath's Downing Street officials acquired great loyalty and respect for their boss which was reciprocated and endured long after the premiership. Nearly twenty years later one of them said: 'Ted Heath was a very serious, very devoted man [who] lived greatly for the job – very straight, much more difficult to know [than other Prime Ministers]. Very shy, very reserved but somebody who every so often the clouds would roll back and you saw that he liked you and depended on you. And those moments were worth much more than more frequent signs of friendship from other people.'[59]

Sadly, those Cabinet ministers who were not close to him rarely if ever saw this side of their chief. Some who were, such as Lord Carrington, knew he was 'a somewhat lonely man ... [who] ... needed friendship yet found it hard to unbutton himself to the affection of others'.[60] His Chancellor of the Exchequer and neighbour, Anthony Barber, recalled that 'if Ted had had a depressing day, he knew that he could always walk through to No. 11 and there would be awaiting him a bottle of his favourite malt'.[61]

Heath meant to be collegial in Cabinet. All his instincts were that way, but he could appear stiff – and he frightened some of his ministers. There is some evidence that this was partly deliberate. Sir Nicholas Henderson, a senior figure in the Diplomatic Service during the Heath premiership, once told to his and Heath's prewar contemporary at Oxford, Woodrow Wyatt, that while at college Heath had been a most amiable and jolly figure. 'He became what we all know him to be now [this was 1987], when he was Prime Minister. He actually said to me, "I want to be feared,"' Henderson recalled.[62]

To Heath's credit, however, he made great efforts to consult his Cabinet colleagues even in the most rapidly moving of circumstances such as the decision to float the pound in June 1972.[63] The veteran political correspondent, James Margach, familiar with every British premier since Ramsay MacDonald, declared (admittedly in 1978 before the onset of the Thatcher years): 'In my experience no Prime Minister rivalled his [Heath's] control. It was a one-man Government. Even those Ministers who were naturally good communicators, with a sympathy for more open government, became afraid to talk even privately about their departmental policies.'[64]

Douglas Hurd reckoned that 'although both of them are irritated if you suggest it, Ted Heath and Margaret Thatcher had rather similar styles. They are both very definite people, not by instinct very patient of dissent . . . They are both, by nature, impatient and authoritative people and that may be one reason why they didn't get on particularly well together.'[65] Those ministers who were close to him, members of his very informal 'Inner Cabinet', as Robert Armstrong put it later,[66] have alluded to this. Lord Carrington recognized that 'Heath could, as Prime Minister, be abrasive and sometimes contrived to seem at the same time both touchy and autocratic . . . He certainly listened. He may not always have been persuaded by what he heard – but that is the top person's prerogative.'[67]

It is difficult to be precise about the nature of Heath's 'Inner Cabinet' because there was nothing formal about it and some of its members were not ministers. It is important, however, as it was the one group, however fluid, where he eased up a little and his rather fierce, almost Gladstonian line, between public duty and private enjoyment blurred somewhat.

I have come closest to pinning it down during a conversation with Douglas Hurd about the desirability (or otherwise) of premiers having 'Inner Cabinets':

HENNESSY: Would you have a Cabinet committee, whether you called it an 'Inner Cabinet' or not, that was a kind of strategic committee of the big hitters . . . ?
HURD: I think it would depend so much on the personalities. I think one would

probably do it as Ted did with a supper at Prunier's occasionally and that would enable you to ring the changes a bit.

HENNESSY: So it would be informal?

HURD: Yes.

HENNESSY: And the Prunier's group was essentially Carrington, Prior, Whitelaw . . .

HURD: Well, it wasn't definite. It varied very much and sometimes it was just the inner folk.

HENNESSY: By the 'inner folk' you mean people like you and Robert Armstrong as well?

HURD: And Michael Wolff [the Prime Minister's senior political adviser and speech writer] and so on, and Jim Prior, yes certainly. But then other people would be brought in as needed. And it was also a recreation for the Prime Minister. There's a great deal to be said for getting a certain amount of the discussion and the thinking done out of No. 10 – away, physically. It could be Prunier's; could be Chequers; it could be somewhere else. Geography is quite important.

HENNESSY: Ted did that more than perhaps outsiders realized?

HURD: Oh much more. He kept it all very private.

HENNESSY: Yes, things didn't leak in your days. Things leaked very seldom in Ted's Cabinet.

HURD: No, we wouldn't have dared! No, of course not. We hugged the secret of these things to ourselves because it made it more fun. No, it was quite a different world . . . absolutely different in that kind of respect.[68]

The Heath years were perhaps the last of the era of relatively private government.

In his memoir written in the late 1970s, *An End to Promises*, Douglas Hurd detected 'a note of genuine puritan protest'[69] which rang through the Heath premiership – a sound which also struck powerfully Hurd's successor in the Political Office, William Waldegrave, who joined it in Heath's last phase after Hurd had gone off to nurse a winnable seat in Oxfordshire. This puritanism, for Waldegrave, was 'an essential element in Mr Heath's character'. It led him to wish not only 'to clean up government' after what he regarded as Wilson's excesses of deviousness and media manipulation, 'but more importantly [to restore a] high moral and intellectual purpose to the process of politics'. If, said Mr (now Lord) Waldegrave while addressing an Institute of Historical Research seminar in 1997 with subsequent Cabinet experience under Mrs Thatcher and Mr

THE SOMERSAULTING MODERNIZER

Major to assist in his assessment, 'that all sounds a little priggish and somewhat asking for trouble – well, perhaps it was. But it was also honourable and genuinely high-minded'.[70] For Waldegrave this explains both why Heath's 'was probably the best prepared new government until that of Blair' and that 'a certain approach or style to government . . . was the defining characteristic of the task Mr Heath set himself' – hence the value he placed in office on 'the process of serious policy analysis in itself more than he did [on] past policy commitments, even Manifesto commitments'.[71]

This singular approach led Enoch Powell to deride him as excessively civil servant-like ('[Ted] believes there is an answer to all problems which can be worked out by proper bureaucratic means').[72] It is something which has always shone through in my conversations with Sir Edward about his Downing Street days. It explains, too, his almost Haldane-like approach to the Cabinet system as an aid to rational decision-taking. William Waldegrave captured this when he concluded: 'Mr Heath approached Cabinet government on the basis that it should be a rational process for policy formation and analysis. He was not naïve – he had been Chief Whip after all – but all I saw of him leads me to the belief that he hoped that the Cabinet and the Cabinet committee structure should fulfil its textbook role as a hierarchy of rational decision, for . . . with the help of dispassionate and largely apolitical policy analysis, previously intractable problems could be rationally solved . . .'[73]

Lord Waldegrave's testimony strikes me as not just an exact evocation of the Heath *mentalité*, but also as an explanation of his distance (both physical and intellectual) from the activist and the partisan in his party and his penchant for dramatic shifts of policy in pursuit of consistent goals if the evidence, as he interpreted it, pointed towards such shifts. Enoch Powell caught this hugely important side of him, too, when he described Heath's belief that: 'If all the relevant facts are assembled and put together by competent people, and logical analysis made, then that will provide the answer.'[74] Directed collegiality might be the phrase to describe this approach to Cabinet government.

Heath's attempts at collegiality helped keep his Cabinet resignation-free and, to a very large extent, leak-free too. But he did by-pass them on occasion, and not just on the traditional nuclear issues such as updating the Polaris missile system with its 'Chevaline' refinement[75] or the intensely secret planning he oversaw to cover what would happen if he and the Cabinet were wiped out by a pre-emptive nuclear strike from the Soviet

Union.[76] The best attuned political commentators such as David Watt picked this up at the time and wrote about Heath's penchant for setting-up 'small *ad hoc* ministerial "task forces", occasionally even containing a senior civil servant, which are constituted to hammer out a policy for a particular purpose and then dissolve'.[77]

The policy David Watt had in mind was Ulster (probably the lead-up to direct-rule in 1972).[78] But the one I have in mind, which had an impact on each and every minister's portfolio, because of both its centrality and its public expenditure implications, was the renewed dash for modernity through state intervention which was tacked on to the 1972 Budget and eventually took the form of the Industry Act 1972, which gave Whitehall increased powers in terms of regional aid. Heath was increasingly frustrated by industry's failure to invest. He has always defended his creation of legislative powers to encourage this and to inject state cash directly into private companies experiencing trouble as 'a sensible, pragmatic and practical response to a disappointing state of affairs' which was intended to be temporary ('Once the industrial climate in Britain had been changed and our companies had acquired some positive momentum, then the government could gradually withdraw and leave it to the entrepreneurs').[79]

As John Ramsden has explained, 'the planning of the policies was taken outside normal departmental channels, and to a quite remarkable extent behind the backs of some key figures. The tilt of policy that led to the Industry Bill of 1972 was known about by the Secretary of State for [Trade and] Industry, John Davies (but not by his more hawkish juniors who had to be moved or removed before the policy could be announced); detailed work was done by a special team of civil servants under William Armstrong, with little input from the DTI, the CBI [the Confederation of British Industry] or the Treasury.'

So secret were these discussions that Tory backbenchers were struck dumb with amazement when the proposals were revealed to the Commons at the end of the 1972 Budget debate. 'What is even more remarkable', John Ramsden has discovered, is 'that the Chief Secretary to the Treasury, Patrick Jenkin, who was responsible for public expenditure . . . and who had to wind up the debate only a few hours after John Davies made the announcement, had no inkling of the new proposals until he heard the announcement in the House, so far was the Treasury kept in the dark.'[80]

In terms of back-channel policy-making, this even outdoes Whitehall's experience of Eden and Suez, though John Campbell indicates that the full Cabinet was informed of the outcome on the morning of Budget Day itself.[81] In general, it could be argued, however, that Heath if anything enhanced the status of full Cabinet by adding Europe and, after the imposition of direct rule in 1972, Northern Ireland to its traditionally regular weekly items on foreign affairs and next week's business in Parliament.[82]

The Cabinet, so far as we know, was unanimous on the application to join the European Economic Community – the policy Heath made central to his own and his government's purposes. In its way, the achievement of membership on 1 January 1973 is without parallel in British history. Neither the acquisition nor the disposal of Empire can be fixed to a particular man or moment. Yet EEC entry was an event of equal, probably greater, significance in the long term.[83]

In the short term, only two very minor members of the government resigned over the terms of entry.[84] But the tactics of piloting the European Communities Bill through Parliament, and the selling of it to Parliament, the Conservative Party and the public, were great absorbers of ministerial time.[85] The passages on Europe are the stretches of Heath's memoir which most came alive. His two-day meeting in Paris in May 1971 with President Pompidou – the bout of intense personal diplomacy which secured the UK's accession to the Community – is recalled with a brio enchanced by intense and personal satisfaction about the outcome and of the way it was unveiled before an unbelieving world. A 'wildly exciting moment',[86] he called it, as he and Pompidou, in the very room in the Elysée Palace where de Gaulle had pronounced his veto in January 1963, jointly told the astonished press and some members of the No. 10 extended family ('I had not even confided in Douglas Hurd or in Michael Wolff . . . to their evident annoyance')[87] that a deal was there for the making.

The slightly vindictive 'I'll show you' side of Heath intrudes among his sentences ('The President and I looked across at each other with delight, for we had secured success and also triumphed over the media'),[88] though in an illustration of a less well-known personal characteristic, Sir Edward manages to laugh at himself and his execrable French accent: 'at Chequers, he [Pompidou] told me (in French!), "If you ever want to know what my policy is, don't bother to call me on the telephone. I do not speak English and your French is awful. Just remember that I am a peasant, and my policy will always be to support the peasants."'[89]

Northern Ireland became, in Paul Arthur's useful distinction, one of the 'required items', as opposed to 'discretionary'[90] issues on the Cabinet agenda and was certainly one of the top three and possibly the greatest absorber of high-level prime ministerial time over the life of the government as a whole (the others being Europe and prices and incomes policy).[91] Though the papers of the Heath administration are still largely retained within the thirty-year rule, we know that its Ministerial Committee on Northern Ireland (NI) was one of the first Cabinet committees he set up on taking office. Trend advising him that: 'We need a small, compact and very senior Committee to keep a close watch on this explosive subject.'[92] Northern Ireland was one of those 'previously intractable problems' to which Heath applied his rational approach to decision-making though, in William Waldegrave's words, plainly 'rationality alone' could not 'dissolve such ancient tangles'.[93] In 1971 Heath asked the Central Policy Review Staff (of which the young Waldegrave was then a member) to bring reason to the Irish question in its latest manifestation.

The 'think-tank' outlined three courses the government might pursue – partition (or a re-partition of the Six Counties to be precise); coalition (power-sharing within the province – the policy eventually adopted); or condominium (a Northern Ireland governed jointly by the UK and the Republic of Ireland 'with its citizens having dual citizenship'[94]). As the crisis and the body-counts worsened in 1972 and the possibility of direct rule from London was mooted, Alec Douglas-Home, the Foreign Secretary, 'was against the move entirely'. 'Fearing that we would end up being stuck with governing the province permanently' and believing that 'no sustainable framework for keeping Northern Ireland within the United Kingdom could ever be contrived,' Douglas-Home advised Heath to 'start to push the people of Northern Ireland towards a united Ireland, rather than trying to tie them more closely into the United Kingdom'.[95]

At no time during his stewardship in No. 10 did the pressure on his NI Cabinet Committee ease, though the committee load generally was something he did try to tackle as the life of his administration progressed. Heath ordered a great cull of Cabinet committees when Sir Burke Trend retired from the Cabinet Office in 1973.[96] Trend's successor, Sir John Hunt, had been involved with the very secret review after the first miners' strike in 1972 which led to the replacement of the old Emergencies Committee with the new Civil Contingencies Unit (which survives to this day, the only one of Heath's 'mixed' committees of ministers and officials to endure).[97] The Civil Service never liked these mixed committees; some officials even thought they were a dangerous blurring of the constitutional divide between the two governing breeds.[98] Heath became a trifle irritated when I put this point to him in 1989, arguing that such bodies educated civil servants in the way politicians thought, 'put them in the picture' and drew them out of their 'ivory towers'.[99]*

One of the problems with Sir Edward, even in his more mellow old age, is the combination of shyness and defensiveness that can, in Roy Jenkins' marvellous phrase, produce the Heath 'affronted penguin' impression.[101] As Colonel Sir Claud 'Toby' Lancaster, one of his backbenchers, put it during the Heath premiership: 'The difficulty with Ted is that you never know him. You can spend hours and hours with him and you never know him any better at the end of it.'[102] The great exception here is Heath on music. Through this medium – and this alone – does Heath's inner warmth flow.

One picture from his Downing Street years captures it to perfection. It is of Heath, with Robert Armstrong in the background, striding through the front door of No. 10 smiling and clutching the score of Elgar's *Cockaigne* on the way to conduct the London Symphony Orchestra.[103] And he once shook the CBI during a negotiating session at Chequers by asking 'Can I play you some Mozart?' before they resumed discussions after lunch.[104] One of the most moving passages of his memoirs is his description of the evening of 28 October 1971, 'my greatest success as Prime Minister',[105] when the House of Commons voted by 356 to 244 in favour of British membership of the European Communities. He returned to No. 10 and, as it were, took to the ivories before taking to the streets: '. . . we returned to my private sitting room . . . and I played the First Prelude from Book I of Bach's "Well-Tempered Clavier" on my clavichord'.[106]

The private Heath was rarely apparent outside his No. 10 household. It certainly did not impinge upon the bulk of his party in Parliament, let alone the country. Sir Edward was not pleased when I put to him the point that he had failed to shine when it came to fraternizing with his backbenchers in the Commons' Tea Room or Smoking Room. 'This unclubbable idea is a myth which has grown up', he insisted.[107] But this view of him proved a handicap when time and chance turned on him after the 1974 election losses and he faced tough criticism as a Tory version of Nye Bevan's 'desiccated calculating machine'.[108]

Enoch Powell was not alone in pushing this line. Angus Maude had

---

* Heath is reluctant to admit any mistakes in his premiership. When pressed hard by Michael Crick of the BBC in 1995 he grudgingly admitted to one: 'Some of my appointments.'[100] It was quite plain who he was talking about!

criticized Heath in 1966, arguing in the *Spectator* that 'a technocratic approach is not sufficient . . . we must have some philosophy', and lost his Shadow Cabinet place for his pains.[109] But it is Powell who has made the sharpest case for the prosecution of Heath the flawed-technocrat-without-a-soul. On one occasion Powell famously declared Ted 'didn't really think, I believe, that the House of Commons had a heart, let alone the British people. At least he's never showed any signs of being able to locate either.'[110]

Private Eye made the same points about Heath's alleged calculating machine where his heart should have been rather more crudely with its caricatures of 'Grocer' Heath – the man who became obsessed with food prices as EEC negotiator in 1961–63 and as the abolisher of retail price maintenance in 1964 – in its stilted parody of him: the regular 'Heathco' strip cartoon.[111] A more apt caricature might have been Heath as stiff and unbending Whitehall Permanent Secretary. He remained proud of having come top in his competition for the old administrative class of the Civil Service in 1946 even though it led to his being posted at the somewhat unfashionable Ministry of Civil Aviation.[112] He soon discovered 'it wasn't really for me. The only thing it did do was give me the satisfaction of saying, if ever I wanted, to a permanent secretary, "Now look here, come along, I could be in your place if I'd wanted to, but I didn't." '[113]

Douglas Hurd, from his close observations of Heath in action, told Michael Cockerell: 'He's an educator, Ted. If he hadn't been a politician I think he would have been a don or a schoolmaster. He believes that people are entitled to the truth.'[114] One of the most impressive examples of this trait, revealed in Nigel Nicolson's memoirs, was Heath's conduct during the Suez crisis. On 8 November 1956, Nicolson, a dissenter, saw Heath who, as Eden's Chief Whip, 'asked me to support the Government in the vote that night. I said that I would do so if he could assure me that the purpose of our invasion was "to separate the combatants", as the Prime Minister claimed, and not to regain control of the Canal by a subterfuge. He held my gaze steadily and said nothing. I thanked him for his honesty, told him that I would abstain and left the room.'[115]

For all the honesty, the technocracy charge levelled at Ted Heath is important. The problems that came in battalions, especially after the 1972 miners' strike, have both obscured the governmental reforms which were central to Heath's so-called 'quiet revolution'[116] *and* discouraged others from emulating his approach on the grounds that those very reforms made no difference at all to his or his administration's capacity to cope with political and economic crises.[117] Heath has somehow become lumped with Wilson's departmental experimentation in the 1960s as a composite folk-memory of how not to do it.[118]

Whitehall's how-not-to folk memory also extends to the US–UK 'special relationship' (whatever its degree of specialness). As Henry Kissinger revealed, Burke Trend was not alone in believing that Heath's determination to be a European had led him to downgrade and under-use unnecessarily the transatlantic advantages which were there for the taking.[119] In 1990, my *Analysis* editor, Caroline Anstey, and I, while preparing a BBC Radio 4 documentary on the 'special relationship', took our tape-recorder separately to Heath and Kissinger. It led to the following extraordinary broadcast exchange after Caroline had juxtaposed the tapes:

HEATH: I've always had my eyes open about the so-called 'special relationship'. I've recognized that our job and Europe's job is to look after our own interests because what the Americans do is to look after their interests.

KISSINGER: Ted Heath was an unusual British leader in that he did not really seem to value the American relationship. I think Ted Heath was wrong in the sense that he threw away an asset without gaining anything corresponding, especially at a time when all the Europeans were very eager to establish a preferential relationship in the United States.

HEATH: What is the asset? First of all, it's been proven again in these last ten years, what it does is to estrange us from our European colleagues because they're insulted by the idea that they're inferior and we can always claim some special relationship.

KISSINGER: We did not submit anything to Europe without first having discussed it with the Heath government. Prime Minister Heath, for very understandable reasons, was eager to demonstrate to the Europeans that he did not have a special relationship with the United States and, therefore, he went out of his way to reject any attempts to work with him on a special basis. But that was not on our side.

HEATH: His whole argument on that respect is quite unsustainable. He created the 'Year of Europe', which never of course came about, without any discussions with us as a special relationship or with anybody else. He just declared he was going to have a 'Year of Europe'. Well, we didn't want a 'Year of Europe'. I said to him, 'Now you've done this, we must have a Year of the United States. Who are you to propose that there should be a Year of Europe? You're not part of Europe. All right, well we'll come along, have a Year of the United States . . .

show you how to do these things.' But what he did afterwards was go and talk to the French, to explain what he wanted and tell them not to say anything to the British – whereupon of course, the French Foreign Minister, as soon as Henry had left Paris, flew over to London and came and told me everything which had happened. You can't carry on diplomacy that way.

KISSINGER: But if I may say one thing. It is easy or relatively easy to go through twenty years of relations and pick out crises. Nobody ever said that the special relationship precluded disagreements and difference of judgement. What the special relationship involved from our point of view is that we had a degree of confidence in British leaders that we did not have in leaders of any other country.

HEATH: What they wanted from the special relationship was to land Britain in it as well. There was the question of the Indo-Pakistan war and what Henry wanted was to land us in that and I was determined not to be landed. We discussed this in Bermuda when President Nixon was there and he opened up the question and said, 'There seems to be a misunderstanding about this. Henry, try to explain why this was what you wanted,' and so then we had a lecture abut the conceptual nature of Kissinger policy. Well we easily dispatched that and Nixon said, 'Well that's the end of that one, Henry, isn't it?' So we didn't go in that war and Harold Macmillan saved us from going in the Vietnam War. Well, thank God, we escaped both of those wars. Did we lose anything by it? No of course not. We gained an enormous amount. I can quite see that it's rather difficult for some Americans, including Henry, to adjust themselves to this, but it's necessary for them to do it. Now, there are some people who always want to nestle on the shoulder of an American president. That's no future for Britain.[120]

One of Jim Callaghan's priorities on becoming Foreign Secretary in March 1974 was to restore the old relationship. He told an aide that he thought the first duty of a British Foreign Secretary was to be on good terms with a US Secretary of State[121] and he put a great deal of effort into building up an excellent relationship with Kissinger which paid off handsomely when Callaghan, as Prime Minister, found himself engaged in a tense process of economic diplomacy in the autumn of 1976.

This is not the place to do more than offer a flavour of the *Sturm und Drang* which weakened the Heath administration before blowing it away in the 'Who governs?' election campaign of February 1974.[122] Yet describing the overlapping, running crises and problems – Northern Ireland; strikes; inflation and incomes policy; Europe; the disturbances and dislocations caused by the Government's industrial relations legislation; the protracted search in 1972 for an accommodation between government, employers and the trade unions; the surge in world commodity prices and, lastly, the chaos in energy markets and the explosion of oil prices associated with the Yom Kippur War and its aftermath in the autumn and winter of 1973–74, combined with industrial action in the pits and the power stations at home – is almost too clinical.

To feel the stress and the overload, particularly when Heath was unwell in his last autumn in office (John Campbell believes he was already suffering from an underactive thyroid[123] though Heath denies this[124]), you have to resort to vignettes and to appreciate that Heath was very much the economic and industrial overlord of his administration. He was the first Conservative Prime Minister to chair the Cabinet's Economic Strategy Committee, ES,[125] and he dominated his Chancellor, the easygoing but far from heavyweight Anthony Barber. As John Nott, one of Barber's ministerial colleagues at the Treasury, later put it. 'The sole author of the dash-for-growth was the Prime Minister, Ted Heath. "The Barber Boom" is misnamed.'[126]

In reality, the pressures were relentless for his last two years as premier. John Campbell has captured the early weeks of 1972, that 'traumatic year for the Heath Government', as he put it, ' – a year of crisis, humiliations and emergencies'.

The pattern of the year was set in the first two months, which must rate as the most dreadful short period of concentrated stress ever endured in peacetime [up to that date]. Two events in particular shook the Government to its core. On 9 January the miners began an unexpectedly determined six-week strike in pursuit of a wage increase of 47 per cent; and on 20 January the monthly figure for unemployment in the United Kingdom reached one million for the first time since 1947 . . .

But these were not the only hammer blows. To understand the pressure Heath and his colleagues were under at this critical moment of the Government's fortunes it is necessary to appreciate that they were simultaneously assailed by two further desperate crises which absorbed the Cabinet's time, drained its energy and stretched its nerves to the limit. First, Northern Ireland was erupting in a new wave of bombings and killings of unprecedented ferocity and the province was slipping closer to the abyss of all-out civil war. Second, the Government was embarking on a perilous parliamentary battle as the enabling legislation to take Britain into the EEC began its fiercely contested passage through the Commons.[127]

Let us dip in now to a second equally fraught period for the Heath administration with the help of Douglas Hurd, whose *An End to Promises* combines the graphic with the reflective. Recalling the period when the oil price quadrupled and the miners moved towards their second strike in two years, Hurd wrote:

A rush of other events prevented senior Ministers from giving the coal crisis the attention which it needed. On Sunday 8 December, for example, the Prime Minister entertained the Italian Prime Minister, Signor Rumor, to dinner at Chequers. The meal was hardly over when Mr Heath flew to Sunningdale by helicopter to preside over the last stage of the conference on the future of Northern Ireland. Three days later it was time for the State Visit of President Mobutu of Zaire. Two days after that the European Summit began in Copenhagen.

These were four major events, two of them (Sunningdale and Copenhagen) of outstanding importance. They were all the kind of diplomatic event which in normal times Mr Heath would much enjoy and at which he would perform very well. They all involved tasks, travel, long meals, extensive briefing beforehand; yet none of them had anything to do with the crisis which was swallowing us up.[128]

As the stress grew, with a state of emergency declared, a three-day week in force and Britain flickering as a lights-on, lights-off nation Heath retreated more and more into his Downing Street shell, closer to his officials than to many of his colleagues (one of whom, William Armstrong, while chairing a meeting of fellow Permanent Secretaries broke down under the increasing strain during the last weeks of the Government).[129]

At such moments Prime Ministers need to call in debts from political supporters and media alike. Here Heath was very thinly endowed, partly for the creditable reason that he had no time for the charlatanries and hypocrisies which are often involved in the accumulation of such credits. He had his party's respect but not its affection in late 1973 and early 1974, and this respect would last until he lost the third of his four general election head-to-heads with Wilson in October 1974. But his credit with the press had largely disappeared long before. 'Heath had the shortest honeymoon of all with the political correspondents', according to Jimmy Margach.[130] Margach dates its demise to the autumn of 1970 when Heath took offence at the lobby's coverage of the Leila Khaled hijacking affair.[131] 'From that moment onwards he more or less broke off relations with the political corps for their lack of co-operation and understanding . . . By the time of his defeat in 1974 he had cut himself off from political reality . . . by his misguided decision to ostracise the media at Westminster.'[132]

Heath, as Margach concedes, continued to see the diplomatic correspondents and, to his credit, he tried Washington-style on-the-record press conferences. In fact, as he told me fifteen years after leaving No. 10, 'I wanted to abolish the lobby system . . . It is a corrupt system.'[133] This is a view with which I have much sympathy, but lobby journalists, like old-style monopoly trade unions, are – or were – a powerful restrictive practice unforgiving to those who cross them. And Heath was no natural communicator who could afford to dispense with the written press thanks to a powerful television persona. As Douglas Hurd has stressed, his ear for musical cadence did not extend to the sound and beauty of words.[134]

Early 1974 found an already isolated Heath, contemptuous of the press, ill at ease with his own party and closer to some of his civil servants – the two Armstrongs, William and Robert, especially – than to many of his Cabinet colleagues.[135] William Waldegrave reckons that Heath 'was perhaps the last Prime Minister – though perhaps James Callaghan was another – who truly respected the British administrative and academic establishment . . .'[136] Reluctantly, Heath was pushed by the miners' ballot for an all-out strike into asking the Queen for a ballot of the electorate.[137] But even the shortest campaign of the postwar period[138] saw his strategy unravel as, inevitably, other issues crowded in to confuse its 'who rules?' thrust. And to make matters ruinously worse, the new relativities mechanism of the Pay Board exposed faulty official calculations of the miners' case, which were promptly leaked.[139]

Far from winning a refreshed majority on 28 February 1974, Heath found himself four seats short of Labour's haul (297 to their 301) though with a wafer-thin lead in terms of the percentage of votes cast (37.8 per cent to their 37.1).[140] He hung on, as we have seen, over a grim weekend, trying and failing to do a deal with the Liberals[141] and some of the Ulster Unionists (who had ceased to take the Conservative whip after the imposition of direct rule in the province in 1972).[142] Finally, after two Cabinet meetings on Monday 4 March, 'poor Ted' as a Palace official put it, brought to an end 'this dicey weekend' and 'came round . . . very very depressed [to resign] . . . and the Queen sent for Harold Wilson which was the only possible thing for her to do'.[143]

A great many things went out with Heath that day in March 1974. Of course the Heath-style mechanics of his 'quiet revolution' were among them. He himself had already begun the break-up of the giant Department of Trade and Industry in January 1974, when energy sprang back into a separate ministerial existence under Lord Carrington.[144] Wilson completed the process the following March, splitting Trade and Industry further into three.[145] Programme Analysis and Review expired gently through the mid to late seventies and was put out of its misery as one of Mrs Thatcher's first acts in 1979.[146] The day after she won re-election in 1983 the Central Policy Review Staff (unlike PAR, a serious loss) followed it into oblivion.[147]

Heath's select committee reforms – a central Expenditure Committee with a constellation of sub-committees around it – were a considerable improvement on the old Estimates Committee and survived until the creation of departmentally related House of Commons committees in 1979.[148] And some of his more secret improvements to the machinery of government, such as a boosting of the Joint Intelligence Committee's capacity for economic analysis, also languished under his Labour successors (though Mrs Thatcher was a keen customer for this kind of intelligence and revived the flow in the 1980s).[149]

But Monday 4 March 1974 has a much greater significance than any of that. I think Vernon Bogdanor is right to treat it as 'the end of the postwar settlement'.[150] It was only as the polls were closing on 28 February that Wilson appreciated he was likely to lead the largest single party.[151] And though he and his successor, Jim Callaghan, were still conditioned by the mid-century political and economic culture that had formed them, British politics coarsened and stretched. (This is the period when Professor Sammy Finer anatomized the malign consequences of adversarialism[152] and Professor Tony King dissected the punishing effects of governmental 'overload'[153]). Equally significantly, the 1970 fall in Labour's core vote of just over a million 'was not to be replaced' for a generation and though, as John Ramsden has put it, 'Labour would still be able to win elections in 1974, on a lowish vote, when the Conservatives were even more unpopular, evidence of the new electoral balance that was to allow Tory dominance in the 1980s was there to be seen in the 1970 result'[154] as well as in the two 1974 elections.

Monday March 4 also saw the iron enter the soul of the great eventual beneficiary of that shift in the electoral geomorphology. At the second of the two Cabinet meetings held to discuss the Liberals' demands before coalition could be contemplated (a Tory replacement for Heath and a commitment to proportional representation),[155] 'Margaret Thatcher', according to Professor Bogdanor, hitherto one of the more silent members of his Cabinet, is said to have burst out, 'Oh, no we couldn't. Think how many seats we would lose.' It was at this point, according to one observer, that her hostility to Heath as a traitor to Conservatism crystallised. For in her view, Heath was prepared to sacrifice any chance of the Conservatives ever again achieving an overall majority on their own for a mere temporary renewal of power.[156]

From then on, the writing was on the handbag.

For Douglas Hurd, himself writing on the cusp of the Thatcher era, 'the years of Mr Heath's government should be regarded as a necessary first attempt, the rough work of pioneers'[157] for the reforms that were put in place in the 1980s. I do not see it like that. For me Heath, from first to last, was attempting to breathe new life, economic vitality especially, into that postwar settlement. In words I suspect Douglas Hurd himself had written for him in 1973, Heath declared:

'The alternative to expansion is not, as some occasionally seem to suppose, an England of quiet market towns linked only by trains puffing slowly and peacefully through green meadows. The alternative is slums, dangerous roads, old factories, cramped schools, stunted lives.'[158]

There spoke a Grade 1 Listed Postwar Settler. Heath was not alone when he called on the Queen on 4 March 1974. The postwar consensus, too, went with him to resign.

14

Centre Half:
Harold Wilson, 1974–76

'Harold Wilson was the orchestrator [of the Cabinet] – very careful to bring people in at certain stages. He didn't take votes but he would make notes of what people said. If he didn't look like getting his way, he would delay it for another meeting or defer it for a Chequers session.'   *Lord Hunt of Tanworth, Secretary of the Cabinet*
during the last Wilson premiership, 1983[1]

'You talk about a messy, middle-of-the-road muddle, but if the Cabinet understand what I mean, I'm at my best in a messy middle-of-the-road muddle.'   *Harold Wilson to the Cabinet when*
placing the 'Agreement to Differ' over the European
Economic Community before ministers in January 1975[2]

'The trouble is when the old problems reappear I reach for the old solutions.'   *Harold Wilson to his Press Secretary, July 1975*[3]

'Is that man crazy? He thinks there's a bug behind all the pictures.'
George Bush, then Director of the Central Intelligence Agency,
after visiting Harold Wilson in No. 10 during his last premiership[4]

'Harold wanted to be a combination of the head of MI5 and news editor of the *Daily Mirror*.'
Downing Street official shortly after Wilson's resignation[5]

'Harold was like a great player of Space Invaders. He would take the first blip to cross the screen whether it was the important one or not.'
Another Downing Street official shortly after
Wilson's resignation[6]

For reasons of balance, any account of Wilson's last, lacklustre premiership has to begin with a statement of the obvious. He was a formidable electioneer – winning four of his five contests – and acquiring or re-acquiring power is, self-evidently, the *sine qua non* of any would-be Prime Minister. Shortly before the 1997 general election, Donald Sassoon compiled an 'Impotency Index' based on the percentage of the period since 1945 in which West European Labour, socialist or social democratic parties had found themselves in opposition. Britain topped the fourteen-strong table with 66 per cent.[7] This, at least, is a failing that could not be laid at Wilson's door. During his thirteen years as party leader, Labour was in opposition for only five of them.

Even he, however, did not expect to win on Thursday 28 February 1974. He had laid elaborate plans, should he lose, to avoid the waiting press at the Adelphi Hotel in Liverpool (his traditional base while campaigning in his Huyton constituency) by slipping off to an obscure hotel on the city's outskirts before flying secretly back to London. These precautions he partly implemented; the Wilson entourage repaired to 'a very depressing little hotel in Kirby' where someone, inevitably, tipped off the press waiting in the Adelphi who rushed there to 'doorstep' him.[8]

Only an hour or two before the polls closed on 28 February did Wilson realize he might become Prime Minister again. It was his aide, the LSE political scientist Dr Bernard Donoughue, who caused and witnessed this last-minute reappraisal:

'I went for a walk with him in Huyton, a dreary wet evening through bleak housing estates, and I was convinced that we would be the largest party. As a pollster, that's what the numbers told me . . . and I told him I thought this would be the result. He perked up a bit and began to discuss the kind of government he would have, and that's when he used his football analogies to me about how he was going to be a sweeper-up at the back and let the other ministers do the attacking and it would be different from 1964 when he had had to score all the goals.'[9]

There were several other contrasts with 1964 which began to appear even before Heath finally left No. 10 to resign on the Monday afternoon.

Oddly enough, it was an older man, his longstanding rival Jim Callaghan, who appeared almost to take charge when the party's National Executive Committee met the day after the poll to decide how to react to Heath's decision to hang on. It was Callaghan's idea, as we saw in chapter 3, that senior Labour figures should sit tight, keep mum and allow Heath to destroy himself.[10] Not that Wilson was a reluctant recidivist. As his press secretary, Joe Haines, put it, Wilson's

'ambition, after losing in 1970 – and I think he would have gone in 1972 or so had he won in 1970 – was really to get back so that he wasn't just another defeated Prime Minister. I think he had run out of ideas on what he could do for Britain.'[11]

But Wilson's return made a sad contrast with the shining hour of October 1964. As he had explained to Bernard Donoughue (who was to accompany him into No. 10 as head of his only innovation, the Downing Street Policy Unit), this time there would be 'no presidential nonsense', 'no "first hundred days"' and 'no beer and sandwiches at No. 10' to solve industrial disputes.[12]

No. 10 was, however, undoubtedly strengthened by the creation of the Policy Unit, an institution adapted and enhanced (never diminished) by Wilson's successors in Downing Street. Wilson was consciously implementing a recommendation of the Fulton Report of 1968 that ministers should have planning units incorporated in their departments.[13] (Interestingly, he ignored the full Fulton recommendation that all Whitehall departments should have such units. Other Cabinet ministers were to be restricted to two special advisers and their names would have to be cleared with No. 10 before they were appointed.)[14]

Wilson's idea was that the Policy Unit should provide him with an alternative and more politically attuned flow of policy analysis on short- and medium-term issues to that produced by the regular Civil Service departments or the Central Policy Review Staff, which, to the surprise of some in Whitehall, he decided to keep, despite its powerful associations with the Heath style.[15]

Apart from these innovations, of interest mainly to Whitehall watchers and Whitehall itself and little noticed more generally, Wilson's return had a lacklustre feel about it. He himself had no illusions, either, about being a renewed hero, even to his own party. Between taking office in March and the second 1974 election in October, when he converted a thirty-four-seat deficit into a slim overall majority of three, Wilson told Sir Nicholas Henderson, UK Ambassador to West Germany (with whom he was staying on a June visit to Bonn) that the Labour Party 'keep me there, not because they love me, but because there is no-one else who can keep the party together'.[16]

This burst of contemporary analysis (and frankness) was but an interlude in an exhausting monologue which convinced Henderson that Wilson was 'living in the past',[17] with talk of prewar Oxford, work with Beveridge in the war, Tony Benn's lack of judgement compared to Stafford Cripps, interspersed with where he would play Billy Bremner in the forthcoming Scotland game with Brazil, the whole scene of banality and reminiscence illuminated by the 'fuel-injector lighter like a flame-thrower' which the Prime Minister used to light his pipe.[18] Joe Haines thought part of Wilson's trouble in 1974 was that he had been at the top too long, working flat-out with scarcely a pause since leaving Oxford to join Beveridge.[19]

The past, however, was not put to good use in 1974–75. In an almost exact re-run of 1964–66, Wilson did not set up adequate Cabinet machinery to deal with his number 1 problem – the economy – until Sir John Hunt, the Cabinet Secretary (retreading Trend's path nine years earlier) finally persuaded him to create a proper Cabinet Committee on Economic Strategy (EY) once the re-negotiation of the terms of EEC entry was completed[20] and the referendum on Britain's continued membership was over (all this at a time when inflation was creeping towards its all-time high of 26.5 per cent). John Hunt (like his mentor, Norman Brook, a great gripper of business)[21] put this tactfully for Wilson's BBC Radio 4 obituary. Speaking of 1974–75, he said:

'The Cabinet devoted a fairly small amount of its time to economic affairs. Partly because it was at first preoccupied with ending the three-day week, getting the country back to work, etcetera, then preoccupied with Europe and preoccupied with devolution, both of which took quite an inordinate amount of time. I think the Prime Minister and other Ministers saw wider economic difficulties looming but they hadn't perhaps the time to grapple with them and I think also to some extent they didn't know what to do about them and were waiting until they were forced to deal with them.'[22]

This could almost be Trend's brief for Wilson for the 'crunch' Cabinet meeting of 19 July 1966.[23]

It appeared that Wilson, the great spawner of 'Inner Cabinets', Cabinet committees and new departments, had abandoned his Mark I tendencies in favour of a Mark II *ad hominem* approach. His Whitehall tinkering was restricted to a breaking-up of the Department of Trade and Industry into three to meet a political need to accommodate the various strands in what Roy Jenkins called his 'coalition of incompatibles ... [this] very uneasy Cabinet',[24] with Tony Benn taking Industry, Peter Shore Trade and Shirley Williams Prices and Consumer Protection. This time there was no Department of Economic Affairs but there was a one-man alternative to it – Harold Lever.

Lever was more gadfly than overlord, but as Chancellor of the Duchy with a seat in the Cabinet, and, in Wilson's words, 'a kind of ministerial general economic adviser in No. 10',[25] he was licensed to roam across the whole range of financial, economic and industrial policy powered by the authority which came from both prime ministerial patronage and Lever's being that great rarity in Labour ministerial circles, a millionaire who both understood the markets and know how to play them. Lever was charming and fun. He may have irritated the regular economic ministers, but he left no bruises.

Lever strengthened Wilson's non-interventionist impulses and was a powerful debunker of Tony Benn's push for economic planning from the Department of Industry. Many years later, speaking of 1974-75, Lever told me (in between doing deals on the telephone from his dazzlingly luxurious Belgravia home): 'I had a very sceptical view about most of our programme. I did not believe in the social policy [the 'Social Contract' with the unions – social improvements in return for voluntary wage restraint] and I did not believe in the so-called industrial strategy . . . all this crap about Benn and his industrial planning . . . The NEB [National Enterprise Board]. I knew it was going to be a dud and the investments would be no good.'[26]

Lever produced one of the most devastating critiques of Wilson Mark I five years after leaving government on the fall of the Callaghan administration. Reviewing Barbara Castle's diaries in *The Listener*, he wrote:

The Cabinet for the period 1964-70 contained an unusually large proportion of highly gifted individuals. Why then was so little achieved? Mrs Castle, by implication, thinks that the failure was due to the defects of individual Ministers, notably Callaghan and Wilson. In my view she is wrong. These governments, like most other modern governments, overestimated their ability to shape and manage the complex drives of a mature economy. They wrongly assumed that they understood all the reasons for its shortcomings and so, not surprisingly, were all too ready to lay hands on superficial remedies for overcoming them. And all this without any attempt to understand the economics of an increasingly interdependent world. It is significant that the National Plans, which were no more than a summary of Labour Party rhetoric, ultimately enjoyed the derision even of the Cabinet itself.[27]

This from a man who had himself served briefly as a junior minister in

1967 in the DEA which he once described as 'a very agreeable form of adult education' as it 'didn't really have either the expertise or the flow of information the Treasury has'.[28]

Wilson, who distrusted the Treasury till his dying day, especially what he once described to me as its 'moles', its 'very skilled chaps in more or less stopping you doing anything',[29] plainly did not share Lever's near total scepticism about intervention but relished his resistance of Treasury orthodoxy.[30] (His Principal Private Secretary during his final year as premier, Sir Kenneth Stowe, recalled that 'Harold Wilson used to say to me that he preferred pirates to policemen. He thought the Treasury were policemen.')[31] Lever, unlike the DEA, immersed himself in the Treasury's core activities – the Budget, public expenditure control and monetary policy. Under both Wilson Mark II and Callaghan he would invite its top officials to tea in his rooms in the Cabinet Office where, using a combination of charm and Socratic method, he would persuade them to tell him much more than they had ever intended.[32]

Denis Healey, Chancellor of the Exchequer throughout the Labour years of 1974–79, 'at first . . . resented Harold's [Lever's] privileged access to the Prime Minister, and his tendency to second-guess my decisions without having any responsibility for carrying them out. When I felt more at ease in my job, I found his understanding of the financial markets invaluable, and I normally accepted about one out of four of his suggestions – a high average for any external consultant.'[33] Healey disapproved of Lever's view that he 'would never have the Government spend its own money if it could borrow someone else's' but he relished the other Chancellor's (Chancellor of the Duchy, that is) 'inexhaustible supply of what I used to call "Leverettes" or "Lever's ripping wheezes", with which to bamboozle the financial markets; this I regarded as a legitimate objective'.[34]

Roy Jenkins, while Wilson's Chancellor between 1967 and 1970, had noticed how 'one of his great qualities was that he had a very good nerve in a crisis. He never recriminated in a crisis and he never panicked in a crisis, and those are two very high qualities in a Prime Minister. It was when things were going better that he got suspicious and difficult.'[35] Denis Healey, like Jenkins, appreciated that 'without the support of the prime minister', the Chancellor's job 'is impossible'. But he found a 'much more relaxed' Wilson as his Downing Street neighbour in 1974. 'He interfered much less in the work of his ministers,' Healey recalled, and he 'was no longer plagued by the demons of jealousy and suspicion which had tormented him in his first two Governments. The prospect of early retirement helped; he had told me during a journey to Helsinki in 1972 that he did not plan to serve for more than three years next time he was Prime Minister'[36] (a matter to which we will return in a moment).

Healey saw a good deal of Wilson, slipping into No. 10 through the connecting door with the Chancellor's residence in No. 11 'at least once a week' for 'a chat'.[37] Roy Jenkins said of that door 'which obviously was controlled from No. 10' that 'sometimes it was locked and sometimes it wasn't locked, so that was a good barometer of the weather'.[38] Healey, with typical bravura, said 'Oh, it was never locked in my time. Wouldn't dare do such a thing to me!'[39] But Healey, I suspect, lacked Jenkins' strange, almost eccentric personal empathy with at least one aspect of Wilson's make-up.

Verbal foreplay is very important in politics, especially at stressful moments. Heath had none of it and always went straight to the point.[40] Wilson, by contrast, invariably managed to embroider his bilateral meetings with his colleagues whether by flirting with his 'little Minister', as he called Barbara Castle,[41] or with that great Cunarder of a Chancellor, Roy Jenkins, with whom he did not flirt but with whom, in Jenkins' glorious phrase, he 'would sort of ramble round some of the ramparts of political reminiscence'.[42] 'He had a very good statistical mind', Lord Jenkins continued, 'and I was rather interested in that sort of detail. He could always remember who lost three by-elections running in what year . . . and liked that sort of gossip. And we also had an interest in railway timetables and railway stations.'[43] The pair of them made a perfect illustration of Orwell's depiction of the English (Jenkins is a kind of honorary Englishman for this purpose) as a nation of crossword puzzlers, a people addicted to hobbies.[44] Jenkins briefly looked set to resume these 'rambles' in March 1974.

Wilson's original plan was for Callaghan 'to take overall charge of industrial relations' with Healey going to the Foreign Office and Jenkins to the Treasury. But, as Wilson put it to Jenkins, 'Callaghan had absolutely declined. He was determined to be Foreign Secretary.'[45] So Jenkins reluctantly returned to the Home Office which he had led between 1965 and 1967 with 'one of the oddest remarks that a Prime Minister can ever have made to a colleague in a new Cabinet' ringing in his ears. 'Maybe the Home Office was the best solution after all, he suggested. If . . . I wanted to be a semi-detached member of the Government, it was the most suitable department from which to play such a stand-off role.'[46] So economic affairs did not return to Jenkins' polished hands but to the rougher ones of Denis Healey and the financially green-fingered ones of Harold Lever. And to do Wilson justice, Jenkins did give the appearance of relative detachment until he left office to become President of the European Commission.

If Harold Lever was Wilson Mark II's surrogate for Wilson Mark I's DEA, Jim Callaghan was his one-man replacement for the 'Inner Cabinet' which Wilson had no desire to re-create, telling a Commons select committee shortly after he retired 'I am not sure that it was a very good idea.'[47] Callaghan, ironically, had, been ostentatiously purged from the Management Committee as the *In Place of Strife* crisis moved to its climax, as we have seen. 'In place of strife' would almost be the perfect summary for the Callaghan–Wilson relationship of 1974–76. Lord Callaghan in retirement took me through his regular session with Wilson as Foreign Secretary (and with senior party managers) which, in their nature and range, strike me as a near replica of the meetings of Wilson's Management Committee in 1969–70:

'Harold and I [would] set aside Friday mornings, and I would go and see him with the Chief Whip [Bob Mellish] and others and discuss the business for the following week with him, because I was working with him very closely politically and he no longer felt . . . that I was trying to take over from him . . . I don't think he really felt that I was a rival so much as a colleague who was ready to aid and support him. And indeed that was true.'[48]

For his part, Wilson told a press conference during the March 1975 Dublin European Summit, which set the seal on the EEC renegotiation, that 'Jim and I are a complete partnership. We pass the ball to each other.'[49] And Callaghan's official biographer has a point in contrasting the relative vigour and political engagement of the older partner – 'as the Prime Minister's energies showed signs of running down, even his famous memory no longer so reliable, Callaghan emerged as all-purpose operator to fill any gaps and give direction to the government. He was almost an alternative prime minister.'[50]

One must not overdo this picture of Callaghan, however. The tone of Barbara Castle's account of a now celebrated Chequers strategy meeting in November 1974 which saw Wilson at his rambling worst (though he later tried to persuade me otherwise, arguing that 'I'd got through all my policies . . . I was quite pleased with it')[51] was disputed by Lord Callaghan.

As the Cabinet wandered despairingly around a paper from the Central Policy Review Staff about the consequences of the quadrupling of oil prices over the previous year, Callaghan, according to Mrs Castle, had 'compounded' the 'gathering gloom' by 'Jim acting Cassandra as usual. "When I am shaving in the morning I say to myself that if I were a young man I would emigrate. By the time I am sitting down to breakfast I ask myself 'where would I go?'"'[52] The Cabinet certainly laughed and Callaghan insisted to me that he was joking. But other attenders are not so sure.[53] Unless one is there oneself, one cannot judge – and there was never any love lost between Barbara Castle and Jim Callaghan.

Europe was the policy area on which Wilson and Callaghan operated most closely together in 1974–76. Their partnership was comparable to Attlee and Bevin's on foreign policy between 1945 and 1950, the rock on which the government survived – and 'survived' is the right word. For Europe had for the first time become a potentially government-wrecking issue (far more so than when Macmillan and Butler speculated about their becoming latterday Peels on the Common Market question). Shirley Williams puts the European renegotiations and referendum as the 1931 issue of the 1974–79 governments (even more so than the 1976 International Monetary Fund crisis). Because if it had gone the other way and the Cabinet had decided to recommend a UK withdrawal from the Community, Mrs Williams and at least some of her fellow pro-Europeans would have quit (whereas, she explained, the Left had nowhere else to go when the Cabinet did not endorse their alternative economic strategy in December 1976).[54]

His management of the European question bids fair to be both Wilson's finest exposition of collective Cabinet government and his final gift to the party whose unity he placed above all other considerations, albeit sometimes resentfully. It was all very well for Roy Jenkins to resign over the referendum idea in 1972, Wilson memorably told a colleague, but he [Wilson] had 'to wade through shit' to hold Labour together on the Common Market question.[55]

What Ken Morgan has called Wilson's 'last notable contribution to his party and his nation'[56] was all the more remarkable because, as we have seen, Wilson's heart never crossed the English Channel. It remained where it always had been – in Britain and the Commonwealth – and he admitted as much to Labour's special conference on the renegotiated terms in April 1975. 'I have never been emotionally a Europe man,' he said.[57] Bernard Donoughue reckoned his boss 'was basically a north of England, non-conformist puritan . . . The continental Europeans, especially from France and southern Europe were to him alien. He disliked their rich food, genuinely preferring meat and two veg with HP sauce.'[58]

In gearing up for his last great political fix, Wilson, too, had to overcome serious health problems. From the beginning of the last premiership, fellow ministers and officials had detected a lassitude that could not be explained away by the Prime Minister's increasing fondness for brandy.[59] He rambled in Cabinet and sometimes failed to sum-up.[60] His deputy, Ted Short, recalls 'a Cabinet meeting one afternoon, an awful Cabinet meeting when we were going to alter the secrecy laws and it got into the most hopeless confusion. Everybody was absolutely exasperated and angry and furious about it. Nothing emerged from it at all.'[61]

Wilson talked a great deal about his health,[62] and on a flight to Paris in December 1974 to see President Giscard d'Estaing as part of the European renegotiations, an unexpected manoeuvre by the pilot as he made his landing affected the Prime Minister. As Bernard Donoughue observed, Wilson 'had some heart racing and the doctor [Sir Joseph Stone] had to intervene a bit'.[63] Ben Pimlott's biography has a rather touching story from the same period when a civil servant, asked by Wilson (who was kindly and concerned in such matters) why he, the official, had not sought Wilson's help on a career matter, replied: ' "I didn't think it an appropriate thing to bother you with, as Prime Minister." . . ."Not even a part-time Prime Minister like me?" said Wilson, his eyes filled with tears.'[64]

Wilson's and Callaghan's European task was to sell to the Cabinet, the Labour Party, to Parliament and to the electorate a largely, though not wholly, cosmetic membership renegotiation. (The European Regional Fund, a very important and valuable development, came out of it, as did important safeguards for New Zealand dairy produce and third-world primary products, though those huge and vexing questions of the Common Agricultural Policy and Britain's contribution to the Community Budget were barely scratched.) Peter Jenkins summed-up Wilson's far from easy purpose as consisting of three objectives: 'to keep his party in power and in one piece and Britain in Europe'.[65] All this was to be achieved on a wafer-thin majority (though most of the Conservatives and Liberals could be relied on in the House of Commons to support Britain's remaining in the EEC) with a party split on Europe with a definite numerical tilt against continued British membership in the Parliamentary Labour Party (apart from the Cabinet itself where there was a jelly-mould full of wobblers), the Party's National Executive Committee and the Party Conference.

In fact, what Donoughue called the 'brilliant combination' of 'Wilson in the party leader role' and 'Callaghan negotiating the policy issues'[66] was reflected in both the mechanics of the Cabinet process and the unusual bonding material used to hold ministers together, given the certainty of a dissenting rump of irreconcilables that would be left whichever way the majority Cabinet decision went. The decision to draw on the 1932 precedent of the National Government 'agreeing to differ' on the question of free trade versus tariffs was essential to the government's ability to hold together during the referendum campaign. It was at the 'historic'[67] Cabinet meeting of 21 January 1975, during which Wilson delivered his ironic 'messy middle-of-the-road muddle' aside, that determined there would be an 'agreement to differ' (which Wilson enshrined, the 1932 precedent included, as an appendix in his *Governance of Britain*).[68] 'Harold', Barbara Castle recorded in her diary, 'announced a fundamental change in our constitutional convention as casually as if he had been offering us a cup of tea.'[69]

Beneath the full Cabinet, Wilson had already established a pair of Cabinet committees which reflected his European job-share with Callaghan. As Donoughue, well placed in the Policy Unit to observe all the intricacies, put it: 'He set up the European Strategy Committee as the senior committee, with himself as Prime Minister in the chair to ensure that the manifesto commitments were met – the classic Wilson party management role. A second and subsidiary, though very important committee (EQS), was established to monitor the details of the renegotiations' with Callaghan in the chair. 'They worked superbly together,' Donoughue continued. 'Given the extent to which they had clashed in the late 1960s, it was quite remarkable how they now worked so trustingly together and held the other ministers in line. But it was an enormous work load for two senior men of around sixty.'[70]

Once or twice the line looked as if it would not hold. On a much quoted occasion, Wilson blew his top when he discovered that the Cabinet's anti-marketeers, licensed to dissent under the 'agreement to differ', were, as he put it, rushing out to hold a press conference and to organize an anti-government campaign.[71] (This had happened on the previous day after the Cabinet, in a marathon two-day session, had finally voted 16-7 to recommend the renegotiated terms.)[72] Michael Foot and Barbara Castle had to console and placate a 'shattered' Prime Minister in the presence of a 'gloomy' Jim Callaghan at a late-night meeting at the House of Commons on 19 March 1975.[73]

The following day at Cabinet Wilson, after warning his colleagues 'it could be 1931 all over again', berated both sides for 'mobilising outside agencies'[74] and, according to Ben Pimlott,

> At one point, apparently close to breaking point, he rose from his seat and strode to the door. Foot and Callaghan pursued him. Eventually he was persuaded to return to the Cabinet table.[75]

Only when Bernard Donoughue published his recollections of the renegotiation was it realized that this had been a deliberate ploy. First Wilson 'banished' the civil servants from the Cabinet Room. Next:

> The Prime Minister attacked the dissenters for their conduct at the NEC [National Executive Committee] and then, in a calculated move arranged beforehand with his Deputy, Edward Short, he withdrew angrily from cabinet. He retreated to his study, where he was periodically visited by colleagues bringing news of the discussion. His withdrawal was intended to convey his willingness to resign over this issue (though it was impossible to establish how serious he was, he was certainly genuinely angry and was anyway beginning privately to plan his retirement).
>
> His various protests worked. Michael Foot persuaded the left to moderate their activities while Shirley Williams rallied additional pressure from the right. The final NEC motion did not commit the party organisation to campaign against the government, simply allowing workers the 'same freedom to support or dissent as ministers had'.[76]

This has always struck me as a significant moment in terms of the old prime ministerial versus Cabinet government debate. The horror which plainly struck those not in on the secret ploy at the sight of a Prime Minister seeming to give up and walk away seems to have been genuine enough. They were like so many unruly children whose distraught mother appears about to abandon them. Tony Benn once said to me 'Cabinets are families',[77] though it is debatable if this particular 'Cabinet family' ever recovered from agreeing to differ.

The NEC, 'a body he grew to loathe',[78] was against Wilson's position on the renegotiation terms;[79] so were the Labour MPs (145 to 137 in the Commons vote on 9 April);[80] the special party conference on 26 April was 2 to 1 against;[81] even the old 'Kitchen Cabinet' was opposed.[82] Yet Wilson did it. He avoided 'doing a Ramsay MacDonald', that most feared of Labour movement nightmares. He achieved exactly the outcome he wanted.

When the referendum result on 6 June showed a 2 to 1 majority in favour of continued EEC membership it was almost as if Wilson had won a fifth general election. Certainly he felt able to demote Tony Benn from Industry to the Department of Energy.[83] A modified industrial strategy of 'picking winners', whereby government aid would go to hopers instead of no-hopers, was announced in the autumn (though the bailing-out of the car manufacturer Chrysler showed the government never learned to choose between social and economic factors).[84] And, at last, Wilson grappled with a counter-inflation policy, resorting once more to a 'voluntary' incomes policy (backed by sanctions if needed) which saw his Policy Unit in the thick of the fighting with a Treasury urging a much tougher statutory regime.[85] Both these incomes and industrial strategies set the pattern for the next three to four years until the arrival of Mrs Thatcher in No. 10.

Nothing compared to the European question in terms of stretching the Cabinet system during Wilson's final premiership. And the stretchmarks remained, some would argue, until Labour lost power in May 1979. Peter Shore, one of the most respected anti-marketeers, does not accept this view, arguing that without the agreement to differ, 'there would have been resignations. The opponents of our membership would have found themselves on the backbenches. In the event it was surprisingly easy. Everyone had a feeling of respect for the other.'[86]

I tend more to the Roy Jenkins 'coalition of incompatibles' view. The 1974 Cabinet began like that – as Wilson's 'semi-detached' line to Jenkins rather corroborates – and I would judge that the 1975 referendum experience exacerbated the incompatibilities. As the Cabinet Secretary, Sir John Hunt, put it: 'The campaign was conducted in a reasonably fraternal and gentlemanly way, but I think the damage which it in fact did to relations within the Cabinet *ex post facto* was very great.'[87] As Hunt added, 'Harold Wilson knew that during the first two years of his premiership – and I think this ties up with the date of his resignation because he wanted it settled before he left office – he had to settle the Europe issue one way or the other.'[88]

Europe was not the only source of friction in Wilson's twilight Cabinets. Industrial and economic strategy, too, caused serious difficulty and in both cases Tony Benn as Industry Secretary (before Wilson shifted him to Energy) was the greatest tension-arouser of them all. Wilson used the fledgling but quickly influential Policy Unit to combat Benn's interventionist industrial strategy. (It substantially rewrote Benn's White Paper on the regeneration of British Industry during the summer of 1974[89] and one of its members, Andrew Graham, became No. 10's special 'Benn watcher'[90]). Wilson supervised the process from a special Cabinet Committee on Public Enterprise which he chaired.[91]

In his largely unsuccessful bid to curb Tony Benn by binding him in the coils of collective Cabinet responsibility, Wilson took to 'waving the rulebook at him every time he stepped out of line'.[92] Wilson noted in his *The Governance of Britain* that 'it became my duty in subsequent months to draw the attention of certain Ministers to the overriding requirements of this code of conduct [*Questions of Procedure for Ministers*], particularly the relationship to their membership of the NEC of the Labour Party . . .'[93] Wilson tightened up especially the sections of *QPM* which dealt with ministerial speeches, press articles and party publications.[94] Benn expressed his dissent to the use of *QPM* by Wilson as an instrument of prime ministerial power by telling him that, 'They have never been collectively discussed with me and I do not accept them.'[95] In a burst of defiance he published his own alternative for the Department of Industry, telling his junior ministers: 'We are still ourselves, Labour Party and trade union members, as well as Ministers; and our accountability is to our consciences, to the people, to the Party and to the [Labour] Movement, as well as to the Government.'[96]

Harold Wilson, constitutionally a traditionalist, was deeply irritated by Tony Benn's attitude towards accountability and responsibility, as was Jim Callaghan (another constitutional traditionalist) after him. Tony Benn shows with pride to visitors at his Holland Park office-cum-archive his considerable file of correspondence with both Wilson and Callaghan on the subject.[97] The slog of business, the difficulties with Benn and the NEC, the lassitude verging on melancholy were important factors in Wilson's decision to go. Once the EEC referendum was out of the way, the counter-inflation strategy was in place and Tony Benn marginalized at the Department of Energy (if not in the councils of the National Executive Committee), Wilson's thoughts turned increasingly towards retirement.

In fact, during that autumn of 1975, contrary to saloon-bar conspiracy theorists who continue to maintain that Wilson dashed for the exit in March 1976 because he discovered MI5 had something on him or because he sensed the pound would collapse that summer or autumn or that an element in his private life was about to surface (all of which I have heard recycled ceaselessly since 1976), Wilson began to plan for his orderly exit on or around his sixtieth birthday.

Wilson told his favourite colleague, Barbara Castle, in March 1976 that he had informed the Queen of the date he would retire when he accepted her invitation to form a government two years earlier. 'She's got the record of it, so no one will be able to say afterwards that I was pushed out.'[98] There are many sources to confirm that Wilson's final hurrah was planned (he was certainly a relaxed man when I called on him in No. 10 a few weeks before the event to talk about how the Cabinet Office worked). The most graphic account I have heard directly is from his press secretary, Joe Haines, who doubled-up as a personal and political assistant in all but name. 'At the Labour Party Conference in 1975,' Haines told me,

'Harold Wilson asked me to draw up the timetable for his resignation the following year, which was to be announced at the end of February, indeed, the afternoon of the last Wednesday in February, the reason for that date being chosen being that the Labour Party National Executive met on the morning of that day and, as he said to me, "I'm not going to let those buggers have anything to say about it." And I drew up the timetable and, although it was to be one copy only, I did actually retain a copy for my own memory . . . It is here in this house.'[99]

In fact, the timetable shifted a little because of a sterling wobble and the government's defeat on its public expenditure White Paper on 10 March 1976, Wilson's sixtieth birthday, put right by a vote of confidence which the government won the following night. Wilson shocked most, but not quite all, of the Cabinet when he announced his intention of going six days later.[100]

In a way it is fitting that the most conspiracy-minded of the eleven post-war premiers should feed the fantasies of conspiracy theorists twenty-plus years after the event. And, sadly, Wilson's ruinous mix of paranoia and conspiracy worsened as his last premiership lengthened. He mistrusted the press (with some reason as shown by the *Daily Mail*'s 'slag heap' campaign against a piece of land speculation on the part of Marcia Williams' brother and the press becoming truly vitriolic when Wilson responded by asking the Queen to ennoble Mrs Williams as Lady Falkender).[101] Within days of my arriving at Westminster as the Lobby Correspondent of the *Financial Times*, Joe Haines, with Wilson's backing, suspended all lobby briefings, which were not restored until Callaghan took over.[102]

Yet even in his closing spell in No. 10, flashes of the old, Eric Morecambe-style deadpan humour could lighten life in the Wilsonian governing circle. Robert Armstrong, whom he inherited as Principal Private Secretary from Ted Heath, recalls an occasion when Wilson alluded to his reputation as a man who sensed plots. The conversation went like this:

WILSON: I was a don in Oxford before the war, as you may know, Robert.

ARMSTRONG: Yes, Prime Minister.

WILSON: But I couldn't stand the intrigue of academic life so I joined the Civil Service. The intrigue in the Civil Service was even worse than at Oxford so I became a politician.

At this point, sensing Armstrong's growing incredulity, Wilson paused. Then,

WILSON: You know Robert, I have a reputation as an intriguer.

ARMSTRONG: Yes, Prime Minister.

WILSON: But I'm not an intriguer Robert.

Another pause. Armstrong's eyebrows were raised to their maximum height.

WILSON: No, Robert. I only counter-intrigue against those who intrigue against me!

Laughter all round.[103]

But, on a more hidden and serious level, Wilson's fascinated ambivalence about the secret services began to turn obsessional in the mid 1970s. On Northern Ireland, for example (which continued to preoccupy him; he toyed with peculiar and vague notions of 'dominion status' within the context of a united Ireland in 1974–75),[104] he once told an incredulous top Northern Ireland Office official to 'ring the number of a callbox in the Mile End Road at a certain time when a certain person would be waiting to give him information he might need to hear'.[105] The official did so and nothing transpired.[106]

Wilson's fear of the secret world seems to have taken three forms: that he was being bugged by hostile intelligence services; that he was under similar surveillance by the British secret services; and that the secret world, in cahoots with former members of the armed forces, were preparing a *coup d'état*. In his last phase as premier he told a startled senior civil servant while being briefed by him in the Cabinet Room to look carefully at the door leading to the No. 10 garden, 'Look. That's where they'll come. They'll come through there.'

'Who Prime Minister?'

'Them. When they come to take over the government.'[107]

It may be that Wilson was piecing together intimations he had about the very small group in MI5 who suspected he was a long-term communist agent[108] and talk which reached No. 10 about a secret plan hatched by former army figures to seize the Cabinet and imprison it *en bloc* on a boat off the Isle of Wight.[109]

George Bush, as Director of the CIA, was not the only one to be told by Wilson that the Cabinet Room was bugged. Wilson left No. 10 convinced of this. In June 1977 his successor, Jim Callaghan, reacted to renewed speculation in the press and, we learn from Callaghan's official biographer, some pressure from Mrs Thatcher (who, it transpired, allegedly had 'misgivings' about Wilson's 'reliability' based on anecdotal evidence), by setting up an inquiry under Sir John Hunt, still Secretary of the Cabinet.

Ken Morgan, drawing on 'uncatalogued personal material in the Callaghan papers',[110] revealed that:

Colourful revelations emerged from its [Hunt's committee's] inquiries. Apparently, Harold Wilson had believed that a hole in the wall of the Cabinet room behind a portrait of Mr Gladstone contained a listening device. He had had a firm called Argon Ltd, run by one who was mixed up with South African intelligence, to check the relevant light fittings. Government electronics experts, however, assured Hunt and Stowe [Callaghan's Principal Private Secretary, as he had been Wilson's before him] that Gladstone's portrait concealed nothing more sinister than the fitting of an earlier wall light, and that the Grand Old Man was in no sense a cover for espionage. An electronic device installed years earlier was, however, removed [no indication is given by Morgan of what this was or what it had been for].[111]

It is very difficult ever to be definite about such matters. It is highly unlikely, unless there are dramatic changes in disclosure practices for intelligence and security related material, that the Hunt report on the alleged 'bugging' of Wilson will reach the Public Record Office in January 2008.

What Lord Hunt did do, however, when asked to make an overall appraisal for Wilson's BBC Radio 4 obituary, was to record as close to a definitive insider's judgement on Wilson's relations with the secret world as it will be possible to get for a very long time. He told me:

'Harold Wilson was a person who, I think, had always been fascinated by the realms of intelligence and spying and security. And his interest, and I suppose his concern, his apprehension, manifested itself not just as to whether MI5 was conducting some sort of vendetta against him, but when one went abroad, he was suspicious and apprehensive that he was being watched or monitored by hostile intelligence services. He had this interest and fascination with that sort of world. When you come to his concern over MI5, which is well documented, I think you have to distinguish between what one knew then and what one had since learnt, through the *Spycatcher* affair, through other people's memoirs and stories. But undoubtedly I think Wilson was concerned – and perhaps increasingly concerned during his second government – that some people in the security services had something against him and were concerned to damage his reputation and possibly even to remove him.

'I didn't think then, and I don't think now in the light of all the evidence and books and things we've read since his government – I don't think that there was anything to smear him with. I've never heard anything against him about his trips to Russia, or anything else, which could possibly throw doubt on him as a security risk. I don't think, either, that there was a deliberate campaign to do him damage. I think it is much more likely that there were a few people – and I really do mean probably two or three – who were in the Security Service at the time who perhaps shouldn't have been there but who were malcontents (a lot of them had been missed over for promotion themselves) who were out of sorts with everyone and who were probably right-wing in their political attitudes and who talked against not just Harold Wilson but members of the Labour government, and who talked to the newspapers.'[112]

This, one suspects, is a story that will never die. In a way, that is Wilson's tragedy. That, and his rather cavalier way with honours (especially his resignation list)[113] and the fantasy stories about the timing of his resignation look set to form a loop which feeds off itself. If so, the popular memory of Wilson may be reduced to almost that alone. Already it flavours his last premiership so powerfully that his considerable European balancing act and his near Baldwinesque pursuit of social and industrial peace at almost any cost has been smothered in the collective memory. Conspiracy plus failed corporatism hardly does him justice. His dreadful 1964 aside to the Westminster lobby correspondents – that 'a week is a long time in politics'[114] – has rebounded cruelly against him; it fits Wilson more than any other postwar premier.

Yet at the moment for departure he was seen by far from credulous observers as perhaps one of a handful of politicians with the form and the skill not only to live without a proper Commons majority, but to reconcile the political and economic forces in play in a disturbed polity with an industrial base spalling under pressure from the oil-price explosion. Those very gifts which David Watt had skewered so effectively when describing a Wilson speech on Europe as 'of the modern gents' rain wear variety – cheap, lightweight and infinitely reversible',[115] were, perhaps, precisely those required at such a juncture in British political life, if indeed the greatest political art, in Bismarck's phrase, is not in 'creating the current of events' but only of 'floating' with them and 'steering them'.[116]

Far from his prime and distinctly below par though he was in his twilight premiership, Wilson could still dazzle on his day on the government front bench, in the Cabinet Room and the television studio. But history tends to be hard on the tactician and admiring of the strategist. And from first to last in No. 10 or leading from the Opposition benches (and he performed opposite no fewer than four Conservative leaders – Macmillan, Douglas-Home, Heath and Thatcher), to adapt Lytton Strachey on Mr Gladstone, 'tactics were the fibre of Harold Wilson's being'.[117]

15

The Sea-Changer:
James Callaghan, 1976–79

His earlier career gave little hint of his later quality. In Opposition he was seen as an opportunist, a reputation which his behaviour over *In Place of Strife* did nothing to modify. He was not particularly distinguished as Chancellor, as Home Secretary (except over Northern Ireland) or even as Foreign Secretary ... Yet when Wilson's resignation offered him the unexpected opportunity, Callaghan pursued it with resolution ... The political skills he had perfected in his unregenerate days were now just what his office needed. Without them the Government would never have survived the negotiations with the IMF, or preserved its fragile hold on Parliament.

Denis Healey, 1989[1]

'I don't claim it's the only way of running a Cabinet but there's a lot to be said for a consensus form of Cabinet in a democratic system ... You can run it as a dictator. You can cow your colleagues, make them afraid of you and not give the opportunity of expressing their views. That will come to an end sooner or later.'

Lord Callaghan, 1996[2]

Although he had a number of more amiable characteristics, I regarded Jim Callaghan as a bit of a bully. This I did not greatly mind for I thought that after the easy-going regime of Wilson's final days a bit of bullying might do the Government no harm. Moreover I did not expect the bullying to be exercised against me ... The reverse side of this coin of prime ministerial discourtesy was however the fact that the Cabinet became more tautly and efficiently run.

Roy Jenkins, 1991[3]

'We in the State Department and in the White House were very sympathetic to Callaghan's problem. We did not want to bring a Labour Government down by bringing pressure of austerity on them and creating the impression that we were doing it for ideological reasons and we valued Callaghan as a man and as a friend.'

Henry Kissinger, recalling Callaghan's IMF
Autumn of 1976 in 1991[4]

'Jim was an old trade unionist who believed that you ought to discuss. The IMF meetings were riveting. He set me up to talk first so that he could knock me down and say there was no alternative.'

Tony Benn, 1999[5]

'He [President Carter] was lying on his bed in his swimming trunks when I walked in – we all had grass huts or something equivalent, and I just walked across ten yards of grass, with the blue sea shimmering almost beneath our feet, and woke him up and said "Jimmy, before we resume tonight, on our next session, I want to have a word with you about the replacement of Polaris." And then I went on to explain that we hadn't taken any decision, that I was trying to find out all the information I could before we had to get to a decision. He was very forthcoming straightaway. He said he had no difficulty about transferring the [Trident] technology, if we decided that we wanted it.'   *Lord Callaghan, recalling the Guadouloupe*
G7 summit of January 1979 in 1988[6]

'I would have liked two things: first of all to have had a majority, which I didn't have and (b) to have had the Office [of Prime Minister] when I was younger and had more energy ... I think I ran out of steam, frankly, in the end.'   *Lord Callaghan, 1996*[7]

'I let the country down.'   *Jim Callaghan to his Principal Private*
Secretary on the late January 1979 phase of the
'Winter of Discontent'[8]

'I doubt if you accumulate much intellectual weight whilst you're in the office [of Prime Minister]. You do some. I think you rather spend your intellectual capital whilst you're in the office so it's important to take some baggage in.'   *Lord Callaghan, 1996*[9]

Jim Callaghan entered No. 10 with a great deal of baggage in terms both of political conviction and ministerial experience. He needed every ounce of it. On his first full day in office, 5 April 1976, 'the government's majority, already virtually invisible, vanished entirely',[10] and the country's gold and dollar reserves were falling alarmingly.[11]

Central to any understanding of his premiership is the fact that Jim Callaghan was, is and will remain a man of 1945. Over twenty years after assuming the premiership he described himself as 'original Labour' on the grounds that the 'old Labour' and 'new Labour' labels show 'rather a failure to understand the historical background'.[12] Lord Callaghan should be listened to on this and many other matters (not least the most effective way of operating a system of Cabinet government under duress) because he is the first and almost certainly the last Labour premier who could truly be said to have emerged out of the bowels of the Labour movement in the century which began with the foundation of the Labour Representation Committee.

MacDonald's formation was as a Liberal trade unionist; Attlee was from the wrong class to qualify for the 'bowel' accolade (though he was, I think, the most left wing of the Labour Prime Ministers in policy terms); Gaitskell was a highly mandarin scion of the old imperial administrative class; Wilson's early tilt was towards Liberalism and he, too, was not of the working class; John Smith sprang from a teacher's household. Mr Blair's roots in the Labour movement, as another 'original Labour' figure put it shortly before the 1997 general election, 'are comparable to those of a stick of celery'.[13] Compared to all of them, even perhaps to Neil Kinnock, Jim Callaghan is the genuine article owing to the poverty of his early life in a widowed household in Portsmouth (his father had been a chief petty officer in the Royal Navy), the shaping and advancement which came as a young trade union official in the interwar period, his service at sea during World War II before, with scarcely a pause, his being swept into Parliament at thirty-three as the MP for Cardiff South on Labour's high tide in July 1945.

If ever the old line about the 'university of life' applied to a politician who reached the very top it does so to Jim Callaghan, though he remained regretful, almost chippy, about not having attended a real one. When the Parliamentary Labour Party elected him Labour leader on 5 April 1976 (he beat Michael Foot by 144 votes to 133),[14] Callaghan's first words to the PLP Chairman, Cledwyn Hughes, were 'Prime Minister of Great Britain. And I never went to a University.'[15] But shortly after entering

No. 10 he said to an aide: 'There are many cleverer people than me in the Labour Party, but they're there and I'm here'[16] – a very Jim-like observation. And as he watched Mr Major's travails in the mid 1990s he said of him that 'John Major, like me, suffers from a lack of higher education. It leaves big gaps in your knowledge which you have to fill from experience. Major's other problem', he went on, 'is that he doesn't have a strong core of philosophical belief against which he can judge things. Added to that, before becoming Prime Minister, he had only been a very short time in senior ministerial positions and had only been in Parliament a very short time.'[17]

By these criteria, Callaghan himself was very well prepared in April 1976. At sixty-four he was four years older than Wilson, had over thirty years of unbroken experience in the House of Commons and was the only premier of the century to have held all three great offices of state before acquiring the top job (the Treasury 1964–67, the Home Office 1967–70 and the Foreign Office 1974–76). As for his philosophy, his intellectual 'baggage', Jim Callaghan remained fixed at about 1948 – a social patriot, a practical, moderate, very British socialist who put careful, sensible improvements to the lives and the life chances of the bulk of people way ahead of any overarching left-wing ideology. For the rest of the century he sounded – and was – a kind of composite of Clem Attlee and Ernie Bevin by another means.

Yet one can overdo the incarnation-of-Labourism line. For Callaghan was also a transitional figure from Attlee's party to Blair's. The assumptions of mid-century centre-left politics had begun to fade and spall under the very man who, by both instinct and experience, embodied them. His rueful words to his senior policy adviser, Bernard Donoughue, as the prime ministerial Rover swept round Parliament Square in late April 1979 during the electoral campaign which heralded a generation-long Conservative hegemony, have entered the lore and legend of British political history.

As Lord Donoughue recalled in his study of the Wilson and Callaghan premierships of the 1970s:

[I] drew Mr Callaghan's attention to the recent improvement in the opinion polls, remarking that with a little luck, and a few policy initiatives here and there, we might just squeeze through. He turned to me and said quietly: 'I should not be too sure. You know there are times, perhaps once every thirty years, when there is a sea-change in politics. It then does not matter what you say or do. There is a shift in what the public wants and what it approves of. I suspect there is now such a sea-change – and it is for Mrs Thatcher.'[18]

Callaghan had, in fact, to tack his politics in anticipation of that sea-change from the very start of his premiership three years earlier. And I would argue that his speech to the Labour Party Conference later in 1976, publicly abandoning Keynes-derived notions about the possibility of governments steering a full-employment, low-inflation economy, made Callaghan an agent of that change himself rather than a mere victim of it.

But the sea-change was not confined to shifts in macro-economic policy-making. It impinged upon a wide range of social policy, too. And interestingly enough, it was in his response to a Donoughue initiative that this first became apparent. (Though there was a hint of things to come in Callaghan's first broadcast as premier on the night he became Prime Minister: 'Do you, like me, sometimes feel that we've been slipping?' he inquired of his viewers and listeners.)[19]

For among the earlier sets of papers placed before him as he settled into the premiership was one entitled 'Themes and Initiatives', printed on the special green paper used by the Downing Street Policy Unit (Harold Wilson, its founder, had suggested this colour as it would distinguish politically attuned Policy Unit material from regular Civil Service briefings).[20] For any premiership-watcher, 'Themes and Initiatives' is a key text, not just for reasons of content but of context too. For its author, Dr Bernard Donoughue, was the first senior policy adviser in No. 10 who could be described as a professional political scientist since Professor W. G. S. Adams headed Lloyd George's Prime Minister's Secretariat in 1917–18.[21]

Donoughue's preamble was, in effect, a treatise on the powers and limitations of late-twentieth-century British premiership. 'Any new Prime Minister', he told his new boss who inherited him from Harold Wilson (and decided to keep him on after consulting his political adviser, Tom McNally, who knew Donoughue from their shared Fabian days),[22]

faces a paradox. He is the pre-eminent Minister and yet – because he has few statutory functions and less policy servicing than any of his Departmental Ministers – he may find difficulty in making a commensurate impact on his Government's policies.[23]

Donoughue's argument was that, to be effective, a premier had to plan his interventions with care:

He is, of course, inevitably drawn into – and shares responsibility for – major policy decisions (especially when they go wrong). He can also choose to take personal policy initiatives, which leave his own stamp on the Government, and possibly on history. But if he is to intervene personally, he should be selective, well informed and visibly effective.[24]

The choice of such interventions, Donoughue continued, 'is partly a question of personal inclination and partly a calculation of where the impact will be most impressive – especially with the next election in mind'.[25]

The rest of the briefing for Callaghan deals with suggested areas for possible intervention, one of which, education, led to the Ruskin Speech later in 1976 in which Callaghan not only gave his version of the traditional approaches to learning which should be sustained or restored but went on to float the idea of a core curriculum[26] which the Conservative governments that followed eventually implemented.[27]

Donoughue knew his man and tailored his 'social responsibility and social cohesion' theme to the new premier's strongly traditional values while recognising, as Donoughue put it, that such an approach 'if done with a heavy hand ... could emerge as indistinguishable from "Thatcherism" '[28] (possibly the first time that particular 'ism' was put down on paper, in high policy-making circles at least). Donoughue's remedy for avoiding such confusion pre-echoed by nearly twenty years Tony Blair's approach to crime and criminality ('... if mixed with a continuing philosophy of reform and a genuine compassion for the under-privileged in our society, this approach of "tough honesty" could evoke wide political support – because there is no doubt that some aspects of the current "permissive" social ethos have produced widespread misgivings')[29] and by five years or so Conservative attempts to stress the pitfalls of a 'dependency culture' ('"Welfare"', Donoughue told Callaghan, 'threatens to produce a corrosive dependency').[30]

Callaghan was receptive to such advice. Once the 'almost ... religious sensation' he felt on entering No. 10 was past ('I stood by the chair in the centre of the Cabinet Table ... I stood there for a moment and it was a very profound feeling. I felt somehow that I'd become a guide to lead the nation into the future and, at the same time, a trustee of all that was best in our past'),[31] he swiftly realized that he could be – and should be – selective in his prime ministerial interventions:

'It was the feeling that you were now the one on whom things pivoted . . . One of the great pleasures of being Prime Minister . . . is that you can pick and choose to some extent. You have . . . room for manoeuvre. You have some space in which you can choose what you're going to be interested in. Of course, there are some things that always come up . . . The economy is always there, like Banquo's ghost, to haunt you.'[32]

It was precisely this – the economic factor – which came swiftly to dominate the political, governmental, national and global weather systems that buffeted and shaped the Callaghan administration and its policies and which led eventually to its loss of office at the polls (though it was a constitutional matter – devolution to Scotland – which was the occasion on 28 March 1979 of the first confidence vote to bring down a government since 1924).

'*Economic policy*', Donoughue declared starkly, 'can destroy a Government. Our problems are deep-seated and daunting . . . You will be inescapably drawn in over the central economic issues and unpredictable crises with wider political implications.'[33] And for students of the conduct of premiership, this – the so-called International Monetary Fund autumn of 1976 – is the terrain that remains of enduring interest. For it is Callaghan's attempts to manage the currency, spending and confidence crises of that year while maintaining the niceties and processes of collective Cabinet government *and* managing a simultaneous and highly secret operation involving personal economic diplomacy at the highest level, which have become a hotly debated and classic case-study of the practice of premiership as well as an intrinsically important benchmark in the (so far) 130-year long march away from economic and financial superpowerdom.[34] The 1976 crisis is also a key element in the picture of Callaghan the sea-changer. In his famous speech to the Labour Party Conference that autumn he spoke hard economic reality to a resistant Labour movement. In a passage drafted by his son-in-law, the economist and journalist Peter Jay,[35] Callaghan declared that:

'For too long, perhaps ever since the war, we postponed facing up to fundamental choices and fundamental changes in our society and in our economy. This is what I mean when I say we have been living on borrowed time . . . The cosy world we were told would go on forever, where full employment would be guaranteed by a stroke of the Chancellor's pen, cutting taxes, deficit spending – that cosy world is gone . . . We used to think that you could spend your way out of a recession and increase employment by cutting taxes and boosting Government spending. I tell you in all candour that that option no longer exists, and that insofar as it ever did exist, it only worked on each occasion since the war by injecting a bigger dose of inflation into the economy, followed by a higher level of unemployment.'[36]

Though Callaghan's Chancellor, Denis Healey, was not impressed by his Prime Minister's apparent outright rejection of Keynesianism ('Never have speeches written by your son-in-law,' was how Healey put it, with uncharacteristic tact),[37] this for me, ranks as one of the great postwar Party Conference speeches comparable, in Labour terms, to Gaitskell's 'fight, fight and fight again' against unilateral nuclear disarmament at Scarborough in 1960,[38] Wilson's 'white heat of technology'[39] delivered from the same boards three years later and Neil Kinnock's evisceration of the Militant Tendency at Bournemouth in 1985.[40]

Speeches are one thing, engineering a shift in entrenched attitudes and hard policy another, and the memory of Callaghan's years as Chancellor (not to mention his unwillingness to back Wilson and Castle in taking on trade union power during the *In Place of Strife* spring and summer of 1969)[41] suggested that as Prime Minister he might not match up to the crisis of increasing magnitude he faced from day one in No. 10. (In fact it began in Wilson's last days when the Nigerians decided to diversify their holdings of sterling.)[42] It ran on virtually unbroken until the days before Christmas.

Callaghan, however, had learned from past experience. He was a genuine autodidact. Though as he admitted ten years later, 'how the City works . . . is a very deep mystery . . . and it isn't probably until you've been in office for a year or two that you really begin to discern the very intangible things that make the City work'.[43] By 1976 'he knew [the] little tricks' of the Treasury especially 'when they were trying to pull the wool over my eyes', as he put it to me.[44] He was from the first as premier absolutely unrecognizable as the nervous tyro Chancellor of the mid 1960s.

As an official well placed to watch him in both periods put it:

'In the 1960s George Wigg [Wilson's Paymaster, or rather Sleuthmaster, General] would turn-up on one of his self-appointed missions to get intelligence from around Whitehall and report to Harold Wilson: "Jim's filleted again; send in a new backbone." At the time of the negotiations with the IMF, Callaghan had confidence, authority, assurance whatever *he* may have been feeling. He seemed to me to be a Prime Minister at the top of his powers in an extraordinary difficult situation.'[45]

At the height of the IMF crisis, sitting in the prime ministerial Rover with a tense, young Parliamentary Private Secretary by his side (Dr Jack Cunningham, the Blair Cabinet's 'enforcer' just over twenty years later), Callaghan said: 'Relax. I know you're feeling the strain. But when you've been through one or two of these, you know how to deal with them. It gets easier.'[46] As Shirley Williams put it succinctly: 'Being Prime Minister became Jim in a way that none of his other jobs did.'[47]

There are several ways of looking at the ingredients of the 1976 crisis. The big picture for Callaghan was of twenty years of fudged decisions which could be deferred no longer because, as he explained a decade later for the television series *All the Prime Ministers' Men*, 'what we were dealing with in 1976 was the delayed reaction to the five-fold [it was four-fold, in fact] increase in oil prices of 1973. That was when it happened and we were trying to put that right. That meant a reduction in the standard of life of the British people . . . We put it right.'[48]

Interestingly enough, a member of John Major's Conservative Cabinet, while trying to convince me in the mid 1990s that the UK's relative decline had halted and that for the next twenty to thirty years Britain would do better economically than Germany and France, said of the halting process in an intriguing backhand compliment to him that 'It started with Callaghan. Margaret did most of the rough stuff. What John Major did was to ensure there wouldn't be a counter-revolution by making the new economic liberalism more humane.'[49]

But that outcome was of course invisible at the time. In the late spring and early summer of 1976 with the pound shaky and depreciating, the future of incomes policy uncertain, the government's majority gone and the Treasury's estimates of the public sector borrowing requirement (current and prospective) rising, the Treasury had to draw on the UK's IMF stand-by credit as the Cabinet went into crisis mode and searched for savings over seven Cabinet meetings between 6 and 21 July. But spending cuts of £1bn, with a further billion coming from extra taxation, did not satisfy the markets, though Denis Healey believed they would: 'I thought enough had been done but . . . there is an area where the markets are supreme . . . the markets decide what is the value of your currency.'[50] Gavyn Davies, at the time an economist in Callaghan's Downing Street Policy Unit, was even more brutal in his recollection: '. . . the markets wanted blood, and that didn't look like blood. We didn't understand that in No. 10 at the time, we didn't know that what they wanted was a humiliation ... trying to avoid the humiliation was a waste of time.'[51]

By the beginning of September, as Callaghan's Trade Secretary Edmund Dell has recalled in his biting study of the postwar Chancellors, 'the Federal Reserve in New York confirmed that up to 30 June, Britain had withdrawn $1.1 billion from the $5.3 billion stand-by. The conviction was growing that the government would have no choice but to make an application to the IMF to fund its repayment obligations ... On 29 September, with the agreement of Callaghan, [Denis] Healey announced that an application was being made to the IMF for support amounting to £3.9 billion, the largest sum ever sought from it.'[52] This was the background to what was arguably the finest display of collective Cabinet government under stress during the postwar period (though Edmund Dell, as we shall see in a moment, disagrees).

Callaghan's strategy was a mixture of the simple, the arduous and the precarious. He knew what he wanted – further cuts. 'There were', he told me later, 'reductions in the proposed expenditure for future years that had to be made, I had no doubt about that, irrespective of the International Monetary Fund or anything else'.[53] But he 'knew it was quite possible for the government to break up, and it could have been another 1931'. '1931' was a powerful code for the Callaghan Cabinet, several of whom had personal recollections of that August crisis when the second Labour government collapsed, unable to agree a set of cuts during another crisis of international confidence, splitting the Cabinet with Ramsay MacDonald leading a small Labour rump into coalition with the Conservatives and Liberals[54] – a political experience that had seared Callaghan's generation.[55] 'So', Callaghan explained, 'I was determined that we should allow the Cabinet to talk itself out'[56] – a very Wilsonian tactic, as we have seen.

Arduous it was. It took twenty-six ministerial meetings (nine of them full Cabinets) to talk it out over two months.[57] Precarious it was because Callaghan had to persuade the money markets and the IMF to give the British Cabinet the leeway to talk it out while he, Callaghan, kept his Chancellor in suspense 'until the very end', as Healey himself put it, about whether he would have his Prime Minister's full backing.[58] Callaghan pushed the IMF as far down as it could go in its demands and engaged in top-level personal diplomacy with the US President, Gerry Ford, his Secretary of State, Henry Kissinger, and the German Chancellor, Helmut

Schmidt, to persuade them to use their political and economic muscle with the IMF in Britain's favour.[59] Harold Lever was dispatched to Washington as Callaghan's emissary.[60] To cap it all, Callaghan was determined once and for all to make sure this was the last currency crisis in which the sterling balances (the debts accumulated within the sterling area during World War II) exacerbated the vulnerability of the pound. Like his permanent secretary during his Treasury days, William Armstrong, Callaghan sensed the sword of Damocles hanging over the British economy in the shape of those balances.[61]

Callaghan eventually pulled off all these tricks. His Cabinet, though, split into four groups. These break down into: the alternative strategists who pressed for import controls and a siege economy as an alternative to the IMF with Tony Benn most prominent and the government's number 2, Michael Foot, sympathetic; the sceptical centre led by Tony Crosland, who argued the July cuts were sufficient; the Chancellor, Healey, with but two allies initially, urging that the bullet be bitten in terms of serious cuts; and the Prime Minister's men who would wait to see which way Callaghan finally jumped.

Callaghan squared all these Cabinet circles. As one aide put it who witnessed Callaghan's very private and highly significant meeting with his two biggest dissenting colleagues, Michael Foot and Tony Crosland: 'They pressed him very hard. Jim told them, "Together the two of you can defeat me . . . A Prime Minister must stand shoulder to shoulder with his Chancellor." All the skills Jim had accumulated were brought into play. It was a bit like Churchill – all his life had been a preparation for this hour.'[62]

The final settlement, embodied in a 'Letter of Intent' sent to the IMF, was of cuts in planned public expenditure (£1.5 bn taken out of the 1977–78 total and £2bn trimmed from the 1978–79 estimates), plus the sale of £500m of government shares in BP and formal targets to be set for money supply and domestic credit expansion.[63] The Cabinet agreed these measures on 2 December 1976, the moment, according to Tony Benn, when the Croslandite social democratic wing of the Labour Party threw in the towel ('an absolute turning point', was how Benn described it)[64] with Crosland going along with a Callaghan–Healey line he was convinced was both flawed and unnecessary for the sake of keeping the Cabinet together and Labour in power. On 1 December Crosland told Callaghan bluntly: 'In the Cabinet tomorrow I shall say I think you're wrong, but I also think that Cabinet must support you.'[65] Benn's point is well made –

and it reinforces my view of Callaghan as an active change-maker rather than the passive onlooker gazing incomprehendingly at a shifting economic scene.

Callaghan's 'never again' requirement was met, too, the following month when a 'safety net' was negotiated for the sterling balances with the IMF and the central banks of the world's leading economies.[66] There are those like Roy Hattersley, a supporter of the Crosland line during the IMF Cabinets, who still maintain Callaghan was unduly and erroneously influenced by forecasts of the public sector borrowing requirement, 'the central economic indicator – on which the IMF's demands for fiscal retrenchment were based'.[67] But as Denis Healey put it later, 'the trouble with theoretical economists [by which I infer he meant Crosland] is that they don't understand that when you have a deficit, you can only finance it by borrowing and you've got to persuade people that it's worth lending money to you and that they'll get their money back ... There is no way of escaping it.'[68] Indeed there wasn't, as Callaghan and Healey realized.

As Morgan notes, the public sector borrowing requirement 'proved to be far less in 1977–8 and 1978–9 than had been forecast: after the imposition of cash limits on departments, it was only £8.5bn in 1976–7 rather than the £10.5bn prophesied by the Treasury'.[69] But, as Hattersley realistically acknowledges, the IMF and the money markets were looking for a change of spending policy on the Labour government's part and would have demanded reductions to a still lower figure even if the Treasury's forecast had been more realistic. 'It is fair to say – in the Treasury's defence', Hattersley continued, ' – that the PSBR is a notoriously difficult figure to calculate. It amounts to no more than the comparison of two aggregates, total government income and total government expenditure. Many of the items which made up the two cumulative figures were either estimates or approximations.'[70]

In reality, Callaghan had no choice but to acknowledge the expectations of the IMF and the markets. It was his misfortune – almost his tragedy – that such a formidable battery of skills were, in the end, largely devoted to holding the line, to buying time rather than to the constructive purposes to which he had hoped to devote himself when he had taken office nine months earlier. As he told me a dozen years later: 'I hadn't intended to get myself immersed in economic affairs. I'd had enough trouble with that when I was Chancellor of the Exchequer, and we had a very experienced Chancellor in Denis Healey ... I just thought that my job would be to support him and allow him to get on with it while I did other things.'[71]

But, in that same interview, in the rueful, self-ironic way Jim Callaghan sometimes has, he said of his Cabinet management in 1976:

'They could talk and talk and talk as long as they liked, everybody had a fair chance, and I told them to put in memoranda; we discussed their memoranda, we rediscussed their memoranda and so on, and eventually, by allowing them to talk themselves out, they all came to a common conclusion, and we preserved the unity of the Cabinet and of the party. It would have been a tragedy if we had split, and it was quite possible we might have broken up as in 1931. I don't put that as an impossibility, and I regard it as one of my minor triumphs – and goodness knows, I had few enough of them – that the Labour Party did not split in 1976, as it might have done.'[72]

Denis Healey rates this, as I do, as much more than a 'minor triumph'. In his memoirs he wrote of 'The consummate skill with which [Callaghan] handled the Cabinet [which] was an object lesson for all prime ministers.'[73] For Shirley Williams, too, it was 'a brilliant operation'.[74]

For Edmund Dell, however, who believed that Cabinets should practise not collective responsibility but 'collective tolerance' at such moments – leaving it to the PM, the Chancellor of the Exchequer and the handful of other ministers who understand the complexities and the realities – the 1976 Cabinet meetings were 'a farce and a dangerous farce at that'.[75] Of the Callaghan 'talk and talk and talk' strategy, all of which he sat through, Mr Dell said:

Nine Cabinet meetings while the market was impatiently waiting for a decision. In a sensible system of government Callaghan would, after discussing with Healey and Foot and possibly, as a matter of *amour propre*, with Tony Crosland, have told the Cabinet 'It is my responsibility. We have to cut public expenditure. Do not be so stupid as to resign, which actually I know you are not going to do anyhow and bring the Government down and let Thatcher in. The party would never forgive you.' If he had said that after a couple of Cabinet meetings I am sure the Cabinet would have accepted it.[76]

I am not so sure, and neither was the former Secretary of the Cabinet, Lord Hunt of Tanworth, who also sat through every meeting.

John Hunt sat beside Edmund Dell at the Institute of Historical Research seminar too when Dell launched into what he saw as the dangerous farce of 1976. Hunt said: 'I do not believe that those nine Cabinets were purely tactical in terms of a rather cynical operation that had to be gone through in order to keep the lads together and to stop them resigning . . . I do not think collective responsibility is a myth. I think it is a reality. It is cumbersome. It is difficult. It has all sorts of disadvantages and it is possible it may need to change . . . probably under any of these systems it is going to be a bit of a shambles. But I do think it has got to be, so far as possible, a democratic and accountable shambles.'[77]

So do I. But where Edmund Dell is undeniably right in his judgement is that 'in days when media attention is greater even that it was in 1976, it would have been impossible to delay a decision so long, with the market waiting and apprehensive, and sterling on the brink'.[78] In the era of electronic news-gathering and the age of twenty-four-hour, instant reaction money markets, a two-month play would very likely have to be reduced to one short, sharp act.

In that sense Callaghan must cease to be the model unless a modern premier were to imitate the intensely secret 'economic seminar' into which market-sensitive discussions were taken in the IMF aftermath. At the suggestion of Callaghan's Principal Private Secretary, Sir Kenneth Stowe,[79] discussion on matters such as interest rate changes or the uncapping of sterling went into this 'seminar'-like forum. With the Central Policy Review Staff, the Policy Unit, the Cabinet Office and that one-man alternative strategist Harold Lever involved, as well as the traditional and narrower configuration of the Treasury, the Bank of England and the No. 10 Private Office, this 'seminar' group was more widely based than the older insider track traditionally followed for such discussions, but much narrower even than the Cabinet's Economic Strategy Committee let alone the full Cabinet itself.[80] As for the normal Cabinet processes, Callaghan used the cuts element in the IMF settlement to alter Wilson's original ruling that appeals from a Cabinet committee to the full Cabinet could only be made if the Chair of the committee agreed. Henceforth, Treasury ministers would enjoy an 'automatic right of appeal' to Cabinet,[81] a change Mrs Thatcher incorporated in her first edition of *Questions of Procedure for Ministers*.[82]

Callaghan was not a collective operator in all circumstances. Like his first mentor, Attlee, he kept his nuclear weapons policy inside the narrowest and tightest of circles,[83] away even (unlike Attlee[84] or his second mentor, Harold Wilson[85]) from the Cabinet committee structure. Callaghan's forum was known as the Nuclear Defence Policy Group.[86] He told me that on matters like the replacement of Polaris, 'it was always traditional, and nothing new, for nuclear issues to be discussed in a small group'[87] (plainly unaware of the Churchill model which had embraced full Cabinet when the decision to make a British hydrogen bomb was taken in 1954).[88]

Naturally on matters to do with intelligence and security he was super-secret. Here, unlike his equally traditional attitude to the maintenance of official secrecy in other, less sensitive areas (where even Denis Healey was critical of him),[89] Callaghan had both a sure and a justifiable touch. He commissioned a still-secret review of recruitment to the Security Service, MI5,[90] which has helped to transform the people-side of that agency over subsequent years. And he used his 'C', Sir Maurice Oldfield, the 'Chief' of the Secret Intelligence Service, MI6, to let the Argentines know in 1977, when a degree of harassment was under-way in the South Atlantic, that a hunter-killer submarine lay undetectable and in wait between the mainland and the islands with two surface vessels positioned within reach as well should their navy try anything serious against the Falklands. Though the Franks inquiry said there was no evidence that the message got through, I have reason to believe that it did. As a former MI6 officer put it: 'This kind of personal involvement was right up Maurice's street. The message would certainly have got through.'[91]

In a manner that should still be a model for his successors in No. 10, Jim Callaghan laid great stress on keeping personally well briefed on the small problems which could suddenly flare up and inflame a government – the Falklands, Gibraltar and Belize were the examples he liked to quote.[92] His naval background was the key here. The essence of Callaghan, the ex-navy man and careful keeper of the watch, came over beautifully when he explained this for the viewers of *All the Prime Minister's Men*. He had, he said,

'my own personal source of information. Because of my background, I asked the Admiralty every week to send me a map of the world, about the size of this blotter in front of us here, which set out the position and disposition of every ship in the British navy, including all the auxiliaries, so that I could know exactly what we could do and how long it would take us to get to the Falklands and where we needed to be. That is the kind of thing I think a Prime Minister must do. There are small things he must do and large things. That's one of the small things he must do that can save a very large catastrophe.'[93]

Callaghan had a sharp sense of where to go in Whitehall to get his information and he liked it to be served up plain and unvarnished. I am sure he appreciated Oldfield's reply when, at his first meeting with the SIS chief as incoming Foreign Secretary in March 1974, Callaghan had inquired, 'Sir Maurice, what is your job?' 'My job, Secretary of State,' said Oldfield, 'is to bring you unwelcome news.'[94]

Callaghan was skilful at making the best use of the policy advice he received directly from the Central Policy Review Staff and the No. 10 Policy Unit as well as the formidable Private Office line-up he enjoyed of Ken Stowe,[95] Nigel Wicks,[96] Tim Lankester[97] and Patrick Wright.[98] Of the CPRS he said: 'I found it very valuable . . . It was useful because it was able to stand back and take a long-range view of some matters and also, because of its wide range of knowledge, it was able to ask probing questions that were placed before ministers when they came to Cabinet. The CPRS didn't have in any way a political role. The Policy Unit did have a political role. It would advise me, for example, about the political consequences of increasing the child benefit or of not increasing the child benefit.'[99] Both the CPRS and the Policy Unit were considerable feeders of alternative advice to the Prime Minister (alternative to the Treasury, that is) during the IMF crisis.[100]

Callaghan also made use of his alternative information systems in the series of bilateral conversations he began with his Cabinet ministers. Unlike Eden's attempts to do this, Callaghan's worked well. He was steeped in domestic, foreign and economic policy and he was good, too, at the personal chemistry involved. He wrote about these sessions in his memoirs:

It had been my experience that Ministers used to ask to see the Prime Minister only when they had a personal problem or had run into a difficulty, and I decided to reverse this. So during the early months after I took office, and in pursuit of my intention not to become over-immersed in the Chancellor's economic problems, I invited other Ministers to come to see me individually and without their officials, to tell me about their work. We sat informally in the study at No. 10 and I put to all of them two basic questions. What were they aiming to do in the Department? What was stopping them? I prepared for these chats by asking Bernard Donoughue and his Policy Unit, in conjunction with my Private Office, to prepare an overview of each Department's activities before I saw them, and Bernard would also suggest certain areas for me to probe.[101]

The memoir describes how the Education Secretary, Fred Mulley, was one of the first to chat *à deux* and how Jim Callaghan, reflecting

Donoughue's 'Themes and Initiatives' paper, steered that nice and under-estimated man across the 'three R's' and 'curriculum' territory about which, he told Mulley, he intended to make a speech.[102]

As with Callaghan the 'original Labourite', one must not paint a monochromatic picture. 'Big Jim', as the more sympathetic tabloids liked to call him, could also be tetchy Jim, especially when he was tired. Journalists and television interviewers were not the only people who could experience the sudden change from soft-edged politician to hard-edged operator and his quite frightening demonstrations of irritated authority. Perhaps the capacity to inspire a little fear is part of any premier's armoury.

It was partly, I suspect, because the mature if not quite hard-baked Downing Street Callaghan had firm views about what he did not like – permissiveness, any sign of disrespect for venerable institutions whether it be the monarchy (he got on famously with the Queen),[103] the Labour Party or, until that ghastly winter of discontent, the trade union movement. He had warm feelings for the armed forces and the Scouts. I mention the Scouts because of a wonderful manifestation of this side of Callaghan when, during a select committee hearing in 1985, he was asked by fellow Labour MP, Austin Mitchell, how ministers should behave towards civil servants.

CALLAGHAN: It is your responsibility to be polite, to be courteous, to listen to what is said to you and absorb it and be loyal to your Private Office so they can serve you to the best of their ability.

MITCHELL: It sounds like a Boy Scout code.

CALLAGHAN: What is wrong with the Boy Scouts?[104]

His respect for institutions, however, did not extend fully to Europe, about which he had, I suspect, an old patriot's ambivalence that vied with a realist's appreciation of the price that would be paid if Britain found itself on the outside edge of an integrating community. His experience of 1967–69 put him off tampering with the House of Lords, and the hours of slog in Cabinet and Cabinet committee on the Welsh and Scottish devolution legislation which eventually brought him down left him with an aversion for the kind of intricate constitutional engineering that successful devolution requires.[105] He believed, and still does, in first-past-the-post for Westminster elections and grew utterly fed up with the weekly, sometimes daily cobbling-together of majorities which he and Michael Foot were required to do especially after the demise of the Lib–Lab Pact in 1978.[106]

Callaghan, though intensely loyal to his Labour movement, was, how-ever, a natural centrist. He found his relationship with left-of-centre Liberal leader David Steel easy and congenial during the Lib–Lab pact (unlike Denis Healey, who could not abide dealing with the Liberals' economic spokesman, John Pardoe, and fobbed him off when he could on to his affable Chief Secretary, Joel Barnett).[107] I have a feeling that Calla-ghan would not have been averse to having Steel in the Cabinet with him if he had found himself leading the largest single party but without a majority after the 1979 election,[108] though not, I imagine, at the price of proportional representation, in which Callaghan has never believed.

A vivid, mixed recapitulation of the pleasures and pains of his premier-ship, prompted by a question from me about the 'misfortune' of losing his majority so soon after reaching No. 10, ended on that very point. 'It's never a misfortune to become Prime Minister,' he said,

'It's always the greatest thing in your life. It's absolute heaven – I enjoyed every minute of it until those last few months of the "Winter of Discontent". But when you lose your majority it's jolly inconvenient, because you have to look at every piece of legislation, every piece of business that's coming up in the following week, to see whose support you're going to get, whether you're going to be able to carry on the Queen's government or not ... It doesn't make for good government. Those who believe that PR is going to improve our form of government are, I think, very much mistaken.'[109]

That 'Winter of Discontent' – how it haunted him. Years later he found it difficult to talk about the sequence of events which flowed from two factors – his determination to squeeze inflation out of the economy by sticking to a 5 per cent pay norm after 3½ years of incomes policy; and his reluctance to call an election in the autumn of 1978 as his private polls indicated that he could expect to achieve no more than largest-single-party status and would be required to undertake still more majority-mongering with assorted Liberals, Scottish and Welsh Nationalists and Ulster Union-ists.[110] To be broken by your own people, the trade union movement, to whose defence he had come in 1969 at the price of losing his seat in Wilson's 'Inner Cabinet'[111] (a group that, incidentally, he was never tempted to emulate or recreate)[112] was unbearable.

His patience snapped in Cabinet, especially with Tony Benn who, in Callaghan's eyes, as in Wilson's, had been leading a kind of internal opposition, using the party's National Executive Committee (which Benn then dominated) for this purpose almost throughout the premiership. Joel Barnett's account of the Cabinet meeting of 1 February 1979 captures both the sourness of the Callaghan–Benn relationship and the bitterness of the 'Winter of Discontent':

The Prime Minister summed up what many of us wanted to say, when he put a question to Tony Benn: 'What do you say about the thuggish act of a walk-out, without notice, from a Children's Hospital?' Tony replied that: 'When decent people become irrational, something else must be wrong if they are driven to such desperate acts.' Jim Callaghan's response was that he 'had never in fifty years been so depressed as a trade unionist'.[113]

So depressed was he at this time that, for a couple of weeks, Callaghan appeared to be almost in self-imposed isolation in his study in No. 10, bereft of ideas on what to do. A sympathetic Cabinet minister told me later, 'I would have said he was having a nervous breakdown if I hadn't known him better.'[114]

For Jim Callaghan really did believe in a tightly United Kingdom with a salt-of-the-earth trade union movement to help keep it taut. But his philosophy was not sectional, hence that outburst in Cabinet against Tony Benn. He was a genuine and a formidable embracer of the middle ground of British politics and he had, to borrow Enoch Powell's phrase, 'a tune to hum'[115] to almost every social strand.

His official biographer, Ken Morgan, captured this in his description of the day he followed his subject on a constituency tour – or rather, a walk – during the 1964 election:

His political skills are of no ordinary kind. They stem from a remarkable control of his variegated constituency base in Cardiff South (or South East). To see Callaghan on the move in Cardiff, subtly adapting his approach as he ambles on from proletarian Splott through the mixed residential population of Llanrumney and on to the genteel villadom of Penarth, taking in myriad ethnic minorities in the old dockside communities en route, is to see a master craftsman at work, his technique tempered by a genuine humanity and directness.[116]

'New Labour' are not the first people to try and embrace those parts that allegedly socialist parties cannot easily reach. As the 1997 general election approached, Callaghan expressed some irritation about both the spurning of the trade unions and the 'number of myths about the way we behaved which have been promulgated by the Conservative government and which somehow our own people . . . have come to accept'. 'I look to history to put it right,' he added.[117]

If, historically speaking, Tony Blair is a celery stick in terms of his Labour movement pedigree, Jim Callaghan was and always will be a rather gnarled tree with huge, sturdy roots, a magnificent piece of political foliage which, in its prime ministerial flowering (except for those last dreadful months), was rather glorious to behold. We can safely say that we shall not see his like again. For the Labour movement – and the Britain – that made him is no more.

But the aspect of his premiership most likely to be examined by students of the history of government is Callaghan the practitioner of traditional Cabinet collegiality rather than Callaghan the last hurrah of 'original Labour'. Here he will always score highly, though there were lapses. Oddly for such a collegial figure, two key decisions broke his normal pattern: the 5 per cent pay policy (noble but doomed and over which he would brook no dissent even from those closest to him in No. 10);[118] and his decision not to go for an election in the autumn of 1978 ('We had twelve months still in power. I hoped that the time would come when we would win. Therefore, why go to the country when I myself was convinced that we wouldn't win and nobody could prove to me that we would?').[119]

These were examples of solo decision-taking, of prime ministerial government even.[120] And, unlike the 'economic seminar' or the Nuclear Defence Policy Group, he did not have a small cluster of colleagues about him with whom to talk over the options. And both these decisions were potentially and in reality of government-wrecking proportions that affected the futures of both his party, his colleagues and the country. Michael Foot, asked by Michael Cockerell in 1997 what had been the biggest mistake made during his time as a minister, replied: 'The way we failed to present and discuss properly the 5 per cent pay policy . . . Terrible things happened in the Winter of Discontent.'[121]

Generally, however, Callaghan demonstrated the virtue of using a consultative style to help avoid overwork and of devolving business as far as possible to his Cabinet ministers. 'Certainly I was not a glutton for reaching out for new work. Unless you had confidence in your people then I think you would overtax yourself.'[122] Douglas Hurd rather admired this side of Callaghan as probably the last Prime Minister to make 'adequate time for reflection'.[123]

Jim Callaghan reckoned he probably picked up his collegiality 'subconsciously' from Attlee. 'But I think a lot of this depends upon your natural commonsense, you know. It depends how you read your fellow men and women as to whether you decide to jump in at the beginning and lay down the law, or whether you stand back, let everybody have a go and see indeed whether what they said is convincing to you,' Callaghan recalled at his most avuncular twenty years on, adding, not entirely convincingly, 'I know there's a belief rulers should always be feared. But I'm not sure I would accept Machiavelli's advice on that, especially [as] he wasn't operating in democratic days and we are.'[124] Callaghan could overplay the 'Sunny Jim' side of his nature. He was tough and he had a temper. Few tangled with Big Jim.

The forces that broke his premiership were collective, not individual. And until these same forces were largely broken by a combination of unemployment and the trade union legislation put through the Commons by the governments of his successor, Mrs Thatcher, Jim Callaghan's party was never in sight of getting one of its own back into Downing Street. Though scrupulously loyal to his successor-but-four as Labour Party leader, Jim Callaghan did feel a little hurt that he was not made more use of during the 1997 election campaign.[125] (He did have a chance to talk to Tony Blair about the virtues of inclusive government when invited to No. 10 for a chat, though it was, perhaps, revealing of the Blair style that Lady Thatcher had had her conversation with the new Prime Minister some time earlier.)[126] When a journalist asked him four months into the Blair premiership if, perhaps, New Labour was keen to avoid any association with the 'Winter of Discontent', all Lord Callaghan would say was: 'Yes, I've been blotted out of photographs, as it were.'[127] Time will take care of that.

16

A Tigress Surrounded by Hamsters:
Margaret Thatcher, 1979–90

'There's not much point being a weak and floppy thing in the chair is
there?'   *Margaret Thatcher, 1993*[1]

'Margaret Thatcher . . . carried the authority of her office always with
her. It was in her handbag . . . She was asserting it the whole time.'
                                                 Douglas Hurd, 1996[2]

She was different. It was partly that she carried with her into No. 10 a
greater baggage of ideology than her predecessors. It was partly that she
was a scientist by training, not, for once, a product of *litterae humaniores*.
It was partly that she was a woman. The combination of femininity and
power intrigued and excited her male interlocutors, from President Mit-
terrand to Anthony Powell . . . She was also intensely serious. The
camaraderie, the relaxed, joky, allusive style, the affectation of doing
things well without trying, the view of politics, and most other things
as a game, these expressions of the ruling male culture, which with
Harold Macmillan had been carried to extreme lengths, all these were
alien to her.   *Sir Percy Cradock, Foreign Affairs Adviser*
                             to the Prime Minister, 1984–92, 1997[3]

'I've always thought there was something Leninist about Mrs Thatcher
which came through in the style of government – the absolute determination, the belief that there's a vanguard which is right and if you keep
that small, tightly knit team together, they will drive things through . . .
there's no doubt that in the 1980s, No. 10 could beat the bushes of
Whitehall pretty violently. They could go out and really confront
people, lay down the law, bully a bit.'   *Sir Charles Powell,*
             Foreign Affairs Private Secretary to the Prime Minister,
                                                 1984–91, 1996[4]

'The Prime Ministers who are remembered are those who think and
teach, and not many do. Mrs Thatcher . . . influenced the thinking of
a generation.'   *Tony Benn, 1996*[5]

Whenever I think of Margaret Thatcher, her place in history, her position
on the spectrum of prime ministerial types that ranges from the presidential
to the collegial, her careful cultivation of her outsiderness even when
commanding the innermost of inner circles, the surging force of her will
and her personality down even the obscurer capillaries of Whitehall, I
think of only one comparable Downing Street phenomenon this century
– David Lloyd George: 'the man from Outside',[6] as A.J.P. Taylor called
him; 'the big Beast', as his contemporaries nicknamed him.[7] And, instantly,
I have to be on my guard. Because my first reaction to both these phenom-
enal premierships is that of a constitutional traditionalist, of someone
who thinks, like Mrs Thatcher's successor, John Major, 'that if you carry
people with you rather than ride through people you will get a better
outcome than otherwise.'[8]

I also share the conviction of Douglas Hurd, her Northern Ireland,
Home and Foreign Secretary at various times, that: 'The main reason
for Margaret Thatcher's loss of the leadership was . . . her failure over
the years to make the best of the Cabinet system . . . [which] . . .
depends on mutual tolerance and mutual support which in turn depends
on knowledge of each other.'[9] Similarly, when it comes to Lloyd George,
I am with Stanley Baldwin who denounced him at the famous Carlton
Club meeting which precipitated the collapse of his coalition as 'a dynamic
force, and it is from that very fact that our troubles . . . arise. A dynamic
force is a very terrible thing; it may crush you, but it is not necessarily
right.'[10]

In other words, I am not neutral about Margaret Thatcher even a
decade after the 'constitutional coup', as she described it to the Soviet
ambassador,[11] which dislodged her in November 1990. I suspect very few
people are. And she herself has made it almost impossible to be so by
claiming frequently, from the moment of her election as Conservative
Party leader in February 1975, to have 'changed everything'.[12] However,
I have come in a strange way to be protective of the lady's significance, if
not her hotly disputed reputation. For almost from the moment of her
demise as Prime Minister, commentators who had commendably resisted
falling under her spell during her ascendancy, such as Alan Watkins,
began to engineer the beginnings of what I like to call the 'Ozymandias

syndrome', whereby the reputations of the once-mighty end up as decaying pillars of stone in the pitiless desert of popular memory.[13]

As early as April 1991, for example, Watkins was writing: 'Large claims were made for Mrs Margaret Thatcher as a great Prime Minister: but they are melting before our eyes like the snows of spring. My prediction is that history will judge her as just above average, below C. R. Attlee and H. H. Asquith, who has better claims than she to being a great peacetime Prime Minister, but above Harold Macmillan and Harold Wilson.'[14] And on the fifth anniversary of her resignation announcement both Hugo Young and Andrew Marr added to the Ozymandias effect. For Young 'time has not accorded her the reputation selective memory sometimes fondly allows to former leaders. Instead, it has removed most of the halo she placed above her. The icon has self-destructed.'[15] While for Marr, 'Five years on, there is no monument to Baroness Thatcher . . . The woman who was once a political iconoclast, a radical force of world class, is reduced to the level of an exiled Stuart, restlessly travelling and remembering past glories.'[16]

I am well aware of the potency of Dr Johnson's judgement that 'Names which hoped to range over kingdoms and continents shrink at last into cloisters and colleges. Nor is it certain that even of these dark and narrow habitations, these last retreats of fame, the possession will long be kept.'[17] As an occupant of a college, if not a cloister, her 'fame', I think, will fight off, rightly, that 'last retreat' (though interest in Lloyd George waned enormously after his death in 1945 and it took the wordpower of A. J. P. Taylor to revivify LG studies in his Leslie Stephen Lecture at Cambridge in 1961).[18]

Because few observers are neutral about her and her possession of a temperament and a style that breed hyperbole, Margaret Thatcher continues to present a problem to would-be rescuers like me even with over several years' perspective plus two bulging volumes of memoirs from her[19] and a veritable shelfful from her former ministers who sat, with varying degrees of pleasure and pain, around her Cabinet Table between 1979 and 1990.[20] These last, of course, do not help. For the most anti-consensual occupant of the Cabinet Room at least since Neville Chamberlain (although modern scholars such as Alistair Parker reckon Chamberlain may have been depicted over harshly in this respect),[21] did not inspire a consensus among her colleagues, either at the time or in their memoir-writing phases.

Just listen to this cacophony. For reasons of balance I will start with a defender, Nicholas Ridley:

Margaret Thatcher was going to be the leader in her Cabinet. She wasn't going to be an impartial chairman. She knew what she wanted to do and she was not going to have faint hearts in her Cabinet stopping her . . . She disliked having votes in Cabinet. She didn't see it as that sort of body. Nor was it suitable to decide matters by vote in view of the constitutional position. She was Prime Minister, she knew what she wanted to do, and she didn't believe her policies should be subject to being voted down by a group she had selected to advise and assist her . . . I myself have no complaints to make about the way Margaret Thatcher ran her Cabinet.[22]

Ridley had not sat in a Cabinet under any other premier, but then neither had Norman St John-Stevas, who declared at the height of her dominance: 'There is no doubt that as regards the Cabinet, the most commanding Prime Minister of modern times has been . . . Mrs Thatcher. Convinced of both her own rectitude and ability, she has tended to reduce the Cabinet to subservience.'[23]

Lord Soames, well placed to observe a range of postwar Cabinet styles as both Churchill's son-in-law and his Parliamentary Private Secretary with full Cabinet experience under Macmillan and Douglas-Home as well as Mrs Thatcher, told me with great passion from his sickbed, clothed in a giant marquee of a dressing-gown, that 'She was not really running a team. Every time you have a Prime Minister who wants to take all the decisions, it mainly leads to bad results . . . The nearest parallel to Maggie is Ted.'[24] (After her very first Cabinet meeting Soames, not the most emollient of characters himself, said to Jim Prior, 'I wouldn't even treat my gamekeeper like that.')[25]

Peter Walker, who *had* sat under Ted Heath, did not care for his successor's Cabinet Room style and made his dissent public, while still in office, by recalling in speeches the Duke of Wellington's amazement after his first Cabinet. ' "An extraordinary affair", roared the Iron Duke. "I gave them their orders and they wanted to stay and discuss them." ' Walker would then pause and say: 'I'm so glad we don't have Prime Ministers like that today.'[26]

For Ian Gilmour, another carry-over from the Heath Cabinet, 'Mrs Thatcher regarded her first Cabinet . . . not as an aid to good government but as an obstacle to be surmounted. Her belief that dialogue was a waste of time rather than a means of arriving at an agreed course of action was part of her rejection of consensus politics.'[27] It was not just bone-bred consensualists like Gilmour who came to regret the gulf this created with colleagues. For Nigel Lawson, 'The practice of taking important decisions in smaller groups and not in Cabinet itself can clearly be taken too far',[28] though he found Cabinet as a discussion-free zone positively beneficial because 'as Chancellor, I used to look forward to Cabinet meetings as the most restful and relaxing event of the week' as 'the Cabinet's customary role was to rubber stamp decisions that had already been taken'.[29]

To be fair to Mrs Thatcher, we were warned. In a now famous interview a few months before becoming Prime Minister she told Kenneth Harris of the *Observer*: 'I've got to have togetherness. There must be a dedication to a purpose, agreement about direction. As a leader I have a duty to try and inspire that. If you . . . choose a team in which you encounter a basic disagreement, you will not be able to carry out a programme, you won't be able to govern . . . it must be a Cabinet that works on something much more than pragmatism or consensus. It must be a conviction government . . . As Prime Minister I could not waste time having any internal arguments.'[30] We also now know that it was after reading this declaration of intent in the *Observer* while on a flight from Geneva to Paris that Ted Heath decided he could not serve under Mrs Thatcher.[31]

It was David Howell, a junior minister under Heath who had had a considerable influence in designing the bureaucratic infrastructure of Heath's new style of government in 1970,[32] who produced the most eloquent summary of how that statement of her intentions actually played out in the Cabinet Room when talking to me for a BBC Radio series on Cabinet government. 'If by "conviction government",' he said,

'it is meant that certain slogans were going to be elevated and written in tablets of stone and used as the put down at the end of every argument, then, of course, that is what indeed happened . . . Of course there is a deterring effect if one knows that one's going to go not into a discussion where various points of view will be weighed and gradually a view may be achieved, but into a huge argument where tremendous battle lines will be drawn up and everyone who doesn't fall into line will be hit on the head.'[33]

No wonder some ministers were actually physically sick[34] before going to meetings with a piece of business likely to be on the receiving end of the most famous handbag in world political history. (Julian Critchley cannot have known quite what he was starting when he wrote as early as 1982 that 'She cannot see an institution without hitting it with her handbag.')[35]

The handbag's importance goes beyond its symbolism as Mrs

Thatcher's weapon (being to her what the chariot was to Boadicea). It served on occasion as the repository of an alternative advice system. As Charles Powell put it: 'It was a great strength to her to get views from different sources and not just from the official machine. Occasionally, the dreaded handbag would open and a piece of paper would be extracted which had reached her through some unofficial channel. She would announce with great triumph that she had an entirely different perspective on a particular problem ... and ... if it had information which contradicted what a minister had told her, that was the greatest joy of all.'[36]

Mrs Thatcher was both self-aware and quite unrepentant about these traits. On one occasion she opened a ministerial meeting by banging the celebrated bag on the table and declaring 'Well, I haven't much time today, only enough time to explode and have my way!'[37] And when she failed to get her way she was furious. 'Why *won't* they do what I want them to?' she fumed to a member of the Cabinet Secretariat once ministers had left after a particularly fractious Cabinet committee meeting.[38]

Mrs Thatcher had no idea of what it was like to be on the receiving end of that handbag and the cumulative resentment it could generate, to the point where some, even some of the other big beasts in the ministerial jungle (Heseltine in 1986, Lawson in 1989 and Howe in 1990), could take it no more. Howe, whom (according to Lawson) she 'treated as a cross between a doormat and a punchbag',[39] said of her outburst in her memoirs against Heseltine's alleged breach of collective responsibility over Westland: 'Coming from the past mistress at marginalising Cabinet committees and deciding issues in bilaterals, this is quite a statement.'[40] In such matters Mrs Thatcher was quite without self-irony. And she was unrepentant to the end and beyond the end. In her televised memoirs, screened in the autumn of 1993, she was as fiercely a conviction person as she had been when talking to Kenneth Harris over fourteen years earlier. 'I think sometimes the Prime Minister should be intimidating,' she told Denis Blakeway.[41]

She was almost Marxian in her sense of struggle. 'Life for me was always a daily battle,' she would say.[42] 'I must govern!' she told a member of her No. 10 staff during her first summer as Prime Minister when he was bold enough to suggest she might need a holiday.[43] 'I still had so much to do,'[44] she declared after nearly two-thirds of her Cabinet had told her she could not go on without risking defeat at Michael Heseltine's hands in the second leadership ballot in November 1990.[45]

'My trouble was', she explained, 'that the believers had fallen away.'[46]

Note that word 'believers'; the famous 'one of us' syndrome (which John Major so disliked)[47] at its perpetual work. No sign here of the tolerance which is traditionally part of the British way of governance, of open discussion before decision, the very bone-marrow of collective government at the top. Dissenters were not honourable men and women. 'There is no consensus,' she told Sir Anthony Parsons (himself a dedicated consensualist who, rather to his surprise, found himself her foreign affairs adviser in No. 10 after the Falklands War). 'I call them Quislings and traitors.'[48] To his intense mirth she once bowled Parsons over by telling him, 'Do you know, Tony, I'm so proud I don't belong to your class?' 'What class would that be, Prime Minister?' Parsons replied. 'The upper middle class who see everybody's point of view but have no view of their own.'[49] (At risk of absurdity, is it too fanciful to say that remarks like that and her January 1996 Keith Joseph Memorial Lecture, built around the political primacy of the middle class,[50] made Margaret Thatcher, in the age of 'New Labour', the leading proponent of the argument that class is the motor of British politics?)

One must be careful not to be swept away by the cascade of post-trauma catharsis in which so many of her former ministers and even some of her Civil and Diplomatic Service advisers have indulged since the night of 'treachery with a smile on its face'[51] as she put it – when Cabinet government really did reassert itself and she realized she could not carry on. ('Have you seen a situation slip away from you?' she said later. 'I'm a politician. I can sense it.')[52] For a very long time the atmosphere in Whitehall gave the general impression that she was, as Harold Macmillan expressed it with characteristic bite, 'a brilliant tyrant surrounded by mediocrities'.[53] And her colleagues' standard if not omnipresent supineness around the Cabinet Table understandably must have given *her* the impression, in John Biffen's vivid phrase, that 'she was a tigress surrounded by hamsters'.[54] Once the 'tigress' was caged in the House of Lords ('a prophet who . . . [occasionally] descends from Concorde rather than the hills', as Peter Riddell put it rather nicely),[55] the hamsters suddenly acquired teeth. 'The revenge of the unburied dead'[56] was how John Biffen described the process which began on that now legendary night in November 1990.

Mrs Thatcher was, after all, a formidable shifter of business, a ruler of the state rather than its servant (to borrow a nice distinction of Roy Jenkins')[57] and, for her, part of this required regular Cabinet purges rather than the softer form of political management-by-reshuffle. Hence the inevitability, in Mrs Thatcher's case, of vengeful catharsis as the deposed reached for their pens. And who is to say that a rough way with 'a cumbrous and unwieldy instrument'[58] like Cabinet government was always and in all circumstances such a bad thing given the political and personal conditions in which Margaret Thatcher found herself presiding over it?

She was never 'house trained' in the Whitehall sense which brought such pride to Harold Wilson.[59] She never wanted to be. This meant that many of the great institutions in the land, especially the Whitehall monuments to cool reason and calm procedure, were in for the kind of storm none of them (unless they had worked in any of the ministries filled by Duncan Sandys) could remember. The Foreign and Commonwealth Office comes particularly to mind. Yet this lack of 'house training' (which was partly the product of her rather narrow earlier ministerial lives at Pensions and National Insurance and Education and Science but mainly the result of that struggle-driven temperament) could be strangely and sometimes productively effective.

Here is that coolest and most rational of Diplomatic Service minds, Sir Percy Cradock, on her early approach to the question of Hong Kong's return to China. 'Casting around at the time for adjectives to define our discussions', Sir Percy recalls in his memoir of *Experiences of China*.

I hit on two: 'unstructured' and 'abrasive'. Abrasive certainly. Unstructured, because the Prime Minister's mind moved in unusual ways. We were accustomed to a frontal approach to the topic in hand, logical and step-by-step, as in eighteenth-century pitched battles. The Prime Minister recognised no such rules and conducted a species of guerrilla warfare, appearing suddenly behind the lines, or firing from unconventional angles.

She also often operated behind a smokescreen of her own, making a series of remarks which were commonplace or even off the point and which induced a false and fatal sense of security on the part of her listeners. Then, amidst the dross and the chaff, would come the missile, a question or comment of such relevance and penetration that it destroyed the opposition. I have seen so many redoubtable visitors and seasoned Whitehall warriors emerge worsted and reeling from such encounters, with a vague sense that there had not been fair play, or that they had not seen fair play, or that they had been somehow prevented from doing themselves full justice.[60]

To cope with Mrs Thatcher in full trajectory did require a very quick, very tough and very high-level form of counter-ballistics of which few were capable and even fewer tried when she was on a high, either after the Falklands victory in 1982, or after her third electoral triumph in 1987 or in her bunker phase, once her deputy and the one-person fire brigade for collective restraint, Willie Whitelaw, had gone into retirement in 1988.[61] With Whitelaw gone, as Nigel Lawson believes, 'there was no restraint on her at all'.[62] Or as Geoffrey Howe sees it, she had succumbed, in her dealings with her colleagues, on European questions especially, to the 'language of the battlefield rather than the language of partnership'.[63]

Even Whitelaw, a genuine deputy Prime Minister (though he never acquired the title) unlike Howe (who did), confined his hosing-down interventions to private bilateral sessions with his boss rather than formal Cabinet or Cabinet committee occasions.[64] And there was simply no one to replace him in this role. Those well placed to observe the shifting geography of power saw still more influence siphoned inside the tight little No. 10 circle after 1988, which is one of the reasons it is difficult to exempt her foreign affairs Private Secretary, Charles Powell, and her press secretary, Bernard Ingham (formidable operators both) from the charge that they were, to some degree, politicized while in her service (a charge from which I exempt the senior Civil and Diplomatic services as a whole).

Powell, candidly, accepts that there is something in the politicization accusation as directed at Ingham and himself: 'I think in Bernard Ingham's case and my own, we were there so long and became so identified, that we both took the right decision to leave the Civil Service at the end of it . . . I never became a political partisan of anyone. I've never belonged to a political party in my life . . . [but] . . . It is true that I developed a great personal sympathy, affection and respect for Mrs Thatcher and I suppose one would say that my views have evolved to be broadly Conservative . . . and there's no doubt that senior members of the Civil Service were very keen to see me depart from No. 10. I understand that. I didn't resent it at the time. I regarded it as part of the great game of life.'[65]

After the 1987 general election the Head of the Home Civil Service, Sir Robin Butler, and the Head of the Diplomatic Service, Sir Patrick Wright, called on Mrs Thatcher and urged her that Powell's secondment from the Foreign Office had been longer than the standard two to three years. It was not in her interests, Powell's or that of the public service generally, for such a figure so personally identified with her to stay on. (Butler and Wright, justifiably, were worried that Powell's profile and presence gave a false picture of a wider politicization of the Civil Service).[66] The Prime Minister would have none of it. She needed Powell. No one understood her thinking as he did. Nobody but him could write the kind of speeches she required. End of interview.[67]

Butler and Wright have kept silent about this. Cradock, who disapproved as they did, has not. 'It was sometimes difficult', Cradock wrote later, 'to establish where Mrs Thatcher ended and Charles Powell began.'[68] Cradock appreciated Powell's 'sharp intelligence . . . remarkable facility for drafting . . . great speed and ease at transacting business generally . . . high linguistic ability, and intense industry.'[69] He was mildly irritated, no more, when the press attributed to Powell his (Cradock's) title of foreign affairs adviser.[70] But

To the Foreign Office, however, his employers, and to the Cabinet Office in the person of the Cabinet Secretary, Charles began to present a more formidable problem. His closeness to the Prime Minister and his influence with her, his willingness to venture into the political world, came to seem as a threat to the balance between No. 10 and Whitehall and even to the constitutional division between ministers and civil servants. It certainly accentuated rather than relieved the strains between No. 10 and the Foreign Office. Charles and the Press Secretary, Bernard Ingham, portrayed as Mrs Thatcher's praetorian guard . . . underlined the dangerous dominance, and loneliness, of their mistress. Ministers and Members of Parliament as well as officials came to resent their influence. It was clearly time for a change of staff. But how was that to be accomplished?[71]

Cradock describes not their meeting with Mrs Thatcher but a 'series of desperate conferences' between Butler and Wright at which: 'A series of embassies was proposed, in ascending order. First Berne, then Madrid, in the end there were even whispers of Washington. But there were no takers. Mrs Thatcher would not let him go . . .'[72] Powell stayed with her until her fall – and with John Major, at Major's request, until the Gulf War was over.

Powell, was – and is – seen as a powerful reinforcer of Thatcher's increasing scepticism about the direction of the European Community (he drafted her September 1988 Bruges speech)[73] and of Germany's role as the driver towards closer integration. Some of the participants at the famous Chequers seminar on Germany in March 1990 were deeply unhappy about the tone and slant of Powell's record of the discussion,[74] though Powell himself has stressed the accuracy of his note.[75] It is plain his record reflected his boss's views. As Nigel Lawson rather doublehandedly put it, Powell was 'the dominant force in her private office . . . as polished as Ingham was blunt. Highly intelligent, he wrote the best and wittiest notes of meetings of anyone in Whitehall . . . He never saw it as his role to question her prejudices, merely to refine the language in which they were expressed. And like Ingham, he stayed at No. 10 for too long . . .'[76]

The Ingham question must be treated in a somewhat different light. Unlike Powell, his job was to cultivate the press and appear as almost the incarnation of the Prime Minister and her views. This he did to great effect. The political correspondents came to see them as indistinguishable. They could hear her speaking through him at his daily lobby briefings.[77] There is always the danger that a career civil servant in the Press Office will appear to be HMV (His Master's or His Mistress's Voice). A powerful case can be made for the job being filled by a political appointee like Joe Haines under Wilson or Alastair Campbell under Blair.

Many of the characteristics of an 'overmighty premiership' were apparent from the start, some time before the Ingham and Powell years, to insiders like Christopher Soames, to the wider political nation after the September 1981 ministerial purge, and by the mid 1980s, they had become part of the standard analysis and almost conventional wisdom. For example, a scholarly admirer of Mrs Thatcher, the historian Professor John Vincent, wrote in 1985–87 that

Mrs Thatcher is an exponent more of presidential than Cabinet government. These things are relative. She has not sought to build up a White House. Indeed, she rejected plans for a Prime Minister's Department and abolished the Think Tank: hardly the actions of a centralizer. Rather, the conduct of business has turned on personality and on faction. By temperament Mrs Thatcher is not a good listener. Her Cabinet technique, it is said, is a brisk exchange of fire with individual ministers on their special topics, not an Asquithian waiting game as discussion unfolds round the table. Moreover, her assertion that her aim is to get things done has to be taken seriously.[78]

The key phrase here is 'these things are relative'. I have never subscribed to the Tommy Cooper school of analysis about Cabinet government that in April 1979 under Jim Callaghan we had such a thing and then – just like that – it went, crushed by Mrs Thatcher's determination to extinguish all things collective including the collectivism of the Cabinet Room.

The 1980s were the period in which what Jean Seaton calls 'the politics of appearances'[79] took a powerful and, so far, irreversible hold on not just the external adornments of politics, politicians and governing, but increasingly on the entire process of government, too. Mrs Thatcher herself had a great deal to do with this from the mid 1970s – from the very moment she became leader of the Conservative Party in the most dramatic and, as it turned out, characteristic fashion. For, as Enoch Powell put it: 'She didn't rise to power: she was opposite the spot on the roulette wheel at the right time, and she didn't funk it.'[80]

She exuded power, purpose and defiant determination from the start in both the office of Leader of the Opposition and the office of Prime Minister. Much of her impact and power rested on the very high degree to which those who sensed it either directly, or as mediated through 'the politics of appearances' took such characteristics at face value, believed them and responded accordingly, whether in an approving, a resentful or a hostile capacity. But, though William Waldegrave took this central point as his start line in a memorable seminar on comparative premiership in 1997, he carefully (and rightly) steered his listeners away from its distorting dazzle. 'In the case of Mrs Thatcher', he said,

'you get what you see. She was by far the most radical "declinist" of my three Prime Ministers [the other two being Heath and Major]; perhaps of any Prime Minister we have ever had. She believed that Britain was in a state of near total political and economic collapse – and this was a view that did not seem absurd by the winter of 1978 to 1979.

'She believed that a huge dose of radical economic liberalism would reverse the economic collapse; that aggressive foreign policy would face down a Soviet Union which she perceived as an immediate threat; that similar firmness would drive back the European Community into its proper trading sphere; and that socialism could be defeated, here and abroad; and that a natural moral regeneration would follow its defeat.'[81]

She was, as Lord Waldegrave made plain, what her *bête-noire*, J. M. Keynes, would have called a 'copy book wisdom' statesman.[82] But it was Waldegrave's coda to her 'copybook' side which was so important: 'There was no private agenda or personal priority which was not quite explicitly her view of what the government's priorities also should be. That not all her colleagues, in particular initially, shared her views; and that it was not clear in the 1979 manifesto quite how radical she intended to be simply reflect the fact that it took her time to establish complete dominance. That only came after the Falklands, after the 1983 [general election] victory, and finally after the defeat of the miners.'[83]

Initially, though her distinctive style and tone were immediately apparent in No. 10, Mrs Thatcher operated like the paratroops dropped behind the German lines in Normandy ahead of the main D-Day invasion force in June 1944.[84] She used her No. 10 Policy Unit (constructed around the radical, strategy-minded businessmen John Hoskyns and Norman Strauss, whom she had come across at the Centre for Policy Studies which she and Sir Keith Joseph had set up in the Opposition years)[85] as a kind of special forces little platoon, on economic and industrial issues especially.[86]

As Waldegrave indicated, she could not trust the economic instincts of many of the former Heathites in her early 1979–81 Cabinet so she adopted a twin-track solution to which both 'wets' and 'drys' have attested. So far, history has tended to remember and stress the semi-clandestine, Cabinet-bypassing element as this fits with the later dominance which has been read back too readily and too far into her premiership. John Nott, her first Trade Secretary, recalls the inner group of 'drys' (himself; the Chancellor, Sir Geoffrey Howe; Biffen, his Treasury number 2; Joseph, then at Industry) who '. . . met informally, outside Cabinet committees, and we . . . gave moral support to Mrs Thatcher that the policies we believed in were right. And so to some extent those who didn't agree with us in the Cabinet were put rather on one side . . . We met sometimes at No. 10, sometimes over a meal, occasionally over breakfast.'[87]

This was the group which, in Jim Prior's phrase, put 'the writing on the wall'. 'It obviously showed', he explained, 'that she was going to go her own way as far as she could. I think I was the only minister in the economic team [Prior was Employment Secretary at this stage] with whom there were likely to be difficulties from her point of view.'[88] Yet in these early phases of what Howe would later call 'her heroic battle against the accumulated causes of British decline',[89] she was verging on the traditionalist in the way she conducted herself in Cabinet and Cabinet committees on most issues.

This was a point Jim Prior made strongly in his memoirs. 'In her early years as Prime Minister,' he wrote, 'Margaret adhered closely to the traditional principles and practice of Cabinet government. She operated very strictly through the Cabinet committee system with the Cabinet Office taking the minutes.'[90] The one exception to this orthodoxy, as Prior acknowledges, was economic policy. Though as Norman St John-Stevas, her Chancellor of the Duchy (and the first 'wet' to be purged – he went in January 1981) observed, even in her more constitutionally impeccable phase in Cabinet government terms, her ministers 'realised very soon . . .

that although those supporting the traditionalist [economic] view were in fact the majority, the weight of the cabinet was not with them'.[91]

On another sensitive issue which, like the economy, was subject to firm Thatcherian views – nuclear weapons – she proved a reasonably collegial Prime Minister. Early on in her premiership she convened MISC 7, an ad hoc Cabinet Committee of five (one more than Callaghan's informal group which oversaw the preparatory studies on Polaris replacement). The decision to go for the American Trident C4 missile only reached the full Cabinet on the morning of 15 July 1980, partly because the word reached Whitehall that the *New York Times* was about to break the story.[92]

Swift technological developments thereafter and a change of administration from Carter to Reagan in the United States led to the US Navy going for the improved Trident D5 and MISC 7 had to re-examine the issue in November–December 1981.[93] This time the full Cabinet was properly involved and was given an informal two-hour briefing by Ministry of Defence officials,[94] led by Michael Quinlan (the leading nuclear theologist of his generation whose intellect and clarity Mrs Thatcher came greatly to admire)[95] and the Chief of the Defence Staff, Sir Terence Lewin (her great prop during the Falklands campaign).[96]

The full Cabinet took the decision to purchase Trident D5 in January 1982.[97] Nuclear weapons policy was not the kind of potential Cabinet-splitting issue it was for the Labour governments of the 1970s in particular. It was for Mrs Thatcher's ministers on MISC 7 and in the full Cabinet pretty well what one well-placed official called an 'of course' decision to replace Polaris on the basis of what Quinlan would later describe as a 'Mark I level of cover'. By which he meant a system bought off the shelf in the USA with operational independence under the Nassau Agreement of 1962 as opposed to Mark II provision – the much more expensive fully home-grown nuclear weapons capacity which did not depend on American largesse, a policy abandoned by Macmillan in 1960 with the cancellation of the all-British Blue Streak rocket and the plan to purchase the American Skybolt missile for the V bombers, itself abandoned in 1962 in favour of Polaris missiles for the Royal Navy.[98]

There was nothing 'of course' about the outcomes of economic and industrial policy matters in 1979–81, however. And it was here that the relative collegiality of the early Thatcher Cabinets was stretched to snapping point. The 1981 Budget was both a showdown in policy terms and a turning-point in the sense of its being the first swerve in a stylistic shift whose full curve carried Mrs Thatcher to her version of a command premiership. The Budget, in which she sought the death of inflation and the birth of financial stability by raising taxes and deflating still further in the pit of the worst recession since the interwar years, sent out certain signals – as it was intended to – to a variety of recipients: to the senior civil servants ('they had absorbed some of the decline');[99] to the money markets;[100] to industry;[101] and to 'the dissenters in the Cabinet'[102] ('the 1981 budget was a shocker', said Prior).[103]

John Hoskyns, keen observer and participant in the No. 10 Policy Unit, said: 'What I think it did do, which was psychologically very, very important – almost regardless of the merits of the budget – it was such a courageous, some might say foolhardy thing to do, that it enormously strengthened the moral ascendancy, the position and power and authority of the Prime Minister and the Chancellor.'[104] The following autumn Thatcher consolidated her internal position with a substantial September purge of three Cabinet ministers (Gilmour, Soames and Carlisle)[105] and by moving Prior to Northern Ireland and bringing in Tebbitt, Lawson and Parkinson. And she exulted to Hoskyns and the Downing Street chief of staff, David Wolfson, at 'what a difference it made to have most of the people in it [the Cabinet] on my side'.[106]

As Hoskyns noted, by demonstrating during the course of 1981 that she had meant what she said in her celebrated 'The lady's not for turning'[107] speech at the previous year's Party Conference: 'That did make the thinking so much easier. People knew that the lines of retreat had been cut off.'[108] Late 1990s Whitehall still treated 1981 as a benchmark.

Despite the polls showing that she was the most unpopular Prime Minister to have held office in poll-taking times,[109] despite the urban riots[110] which punctuated the months between the Budget and her ever-defiant Party Conference performance,[111] the autumn of 1981 is seen as the moment the true Thatcher governing style began to take its distinctive (and most powerfully remembered) shape. One senior civil servant, whose closeness to events spanned the seventeen years between 1981 and the late 1990s, declared to me in the summer of 1998: 'I believe the form of the Blair government is not going to be apparent for about two years . . . Just think, when did we really know what Mrs T's government would be like? Not until 1981.'[112]

I would place that moment not in 1981 but in the summer of 1982 after she had faced a test of her no retreat, no surrender philosophy far tougher than anything she had encountered before or was to experience later (including the miners' strike of 1983–84) until that great destabilizer of both her psyche and her Cabinet – Europe – began like the 'incoming tide' of Lord Denning's imagination,[113] to flow into all the crevices of her government and her governing practice in a way which, in the end, undermined her ascendancy and destroyed her premiership. For it is the Falklands War which remains her own abiding memory of her premiership and certainly was the fulcrum around which her power and her style most significantly revolved. Had she fallen with the Islands (and she almost certainly would have if the Falklands had proved unregainable), her brief three-year premiership would have featured in a book such as this as 'as study in failure', to borrow the title of Robert Rhodes James's study of Churchill's life pre-World War II.[114]

As she expressed it in her memoirs: 'Nothing remains more vividly in my mind, looking back on my years in No. 10, than the eleven weeks in the spring of 1982 when Britain fought and won the Falklands War. Much was at stake . . . When I became Prime Minister I never thought that I would have to order British troops into combat and I do not think I have ever lived so tensely or intensely as during the whole of that time.'[115] Indeed, her memoirs reflect this in another sense: her two chapters on the war are the most compelling of all twenty-eight in the book. She says there that had the 'War Cabinet' accepted the plan brokered by Al Haig, the US Secretary of State in late April 1982 (whereby both Britain and Argentina would have withdrawn their forces from the area to pave the way for a Special Interim Authority on which the Argentine would be represented) as her Foreign Secretary, Francis Pym, wished, 'I would have resigned.'[116] I believe her.

The Falklands War was the defining event of her premiership. Sir Frank Cooper who, as Permanent Secretary at the Ministry of Defence in 1982, saw a great deal of Mrs Thatcher during the war, is 'sure she does regard it as the high peak of her whole prime ministerial life and she'll be with it as long as she lives'.[117] The more so because, thanks to intelligence failures and lack of ministerial attention at Cabinet and Cabinet committee level (all carefully and vividly laid out in the postwar Franks inquiry),[118] it was both 'very sudden'[119] and unlike anything she had had to deal with heretofore in difficulty, unpredictability and lethality (both to her and to others). We have seen in chapter 6 how she called in Sir Frank Cooper on the Sunday after the invasion for advice on how to run a war and how Harold Macmillan came in two days later with virtually identical advice. We have seen, too, why it was decided not to declare war on Argentina.

The first few days of the Falklands conflict were very illuminating of the Prime Minister's character but with Mrs Thatcher under severe duress they were also, in a way, counter-cultural. For they revealed her as a punctilious traditionalist in her dealings both with her Cabinet and with Parliament even when her Boadicea qualities were most in demand. Mrs Thatcher had become increasingly worried about the security of the Falkland Islands in the early months of 1982. A group of Argentinian scrap-metal merchants had been busy dismantling an old whaling station on the Falkland Islands Dependency of South Georgia since December; talks about the Falklands with the Argentine government had begun to hit problems at the United Nations in New York. A sense of urgency began to intrude in early March 1982, when preparations were made to update the Joint Intelligence Committee's assessment of the invasion threat and the Prime Minister called for contingency plans to be prepared[120] (though the dispatching of a hunter-killer submarine to the waters between the mainland and the Islands was only decided upon when it was too late).[121]

It was only on the evening of Wednesday 31 March that Mrs Thatcher came to appreciate that she had a crisis of potentially premiership-wrecking proportions on her hands – a dreadful position for which the 'C' of her late premiership, Sir Colin McColl, accepts that much of the blame must fall on the UK's intelligence apparatus for lacking a methodology for 'balancing' the 'forces' of risk.[122] Though others, such as Jim Callaghan, have always (and justifiably) believed that lack of timely ministerial attention was also a powerful factor – not least because of his conviction, as we have seen, that the Falklands is one of those 'small things' to which a premier must pay attention to 'save a very large catastrophe'.

Such a catastrophe plainly faced Mrs Thatcher on that Wednesday evening 'I shall not forget', as she wrote in her memoirs:

I was working in my room at the House of Commons when I was told that John Nott [Defence Secretary] wanted an immediate meeting to discuss the Falklands. I called people together . . . John was alarmed. He had just received intelligence that the Argentinian Fleet, already at sea, looked as if they were going to invade the islands on Friday 2 April. There was no ground to question the intelligence. John gave the MOD's view that the Falklands could not be retaken once they were seized.[123]

Sir Frank Cooper, one of the people summoned to her room that Wednesday evening, recalled that 'she was very shaken . . . She was cross with the Foreign Office who were put in a corner. She was deeply angry that this had come and there had been no warning. She was quick to recognize that this was a major crisis . . . She didn't have an instant answer to that other than that we had to do something. No one had an idea at first of what that should be . . . I think that we were moving quite quickly towards the idea that we would have to make military moves . . . when Henry Leach [the First Sea Lord] arrived [in full naval uniform], a joy to the eye and the ear.'[124]

Leach was the kind of 'quiet, calm and confident'[125] member of the officer class for which Mrs Thatcher has always demonstrated respect of a kind rarely forthcoming for crown servants in civvies. Two days earlier Sir Henry had instructed his staff to draw up a contingency plan in case the islands were invaded.[126] This he placed before Mrs Thatcher, who had already made up her mind that the MOD view that recapture was not on 'was terrible and totally unacceptable'.[127] 'If they are invaded, we have got to get them back,' she told the meeting just before Leach arrived. Leach laid out before her a naval 'task force' which could leave for the South Atlantic within forty-eight hours and, he believed, retake the Falklands.[128]

The Prime Minister clambered aboard and did not disembark until the white flags appeared round Port Stanley nearly three months later. 'All he needed', she wrote of Leach, 'was my authority to begin to assemble it. I gave it him, and he left immediately to set the work in hand. We [an early example of her propensity to pluralize herself] reserved for Cabinet the decision as to whether and when the task force should sail.'[129]

I was very impressed when I learned of this from one of her most astringent critics inside her Cabinet. 'That task force would never have sailed without Cabinet approval. There is no question of that,' he told me.[130] The next week, in fact, showed Mrs Thatcher to be almost Churchillian in the punctilio she showed to Cabinet and Commons.

Mrs Thatcher held two Cabinets on Friday 2 April. At the first, at 9.45 in the morning, she told her ministers of the imminence of the Argentine invasion: 'We would meet later in the day to consider once more the question of sending a task force – though to my mind the issue by this stage was not so much whether we should act, but how.'[131] They reconvened at 7.30 p.m. and the decision was taken. The Fleet would sail.[132]

Parliament met the following morning for its first Saturday debate since Suez.[133]

'It was the most difficult [debate] I had to face,' Mrs Thatcher recalled in her memoirs and, having announced the dispatch of the task force, she was powerfully affected by Enoch Powell's reference to the 'Iron Lady' sobriquet afforded her by Tass, the Soviet Union's official news agency, in her Opposition years.[134] 'In the next week or two', said Powell, 'this House, the nation and the Right Hon. Lady herself will learn of what metal she is made.'[135] Powell later delivered a favourable verdict on her metallic qualities in a Parliamentary question. 'Is the Rt Hon. Lady aware that the report has now been received from the public analyst on a certain substance recently subjected to analysis and that I have obtained a copy of the report? It shows that the substance under test consisted of ferrous matter of the highest quality, and that it is of exceptional tensile strength, is highly resistant to wear and tear and to stress, and may be used to advantage for all national purposes.' Her Parliamentary Private Secretary, Ian Gow, had the pair of them framed and they still hang on her office wall.[136]

That House of Commons debate was the most extraordinary I can remember (I was too young in 1956 to have had more than the vaguest notion of the parliamentary end of the Suez Crisis). It was, for once, a quite genuine debate in which there were no preset tramlines. It could not be shaped – and was not – by the orthodox line-ups of Left and Right or pro-Empire or anti-Colonial as became familiar in the 1950s. For once the House had to think its way through a breaking issue, as well as indulging in the inevitable criticism of an administration which had allowed such an issue to roar in from the periphery to dominate events and to make the political weather as it did throughout the spring and early summer of 1982.

The Prime Minister, however, got her majority for sending the task force, albeit on a technical motion. A proposal to continue the debate beyond the planned adjournment time was defeated by 204 to 115.[137] 'I obtained the almost unanimous but grudging support of a Commons that was anxious to support the Government's policy, while reserving judgement on the Government's performance,' she wrote later.[138] She did lose her Foreign Secretary, Lord Carrington, three days later – and almost lost her Defence Secretary John Nott as well.[139] Carrington's departure (against her wishes), with his Cabinet and Foreign and Commonwealth Office colleague, Humphrey Atkins, and their junior minister, Richard Luce, continues to shine like a beacon of honour in an era when most ministers in trouble appear to hang on to their office as if it were a personal freehold rather than a crown possession.

After consulting Frank Cooper and Harold Macmillan, Mrs Thatcher set up a Falklands war machine which held good throughout. A small 'War Cabinet', technically an offshoot of the standing Cabinet committee on Overseas and Defence policy and known as OD(SA) – Overseas and Defence (South Atlantic) – was created to bring together an inner group of war-waging ministers with their technical advisers from the politico-military, diplomatic and intelligence worlds.

She followed Macmillan's advice and kept the Chancellor, Geoffrey Howe, off it. He was understanding enough about this in his memoirs ('It was no part of the Chancellor's duty at such a time to argue against the use of the defence forces for the very purposes for which they had been provided . . .').[140] OD(SA) consisted of Francis Pym, Carrington's replacement as Foreign Secretary, Nott, Willie Whitelaw 'as my deputy and trusted adviser'[141] and Cecil Parkinson 'who not only shared my political instincts but was brilliantly effective in dealing with public relations'[142] (not a view generally shared; hc was seen as a safe vote for her should the 'War Cabinet' encounter serious disagreement).[143] The Chief of the Defence Staff, Lewin, was a constant attender, as was the Attorney General, Sir Michael Havers,[144] described by one participant as 'a very good hand-holder – he'd been in the Navy as well and was really rather good at it',[145] who also gave advice on the legality of the operations in terms of United Nations resolutions and the royal prerogative (which, as we have seen, is of central importance if war is not formally declared).

The 'War Cabinet' met at least once, sometimes twice a day throughout the war, usually in No. 10 but occasionally at the joint operations headquarters in Northwood and often over weekend sessions at Chequers. It is quite plain that Suez served as a 'how not to' guide for Mrs Thatcher. Frank Cooper recalled that during their 'Falklands Sunday' conversation

'She said something like "I'll have to tell the Cabinet from time to time what's going on down there and if it does come to something, obviously they'll have to be involved." I don't think she ever envisaged evading or had any fundamental stand against going back to full Cabinet. I think I certainly used Suez to stress the need to keep everybody in line – and you mustn't let the whole thing get out of control at any place, because once it's started it would have a dynamo effect.'[146]

Mrs Thatcher did keep 'control' but not – and it is a significant 'not' in terms of the 'she who must be obeyed' (as a senior official once called her)[147]

image that has come down to posterity – in a stark and caveat-free fashion – at the expense of Cabinet government.

In her conduct of OD(SA) meetings she was markedly non-strident, though as one attender put it, the role of the Foreign Office and their 'attitude of mind' continued to irritate her ('It took some time for her to understand . . . that they were doing their duty and that the Foreign Office task was to see if you could achieve an honourable peace').[148]

Apart from animus towards a department she later said always took the view 'that a little bit of appeasement is no bad thing'[149] ('When I'm out of politics, I'm going to run a business called "Rent-a-spine",' she contemptuously remarked in the context of her views on the Foreign Office during the television version of her memoirs),[150] 'War Cabinet' meetings were, as one insider recalled, 'pretty relaxed on the whole':

'She was scrupulous throughout. Everybody had their say – the chance to ask questions – and she was a much better listener than she was on many occasions. The public person was very different from the working persona.'[151]

It is plain from insiders that, although determined to win, Mrs Thatcher was far from sanguine about the loss of life likely to be involved, and the memoirs are an almost tangible account of her sense of the precariousness of the operation from start to finish. The World War II veterans amongst her ministerial colleagues, her military and her Civil Service advisers were very sensitive to this side of her: 'People very much wanted to help her. People were aware this was something new to her. They probably had some sexist things [in mind] – here is a woman who doesn't know anything about . . . war anyway. And there's no doubt in my mind that people went out of their way to try and say this could be very difficult, this might be very nasty . . . she was terribly grateful to people like Willie and Michael Havers . . . He [Whitelaw] would say "Are you *sure* that's all right?" in response to something one of the Chiefs had said . . . People went out of their way to tell her that people would get shot, aircraft downed or ships sunk.'[152]

The Prime Minister reserved all serious and detailed operational decisions to OD(SA). It was a 'War Cabinet' meeting at Chequers, for example, in early May which took the decision that the Argentine cruiser, *General Belgrano*, should be sunk by its shadowing submarine, HMS *Conqueror*, as in her own words 'We had received intelligence about the aggressive intentions of the Argentine Fleet'[153] towards the task force now vulnerably placed off the islands, despite the *Belgrano* being outside the total exclusion zone when it was sunk on 2 May with the loss of 368 lives. An additional, publicly unacknowledged reason for *Conqueror*'s attack was, in the words of a figure closely involved, 'that the *Belgrano* had the capacity electronically, radar etc., to help locate the Fleet or, indeed, guide attacking Argentinian aircraft towards it. [But] the major element was that there was concern that the *Belgrano* and other units of the Argentinian navy could have made a serious assault on the [Royal] Navy and particularly on the supporting vessels . . . They never came out again. None of the Argentinian navy reappeared . . .'[154]

In keeping such operational matters to her inner war group, Mrs Thatcher was firmly in accord with the prescription laid down by Sir Maurice Hankey in his classic paper for the Committee of Imperial Defence some fifty-four years earlier. She did, however, take the need to keep the full Cabinet abreast of the wider picture sufficiently seriously to establish a second weekly meeting of the full Cabinet solely for this purpose.

Nigel Lawson, as Energy Secretary, was not closely involved in the war, but his memoirs provide a precise account of the special Falklands full Cabinets, as one might call them:

Margaret introduced the practice of holding a second weekly Cabinet . . . Throughout the critical weeks of May and June, there was a full Cabinet meeting every Tuesday after the daily War Cabinet.

The Chiefs of Staff were present and, although sensitive military matters were not discussed, it was possible always to gauge the balance of the conflict.[155]

Lawson hints at less than total unanimity in the Cabinet about victory at all costs, which throughout was the Thatcher line. 'What was the alternative?' she inquired in her memoirs. 'That a common or garden dictator should rule over the Queen's subjects and prevail by fraud and violence? Not while I was Prime Minister.'[156]

Lawson was a recapturer, too: 'I was convinced from a very early stage in the conflict that the various diplomatic manoeuvring would amount to nothing and that it would be necessary to retake the islands by force, and said as much. This view may not have been universally shared.' Lawson reckons that if the Argentine Junta had been persuaded 'to place the islands under the indefinite jurisdiction of the United Nations, it is possible that the recall of the Task Force would have commanded a majority in

36. Ted Heath in Slough with a less-than-radiant young candidate, Nigel Lawson, during the 1970 general election campaign.

37. Heath with Willie Whitelaw in Belfast, November 1972: Northern Ireland was the single greatest absorber of his Cabinet's time.

38. Margaret Thatcher with Heath:
He placed her out of his eye-line in
the Cabinet Room on the other side
of the Cabinet Secretary.

39. Heath leaving No. 10 to conduct
Elgar's *Cockaigne* with the London
Symphony Orchestra at the Festival
Hall, November 1971.

40. Sir Burke Trend: Speaker of truth unto power.

41. Jim Callaghan with a fading Harold Wilson, February 1976: Itching to hand over to the older man.

42. Harold Wilson with Lady Falkender and George Thomas MP: When it was over, Marcia would remain.

43. Prime Minister most precarious: Labour lost its Commons majority on Callaghan's first full day in No. 10.

44. Jim with his own generation: Jessie Matthews and Vera Lynn.

45. Callaghan arrives at the back door of the Blackpool Winter Gardens in
September 1976 to announce the death of Keynesianism before the Labour
Party Conference.

46. Jim Callaghan makes a clarion-call for educational reform at Ruskin College, Oxford during the 1976 IMF crisis: The Left were not impressed.

47. The bowels of the Labour movement: Callaghan with Jack Jones of the Transport and General (there was serious trouble with the unions once Jones had retired).

48. 'I let the country down': A sombre Callaghan out of his office in his 'JC'-stripe suit.

49. Margaret Thatcher: 'The facts? The facts? I have been elected to change the facts!'

50. Shouting at the Europeans from the start: Mrs Thatcher in Strasbourg with Helmut Schmidt, June 1979.

Cabinet. Very foolishly it did not do so. As a result, there was no dissension within Cabinet throughout the war, even if one or two members may have nursed private doubts.'[157]

As we have seen, it was within the confines of OD(SA) rather than the full Cabinet that Mrs Thatcher faced the most precarious moment in her pursuit of complete victory over the invaders. For the Prime Minister 'Saturday 24 April was to be one of the most crucial days in the Falklands story and a critical one for me personally.'[158] Pym wanted the Haig plan accepted as the basis for a settlement. She thought its contents 'were totally unacceptable', as she told her Foreign Secretary early that morning. Havers, the Attorney General, confirmed her view that acceptance would make impossible a return to the *status quo ante* and be an abandonment of 'our commitment to the principle that the islanders' wishes were paramount'.[159]

OD(SA) was to meet that evening. Her fury at Pym's advocacy (which was entirely consonant with his beliefs and prerogatives as Foreign Secretary) seared the pages of her memoirs a good ten years after the event:

Despite my clear views expressed that morning, Francis put it in a paper to the War Cabinet recommending acceptance of these terms. Shortly before 6 o'clock that evening ministers and civil servants began assembling outside the Cabinet Room. Francis was there, busy lobbying for their support. I asked Willie Whitelaw to come upstairs to my study. I told him that I could not accept these terms and gave him my reasons. As always on crucial occasions he backed my judgement.[160]

A majority of OD(SA) backed her, too, but it was John Nott who suggested a way out. Haig should be asked to put his plan to the Argentinians first. If they accepted, the Thatcher position would be very difficult. If Galtieri and the Junta rejected it, the Prime Minister would ask President Reagan to bring the United States firmly down on Britain's side (which is exactly what happened). 'And so', she wrote, 'a great crisis passed. I could not have stayed as Prime Minister had the War Cabinet accepted Francis Pym's proposals.'[161] On 29 April the full Cabinet was briefed on the outcome after the deadline had passed for a reply from Buenos Aires.[162] The following day Reagan came out in support[163] of the UK's determination to recapture what he quaintly, if erroneously, called 'that little ice-cold bunch of land down there'.[164]

After what one insider called 'the one time' she had an argument with

Francis Pym 'on grounds that he was trying too hard to find a negotiated settlement', Mrs Thatcher's relationships were essentially harmonious.[165] On Tuesday 18 May OD(SA) took the decision to authorize an assault on the islands subject to the Cabinet's final approval two days later which was forthcoming.

'They were proper Cabinets with proper decisions', a collectively minded Whitehall figure attested. 'She was aware that the nearer she got, the surer she had to be that people were with her . . . She was seen as an able and acceptable leader of a team of people . . . she spent much more time asking questions and weighing up the answers than she is reputed to have done in all other areas. With hindsight, the fact that she was a woman, that she did not have military experience and that she had a clear and penetrating mind were all pluses.'[166]

What Mrs Thatcher and her OD and, later, OD(SA) colleagues did not have was good intelligence material on the Falklands. As Prime Minister she had a soft-spot for the intelligence world, MI6 especially, whose dashing officers she always contrasted favourably with those detested 'appeasers' in the Foreign Office. At dinners or parties where both breeds were present this could become painfully apparent.[167] I have heard from more than one source how after top-level Whitehall meetings in which the Treasury appeared to have successfully resisted a bid for, say, a highly sophisticated and expensive addition to GCHQ's computer armoury, '"C" and Robert Armstrong [her Cabinet Secretary] would go in and see her and she would reverse it.'[168] She exempted MI5 and MI6 from her public service recruitment freeze in the early 1980s and later agreed that the state's secret servants should be paid a top-up of some 10 per cent above comparable grades in the overt services of the crown.[169] One of her later acts as Prime Minister was to agree to new and technologically highly sophisticated headquarters for MI5 and MI6 at Thames House and Vauxhall Cross, respectively, a piece of largesse for which the sustainers of what became the Single Intelligence Vote in the 1990s reckon ruefully that they have been paying in terms of Treasury fierceness ever since.[170]

The Franks Report was graphic in its account of the shortcomings of both the Joint Intelligence Committee and its Latin America Current Intelligence Group before the invasion. Once the islands were captured matters improved very slowly, partly because Ted Rowlands, a former junior Foreign Office minister in the Callaghan government, let it be known in the great Falklands debate in the Commons on 3 April that, in his time, the UK had been reading Argentinian diplomatic traffic. (For this breach of security, the secret world has never forgiven him – reprising the tale as a horror story for new ministers and new recruits.)[171] The Americans had left the South Atlantic largely to British intelligence. But the UK owns no spy satellites. Only later did material arrive at GCHQ from a repositioned American satellite.[172] In the meantime, 'everybody was told to beam in and pick up what they could from anywhere. One of the problems with intelligence is that you can't just conjure the stuff out of the air.'[173]

The intelligence flow did improve as the campaign progressed, and before the San Carlos landings the intelligence community had 'built up progressively a sort of order of battle of people on the islands that did come out of intercept. Gradually they began to get better on what type of equipment they had.'[174] Criticism was heard within Whitehall, too, that the JIC's feed into OD(SA) decision-making lacked timeliness.[175]

Ironically, by the time of the approach of the Gulf War in the last days of Mrs Thatcher's premiership, the intelligence organization and flow was much better. But by this time her aversion to collegiality meant that she eschewed an equivalent to OD(SA), which had to await John Major's arrival, and ran the British end of the build-up through a tiny group at which Charles Powell took the minutes, leaving several of Whitehall's biggest players, such as the Cabinet Secretary and the head of the Diplomatic Service, out of the loop – to their considerable consternation, as we shall see in the next chapter.

Her Falklands experience left Mrs Thatcher a changed premier. Following the Franks Report of January 1983 she tightened up the JIC and its apparatus.[176] She toyed with the idea of a Prime Minister's Department to ensure that never again would she be caught unawares by a serious crisis. She rejected this idea and settled instead for having her own foreign affairs adviser in No. 10 – the first a somewhat reluctant Sir Anthony Parsons; the second Sir Percy Cradock, who later assumed the chair of the JIC as well. Ironically, both were from the despised Foreign Office but she seemed to exempt them from the appeasers' stigma on the grounds that, in their different ways, each was a free and independent spirit (which was true in Parsons' case, and remains so in Cradock's).

There was an unstoppable quality about Margaret Thatcher following the Argentine surrender on 14 June 1982. In a vintage example of what you see is what you get, she distilled her essence of Falklands in a speech at Cheltenham on 3 July which linked all her battlefronts:

'We have ceased to be a nation in retreat. We have instead a new-found confidence – born in the economic battles at home and tested and found true 8,000 miles away . . .'[177]

This upfront aspect of Mrs Thatcher's is worth emphasizing. As an official who saw her in action in the early 1980s put it: 'Most ministers have two personalities – a frontstage and a backstage. After a speech or a presentation they will say things like, "My God, we got away with that!" or "Thank God, they didn't see through this!" Mrs Thatcher wasn't like that. Her backstage was exactly the same as her frontstage.'[178]

From the Falklands summer on, even before plans carefully laid in a highly secret Cabinet committee, MISC 57[179] (a group of civil servants chaired by Robert Wade-Grey, head of the Cabinet Office's Overseas and Defence Secretariat tasked to find ways of increasing the capacity of the power stations to resist the impact of picketing), helped her to create an instrument to break both the National Union of Mineworkers and the spectre of wider trade union power in 1983–84, the high Thatcher years took hold. With them came a decline in collegiality and a waxing of an appetite for a very personal style of government. From early 1983 onwards as *The Times* Whitehall correspondent I became the ever more frequent recipient of tales from the frontline (from both ministers and officials) and began to prepare my first stories and articles on Mrs Thatcher and Cabinet government.

The hours and days after the general election of June 1983 were revealing both at the time and subsequently. Enoch Powell's roulette wheel was in action again. She was very fortunate in her opponents in the early 1980s, whether scholarly and charming (Michael Foot as Labour leader), sinister (General Galtieri), or menacing (Arthur Scargill). Her new majority of 144 seats over all parties reflected this. Once it was in the handbag, Mrs Thatcher's high and very personal governing style truly became apparent and the new politico-economic weather system that Jim Callaghan had sensed was on the turn four years earlier really began to take hold over the United Kingdom.

In the early days of her premiership she had told a CPRS team which included Professor John Ashworth, its Chief Scientist, that their report on unemployment (commissioned by Callaghan but delivered to her) was unacceptable. 'But, Prime Minister, it's based on the facts,' said Ashworth. The famous withering, slightly manic gaze was turned on. 'The facts. The *facts*,' she declaimed. 'I have been elected to *change* the facts!'[180] By the summer of 1983, in the political sense at least, she thought she had done just that. By the time of the 1987 general election, that view was almost baked solid as a generally held conventional wisdom. The Cabinet was remade once more to bring it closer to her temperament and ideological requirements.

It has to be remembered that she was not a Tory. This was one of the reasons why her worshippers, such as her confidant Woodrow Wyatt, loved her – 'because she is not a Conservative . . . She is a radical making a revolution which horrifies many Conservatives.'[181] Milton Friedman, one of the free-market intellectuals whose stars she steered by, recognized this instantly on first meeting her. She is, he said, '. . . not a typical Tory. She really is the closest thing there is equivalent to a nineteenth-century liberal in British political terms . . . What you had [in Britain] is an alternation between groups that wanted to construct different aristocracies. In the one case it would be an aristocracy of Labour, in the other it would be a case of the wise, the well born . . . So Mrs Thatcher's ideas and approach represent a sharp break.'[182]

The post-election reshuffle in 1983 reflected that Friedmanite analysis. Out went Pym; belated revenge for that Saturday evening in the 'War Cabinet' ('In following Peter Carrington with Francis Pym as Foreign Secretary I had exchanged an amusing Whig for a gloomy one')[183] and for opining during the election campaign on the undesirability of a large majority.[184] Most important of all, Howe moved from the Treasury and was replaced by Nigel Lawson – 'an enormous and to most people unexpected promotion', she wrote in her memoirs. 'Whatever quarrels we were to have later, if it comes to drawing up a list of Conservative – even Thatcherite – revolutionaries I would never deny Nigel a leading place on it.'[185]

In the afterglow of the election, she rejigged the infrastructure of her command post. The Central Policy Review Staff was culled. She thought it had never lost its Heathite DNA. Heath, she believed, had created it in an era when there existed 'a widespread belief that the great questions of the day could be resolved by specialised technical analysis. But a government with a firm philosophical direction was inevitably a less comfortable environment for a body with a technocratic outlook. And the Think-Tank's detached speculations, when leaked to the press and attributed to ministers [she had in mind a spectacular leak to *The Economist* in September 1982 of a long-term CPRS options paper on public expenditure],[186] had the capacity to embarrass.'[187]

She concluded that the world had changed and that the CPRS could not.

'I have to say that I never missed it.'[188] Instead she built up her Policy Unit (always *her* instrument; never an allegedly shared Cabinet asset like the CPRS) into what was in effect a proper Downing Street version of a French prime ministerial *cabinet*. Hoskyns and Strauss had left, disappointed that she had not seriously broken Civil Service power by tackling its consensual instincts and dominant role in policy advice,[189] confining herself instead to managerial changes in its processes under the guidance of Sir Derek Rayner of Marks and Spencer (by whom she swore)[190] in an Efficiency Unit attached to her office though located in the Cabinet Office.

Hoskyns, who had worked effectively with Alan Walters, Mrs Thatcher's Downing Street economic adviser, was replaced in 1982 by the journalist, novelist and constitutional scholar, Ferdinand Mount. After the 1983 election, Mount was joined by two members of the disbanded CPRS.[191] Gradually the Policy Unit mutated into a group of experts who shadowed clusters of Whitehall work on the economic, industrial and social side (though foreign policy and intelligence was left to Parsons, then Cradock). The enhanced Policy Unit fed Thatcher with alternative analyses,[192] filtering in material from outside bodies such as the Centre of Policy Studies and others,[193] and taking part in the famous 'judge and jury' sessions in which ministers would be called to No. 10 and interrogated on their policies and performance and which by the mid 1980s had become a feared and hated part of their lives.[194]

Under first the merchant banker turned politician, John Redwood (who replaced Mount in January 1984) and Professor Brian Griffith (the City University economist who succeeded Redwood in 1985 when he was adopted as a prospective parliamentary candidate), the Policy Unit took on the shape it has maintained to this day. No other minister has been allowed to acquire anything approaching it. Once Charles Powell was in place as foreign affairs Private Secretary (he replaced John Coles in 1984) and with Bernard Ingham at his most effective in the Press Office, Mrs Thatcher had in her No. 10 team an outfit which, in Powell's phrase, really 'could beat the bushes of Whitehall pretty violently'[195] – a squad the like of which had not been encountered in peacetime and which was not to be surpassed until the installation of Tony Blair's team in May 1997 with, interestingly enough, Charles Powell's younger brother, Jonathan, as its chief of staff.

Policy reflected the enhanced potency of Mrs Thatcher's Downing Street. After a peculiar post-election lull – which Mrs Thatcher acknowledges in her memoirs as 'a somewhat troubled six months'[196] while, strangely blaming it on a critical press (it certainly did not look 'critical' to me from where I sat on the still recently Murdochized *Times* newspaper) and on there being 'still too much socialism'[197] around – what she called the 'revolution still to be made'[198] was set in train. By this she meant both more trade union legislation as part of the rolling programme of reform which, coupled with high unemployment, progressively broke their power; further council house sales; and serious and substantial privatization. These were the political economy transformers – and they were hers. No other Prime Minister (except perhaps Nigel Lawson had he made it to No. 10) would have pushed these policies so far, so firmly or so swiftly. From 1984, with British Telecom, the big privatizations rolled off the Whitehall, parliamentary and City production lines – British Aerospace (1985), the shipbuilding industry (1986), National Bus (1986), British Gas (1986), British Airways (1986), Rolls Royce (1987), British Airports (1987), Leyland Bus and Truck (1987) and BP (1987). Here was the undoing of substantial slices of the Attlee nationalizations.[199]

This was the period which established new expectations of prime ministership – what one might call the stretched premiership of late-twentieth-century Britain. In William Waldegrave's judgement, we had 'not had such all-pervasive personal government since Churchill as a war leader; perhaps, in fact, since Lloyd George as a war leader, since there were large areas of policy on the home front about which even Churchill did not much concern himself. There were no such areas under Mrs Thatcher.'[200]

This, too, was the phase of the Thatcher premierships when, in Douglas Hurd's phrase, it came to be expected that the occupant of No. 10 always had 'to be the head of the rush' in a kind of malign symbiosis with the media. Under Mrs Thatcher this syndrome, this aspect of Jean Seaton's 'the politics of appearances', surpassed even the Harold Wilson of 1964–66. Hurd regards this aspect of modern prime ministership – 'of putting himself, herself . . . at the front of the rush of events; having to be the one who is out front waving his or her sword at the beginning of every charge' as 'somewhat dodgy'.[201]

Hurd recalls that during his time as her Home Secretary, 'I constantly saw on the poster of the *Evening Standard* . . . "Maggie Acts!" on something. Often in those cases she wasn't even aware of the situation. But the whole ethos of No. 10 was that it had to be "Maggie Acts!" and everybody, from Bernard [Ingham] on, everybody had to keep up with that.'[202] Media management during the Thatcher–Ingham years acquired a centrality to policy-making and political weather-setting that, once again, was not to be surpassed until the Tony Blair–Alastair Campbell partnership of the late 1990s.

Not that Mrs Thatcher, unlike Major after her or Wilson before her, was a compulsive consumer of newspapers. Nigel Lawson, himself an ex-journalist, is very funny about the Ingham–Thatcher partnership, which he regarded as 'one of the most self-defeating aspects of the Thatcher regime . . .'[203] Lawson claimed that Ingham, despite his background as a labour correspondent on the *Guardian*, 'was only really at home with the tabloids – above all the *Sun*' and that he had rebuked Lawson's press secretary for lunching a senior *Financial Times* writer instead of the journalists that counted. 'At quite an early stage', Lawson observed,

Margaret decided that she had no time to read the newspapers during the week. Instead, Ingham would get into No. 10 very early each morning, go through the papers himself, and prepare her a crisply written press summary. This had a selection and a slant that was very much his own. It would usually start with the *Sun*, the paper he himself was closest to and which he had taught Margaret represented the true views of the man in the street. It was also the paper whose contents he could most readily influence.

This led to a remarkable circularity. Margaret would sound off about something, Ingham would then translate the line into *Sun*-ese and feed it to that newspaper, which would normally use it. This would then take pride of place in the news summary he provided for Margaret, who marvelled at the unique rapport she evidently enjoyed with the British people.[204]

It has to be remembered, however, that critical press coverage upset her. Woodrow Wyatt's diaries are littered with her Sunday morning words of gratitude for his 'The Voice of Reason' column in the *News of the World* which, it seems from her simpering to her adoring friend on the other end of the telephone, was the only one she could really rely on to understand what she was trying to do. Even at my level – as a leader writer and Whitehall columnist on *The Times* – it was made apparent to me by my editor, and by at least one of Mrs Thatcher's people in Whitehall, that it mattered to her what was written. The Whitehall figure even suggested, to my amazement, that I try to be more understanding of the hurt that could be caused.

This combination of assertiveness and sensitivity was at the heart of her style throughout the days of her ascendancy. 'People don't realize', wrote Wyatt in the summer of 1986, 'that she's very sensitive underneath and it takes a lot for her to screw herself up to face all the hostility she is getting unjustly.'[205] For her part (the episode concerned was a *Sunday Times* story which claimed she had a difficult relationship with the Queen),[206] Mrs Thatcher told Wyatt 'she was determined to grit her teeth and not show any dismay . . .'[207]

This gritted style increasingly permeated her Cabinet Room performances post-Falklands and the 1983 electoral triumph. Now she began to downgrade the full Cabinet (though nowhere near to the level Mr Blair did from day one in 1997).[208] By early 1984, Sir Geoffrey Howe, referring to the decision the previous month to ban trade unions at GCHQ, told the *Daily Mail* quite openly: 'There are very few discussions of Government decisions by full Cabinet.'[209] She did, however, sustain to quite a high degree the use of Cabinet committees as decision-taking fora. The complete retreat from the principles of the 1945 Anderson Report also had to await the Blair years.[210]

The real trouble arose when she resorted to little ad hoc groups that were strangers to the Cabinet Secretary's Committee Book and which she stacked to achieve a particular outcome. There had been signs of this early on. Michael Heseltine carried for years the incendiary memory of the group she had convened to kill off his, to her mind, overly interventionist plans for urban regeneration which followed the disturbances of 1981 and which he evocatively entitled *It Took a Riot*.[211] Another long fuse was lit when she confined the question of the UK's membership of the exchange rate mechanism of the European Monetary System first to a seminar and then an informal ministerial group in the autumn of 1985[212] and declined to bring it to proper Cabinet discussion until Lawson as Chancellor and Howe as Foreign Secretary forced her hand (the 'ambush', she called it) by a threat of joint resignation ahead of the Madrid Council of the European Community in June 1989.[213]

Lawson subsequently laid great stress on the November 1985 gathering not being a proper Cabinet committee and, therefore, 'it was not a meeting that had any constitutional significance'.[214] He also stressed the fact that though Mrs Thatcher was in what she later acknowledged to be 'a very small minority' inside her Cabinet on this issue,[215] her resignation threat ('If you join the EMS, you will have to do so without me')[216] made it simply unthinkable that the issue could be forced in a way that would propel her from No. 10. As in April 1982, she meant, I am sure, what she said – and her colleagues believed her.

Lawson was careful to stress that proper Cabinet or Cabinet committee discussion did not preclude potentially premiership-wrecking problems. He has always pointed out that one of the other great policy destabilizers of her last days in No. 10, the poll tax, *did* enjoy a lengthy and proper Cabinet committee treatment in E(LF) [Economy (Local Finance)], passing 'through vigorously all the text books said it should and more', though it still turned out to be 'the most disastrous single decision which the Thatcher Government took'.[217]

By late 1985 and the November ERM meeting, the elements of the Thatcher style which were eventually to prove its undoing were plainly there, and I tried to capture them as I drafted what became my *Cabinet* book: an overmighty Prime Minister at the centre of an assertive and intrusive No. 10 pushing prime ministerial influence more deeply into the departments while siphoning the collective spirit ever more effectively from the Cabinet and Cabinet committee structure and seeking increasingly to by-pass its confines. That other great destabilizer – the European question – was about to fuse with the command premiership issue to produce the first of the three great resignations from her Cabinets, all of which were stimulated by varieties of that fissile combination. These two elements together caused her more difficulty than any form of parliamentary opposition or the traditional kind of scrutiny of the new select-committee-driven variety between May 1979 and November 1990.

With 'the wisdom of hindsight . . . sadly denied to practising politicans',[218] she herself had no doubt that the years 1983–87 were the watershed for European policy. 'Looking back', she wrote in her memoirs,

it is now possible to see my second term as Prime Minister as that in which the European Community subtly but surely shifted its direction away from being a Community of open trade, light regulation and freely co-operating sovereign nation-states towards statism and centralism.[219]

Late in life she came to treat Europe as a matter not just of politics or economics or even of geopolitics but of theology. Listen to her in 1998, for example, in an extraordinary interview crafted for an audience of her fellow elderly in *Saga* magazine. 'In my lifetime', she declared, 'Europe has been the source of our problems, not the source of our solutions. It's America and Britain that saved the world.'[220] This is millenarian talk. Back in the mid-1980s, as she herself admits, '. . . it did not seem like that at the time. For it was during this period that I not only managed to secure a durable financial settlement of Britain's Community budget imbalance and began to get Europe to take financial discipline more seriously, but also launched the drive for a real Common Market free of hidden protectionism.'[221] The deal was a liberalized internal single market in return for qualified majority voting in important European decision-taking.[222] She knew what she was doing. As David Williamson, then head of the Cabinet Office's European Secretariat, later recalled: 'I was present in No. 10 Downing Street on one occasion when Mrs Thatcher came down the stairs and said to me, "I have read every world of the Single European Act" '[223] (which passed through Parliament in the spring of 1986). She certainly knew 'from the start that there were two competing visions of Europe' but at that stage she 'felt that our vision of a free enterprise *Europe des patries* was predominant'.[224]

For Mrs Thatcher the Westland crisis of December 1985 to January 1986 was not about Europe or proper collective Cabinet responsibility, as Michael Heseltine, her Defence Secretary, saw it, but about free enterprise and Cabinet discipline. He felt his European alternative to an American rescue bid for the troubled Westland helicopter company (an important defence supplier) had been prevented by her from getting the consideration it deserved both in the Cabinet's Economic Committee, EA, and the full Cabinet itself.[225] She felt he was breaching 'collective responsibility, because one person was not playing as a member of a team'.[226] She had refrained from sacking him before the Cabinet showdown on 9 January 1986 because 'the press would have said: "There you are, old bossy-boots at it again." '[227] She was a great stickler for the rules and had indeed tightened up the drill on the proper early circulation of Cabinet papers and the care ministers had to take over statements to the press in her revised *Questions of Procedure for Ministers* following the 1983 election.[228] But as Amy Baker has pointed out, by the time of the ERM meeting in November 1985 and the Westland crisis which erupted shortly afterwards, Mrs Thatcher's 'methods clearly contradicted the written guidance in *QPM*' to the effect that:

Cabinet and Cabinet Committees' business consists in the main of:

(i) Questions which significantly engage the collective responsibility of the Government, because they raise major issues of policy or because they are likely to occasion public comment or criticism.
(ii) Questions on which there is an unresolved argument between Departments.[229]

Woodrow Wyatt comforted Mrs Thatcher at the height of the Westland crisis with the words 'Have you got a copy of the British Constitution? I would like to see one.'[230] Having consulted, of all things, the Crossman Diaries and Crossman's 1970 Godkin Lectures at Harvard,[231] Wyatt took it upon himself to tell Mrs Thatcher that she 'had done nothing unusual for a Prime Minister' in her handling of the Westland question. 'The real criticism of you is you have been far too tolerant and you should have acted sooner.' 'I suppose you are right,' she replied. And Wyatt took up his pen to offer her consolation through journalism. 'A good article in the *Times* on Saturday about the constitutional powers and rights of Cabinet Ministers being zero . . .' he wrote in his diary for 18 January 1986.[232] 'Most Prime Ministers have a kind of permanent toady and I suppose Woodrow Wyatt was Mrs Thatcher's,' said one of her Downing Street advisers after the Wyatt journals had appeared.[233] Toady maybe, but a revealing one, certainly.

One must beware, once more, of the Tommy Cooper syndrome. It would be wrong to think that by early 1986 all the vestiges of collegiality had disappeared from No. 10. There remained, for example, that formidable lifebelt for Cabinet collectivism in the considerable form of Lord Whitelaw, who had urged Lawson not to resign amid the wreckage of the ERM meeting in November 1985.[234] And just think what could have happened if the 'core executive' had become a personal adventure playground for Mrs Thatcher in terms of her being able to drive through her preferred polices by sheer force of personality at full Cabinet, by packing Cabinet committees with the pliable and by using her No. 10 Policy Unit as a counter-Whitehall backed by her patronage and her will. Would there have been a Hillsborough Agreement on Irish matters in 1985? Would healthcare have continued to be provided by a national, taxpayer-funded service free at the point of delivery? Would the BBC licence fee ('taxation without representation', she liked to call this),[235] let alone the BBC itself, have survived?

She was, in this sense, a sensitive politician. She knew, most of the time, what would run at Cabinet, party and parliamentary level and what would falter or crash. And if the collective spirit had flown the Cabinet Room most Thursday mornings on most weeks, surely it is as much the fault of the other figures around the table – the Downing Street 22, as one might call them – as of her. Nigel Lawson has a very revealing (and convincing) passage in his memoirs about the all too human reasons for this apparent timidity. His account in part explains, too, I think, why neither he nor Geoffrey Howe went to Heseltine's rescue when the Westland helicopter crashed through the Downing Street ceiling on to the Cabinet Table at the turn of 1985 and 1986. It also helps us to understand why Howe did not lift much of a finger for Lawson himself in 1989 over the Walters affair (the degree to which Thatcher was permitting the Walters view of European monetary matters to shape her views in preference to those of her Chancellor) – not that she would have listened. She did not consult Howe about Lawson's successor and he was taken by surprise by the appointment of John Major.[236]

In a section evocatively titled 'Consent of the Victims', Lawson asked:

Why did the colleagues allow her to govern in the way she did? While spinelessness or careerism may be adequate explanation in the case of some, it will not do for all. And belief in her infallibility was even more narrowly shared. Of course all Prime Ministers are in a position of great power, so long as they can retain the office; and she was a particularly formidable Prime Minister who, over the years . . . had acquired considerable experience.

But beyond this, her method of Cabinet Government was accepted because in many ways it was highly convenient to her colleagues. Most Cabinet Ministers, particularly after a longish period in government, tend to be preoccupied with fighting their own battles and pursuing the issues that matter within their own bailiwick, and lose interest in the wider picture. Most of the time it is comforting for them to feel that all they need to do is strike a deal with the Prime Minister, and not have to bother overmuch about persuading their other colleagues. (And if they are fighting the Prime Minister on an issue that means a great deal to them all the more reason to concentrate on that.) It was noticeable that, towards the end, those colleagues who most bemoaned the lack of collective discussion of issues outside their own departmental field were busy making private bilateral deals with Margaret over issues within their own departmental responsibility.[237]

This 'creeping bilateralism', as Lawson called it on another occasion,[238] is corrosive of the collective spirit and a powerful contributor by the victims to the overmighty premiership which so bruised their psyches. By the time Lawson went in October 1989, having warned the Queen some eighteen months before (during the Chancellor's traditional pre-Budget briefing of the Monarch), as 'the one person to whom I could unburden myself in complete confidence' that 'I thought the 1988 Budget would be my last, because the Prime Minister was making the conduct of policy impossible',[239] Mrs Thatcher was beginning to reap the consequences of her overmightiness, her increasing reliance on her No. 10 entourage and the apparent belief that her longevity in office meant that she was mistress of all her ministers' briefs, having been round all the policy courses so thoroughly for so long.

Howe had already paid the price for their joint démarche to her before Madrid that once the economic conditions for entry were met, Britain would join the Exchange Rate Mechanism (which it did in October 1990, just one month before her demise). Mrs Thatcher demoted him from the Foreign Office in July 1989 to the Leadership of the House of Commons with a meaningless consolation prize – the title of Deputy Prime Minister. Willie Whitelaw had resigned through ill health in January 1988, leaving her dangerously exposed in her self-belief and Downing Street isolation. The DPM's title 'never conferred the status which he hoped', she recorded acidly of Howe. 'In practical terms it just meant that Geoffrey sat on my immediate left at Cabinet meetings – a position he may well have come to regret.'[240]

There were many admirers inside her Cabinet and her party who wished she had taken her tenth anniversary as Prime Minister in May 1989 as the moment to leave with dignity and a degree of glory untarnished before her increasing unease at events in Europe and her own Cabinet's European policy verged on the unbearable. But in the summer of 1989 she had her sights on 'half way into the next Parliament' – beyond a fourth election victory – 'to see through the restoration of our economic strength, the fulfilment of our radical social reforms and [the] remodelling of Europe' when, too, there would be 'several candidates with proven character and experience from whom the choice of my successor could be made'.[241]

It was around this time that a former senior civil servant who knew her well and admired her greatly talked to me about Mrs Thatcher in a way which had a considerable and enduring impact. 'Remember', he said, 'how close the IRA came to killing her at Brighton in 1984. I have a sense that she feels she has been living on borrowed time *and* that she has so much left to do ever since. As you know,' he continued, 'she needs very little sleep and sits up there in that study of hers on the first floor of No. 10 until the small hours. It's as if she looks out the window and sees the camp fires of her enemies who are surrounding her, just waiting for her to go. And she knows that so many of the old ways and policies she despises will begin to reappear the moment she does.'[242]

She may have been placed on the first floor by my interlocutor – but this was a portrait of a bunker with a mentality to match. Yet, in a way, it contained within it a foresight of reality. For it took a quite unpredictable concatenation of events and personalities to prise her out and, once in train, those events did so with a breathtaking swiftness only matched in the twentieth century by Asquith's fall in December 1916 and Chamberlain's demise in May 1940.

One of her Cabinet ministers had foreseen it – and that was as long ago as 1980. Over lunch one day he said two things that stayed with me throughout Mrs Thatcher's Downing Street years:

'I don't know why you're always banging on about open government. She doesn't believe in open government for the Cabinet let alone for people like you.'

and

'When she goes she will go very fast. Our wives will have soaped the stairs for her.'[243]

Contrary to the wisecracks of the time, it was not Geoffrey Howe's wife – the formidable Elspeth – who wrote his killer of a resignation speech for him. If she had, the anonymous minister of 1980 would deserve a guaranteed place in history as the Mystic Meg of the Thatcher years. But the Howe resignation, the third entwining the questions of Europe and the proper conduct of Cabinet government,[244] was the trigger for the Heseltine leadership challenge, thereby completing a deadly symmetry with the first. And it was the first ever significant resignation speech to be relayed live from the then newly televised chamber of the House of Commons. It saw the second-round resigner, Lawson, sitting beside Howe, nodding grave approval, as the knife went in, with the camera, inevitably, capturing its victim's face a few feet below. It was the most dramatic example of televisual politics in the United Kingdom in my lifetime.

Narrowly failing to achieve a first-round win over Heseltine, she was sufficiently wounded for her Cabinet to thwart her original intention of fighting on. The price of an overcommanding premiership was an accumulation of resentments and resistances which caused her to lose it. For it was the Cabinet – that ancient instrument for dispersing power and preventing the growth of a single chief executive – which undid her (albeit in dribs and drabs as they came in to give her their views that Wednesday night in November 1990 rather than *en masse* in a single Cabinet Room showdown).[245]

Poignantly enough, it was her campaign manager of November 1990, John Wakeham, who placed the epitaph on the tombstone of her command premiership in a lecture on 'Cabinet Government' two years after her departure. The process of Cabinet government 'has to work by building consensus. Colleagues must be able to support collective decisions. It is not possible to conduct business by putting them in a position where the only options they have are to submit or resign,' he said.[246] As Geoffrey Howe put it even more pointedly:

Margaret Thatcher was beyond argument a great prime minister. Her tragedy is that she may be remembered less for the brilliance of her many achievements than for the tenacity, the recklessness with which she later defended her own, increasingly uncompromising views. The insistence on the undivided sovereignty of her own opinion – dressed up as the nation's sovereignty – was her undoing.[247]

In short, to adopt Lawson's phrase, she finally lost the 'consent' of a majority of her 'victims' in her Cabinet. This was a linkage she was unable to make, let alone anticipate, at the time – or not until it was too late.

What was that lesson? Simply this – set aside the traditional practices of Cabinet government and you have instead pressure-cooker government. On some occasions steam can burst through with the valve taking the strain, as happened over the Heseltine and Lawson resignations. But the Howe resignation was the final build-up of pressure which was to cause her premiership to blow once and for all. As she explained in her memoirs, 'a prime minister who knows that his or her Cabinet has withheld its support is fatally weakened'.[248]

Yet, deep into retirement, she still could not make the connection between the first reflections in her memoirs of her Cabinet life and her last. She talked of the 'culture shock' of her officials at the Department of Education and Science in 1970 which stemmed 'from the opposition between my own executive style of decision-making and the more con- sultative style to which they were accustomed'.[249] But the Cabinet is a 'collective executive'[250] above all else. Cabinet government simply cannot work properly without it. The key to successful premiership is a Prime Minister's ability to combine the jobs of both chairman and chief execu- tive, tilting towards one rather then the other according to circumstances.

But would she have achieved so much if she had conducted her version of Cabinet government differently? Or might she have lasted deep into the 1990s, perhaps even outstripping Walpole's record of twenty-one years in the post? Who knows. Despite that Ozymandias syndrome, achieve she did. What will endure to be dissected inside the scholarly cloisters as Margaret Thatcher passes through on her way to 'the last retreat of fame'? I had a stab at answering this on the very day John Major arrived on the steps of No. 10. By a bizarre coincidence I had long been booked to deliver a lecture at Georgetown University in Washington on 'Mrs Thatcher as History'.[251]

'History is a ruthless sifter,' I declared grandly. 'Time reduces even the greatest reputations to a few sentences on a single side of A4. What will remain on the Thatcher ledger?'[252] Five entries I suggested:

1: The breaking of trade union power. The balance will never again tilt so far in favour of the Labour Movement as it had by the late 1970s.

2: The public–private boundary will not return to the *status quo post* Herbert Morrison or *ante* Margaret Thatcher. The argument from now on will be more about regulation than ownership.

3: With two thirds of state assets sold off in her first 10 years, the spread of shareholding from 3 million individuals in 1979 to 9 million in 1989 will have a significant permanent place in British economic history.[253]

4: That other significant form of public asset disposal – council house sales – saw a million homes transferred to private ownership on very favourable terms,[254] a substantial shift towards that long standing Conservative ideal of a 'property owning democracy'.

5: By playing midwife to the 'Next Steps' executive agencies inside the Civil Service, the most important of all her Civil Service reforms, whereby large portions of Civil Service work were placed in what were, in effect, free-standing public businesses from 1988, Mrs Thatcher put the kind of mark in Britain's 'permanent government'[255] that Gladstone left when he turned Whitehall from a patronage society into the country's first meritocracy by establishing the principle of recruitment by competitive examination in the late nineteenth century.[256]

I would stand by that – and it is a formidable list by any criterion. And it might have been more widely appreciated if only she had modelled herself on Alec Home or Jim Callaghan in their retirements and curbed her desire to descend firing thunderbolts upon political battlefields old and new. But if she had not been like that post-1990, she could not have been what she was between 1979 and 1990. Perhaps the earth-movers among politicians have to be of the unchangeable and unchanging kind and beyond the possibility of a true mellowing.

Her impact while in office was less only than that of Lloyd George and

Churchill. Perhaps she was even their equal in this. Friends in the Health Service told me that by the mid 1980s, psychiatrists engaged in the early diagnosis of their more disturbed patients ceased asking them for their own names and birth dates and so on, and asked instead for the name of the Prime Minister. If patients failed to remember that, they knew they were properly sunk.

There is only one thing I can safely say that I got right when she was at the height of her powers. As the sounds of the Westland affair died down early in 1986, I penned my last words on her 'Conviction Cabinet' in my study of *Cabinet* which was published later that year. 'At worst', I wrote, 'she has put Cabinet government temporarily on ice. In a political and administrative system as riddled with tradition as the British, the old model could, and probably will, be restored in the few minutes it takes a new prime minister to travel from Buckingham Palace to Downing Street.'[257] And so it proved.

17

The Solo-Coalitionist:
John Major, 1990–97

'He was . . . as tough as old boots. The strength of his character is . . . more remarkable given how easily hurt he can be and how socially vulnerable he is.'   *Chris Patten, 1999*[1]

'I like my Prime Ministers to be a bit inhumane. The PM has insufficient inhumanity. It's a government-of-chums. He wants to be liked. He cares deeply about what the papers say about him. He can't walk past a paper without picking it up. Mrs T never read newspapers. She only read what Bernard Ingham told her was in them.'
Very senior civil servant shortly after Major
succeeded to the premiership[2]

Margaret had often introduced subjects in Cabinet by setting out her favoured solution: shameless but effective. I, by contrast, preferred to let my views be known in private, see potential disasters ahead of the meeting, encourage discussion, and sum up after it . . . Margaret had been at her happiest confronting political dragons; I chose consensus in policy making, if not always in policy.   *John Major, 1999*[3]

'It was much more what Cabinet government is supposed to be like. It was much more rational . . . the problem was that when people began to be disloyal later on, they were not very frightened of him.'
William Waldegrave, 1999[4]

'I was detached from everything other than how we dealt with the problem immediately in front of us. But the price to be paid for that was that once the crisis was over, I often became very depressed . . . and I think those depressions were a serious problem.'
John Major, reflecting on 'Black Wednesday',
September 1992, in 1999[5]

'He demonstrated the greatest self-control at Cabinet even when he was enraged to distraction by the latest series of leaks or briefings against him. The most irritated gesture he would allow himself was to throw his pencil down. I have often wondered what the effect would have been if he had really given vent to his feelings – ruinous leaks in the press, I suspect, of the "Major lost it" variety, and I have no doubt that is why he never did.' *Gillian Shephard, 1999*[6]

'John Major tended . . . to agitate about the smaller things, particularly about the wretched media. But on the bigger things he was pretty calm.' *Douglas Hurd, 1997*[7]

'There was this odd mixture of misery and the limpet – the miserable limpet if you like – which was a great inhibition to his premiership.' *Robert Cranborne, 1999*[8]

It was always been easy to underestimate John Major when he was in office and it has been the same since he left it – the 'risen without trace' premier; the most underwhelming figure to occupy No. 10 since Attlee; 'the only surviving charisma-bypass patient in British medical history' – that sort of thing. Partly, of course, it has to do with the voice and vocabulary (as verbal foreplay goes his tendency to open his remarks with 'As far as the XYZ is concerned, I've made my position absolutely clear' is about as exciting as a recitation from the Huntingdon telephone directory) and the overall greyness attributed to him. These should not matter. The compounds which make up a premier's chemistry ought to be assessed and estimated differently. But superficial impressions and appearances count in politics. And the manipulation of words, the ability to make the language sing, is a necessary part of the great politician's armoury. The best, perhaps the only defence available to those at the monochromatic end of the spectrum is to turn these disadvantages into a political art form as Clem Attlee managed to do.

But Major is no Attlee in the sense that he might somehow grow in stature as the years pass to the extent of almost becoming an exemplar, as Attlee did. Major's reputation will accrue in a manner that it was just possible, although difficult, to appreciate during his battered twilight days in Downing Street in 1996–97, at the very fag-end of what Gillian Shephard called his 'end game government'.[9] Some of those who worked closely with him already sensed this, and the more thoughtful of them began to place him tentatively within the matrix of factors which contribute to an assessment of a Prime Minister's statecraft and his or her place in the pantheon of the practitioners of premiership. For example, even at this late stage he continued to score highly on the Cabinet collegiality index. As one experienced Cabinet minister put it when comparing Major to his two Tory predecessors:

'He has always been and remains a good chairman of Cabinet and Cabinet committees. Though sometimes he drives me round the bend when he won't wrap-up a discussion until he has made sure that everyone has had a chance to speak. Ted was much closer to Margaret than to John. They both were *führerprinzip* leaders, whereas he's a proper democratic leader.'[10]

This deeply ingrained and admirable trait was apparent from the very first moments of John Major's very first Cabinet meeting in the PM's chair. Chris Patten emerged on that occasion to brief his favourite lobby correspondent and compared the Cabinet's mood to that of the prisoners released from the dungeons in Beethoven's opera *Fidelio* who emerged into the sunshine blinking and singing of freedom.[11]

For weeks afterwards, ministers and senior civil servants, as part of their post-Thatcher catharsis, would talk freely like so many veterans of the Somme back safely in Blighty with no prospect of ever returning to the front. As one Whitehall deputy secretary put it to me, wearing a huge grin, at a Christmas party less than a month after Mrs Thatcher's demise: 'Discussion is allowed; argument even.'[12] Early in the New Year of 1991 a very senior Cabinet minister said:

'The Prime Minister sums up but he doesn't prejudge the question. So that changes the discussion. It has a rather odd effect on ministers. In the old days, a Secretary of State would discuss a proposal with the Prime Minister [Mrs Thatcher]. If after one meeting or perhaps two he had persuaded her it was right, she would say: "We'd better put it to Cabinet." Then he wouldn't have to worry about it *because he'd gone through the difficult part* [my emphasis]. Now he has to persuade the Prime Minister *and* he has to persuade a lot of other people in the Cabinet as well. It's all to the good, but it's going to produce a lot more effort.'[13]

This was early January 1991 and this minister, like his chief, was heavily involved in preparations for the then imminent military action against Iraq in the Gulf. In fact, he wondered if Mr Major needed to be slightly less accommodating as a certain distance between the *primus* and the *pares* was necessary, not least at times of difficulty or emergency.[14]

The imminence of war raised immediately the question of Major's readiness for the premiership. He admits that as the prospect suddenly became very real the night before Mrs Thatcher announced her intention to resign, he 'thought it was too soon for me[15] . . . I would have preferred more time in a senior Cabinet post before seeking the leadership . . .'[16] This is entirely compatible with the portrait of a man of calculating ambition penned in her diary by his political adviser, Judith Chaplin, as he took the job. 'He is certainly tough enough' to be Prime Minister, she wrote.

It is possible to understand if you recognise that every decision is taken on how it affects and promotes him. This doesn't mean he is not a very nice man, as everyone says he is, but he is ruthless. Is he experienced enough? Difficult to say.[17]

On balance, he was not. His Treasury experience as both Chief Secretary and Chancellor was deep enough and he had a feel for social policy as demonstrated during his time as a junior social security minister. But he had been somewhat overwhelmed during his brief, ninety-day spell as Foreign Secretary between July and October 1989. He admitted his 'heart sank' when he was asked to do the job by Mrs Thatcher.[18] As Douglas Hurd put it tactfully: 'He was dismayed by the number and complexity of the things that came at him out of his Foreign Office boxes.'[19] By contrast Major liked the Treasury ('it was like a home coming'[20] when he returned as Chancellor) and the Treasury liked him.[21]

Yet, like any successful aspirant to the premiership, he had to eschew the doctrine of unripe time: '. . . with the Foreign Secretary [Hurd] already in the contest, and a challenger from outside the Cabinet [Heseltine], I could not credibly stand aside without giving the impression that I had no stomach for the top job'.[22] In many ways it is to his credit that, as Gillian Shephard put it, he 'felt so constrained by the fact that his inherited Parliamentary majority, a healthy one of ninety-five overall, was not his own . . .'[23] Major himself said that until he won his own twenty-one-seat majority in April 1992, he 'had the sneaking feeling that I was living in sin with the electorate'.[24]

His memoirs have a curiously endearing passage, too, about wanting to provide an 'antidote' to 'the pomp and circumstance' of the Thatcher years and to exercise power 'in a way that did not make you different from other people . . . I think I felt quite differently about power than any prime minister this century.'[25] Some manifestations of his ordinariness – the McDonald's–Little Chef–Harry Ramsden aspect of him in particular – laid him open to the kind of 'little man', 'nerdy' disdain which was discernible both within, in parts of the government, and without, in the press. The genuinely grand in the Cabinet quite liked this side of him. 'Funnily enough, the nice snobs did not give a monkey's where Major came from. It was the people from the slightly meaner streets who sneered,' said one.[26]

Yet it was the old aristocratical side of the ancient core state – diplomacy and defence, where Major was at his rawest and most inexperienced – which provided an immediate, time-consuming and unavoidable test in the move towards war in the Gulf. Intriguingly, he soon won the respect of the permanent practitioners in these fields and in the intelligence world. He had scarcely got to know the intelligence community or they him during his truncated tenure at the Foreign Office. They mainly remembered him as the Chief Secretary who had run the Treasury's absurd argument that the intelligence services should be subjected to a kind of internal market – the agencies would mount only those operations which their Whitehall customers wanted and were willing to pay for.[27] As Prime Minister, Major quickly learned that if you aspire to a global intelligence reach, 'it's like the sea; it's one'[28] and cannot be reduced to a kind of customer–contractor business.

Major impressed the overseas, defence and intelligence sides of White-hall partly, ironically, because Mrs Thatcher's Gulf style made it easier for him to do so. For by the summer of 1990 the victrix of the Falklands had forgotten some of the lessons learned when Whitehall had had so swiftly and unexpectedly to revert to a war footing in the spring of 1982. Major's memoirs are misleading about this, partly because in the build-up to the Gulf War Mrs Thatcher had once again, as she told what she called her 'War Cabinet', followed Harold Macmillan's advice and kept the Chancellor of the Exchequer off her inner group.[29]

In *The Autobiography* Major writes that 'Margaret had already established the Overseas Defence (Gulf) – OD(G) – Cabinet committee to oversee the crisis.'[30] She had not. She had created a ministerial group consisting of herself in the Chair, Hurd (Foreign Secretary), Tom King (Defence Secretary), Sir Patrick Mayhew (Attorney General), John Wakeham (Energy Secretary) and Sir David Craig (Chief of the Defence Staff). Also in attendance were Sir Percy Cradock (Chairman of the Joint Intelligence Committee and her foreign affairs adviser in No. 10), and Charles

Powell (her foreign affairs Private Secretary), who took the minutes. Not only were senior Cabinet Office people such as the Cabinet Secretary, Sir Robin Butler, and the head of its Overseas and Defence Secretariat, Len Appleyard, kept out of the group (as was Sir Patrick Wright, the top official in the Foreign Office), but copies of Powell's minutes did not reach all of those who needed to know what was going on.[31]

As one insider put it, contemplating Mrs Thatcher's general governing style in her last years: 'She became even odder over the Gulf and it was getting pretty chaotic. Bureaucratically it was getting into a tangle. It was constitutionally pretty dangerous.'[32] Butler and Wright were reduced to calling their own meeting at which highly placed officials pooled what they knew.[33] Patrick Wright, ever jovial even under duress, sent Percy Cradock (who had a taste for such things) a limerick based on 'There was a young Man from Khartoum' about such 'what-is-she-up-to?' meetings.

The outward Limerick ran:

> Robin Butler, preparing for doom
> Called the mandarins into his room.
> As he turned out the light
> he said 'Let's get this right.
> Who does what and with what and to whom?'

Cradock's reply was as follows:

> 'Dear Robin', the mandarin said,
> 'There are letters that may not be read.
> There are minutes as well
> Which no man may tell.
> And which all must be kept in the head.
>
> And from this the conclusion is stark
> That we all must remain in the dark
> While our Masters decide
> Without briefing or guide
> Who does what and to whom in Iraq.'[34]

Butler, a less whimsical figure than Wright or Cradock, did not join in. But once Major was installed, the new Prime Minister swiftly regularized the position, thanks, no doubt, to his Cabinet Secretary's briefing and guidance.

A proper Cabinet committee, known in fact as OPD(G) – Overseas Policy and Defence (Gulf)[35] – was set up by Major. It consisted of Mrs Thatcher's group plus Butler, Appleyard and Gus O'Donnell, Major's press secretary.[36] His Principal Private Secretary, Andrew Turnbull, was there the day the official photograph was taken.[37] The Treasury, in the person of David Mellor, the Chief Secretary, came occasionally. Mellor was present on 7 February 1991 when IRA mortar bombs landed in the garden of No. 10[38] (the first time a 'War Cabinet' had met within the sound of actual fire since World War II). Whitehall judged Major's conduct of Gulf War cabinetry a success. It was rational, measured and made good use of its own and America's intelligence flow.[39] Once the war was over, President Bush sent Major a message for onward transmission to the British intelligence community expressing his appreciation and saying later he found the JIC's daily assessments of more use than his own intelligence feed.[40]

Major's conduct of the British element in UN, and later NATO, operations in Bosnia is much more difficult to assess given the nature and duration of the problem and the splits inside the Cabinet on the issue in August 1992, when the decision to deploy British troops was taken. Major and Hurd were full believers in committing UK forces; Clarke, Portillo, Rifkind and Cranborne were uneasy. Heseltine was 'supportive but troubled'.[41]

Major came to console himself more and more with Harold Macmillan's 'events, dear boy, events' (in the formulation Major would use) as the distractor of premiers from the course which they have set for themselves.[42] Looking back, one can discern a pronounced hinge in the late summer/early autumn of 1992 when 'events' conspired powerfully against a John Major with his own parliamentary majority (albeit a slimmish twenty-one) in ironic contrast to his living in sin with the electorate phase when he felt unable to 'stamp his own authority' on what he felt was not really his majority or his Parliament.[43] It is important to remember, therefore, that those closest to him in his very first days as premier felt such powerful and distracting sidewinds from the start.

The memoir written by Sarah Hogg, head of his Policy Unit, and his Political Secretary, Jonathan Hill, *Too Close to Call*, brings out very well his *intended* priorities for the 'society at ease with itself' which he promised on the steps of No. 10 on 28 November 1990 (they reproduce the note he had scribbled in the prime ministerial car between the Palace and Downing Street)[44] to his priorities as Prime Minister as outlined during his first,

'Fidelio' meeting of his full Cabinet on 29 November 1990. He had, they recalled,

beneath his folder, a list scribbled on one of the scruffy pads provided at each place around the table. On it, he had noted four issues on which he was determined to make an impact: inflation and unemployment (the predictable preoccupations of a former Chancellor); but also perhaps more revealingly, Northern Ireland and public services. To the Cabinet, however, he pointed up three different and more urgent questions: Europe, the poll tax – and the Gulf. None could wait. Between them they would absorb most of the energies of John Major's pre-election Government.[45]

How he set about tackling these priorities in that November 1990–April 1992 phase is genuinely revealing about Major's preferred style of premiership – much more so than the end-game years from 'Black Wednesday' in September 1992 up to the Tories' worst electoral performance since 1832, in May 1997.

Looking back, Major himself saw the irony of 'The eighteen months leading up to the general election in April 1992 [being] the time of greatest promise for me in government. There was much I hoped to do after the election, but which, as things turned out, I would not achieve. I shall regret this all my days.'[46] Those eighteen months were indicative of the real Major not just in policy terms (the Citizen's Charter; the apparent achievement of a compromise within the European Community and his own party on the great political wrecker of the 1990s – the question of Europe) but in process terms, too.

These were the high days of Major's consensual, consultative style in the Cabinet Room and in his bilaterals with ministers. Neither would wholly survive the traumas of late 1992. After that he would bring less and less to full Cabinet for fear of leaks and would skip through the regular business item of European affairs (which with parliamentary business, foreign affairs and home affairs were the staple opening items of his Thursday morning Cabinets) for fear of the party's civil war on Europe erupting and poisoning the entire proceedings.[47]

Kenneth Clarke was especially eloquent on this shift during that strange memoir-autumn of 1999 when the survivors of the Major Cabinets compared scars and, in the case of Norman Lamont, sought to wrench open old wounds.[48] 'The Cabinet', the former Home Secretary and Chancellor of the Exchequer recalled, became an unhealthy place after the early years of the Major Government when it had been a delight to be in it because it had been secure and cohesive and rallied behind John to deliver what he wanted to deliver. Eventually the Cabinet became as leaky as a sieve and no minister wished to raise any serious business there. The Cabinet Secretary [Butler] became concerned that ministers would not bring their business to Cabinet.[49]

Robin Butler had referred obliquely to this in a public lecture earlier in 1999 when he said: 'I used to think that the phrase "too sensitive to discuss in Cabinet" would make some of my predecessors turn in their graves, but I heard it used on more than one occasion during my time as Cabinet Secretary.'[50]

Major enhanced his push for collegiality by developing, as we have seen, the occasional practice of 'Political Cabinets' (to which PMs had long resorted when the date of elections would be discussed) as a regular feature of his style of government. His Political Secretary would take the minutes and other party officials would enter the Cabinet Room as Butler and his team left. These were valued by his ministerial colleagues. As one explained:

'I think he started them as a regular thing. They should become a regular part of government. It meets that old Dick Crossman problem – that in Cabinet you never talk as politicians but as satraps of great departments of state.'[51]

There was an occasional problem, however, with Major's 'Political Cabinets'. In the heat of discussion, ministers could sometimes fail to distinguish between the grandeur of the real Cabinet and the how-to-screw-the-Opposition nature of the Political Cabinets (even though formal titles were forsaken for first names once the Cabinet Secretariat had gone). Decisions were sometimes taken in the 'Political' which belonged to the 'real' Cabinet and ministers were left wondering later why Whitehall had taken no action on them.[52]

The atmosphere in No. 10 can be a powerful tone-setter for the rest of Whitehall and the Cabinet as a whole. Signals – personal and presen-tational as well as policy tones – are always carefully watched by those in the penumbra of departments, both ministers and officials. Norman Lamont, later so critical of Major across all these areas and generally for giving 'the impression of being in office but not in power' (as he put it his resignation speech after being sacked as Chancellor in May 1993)[53] was warm in his initial assessment of the Major style. 'Like everyone else', he wrote later, 'I appreciated the more consensual style of conducting business compared with Margaret's.'[54]

The Downing Street team, too, reflected the shift of personality at the top, especially on the media side where Gus O'Donnell swiftly established a less combative and partisan relationship with the political correspondents than Bernard Ingham, who left with Mrs Thatcher.[55] Charles Powell, the other great warrior-courtier in her entourage, stayed on until the Gulf War was over when he was replaced by Stephen Wall, whose relationship with his parent department, the Foreign and Commonwealth Office, reverted to one of full mutual co-operation.[56]

Andrew Turnbull, whom Major inherited from Mrs Thatcher as Principal Private Secretary, was from the classic mould of the highly politically attuned yet neutral official – a great dispatcher of business who does not go native on his ministers. He was replaced in 1992 by Alex Allan, who saw Major through all his trials and became one of his closest and most trusted confidants before seeing him out and Blair in in 1997. Allan, the son of Bobby Allan, the Parliamentary Private Secretary who had seen Anthony Eden through the ghastliness of Suez, receives the warmest of plaudits in Major's memoirs as 'by no means an indentikit civil servant. A fan of the Grateful Dead rock band, he had once windsurfed down the Thames . . . He worked the most unbelievable hours, and was universally popular as well as effective.'[57]

Major wanted – and very largely enjoyed – a warm relationship with his official Downing Street family. He brought out the protective side in people. They worried about his solitary late-evening existence in No. 10 (his wife, Norma, preferring to be with the family at home in Huntingdon on most weekday nights) and the unhealthy junk food he would have brought in, if he ate at all. They were much relieved when in 1992 'It was arranged that someone from Chequers, traditionally staffed by the Royal Navy and WRNS [Women's Royal Naval Service], would come up to Number 10 on rotation.'[58]

As time passed, Major made other changes to Mrs Thatcher's Downing Street configuration. Her post-Falklands arrangement of having a foreign affairs adviser in No. 10 did not last long once the austere (though limerick-loving) Percy Cradock retired in 1992. His successor, the former ambassador to Moscow, Sir Rodric Braithwaite, chaired the Joint Intelligence Committee as Cradock had done (which was odd for a man so sceptical about the uses of intelligence – opinions which he did not conceal from insiders when *en post* or from outsiders once retired).[59] Braithwaite was not replaced in No. 10 when he left in 1993, having persuaded Major that the diplomat traditionally in charge of the Cabinet's Overseas and Defence Secretariat should chair the JIC and that the foreign affairs Private Secretary in No. 10 could cope with the remainder of the Cradock portfolio[60] (not a view universally shared, not least by the formidable Sir Percy now in retirement).[61]

The most personal piece of a premier's No. 10 back-up, the Policy Unit, was headed by the economics journalist Sarah Hogg. Of the political purple herself (a Boyd-Carpenter who had married Lord Hailsham's son Douglas), Mrs Hogg, like Mrs Thatcher, has a mixture of intelligence, personality, word-power and sense of domain which leaves nobody neutral about her.[62] She was a powerful shaper of Major's detailed thinking not just on the economy, but on Europe and social policy too. There has always been a touch of the social market philosopher about Mrs Hogg, which led some of her detractors to parody her views too crudely as closer to the Continental Christian Democratic tradition than to native British Toryism. Certainly she reinforced Major's own instincts on the need for a caring Conservatism.

There could be friction around Sarah Hogg, and Judith Chaplin, the adviser Major brought with him from the Treasury to run his Political Office, felt it acutely. As Anthony Seldon has noted: 'Chaplin had little stomach for a turf-war; she continued to enjoy a trusting relationship with Major, but with a dense atmosphere at Number Ten, she increasingly withdrew to nurse her constituency [Newbury], which was under Liberal Democrat attack.'[63]

Major generally got on well with the senior Civil Service, especially with the cricket-loving Cabinet Secretary, Robin Butler. The Cabinet Table immediately to Major's right became the cricketers' pitch. To Butler's left was the PM; to Butler's right was Peter Brooke, Secretary of State for National Heritage. Test scores would be brought in regularly during Cabinet meetings, with Butler informing first Major then Brooke of what was all too often England's plight.[64]

But word would occasionally emerge of Major's sensitivity towards the manner and over-confident intellects of the grander members of the Civil Service *grand corps* (how they seemed to rise above failures and get away with it in a manner not permitted to the juniors).[65] In the very first section of his memoir, as part of a highly revealing Foreword, Major alludes to this ambivalent attitude towards the profession whose minister, as First Lord of the Treasury, he found himself for seven and a half years:

I did believe in public service and public obligation, and if I'd had a double first I would have been attracted to a career in the Civil Service. But I had no wish to be a second-rank civil servant, and my background and lack of paper qualifications would more or less have dictated that fate, irrespective of any talent I might have shown. Being insufficiently educated to advise ministers, I decided early on to be a minister myself, and to harness others' learning to my native good sense.[66]

And, interestingly enough, it was on Whitehall matters where his greatest and most lasting impact on British governing processes (as opposed to policies) was perhaps left.

The most famous of Major's public service initiatives or reforms was the Citizen's Charter. It was also the most derided. Ever super-sensitive to criticism and disdain, he almost anticipated this when he decided not to call it the 'People's Charter' as 'such populism was thought to be risible, and likely to be taken as a gimmick'.[67] There were those who did laugh at it. The 'motorway cones hotline' alone ensured it would enter the nation's stock of standard humour. As Hogg and Hill recall, this 'rabbit out of' the Department of Transport's hat 'came to haunt tabloid coverage of the Charter . . . [as] . . . almost unbelievably, Transport launched this service simply by feeding the hotline into the departmental switchboard. Frustrated drivers would expect to get no more informative answer than from any other busy telephone operator.'[68]

Others simply found the Citizen's Charter boring – the kind of 'big idea' a mediocre mind would produce with a title to match. One of the more interesting entries in Gyles Brandreth's rather underestimated diaries of a (generally) loyal backbencher and later whip, is a passage from the difficult, immediately post-Black Wednesday days in the autumn of 1992:

Lunch with the Prime Minister. Because Number 10 is being rewired and double-glazed (not to keep the heat in: to keep the bombs out), the PM has decamped and is now ensconced half-way up Whitehall in Admiralty House. There are ten of us for lunch, eight assorted backbenchers, the Chief Whip and the PM. He's down: feels it, shows it. There's no bounce. He may be letting us see this deliberately, to remind us that he's human, to take us into his confidence, to make us realize he's just like us. But we don't want to be led by someone who's just like us. We want a leader who is *extraordinary* – and decent, determined, disciplined, convincing as he is, JM isn't that. The party is profoundly divided, our economic policy is discredited, we're on the brink of being dragged into a Balkan War, and the PM talked about the Citizen's Charter!

Of course, he believes in it, passionately, believes it will change the quality of life of ordinary people. Inevitably, though we all must have thought it, not one of us dared say, 'No one gives a toss about the Citizen's Charter, Prime Minister!'[69]

A note of passionate defiance has always characterized Major on this issue since he first floated his philosophy in a little-noticed speech to the Audit Commission when Chief Secretary. This speech was the basis from which Hogg, Hill and Nick True, the Policy Unit adviser on public service reform, started when they began in the Policy Unit to work it up into Major's 'big idea' in early 1991 – the eventual name came to them over curry in an Indian restaurant in Horseferry Road, and Major launched it during a speech in Southport on 24 March 1991.[70]

His 'Raising the Standard' is, in policy terms, the most passionate single chapter in Major's memoirs. He scorns the mockers – the cynics 'on both the right and left' who declared 'from the comfort of privilege and the cushion of an expense account, that these were trivial issues, or somehow evidence that I had a chip on my shoulder'.[71] He made the chapter the centrepiece of his softer, non-Thatcherite ideology and his re-emphasis of what he called the 'compassion . . . [which] . . . the best of the Conservative Party has long lived by',[72] underpinned by his own memory of the degree to which 'my family had depended on public services'.[73] Major singles out his Charter, too, as an example of where the pushing forward of a new policy 'needed the unique influence of Number 10 to put right'.[74] With the assistance of a middle-ranking minister at the Treasury, Francis Maude, his Policy Unit and a Cabinet Office team led by Andrew Whetnall, he drove it through the sceptical resistance of Whitehall generally.[75]

When the White Paper was finally launched on 22 July 1991, it was in many ways a classic 'new public management' Whitehall production – shiny, glossed with rhetoric, brimming with performance indicators, but it was not justiciable in the courts and there was to be no shot of extra public spending to propel it.[76] It was not, therefore, a citizen's charter – the beneficiaries remaining subjects and the contents more a set of hopes. 'Aspirations for Consumers' would have been a more accurate title for the White Paper. The charter rested on four themes – a steady improvement in the quality of public services; an extension of choice within them; published standards for performance against which consumers could assess the performance of producers; and the squeezing of greater value out of each taxpayer pound.

There was a feeling in Whitehall and the Cabinet that Michael

Heseltine's competitiveness agenda came to overshadow Major's chartery in the last phase of his government[77] (which, to some extent, was a dual agenda administration once Heseltine was made Deputy Prime Minister in June 1995 and given sway over a huge range of Cabinet committees). [78] Yet the Citizen's Charter did matter to the premiership both at the time and subsequently. It was a useful development in terms of transparency and accountability across the whole Civil Service and public sector, including the NHS and transport. The concept of customer care was infiltrated into state services.

As William Waldegrave put it, Major 'sensed that the electorate now wanted to find a way of humanizing the irreversible Thatcherite revolution'[79] – a matter of personal conviction for Major but also a useful selling pitch at the polls for a party which had rebranded itself when the premiership passed from Mrs Thatcher to her Chancellor in November 1990. As Lord Waldegrave recognizes, Major 'never found the language' in which to capture fully his Thatcherism-humanized philosophy.[80] Chartery ploughed on doggedly until the end. By the time the government fell, the programme had spawned forty-two national charters and around ten thousand local ones.[81]

In one area of public service reform, Major out-Thatchered Thatcher by shifting Civil Service activity almost certainly permanently from the public and into the private sector. His *Competing for Quality* White Paper, also published in 1991, established a programme whereby 'departments and Executive Agencies will in future set targets for testing new areas of activity in the market to see if alternative sources give better service and value for money'.[82] Over the first two operational years (1992–94) of the 'market testing' programme, as it came to be called, some £1.8bn of state activity was subjected to the process, and 55 per cent of it eventually shifted to the private sector.[83]

Combine chartery and market testing with Major's remodelled public spending Cabinet committee, EDX, created in 1992, which under the Chancellor's chairmanship tried with some success to bring a more collegial approach to expenditure allocation with closer attention to implementation and outputs, and one can discern a distinctive Major approach to state resources as prosaically important as it was personally unheroic. Sarah Hogg, in retrospect, rated EDX (with some justification) as the 'most important' of Major's Cabinet-level innovations. It was, she said, the 'filter for all the Government's big public spending decisions' and balanced out Treasury power with a collection of non- or small-spending ministers whose binding-in as members of EDX helped ensure its decisions held at full Cabinet level.[84]

In the same 1995 *Sunday Times* Lecture in which she emphasized the importance of EDX, Sarah Hogg reckoned that her former boss had 'been given far too little credit for what he has done to shed light on the working parts of Government. This, I think, is partly because of the typically British, unglamorous nature of the important constitutional documents which he has – for the first time – made public.'[85]

I am an interested party here because I had lobbied Major for the declassification of both *Questions of Procedure for Ministers* and the *Ministerial Committees of the Cabinet*.[86] Robin Butler had been instrumental in pressing from the inside the case for their disclosure.[87] Major pledged to do so in the Conservative manifesto in the 1992 election.[88] And, after a bit of resistance in the Cabinet,[89] they were duly published in May 1992.[90]

His liberal impulses did not stop there. A case can, in fact, be made for Major as the most open-government minded of all eleven postwar British premiers (including Tony Blair, despite the somewhat watered down Freedom of Information Bill his government produced in November 1999: a great deal of the watering down had to do with No. 10's scepticism about FOI).[91] There were early signs of a more comprehensive approach to government shortly after the 1992 election pledges were promulgated. William Waldegrave, the newly appointed Chancellor of the Duchy and Minister for the Office of Public Service, acceded to another request of mine in an interview for the Radio 4 *Analysis* programme 'The Last Right?' on 17 June 1992[92] that thirty-year-old JIC assessments should be removed from the blanket ban on the release of intelligence-related documents. In doing so, he said two things: first, that he wanted historians to let him know of other files retained for longer than thirty years which they wished to examine, to write to him and he would see if he could release them. The historical profession immediately picked up on what we called the 'Waldegrave initiative' which by the end of the century had led to some 96,000 formerly closed files, some of the greatest sensitivity on nuclear matters, reaching the Public Record Office.[93] Secondly, to the visible shock of his Private Secretary who was taking a note of the meeting, Waldegrave said he thought the time was ripe for the preparation of a White Paper on open government generally.[94]

The White Paper, which appeared the following year,[95] would not have got through a cautious Cabinet but for the support of Douglas Hurd, the

Foreign Secretary (who said 'Why can't we for once do something we *want* to rather than because we *have* to?')[96] and the Lord Chancellor, James Mackay (who wondered if doubting colleagues were, in effect, saying that they wished to deceive Parliament)[97] and, above all, the Prime Minister himself.[98] The following year, a *Code of Practice On Access to Government Information* was promulgated which implemented the White Paper's policy of restricting the inner ring of secrecy to defence, intelligence, foreign relations, relations with the Palace, internal ministerial discussions and law enforcement, and also undertook to publish information on the factual and analytical background to major policy decisions. For the first time a figure from outside the inner loop of government – the Parliamentary Ombudsman – would be involved in adjudicating disputed cases (though his advice to ministers in favour of publication would not have to be acted upon).[99] Interestingly enough, Major placed the code within the remit of the Citizen's Charter.[100]

If you add to these changes *The Civil Service Code* which Major promulgated in 1996 in response to the concerns of the House of Commons Select Committee on Public Service about dangers of the politicization or improper use of Whitehall,[101] and the increasing focus on the now public *QPM* (both the Nolan Inquiry on Standards in Public Life and the Scott Inquiry on Arms to Iraq made important play on this document as the bedrock of ministerial probity and accountability),[102] the Major premierships take on a considerable constitutional importance. For under him the British Constitution began to move from the back of an envelope to the back of a code. In virtually all of these areas, Mrs Thatcher had proved resistant to calls for reform.[103]

The political storms which were to follow distracted attention almost totally from Major the incremental constitutional reformer – and continue to do so. These reforms are, however, important both intrinsically and as an indicator of the style of premiership he would have liked to sustain had not 'events' unseated his intentions. There are other aspects of his conduct of the office of Prime Minister from his 'living in sin with the electorate' phase which are worth commenting upon, almost in isolation from what followed after the autumn of 1992. Some of these are human, others procedural.

It was apparent from the outset of his premiership that Major was a Prime Minister who needed close political friends around him whom he could trust. Graham Bright, his Parliamentary Private Secretary, was very important to him. 'Major relied on and trusted' Bright.[104] But the central relationship of 1990–92, to the surprise initially of some, was the Major–Patten axis. Chris Patten remembers Major seeming a young (he was forty-seven) and inexperienced man, saying on his first morning in No. 10 'I don't know if I can do this job. I wasn't really expecting it yet.'[105] Major made Patten his Party Chairman and he swiftly became, in Anthony Seldon's words, 'the political ally who stood out'.[106]

Patten, the polished, fluent, classical Oxbridge product, and Major, the pedestrian striver with jagged and chippy social edges, made a vivid contrast. If told that of the 1979 intake of Conservative MPs, one of these two would have been Prime Minister for the bulk of the 1990s, all the smart money would have been on Patten. Yet their regard for each other was high and genuine, with a strange complementarity at the heart of it. Patten said of Major and the class of 1979: 'He had a drive and a commitment and an energy . . . which put him in a completely different league from the rest of us.'[107] Major described Patten as 'an old friend with whom I could work easily'.[108]

The Prime Minister became increasingly dependent on Patten's advice and friendship. Patten, who had been central to Hurd's leadership campaign, not Major's, in November 1990, said later: 'There was every conceivable reason why he should have mistrusted me, but I don't think I have ever been trusted as much by anybody in my entire life.'[109] Once Patten had lost his Bath seat at the 1992 election and had taken the Governorship of Hong Kong, Major pined for his old friend and the phone calls were plentiful from No. 10 to the Governor's Mansion in the autumn of 1992 and beyond as the Prime Minister sought solace and counsel as his troubles intensified.[110]

It was plain to his colleagues that Major never found a surrogate for Patten. It is difficult to speculate about the difference Patten might have made had he retained Bath. Major's personal tranquillity index would have been higher. And Patten at the Treasury could well have cut a more Chancellorial figure than Norman Lamont, whom Major planned to move after the 1992 election to make way for his friend, as we shall see. Gillian Shephard recalled that 'as difficulties thickened, one was left with the strong impression that Major had come to feel he could trust very few and those he could were not Cabinet colleagues. This feeling of isolation inevitably made his task harder . . . To be Prime Minister at a difficult time is intensely lonely.'[111]

Within his first month as Prime Minister Major confronted one of the most solitary aspects of the job – the need to take international decisions in advance of discussion with Cabinet colleagues in emergency or fast-moving circumstances. On a car journey on snowy roads between Washington and Camp David, President George Bush and Major, with only Powell and Brent Scowcroft (Bush's national security adviser) beside them, agreed the military strategy to be used against Saddam Hussein and the date (16 January) which would mark the start of the air assault on Iraq.[112]

Those special prime ministerial functions on matters of war-making left a mark on Bush. 'The thing that impressed me', he said later, 'was Major could well have said "Look, I've just taken over. Let me call my Defence Minister . . . Let me . . . get the Cabinet together when I get back. I'm sure we'll be with you, but I'd feel more confident if I had my team on board." No. He said, "Absolutely. You can count on us 100 per cent." Never flinched.'[113] And after leaving the premiership, Major hinted very strongly that as 16 January 1991 approached, he had had to contemplate the most awesome prime ministerial decision of all – authorizing the use of British nuclear weapons – if Saddam Hussein had used his own chemical and biological weapons of mass destruction. With the Americans, Major used diplomatic channels to warn the Iraqi leader of 'precisely the scale of the response there would be' in such an eventuality.[114]

Sarah Hogg quickly noticed another aspect of what might be called unavoidable prime ministerialism – the increasing need during protracted and often nocturnal European Community negotiations for Major to reach deals on behalf of the government on which he would subsequently report back to Cabinet and Parliament.[115] War-making and deal-making were reserved, at the initial phase of decision-making, to the prime ministerial annex of Major's otherwise studiously collegial attitude to the job.

Collegiality was to be the healing ointment of his approach to the rawest scars left by his predecessor – the poll tax and Europe – both made more livid by the manner of Mrs Thatcher's departure *and* her famous promise (which caused him real alarm from the start) to be 'a very good backseat driver', a remark, according to Major, which 'would cast a very long shadow indeed . . . the first part of the wedge that was to come between us'.[116] In a very shrewd move, Major had brought Michael Heseltine back into the Cabinet as Environment Secretary to find a more acceptable and graduated version of a property tax to replace the hated, Thatcherian imposition. Major took his time and personally oversaw the process of creating what became the council tax from the chair of the special Cabinet Committee he established for the purpose.[117]

Major was, in many ways, a reflection of the country he surprisingly came to lead. I remember a successful businessman out of very much the same mould reflecting that for all his greyness (another Major sore spot, it dominates no less than a sixth of the Foreword to his memoirs)[118] perhaps he was truly representative of the kind of country Britain had become. This conversation at Templeton College, Oxford depressed me somewhat at the time. But I have come to think that on some key aspects – Europe in particular – there was something in it.

Once Europe had helped destroy his premiership leaving him on the back benches surrounded by a shrivelled and emotionally exhausted parliamentary party, he would liken himself to Balfour who had been similarly wrecked (and his party with him at the 1906 election) by the free trade versus protection issue about which Balfour, like him, had been furiously criticized by the partisans for not having firm views and for placing party unity above the more ideologically pure notions of political economy.[119]

Major's first practical European impulse was to reposition the UK within the Community, firmly and publicly. His wish, announced before a German audience in March 1991, for Britain to be 'at the very heart of Europe' was hung round his neck by both the inflamed wings of the European debate for the rest of his premiership, wreaking a 'havoc' he did not foresee.[120] And, indeed, it was misleading both of the possibility of his country in effect turning a dual Franco-German axis into a trilateral one embracing the UK *and* of his own Euro-opinions which, his detractors would say, were always carefully crafted in private to suit the tastes of his particular listeners.[121]

His memoirs, without placing the word 'chameleon' in neon above the relevant passages, bring this out rather well:

I was a pragmatist about the European Community. I believed it was in our economic interests to be a member. I welcomed sensible co-operation. I had no hang-ups about Germany. I accepted that being one of a Community of fifteen meant that sometimes we had to reach a consensus that was not entirely to our taste. I was keen to rebuild shattered fences, to prevent Britain from being seen forever as the odd man out to be excluded from the private consultation that so often foreshadowed new policy in Europe.[122]

In other words, Major wanted to be anybody but Margaret.

Yet I shared many of her concerns. I recoiled at the prospect of a 'federal' Europe. I was deeply suspicious of political union. I did not wish to ditch sterling. I believed the conditions the Social Chapter [elements of what would become the Maastricht Treaty] sought to impose would add to employer's costs and push up unemployment. I did not wish to see a more powerful Commission. I did believe it was right to enlarge the Community and bring in the nation states of Central Europe . . .'[123]

These A and B twin pulls would later stretch and nearly break Major's position – A leading him to enrage an increasingly influential and vocal section of his party and the press by not ruling out eventual British participation in a single European currency and B to distress an unbelieving sector of the political nation when launching a 'beef war' on the back of a policy of non-cooperation with the UK's partners.

But, initially, the Major way appeared to yield dividends. He took immense pains to increase the chances of the UK satisfying both A and B Major during and after the piecing together of the Maastricht Treaty. As Gillian Shephard recalled:

'Major recognized from the start the importance of the Maastricht negotiations of December 1991 for his own political survival and for the forthcoming election. Elaborate arrangements were put in place to get instant feedback and briefing for the parliamentary party as the negotiations drew to a close. Francis Maude, under Tristan Garel-Jones's [Foreign and Commonwealth Office Minister for Europe] direction, was put in charge, and a very long night of brief preparation, ringing round colleagues, foreseeing and blocking of loopholes, and dealing with the British and foreign press took place.'[124]

A clever blending here of the prime ministerial and the collegial. Yet, as Mrs Shephard recognizes: 'The opt-outs of EMU [Economic Monetary Union] and the Social Chapter were enthusiastically received domestically but, as things turned out later, the enthusiasm was only a deferment of the difficult inheritance that Europe was for Major.'[125]

To a remarkable extent, Major's 'living in sin with the electorate' phase, on which he would look back with regret that he had not been bolder during it,[126] prepared the ground for a spectacular and unexpected election victory in his own right. He had temporarily silenced the siren sounds aroused by the European question. What Kenneth Clarke called his 'Thatcherism with a human face'[127] approach to policy enabled him both to overcome the potentially ruinous electoral consequences of the recession-hit economy over which he had presided and to present a twin image of decency and unspectacular competence with which to confront

Neil Kinnock and his still only partially reformed Labour Party. The McDonald's-munching, soap-box orating Major on the stump showed the voters the acceptable face of greyness.

In the 1992 election Major and his party achieved an overall majority of twenty-one, taking 42.8 per cent of the votes cast to Labour's 35.2 per cent. Normally the UK's first-past-the-post voting system would have converted that differential into a winner's bonus, giving the Conservatives a majority of around seventy (as Major well knew).[128] But Britain was learning to vote tactically – especially in the Greater London area. However, at the time, twenty-one seemed like a personal and political triumph. It was five more seats than Churchill had enjoyed as his majority forty-one years earlier. But it was not to be enough.

Governing in his own right gave Major the opportunity to innovate in the mechanics. He was a believer in making greater use of his standing Cabinet committees and their offshoots as handlers of policy detail. This enabled him to keep his ad hoc committees down to forty or so in six years, a feat managed by no other premier since 1939; even Mrs Thatcher accumulated around 120 of them over a comparable period.[129] As we have seen, he created a new standing committee on public spending, EDX, after the 1992 victory, to improve the quality of policy analysis and ministerial decision-taking.

Like his predecessors, he operated a mixed approach to his Cabinet committees. Irish policy (an area of increasing initiative after an MI6 back-channel to the Provisional IRA conveyed to Major in February 1993 a message from their leadership that 'The conflict is over but we need your advice on how to bring it to a close')[130] was handled by the Ministerial Committee on Northern Ireland which consisted of eight regular attenders, over a third of the full Cabinet,[131] though, as always with Irish affairs, the really sensitive intelligence would be kept to a very small inner circle.[132]

Nuclear weapons matters (such as how many warheads the new Trident missile submarines would carry[133]) were confined to his OPDN, the Ministerial Committee on Nuclear Defence Policy, which was quite close to the minimum number of ministers required (Prime Minister; Deputy Prime Minister after June 1995; Chancellor of the Exchequer; Foreign Secretary and Defence Secretary);[134] while market-sensitive issues, such as the raising or lowering of interest rates or exchange rate policy, saw Major acting very much in the traditional mould, confining discussions to himself, the Chancellor of the Exchequer and, sometimes, the Chief Secretary to the Treasury.[135]

John Wakeham, in his Brunel Lecture stressing the return to collegiality and consensus in the Cabinet Room, made public another strand of Major-style prime ministerialism. Recalling his own practice as chairman of several home front Cabinet committees, Lord Wakeham said: 'On rare occasions, where opinion is evenly divided, the issue will be referred to the Prime Minister for decision. I try hard not to do that. He has enough to do, and it puts him in an invidious position. But sometimes there is simply no option.'[136]

Some of the examples of Mr Major's solo policy-making are quite substantial, politically sensitive or symbolic. The decision not to dump nuclear waste at sea was his,[137] as was the decision to keep May Day a Bank Holiday.[138] And though the decision to replace the Royal Yacht at public expense was taken in an ad hoc Cabinet committee,[139] it was very much the Prime Minister's own, based on a Cabinet Office briefing by the Cabinet Secretary, Sir Robin Butler.[140] But for the intervention of the Prime Minister and the Cabinet Secretary, the Chancellor of the Exchequer and the Treasury would have maintained what seemed almost a veto on the disbursement of £60m of public money on the *Britannia* replacement. As one insider put it: 'Ken Clarke could have blocked that for ever if the PM hadn't taken the view that we had to do it. He decided that we would have to wind this [discussion] up because it had to be done. He does that very seldom.'[141] Interestingly enough, because Major was so restrained in his use of prime ministerial override, his Cabinet colleagues did not seem to mind episodes such as the nuclear waste, May Day or the Royal Yacht decisions.[142]

Fresh from the electorate in the spring of 1992, Major sought to tread where many previous premiers had ventured before him into the strategic gap at the centre of government. He established a new body intended to raise the strategic consciousness of the Cabinet. The ministerial Cabinet committee at the top of the first ever complete list to be officially published was EDP, the Ministerial Committee on Economic and Domestic Policy.[143] It remained in pole position throughout.[144] It stayed steady, too, at a dozen members with the PM in the chair and its terms of reference constant: 'To consider strategic issues relating to the Government's economic and domestic policies.'[145]

Major created EDP because his experience of the premiership so far had convinced him of the need for a body under his chairmanship that would catch and examine strategic issues before they reached full Cabinet.[146] It was a gap that needed plugging but it was never properly filled.

Why? Partly, I suspect, because the bias towards the short term (which a small and falling majority and the European question underscored, on an almost daily basis) militated against full and effective use of the new committee.

But there were other reasons. Mr Major did not feel the need for a special underpinning for EDP in the form of its own, extra information flow. Its longstanding twin on the foreign and defence side, OPD, the Ministerial Committee on Defence and Overseas Policy, enjoyed the services of the Joint Intelligence Committee and its own, customized Assessments Staff in the Cabinet Office. EDP had precisely nothing by comparison.

There easily could have been. A model was to hand in the Central Policy Review Staff culled by Mrs Thatcher in 1983. As one minister put it (he was speaking towards the end of the Major years)

'EPD hasn't really been a strategic committee. It's just been an ordinary committee. It needed a staff like the CPRS. He's not getting that kind of service from his [Downing Street] Policy Unit. And you do need someone close to the PM who is not a rival to generate ideas. Michael [Heseltine] doesn't. He's not a broad policy man.'[147]

A strategic policy committee was just what Major needed as summer turned into autumn in 1992 but, paradoxically, the two issues EDP should have caught, but did not, were the currency question (kept to the customary Prime Minister–Chancellor duet)[148] and pit closures (which were deemed too sensitive to bring before ministers collectively, even in a smaller Cabinet committee, to the eternal regret of the Cabinet Secretary, Butler, who later used this before his Whitehall colleagues as an example of how fear of leaks preventing proper collegial discussion can lead to bad decisions[149]).

There was a poignant personal symmetry to the issue which permanently altered the internal ecology of the Major government, the general political weather and the Prime Minister's position, personal contentment and individual authority – Britain's entry into the exchange rate mechanism (ERM) of the European Monetary System in the autumn of 1990 and her humiliating departure from it two years later.

Throughout his political life, Major has had a loathing of inflation. This was his main reason for wishing the pound to be part of the ERM as it would be linked to a system driven by the stiffest-backed and most

inflation-resistant currency in Europe, the deutschmark – 'a form of mone-
tarism by proxy, linked to the mark', in Sir Samuel Brittan's intriguing
analogy[150] – just as the pound under the old Bretton Woods system of
fixed exchange rates had been chained to the dollar which, until the late
1960s, was the hardest of the world's currencies.

From the spring of 1990, Major and Hurd plotted to 'coax' rather than
'browbeat' Mrs Thatcher into agreeing a date for entry.[151] Just such a
Chancellor and Foreign Secretary combination had enraged Mrs Thatcher
and stiffened her resistance to entry during the Lawson–Howe partnership. But she could not risk losing two Chancellors within a year. On 4
September 1990 she conceded – she would agree to ERM entry provided
there was a simultaneous cut in interest rates.[152] On 5 October 1990 Major
announced Britain's entry at DM2.95 to the pound – too high in the views
of many but the only realistic level which the ERM partners would
have permitted, according to Major.[153] Thereafter, Britain's membership
became the central pillar of Major's economic strategy through the last
few days of his Chancellorship and throughout his premiership until the
afternoon of Wednesday 16 September 1992.

During that period, a number of misfortunes began to afflict the key
to Major's counter-inflationary desires. Thanks to the costs of German
reunification and the Kohl government's decision in the summer of 1990
to unite the East and West German marks 'at the ludicrous rate of one for
one',[154] and Kohl's refusal to cut spending or raise taxes, Germany ceased
to be the proxy guarantor of UK counter-inflation. At home the recession
deepened. Major's Chancellor, Norman Lamont, nurtured growing
doubts about British membership of the ERM. He was not close to Major,
who did not care for his 'great mood swings',[155] and Lamont found it
difficult to share his doubts and the Treasury's options with its First
Lord.[156] At a seminar in No. 10 on 28 July 1992, Major gave Lamont
the clear impression that withdrawal from the ERM was 'unthinkable'
(Lamont's word).[157]

Major continued to assert in private and semi-public (to a lunch at *The
Sunday Times*, which promptly ran the story) that linked to his 'loathing of
inflation' was his belief that provided the UK 'followed the right policies,
there was no intrinsic reason why sterling should not become stronger than
the deutschmark'.[158] 'Events' quickly disposed of this fiscal mirage. This is
not the place to trace the sequence which led to Black Wednesday – pressure
on the pound in the markets; general market instability in the days leading
up to the French referendum on the Maastricht Treaty; the deeply unhelpful

remarks of Helmut Schlesinger, President of the Bundesbank, that there needed to be a wider realignment of currencies within the ERM; Chancellor Kohl's reluctance to help by acceding to Major's personal economic diplomacy and urging lower German interest rates.[159]

It has to be said that with his policy and sterling's position under increasing strain, Major 'went much further than the ritual "no devaluation" protestations required by a fixed exchange rate regime'.[160] This was especially true of his speech to the Scottish CBI on 10 September 1992, which left Sarah Hogg 'extremely nervous'.[161]

Sarah, Major recalled, was

well aware of the fragility of sterling, and with my personal interests as her main concern, urged caution. I hesitated, but concluded that I had no choice but to robustly defend the exchange rate. I took the view that if sterling were devalued it would be catastrophic anyway, and a little more egg on my face would barely be noticed. So, to Sarah's dismay, I went for broke.[162]

Major likes to regard himself as a gambler. He has been known to press this aspect of his self-image upon his friends with great animation.[163] Though I doubt whether a more cautious approach in Glasgow on 10 September would have made any real difference to subsequent events, this kind of 'going for broke' in such precarious circumstances was self-indulgent folly.

On the shiny late-summer morning of Wednesday 16 September 1992, with the *Financial Times* carrying Schlesinger's remarks, the market began to move powerfully and irresistibly against sterling. By the end of the day, the Bank of England had made the largest intervention in the currency markets in its history, having sold over £15bn of its reserves (over the Tuesday and Wednesday combined), and interest rates had shot up from 10 to 15 per cent before sterling's enforced exit from the ERM announced in the street outside the Treasury by Lamont at 7.30 p.m. brought them back to 12 per cent.[164] (The final cost to the British taxpayer was between £3 and £4bn[165] – the latest estimates veer towards the upper figure, equivalent to £20 for every man, woman and child in the UK.[166]) And Major finally retired to his flat after the most humiliating single day any British Prime Minister had experienced at the hands of the markets, contemplating what was unarguably 'a political disaster' of the first magnitude and uncertain 'that I could, or even that I should, remain as Prime Minister', his policy and his personal standing in ruins.[167]

As a case-study of Cabinet government under crisis, Black Wednesday, though of far shorter duration, has acquired the status of Callaghan's IMF autumn. Initially, lurid stories were attached to it of a desperate Major on the verge of collapse, of him even hiding in the loo at one stage. All sources point to this being 'absolute junk', as one of the officials who was present at Admiralty House throughout the day put it.[168] The evidence supports Major's own description of himself as 'detached from everything other than how we dealt with the problem immediately in front of us'[169] and Sarah Hogg's observation about his 'calm'[170] (the 'price to be paid' came later in the form of the doubts, depression and if-onlys that afflicted him).[171]

Major handled Black Wednesday with what I would call improvised collegiality. His Principal Private Secretary, Alex Allan, warned the Prime Minister in his flat at 7 a.m. that the position was 'very bad', the Bank of England had intervened but sterling was being widely sold.[172] At 9 a.m. Major and Lamont agreed on further intervention, anticipating a hugely difficult day.[173]

Soon after the event, I was told that the Treasury's usually formidable tradition of preparing 'sterling war books' against the direst of contingencies had slipped a little in September 1992. There were elaborate contingency plans, but they were focused on what might happen to the pound if the French voted 'no' on Sunday 20 September in the Maastricht referendum and not on the desperate possibilities should a currency storm attack sterling in the run-up to the French poll.[174]

Major's account of the events of 16 September rather corroborate this. 'With one eye on the value of sterling', he wrote,

I chaired a meeting at Admiralty House on how to respond to the result of the French referendum, due that weekend. In attendance were Douglas Hurd [Foreign Secretary], Kenneth Clarke [Home Secretary], Michael Heseltine [President of the Board of Trade], Richard Ryder [Chief Whip], John Kerr [UK ambassador to the European Communities], Alex Allan, Stephen Wall and Gus O'Donnell. The outcome still looked too close to call. We knew a 'no' vote would up-end policy all over Europe, but my immediate concern was the markets. Bad news filtered in, and a note of gallows humour spread into our exchanges.[175]

The 'cabinet's big beasts ... Hurd, Heseltine and Clarke, readily endorsed' the decision to raise interest rates from 10 to 12 per cent agreed by Major and Lamont over the telephone at 10.30 and implemented by the Bank half an hour later.[176]

Lamont, intently watching the Reuters screen in his Treasury Private Office, saw that sterling had not moved above its floor of DM2.7780 despite the interest rate hike and concluded 'the game was up . . . I wanted to suspend our membership of the ERM as quickly as possible and stop the haemorrhaging of our reserves.'[177] He asked his Private Secretary, Jeremy Heywood, to arrange an immediate meeting with Major at Admiralty House.[178]

At this point the crucial relationship between the Prime Minister and the Chancellor went into irreversible decline. Major insists that no message reached him that the Chancellor was waiting on him urgently.[179] Lamont insists that the Prime Minister kept him and senior officials from the Bank and the Treasury waiting for between a quarter and a half an hour while he finished a meeting with backbench MPs.[180] Mystery still lingers around this meeting. Philip Stephens says it was 'long-planned'.[181] But one of the backbench attendees, Stephen Milligan, confided to his friend, Gyles Brandreth, that 'he was summoned to see the PM simply because he was a backbencher who happened to be around and the boss wanted "to settle the troops", show his steady hand at the tiller, prove to us other ranks that – though under fire – as ever he was cool, calm and collected'. (If this was so it ranks as probably the most futile attempt at party management in recent times.) 'Stephen was excited, delighted to be in at the kill,' Brandreth added.[182]

But it was not quite 'the kill'. Major, to Lamont's increasing fury, asked him to wait for Hurd, Clarke and Heseltine, who had been asked to return to Admiralty House.[183] Just after one o'clock, the trio of big beasts, plus Ryder, the Chief Whip, reappeared as, in Major's words, 'decisions were needed speedily and there was no time to call a full Cabinet . . . We knew that history was in the making, and the atmosphere was sombre and calm.'[184] Lamont by his own account was 'astounded. I could not see why it was necessary to involve all these Ministers'[185] – plainly failing to appreciate at the time both that the magnitude of these exchange rate policy matters was sufficient to lift them way beyond the customary Prime Minister–Chancellor duopoly of decision-making and Major's understandable desire for political insurance by spreading the guilt.

This divergence of view, so powerful a contributor to the enmity which poisoned their relationship and which caused them never to exchange another word after Lamont was sacked the following May,[186] produced one of the most vivid pieces of inter-cutting in the television series which accompanied the publication of Major's memoirs in the autumn of 1999:

LAMONT: I was completely flabbergasted! They had nothing to do with the Treasury and, frankly, they did not understand the issues at all. I rather came to the conclusion that he just couldn't face it – he couldn't bring himself to make the decision . . . and the results were disastrous.

MAJOR: That is absolutely outrageous! The senior members of Cabinet . . . had a right to be involved. This involved a very important matter of future European policy as well. Moreover, I thought Norman was wrong about suspension, and so did all the rest of our colleagues.[187]

Despite Lamont's wishes, it was agreed that a further rise in interest rates to 15 per cent would be announced, to come into effect the following morning. Major would engage in economic diplomacy-by-telephone with the Germans and the French in a last effort to persuade them to intervene helpfully.[188] But the blood lust of the market was beyond appeasement. As Clarke put it later: 'The Prime Minister, the Chancellor, the leading members of the Government were utterly out of control of events. The market was going to devalue the pound, which it sure as hell did.'[189] At 4.40 Lamont returned to Admiralty House with the news that the announcement of 15 per cent had made no difference. At 5 p.m. the 'big beasts' assembled for the third time and the inevitable was faced. Britain would withdraw from the ERM.[190]

For Douglas Hurd, something of a connoisseur of the practice of Cabinet government, the day's events were not without a wider, rueful and somewhat historical significance. As he told me many years later:

'When you have a war, whether it's Kosovo or the Gulf or Bosnia, you have a proper system of War Cabinet – advice from the Chiefs of Staff, Cabinet consulted at certain times. And it's an orderly system – statements to the House of Commons. The thing works impressively and I would say in a democratic way. Decisions may be right, may be wrong. But at least they're properly produced and paraded.

'Handling of the pound sterling in my experience was entirely different. As a minister for sixteen years and a Cabinet minister for ten years, I never felt – as Northern Ireland Secretary, Home Secretary, even as Foreign Secretary – that I was privy to the handling of the British currency except on one day when I was summoned, as it were, to sign the death certificate but not really to influence the policy.'[191]

Kenneth Clarke put it more brutally. He knew why the 'big beasts' were thrice summoned to Admiralty House (which, given Macmillan's running of the British end of the Cuban missile crisis from there, has come to have an awful association with drama) on Black Wednesday: 'One of the reasons why Douglas, Michael Heseltine and myself stayed in the meeting during the day once the subject matter had changed was because it meant that here were the senior members of the government – all of us – with our hands dipped in the blood . . .'[192]

Major was punctilious about his relations with the Queen. (They got on well. In the summer and autumn of 1992 they had been transacting extra and unusual business – the mechanics of the Sovereign's desire to pay tax and matters relating to the eventual divorce of the Prince and Princess of Wales.)[193] Before Lamont made suspension of British member-ship of the ERM public, the head of government rang the head of state from the Cabinet Room. He told her he would recommend the recall of Parliament when the Cabinet met the following morning, though he did not expect the government to lose a confidence vote that 'would precipitate a general election . . . I was, as always, frank with the Queen, and set out the extent of the reversal for the government. "With the markets as they were," I said, "we could not have gone on – it would have looked like King Canute." '[194] Which is exactly what he and his government came to resemble as the experience of Black Wednesday unleashed tidal waves of criticism and attack, not least from within the Conservative Party, the most damaging assaults soon coming to be associated with the lady likened by Douglas Hurd to 'the Queen over the Water', Mrs Thatcher – an image which in Hurd's view 'she did nothing to discourage and certainly made his [Major's] life very difficult'.[195]

Few political watersheds have been as dramatic as Black Wednesday. The political landscape for Major before and after was dramatically different – and so were that intensely scrutinized patch of the political terrain, the opinion polls. The government never recovered, its reputation for economic competence beyond repair.[196] At the Party Conference which followed swiftly upon it, Norman Tebbitt turned on Major and linked all the Prime Minister's failings with the European question, leaving his victim 'astounded . . . he spoke in absolutely demonic mode', yet the conference rose to him.[197] Two days later, Mrs Thatcher published an article in the *European* 'in which she claimed that "Maastricht will hand over more power to unelected bureaucrats and erode the freedoms of ordinary men and women" '. To Major, the sub-text was clear: 'She would not have agreed to Maastricht, whereas I had. She would have protected "the freedoms of ordinary men and women", whereas I had not.'[198] From this passage on, Major's memoirs are written on scar-tissue, not paper.

Looking back from the Conservatives' defeat in the general election of May 1997, it is possible to argue that the pressures which plunged the Tories' share of the vote to such an extraordinary low of 31.4 per cent might not have combined in such a ruinously depressive fashion if John Major had shown himself to be a Prime Minister of different and exceptional mettle in the autumn of 1992. Professor Stuart Ball, the analytical undertaker of Conservative demises at the polls, has demonstrated that on his nine key indicators (policy direction; media and intellectual climate; public perception of economic record; 'time for a change'; credibility of opposition; Tory organizational strength; leader's image; party finances), Major and his party were in a worse position even than Balfour and his Unionists in 1906 and Churchill and his Tories in 1945.[199]

Many of these, in their acute and most vote-sapping form, can be traced to the autumn following Black Wednesday, the pit closures and the starting-gun for serious and searing Euro-divisions. Could a differently constituted Major – a tougher, more self-confident and assertive Major – have turned setbacks into triumph (personal and electoral) as Mrs Thatcher's admirers like to claim that she did between the March 1981 Budget and the white flags going up in Port Stanley in June 1982?

One option was to resign, taking Lamont with him and freeing the government of the taint of a failed duopoly at its head. Major considered this for several days after Black Wednesday. The following Tuesday, his party chairman, Norman Fowler, called on him in Admiralty House to discuss parliamentary tactics and negotiations on Europe. 'As I was leaving John Major walked with me to the lift,' he recalled.

'I wonder if the negotiations should not be done by someone else,' he said suddenly.

'You mean a new leader?' I asked.

'Yes,' he said bleakly.

'That would be absurd,' I replied immediately. 'There is no one else who could do remotely as well.'

'That's what the others say,' John replied gloomily.[200]

Lamont, too, had considered resignation.[201] Major would not have retained him at the Treasury beyond April 1992 had not Patten lost his seat in Bath and become unavailable for the Chancellorship.[202] Yet he asked Lamont to stay in the aftermath of Black Wednesday. 'You are a lightning conductor for me,' the Prime Minister explained.[203]

Lamont was anything but, as it turned out, and it was quite plain to any Whitehall observer from the autumn of 1992 to Lamont's eventual sacking in May 1993 that a never-commanding Chancellor was reduced to a weaker figure in the governing constellation than is good for any administration, let alone one in deep trouble as was Major's.[204] Lamont's parlous position was immediately apparent within Whitehall and graphically illustrated a month after Black Wednesday. The 'big beasts' whose power was waxing as his waned – Clarke and Heseltine – took him on in EDX and flattened him on spending cuts. Lamont could take no more at this 16 October 1992 meeting of the Committee. He picked up his papers, walked out and went home. Sarah Hogg was sent as an emissary by Major to prevent Lamont from resigning.[205]

'Sleaze' entered the political vocabulary that autumn too. Had Major sacked David Mellor from his Heritage portfolio once the details of his personal difficulties became apparent, rather than first being persuaded that this would look like weakness in the face of an aroused media only to succumb to their feeding frenzy eventually, he could, so some of his more thoughtful ministerial colleagues believe,[206] have set a pattern for decisive, disciplinary action that might have prevented another electorally ruinous impression (what Worcester and Mortimer call 'the swamp of sleaze')[207] from taking hold. (In fairness, Mellor's case was a complicated one; it was only when it emerged that he had accepted a free holiday from a friend who was the daughter of a prominent member of the Palestine Liberation Organization that he appeared to be in breach of *Questions of Procedure for Ministers*.)[208]

In a cruel irony, Major's wholly virtuous decision to declassify *QPM* did not help him here. In the long string of ministerial resignations from Mellor in September 1992 to the Neil Hamilton case which dogged Major right up till the moment he lost office, *QPM* featured as part of the public story in a way, of course, it could never have done in its thirty-seven years as a classified Cabinet paper. As Amy Baker has written:

The publication of *QPM* had immediate implications for the accountability of Ministers. One High Court judge has privately described *QPM* as a statement of the terms of ministerial office. In many ways the public at large have treated it as such, by expecting either a valid explanation for the Minister's conduct, or a resignation, when the rules appear to have been breached.[209]

Major had weakened his position as the enforcer of the rulebook by adding what has been called 'a get out of jail free card' for ministers[210] in a key opening Clause placed in *QPM* before it was released in May 1992. This declared that: 'It will be for individual Ministers to judge how best to act in order to uphold the highest standards.'[211] The Nolan Committee on Standards in Public Life, the 'ethical workshop', as Major called it,[212] which he set up in the autumn of 1994 to advise on sleaze-related matters, expressed considerable concern about the escape-clause nature of paragraph 1 of *QPM*.[213]

On 'sleaze', Major could certainly have been more Attlee-like in dispatching ministers to the back benches. On pit closures, too, he could have and should have insisted on a proper political discussion of the programme at full Cabinet level. Here, as Gillian Shephard (Employment Secretary at the time) has recognized, the operating style of one of Major's 'big beasts', Michael Heseltine at the Board of Trade, did require a strategic intervention from the Prime Minister which was not forthcoming. 'Michael Heseltine's qualities', she told an audience at Queen Mary and Westfield College some years later, 'did not include a grasp of detail nor even a recognition that such a grasp could help one's cause. At the time of the mine closures, I well recall meetings when neither he nor his junior ministers were clear about which mines were affected. Yet what he could see was the end of the line for the coal mining industry – a great shift in the industrial economy that had to be faced.'[214]

'Back to Basics', his big idea for the 1993 Party Conference, was another Major idea which needed and was not accorded the refining fires of proper Cabinet discussion. 'It is time to return to those old core values. Time to get back to basics,' he declared, to the evident approval of his audience.[215] 'It was never for me a question of individual morality,' he explained later. 'I would have shied away from that.'[216] But that, inevitably, is how it played in the press – as a hypocritical accompaniment to the symphony of sleaze then in full performance. To their credit, Richard Ryder and his whips made their disquiet known,[217] but 'Back to Basics' made its journey from Policy Unit and speechwriters' wordprocessors to the public domain with not a trace of proper collective discussion in between.[218]

But the European question was the real, the relentless destabilizer of post-Black Wednesday Major. Could a premier of the first rank have coped with this version of it in those circumstances, not least the shrivelling parliamentary majority which 'meant that small groups of colleagues, even individuals, with axes to grind, gained a disproportionate importance in the scheme of things and took up unimaginable amounts of John Major's time'?[219] There are those who argue that on Europe after September 1992,

Major should either have done a Peel or a Wilson; split his party by sacking one or other group of the conviction politicians in his Cabinet (as Michael Portillo once urged him to do)[220] or offending the Europhiles, Clarke in particular, by calling for a referendum on the Maastricht Treaty in 1992 and taking 'the chance to transfer responsibility for Europe from [the Conservative] party to the people of Britain . . . thereby [sidestepping] the divisions over Europe that tore the party apart'.[221]

Instead, in a vain attempt to reconcile Major A and Major B, and to hold his Cabinet and party together, he staggered on through a year's-worth of parliamentary infighting on the Maastricht legislation and still more anguish over the European Communities (Finance) Bill. Between them these produced two moments when he might have had to resign or call on the Queen to ask for a dissolution (the Maastricht 'paving' motion in October 1992, when he considered resignation if it were lost;[222] and on the European Budget legislation in November 1994 when 'all the most senior members of the Cabinet' agreed that, should the vote be lost, 'the government would resign and I would ask the Queen for a dissolution of Parliament'[223]). It was this same European question and its capacity to reduce such leadership skills as he possessed to near rubble that caused him eventually to resign his leadership and call a 'put up or shut up' contest on June 1995[224] which, even though he won it, left him, in the words of Robert Cranborne, his campaign manager in that poll, an 'emotional vampire'.[225]

On the one occasion I encountered Major himself during his premiership, this was his most prominent characteristic. It was in July 1993, in the last days of the Maastricht Bill's passage through Parliament. We were introduced by Peter Brooke at a party to celebrate the official opening of the Department of National Heritage's building just off Trafalgar Square. The Prime Minister asked me what book I was working on. I described the preparation of this volume. 'It starts with Clem Attlee and finishes with you,' I said. 'Oh, I *do* hope so,' he replied.[226] I have talked at least once to all British prime ministers since Harold Macmillan at some stage in their political lives and this was the first and only time when my reaction was almost to wish to mother one of them! It was sad, rather than pathetic. But his self-pitying could make him seem even that, pathetic, to those who watched him closely from the inside. They would notice how at moments when the gambler's survival instinct took over, as in June 1995, he would be animated only to sink back into enervating self-doubt and brooding once the immediate excitement was over.[227]

An impression of helplessness in a premier can be contagious – depressing one's friends and arousing one's enemies. One of the former, Gillian Shephard, has described how 'as difficulties thickened, one was left with the strong impression that Major had come to feel he could trust very few and, those he could were not Cabinet colleagues. The feeling of isolation inevitably made his task harder and also made it difficult for his colleagues themselves to feel they enjoyed his trust except intermittently and when he had time to focus on them. Thus some of us who did support him throughout could not always find the means to do so.'[228]

For Major, therefore, Europe was a wrecker in both policy and personal terms as his famous and, as he thought, off-camera outburst against the 'bastards' on 23 July 1993 captured to perfection. 'Utterly exhausted and drained of all energy' by 'a year of gruesome trench warfare in the Commons' over the ratification of the Maastricht Treaty, Major confided his frustrations to Michael Brunson, the Political Editor of ITN, with, unknown to either of them, a live feed from an earlier interview still open to the BBC's studios at Millbank. Brunson suggested that three Eurosceptic Cabinet ministers had threatened to resign over European policy. Peter Lilley, Michael Portillo and John Redwood were the names circulating at the time (Major said it was not so).[229] The Prime Minister invited the respected trust of Brunson to:

'Just think it through from my perspective. You are the Prime Minister, with a majority of eighteen, a party that is still harking back to the golden age that never was and is now invented. I could bring in other people. But where do you think most of this poison is coming from? From the dispossessed and the never-possessed. You and I can think of ex-ministers who are causing all sorts of trouble. Do we want three more of the bastards out there?'[230]

Looking back, Major alluded to the fact that his administration had ceased to be a government-of-chums and that his full Cabinet had become a place where serious and sensitive issues could not be securely discussed:

Rereading the exchange with Brunson, it is easy see why it was assumed that I was referring to existing Cabinet Ministers. In fact I was not. Exhausted as I was, my words and my meaning became disconnected. Insofar as I had anyone in mind, it was former ministers who had left the government and begun to create havoc with their anti-European activities, given free rein by their release from collective responsibility.[231]

The poison Major referred to was a compound enemy – Eurosceptic political critics of his attempted middle way on Europe in both his government and his party in alliance with influential, fluent and highly ideologically charged press columnists such as Simon Heffer, a pet hate of Major's.[232]

The *Daily Express* political columnist, Peter Oborne, has developed a theory of what he calls 'the rise of the media class' which 'by the 1980s . . . had established itself as the most powerful force in British national life, comparable in a number of ways to the over-mighty trade unions in the 1970s', acquiring a capacity to 'destroy with a pitiless and awesome brutality'.[233] Mrs Thatcher, Oborne believes, 'rode the monster', partly thanks to her special relationships with the proprietors of the right-wing newspaper conglomerates such as Rupert Murdoch's News International:

And Margaret Thatcher's extraordinary personality fitted like a glove with the screaming Media Class demand for heroics, for confrontation and for drama. The eventual downfall of Thatcher, however, created an entirely new state of affairs and in due course unleashed the Media Class in a new direction. Under the bland and weak . . . John Major, the Media Class finally came of age.[234]

I am not entirely with Oborne on this. I do not believe that, even at their worst, the 'Media Class' make the political weather. Once a new pattern has set in, they make it better or worse, depending on whether the resulting storms are or are not in your political favour.

Where Oborne is absolutely right is in his analysis of the determination of the emerging Blair circle, Alastair Campbell and Peter Mandelson in particular, not only to avoid the ravaging of a hostile 'media class' but to ride it, tiger-like, as they, too, believed Mrs Thatcher had done.[235] The emphasis on a personalized, strong and prevailing individual leadership was there from the very first once Blair has been elected to replace John Smith in the summer of 1994.

At the height of the Prime Minister's agonies with his Eurosceptic diehards on the backbenches in early 1995, 'Tony Blair', wrote Major, 'made full use of the ammunition they handed him. "I lead my party, [you] follow yours," was his wounding jibe, the best one-liner he ever used against me.'[236] And it is this desperate weather pattern of 1994–95, when he deprived eight of them of the Conservative whip (a ninth, Richard Body, resigned the whip in protest), thereby depriving himself and his government of an absolute majority, that leads me to wonder whether even the most titanic of leaders could have held the line on that issue with the parliamentary arithmetic as it was and party and Cabinet opinion in such a condition. Added to this, every private criticism of him uttered by Lady Thatcher, each example of private encouragement she gave to the Eurosceptics, was relayed to Major, whose vulnerable skin took every slight through each available pore. 'I had no material majority at all and yet she seemed to be actively persuading new and relatively impressionable Members of Parliament to vote against the Government . . .' He found his predecessor's behaviour intolerable.[237]

The 'whipless wonders' were out of control and several of them appeared to be on a permanent high. And in Teresa Gorman, they possessed a telegenic, funny and fluent card of a character who guaranteed permanent media visibility. As another prominent whipless one, Teddy Taylor, put it, they 'changed chair at each weekly meeting . . . We'd say "Who's the Prime Minister this week?" . . . We would consider the government's business and decide how we were going to vote.'[238]

No Prime Minister in the postwar period has had to face a rebellion quite like this on the issue of the day. It drew forth from Major one of the most embittered threnodies of the television version of his memoirs:

'Every time the Eurosceptic MPs scratched their political sores in public we became more unpopular . . . [they] . . . were absolutely unbiddable on any subject to do with Europe . . .

'They were in very great demand. College Green [the patch of grass across the road from the Houses of Parliament much favoured by television interviewers and crews] was permanently booked. There was nothing I could do about their behaviour before they lost the whip . . . and, of course, when they lost the whip there was even less I could do about it.'[239]

What he could have done was not to restore the whip without conditions. His decision to do so in March 1995 was treated not as an act of magnanimity but as a sign of irreparable weakness – which depressed him still further ('You may say I was gullible and foolish and I could scarcely disagree with that judgement').[240]

In the spring and summer of 1995 he brooded on a fightback. Tired, as he told his fellow heads of government at the Halifax summit in June, of being 'a coalition government on my own' (once again not realizing the microphones were on), he decided on the plane home and, finally, once home at The Finings, to bring forward what he thought would be an inevitable challenge to this leadership the following autumn.[241]

It succeeded on one level (218 votes to Redwood's 89 – a mere three votes above the minimum he had set to prevent him resigning the premiership as well as his party leadership);[242] but not on another and more serious plane – the real terms of parliamentary and political exchange. As Gillian Shephard has put it, 'It was . . . too late to help the party recover its fortunes.'[243] In Kenneth Clarke's words: 'The party had gone beyond hope and was not capable of having its divisions healed.'[244]

Cabinets can have a smell of death abut them long before the electorate as undertaker produces the shroud. Major's did during the last two years of its life – with one prominent exception in its ranks: Michael Heseltine. Major had for a long while toyed with the idea 'that a big hitter was needed at the centre to chair cabinet committees and co-ordinate presentation of government policy'.[245] In the weeks before his leadership surprise in June 1995, he had scouted the possibilities with the 'warrior politician' Heseltine.[246] The battle with Redwood over, the 'warrior' was granted a most extraordinary swathe of governing territory and the title of Deputy Prime Minister.[247] His sway over the Cabinet committee world was such that he could pursue his three passions – competitiveness, presentation and bashing the Opposition – almost at will.

Heseltine had his mockers amongst his colleagues. They bridled and laughed a bit when in his first week as DPM he told them all to read Correlli Barnett on successive governments' roles in Britain's relative economic decline.[248] And they could be very funny about his new Cabinet committee which met every morning to do something about the 'media class' – EDCP [Economic Domestic Co-ordination and Presentation]. 'EDCP is a completely absurd thing,' one Cabinet minister told me.

'They don't know what's happening when they are sitting. They sit for quite a long time. They are out of date even before they finish, as the first edition of the *Evening Standard* has come out and the news bulletins have moved on. It was part of Michael's settlement with the Prime Minister . . .'[249]

Major never seems to have regretted that settlement. Heseltine was a force of political nature. He derided the press to his colleagues – telling them to take no notice as journalists were very largely the kept men and women of their proprietors.[250] He believed until the end – even in private, so his colleagues said – that economic recovery could turn the election the

Conservatives' way.[251] And, as one Cabinet colleague put it: 'By the end Major loved him because he relied on him and because he could handle things Major couldn't. It was partly his mane-waving in the House of Commons and partly because Heseltine simply adored crises and Major didn't.'[252]

The crisis to the Prime Minister appeared continuous and the press unrelenting. Virtuous progress on public service reform continued and his openness programme proceeded. (He built on his avowal of the existence of the Secret Intelligence Service and the naming of its chief in 1992 with the Intelligence Services Act of 1994 – which set MI6 on a legal basis for the first time – and the creation of a parliamentary oversight committee for the secret world as a whole).[253] But he regretted mightily the might-have-beens of those last four and a half years in office when he was 'too often on the back foot'.[254]

The media obsession never abated – from 1992 it was a huge contributor to 'overload', not just on the Prime Minister but on the Cabinet as a whole. As Douglas Hurd put it a year after leaving government (he left when Major reconstructed it after seeing off Redwood's challenge): 'Nowadays ministers . . . fret infinitely about the media. A huge amount of time is given to this fretting . . . The Cabinet may no longer have to worry abut India but it may, from time to time, worry itself sick about the *Daily Mail*.'[255]

I asked a well-placed senior civil servant in the last days, as the government held on grimly until the last moments of the full stretch 1992–97 Parliament, to capture 'late Major' for me. 'What's the hallmark of the Major premiership?' he replied.

'Bunker mentality and short-termism. It's extraordinary the degree to which the PM reacts to what's in the *Daily Mail* or the *Daily Telegraph*. On Prime Minister's Question days, private offices across Whitehall scan them with particular attention because if their department is mentioned, as like as not, it will be rung-up by the No. 10 Private Office . . . asking for a brief in case the Prime Minister is asked about it.'[256]

This was not a case of No. 10 being able, in Charles Powell's phrase, 'to beat the bushes of Whitehall',[257] quite the reverse.

The size and the trauma of defeat when it came was worse than Major had feared. He watched the first results at home at The Finings 'with a certain amount of disbelief'.[258] When it was all finished he turned over in his mind again and again what he could or should have done differently.[259] While writing his memoirs, he told friends he found it 'cathartic'.[260] They do not read that way.

Nearly two and a half years after the loss of office, I asked a well-disposed and historically minded Cabinet colleague to sum up Major as Prime Minister. After pausing for thought, he replied:

'A very good tactician . . . with a great many honourable prejudices but I didn't think with any fixed points to steer by in the end. And when events rushed down on him, he didn't have the strength to see what was important and took refuge in minutiae. A decent, honourable man who was screwed up, frankly, by not being up to the job.'[261]

Though matters might have been different if Major had enjoyed the longer Cabinet apprenticeship he would have liked, it is very hard to better that. And the innate decency of the man only adds to its poignancy.

18

Command and Control:
Tony Blair, 1997 –

'People have to know that we will run from the centre and govern from the centre.' *Tony Blair, March 1997*[1]

'It will be Blair, Blair, Blair just as it was Thatcher, Thatcher, Thatcher. Wilson and Callaghan were a bit more collective in their thoughts.'
Tony Benn, replying to a student's question on
the supremacy of prime ministerial power, March 1997[2]

Goodbye Cabinet Government. Welcome the Blair presidency. The *Ministerial Code* . . . is the most revolutionary publication produced by the Government since the election. It sets out in a formal code of conduct, to be obeyed by all ministers, the biggest centralisation of power seen in Whitehall in peacetime. All the familiar textbooks about the cabinet system will have to be rewritten. The idea that heads of department have an independent standing has been torn up.
Peter Riddell, August 1997[3]

'The idea that the Prime Minister is *primus inter pares* is wrong. The Prime Minister is not *pares*. He's way above that. Like Caesar, he bestrides his world like a Colossus.' *Senior Whitehall figure,*
shortly after the end of the Balkans War, 1999[4]

'. . . most Prime Ministers who have got a strong programme end up expecting their Secretaries of State to put it through . . . if you have a strong idea of what you want to do and believe in pushing it through, then you're, in inverted commas, a "dictator". And if you're not, then you're "weak". And, you know, you pays your money and you takes your choice on that one.' *Tony Blair, January 2000*[5]

'Do we need a Prime Minister's Department? It's largely an academic debate now because we already have one. It's a properly functioning department with a departmental head [the chief of staff, Jonathan Powell] with a sense of being *the* central machinery of government.'
Prime ministerial adviser, March 1999[6]

'The idea that the PM gets integrated advice is nonsense. You could not see a more *unjoined* system. To say they have imported the White House to No. 10 – Washington to Downing Street – is absolutely right.' *Senior Whitehall figure, January 2000*[7]

'I will decide the issue of monetary union. I'm the Prime Minister who's got responsibility for it, according to the British national interest.' *Tony Blair, January 2000*[8]

When Tony Blair asserted what he saw as his primacy over the timing and the nature of the euro decision as a first person singular responsibility which fell to him as premier, I treated this as a significant expression of his view of the functions of being Prime Minister, and one that did not accord with traditional notions of the constitutional limits of the job. Yet his words occasioned no great surprise. For even before he formed his government on 2 May 1997, debate began about Mr Blair's construction of a 'command premiership'. Signs aplenty existed to suggest that command and control would be the Blair style in government as it had been in opposition.

Tony Blair and his inner group of advisers seemed determined to operate inside No. 10, once they got there, as they had within the Labour Party – driving policy and presentation from the centre around a core of delivery musts, and brooking no serious resistance either from ministerial colleagues or from cumbersome, traditional government mechanics. The one great exception to this was the Chancellor of the Exchequer-in-waiting, Gordon Brown. For the deal at the heart of the Blair style was that a command premier would operate alongside a command Chancellor licensed to dominate across a wide range of economic and domestic policy. It was plainly going to be a centre-driven administration with the 'centre', as later defined publicly by Mr Blair, as 'my own office, the Cabinet Office and the Treasury'.[9]

I sensed a good deal of this when chairing private training sessions organized by the Fabian Society for Labour shadow ministers.[10] But it was when I was chairing a non-Fabian breakfast meeting of senior figures from Whitehall and the private sector in March 1997 that the most graphic statement of intention was uttered by a figure then as now very close indeed to Mr Blair. Sitting in our Westminster attic almost within sight of the Whitehall Blair's people were expecting to inherit inside two months, he said: 'You may see a change from a feudal system of barons to a more Napoleonic system.'[11]

Instantly, the senior civil servants present switched to a condition at which they are expert – disguised animation. It was as if radar scanners had suddenly sprung from their heads. The import of the metaphor was absorbed. The word got round. Mr Blair's public version of it was also delivered in March 1997. 'People have to know that we will run from the centre and govern from the centre', he told a meeting of the Newspaper Society.[12] We were warned. Place Mr Blair's words together with those of his aide and we have a declaration of intent comparable to Mrs Thatcher's remarks in February 1979 that hers 'must be a conviction government. As Prime Minister I could not waste time having any internal arguments.'[13]

I was sufficiently alarmed by this to throw of a fit of constitutionalism-in-advance. 'Command premiership of a highly personalized and driven kind', I declared in the *Financial Times* on 26 March 1997, 'usually ends in tears. Sir Anthony Eden's and Mrs Thatcher's did in 1957 and 1990 respectively. Getting your own way simply by stamping the prime ministerial foot is conducive neither to good government nor to personal survival, nor to a contented retirement.'[14] A month later, during a BBC Radio 4 *Analysis* discussion with William Hague and Donald Dewar among others, I was even more Savonarola-like. 'You have a commanding figure in Mr Blair,' I said. 'It's going to be a command premiership. I just hope there's a bit of freedom of information and democracy in the Cabinet.'[15]

The significance of the Blair aide's words about a Napoleonic rather than a feudal approach to government from the centre is that such a style was planned for long before the election. It did not depend on the electorate granting Mr Blair and his party a 179-seat majority on 1 May 1997. It would have been put into operation if the majority had been closer to the fifty Blair and his people privately expected.[16]*

---

* Despite my warnings of the perils of a 'command premiership' from the last days of Blair's opposition phase, I was worried from the beginning of his governing years about the dangers that befall political historians after the once-mighty have departed. We have a tendency to place overly neat patterns on premierships when finished, creating a misleadingly tidy picture of Downing Street incumbencies. From the early days of the

Yet it would be misleading to assert that anything meriting the description of an overarching plan to remodel Whitehall, the premiership or the Cabinet system was ready for implementation on 2 May 1997. Certainly Mr Blair's vanguard roared into No. 10 like a through train, greatly impressing the waiting civil servants with their push-and-go and team-like qualities.[18] Similarly, Gordon Brown's very personal coterie hit the ground running in policy terms in the Treasury, too.[19] But *process* – the mechanics of decision-taking and implementation – was another matter entirely. People deeply embedded in the Blair centre from the beginning were warning me over two years after they entered into government against notions that the new Prime Minister and his people had arrived with a grand design to put to the Cabinet Secretary, Sir Robin Butler, or to Alex Allan, Principal Private Secretary in the No. 10 Private Office. It was more a matter of trying to remedy weaknesses in capacity and method as they encountered them.[20]

Early in this book, I emphasized how important it was to examine closely the transition from one Prime Minister to another. The early days of the Blair administration underscore this. Blair's inner corps, Jonathan Powell (chief of staff), Alastair Campbell (press secretary) and David Miliband (acting, later confirmed, head of the Policy Unit) 'came in as a package', said one old No. 10 hand, who had never seen anything quite like it. 'They had all worked so closely together in opposition on the policy and press side, they just came in as they were. Within forty-eight hours it was all in place. Very impressive.'[21]

On the morning of 7 May, Sir Robin Butler brought the new premier into his (Butler's) regular ten o'clock Wednesday meeting of Permanent Secretaries, the 'College of Cardinals'. Several of them were hugely impressed when Blair told them he was going to run his government on the basis of ethics, not ideology (and one or two became quite cross with me when, at a private gathering shortly afterwards, I expressed shock at their desire to be illusioned and dismay at the abandonment of their traditional scepticism).[22]

Blair premiership, therefore, I decided to take to the air, like a battered old reconnaissance aircraft, every six to nine months or so to overfly Whitehall and to publish the resulting snapshots as a kind of insurance against excessively precise or teleological retrospective explanation of an inevitably messy scene.[17] As far as possible, this chapter will be constructed around these 'overflights', reflecting the picture the Blair premiership presented *as* it unfolded – including those impressions which had to be modified when later rolls of reconnaissance films were developed.

Over in the Treasury, the reception of the Brown team (Ed Balls, economic adviser; Ed Miliband, brother of David and personal adviser to Brown; Charlie Whelan, press adviser) was warm enough on the afternoon of 2 May when 'officials lined the staircase of the Treasury's monumental chambers ... to cheer ... the new chancellor into office.'[23] But it soon cooled when it swiftly became apparent that the Brown style would be to work as tightly as possible through his politically appointed temporary civil servants at the expense of the regular officials he had inherited, with the Permanent Secretary, Sir Terry Burns, and the head of Information, Jill Rutter, as particular losers. The career Treasury, as it might be called, felt very definitely 'sidelined in favour of the chancellor's personal appointees' in these early days.[24]

From the beginning it was plain that the Blair–Brown axis would dominate economic policy, that the full Cabinet would be nowhere and that its main economic committee (which Brown would lead, the first time a Prime Minister had vacated the chair since 1966) would be scarcely better placed. The decision-taking circle that mattered on economic strategy was described simply by the bilateral meetings between Blair and Brown. Yet Moira Wallace, the Private Secretary for economic affairs in No. 10, initially found it difficult to get into these meetings to take a note and record what was agreed (Blair's people say the solitary, broody Chancellor was the problem here).[25] Things improved, and by the time Jeremy Heywood had succeeded Moira Wallace in the post, Private Secretary access to the PM/Chancellor sessions had become much easier.[26]

One of the most significant economic decisions of the Blair administration was also taken during the first week of its life – the shifting of responsibility for setting interest rates from what had effectively been a chancellorial/prime ministerial prerogative in consultation with senior figures from the Bank of England and the Treasury, to the Monetary Policy Committee of the Bank of England alone. Sir Alan Budd (who as the Chief Economic Adviser to the Treasury Brown inherited, spent the bulk of Labour's first weekend in office piecing together the mechanics and details of this transition with Terry Burns)[27] was right to stress the boldness of this move, the degree to which it took politics *out* of interest rate setting and put economics *in* as well as the 'wonderful moment of political drama' involved[28] when Brown announced the decision to an unsuspecting world on 8 May 1997.[29] Only two other Cabinet ministers were in the loop of prior knowledge on the shift to an independent Bank of England – the Deputy Prime Minister and Secretary of State for

Environment, Transport and the Regions, John Prescott, and the Foreign and Commonwealth Secretary, Robin Cook.[30] Not only was the full Cabinet left unconsulted, it had not even met for the first time when the decision was announced.[31]

At the beginning of the administration, I attached great significance to the existence of this 'Big Four' of Blair, Brown, Prescott and Cook.[32] I thought they might constitute a shrunken equivalent of Major's 'Political Cabinets', meeting as they did before full Cabinet on Thursday mornings.[33] These, I thought, were major figures in their own right and might comprise a kind of counterbalance to excessive prime ministerialism. Only later did I discover that the 'Big Four' sessions did not survive 1997 (though Prescott continues to have his meetings with Blair pre-Cabinet and Brown and Cook had their own bilaterals at other times[34]) as 'too many of them can't stand each other's company', in the words of a fellow Cabinet minister.[35]

The need for a dash of collegiality and the restraint that comes with it was swiftly apparent in the summer and autumn of 1997. For as one well-placed official put it quite starkly: 'This is not a collective government. We have to accept that the old model of Cabinet government is dead as a doornail'[36] (though, as we shall see, it enjoyed an important revival in Mr Blair's conduct of his 'war cabinets').

Early observations did indeed suggest that the Blair Cabinets were extraordinary affairs and not just because of their brevity. A thirty-minute one just before the 1997 summer recess may well have been a postwar record for a full-dress, as opposed to an emergency, full Cabinet. They rarely lasted more than an hour.[37] There was (and remains) no proper agenda, merely regular items – 'parliamentary affairs', 'economic and domestic affairs', 'foreign affairs' (initially a fourth, 'European affairs', existed but, by the turn of the century this had been chopped, European matters coming up wherever deemed appropriate under the other three headings). The three regular headings are supplemented by a very New-Labourish addendum – 'The Grid' – a plan for the forthcoming week linking the timing and presentation of ministerial and departmental announcements and initiatives with political, cultural and even sporting events generally.[38]

From the preparations for the famous so-called 'call me Tony' (not quite his exact words[39] which were: 'Now what do we call each other? I suppose as we've called each other by our first names all our lives we should just carry on doing that') first full Cabinet of 8 May 1997, it became clear that Blair would not use a formal agenda as had been the norm since Lloyd George and Hankey invented the Cabinet Secretariat in 1916. Nor did Blair necessarily keep to the order in which the regular business items appeared. The Cabinet Office's note-takers followed the discourse wherever it went and wrote it up as best they could.[40] Non-Cabinet ministers found the Cabinet minutes among the least important parts of their weekly reading.[41] One particularly longstanding customer of the Cabinet minutes noted that they 'are different under this Government. There is much more in them about presentation and how to do down the Opposition'.[42]

The Blair editions of the long-established but previously unpublished Cabinet Office document, *Cabinet Committee Business: A Guide for Departments*, continued to open, beneath the heading 'Cabinet and its Committees', with the declaration that: 'The Cabinet reconciles Ministers' individual responsibility. It is the ultimate arbiter of all Government policy.'[43] In some areas, however, this was not entirely a fiction after May 1997 (though at full Cabinet level it certainly was). The January 2000 edition of *Cabinet Committee Business* listed sixteen standing ministerial Cabinet committees, fourteen sub-committees of those sixteen plus six MISCs (or ad hoc) ministerial groups.[44] Yet only the legislative-planners (QFL – Queen's Speech and Future Legislation; and LEG – Legislation) and the constitution-changers, the great swathe of ministerial groups chaired by Lord Irvine, the Lord Chancellor, under CRP, the strategic committee on Constitutional Reform Policy which Blair himself led, could be seen as representative of the old, Cabinet committee system for collective policy-making and the collegial treatment of disagreement or case-work.

Perhaps the public spending committee chaired by Brown could be seen as a traditional instrument, especially during the preparation of comprehensive spending reviews which occurred on a three-year cycle. And it is true that a degree of collegiality by other means was handled by ministerial correspondence,[45] a practice that had been growing since the beginning of the Thatcher years, as Sir Richard Wilson (Butler's successor as Cabinet Secretary) was at pains to point out to a concerned House of Commons Select Committee on Public Administration in February 2000.[46]

But by the time Sir Richard sought to soothe MPs' fears about excessive prime ministerialism, it was plain that the system of Cabinet government by Cabinet committee as developed during the two world wars, adapted by the Anderson Committee of 1945 for application in the peace[47] and operated by all Prime Ministers in varying mutations until May 1997 as part of a kind of governing norm, was, for all practical purposes, dead. Its demise was linked, powerfully and inevitably, with what became known, however, crudely or regrettably, as the 'Blair Presidency' question.

As early as September 1997, that most scholarly of political columnists, Peter Riddell of *The Times*, was floating the concept (albeit slightly tongue-in-cheek) at a gathering of political scientists, some of whom, he knew, would recoil at the crudity of a 'presidential label':

'I can already hear veterans of the academic debate over the premiership tut-tutting over such journalists' laxity and ignorance. That phrase is never uttered publicly by any of the Blair inner circle, but it is often used by them privately . . . This is not just a matter of style . . . There has also been a deliberate attempt to change the way Downing Street and the Cabinet Office work to allow the Prime Minister to exercise more control over the Whitehall machine. This has not occurred out of the blue. Mr Blair's close advisers have studied the debate over the size and scope of the Prime Minister's Office which has developed since the 1960s.'[48]

By this stage there were some substantial primary sources, as well as anecdotal evidence, to illuminate the Riddell portrait of a developing 'control freak' premiership.

As early as June 1997, the Whitehall editor of the *Daily Mail*, Sonia Purnell, had got hold of a Prime Minister's personal minute on the subject of 'Press Handling'. 'An interesting idea injected into the media', Blair told his ministers, 'will be taken as a statement of Government policy. All new ideas or statements of this sort must be cleared with No. 10.'[49] It would be wrong to see anything clandestine about this approach, for all the confidentiality that attaches to a prime ministerial minute. When the *Ministerial Code*, Blair's updated version of *Questions of Procedure for Ministers*, was published the following month, there it was – openly proclaimed in black and white.

It was the soon to be notorious paragraph 88 of the *Ministerial Code* which became swiftly treated as the classic statement of 'control freakery' and which led Peter Riddell to declare: 'Goodbye Cabinet government. Welcome the Blair presidency' in his *Times* column.[50] Under the heading 'Co-ordination of Government Policy', it reads:

In order to ensure the effective presentation of government policy, all major interviews and media appearances, both print and broadcast, should be agreed with the No. 10 Press Office before any commitments are entered into. The policy content of all major speeches, press releases and new policy initiatives should be cleared in good time with the No. 10 Private Office; the timing and form of announcements should be cleared with the No. 10 Press Office. Each Department should keep a record of media contacts by both Ministers and officials.[51]

For Peter Preston of the *Guardian*, adherence to 88 would reduce any minister to a 'diminished, drivelling figure'.[52] For Peter Riddell, the Blair version of the old *QPM* represented 'the biggest centralisation of power seen in Whitehall in peacetime'.[53]

To most veterans, the ambition of paragraph 88's reach was very striking. Sir Bernard Ingham, for example, sustained a nice line in mock innocence at the audacity of Alastair Campbell: 'this lot believe the impossible is achievable – the co-ordination of the presentation of the work of this Government – because ministers have minds of their own. They all have their own spin-doctors and special advisers.'[54] But there was another intriguing interpretation from a very well-placed insider which argued that the assertiveness of No. 10 over policy and presentation stemmed from a sense of weakness rather than potency.

'The Blair centre in opposition', he explained to me, 'had wielded much more control. So, when the new Government took office, departments took their lead from the way their Ministers seemed much more willing to do what the centre wanted, particularly in terms of presentation. That has made it more effective – though it was very noticeable in the early days how the incoming team at No. 10 felt they were very much less in control than they had been. Hence some of the directives to departments, such as that on clearing announcements, etc.'[55]

There is much in this. Whenever you talk to those who live at the 'Blair Centre', they all give you the impression of how powerful everybody else in Whitehall seems to them. They tend to go on to make the case for an even more forceful centre, as Philip Gould, the Prime Minister's pollster and political strategist (with whom he starts the week every Monday morning when in town) has done publicly. 'Number 10 Downing Street', Gould wrote in the Preface to the paperback edition of his *The Unfinished Revolution*, published during the 1999 party conference season,

does not need fewer communications resources but more ... to ensure that government is competent and effective ... The centre actually has far less power than is typically ascribed to it. Anyone who speaks any time at Number 10 quickly realises that it is a tiny corner of a huge government machine, staffed with talented people but lacking the resources necessary to be a commanding and dominating nerve centre ... For the most part they are over-worked, over-stretched and desperately trying to cope with a constant stream of difficult and challenging circumstances.[56]

Gould, the great evangelist *for* a more 'commanding' centre, believes that without a greater capacity 'to integrate and reform' at the centre through a Prime Minister 'supported by his own department that is powerful, talented and fast enough to cope with the speed of changing circumstances ... good government will become increasingly elusive'.[57]

A very senior Whitehall official consistently argued from the start of the Blair premiership that 'the form of the Blair government is not going to be apparent for about two years. We are doing a lot of re-engineering in flight. Just think, when did we really know what Mrs T's government would be like? Not until 1981.'[58] There was a great deal in that remark and it has vitality still. But, on the Gould point, did we not see the beginning of the Prime Minister's *Office* shifting to an unavowed Prime Minister's *Department* from those earliest days when paragraph 88 was being minted and the talk of a 'presidency' began *sub rosa*? There may not have been a grand design ready for Blair-as-Napoleon or his No. 10 commanders to implement, but the instinct was there.

Listen to a member of the 'Blair Centre' not long before the second anniversary approached:

'Do we need a Prime Minister's Department? It's largely an academic debate now because we already have one. It's a properly functioning department with a departmental head [the chief of staff, Jonathan Powell] with a sense of being *the* central machinery of government. We do now, in effect, have a PMD *but* (and it's a crucial "but"), it is not formalised. This is an advantage because it makes it extremely flexible.

'It makes it possible to bring in large numbers of advisers at very short notice. Almost all the people in this structure hold office at the pleasure of the PM. It is *sui generis* – a case apart from the rest of the Whitehall machine. The centre is now not just a person, the Prime Minister and a small staff – it is machinery around him.

'The key part of the job is to keep the PM informed – to be the PM's early-warning mechanism on policy developments. And when the government changed, No. 10 became much more central to the presentation of policy. The area where there has been a big increase in staffing is the Press Office and the

Strategic Communications Unit. That represents a determination that No. 10 shall not just be *primus inter pares*, but the dominant department in putting forward the message of the government.'[59]

This is the most vivid insider word-picture I have encountered of the Blair style. And it helps explain many of the concerns of the Neill Committee on Standards in Public Life[60] and the Select Committee on Public Administration[61] about the constitutional and the patronage implications of the 'new centre', not least the doubling of the number of special advisers to seventy-four in Whitehall as a whole between May 1997 and early 2000 and the trebling to twenty-four of the No. 10 quotient over the same period.[62]

The notion of a Prime Minister's Department that dare not quite speak its name increasingly found an echo on the part of those in Whitehall who felt themselves to be on the receiving end of its *esprit de corps* and its clout. 'Does the man in Whitehall know best? Probably not. Do the men in No. 10 know best? I think they think they probably do' was how one senior figure, well known for his irony, put it.[63] Intriguingly they were seen as operating a mini-collegiality of their own within a far from collegial overall system. 'Some members of the Policy Unit are quite often important individual players,' according to one observer. 'What tends to happen is that they will discuss a question among themselves and then – snap! They will decide. They are very loose within and very tight without when dealing with the rest of Whitehall.'[64]

The Policy Unit was very much part of the 'Tony wants' phenomenon (which one of his ministers described to me as 'the two most powerful words in Whitehall').[65] But it would be wrong to suggest that the members of the Miliband team were the sole conveyors of what Tony wanted, any more than were Powell or Campbell. The career officials in the Private Office, such as Allan's successor as Principal Private Secretary, John Holmes, and his successor, Jeremy Heywood, who continued to perform that role, as did John Sawers, who inherited Holmes's foreign affairs brief.[66] It was the degree to which lifers and temporaries were flung together, the increase in the proportion of special advisers within that mix, the competition for the Prime Minister's ear and the combined force of Blair's people (whether Whitehall regulars or irregulars) which gave the justified impression of No. 10 becoming more like the White House.

Much was made, too, not least in Parliament, of the power granted to Powell and Campbell through a special order in council to 'manage' career civil servants in the No. 10 Private Office and Press Office, respectively, as Sir Richard Wilson explained to the Commons Public Administration Committee. And when the number 1 figure in Brown's special adviser court, Ed Balls, was made Chief Economic Adviser in 1999 (albeit *without* the power to manage Treasury staff), Wilson sought to reassure anxious MPs that 'no constitutional problems' arose.[67]

The Cabinet Secretary stressed the view that such things were a matter of 'scale'. We were neither moving to an American 'spoils' system where hundreds of top civil servants' jobs change with incoming presidents who fill them on a political basis, nor to a French *cabinet* system where ministers had sizeable staffs of outsiders mixed with insiders in the circles immediately around them.[68] Sir Richard took the view that seventy-plus special advisers 'could not swamp' the 3,000 or so senior career civil servants involved in advising ministers.[69]

It struck me that the Blair-style No. 10 was noticeably akin to a French-style *cabinet* and that Brown, because of his preferred way of working, was close to running a *cabinet* system, too, not least because Ed Balls acted as the gatekeeper to the Chancellor. 'Officials who wished to persuade the latter had first to carry the former', as David Lipsey elegantly expressed it.[70] It was important, however, to trace the growth points of special adviserdom in No. 10 within the context of an overall increase from eight to twenty-seven between 2 May 1997 and the end of 1999.

The Policy Unit had grown from eight special advisers under Major to twelve under Blair. By the end of 1999 they had been joined by two career officials (Jim Gallagher from the Cabinet Office and Brian Hackland from the Department of the Environment, Transport and the Regions). Four of the special advisers worked within the Private Office, which in the postwar period had very largely been a fiefdom of the career Civil Service (Powell; his deputy, Pat McFadden; Anji Hunter, Mr Blair's personal assistant in opposition and government; and Fiona Millar, who ran the social side of the office and assisted Mrs Blair). Ten other special advisers were distributed across what might be called the enhanced communications capacity of No. 10 – the Campbell-led Press Office; the Strategic Communications Unit headed by a career official, Alun Evans (succeeded by Campbell himself in early 2000); and later the Research and Information Unit run by another special adviser, the psephologist and political analyst, Bill Bush.[71]

It was the qualitative, if not the quantitative, increase in special advisers – their prominent position in what one former chief economic adviser to the Treasury called 'the geography of power'[72] – which led one seasoned and balanced Whitehall figure to worry lest 'this is not a way into the American system by the back door'.[73] These private concerns found an equivalent public expression across the first three years of the Blair administration in both government, 'good and great', and Parliamentary inquiries.

The initial area of inflammation followed by investigation was the activity where the Blair Centre's focus, drive and near obsession eclipsed that of any previous administration – presentation and communication, bundled together under the somewhat coarse label of 'spinning'. Two factors combined to give it lift-off: Alastair Campbell's position as arguably the closest and most influential individual within the Prime Minister's innermost circle; and what its members came to call the 'great purge' – the cumulative removal of the senior departmental heads of information from the top of the Government Information Service inherited by the new administration. One of the most senior of the departees, Romola Christopherson (who left the Department of Health in January 1999), captured this very neatly when she dubbed Campbell 'monarch of all he surveys'. The Prime Minister, she said, 'turns to him on policy as much as presentation. He is more at the centre of the "big picture" than anyone else in the cabinet . . .'[74]

Sir Robin Butler tackled the Campbell/GIS problem in two stages. In July 1997 he published a revised version of *Guidance on the Work of the Government Information Service* which underscored the longstanding 'basic conventions, which successive Governments have applied' requiring that the activities of the GIS should, amongst other things, 'be relevant to Government responsibilities; . . . objective and explanatory, not tendentious or polemical; . . . not be, or [be] liable to misrepresentation as being, party political'.[75] The following September, Butler asked his number 2, Sir Robin Mountfield (who headed the Office of Public Service within the Cabinet Office), to review the GIS on an efficiency as well as a propriety basis. Campbell sat on the Mountfield group as did Mike Grannatt, Head of the GIS, four more career officials and one special adviser, Conor Ryan, from the Department for Education and Employment.[76]

Mountfield stressed the need for the GIS to reflect the non partisan, impartial essentials which lay at the heart of the *Guidance* document and the *Civil Service Code*.[77] Yet, as Butler himself had already put it to the House of Commons Public Administration Committee, the GIS needed to 'raise its game'.[78] Hence the Mountfield recommendations that a new

Strategic Communications Unit be created in No. 10, plus a new capacity for co-ordination and media monitoring across Whitehall (the Research and Information Unit of No. 10 emerged out of this). Departmental press offices needed to be modernized and their reflexes sharpened, the report continued. Heads-of-information jobs should be filled from within the GIS or as a result of internal or external competitions overseen by the Civil Service Commission. The whole new modernized entity should be renamed the Government Information and Communication Service – which it duly was.[79]

As for Romola Christopherson's monarch-of-all-he-surveys, Mountfield (reflecting his, Butler's and later, Wilson's view) told the select committee that 'the appointment of Alastair Campbell with an explicitly political role actually clarifies the position, it is a more honest position . . . We are all very jealous, particularly those of us who have been permanent civil servants for a very long time, . . . of preserving the non-political status of the career Civil Service and I think Alastair Campbell's position as a Special Adviser actually helps to preserve that by clarifying the distinction between the two positions.'[80] I agree with the Mountfield position. Just as it was healthy for the openly partisan Joe Haines to be a temporary civil servant when he was Harold Wilson's press secretary, and unhealthy for Bernard Ingham to be such a political career civil servant under Thatcher, so the transparency of Campbell's position had its virtues.

It took rather longer for the special adviser question as a whole to receive its necessary constitutional probing. This came with the Neill Report, on *Reinforcing Standards*, presented to the Prime Minister by the Committee on Standards in Public Life on 12 January 2000,[81] and the *Making Government Work* inquiry launched by the Commons Public Administration Committee eight days later.[82]

Between Mountfield and Neill, a great deal of rejigging of the centre had begun, with plans for ever greater 'joining-up' (a Mountfield catchphrase which he publicly[83] and Richard Wilson privately[84] came to dislike) to follow. Of equal importance, considerable experience of the Blair style in action (not least in warlike circumstances in the Gulf and the Balkans) had fleshed out first impressions. To some extent the succession of papers and action plans either prepared directly or overseen by Sir Richard Wilson as Cabinet Secretary have been efforts at marrying the *de facto* ruling style of Tony Blair with the traditional essences of government as well as attempts to plan for a more efficient, streamlined, integrated and focused style of government for the future.

Sir Richard, who replaced Sir Robin Butler on his retirement in January 1998, was different in style though not philosophy (both were wedded to what one of their Permanent Secretary colleagues called 'the eternals' of a career Civil Service, recruited and promoted on merit) from his predecessor. Wilson gives the impression of suppleness, of thinking aloud and sometimes elliptically, where Butler practised a terse briskness, his conversation, though engaging, driven by a capacity to speak in paragraphs in the manner of an oral memo. In the autumn of 1997 Lord Irvine interviewed the three contenders for the apostolic succession to the Cabinet Secretaryship (Wilson, then Permanent Secretary at the Home Office; Andrew Turnbull, at that time Permanent Secretary at Environment, Transport and the Regions; and Richard Mottram, then Permanent Secretary at Defence). Wilson was judged the most likely to fit in with the Blair style.[85]

Blair's people invested high hopes in the first task assigned to Wilson by the Prime Minister – a review designed to map out and create that more dynamic centre, on which Blair was set, along the lines described by Peter Mandelson and Roger Liddle in their pre-election study, *The Blair Revolution*.[86] Sir Richard was confronted by what might have seemed an insoluble dilemma for a man of great experience who is neither feudal nor Napoleonic by temperament, but collective; more a servant of the Cabinet as a whole than the Prime Minister's 'Whitehall Chief Whip', as one of Mr Blair's people envisioned him becoming.[87] Sir Richard expressed it rather differently. He described as 'a key role' of the Cabinet Office that it 'holds the ring'. As he put it to a conference of senior civil servants in the autumn of 1998, 'the Cabinet Office ought to be available for the Centre to communicate to Departments and for Departments to communicate to the Centre. I want No. 10 to feel that they can say to us "What is happening in Department X" or "I'd like to give them this message." And I'd like Department X to feel that they can say to us "What is No. 10 thinking on this issue? Can you help us get this through?"'[88]

Those who knew Wilson well quickly observed two parallel tracks at work. It was quite plain from the way he operated day-by-day that he would try to bridge the old and new in a palpable if unobtrusive way. As one close observer put it: 'Richard would almost wait around, seeming to be useful. He played it brilliantly and waited. And, bit by bit, as ministers continued doing things without consulting each other, and getting into trouble, he began to offer a brokerage – almost a conciliation – service. He could not have produced these ways of preserving much of the old system while fitting in with the wishes of the new Prime Minister if he hadn't waited.'[89]

The Wilson review of the centre was expected to be completed swiftly, but it was not finished until Maundy Thursday 1998 and the Prime Minister did not get round to publishing his thoughts upon it until just before the summer recess. It would be wrong to think that Blair finds the mechanisms of state interesting. He has a powerful instinct about what he wants. But for the detail, and the hidden wiring that needs to be laid down on the way to getting there, he has no feel (and deepening experience of the prime ministerial function did not alter this, as we shall see).

So what was the essence of the Wilson solution? It was, as a close colleague put it, to fashion 'new corporate bricks' from the masonry of the traditional Cabinet system.[90] Stripped to its essentials, the Wilson philosophy was that the Cabinet Office had to provide a service to the collective *through* the Prime Minister, who is not only the keeper of the government's strategy but the Minister for the Civil Service as well – hence Sir Richard working for the PM as both Cabinet Secretary and Head of the Home Civil Service. The Wilsonian view of the central architecture thereby saw no need for a formal Prime Minister's Department nor for any tampering with the constitutional or legal position of Secretaries of State. For him, No. 10 and the Cabinet Office will always have separate but complementary functions, with the collective purposes of the Cabinet Office rooted strongly in departments and the Cabinet, its committees and what one might call collective government via correspondence, remaining the formal, symbolic centre of decision-taking.[91] This was very much part of what a sympathetic observer described as Wilson bending, but not breaking, in his efforts to reconcile traditional and tested practices and virtues with the 'Tony wants' phenomenon.[92]

By autumn 1998 this attempted reconciliation was quite apparent,[93] partly because of the Prime Minister's Commons statement on the Wilson Report (which has never been published) in reply to a question from Mrs Gwynneth Dunwoody on 28 July 1998 requesting that he make such a statement 'on the future of the Cabinet Office'.[94] The opening section of Blair's reply was pure Richard Wilson in its approach: 'The role of the Cabinet Office has traditionally been to help the Prime Minister and the Government as a whole to reach collective decisions on Government policy. Since the election, the three principal parts of the centre – my own office, the Cabinet Office and the Treasury – have worked closely and effectively together, and with other Departments, to take forward the Government's comprehensive and ambitious policy agenda.'[95]

Plainly, a deal had been struck between old and new in this very un-Bonapartist preamble. However, the status quo was not enough. The Cabinet Secretary, the Prime Minister told the Commons, had identified weaknesses in the linkages between centre and periphery; policy formulation, implementation and monitoring; Whitehall mechanics and delivery on the ground; forward looks that embraced both difficulty and potential.[96] (Blair has had a considerable and sustained interest in risk and its management and the task force on regulation – under its various guises – led by the businessman and Chairman of Northern Foods, Chris Haskins has produced some valuable material for him on this theme.)[97]

It was during this reshaping the centre phase that the Blair/Wilson approach took a distinctive institutional form. Although it was to be another year before the long-awaited White Paper *Modernising Government* appeared,[98] certain important changes to both the formulation of policies which crossed the boundaries of several departments and the public service itself were put in place long before the document which was expected to pull it all together appeared. (Partly because, in that nasty way the political class has, the black spot was on the Minister for the Civil Service, Dr David Clark, from the moment he entered the Cabinet in May 1997 until the hour of his departure in the summer 1998 reshuffle when he was replaced by the so-called 'Cabinet Enforcer', Dr Jack Cunningham, who himself only lasted a year).

Key to the ever closer fusion between the Prime Minister's Office and the Cabinet Office was to be Mr Blair's version of that Thatcherian phenomenon – government by unit. There was a difference, though, which was evident almost from the moment the Social Exclusion Unit and the Performance and Innovation Unit were created by the Prime Minister (in late 1997 and the summer of 1998, respectively). They were housed in the Cabinet Office but they belonged to Tony Blair, who laid down the tasks and to whom they reported through Richard Wilson. Though similar in many ways to aspects of the old Central Policy Review Staff, not least in the mixture of Whitehall insiders and outsiders who peopled them, they were not constructed as a shared resource for the Cabinet. By autumn 1998 it was widely appreciated that if these two units worked effectively as joiners-up of especially knotty problems which crossed departmental boundaries, they could well be the models for future Cabinet Office operations rather than the traditional Cabinet Secretariat.[99]

This period, too, saw a sharpening of that most brutally effective instrument for scything through departmental autonomy – the public expenditure process. The original PX Cabinet Committee (very similar to

EDX under Major) was to be replaced by a new Cabinet Committee on Public Services and Public Expenditure, PSX. PSX would monitor the public service agreements conducted between the Treasury and departments under the first of the triennial comprehensive spending reviews whereby money was only to be released to departments if they had reached already agreed targets[100] (a hugely important element in the 'command chancellorship' Gordon Brown had constructed alongside Tony Blair's 'command premiership'). The seeds of possibly institutionalized tension between the world of PSX and the kingdom of units in the Cabinet Office was apparent from the moment the Committee was established.[101]

Richard Wilson's Maundy Thursday brief for the Prime Minister also needed to address another area of concern to Blair's people – his own service. Very early on in the Blair years, a seasoned figure in the senior Civil Service said to me: 'If we don't show we can deliver in a couple of years, they will find their own ways of delivering what they want.'[102] This theme kept reappearing in my rolling conversations with the well-placed over those first two years. Another version ran like this: 'The trouble with No. 10 is that they only think of loyalty to Tony. They cannot see civil servants as having loyalty to something higher – the government or the Cabinet collectively (although there is precious little of that)'.[103] Another private appraisal in early 1998 was that the 'one of us' climate ran on from the Conservatives' years in government,[104] though under the Blair team, the emphasis was different – more a thing of 'personalization rather than politicization', as an especially well-placed observer expressed it.[105]

Richard Wilson was sensitive to such matters – and to the relative neglect of his service's craft as policy analysts during the Tory years (though when the guide to good policy-making eventually appeared in the autumn of 1999, it was a disappointingly uninspired and acronymia-laden production).[106] Ahead of this Wilson had, through the Prime Minister's reply to Mrs Dunwoody, announced the setting up of a new Centre for Management and Policy Studies in the Cabinet Office to help create a revived sense of common Whitehall citizenship among senior civil servants while drawing in new thinking from the academic and policy-analysis worlds outside. The Civil Service College was to be moved inside its orbit.[107] There was to be a fusion of the Civil Service management side of the Cabinet Office and the Cabinet Secretariat.[108] A new Civil Service Management Board was to be spun out of the Cabinet Secretary's Wednesday morning meeting of permanent secretaries.[109]

By the autumn of 1998, I had begun the practice of including in my 'overflights' depictions of the circles of influence around the Prime Minister. The trigger for this was the comments of a well-placed insider who had read my first, December 1997, 'overflight'. He suggested that I might consider an entirely different geopolitical model when mapping the geography of power around Tony Blair. 'The real core is No. 10 and No. 11,' he said. But even allowing for the overwhelming importance of what one might call the Downing Street axis, my highly experienced observer suggested that a model of concentric circles fitted the general reality of relationships more than a pyramidical, hierarchical arrangement of the kind usually produced when the traditionally collective Cabinet system is described.

At the turn of 1997/98 he placed the following around the Prime Minister in circle one: Alastair Campbell, Jonathan Powell, John Holmes (the foreign affairs Private Secretary who had replaced Alex Allan as Principal Private Secretary in No. 10 on the latter's departure to Australia as High Commissioner) and David Miliband, head of the No. 10 Policy Unit. In circles two he placed Brown, Irvine and Mandelson (at that time in the Cabinet Office as Minister without Portfolio with a roving, co-ordinating brief). In circle three sat the Deputy Prime Minister and Secretary of State for the Environment, Transport and the Regions, John Prescott. In circle four he placed the Foreign Secretary, Robin Cook, and the Home Secretary, Jack Straw. Circle five contained the remaining members of the Cabinet.[110]

Perhaps unsurprisingly, given the perpetual fascination of both ministers and civil servants with who is up and who is down in Whitehall, the circles of influence attracted a good deal of attention when I first published them and have continued to do so. All agree, including myself, that as geographical expressions of power go, they are imperfect (it depends very much on the matter concerned and what is the issue of the moment). Nevertheless, well-placed figures were keen to help me amend or update the geometrical placings and I was happy to co-ordinate their intelligence. When placed in sequence, the circles of influence were a crude guide to form.

By the time I drew another set in the summer of 1999, a number of quite significant changes were apparent. I reckoned that I should have placed the Cabinet Office minister, Lord Falconer, in circle one the previous autumn even though he was, in terms of the ministerial hierarchy, below the Chancellor of the Duchy of Lancaster and Cabinet 'Enforcer', Dr Jack Cunningham. I should also have included (albeit in brackets, as

Circle one
PM,
Campbell, Powell,
Private Office
and Policy Unit

Circle two Circle one plus Brown, Mandelson and Irvine

Circle three Circles one and two plus Prescott

Circle four Circles one, two and three plus Cook and Straw

Circle five Circles one, two, three and four plus everyone else

Circles of influence: late 1997/early 1998

he held no crown position as either a minister or a civil servant), Philip Gould, the Prime Minister's pollster, focus-grouper, adviser and friend.[111]

Peter Mandelson had gone in the ministerial sense, having resigned over the question of the home loan he had received from his fellow Labour MP and later ministerial colleague, Geoffrey Robinson. Yet I noted in my summer 1999 'overflight' that 'the phone links he has with the Prime Minister continue, I suspect, to be influential'.[112]

In the court model, for that is what the concentric circles implied, I rated as 'important as ever' in circle one, Campbell, Powell, Miliband and the No. 10 Principal Private Secretary (by this time the one for economic affairs, Jeremy Heywood, who had replaced John Holmes on his appointment to the Lisbon embassy).[113] At this stage, I believed Brown to be standing alone in circle two. Irvine was judged to have lost a good deal of influence (for example, on freedom of information, though he chaired the Cabinet committee in which the 1997 White Paper was gelded, the outcome was thought to have illustrated his slipping as he had been unable to resist the bladework of Straw after the Home Office had grabbed the lead on FOI from the Cabinet Office when Clark was sacked and No. 10 had backed Straw on the issue). For when it came to full-blooded freedom of information, it was very much a question of what Tony does *not* want.[114] In circle three I placed Prescott and the Cabinet Secretary, Richard Wilson, as hugely important figures but not exactly 'one of us', or one of 'Tony's people' as its Blairite manifestation was best described. Irvine, I reckoned, had joined Cook and Straw in circle four. The rest remained in circle five.[115]

As the century turned, little had changed in the land of the circles apart from the return of Peter Mandelson, who had rejoined the Cabinet as Secretary of State for Northern Ireland the previous October. There was some debate about where he was best placed. Some put him in circle two with Brown; others in three 'as he's still doing his time' to some extent.[116] I plumped for three. There were those who argued that Robin Cook's place in circle four was tenuous, given what I suspected would be his temporary isolation on Britain and the euro (as a convinced single-currency man) as this was a matter of enthusiasm and emphasis rather than fundamental policy differences.[117] Circle one was the same as in the previous 'overflight'. Lord Falconer, though still only a middle-ranking Cabinet Office minister and for all the flak he was enduring as 'Minister for the Millennium Dome', was as centrally placed as ever. People tended to put Campbell in pole position above all others in terms of policy and

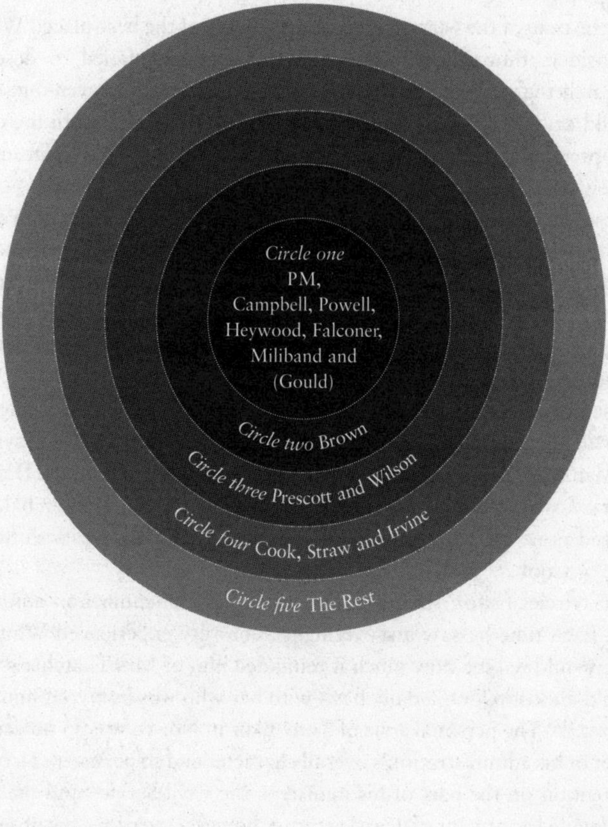

Circle one
PM,
Campbell, Powell,
Heywood, Falconer,
Miliband and
(Gould)

Circle two Brown

Circle three Prescott and Wilson

Circle four Cook, Straw and Irvine

Circle five The Rest

Circles of influence: summer 1999

presentation influence,[118] but Charlie Falconer, the PM's old flat-mate, was widely thought to be 'the one above all others that the Prime Minister opens up his heart to'.[119]

Taking to the air in the spring 2000, the circles looked to me as shown on page 500.

By the time of the March 2000 Budget, some of the best-placed White-hall insiders thought that my geometric approach failed to describe adequately the very special position of Gordon Brown. One even suggested I should draw a dumbell with circles of influence around both the command premier and the command chancellor.[120] Instead I have placed him in a new pattern – circle one-and-a-half.

Peter Mandelson, my observers told me, was further in now than circle three and would remain so, given his role as strategist for the election widely expected for the spring or early summer of 2001. Furthermore, his regular early morning phone call from Belfast to No. 10 indicated a policy and general advice role far beyond that associated with his Northern Ireland Secretaryship.[121]

One or two contenders for circle four had been mooted, including two of the 'delivery ministers' – David Blunkett at Education and Employment and Alan Milburn at Health. On party matters, Geoff Hoon, the Defence Secretary, was also thought to be increasingly influential. But, on balance, I judged none of these three yet to be on an influence par with Straw, Irvine or Cook.[122]

The 'circles factor' should not be treated as a phenomenon unique to Blair. Each time he saw an 'overflight', one very experienced Whitehall figure would tell me how much it reminded him of Mrs Thatcher's time: 'I could almost tell on a daily basis with her who was in favour and who was not.'[123] The personal style of Tony Blair in No. 10 was so powerful a shaper of his administration's overall character and so persistent an object of attention on the part of his ministers, the Civil Service and the press that detailed treatment of it is imperative, however overdone the obsession with personality may or may not appear with hindsight. What of those other, more concealed 'inner loop' factors that are so often revealing about the flavour of a premiership?

On nuclear weapons policy, Blair and his ministers had some serious decisions to take as part of the Strategic Defence Review which absorbed significant time during their first year in office. He used a ministerial group, not a Cabinet committee, rather in the style of Jim Callaghan.[124] It consisted of himself in the chair; George Robertson, Defence Secretary;

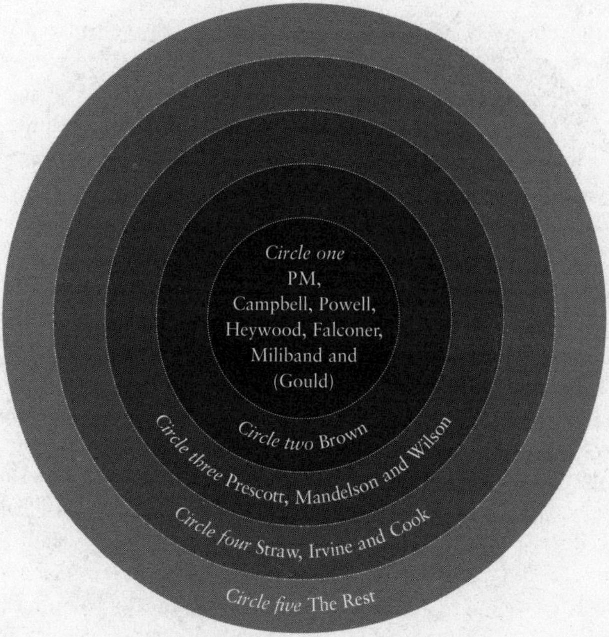

Circle one
PM,
Campbell, Powell,
Heywood, Falconer,
Miliband and
(Gould)

Circle two Brown

Circle three Prescott, Mandelson and Wilson

Circle four Straw, Irvine and Cook

Circle five The Rest

Circles of influence: late 1999

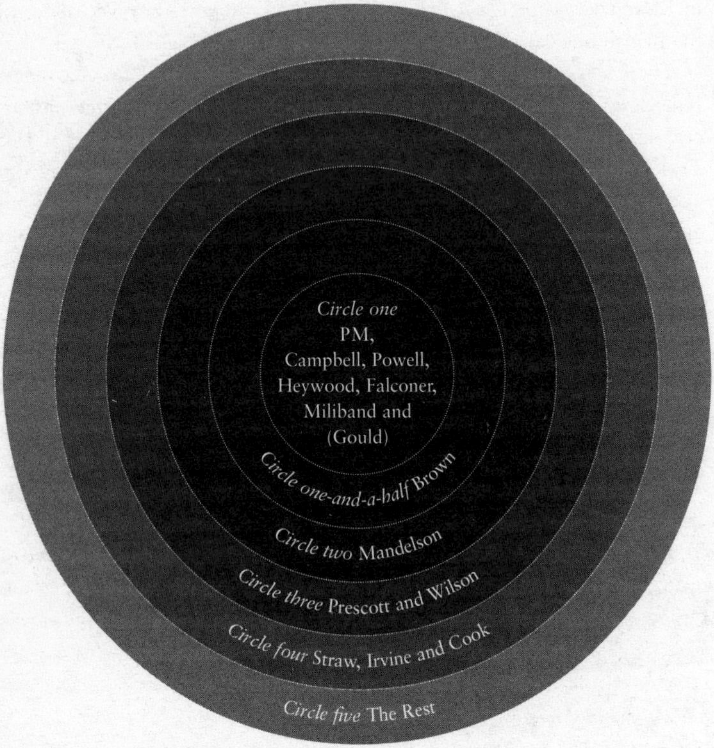

Circle one
PM,
Campbell, Powell,
Heywood, Falconer,
Miliband and
(Gould)

Circle one-and-a-half Brown

Circle two Mandelson

Circle three Prescott and Wilson

Circle four Straw, Irvine and Cook

Circle five The Rest

Circles of influence: spring 2000

Robin Cook, Foreign Secretary; Gordon Brown, Chancellor of the Exchequer; and John Prescott in his capacity as Deputy Prime Minister.[125] Once the RAF decommissioned the last of its WE177 gravity hydrogen bombs in March 1998, the Trident submarine force became the sole carrier of the British nuclear weapons capability.[126]

There was never any doubt about the continuation of a strategic deterrent, despite the presence in Blair's ministerial group of the former unilateral disarmer, Robin Cook. The group authorized the completion of four Trident boats but reduced their planned warhead stock by a third from 300 to 200,[127] and disclosed the size of the UK stockpiles of plutonium and uranium available to prime them[128] (this was a first) when the review's results were presented to Parliament in July 1998.

There was also a change in 'operating posture' that was announced with another dash of unaccustomed openness. 'We intend', the *Strategic Defence Review* White Paper declared,

to maintain continuous at sea deterrent patrols, not least to avoid misunderstanding or escalation if a Trident submarine were to sail during a period of crisis. But the relaxation of tension and vast improvement in current strategic conditions since the end of the Cold War also permit us to adopt a reduced day-to-day alert state.

We will have only one submarine on patrol at a time, carrying a reduced load of 48 warheads. This compares with the previous Government's announced ceiling of 96 ... Although Trident is now our only nuclear weapon and covers both strategic and sub-strategic requirements, the potential explosive power deployed on a Trident submarine is one third less than a Polaris submarine armed with Chevaline [the improved Polaris system].[129]

No longer would the Royal Navy target its nuclear warheads on the former Soviet Union. Henceforth it would sail with 'several days' "notice to fire"' required, though the Navy would ensure 'that we can restore a higher state of alert should this became necessary at any time'.[130] In Ernie Bevin language, there would be 'a bloody union jack' atop a British-owned nuclear weapon well into the 2020s (unless a decision to disarm completely should be taken in the meantime).

On intelligence matters, Tony Blair is perceived as a thoughtful and generally appreciative customer of the product of the secret world.[131] For obvious reasons, the intelligence feed on Northern Ireland has been a swift and continuous element in his special intelligence box. And on Irish policy, an element of prime ministerialism was necessary and justifiable in the long slog to the 1998 Good Friday Agreement and the precarious process towards the creation of a devolved executive in Belfast in December 1999, its temporary 'collapse' of the following month, its restoration in June 2000 and beyond. Like every Prime Minister since Wilson set up his special Cabinet Committee on Northern Ireland in 1969 and rejigged intelligence arrangements to supply it, Blair had to keep a constant eye on the great intractable.

He had a bespoke Cabinet committee on Northern Ireland (IN) which consisted of himself, Brown, Cook, Straw, the Secretary of State for Northern Ireland Mo Mowlam (and her successor Peter Mandelson, from October 1999) and Robertson (Geoff Hoon from October 1999).[132] Much of the policy, however, was formulated (again justifiably) outside the formal Cabinet committee with several of Blair's No. 10 people (Jonathan Powell throughout; John Holmes and John Sawers as the foreign affairs private secretaries) having a personal input and role.[133] Blair created a Cabinet Committee on the Intelligence Services (CSI) but, as far as I have been able to discover, it has never met,[134] its business being conducted by correspondence between its members (Blair, Prescott, Brown, Cook, Straw and the Secretary of State for Defence George Robertson, and later his successor Geoff Hoon; strangely, the Northern Ireland Secretary was not a member in either the Mowlam or the Mandelson era).[135]

At the end of 1999 there were signs that Mr Blair was toying with the idea of ending the traditional (and much-prized) distinction between intelligence analysis and policy advice, the absence of which the British intelligence community has long believed weakened the business (for different reasons) in both the United States and the USSR (and its successor states).[136] It was consistent with the Blair style for him to want material which presented a point of view, but there were distinct signs in early 2000 that the foreign, defence and intelligence communities were determined to resist this.[137] Overall, however, Blair and his ministers within the intelligence loop showed during the first comprehensive spending review in 1997 that they wanted at the very least to maintain the UK's existing global intelligence reach, albeit on a slightly reduced budget.[138]

For reasons quite separate from Northern Ireland, Blair acquired a swift familiarity with the fusion of foreign and defence policy and intelligence that is triggered by military conflict. He was the first post-1945 premier to have presided over two wars in the space of six months (if you exclude the kind of colonial emergencies which were running at the same time as Korea or Suez). And wars, as we have seen, have often proved both testers of prime ministerial mettle and considerable revealers of prime ministerial style. Since Whitehall was caught short by the Argentinian invasion of the Falklands, what might be called a 'War Cabinet War Book' has been kept in good condition in the Cabinet Office.[139]

Would Tony Blair, not a natural Cabinet committee type as the Cabinet Secretariat well knew, revert to the more traditional practices for the very serious business of managing a crisis which might involve the deployment of British armed forces in hostile circumstances? It transpired that the War Cabinet equivalent of a mixed economy was adopted – a special hybrid of Hankeyism and the Blair style. It was a classic manifestation, too, of the Richard Wilson approach of marrying the requirement of clear, crisp and properly minuted decision-taking to the faster, looser policy-making groupings the Prime Minister prefers.

To his credit, Blair had sought and received the specific approval of the House of Commons in February 1998 for the use of military force against Iraq should the need arise (to the conspicuous approbation of Tony Benn, who pointed out that no previous post-1945 premier had done this).[140] But he did not seek to refresh it as the crisis recrudesced towards the end of the year.[141] Before the RAF Tornados flew against Iraq in Gulf War II in December 1998 (though constant sorties and frequent engagements were a feature of the RAF's part in enforcing the 'no-fly' zones in Iraq before and after this), the Cabinet's Defence and Overseas Policy Committee met more than once on the crisis and approved the use of force against Iraq.[142]

During the four days of military action, decision-taking moved into smaller groups in accordance with plans already laid (part of Richard Wilson's hybrid approach). The first gathering of the day took place at 8.00 a.m. in PINDAR, the underground operations room beneath the Ministry of Defence main building. Known as 'The Secretary of State's Meeting', it was chaired by Robertson and included the Chief of the Defence Staff, Sir Charles Guthrie, senior military, defence officials and senior figures from the intelligence community. The meeting had before it the latest assessment from the Joint Intelligence Committee's Middle East Current Intelligence Group which worked through the night to prepare it.[143] PINDAR has a direct televisual link with the joint operational headquarters in its Northwood bunker under the Chilterns.

At the conclusion of this session, Robertson and Guthrie crossed Whitehall to No. 10 to take part in what was known as 'The Prime Minister's Group on Iraq'. Effectively this was a slimmed-down version of the

Cabinet's Defence and Overseas Policy Committee. Though it was not designated as a sub-group of that committee (as Thatcher's Falklands 'War Cabinet' and Major's during Gulf War I had been), the Cabinet Secretariat, led by Richard Wilson and the head of the Overseas and Defence Secretariat, Michael Pakenham, serviced it and took the minutes, thereby cladding the Blair style in the traditional masonry of the more collective processes of old.[144] The group met in Mr Blair's study, the old Principal Private Secretary's Office which adjoins the Cabinet Room. It consisted of the Prime Minister in the chair; the Foreign Secretary, Robin Cook; plus Robertson and Guthrie. Also in attendance were Powell, John Holmes and Campbell. The Attorney General, John Morris, and the Deputy Prime Minister, John Prescott, occasionally joined the group.[145]

As one insider suggested: 'You could say it was a mini version of a War Cabinet. Only the people who needed to be were there but with a proper organic link to the Cabinet. Everything was properly minuted and all the proper processes were followed.'[146] Note the emphasis placed on the word 'proper'. On the last day of the air attacks on Baghdad and areas outside the southern no-fly zone, the Prime Minister joined the 8.00 a.m. meeting in PINDAR and had his photo taken.

It was evident that the Balkans War was likely to be both a bigger and a more perilous matter. It appears that the Whitehall intelligence machine did its job, though some of its customers say it was, like everyone else, less good on end-games. As one insider put it: 'The intelligence was spot on but it wasn't always welcome.'[147]

Of pre-war Balkans intelligence another insider said a variety of threats and uncertainties were envisaged but the notion of a quick, two-day air war was 'not a view strongly espoused over here' (i.e., as opposed to Washington).[148] A third said: 'Ministers went into this with their eyes open.' He paused and added, 'You have to remember that the PM is a conviction politician.'[149] This preaching-heavier-than-our-weight was a hugely important factor throughout the war against Milosevic, and commentators such as Peter Riddell were right to stress the wider importance of the Blair approach to the spectrum that runs through diplomacy to war as outlined in the Prime Minister's 'doctrine of international community' speech in Chicago on 22 April 1999.[150]

So how did Mr Blair run his Balkans War machine? Essentially it was another version of the Wilson hybrid. The Cabinet's Defence and Overseas Policy Committee met more than once in the weeks before the air raids began to approve a British contribution to the use of NATO force against

Serbia if Milosevic failed to meet the terms laid out at the second Rambouillet Conference.[151] The full Cabinet was reported to by the Prime Minister and the Foreign Secretary regularly as Rambouillet II proceeded and in the period between the end of the talks in Paris and the first NATO air strikes on 24 March.[152] As one Cabinet minister, who was not a member of the Defence and Overseas Policy Committee, put it to me a trifle ruefully as the air war was about to begin: 'Like everyone else, I didn't expect to find myself sitting in War Cabinets. But we have had more discussions on Serbia/Kosovo than anything else. Tony has made sure there have been regular updates. We have had far more opportunity for discussion in Cabinet on Kosovo than on the Budget.'[153]

Once the war began, a daily sequence of meetings managed the British input into NATO operations and the media presentation of the conflict. This time the Balkans Current Intelligence Group of the JIC provided the continuous assessment service (and the full Joint Intelligence Committee had special extra meetings on the war in addition to its regular Wednesday afternoon sessions).[154] At 8.00 each morning the Chiefs of Staff met in PINDAR with senior Defence Ministry officials and intelligence figures.[155] (By tradition, all four chiefs had briefed the full Cabinet together before previous substantial wars. But the tradition was broken on this occasion and no such briefing took place.)[156]

At 8.30 George Robertson would join them and the group would transmogrify into 'The Secretary of State's Meeting' with officials present from the Foreign Office, the Cabinet Office and the Treasury. Sometimes Robin Cook would be there, as would Clare Short, the Secretary of State for International Development, if refugee issues were to be discussed. A range of questions would be covered including preparations for the Prime Minister's meeting at 10.00 and the Ministry of Defence's daily press conference at 11.30, in which a variety of ministers and senior military figures took part as the conflict progressed before a worldwide television audience which was estimated to be 200 million at its peak. At the conclusion of 'The Secretary of State's Meeting', Robertson and Guthrie would pass beneath Whitehall, using this time the underground tunnel which links the MOD with the Cabinet Office, thus avoiding demonstrations in the street above.[157]

'The Prime Minister's Group on Kosovo' was, like its Gulf War II equivalent, essentially a slimmed-down Defence and Overseas Policy Committee, another Wilsonian hybrid, with the Cabinet Secretariat organizing the business. It met either in the PM's study or in the Cabinet Room, according to the numbers involved. Once more at its core were the War

Cabinet quartet of Blair, Cook, Robertson and Guthrie. Morris, the Attorney General, would attend when certain legal or targeting matters were under discussion. Powell, Campbell and John Sawers, the PM's foreign affairs Private Secretary, also attended.[158]

For the first three weeks of the war, meetings of the Prime Minister's Group were punctuated by absences for the Special European Council, for Mr Blair's negotiating sessions in Northern Ireland and by the Easter weekend. Thereafter, the morning sequence was more constant and it was supplemented by a once- or twice-weekly meeting of the full Defence and Overseas Policy Committee, which consisted of the PM's War Cabinet quartet plus John Prescott, Clare Short and a Treasury minister (either Brown himself or, as often as not, the Chief Secretary, Alan Milburn, who deputized for him). The Chancellor did not seem to take much direct interest in the prosecution of the war, though the Treasury kept a close eye on its costs, immediate and long-term.[159] The weekly meetings of the full Cabinet devoted about a quarter of their time to the war. Blair, Cook and Robertson would report. Discussion was lively but in a spirit of inquiry rather than dissent. At no time did a Cabinet Minister speak out in the Cabinet Room against the military-political action being taken during the eleven-week campaign, though some were seriously worried in private.[160]

So what did the handling of the Balkans War tell us about the Blair style? It underlined the blend of custom and practice and the desire for smaller, leaner decision-taking patterns. As one careful observer expressed it:

'Although the operation showed the PM's preference for operating on a daily basis in small groups, it also showed the endurance of the entrenched constitutional system whereby the "inner war cabinet" was linked continuously by less frequent meetings of DOP and the Cabinet itself overseeing a variety of subject-specific official groups.'[161]

In terms of the wider picture of the Blair style, the Balkans War had another impact which cut against the norms of that 'entrenched constitutional system' based on collective government.

For quite simply, as one insider connoisseur put it, despite the Prime Minister's careful avoidance of postwar triumphalism, his conduct of the British part of the conflict and his prominence within the NATO coalition showed that any residual notion of Tony Blair as *'primus inter pares* is wrong. The Prime Minister is not *pares*. He's way above that. Like Caesar, he bestrides his world like a Colossus.'[162] Another seasoned figure said simply, 'Because of the war, presidential government is more extreme than ever now.'[163] For a third very well-placed witness: 'In the early days of the war, Blair was flying blind. But by the middle to the end of May [1999] he knew exactly where he wanted to go and had created the means of getting there in a hugely impressive way. He was tired and he was impatient, but it was the making of him as Prime Minister. Awesome.'[164]

Awesome, perhaps. But worrying, certainly. When the Gulf and Balkans war-dissenter, the incomparably independent Tam Dalyell, raised the Blair tendency towards the Napoleonic in a critical spirit and called for the restoration of Cabinet government at a meeting of the Parliamentary Labour Party in June 1999, the Prime Minister merely smiled and raised his eyes as if to say 'it's just Tam being Tam'.[165] When the political correspondents heard about it, they were informed by 'Labour officials' that all the eighteen other MPs who spoke at the gathering had 'backed' Mr Blair,[166] underscoring rather neatly, I thought, the point Mr Dalyell was making.

There are several worrying features about excessive prime ministerialism in the conduct of British central government. It cuts against the collective grain, which runs that way for a purpose – as just about the only barrier against undesirable accumulation of power which can all too easily accrue around a single figure under Britain's constitutional arrangements. An excessive focus on the premier can both overburden the Prime Minister (Mr Blair acknowledged publicly that he found the job 'remorseless' just before the Balkans War began)[167] and, in the words an American journalist applied to President Clinton during the conflict, 'threaten to drain the political oxygen available for other projects'[168] if the head of government is faced by too many huge sappers of time and energy simultaneously. Mr Blair had no shortage of these in the spring of 1999. Kosovo and Northern Ireland alone were enough to induce the oxygen starvation effect. The Prime Minister was in danger of wearing himself out, as Roy Jenkins wrote of Mr Gladstone, in 'fighting his endless battle for the victory of activity over time'.[169]

Peter Mandelson himself said shortly after losing office in December 1998 that he had learned 'that it is departments [rather than the centre] that deliver 90 per cent and more of the Government's policies. That's where the officials are. That's where the leadership needs to be shown.'[170] It was this aspect of the Blair style that worried Jim Callaghan. According to Lord Richard, who led the Lords for the Blair government until the summer 1998 reshuffle when he was replaced by Callaghan's daughter, Margaret Jay, 'Jim does not approve. He does not approve at all. He doesn't think that is what a Prime Minister should do. He thinks the departments should be left to get on with it and the Prime Minister should watch. The risk is that Blair could burn himself out.'[171]

Callaghan, who has had more than one chance to put his points directly to his young successor-but-four as Labour Leader (even though Blair summoned Lady Thatcher to No. 10 for a chat before he called in Callaghan – 'Always leave yourself a way out', she told him),[172] went public with his concerns about the Blair style as the century turned. He urged Mr Blair to give Cabinet ministers a greater role in decision-making as he would need their support and loyalty when times got hard.[173]

There is a paradox at the heart of the Blair style, however, which his insider defenders deploy at such moments of serious criticism from experienced figures. How can he be a control freak running a command premiership, their argument runs. Hasn't he presided over a government which has dispersed more power in its first three years than any in history? And don't forget the Brown factor. Has there ever been a greater degree of *de facto* power-sharing between a Prime Minister and a Chancellor of the Exchequer? To which I think the answer is 'True – but.'

Let us consider constitutional reform first, the factor which makes the Blair administration utterly and unarguably different from all its predecessors. A year into the life of the government, I took to the boards at the Burrell Collection in Glasgow to do an assessment for a Lloyds TSB Forum on progress so far and the long-term implications of what I called the 're-engineering of the state in flight'. There was, I declared, no precedent since 1688 for such a concentrated and deliberate rebuilding of the constitutional architecture which equalled, perhaps surpassed, the nineteenth- and early-twentieth-century surges of franchise reform.[174] I wondered why this extraordinary enterprise lacked the central position it deserved in both the popular impression and self-image of this most image-conscious of administrations.

Before setting out to tackle this question, I simply listed the changes already in place, in the process of implementation or planned. They were:

- Devolution to Scotland and Wales.
- Incorporation of the European Convention on Human Rights into domestic UK law.

- A possibility of an entirely new configuration within the British Isles that reflects a transformed relationship between the north and south of Ireland overseen by both the Irish Republic and the reshaped United Kingdom.
- A Freedom of Information Act for central and local government and virtually all public bodies.
- A strategic authority and an elected mayor for London.
- Regional development agencies for England as a precursor of possible devolution to English regional assemblies during a second Parliament should Labour win again.
- Reform of the House of Lords in at least one and perhaps two or more stages.
- A rolling programme of modernization for the House of Commons.
- A commission on electoral reform for the Westminster Parliament.
- A Joint Consultative Cabinet committee with the Liberal Democrats on matters of mutual (and largely constitutional) interest as a stop short of the coalition Mr Blair toyed with before and, for a time, after the 1997 election.[175]
- A reshaping of the practices of the centre of central government to reflect the Blair style of administration.

On top of this mighty agenda, I noted, we already had:

- A new, more proportional system of election to the European Parliament.
- The Neill Committee, Mark II of Nolan, engaged upon a rewriting of the rules governing the funding of British political parties.[176]
- The incorporation of the European Union's Social Chapter.
- Preparations for the pound's eventual disappearance into a single European currency of which phase one – the transfer of responsibility for setting interest rates from the Treasury to the Monetary Policy Committee of the Bank of England – has already produced the greatest single change in the UK's economic policy-making since, in Keynes' words, 'we threw good housekeeping to the winds'[177] during World War II.

Merely to list the agenda – in the style of a recitation from a telephone directory – is to take the breath away. These reforms, as Sir Richard Wilson aptly put it, would have a 'perpetually profound' effect on government.[178]

Senior civil servants and the judiciary had an acute sense of the combined effect of these reforms, so why not the political class (including a high proportion of the membership of the Blair government)? There were several reasons why the magnitude and enduring significance of this combined endeavour were not, at the end of Blair's first year, widely appreciated. Strangely enough, one has to start with its political engineers – ministers themselves from the Prime Minister (who chairs the overarching Cabinet Committee on Constitutional Reform Policy, CRP)[179] down. CRP's terms of reference describe it as a 'strategic' body yet, quite deliberately, ministers decided not to issue a declaratory White Paper embracing, describing and linking the whole rolling process.[180] One insider told me it was as well that they did not, for ministers might well have recoiled from the purpose and the prospect had they appreciated the programme *in toto*.[181]

Why was this? As another well-placed Whitehall insider put it: 'Most of the senior ministers involved in constitutional reform either don't believe in it, aren't interested in it or don't understand it.'[182] Interestingly, the Prime Minister himself was included amongst the sceptics by this source as was the Home Secretary, Jack Straw.[183] 'Derry Irvine', my informant continued, 'didn't know very much about it at the start but has become very much excited about it.'[184] Lord Irvine indeed confessed to Marcel Berlins in 'A Man for All Roles', a highly revealing BBC Radio 4 documentary on the 'Derry phenomenon' broadcast in April 1998, that 'I'm having the time of my life doing it.'[185]

The root of the problem, I think was this: ministers and the political class generally were treating the government's constitutional reform programme as a restructuring of an *existing* political culture rather than seeing it as the cultural transformer it was almost certainly going to be. There was an element, even among those on the Cabinet committee, of 'we've sorted devolution, now let's move on to human rights and freedom of information and, when they're in the bag, we'll fix the House of Lords, or at least the blue bloods deliquescing on the red benches'. This is the Tommy Cooper – or the 'just like that' – school of reform at work.

But it was not, will not and cannot be like that. Take the creation of a Scottish Parliament in 1999. It marked only the beginning of a protracted negotiation and a series of adjustments between Westminster/Whitehall and Edinburgh. From the outset one had a sense of this from the 'Concordats' drawn up by the Cabinet Office to map out the procedural side of the relationship between Westminster/Whitehall and the devolved assemblies for the purpose establishing, as the Concordats put it, 'the confidence that working relationships will be conducted properly and in accordance with agreed processes such as adequate consultation'. (I'm quoting here from the Welsh Concordats, which, like the Scottish ones, were made available in the House of Commons Library.)[186] They covered legislative and executive action, a policy of 'no surprises', exchange of information and data, joint working on Whitehall and other official committees, liaison on European Union matters, financial relationships, confidentiality and arrangements for resolving disagreements about any matters related to the concordat. They were 'non-statutory and are not intended to be legally enforceable contracts between the parties'.[187]

This area was hugely significant yet scarcely mentioned. Why were the Concordats important? First, the ultimate arbitrator in the Scottish–Whitehall/Westminster context – the Judicial Committee of the Privy Council – was intended to be a body of last resort. It was the Concordats which were meant to take the strain. And yet they only will if relationships are relatively harmonious. The edifice of devolution is very largely constructed on the harmony model. But that desirable state of affairs cannot be guaranteed. Far from it. And, if it does go wrong, the Prime Minister will be central to the resulting conflict management as the *Memorandum of Understanding* on the operation of the Joint Ministerial Committee made plain when it was published in October 1999, describing Blair's role as chairman of the plenary sessions of the JMC.[188]

Already in the late summer of 1998, the Prime Minister's spokesman, Alastair Campbell, was reflecting his boss's sense of 'constitutional overload'.[189] A year later the avoidance of 'gridlock' was the great phrase one heard in No. 10, which boded ill for the prospects of electoral reform for Westminster (Mr Blair was very irritated by those coalition governments among the NATO allies who had to broker deals back home before deciding on the line to take on Kosovo).[190] The 'gridlock' aversion was powerfully fed in late 1999 and early 2000 by disagreements with the Scottish Executive about student fees and beef and with the Welsh administration over both beef and the travails of its first Chief Minister, Alun Michael.[191] And 'gridlock' avoidance was a hugely powerful factor in watering down the proposed freedom of information legislation to maximize Whitehall's continuing control over disclosure.[192]

Robert Hazell, the former Home Office civil servant who directs the Constitution Unit at University College, London, told the Commons Public Administration Committee in the summer of 1999 that: 'The Government still does not fully understand the difference between open government and freedom of information. Open government means the Government publishing information largely for its own purposes: information that the Government thinks we need to know or might like to know. Freedom of information requires the Government to disclose information which we decide for ourselves we want to know.'[193]

I think the Prime Minister and Jack Straw understood the difference only too well. As Straw put it privately: 'Freedom of information is for oppositions, not for governments.'[194] And a very senior Whitehall official, reflecting the centre's view, said of the FOI question and the retreat from the 1997 White Paper: 'We only just got it back in time.'[195] Mr Blair is not known for his sense of history (political biographies apart). What he most certainly could not contemplate is what Sir John Browne, Chief Executive Officer of BP Amoco (whom he much admires), describes as 'accelerated history'[196] (which is my own favourite definition of freedom of information, implying as it does sufficent release of policy material to avoid the gaps in knowledge which, under the British system, have all too often yawned until files are opened under the thirty-year norm).

The reaction to what he saw as excessive openness was illustrative of the Blair approach to constitutional reform – his spasmodic attention to it often, though not invariably, stimulated by irritation. As Peter Riddell put it in March 2000, the Prime Minister

has an aversion to talking about the constitution. In nearly three years as Prime Minister, he has not made a single speech on the programme which has been the subject of at least 20 major Acts or Bills since 1997. He refers sometimes to the end of the hereditary peers and to what he calls 'the biggest ever decentralisation of government', but never to the constitution as such.

This glaring gap can be explained by Mr Blair's lack of interest in pledges largely made by his predecessor [John Smith], his confidence in Lord Irvine . . . and Jack Straw to handle these matters, and his belief that voters do not really care about constitutional matters . . .[197]

The voters in England may not, but a premier who has presided over the writing of a new Constitution (the constitutional statutes themselves plus development of a process under way in Major's time of shifting conventions from the back of an envelope to the back of a code) shows a remarkable insouciance in giving this transforming scene such a low salience in his public utterances.

Power-sharing with his Chancellor of the Exchequer, however, was a matter of daily importance, and the Blair–Brown partnership was as much the bedrock of the government as the Attlee–Bevin axis between 1945 and 1950. We have already seen the centrality of their regular bilaterals to the government's economic policy. But there is much more to it than that. Brown is, in effect, overlord of the economic and domestic front. It is a bi-stellar administration with policy constellations revolving round the two stars in Downing Street. It was an old Cabinet Office hand, Jonathan Charkham, who first alerted me to the policy range encompassed by Brown's Budgets – a scope imaginable only for Prime Ministers before the late 1990s. Mr Charkham saw Brown as comparable to a French Prime Minister with Blair as a kind of Fifth Republic President,[198] an impression powerfully underscored in the Chancellor's speech to the Institute for Fiscal Studies in May 1999.[199]

The *operational* key to Brown's reach, as opposed to his *personal* power as the second biggest beast on the New Labour terrain, was the new wiring of control installed as part of the triennial comprehensive spending reviews. The public service agreements that underpin the implementation of the CSR process ensure that departments only receive their next tranche of finance if the Treasury is satisfied they have already achieved the policy outcomes outlined by their time-table agreed in advance and monitored by the PSX Cabinet Committee which Brown chairs.[200] This leaves Brown with the most detailed power over policy of any Chancellor since 1945, with the Treasury's tentacles exerting an unprecedented sway within departments.

The rival Blair and Brown courts may engage in a good deal of mutual bad-mouthing, and Brown has always been a somewhat solitary, moody and prickly politician, but the two principals make an extraordinarily effective combination. The final stages of the first Comprehensive Spending Review in 1998 was very much a No. 10–Treasury business.[201] There was precious little collegiality about it, despite the existence of PSX (and the Cabinet's Economic Committee, EA, which is supposed to consider issues affecting the government's wider economic policy, rarely meets).[202] As David Lipsey put it:

the CSR was a triumph for a strong prime minister and a strong chancellor, working together. Nothing illustrates this more clearly than the brutality of its execution. The two just called in ministers and told them how much they were getting. There was no appeal.[203]

For all the plethora of governmental departments and units active on welfare-to-work questions (including the hugely productive Social Exclusion Unit in the Cabinet Office),[204] the reality is that Gordon Brown's 'command chancellorship' is the ultimate arbiter of what does or does not happen domestically on any serious scale unless the Prime Minister chooses to moderate the Treasury's wishes to some degree.

It took some time for the nuances, though not the prevailing style, of the Blair approach to become apparent – as with all new and would-be transforming administrations. ('We do not simply exist to govern. We are there to transform,' Blair told the activists gathered to celebrate the centenary of the formation of the Labour Representation Committee in February 2000.)[205]

In fact, it took longer than the two years that key insiders had envisaged for the internal Whitehall operating patterns of the Blair premiership to become apparent. The *Modernising Government* White Paper was a considerable disappointment in this regard when it finally appeared at the end of March 1999, with all eyes on Kosovo rather than on the alleged beauties of joined-up government.[206] Blair's people insisted that it contain a scattering of eye-catching pledges (they rewrote its front end almost at the last minute) and it is replete with both new public management argot and Billy Graham-style testimonies of various breakthroughs on the customer-care front. The whole production smacked of a mixture of Pollyanna and piety which caused in me an almost involuntary recoil, not least because it poured shamelessly and unforgivably off the wordprocessers of what is probably the most literate Civil Service in the world.[207]

Yet some nine months later, a degree of relative clarity was possible. It was not until the New Year 1999–2000 that the new style of government was anything like fully fleshed out, in a revealing pair of documents, the first a report from Sir Richard Wilson to the Prime Minister on *Civil Service Reform*,[208] the second, *Wiring It Up*,[209] the study Tony Blair had commissioned from the Performance and Innovation Unit on 'Whitehall's Management of Cross-Cutting Policies and Services'.[210] Sandwiched between these two significant publications there came, interestingly enough, a document from the Neill Committee on Standards in Public Life entitled *Reinforcing Standards*[211] (Lord Neill of Bladen had replaced Lord Nolan in the chair) which analysed and tackled head-on several of the post-May 1997 changes which brought with them a range of awkward constitutional and procedural implications. Lord Neill and his colleagues were concerned about the extension of special adviserdom within the policy-making structures of government and the downgrading of traditional Civil Service advice which some insiders saw as its accompaniment.

The first weeks of the new century, therefore, marked a good point at which to reach some interim conclusions about the Blair impact on the practices of British central government. This was a moment of added piquancy given the conjunction of the Prime Minister's first thousand days[212] with largely (though not wholly) inflated claims both that we were dealing with a peacetime Prime Minister like no other in his focus on outcomes and ruthless disdain for traditional government practices in pursuit of them,[213] and newspaper stories arguing that the bloom had finally worn off the shining hours of May 1997. The Prime Minister's tetchily defiant speech on 21 January 2000 at a school in Forest Gate, East London – during which he declared that he would not be distracted by the 'forces of conservatism and reaction, left or right'[214] – will be treated, I suspect, as a milestone in the progress of his premiership. And Blair's people, not too long before, had firmly linked his governing style with his determination not to be deflected.

The view in No. 10 is that the purpose of the Prime Minister's personal involvement in the annual work programmes he agrees with each Cabinet minister and their Permanent Secretaries is a deliberate and important method of avoiding drift and distraction. For example, though the war in the Balkans had absorbed about 90 per cent of the Prime Minister's time at its height, it was regarded by those in the inner loop as a vindication of the Blair style of government because, thanks to the agreements with ministers and Permanent Secretaries at the head of each department, they could forge ahead on agreed policy lines even when the Prime Minister's thoughts were devoted to the skies above Kosovo and Serbia and tackling gridlock within NATO's decision-making processes.[215]

The centrality of public service reforms to the effectiveness and durability of the Blair style (and the high level of No. 10's input into their shaping) means, I think, that we are witnessing a fusion, albeit unplanned and far from joined up, of several governing approaches – a mixture of the Wilson–sponsored Fulton Report on the Civil Service of 1968,[216] Heath's *The Re-organisation of Central Government* White Paper of 1970,[217] Mrs Thatcher's approach to innovation through unit (her Rayner-designed Efficiency Unit being the most glowing memory here)[218] and Major's Citizen's Charter-style emphasis on improved service delivery on the ground.[219] The whole programme has been driven through without regard to the niceties of traditional Cabinet structures, the differences of function between permanent officials and temporary special advisers or any great sensitivity towards Parliament.

Quite apart from the critical question of 'will it work?', the 'revolutionary' adjective could be applied by the turn of the century to certain sustained aspects of the Blair approach, notably the demise of anything approaching a genuine system of Cabinet government. We have seen, too, the tacit abandonment of the robust idea that the Cabinet Office, unlike No. 10, is a shared resource belonging to ministers collectively rather than the Prime Minister exclusively. It has been a question of ever closer fusion since May 1997, though Sir Richard Wilson continued to see himself as the servant of the Cabinet as a whole, as a hyphen linking the Blair Centre with the departmental periphery and a holder of the ring when disputes require resolution.[220] His hyphenating role, as one might call it, placed Sir Richard in an awkward position (albeit one which has fallen, to some degree, to all previous holders of the Cabinet Secretaryship). To some traditionalists he is seen as too much of a flexible friend of the Prime Minister and Blair's people ('the kids in No. 10', as the more acid old sweats in Whitehall call them).[221] To some of the young and politically upwardly mobile who have done well out of Mr Blair's patronage, Sir Richard, far from being a courtier of the new, is, for all his charm, a ruthless sustainer of the old beneath that engaging smile and modernizing language.[222]

The *Modernising Government* White Paper and Sir Richard's evidence to the Neill Committee on the *non*-politicization of the senior Civil Service,[223] and the revarnishing in the Neill Report of a career profession recruited and promoted on merit,[224] *and* Sir Richard's reform action plan for the Prime Minister[225] can all be seen (and are seen) by several of his colleagues as a brilliant preservation job. As one seasoned Whitehall figure put it: 'We were right to respond to their [Blair's people's] concerns, and we were right to grab it back.'[226] And when it comes to 'speaking truth unto power', Sir Richard has said publicly that if the need arose, 'I'd simply say "bollocks" to the Prime Minister'.[227]

In the context of Whitehall reform, Sir Richard's making a firm ally of Lord Simon of Highbury, former Chairman of BP and the Prime Minister's informal adviser on Civil Service reform, was seen as highly significant.[228] At the session in No. 10 in November 1999 when Sir Richard and his Permanent Secretary colleagues responsible for working-up the different chunks of *Civil Service Reform* ('vision and values'; 'diversity'; 'performance management'; 'talent') presented their findings, Mr Blair turned at the end to Lord Simon and asked if the changes proposed accorded with best private-sector practice? Lord Simon said they did, which plainly was quite enough for Mr Blair as the proceedings ended shortly afterwards.[229]

Any close observer of the push for modernity in the mechanics of government could not help but notice considerable confusion and overlap even after a thousand days. Shortly before Sir Richard and his colleagues went in to see Mr Blair with their reform plan, a particularly well-placed figure offered an explanation for the anything but joined-up approach of No. 10 despite some of 'Blair's People' and Lord Simon attending the autumn Sunningdale Conference of the Civil Service Management Board, the twenty-five senior officials who make up his inner group[230] devoted to bringing coherence to the 'Tony wants' phenomenon[231] and the realities of administration. 'Blair confuses the civil servants around him', he said:

'On the Civil Service, he doesn't know what he wants. They say, in effect, "Tell me, Prime Minister, what *you* want and *we'll* do it." But he keeps saying different things. Richard Wilson finds it very difficult the way the Prime Minister jumps around. It's a succession of knee-jerks . . . They are not standing back and defining what they mean. Phrases like "joined-up government", and the "Third Way" don't mean anything.'[232]

So what *does* the Blair approach mean?

In some ways, we are replete with detail. Sir Richard Wilson's plan is brimming with items, many of which can be measured in terms of their implementation (pay and appraisal systems, greater diversity in recruitment; increased two-way interchange with senior people in outside professions), though any improvements in the quality of policy formulation along the hugely complicated and new public management-infected lines of the autumn 1999 document *Professional Policy Making for the Twenty First Century*[233] will be far harder to measure. The Performance and Innovation Unit's *Wiring It Up*, too, contains some potentially very fruitful ideas on how to adapt decision-taking and budget-holding procedures to suit knotty problems whose complications transcend neat departmental boundaries.[234] Here, too, improvements in techniques and performance should be more transparent and, therefore, measurable. The same applies to many of the social and anti-poverty proposals emerging from the Social Exclusion Unit.[235]

But is there a bigger, new style of picture to be discerned here? I am inclined to think there is. It links Mr Blair's disdain for the old collegial Cabinet- and Cabinet committee-driven model with the great variety of new approaches to policy advice and policy-making (including those hard-to-map 'task forces' on which the Neill committee had some valuable things to say, both on defining them and curbing their capacity for patronage of the more unaccountable kind)[236] and on the propensity for 'Czardom' – the 'Drug Czar', Keith Hellawell, being part of the Blair-fashioned Cabinet Office until the start of the second term). It also helps to explain the impatience and conflicting signals Mr Blair displays when his attention turns to administrative reform and matters of delivery.

As one insider said of the Prime Minister:

'What he wants is results. He has a feel for the policies but not how the results come. He finds it hard to understand why things can't happen immediately. There is a frustration in waiting for the pay-off and he doesn't have time. He comes back to this when one or other of the policy areas gets hot: education, then transport and now health. He comes back to all this when the delivery focus changes. This is the real-time political management which the administrators don't like. (They didn't like it under Mrs Thatcher either.)'[237]

The Blair-approved Wilson reform plan, and the work of the Cabinet Office units, are the way, according to this interpretation, to reconcile the Blair style of 'real-time' political operation with improved administrative delivery.

The great problem, however, is the messy and confusing gap between old structures (Cabinet system, Whitehall departmental 'silos') and the reality of political and policy decision-taking (Prime Minister's Department in all but name; bilaterals between the Prime Minister and individual ministerial colleagues; the Brown-led Treasury push to steer departmental policy outcomes through public service agreements bristling with tight and plentiful performance indicators). The nearest parallel, according to a particularly persuasive explanation from a shrewd observer, is business. Everybody knows that real decisions are taken in Blair's preferred way some distance from the Cabinet and its apparatus. But full Cabinet, and some of its committees, are used for the purposes of laying down an 'audit trail' in the manner of company boards.[238] According to this view, what Wilson and Simon are about is trying to marry the reality of Blair-style governance with the shell of the old and to link the government's strategy of policy priorities with effective delivery through a sharpened and reformed administration system.

Two conclusions emerge from this analysis and one running question. The first conclusion is that as the new century began there was still a long way to go before the new system based on a blending of the traditional and the novel, the audit trail and variable-geometry policy-making bedded down and was tested against reality. The second was the degree to which the new model depended on the Prime Minister. And linked to this was the continuing debate about prime ministerial power, the importance of being Tony. For driving this new hybrid system, it could be argued, both generated excessive prime ministerialism and depended upon it if momentum was to be sustained.

Such accusations of overmightiness at the centre have long annoyed Tony Blair and his people. Rebutting them at regular intervals has been a recurring feature of his premiership.[239] They are usually allied, as we have seen, with observations about the historically unparalleled force, scope and organization of the press, communications and information rebuttal capacities available to him, presided over by the most influential press secretary in Downing Street history, Alastair Campbell.[240]

The most sustained questioning Tony Blair has faced about the 'command premiership' he was expected to and, indeed, has operated since May 1997 came in the interview he gave Michael Cockerell for the BBC2 *Blair's Thousand Days* programme. Mr Cockerell put to him the idea that his individually agreed aims with each Cabinet minister and Permanent Secretary represented an extension of prime ministerial power not seen before. 'It's not that I want everything done via me', Mr Blair replied,

'but we have a programme and it's my job as Prime Minister to deliver it. And so inevitably if you don't have a strong centre . . . You're not running the government properly. But, I think there's a dichotomy here that is false really because most ministers want the support of the centre in driving their programme through. But the idea that I sort of, you know, for example in Education or in Health, or in the Treasury, you know, just sort of issue edicts or diktats from here [No. 10 Downing Street] that others carry out, I think is absurd.'[241]

At this stage, Michael Cockerell brought Mr Blair back to his personal agreements with Secretaries of State and Permanent Secretaries which made them more accountable to him than to any previous Prime Minister. 'I doubt that very much', said Mr Blair.

'I mean I think most Prime Ministers who have got a strong programme end up expecting their Secretaries of State to put it through; and you've always got a pretty direct personal relationship as Prime Minister, you appoint the Cabinet ministers. I'm not sure – I mean – I don't know about this. I've got a feeling with this thing that if you have a strong idea of what you want to do and believe in pushing it through, then you're, in inverted commas, a "dictator". And if you're not, then you're "weak". And you know, you pays your money and you takes your choice on that one.

'. . . this idea . . . that . . . I don't discuss things with ministers . . . is just not true . . . People often say in relation to Cabinet government, look I would be pretty shocked if the first time I knew a Cabinet minister felt strongly about something was if they raised it at the Cabinet table. I would expect them to come and knock on my door and say, "Look, Tony, I've got a problem here. I disagree with this" or "I disagree with that". And that happens from time to time. And people do that. And then you sit down and you work it out.

'But, you know, the old days of Labour governments where, I think, the meetings occasionally went on for two days and you had a show of hands at the end of it. Well, I mean, I shudder to think what would happen if we were running it like that.'[242]

Allied to this fascinating reply was Mr Blair's assertion that he kept a 'pretty iron grip' on his diary as 'one of the greatest dangers in this job is that you lose the big picture because . . . if you're not careful, you'd have meetings from six in the morning till midnight, and you might in the end achieve very little'.[243]

There are a number of important and revealing aspects to the Prime Minister's long reply to Michael Cockerell. First, note the stark portrayal of the alternatives. You either have a strong and determined approach to the job or, just like that, you have weakness, indecision and chaos, as if the operating of Cabinet and premiership were an either/or matter, a question of primary colours rather than more subtle and variable shades. Secondly, notice that oversimple parody view of previous Labour styles – Attlee's, Wilson's and Callaghan's – as if they were all the same. Thirdly, note too the similarity to late Mrs Thatcher, the era Nigel Lawson characterized as 'creeping bilateralism' or the 'consent of the victims' in which Cabinet ministers settled for doing individual policy deals with the boss in return for acquiescence in collective meetings of the Cabinet or its committees.[244]

Will matters change? It was known by early 2000 that Lord Simon, in his attempt to marry the old and the new along lines adapted from business, had suggested to Blair and his people that some kind of inner group consisting of the Prime Minister and half a dozen key ministerial colleagues and holding regular meetings might be the way forward.[245] But equally there were indications that Blair did not warm to this. It was not his style. Bilateral rather than collective dealings with his ministers remained the preferred way of doing business.[246]

'It's very personal. It's very instinctive', as one insider put it to me.[247] Yet the most experienced figures in Whitehall reckoned that unforeseen setbacks would be the most likely trigger for a shift towards the collegial, when a shock would make Tony Blair realize the utility of what Kenneth Clarke called the 'dipping the hands in the blood' aspect of political insurance.[248] 'All the old bits are in place. Nothing has been thrown away,'[249] explained a figure with a sense of the past and an instinct for anticipating the day when the phrase 'Tony wants' would not be enough.

The weeks leading up to the third anniversary of the Blair government's creation found the Prime Minister in an intriguingly reflective mood both about his place in history and the stress related to his job. He gave his friend, the writer and political commentator Robert Harris, an interview in which he confessed that the 'reality' of the premiership

'is different from anything that you might have anticipated. The reality itself is more intense and more endless, even though in theory you would have anticipated that it would indeed be intense and relentless. And there are things that come and knock you about.

'But I have a very fixed view as to what I want to do for the country, and I haven't really shifted on that, and I haven't shifted in my belief that I can do it. But keeping a grip of that big picture and following it through is the toughest part of it.'[250]

Blair made plain to Harris that two of the big canvases he had in mind were the mending of the Liberal/Labour split on the centre left during the Great War (of putting that right he said 'I've never given up on that goal, and I still believe it can be achieved')[251] and steering Britain into Euroland (though he would go no further with Harris than saying his 'objective' was for 'Britain to be a key and leading player in Europe').[252]

Stung by criticism of such linguistic caution from Roy Jenkins, the man Peter Riddell has described as Blair's 'political father figure',[253] Blair invited himself to dinner with the grand old man of the progressive centre and reassured him of his determination to leave his mark on the twin causes dear to Jenkins' heart.[254] Jenkins sent out a signal of continuing approval of Blair's credentials as the restorer of 'Lib–Lab co-operation' and the construction of 'an enthusiastic Left-of-centre constituency' in a newspaper article to mark the third anniversary of the government's creation. On the euro, however, Blair had not entirely reassured the fastidious former President of the European Commission ('He is the most

European Prime Minister since Edward Heath left office ... although Blair in my view has been over-cautious about his European timing and is not sufficiently making the political weather on the issue').[255]

Yet power is a wasting asset, as virtually all premiers have found – even those blessed with three-figure majorities in the House of Commons. Matthew Taylor, Labour's former Director of Policy, accurately reflected the countervailing reactions produced by the 'political command culture' built around the 'centralized duopoly' of Blair and Brown which continued to diminish most other ministers in the Cabinet three years on.[256] Resentment had yet to crystallize into resistance in the Cabinet Room though by the spring of 2000 it was inconceivable that Blair could bounce a sceptical Cabinet into spending £750m on a *grand projet* such as the Millennium Dome.[257] And as for a coalition with the Liberal Democrats, Mr Blair would have to be prepared for the resignation of the Deputy Prime Minister, John Prescott,[258] if the pleasures of Lord Jenkins' table were to trump the wishes of the Labour Party (a body Blair has always given the impression of borrowing rather than owning).

It was Blair's Home Secretary, Jack Straw, who put the Blair style in Labour perspective most effectively when asked by my students shortly before Easter 2000 to compare his boss with Harold Wilson (last phase) and Jim Callaghan, whom Straw had observed from what he described as his 'ringside seat' as a special adviser first to Barbara Castle and then to Peter Shore between 1974 and 1977.

In 1974, he said,

'a lot of decisions went to Cabinet. The fundamental distinction is between Cabinet now and then. Cabinet still has an important role but fewer decisions are formally endorsed there. The key fundamental difference is that the Labour Party in the 1970s had a pretty schismatic division inside it. And the leadership, therefore, in a fundamental way, was unstable.

'Overall the political position was dire when Callaghan became Prime Minister. There was quite a lot of goodwill for Jim. But his government was in dire straits on the economy and public expenditure, so he felt the need to run the system in a more open and collegial way than Wilson had done.'

Turning to Tony Blair, the Home Secretary said 'our Prime Minister has adapted the mode' developed by Mrs Thatcher in the 1980s, whereby fewer decisions were made at full Cabinet level with more devolved to Cabinet committees. And 'what Mrs Thatcher did was develop the idea of bilaterals with ministers', an approach extended by her successor-but-one in No. 10.

Summing up the Blair style, Jack Straw said:

'The Prime Minister is operating as chief executive of ... various subsidiary companies and you are called in to account for yourself.'

'A good process,' the Home Secretary added, loyally.[259]

As for Blair's own overall assessment in the spring of 2000, he told Robert Harris he agreed that most political lives ended in failure. Why? 'It's because the public is always encouraged to be cynical about people. And ... in the end ... whatever the expectations are, you can't meet all of them.'[260] Whatever else might be said of him, Tony Blair is a command and control premier with a sense of political mortality.

Within four months of his conversation with Harris reaching the book-stands, that sense, I suspect, became his most dominant emotion for a few, fraught days in September 2000 when a curious, unanticipated coalition of the semi-organized effectively closed down much of the UK's oil and petrol distribution system.[261] From the moment the Prime Minister was warned by the contingency planners in the Cabinet Office early on the morning of 12 September that 'the situation is near breaking point' and that 'MOD [is] looking at options for military assistance',[262] an autumn of fretfulness began to afflict the Government and, for a few days, none of those around the Prime Minister 'knew what the petrol scare meant. Is it the end? Have we lost it? This went on for three or four days', as one of them recalled.[263] The normally phlegmatic Home Secretary, Jack Straw, declared at a meeting of the Civil Contingencies Committee in the Cabinet Office at the height of the crisis: 'This is our poll tax.'[264] Over the coming days the opinion surveys suggested Straw may have not entirely succumbed to anxious overreaction by giving the Conservatives a lead over Labour for the first time since the 'Black Wednesday' crisis eight years earlier.[265] 'The focus groups failed' was the blunt conclusion of a highly intelligent Labour movement veteran.[266] In fact, this was not quite the case. Philip Gould had been briefing Blair on rising anger about the price of fuel since the beginning of the year.[267] The problem flowed partly because, as we have seen, Whitehall's capacity for contingency planning had been dispersed and allowed to lose its sharpness. Sir Richard Wilson and Sir David Omand, Permanent Secretary at the Home Office, swiftly set about reviewing this in the wake of 'petrol September',[268] only for its shortcomings to be shown up in a still more acute and protracted fashion when the foot and mouth crisis began to bite in late February 2001.[269]

Briefly, it looked as if the events of September 2000 had fuelled a mini-revival of collective government. 'There is more challenge to the PM', an insider explained. 'They realize that they are not going to win an election just on his face.'[270] This impression of mildly waxing collegiality was reinforced by two other factors. As the preoccupation with winning a second term grew (not that it had been absent for one moment since 2 May 1997: hence the relentlessness of the permanent election campaign over the subsequent four years which had, I believe, much to do with the fifty-nine per cent turn-out when the real election campaign ended on 7 June 2001), there appeared to be a little more space at the centre in which the career civil servants could operate. This included the Prime Minister's Department-that-will-not-speak-its-name as the regulars in the No. 10 Private Office began to take over more of the day-to-day running of business from the special advisers.[271]

In addition, close observers of the Cabinet Office noticed a burst of Cabinet committee activity. The Deputy Prime Minister, John Prescott, had always liked operating through them and the autumn of 2001 found him particularly active in the chair of MISC 10, the Ministerial Committee on the Millennium Dome.[272] Sir Richard Wilson, too, was at his collegiate subtlest in encouraging that mini-revival of Cabinet committeedom and bringing together clusters of informal groups into a proper Cabinet committee shape. MISC 9 on children's and young persons' services was an example.[273] He was also skilled at offering the Cabinet Secretariat as minute-takers even if a particular ministerial group did not feature formally in his Cabinet Committee Book.[274]

This phenomenon of the late first term should not be exaggerated, however. In October 2000, a Cabinet minister said greater collegiality was not apparent on Thursday mornings as the full Cabinet could neither tackle difficult issues on which there might be disagreement nor go on much beyond an hour for fear of the press reporting splits.[275]

Such a self-defeating preoccupation with the media's obsession for personality and clash stories, in the view of another Cabinet minister, is what, in the longer-term perspective of the first term as a whole, had stymied what might have been a natural growth in collegiality as ministers became more experienced:

'We all went in [in May 1997] nervous. There was a high degree of ignorance. There was a degree of silence round that table. Then we got a bit more verbal and things began to improve. Then we got into trouble with the press and Tony took more control.'[276]

In the last months of the first term, just before the outbreak of foot and mouth, a very senior Whitehall figure thought that over the past three and three quarter years a more profound factor had been at work virtually trumping all else: 'It's not the fear of the press going on about splits that stops the Cabinet from discussing things, it's because the PM doesn't like argument. Cabinet these days is just a series of self-congratulatory remarks.'[277]

When Jim Callaghan had been to see Blair in the early months of his premiership, he had added a rider to his arguments about the importance of collegiality. He told Blair to find about six really good ministers on whom he could rely,[278] which is rather different from advancing the idea of an 'inner cabinet' in which, as we have seen, Callaghan never believed. It was a version of a collective apex nonetheless. As the 2001 election approached, despite 'petrol September' and the stresses caused by foot and mouth searing large tracts of the rural kingdom, Blair would have none of the Callaghan or David Simon notion of an inner group. And he was publicly unrepentant about this telling Anne Applebaum in March 2001:

'People sometimes say, well, Cabinet sessions don't last for hours and days, but that's just a function of modern government. It's also that you do more through Cabinet committees and through informal groups of people.

'I remember Roy Jenkins telling me about the 1960s Labour Cabinets, when they would have Cabinet for two days. Can you imagine trying to conduct business today like that? The Government would go into freefall.

'I think a lot of the things that I've done – a strong centre, making sure that the writ of the Prime Minister runs throughout – I think that's just an inevitable part of modern government. I don't apologize for it at all. The crony stuff is just a piece of abuse dressed up as political argument.'[279]

'. . . [M]aking sure that the writ of the Prime Minister runs throughout;' the aspiration was plain enough. But this was not happening in the spring of 2001 and had not at any stage since May 1997 because of the twin peak of the Blair administration, the Chancellor of the Exchequer, Gordon

Brown, a great crag standing in the way of a thoroughly monocratic government.

The 'King Tony' phenomenon, as I have heard another very senior Whitehall figure put it,[280] has to be seen more in the context of a dual monarchy, the rivalry and sustained malice of whose courts inspired one of the most racy and readable political books of recent years, Andrew Rawnsley's *Servants of the People*.[281] For throughout its first term, the Blair Administration was 'a bi-polar government,' in the words of another Whitehall veteran,[282] to a degree not experienced in modern times.

In fact, the extent to which Whitehall was shot-through by the influences of the Blair–Brown axis led me, as the first premiership deepened, to abandon the concentric-circle model for a different geographical expression. Because probably the best way to depict the Blair and Brown domains up to the 2001 election was to map the policy fiefdoms where an individual dominance could be discerned, though a caveat is needed here. Such dominance was nowhere absolute. As Peter Riddell has expressed it, there is a case for a trilateral model as the Treasury has usually been involved as a central player in the most important No. 10 initiatives.[283] Perhaps areas of special interest would be a better way of describing the particular policy concerns of No. 10 and No. 11.

For the Prime Minister they were these:
Schools
Health
Crime
Transport
Northern Ireland
Foreign and Defence
Intelligence (in so far as he takes an interest in it).

The Cabinet Office, once meant to be a collective resource shared by the Cabinet as a whole, was in a feudal relationship with the overlord next door; a case of ever closer fusion.

For Brown, the policy cartography looked like this:
Pensions
Child and youth policy
Welfare to work
Enterprise
Science and technology transfer
Structural change and regional development

Here Treasury policy pervaded and, through the comprehensive spending reviews and the public service agreements which underpin them, the Chancellor exerted a sway no predecessor in the Treasury has ever matched over his colleagues and he 'stuffs their mouths with gold if they do things that are on his agenda', as an admiring insider put it.[284] For example, the Department of Social Security, by the end of the first term, was virtually a Brown satrapy.

All this was (and remains) a constitutional issue insofar as it subverts what is supposed to be a government of departments which adheres to collective responsibility in return for a shared say in serious decision-taking. For a combination of commanding premier and overmighty Chancellor leaves a residue of considerable resentment on the part of the dominated ones about the degree to which the 'Tony wants' and 'Gordon requires' phenomena drive policy and suppress collegiality across Whitehall.

One needs to construct an RI (or resentment Index) for the first Blair administration. And here the Chancellor outstripped the man who won the leadership crown after the death of John Smith. As one minister put it privately:

'The PM's bilaterals are a very important aspect of the Blair Government. It's his way of keeping the pressure on. Cabinet Ministers tend not to like them; nor do their permanent secretaries. But they are taken seriously.

'They involve a much easier relationship, however, than Cabinet ministers' dealings with Gordon Brown. There it is much more "do as you're told". It's much more a paper relationship. The Chancellor is a paper man – solitary. It's as if he sits there in his own room poring over his papers with a cold towel round his head. Cabinet ministers, when they get no further with Gordon Brown, try to line-up with No. 10 against the Treasury.'[285]

This remained a tension-raiser between No. 10 and No. 11 Downing Street. And so was, and is, the euro, a question the PM and the Chancellor are both profoundly interested in and over the nuances of which they both wish to prevail. And here one detected the Mandelson factor at its most destabilizing before his second exit from the Cabinet in January 2001.[286] It wasn't just the Chancellor's people who knew about the daily early morning phone call from the Prime Minister to his Northern Ireland Secretary when in Belfast which ranged across issues far wider than the great unresolvable of the nineteenth and twentieth centuries. They noticed, too, how often Mr Blair invited Mr Mandelson into his office for a chat after Cabinet meetings.[287]

The Prime Minister's people blame the Chancellor for some, though not all, of the absence of procedural collegiality in the Blair government. 'Tony is not a particularly command-and-control person,' it has been put to me.

'He is bugger all interested in the detail. That's Brown. Tony has a great sense of the big picture. But he knows how to take a barrister's brief and he does have a strong sense of what the Government is about. Gordon hates collective discussion. As a result, they tend to have to be bilaterals, not just with Gordon Brown but with other ministers too.'[288]

I'm not sure that Blair is a natural collective Cabinet government man distracted from this approach by a rival imperium in the Treasury. Though it is true that 'Tony will not take Gordon on', as a neutral observer in neither camp put it.[289]

It's partly that Blair is not a systems man. I have heard it said that since his Kosovo-related experiences during the Balkans war of 1999, 'the only system and institution the PM empathizes with is the Armed Forces'.[290] Hence the influence of the Chief of the Defence Staff, Sir Charles Guthrie, generally and in particular when he strode across Whitehall in the summer of 2000 to persuade the Prime Minister to see off the Treasury's demands to trim back the defence budget to a point where, in Guthrie's view, it would renege on the deal struck during the Strategic Defence Review of 1997–8 on which he, Guthrie, had expended much personal capital in selling it to the Armed Forces.[291]

The consequences of Blair's lack of feel for what Clem Attlee called the 'architectonics' of state, have been captured by two of the businessmen brought in to help him in 1997. Chris Haskins, who headed the Regulatory Impact Unit in the Cabinet Office, said in the early autumn of 2000 that the Government was 'in the worst of all worlds now where we've sort of abandoned the Cabinet committee. We've got a sort of Prime Minister's Office, including the Cabinet Office, which really hasn't got the teeth to deliver what the Prime Minister wants. And I'm not too sure that it's the institution that should be delivering'.[292] David Simon, who advised Mr Blair on his modernizing government agenda, attempting to reconcile the real-time policy-making practices of the Government with the need to lay an audit trail of properly minuted decisions taken in what remains of a collective system, was even more candid when writing earlier in 2000, as a member of the Treasury's Public Services Productivity Panel. 'The process', he said, 'by which Cabinet Government develops effective policy and the Civil Service and executive agencies work to achieve improving results is both complex and currently inadequately co-ordinated and reviewed.'[293]

Lord Simon said more consistent leadership and focus was needed from ministers. There were 'too many' objectives 'and they change often'.[294]

This has certainly been a problem for Mr Blair and the importees – the penumbra of special advisers – around him in No. 10. As Chris Haskins explained: 'He is a lawyer – you have to start with that – so he never actually ran anything before he became Prime Minister. I think he's learnt reasonably quickly that running government is pretty complicated.'[295] And, as David Simon indicated, ministers need to realize that 'culture change is a marathon not a sprint'.[296] One close observer of Blair's inner circle underscored the Haskins/Simon analysis. 'The PM,' he said,

'has never run a department. That shows through and in the people around him. They have no real sense of how departments think things through and the brokerages they have to operate and implement. He and the Policy Unit always want instant action.'[297]

And it is not always plain to senior figures out in the departments that when Tony's people say 'Tony wants' whether Tony really does want it rather than his Policy Unit people wishing it to be so.[298]

The Blair style had aroused some intriguing resistances by the time the first term approached its end. The Commons Select Committee on Public Administration, building on the anxieties about the spread and roles of special advisers by the Neill Committee on Standards in Public Life,[299] followed Neill in urging the Government to draw up a separate 'Code of Conduct for Special Advisers' and Parliament to control the overall number of special advisers an administration can appoint by voting a special sum for this purpose that cannot be exceeded.[300]

The select committee, too, persisted with its inquiry into the *Ministerial Code* despite the Prime Minister's disdainful remarks in the House of Commons during the summer of 2000 to the effect that 'no one will be better governed through fine-tuning the *Ministerial Code*. Those are good issues for academics and constitutional experts, but they are not the big issues that Parliament should debate when we consider our role in the modern society . . .'[301] In its February 2001 report, *The Ministerial Code: Improving the Rule Book*, the select committee recognized the increasing salience of QPM and its successor to the country's constitutional arrangements since John Major first published it in 1992 and the centrality of the Prime Minister to its proper application:

'We believe that the development of codes of conduct across public life reinforces the need for the constitutional status of the *Ministerial Code* to be properly recognized. It is not a legal document but a set of guidelines. It does not necessarily cover all aspects of what should be considered acceptable Ministerial practice or behaviour and should not substitute for the Prime Minister's judgement, for which he must account to Parliament. It is unsatisfactory for its status still to be in doubt. It is the rulebook for ministerial conduct, including the responsibilities of Ministers to Parliament, and its status should reflect its importance. It may have developed in a private and *ad hoc* way, but it is now an integral part of the new constitutional architecture. It is time for it to be recognized as such.'[302]

No acceptance here of the Blair line that such affairs should be the concern of my seminar room rather than the chamber of the House of Commons.

For good measure, the Public Administration Committee reminded Mr Blair directly of what they regarded as a first order prime ministerial concern:

'The Code is the Prime Minister's document; and it is with the Prime Minister that the buck must finally stop. This closes the accountability gap . . .'[303]

Such a closing of the gap did not appeal to Tony Blair. Twice he refused to give evidence to the PAC on the code of which he was custodian-in-chief. The select committee appended the exchange which follows to its report.[304]

On 10 May 2000, Dr Tony Wright, the Committee's Chairman, wrote to the Prime Minister, noting

'your own contribution to the development of the Code, and in particular, your declaration in the foreword to the current edition in which you say "openness is a vital ingredient of good accountable Government . . . I believe we should be absolutely clear about how Ministers should account, and be held to account, by Parliament and the public." It is in this spirit that the Select Committee invites you to give evidence to us. As the Code is the Prime Minister's document, you will understand that your evidence is indispensable to the Committee's inquiry.'[305]

Blair's dismissal of this request was curt: 'As you know, evidence to Select Committees is normally provided by "line" departments or via a Government memorandum. Prime Ministers have not themselves, by long-standing convention, given evidence to Select Committees. That remains the position.'[306]

'. . . [B]y long-standing convention.' The Cabinet Office primed No. 10 on how to fend off Wright's assertion of all-party select committee power. They rested on the argument that when premiers ceased to be Leader of the House of Commons during the Second World War select committees lost the power to summon them. The last premier to appear, Neville Chamberlain, had gone as Leader of the House not Prime Minister. This was the defence 70, Whitehall provided for the Prime Minister's Office.[307] It ignored completely the changed world of select committeedom since 1979 and that it was Mrs Thatcher who simply invented the convention under the post-1979 dispensation that premiers do not attend as she wished to avoid giving evidence to the Defence Select Committee on the Westland Affair in 1986, sending her Cabinet Secretary, Sir Robert Armstrong, instead.[308]

Tony Wright persisted. On 8 June 2000, he told Blair: 'There is no one apart from the Prime Minister who can account to Parliament for it [the *Ministerial Code*]. You will understand that there is an important issue here in relation to Parliament and the Executive. This was put to the Committee forcibly by Professor Peter Hennessy in his evidence on 24 May . . . Referring to the convention of the Prime Minister not appearing before the Committee to discuss the Code he said "I think . . . the greatest single gap in the Select Committees' reach now is that of the Prime Minister. We have long passed the point when Prime Ministers can shelter under the convention that they do not appear." '[309] Blair was unmoved: 'I have looked at this again, but I am afraid I can see no case for departing from the long-standing convention that Prime Ministers do not themselves give evidence to Select Committees, a position always adhered to by previous administrations.'[310]

The House of Commons Liaison Committee (the 'shop stewards' group consisting of all select committee chairs) took up the cause at the end of the year. Writing to Blair on 14 December 2000, its chairman, Robert Sheldon, produced an ingenious suggestion:

'The Government has made it its practice to produce an Annual Report. What the Committee has in mind is that this document should be the basis of an annual appearance by the Prime Minister to discuss with the Liaison Committee the main elements in this Report . . . For its part the Committee would undertake that no further requests for your appearance would be made by any Select Committee that year, and that, so far as possible, you should be given an indication of the main themes to be covered.'[311]

Blair's reply was a collector's item, coming as it did from the Prime Minister who has given less space to his individual ministerial colleagues than any other since 1945:

'It is right of course that the House of Commons should have an opportunity to question me as the Head of the Government, and it does of course have that opportunity in weekly Prime Minister's Questions. More detailed questioning of the kind that you propose would, however, inevitably mean trespassing on other ministers' responsibilities and would, I believe, risk obscuring the present lines of accountability in our system where statutory powers are conferred directly on Secretaries of State and other Departmental Prime Ministers, and not on the Prime Minister.'[312]

A third 'no' from No. 10. Less than three months later, Blair was giving away *en clair* the true position to Anne Applebaum claiming credit for his creation of 'a strong centre, making sure that the writ of the Prime Minister runs throughout'[313] – no reluctance here to 'trespass' on other ministers' patches. Tony Wright's Public Administration Committee had not abandoned their scrutiny on this terrain either. In the last days of the 1997–2001 Parliament, their report on *Making Government Work: The Emerging Issues*, sensitive to the thinking taking place inside No. 10 and the Cabinet Office about machinery of government in the second term, declared that: 'Our preference is for a model which strengthens Cabinet government as a whole, rather than for one which supplants it with something else, although the case for a Prime Minister's Department needs to be properly assessed.'[314]

As the ink dried on *Making Government Work*, the first press stories about how a determined 'Blair plots revenge on the Civil Service' were appearing on the front pages of the quality press.[315] Neither top civil servants nor traditional departmental boundaries were to get in the way of delivery after 8 June 2001. What would this mean? A Prime Minister's Department that really would speak its name? Unlikely. Sir Richard Wilson, a consistent opponent of such a notion, was thought to have won that argument in advance, if only because of the row such a development would cause in Parliament and among the commentating classes and, perhaps equally importantly, on the part of Gordon Brown who was, in private, quick to point out the threats to collective government if a development threatened his fiefdom.[316] It was plain, however, that the 'centre' would indeed be strengthened to try yet again to ensure Blair's writ really did run throughout Whitehall.

Senior journalists at *The Times* got furthest in persuading the Prime Minister to think aloud about this ahead of the 2001 election.[317] During the conversation at Labour's headquarters in Millbank Tower on 31 May 2001, the Prime Minister said:

'... I want to focus the centre of government on delivery particularly. I will establish what will in effect be a ... specific policy delivery unit in the Cabinet Office but the head of it will report directly to me and we will use that in order to make sure that across the public service areas, we're driving through the change and reform that is necessary. And, in particular, that we are refocusing the civil Service on what I think is their task today which is less to do with detailed day-to-day policy advice and more to do with project management and delivery.'[318]

Did this mean that Washington really would come to Whitehall – that politically appointed special advisers would dominate policy advice with senior officials more and more becoming managers and executors?

Shortly before Blair's *Times* interview, one Whitehall veteran judged that 'the public may not like the Civil Service very much but they like the idea of "Tony's cronies" even less'. He was sympathetic to the predicament in which Sir Richard Wilson had already found himself as a defender of Northcote–Trevelyan notions of a Civil Service inoculated against politicization:

'This lot push out against boundaries all the time, though sometimes they don't realize they are. It's about four times as difficult for Richard as it was for Robin Butler. Richard constantly treads the fine line between losing the Service, losing the Government and losing the commentators.'[319]

Should Mr Blair alter the basics of what one permanent secretary called 'the arranged marriages between permanent secretaries and ministers'[320] transgressing what another called 'the thin golden line that must not be crossed',[321] his second term could be hugely constitutionally significant in a hotly disputed fashion.

Already by the end of the first term there were grave anxieties about the precedent created by Ed Balls's promotion to the role of Chief Economic Adviser to the Treasury (though without management responsibilities over career officials). As one shrewd judge of Treasury form put it in early 2001: 'Ed Balls is not just a minister, he's a permanent secretary as well. The Chief Secretary [Andrew Smith] is just a personnel officer.'[322] Though the real Permanent Secretary, Sir Andrew Turnbull, remained a hugely respected figure throughout Whitehall, this was undoubtedly true. Balls was commonly referred to as 'the Deputy Chancellor.' Should Blair go for an Americanization of the Whitehall advice systems, he may find a considerable – and public – road block in a revitalized Civil Service Commission under Usha Prashar, the First Commissioner. As one of her first acts, Baroness Prashar appointed twelve new commissioners by open competition (the first time this has ever happened). They took up their posts in the spring of 2001 and were undoubtedly alert to the dangers of politicization and determined to ensure that in the Civil Service Bill the Government seemed likely to bring forward at some point in its second term that their Gladstone-devised independence and answerability to the Monarch alone would remain intact and embedded in the legislation.[323]

Mr Blair won his second term with an extraordinary 167-seat majority. He rejigged several Whitehall boundaries instantly and substantially (though without any attempt to mount a Haldane-style inquiry first – the indispensable precondition of a lasting settlement). There was much remixing and retitling with new combinations such as the departments of Work and Pensions; Environment, Food and Rural Affairs (Social Security and Agriculture, Fisheries and Food disappearing into the bureaucratic waste basket of history). DETR was completely dismembered with a strange mixture of Transport, Local Government and Regions as a rump. Education lost Employment to Work and Pensions and was renamed Education and Skills. The Home Office lost important and longstanding functions – elections, incongruously to Transport, Local Government and Regions; and human rights/freedom of information rather more logically to the Lord Chancellor's Department.

The Prime Minister's Office and the Cabinet Office went into ever tighter yet ever untidier fusion. No. 10 was reconfigured under three commands:

1. Jonathan Powell and Jeremy Heywood would henceforth run a merged Policy Unit and Private Office in the shape of a government and policy division.
2. Alastair Campbell would oversee communications and strategy combined and remove himself from the Press Office where the career officials, Godric Smith and Tom Kelly, would deal day-to-day with the media.
3. Anji Hunter would lead government relations division liaising with the devolved administrations, the Labour Party and business.[324]

In a way, a fourth strand was added in the shape of two amphibians shared between the Cabinet Office and No. 10. Sir David Manning was recalled as Ambassador to NATO to head the Cabinet Office's Overseas and Defence Secretariat *and* to act as the PM's Foreign Affairs Adviser in the way Sir Percy Cradock had under Mrs Thatcher and John Major. Sir Stephen Wall continued to act as head of the Cabinet Office's European Secretariat while serving as Blair's principal adviser on European Affairs in No. 10. The promised Policy Delivery Unit appeared in the Cabinet Office led ministerially by Gus Macdonald and day-to-day by Professor Michael Barber, brought over from Education. Lord Macdonald's boss in DETR days, John Prescott, moved into a new Office of the Deputy Prime Minister in Dover House to head up the clutch of ministers in the Cabinet Office.[325]

To confuse matters still further, two weeks after winning his second term, Mr Blair announced three new appointments 'to strengthen the Government's ability to deliver change in the public sector'. In addition to Professor Barber, Wendy Thompson was brought in from the Audit Commission to lead a new Office of Public Services Reform 'to advise the Prime Minister on how the Government's commitment to radical reform of the Civil Service and public services can be taken forward.' Yet another accretion had been added which appeared to be the cutting edge of change and bureaucratic regeneration. A third and promising development was a Forward Strategy Unit, headed by Geoff Mulgan (who would continue to run the Performance and Innovation Unit) for the purpose of mounting 'blue skies policy thinking for the Prime Minister' and undertaking 'strategy projects at request'.[326]

The Cabinet Office, already groaning with overlapping functions and units, thereby acquired still more in a way which suggested Mr Prescott and Sir Richard Wilson would be stretched to co-ordinate *it* let alone the rest of Whitehall though Sir Richard told his colleagues that, in fact, the reshaping of the centre amounted to a streamlining.[327] In the run-up to the election, an especially thoughtful Cabinet Office hand had inquired of me: 'Do you know, there are thirty-two separate management units? It's *Gormenghast* in there!'[328] As another Cabinet Office figure had predicted, Gordon Brown would fiercely resist any Cabinet Office encroachment on his conduits of money and power – the public service agreements. And so he did. The Treasury made it swiftly plain in the first days of the second term, after Blair and Brown had discussed the new dispensation,[329] that the Policy Delivery Unit would report to Mr Blair but it would answer also to the PSX Cabinet Committee, Gordon Brown's public spending instrument, part of whose secretariat it would provide.[330]

The special and most central relationship of Blair I seemed to have carried over intact and substantially unaltered into Blair II. Much else remained to play for in terms of the bedding-down of the new departmental configurations and the possible shift of the senior Civil Service away from policy and strategy. The degree to which the passage of time and the accumulation of vicissitudes would weaken the Prime Minister's capacity to command his extraordinarily pliant Cabinet colleagues remained to be seen.

But it was now possible, as the second term began, to ponder more fully the kind of political animal who was exerting such sway from Downing Street. Mr Blair has confided in his mentor, Lord Jenkins of Hillhead, his 'regret that he read Law and not History at Oxford', and, in Jenkins's words, that he 'has become a considerable addict of political biography'.[331] The Prime Minister plainly cares about his place and that of his administration in the 'big picture' of political history. So, on the evidence of the bulk of his first premiership, what kind of politician are we dealing with? For one well-placed observer, it's quite simple:

'Blair is the best Liberal Prime Minister the country has had since Lloyd George but he doesn't lead the Liberal Party. He leads a Party that is not Marxist, not socialist, not even Croslandite. It doesn't really know what it believes in . . . It's a New Labour Government which has a very small cadre of New Liberals in No. 10 [New Liberal in the sense of Asquith, Lloyd George and Churchill during their reformist phase in 1906–14]. This is more important than the Napoleonic/presidential-style question.

'The problem is that very few Cabinet ministers understand this. They were building their careers in Michael Foot's time. Tony built his career at that time too, but he never believed a word of it . . . He's basically leading a party which is very disconcerted. It doesn't know what to believe in. It can never quite decide if he's one of them. He isn't one of them. He's a younger version of Roy Jenkins and all of Roy's big agenda items are the Liberal ones.'[332]

And what does the old Asquithian himself make of the his young protégé? According to Jenkins, Blair 'has clearly shown himself a competent Prime Minister'. He is the most European-minded since Ted Heath and has 'manifestly rid the Labour Party of much of its ideological baggage and laid to rest the view that it is essentially a class party. He has broken the constitutional log-jam, and has reformed the voting system for nearly all the subsidiary elections: the European Parliament, Scotland, Wales and London'.[333] But for Jenkins, whether Blair will turn out to be 'a great [Prime Minister] remains to be seen'[334] depending on truly tough tests such as eventual British membership of Euroland and a degree of proportionality for elections to the Westminster Parliament.

The grand old centrist is a considerable connoisseur of premiers having already written biographies of Gladstone, Asquith, Baldwin and Attlee, with a fifth, a life of Churchill, on the way. He has plainly fallen for the Blair promise and, according to his friends, did so at one of their private meals together before the 1997 general election when Blair confessed that two worries would occasionally afflict him on waking early in the morning − one that he failed to make it to No. 10; the other that he did make it but proved not up to the job. Jenkins found such candour attractive[335] − as indeed it is, or rather was.

One must, however, be a touch careful of treating Blair as early-twentieth-century New Liberalism reincarnate and freshly spun. Michael Young, author of the 1945 Labour Manifesto, *Let Us Face the Future*, once described its contents as 'Beveridge plus Keynes plus socialism';[336] in other words, developed New Liberalism plus a dash of public ownership. But Blair goes neither for nationalization, demand management nor a universalist welfare state. Though Gordon Brown is more 'a man of 1945'[337] (to borrow Tom McNally's typology) in instinct, emotion and rhetoric than his Downing Street neighbour and the wider Labour Party has a real sense of this. There is, however, one element of the older tradition of British politics that is part of the Blair make-up which it is important not to forget − religion. He does not flaunt it, but it's there. He travels with a bible among his boxes and is disturbed if he cannot attend Holy Communion on a Sunday.[338]

But it is another aspect of Blair which *is* very public and consistently expressed that both links him with Mrs Thatcher and Harold Wilson and adds coherence to his policy stances, if not to his kaleidoscopic approach to government. It is his espousal of the notion of 'meritocracy,' the word invented in the mid-1950s by the same Michael Young who had drafted Labour's election manifesto a decade earlier. Mr Blair made it the centrepiece of the speech he delivered in his Sedgefield constituency accepting the local party's nomination of him as their candidate on 13 May 2001.

'We are not crypto-Thatcherites. We are not old-style socialists. We are what we believe in. We are meritocrats. We believe in empowering all our people. We should celebrate not just those who are born well, but those who do well.'[339]

The Prime Minister, it seemed, had no conception that Young's *The Rise of the Meritocracy, 1870–2033*,[340] was both a satire of such attitudes and a terrible warning of the consequences of such a philosophy both to the UK and to the Labour Party. Young warned against turning away from R. H. Tawney-style notions of equality[341] in favour of the overriding principle that IQ + Effort = Merit. Intriguingly, he also noted that the Civil Service reformed along Northcote-Trevelyan lines was the first meritocracy – hence the starting date of the book in 1870 – and the exemplar of what was to follow.[342] It would be enormously ironic if the determined meritocrat in No. 10 diluted the principle of a politically neutral career civil service in the name of 'efficiency'.

PART FOUR
CODA

19

The Premier League:
The Inevitability of Disappointment

All political lives, unless they are cut off in midstream at a happy juncture, end in failure, because that is the nature of politics and of human affairs.   *Enoch Powell, 1977*[1]

The historian is not a kind of celestial chief justice sentencing the guilty and setting free the innocent. He is part of the process he describes, and his judgements can never be more than provisional.
                                    Professor David Marquand, 1977[2]

> The Past is a strange land, most strange.
> Wind blows not there, nor does rain fall:
> If they do, they cannot hurt at all.
> Men of all kinds as equals range
> The soundless fields and streets of it.
>   *Edward Thomas, 'Parting'*[3]

'It's very difficult to be a major Prime Minister unless you're there for four or five years.'   *Lord Jenkins of Hillhead, 1999*[4]

'I've known every Prime Minister to a greater or lesser extent since Balfour, including Balfour, and most of them have died unhappy . . . It doesn't *lead* to happiness.'   *Lord Hailsham, 1989*[5]

There is something haunting about both the Powell and the Hailsham view of contentment and premiership. Both men, being top-flight classical scholars in their precocious youths,[6] had an acute sense of time and tragedy. One can understand the poignancy of their points for those who have held the highest non-hereditary office in the land, who have possessed for a time the most potent cluster of public power within the United

Kingdom, only to discover in their deepening years beyond the premiership just how slim was the impact they had, how relatively faint their trace on an ancient, settled nation that is so difficult to move.

For most of them – Attlee and Douglas-Home were probably the exceptions – rolling, fitful regret would perhaps inevitably be the accompaniment to retirement. As Margaret Thatcher put it when looking back on the events of November 1990: 'There was still much that I wanted to do.'[7] Her successor was even more eloquent (with considerable reason) for things undone. 'Of course there are regrets', John Major wrote.

I shall regret always that I rarely found my own authentic voice in politics. I was too conservative, too conventional. Too safe, too often. Too defensive. Too reactive. Later, too often on the backfoot ... I made only a beginning [on educational and social changes], and it was not enough.[8]

Jim Callaghan, though closer to Attlee and Douglas-Home in terms of retirement tranquillity, wishes 'I'd become Prime Minister ten years earlier – or fifteen years earlier when I was fifty ... I would have had much more energy.'[9] He wished, too, that he had had a comfortable majority and that he had not had to spend so much time on economic affairs while in No. 10.[10]

But, as Harold Macmillan once said of Ramsay MacDonald, 'complaining that he felt like "a weary Titan" ... the answer is easy. Nobody asked you to hold up the world. If your shoulders are tired, there are others ready and anxious to sustain the burden ...'[11] One should not feel too sorry for those who seek to exercise considerable power over their fellow countrymen and women and, through a set of curious chances, are finally placed in a position to do so.

Yet David Marquand's warning to historians is also salutary: *we* play the game of 'celestial chief justice' at our peril. But it is possible to draw up the ingredients of assessment for premiership performance, and I did so on one occasion for an Historical Association lecture.[12] Political scientists like to do this kind of exercise.[13] I think it has serious limitations. But, if pressed, these would be the criteria I would apply based upon an historical observation of the job as it has been conducted since 1945:

1. Backdrop to the premiership
   - Condition of the economy and society
   - Parliamentary arithmetic
   - Internal condition of premier's party

- Disposition of the media to the premier, his/her government, his/her party

2. Management capacity
   - Premier's skills at managing the status quo (i.e., the prosaic but necessary on-going functions of central government)
   - Handling crises (including the media aspects of crisis management)

3. Insight and perception
   - Personal (including self-awareness)
   - Political (sensitivity towards colleagues, official and party)
   - Policy (a capacity to see beyond the shibboleths of established or manifesto positions)

4. Changes and innovation
   - Planned
   - Improvised
   - Contingent upon unforeseen events

5. Constitutional and procedural
   - The running of No. 10 and the balance within it between the political and the administrative
   - The handling of Cabinet and the apparatus of collegiality
   - Managing Whitehall and the career Civil Service
   - The personal handling of the House of Commons; the care and attention paid to the institution of Parliament and the management of his/her party in both Commons and Lords
   - Probity and decency of the system (Prime Minister as manager of codes, ministerial and Civil Service)

My doubts about this approach to premiership stem from it not being a tick-in-the-box operation. If it was, it would make the construction of a performance table – a premiership league, if you like – an easier proposition.

Other problems, too, intrude between such a chart and the would-be simplifier. Roy Jenkins is interesting here, and not just in the 'four years needed to show mettle' sense. There are 'suffix'[14] premierships in his terms – Douglas-Home and Callaghan being the classic examples. It plainly does matter to such Prime Ministers that they held the top office without having won an election in their own right.[15] And leaving office by other means than the hand of the electorate counts too. Mrs Thatcher was well aware when she left Downing Street in November 1990 that she did so undefeated, having led her party 'to victory in three elections'.[16]

Above all, the conditions in which the postwar first eleven have had to operate have varied enormously for all the indispensable functions that fall into the sump of a job we call the premiership. With all those caveats in mind, it is possible to compile a crude taxonomy of postwar Prime Ministers which is itself an index of performance.

The very top flight contains two names. There would be three if Churchill's two premierships were treated in combination. As this is a *post*war exercise they are not, and so two it is – Clement Attlee and Margaret Thatcher. To adapt – again – Churchill's famous phrase about Joe Chamberlain,[17] Attlee and Thatcher were the two great 'weathermakers' of the postwar years in that they set the terms of political trade, as Nigel Lawson recognized when he said of Mrs Thatcher (while they were both still in office) that she had 'transformed the politics of Britain – indeed Britain itself – to an extent no other Government has achieved since the Attlee Government of 1945 to 1951 . . . [which] . . . set the political agenda for the next quarter of a century'.[18]

Attlee can be seen less as a weathermaker than as the beneficiary of a new weather system created cumulatively by the experience and circumstances of World War II. Using a different metaphor, Paul Addison sensed this in his classic study of *The Road to 1945* when he wrote that as 'Labour swept to victory in 1945 the new consensus fell, like a branch of ripe plums, into the lap of Mr Attlee'.[19] Mrs Thatcher forged her new consensus; Mr Attlee refined his.

Yet he did it inside six years on very few resources within a war-exhausted nation and without taking any constitutional shortcuts (nuclear weapons policy-making, perhaps, the exception) in the process. The Attlee and Thatcher styles, as well as their policies, could not be further apart (though both were great patriots with a certain kind of patriot's antipathy towards being inside an integrating Europe). Yet both, in a way, serve as the bookends of the postwar years. I have an aversion to postism (whether it be post-modernism or post-structuralism), but Major and Blair can be seen as post-postwar figures in a way that none of their predecessors could (the ending of the Cold War, the great unfinished business of 1945, being a factor here, too).

Below Attlee and Thatcher belongs a special category of premier – the nation- or system-shifters. Ted Heath is the classic example. Though deficient in many of the skills of political (as opposed to administrative) management, he none the less moved his country into an utterly different geopolitical position. But for the Heath–Pompidou relationship, I am not convinced that Britain would have joined the European Communities (though it is impossible and foolish to be dogmatic about these matters). For all the ruination of his powers and eventually his policies that befell him in the weeks before his fall in 1974, Heath's will always be a special, system-shifting stewardship.

So, too, will be Tony Blair's. It is too early to place him in other categories, and though he may well have played fast and loose with some of the more venerable constitutional conventions of the traditional Cabinet government variety, he has shifted the system within to a degree that quite simply has no precedent. The combination of devolution and the construction of a rights culture, though he rarely trumpets them (and, in his first two and a half years, had still to make a speech on the new constitutional architecture as a whole), do already put Blair in the Heath category as a remaker of the country in a significant, substantial and almost certainly irreversible fashion. Beyond this, wider judgements on Tony Blair can only be interim ones.

A kind of obverse to the scene-shifters are Churchill and Callaghan – seasoned copers but not transformers. Traditionalist in method and constitutional thought, both had the air of an entr'acte about them, though in Churchill's case the singularity and the magnificence of what had gone before coloured and infused his every utterance and judgement, and the perception of those to whom they were directed. The dreadful dislocations surrounding Callaghan's demise should not obscure the steel he showed in bringing his difficult Cabinet around to accept tough notions of financial stability in 1976. Similarly, Churchill's fading after his 1953 stroke should not diminish the bravery of his attempts to mitigate the Cold War on the threshold of its thermonuclear-threatened phase.

The two most difficult premiers to place are Macmillan and Wilson. Macmillan can lay claim to being a system-mover thanks to the final dash for decolonization which he authorized and oversaw. And, like Wilson, he sought to engineer the great shift from Empire/Commonwealth to Europe. Yet both fall into the promise-unfulfilled category.

They were known as 'the two Harolds' in the brief period during 1963 when they faced each other as Prime Minister and Leader of the Opposition, and as Alistair Horne has noted, they 'formed, to the end, a curious mutual admiration society for each other, based chiefly on parliamentary prowess'.[20] Both took the use of the electronic media to new heights. Both could be very funny. Both had style. Both were prone to nervousness about their position. And both were highly intelligent men who came to the premiership with a great deal of political and administrative experience.

But the 'two Harolds' suffer in the ratings, I fear, because they both set out their stalls (Wilson from his first day in office and Macmillan from 1961) as modernizers of the British economy and, on the back of that, of their societies as a whole. They had an acute sense of the deficiencies of their economic and industrial inheritance and both, in their different ways, undertook to transform them with growth through planning – in short to reverse a deep-set relative economic decline. Neither can be said to have done more, at best, than to identify part of the bundle of near-intractable problems – and to hold still further decline at bay. In their own terms, therefore, they were victims of Powell's Law of political failure. The man who bridged the Macmillan and the Wilson years, Alec Douglas-Home, though charming and funny, straight and shrewd, could only be a punctuation mark between the two Harolds, given the length of his tenure. If decency were the only criterion for a premier league position, Douglas-Home, Major and Attlee would top it.

John Major, however, has to rank below the system-shifters, the copers and the promise unfulfilled. He had neither the perceptiveness of the two Harolds nor their sustained political and parliamentary skills. He could be good on his day and where circumstances were propitious, but he was not in their league. He succumbed to the political weather rather than made it. He falls into a category of the overwhelmed. It might, however, have been different had he enjoyed a longer spell in the ministerial tier just beneath the premiership and had circumstances not been so punitive, almost cruel, for him after September 1992. But doubt would remain about the fireproofing needed to be a premier under duress. He was too sensitive, too easily bruised to be number 1.

The tragedy of Anthony Eden is that, despite the exonerating circumstance of Jenkins' Law (four years at least is needed in No. 10), he falls into a catastrophic category of his own. For his own honourable motives, he took great and eventually fatal shortcuts with procedure (even allowing for his telling the Cabinet far more than previously thought about the collusion with France and Israel). He none the less deceived his party, Parliament and the public about his war plot. He brought his party, his country and the office of Prime Minister to an albeit temporary low and all over an area of governance, foreign policy and diplomacy, where he had once shone to the point of near radiance.

Yet Eden has my sympathy. All holders of the premiership do. There may be hubris lurking in anyone who believes they are up to the top job and who seeks, in Othello's words, to do the state some service at the highest level. Certainly nemesis in a thousand forms awaits those who make it. Could it be different? Do we – and they – expect too much from the office of Prime Minister? How might it be constructed in the twenty-first century to increase the chance of improved performances?

20

Towards a New Specification: Premiership for the Twenty-First Century

'There's a very fine line between sinking into a Hamlet-like sea of indecision, and being so self-righteous you pay no heed to anyone else, of which Margaret Thatcher was the extreme.'

Roy Jenkins, 1997[1]

It often occurred to me that no man ought to be Prime Minister for longer than five years. I doubt whether any man is capable of standing the strain for longer than that period – at any rate without sinking into a far more negative attitude towards things than is good for the conduct of human affairs.

Sir Edward Bridges, Permanent Secretary to the
Treasury and former Secretary of the Cabinet, 1948[2]

'When you become Prime Minister the first thing they do – after telling you how to launch the nuclear bomb – is to take your passport from you, and then the rest of the time trying to get you to travel round the world.'

Tony Blair to the 1998 Labour Party Conference[3]

Does my boss [Mr Blair] work harder than Mr Gladstone? He does different things. Lots of time on planes, in meetings and doing media interviews – but little time in the House of Commons and virtually no debating. He also has a staff, where Mr G had two private secretaries. But that doesn't affect my point – that the weight of the premiership is no heavier than in the past, and that the difference between Prime Ministers lies in personal temperament and ambition, not the weight of the office *per se*.

Dr Andrew Adonis, Downing Street Policy Unit, 1999[4]

History is a discipline that sobers up its practitioners. It prevents them, or it should prevent them, from imposing oversimple and, therefore, misleading patterns on the past. Of equal importance, it should divert them from making overconfident or overprecise predictions about the future. I do believe that the speed and pressure of modern government driven by both the media and 'events' have changed the metabolic rate of the turn-of-the-century British premiership. I am also convinced that the temptation aroused to recognize this new reality by moving to a command model of central government presided over by a single (or chief) executive in the person of an unashamedly dominant Prime Minister, with an administrative back-up to match, should be resisted.

My reasons for this are, I hope, plain from earlier chapters. But, as these assumptions – these first-order continuities – infuse my thinking about premiership in the future, I should state why I regard such require-ments as essential. There are two reasons – one philosophical, the other related to the nature of the British governing culture.

First, command models sit ill with open societies. The excesses of personality politics – Michael Foley's notion of 'leadership stretch'[5] – may be inevitable in media-driven politics. But this no is reason for winding up the pluralism which open societies must have in their institutions which process, arbitrate and, when necessary, constrain the flow of government power. The second reason is that British political culture reflects the compost in which it has grown. It is essentially a parliamentary system.

A very seasoned former Whitehall hand, Sir Patrick Nairne, put this point with great clarity when considering the 'Functions of the Prime Minister in the Next Century', just before Labour took office in 1997.[6] For Sir Patrick, two important factors would continue to fashion the job and its requirements:

First, the character, personality and personal style of different Prime Ministers may well determine the development or importance of particular functions and the way in which they choose to perform them – or even whether some function is accepted as a task for the Head of Government.

Secondly, so long as Parliamentary democracy in its present form continues to exist in the UK, the Prime Minister must continue to undertake the functions of political party leader, of exercising power through Cabinet government, and of being accountable to Parliament.[7]

The subsequent Blair experience has added bite to these observations and worries for those, like myself, who subscribed to the Nairne norms.

Among this group is Shirley Williams, who has watched the developing Blair experience partly from 200 yards away in the chamber of the House of Lords and partly from a distance of 3,000 miles in the Kennedy School of Government at Harvard University. In the autumn of 1999, she confessed to a Gresham College dinner audience consisting of City, Whitehall and university people that: 'I worry about prime ministerial power because the British parliamentary system does not work as a prime ministerial system . . . In the United States, the checks and balances are built into the presidential system.' Parliament, Lady Williams added, 'is not an effective check any more. All the checks on the executive are very weak at the moment.'[8]

I no more believe in a weakening of the instruments of parliamentary accountability than I do in the strengthening of prime ministerial power as a task for the early twenty-first century. Yet an adjustment to the office of Prime Minister and its supporting systems is necessary. And the reasons for this are not novel. They resonate from the past – since Sir Robert Peel first briefed his promising protégé, a certain W. E. Gladstone, on the hugely burdensome nature of the premiership in the 1840s.[9]

Indeed, in his February 1999 letter to me about the 'myth' of an increasingly burdened contemporary premiership, Andrew Adonis took as his 'starting point . . . the Gladstone diaries, which give a brilliant day by day account of the job in the late 19th century'.[10] For the purposes of comparing the No. 10 of the 1890s with what he was observing from inside Mr Blair's Downing Street in the 1990s, Dr Adonis pulled a volume of the Gladstone diaries

from the shelf and took a Gladstonian 'working' month at random – February 1893. From a quick scan I notice 17 days when Mr G spent long periods (typically five hours or more) on the front bench in the Commons as Leader of the House, including seven major speeches. I also note five meetings of the Cabinet (all at least two hours long), a party meeting and 94 official letters (all of which he would have written by hand, many of them long and technical). Then there are interviews and deputations. All this was before the Irish Home Rule Bill (which G played a large part in drafting) reached Committee in the Commons, when G spent night after night steering the Bill through personally aged 83![11]

Adonis's boss, of course, is famously not a great one for spending his hours at Westminster, as we have seen, nor does he have to write his own letters or draft his own legislation.

The load on the Prime Minister is like mercury – it shifts but is always heavy. In the postwar years, it has appeared to be increasingly relentless. And any thinking about the future of the job has to start by addressing it. Between them Roy Jenkins and Edward Bridges capture the premier's dilemma. You need at least four or five years to have a serious chance of shifting your polity and your country. Yet such is the punishing nature of the job that exhaustion, negativism and (I would add) often overmightiness, too, set in around this point. Herein lies the centrality of the overload problem and the reason why tackling it is a first-order question.

Immediately, however, one is struck by a forecasting problem. What kind of demands are likely to fall upon the holders of the office of Prime Minister? Looking back to the turn of the nineteenth and twentieth centuries, Sir Patrick Nairne reflected 'that, compared with today, the *beginning* of the century* offered a greater possibility of range – the notable agenda of the Asquith Government, the threatening rise of German power, the European prospects of coming revolution'.[12] Yet, Sir Patrick continued:

the Prime Minister and his advisers would not have foreseen then the vast extension of the role of government; the changed international role and the entry into Europe as the country's power declined and the Empire was transformed into the Commonwealth; the development of air travel, modern communications systems, and information technology; and the increasing pressure of the media. The substance of the Prime Minister's functions and the daily life at No. 10 have been hugely affected by these changes.[13]

Sir Patrick quite rightly wondered whether there were not bound to be changes of a comparable magnitude in the twenty-first century. 'Possibly', he concluded,

but at the start of this century nobody could have forecast with confidence that the Prime Minister's functions relating to party leadership, Cabinet government, Parliamentary accountability, international responsibilities, relations with the Sovereign and the national press would be basically unchanged at the century's end. *Plus ça change . . .*[14]

The Nairne analysis coincides very closely with Harold Wilson's notion

---

* Sir Patrick was writing in 1997.

which I quoted at the beginning of the book, of the job being 'organized by history'.[15]

For all the perils of prediction, some forecasting is possible of future shapers of the premiership.

- The amount of time a Prime Minister must spend on foreign affairs is unlikely to diminish except in the improbable event of a government consciously withdrawing the United Kingdom from the business of trying to influence the world.
- Even if that occurred, the hybrid arena where the domestic and the external fuse – the European Union – will continue to be a great absorber of prime ministerial time, personal energy and national political capital, even in the unlikely event of a UK withdrawal (which itself would make huge and continuing demands on a premier of a country engaged in a profound refashioning of its economy and its geopolitical position).
- What Douglas Hurd calls 'the avalanche of information'[16] which flows across a Prime Minister's desk, has not – and will not – be diminished by changes in IT. If anything, the information revolution has made this worse.
- The intrusions, pressure, pace and relentlessness of media demands on the head of government will not cease even if a future premier wanted his or her No. 10 to be more like Mr Attlee's than Mr Blair's.
- The reconfiguration of the British state from within – devolution together with the human rights and freedom of information regimes – are going to add to a Prime Minister's burdens. Semi-federal states are harder to keep on the road than unashamedly centrist ones.

Douglas Hurd has long believed that one of the best kept secrets in Whitehall is that a Prime Minister does not have to be a hugely overburdened figure. For him, the key is to have 'someone . . . at the centre who allows himself or herself to be reflective', someone who does not 'feel temperamentally compelled to be the head of the rush'. Therefore 'a Prime Minister in the twenty-first century should clear space around him and make sure that he has adequate time for reflection'.[17]

This prevents Hurd, as it prevents me, from being an advocate of the Prime Minister's Department solution. I would proffer instead what might be called the small-but-smart remedy for the lack of prime ministerial back-up, appropriate for a non-presidential premiership. This approach goes with the traditional collective grain rather than the command model. Cabinet colleagues must be given space and accorded the face to be serious and substantial political players and policy deliverers. An overmighty

No. 10 does not allow for this except at moments of serious trouble and dislocation when events oblige a Prime Minister to be more consultative.

So what would the job specification of a twenty-first century Prime Minister be inside the small-but-smart model of a No. 10, and within the context of a proper system of Cabinet government which affords Cabinet ministers the independent status and scope their office requires, while, at the same time, avoids excessive overload on the premier? First of all, the head of government has to be the keeper of the big picture, the guardian of the government's overall strategy. Such a function carries with it a prime and inevitable presentational function (though this does not have to be fulfilled continuously and obsessively with every day a battleground in a relentless information war).

The constitutional side of the job displays characteristics of both deep continuity and demanding novelty. Relations with the Monarch, accountability to the House of Commons and tone re-setting within it, a genuine sense of the collective Cabinet and Cabinet committee, a sensible and careful use of a traditional career Civil Service and a sense of difference between it and special adviserdom in all its forms – all these functions must be carried out within the context of procedures and conventions that afford what few internal checks and balances the British system of central government provides. The novelty arises in the area of the new constitutional settlement as part of a process of adjustment, which will be acute in the early years of the twenty-first century but will never entirely cease thereafter.

The special foreign and defence functions will remain, as will dealings at the heads of government level. Allied to this will be the special role of the Prime Minister as the overseer of the country's intelligence and security apparatus. Even without the very special nuclear weapons function (in the again unlikely event of a future premier abandoning such a national capability), these areas of necessarily high prime ministerial input will remain continuous and sometimes extremely stretching.

Where a new approach might help incumbent Prime Ministers and shift the job towards something closer to the Douglas Hurd model is a notion which sees the premier as what might be called the nation's risk manager in chief and, when 'events' intrude in an acute form, number 1 crisis manager. This specification argues for a continually well informed but not normally over-intrusive head of government and keeper of strategy. Prime Ministers have to have a sense of when to draw a particular policy into No. 10 and when to return it to the departmental minister normally in charge. Again, there is nothing new about such an analysis.

Reading the files of the first Wilson premierships as they were declassi-fied in the 1990s, I sensed an insider analyst I greatly admired – Sir Burke Trend – continually trying to steer his Prime Minister into a recognition of this, often, though not invariably, on the back of a crisis. He did it, as we have seen, in 1966, when he told Wilson, in effect, that he should not bounce his Cabinet again by requiring them to take serious economic decisions swiftly and unbriefed *and* that they had to confront realities if permanent remedies were to be found.[18]

Sir Burke addressed the problem of risk management in 1967 during the aftermath of the oil tanker *Torrey Canyon* running aground off Land's End, when he worried about the centre's capacity to handle emergencies. 'What has always bothered me about our emergencies organisation', he wrote, 'is that fact that, if something goes wrong we can usually improvise administrative arrangements pretty quickly, but we are much less efficient in mobilising the professional and technical advice which is required. We go to a good deal of trouble to keep up to date an organisation to deal (we hope!) with a nuclear war if one ever developed – even though most of us would put the risk pretty low. But we take no similar steps to try and anticipate in any organised way the results of the various kinds of peacetime disasters which are far more likely to happen.'[19]

During this same period when, as we have seen, a combination of overload and events was having a serious effect on the capacity of the Wilson variant of government (which his experiments with 'Inner Cabi-nets' did little or nothing to mitigate), as were the convulsions associated with successive defence reviews which the faltering economy obliged ministers to undertake, Trend also turned his attention to the need for a refashioning of the UK intelligence machine. Rightly surmising that Wil-son and his ministers within the intelligence loop did not wish to opt out of this aspect of the 'great game', Trend reminded the Prime Minister that: 'After the Second World War, it became apparent that we should henceforward have to make our way in the world by influence rather than by power and that political intelligence would henceforward be at least as important as military intelligence, if not more so.'[20] Out of these concerns in 1968, as we have seen, came a refashioning of the Joint Intelligence Committee with its own sharpened, bespoke, all-source analytical capacity in the form of the Cabinet Office Assessments Staff.[21]

Ted Heath's creation of the Central Policy Review Staff in 1970–71, in which Trend was also closely involved, embraced an attempt to remedy such governing defects in all areas but intelligence. To some extent, as we have also seen, Tony Blair's construction of his Cabinet Office-based but prime ministerially directed Performance and Innovation Unit and Social Exclusion Unit are his version of an attempt to build extra capacity for himself on part of his terrain to reach those problems that neither his Policy Unit nor the Cabinet Secretariat can handle to his satisfaction.

A variable-geometry approach is inevitable and desirable here. Though I worry if the loci of decision-*making* become confused and non-collective, a plurality of analytical capacities is compatible with proper Cabinet government and the range of them can and should be determined by prime ministerial styles and ways of working.

'Inner Cabinets' as they have operated formally or informally since 1945 have *not* proved an aid to good or effective government. But *if* one could be constructed that was a genuinely strategic body, it might have real utility as a way of linking Cabinet government to the big picture of the day by serving as the forum where the long-term, the vexing and the seemingly intractable could be pondered. This is an approach as yet untried by any premier. Though I can appreciate the human and procedural difficulties the Wilson experiments and other less formal variations have encountered in the past. And, as we have seen, Tony Blair has been resistant to such notions even when the idea of an inner group of senior ministers has been advocated by as influential a figure as Lord Simon.

This idea is unlikely to be a serious runner as a helper of the twenty-first-century premiership. So what would I propose? Simply put, an enhancement of No. 10's capacity to serve the Prime Minister as the government's strategy maker *and* blame carrier in chief. There are two ways in which this might be done. The existing Assessments Staff in the Cabinet Office could have its remit extended substantially to embrace a wide swathe of possible risks including domestic, health and environmental matters. This would involve a rethink and a reorganization even greater than the late-1960s review out of which the Assessments Staff was born.

Alternatively, a Prime Minister's risk assessment unit could be placed alongside the No. 10 Private Office and the Downing Street Policy Unit *and* the Cabinet Office's Assessments Staff to update, filter and present risks of all kinds to the PM. Its range would be very wide – all those areas and activities where setbacks, catastrophes or unforeseen developments can (rightly or wrongly) be laid at a PM's door.

How might such a unit be constructed? It should be fairly small – no more than a dozen people at any one time, drawn largely but not wholly from Whitehall insiders on secondment from relevant departments and agencies. The staff should rotate at eighteen-month to two-year intervals. It should provide the Prime Minister with a regular weekly risk assessment to supplement, but not replace, the JIC's 'Red Book'. It would be up to the Prime Minister to decide which ministerial colleagues and which officials should be on its circulation list.

The unit's staff should all have the highest security clearances and be backed up by a charter in the PM's name giving them access to people and data wherever it is located in the crown and public services. The unit's head should have access without hindrance to the Prime Minister at all times if urgent warning is required. The PM, if he or she wished, could commission specific assessments of a short-, medium- or long-term character from the Downing Street risk people.

Such a unit could have its dangers, of course. Risk assessment should not become risk obsession. As the great Marquess of Salisbury once said of his senior military advisers at the height of the 'Scramble for Africa': 'If these gentlemen had their way, they would soon be asking me to defend the moon against a possible attack from Mars.'[22] Doomwatchers need a sense of proportion and Prime Ministers a healthy dose of Salisbury-style scepticism. Nothing in the twenty-first century, I fear, will alter the more irrational expectations of what government can or cannot be expected to do or raise substantially the level of trust on the part of the electorate for the politicians voted into office. But that is not an argument in favour of being supine or resigned in the face of those famous 'events'.

For the buck will continue to stop in No. 10 when matters go awry. And whatever developments there are in Europe, the United Nations or any other supranational body, the premiership will remain the glittering prize bar none that attracts the ambitious and the politically highly charged in the United Kingdom. The office of Prime Minister will not cease to be an object of fable, fascination and concern to those who observe it, and of lust for those who aspire to it. But would even such aspirants sacrifice so much in terms of energy and private life to achieve it if they sensed the precarious realities of the job: the stress, the relentless demands, the constraints on action, the corrosive 'what ifs' when it was all over? Almost certainly the answer is yes. For with occasional exceptions, such as Attlee or Douglas-Home, premiers tend to be the sort of figures who believe it will be different this time because it's they who are there. In other words, self-belief is the greatest spur, and in that lies the potential temptation – and deformation – of excessive prime ministerialism.

Notes

1 The Platonic Idea and the Constitutional Deal

1. John Morley, *Walpole* (Macmillan, 1889), p. 157.
2. Earl of Oxford and Asquith, *Fifty Years in Parliament* vol. 2 (Cassell, 1926), p. 185.
3. Lord Butler was speaking on 'Cabinet Government Since 1970' at the Twentieth Century British History Seminar, Institute of Historical Research, 16 December 1998. This was a private occasion but Lord Butler has given me permission to reproduce this particular section of the question-and-answer session which followed his presentation (conversation with Lord Butler, 14 February 1999).
4. Lord Armstrong was addressing the 'Hidden Wiring' seminar of the MA in Contemporary British History programme at Queen Mary and Westfield College, University of London, on 'The Practice of Cabinet Government' on 20 January 1999.
5. Professor Jones was speaking on 'The Role of No. 10' at the ESRC/Goldsmiths/Civil Service Public Service Seminar at the British Academy on 2 October 1998. This was a private occasion but Professor Jones has given me permission to attribute this to him.
6. See chapter 4.
7. Armstrong, 'The Practice of Cabinet Government'.
8. Ibid.
9. Ibid.
10. Lord Butler of Brockwell, 'Cabinet Government'. The 1999 Attlee Foundation Lecture delivered at the Mansion House on 18 February 1999. I am grateful to Lord Butler for providing me with a copy of his text.
11. Ibid.
12. Ibid.
13. Ibid.
14. Peter Riddell, 'You'll never walk alone, Mr Blair', *The Times*, 22 February 1999.
15. Private information.
16. Butler, 'Cabinet Government'.

17. Discussion following Lord Butler's 'Cabinet Government Since 1970' presentation.

18. Peter Hennessy, 'The Blair Style of Government: An Historical Perspective and Interim Audit', *Government and Opposition*, vol. 33, no. 1 (winter 1998), p. 19. The former Cabinet minister's actual words were: 'Yes, but you can get away with it for a very long time.'

19. Discussion following Lord Butler's presentation 'Cabinet Government Since 1970'.

20. See chapter 16.

21. The phrase widely attributed to Harold Macmillan; see Peter Hennessy, *The Hidden Wiring: Unearthing the British Constitution* (Gollancz, 1995), p. 165.

22. Armstrong, 'The Practice of Cabinet Government'.

23. The proofs became Peter Hennessy, *The Blair Centre: A Question of Command and Control?* (Public Management Foundation, February 1999).

24. Private information.

25. Private information.

26. House of Commons, *Official Report*, 1 February 1999, col. 626.

27. Tony Benn addressing the QMW MA in Contemporary British History programme and the undergraduate Cabinet and Premiership course, House of Commons, 27 January 1999.

28. When published by the House of Commons, Mr Benn's measure was cited as the Commonwealth of Britain Bill, 1991 (HMSO, 1991).

29. Tony Benn to Peter Hennessy, February 1999 (no day given).

30. Tony Benn to QMW students, 27 January 1999.

31. Tony Benn MP, 'Modernization of the Premiership Bill, 1999', February 1999 draft. It was later published, after some redrafting in the House of Commons Table Office, as the Crown Prerogatives (Parliamentary Control) Bill 1999 and presented to the House of Commons on 3 March 1999.

32. Hennessy, *The Blair Centre*, p. 7.

33. Michael Prescott, 'Thatcher calls Blair "bossy"', *The Sunday Times*, 31 January 1999.

34. Roland Watson, '"Blair Unedited" comes unstuck', *The Times*, 2 February 1999.

35. Julia Hartley-Brewer, 'I'm not bossy just firm says Blair', *Evening Standard*, 1 February 1999.

36. *The Jimmy Young Show*, BBC Radio 2, 9 February 1999.

37. See chapter 16.

38. Peter Hennessy, 'View from Here', *Independent*, 4 March 1999.

2 Continuity and Cottage Pie

1. Lord Callaghan, interviewed for the BBC Radio 4 *Analysis* programme, 'The Back of the Envelope', first broadcast on 20 June 1991. The script is reproduced in Peter Hennessy, *Muddling Through: Power, Politics and the Quality of Government in Postwar Britain* (Gollancz, 1996), p. 44.

2. Margaret Thatcher, *The Downing Street Years* (HarperCollins, 1993), p. 17.

3. Conversation with Sir Kenneth Stowe, 8 March 1997.

4. Private information.

5. Conversation with Sir Kenneth Stowe, 8 March 1997.

6. Private information.

7. Private information.

8. Private information.

9. Thatcher, *The Downing Street Years*, p. 18.

10. Conversation with Sir Kenneth Stowe, 8 March 1997.

11. Thatcher, *The Downing Street Years*, p. 18.

12. Conversation with Sir Kenneth Stowe, 8 March 1997.

13. Thatcher, *The Downing Street Years*, p. 19.

14. Private information.

15. Thatcher, *The Downing Street Years*, p. 19.

16. Ibid., pp. 25–6.

17. Private information.

18. Conversation with Sir Kenneth Stowe, 8 March 1997.

19. Ibid.

20. Roy Jenkins, *The Chancellors* (Macmillan, 1998), p. 10.

21. David Knowles, *The Historian and Character* (Cambridge University Press, 1955), p. 4.

22. Eric Hobsbawm, *On History* (Weidenfeld and Nicolson, 1997), p. vii.

23. Michael Young, *The Rise of the Meritocracy* (Allen Lane, 1961).

24. Ross Terrill, *R. H. Tawney and His Times: Socialism as Fellowship* (Harvard University Press, 1973).

25. Conversation with Lord Young of Dartington, 24 March 1994.

26. For a useful and succinct study of this approach see R. A. W. Rhodes, 'Introducing the Core Executive', in R. A. W. Rhodes and Patrick Dunleavy (eds.), *Prime Minister, Cabinet and Core Executive* (Macmillan, 1995).

27. Percy Cradock, *In Pursuit of British Interests: Reflections on Foreign Policy Under Margaret Thatcher and John Major* (John Murray, 1997) p. 37. Sir Percy, in this passage, was talking abut the world of the Joint Intelligence Committee which he chaired 1985–92.

28. Ibid., p. 34.

29. Bryan Magee, *Confessions of a Philosopher* (Weidenfeld and Nicolson, 1997), p. 25.

30. Ibid., p. 24.

31. Morrison declared, probably at an LSE seminar, that 'Socialism is what the Labour Government does'. Peter Hennessy, *Never Again: Britain 1945–1951* (Vintage, 1993), p. 196.

3   The Double-Headed Nation

1. Public Record Office (hereafter, PRO), CAB 21/1638, 'Function of the Prime Minister and His Staff', 1947–9.

2. Conversation with Sir Kenneth Stowe, 8 March 1997.

3. Letter from Lord Charteris to the author, 8 March 1997.

4. For a short but atmospheric re-creation of the background to the general election of February 1974 see Phillip Whitehead, *The Writing on the Wall: Britain in the Seventies* (Michael Joseph and Channel 4 Television, 1985), pp. 99–115.

5. Private information.

6. Vernon Bogdanor, *The Monarchy and the Constitution* (Clarendon Press, 1995), p. 27.

7. Ibid., p. 148.

8. Interview with Lord Charteris for the Wide Vision Productions/Channel 4 television series *What Has Become of Us?*, 6 June 1994.

9. Lord Callaghan speaking on the BBC Radio 4 *Analysis* programme, 'The Back of the Envelope', first broadcast on 20 June 1991 and quoted in Peter Hennessy, *Muddling Through: Power, Politics and the Quality of Government in Postwar Britain* (Gollancz, 1996), pp. 35–6.

10. Bogdanor, *The Monarchy and the Constitution*, p. 149; John Ramsden, *The Winds of Change: Macmillan to Heath 1957–1975* (Longman, 1996), pp. 387–9.

11. Jeremy Thorpe, *In My Own Time: Reminiscences of a Liberal Leader* (Politicos, 1999), p. 115.

12. Interview with Lord Charteris, 6 June 1994.

13. Ibid.

14. Ibid.

15. Ibid.

16. Ibid.

17. The official life appeared as John W. Wheeler-Bennett, *King George VI: His Life and Reign* (Macmillan, 1958).

18. Balfour is quoted in W. Ivor Jennings, *Cabinet Government* (Cambridge University Press, 1936), p. 427. Jennings does not cite the original source.

19. Interview with Lord Charteris, 6 June 1994.

20. Hennessy, *Muddling Through*, p. 37; Bogdanor, *The Monarchy and the Constitution*, p. 149.

21. Vernon Bogdanor, 'The Fall of Heath and the End of the Post-war Settlement', in Stuart Ball and Anthony Seldon (eds.), *The Heath Government 1970–74* (Longman, 1996), p. 373.

22. Lord Elwyn Jones, *In My Time: An Autobiography* (Weidenfeld and Nicolson, 1983), p. 260. I am grateful to my colleague Professor John Ramsden for pointing out this reference to me.

23. Private information.

24. Interview with Lord Charteris, 6 June 1994.

25. See 'The Back of the Envelope' as quoted in Hennessy, *Muddling Through*, p. 50.

26. Stephen Sedley, 'The Sound of Silence: Constitutional Law Without a Constitution', *Law Quarterly Review*, April 1994, pp. 220, 272.

27. Sidney Low, *The Governance of England* (Fisher Unwin, 1904), p. 12.

28. This principle is enshrined as the heading to the No. 10 Downing Street planning papers for both the 1959 and the 1964 general elections. See PRO, PREM 5/232, 'Deadlock. The Queen's Government Must Be Carried On', Bligh to Macmillan, 'Top Secret and Personal', 5 October 1959 (I am grateful to my research student David Welsh for drawing this file to my attention); PRO, PREM 11/4756, 'Top Secret and Personal. Deadlock. The Queen's Government Must Be Carried On', DJM [Derek Mitchell, Principal Private Secretary], 16 October 1964.

29. I am grateful to Bridget Wright of the Royal Library at Windsor Castle for bringing the original source of the phrase to my attention. During the change of administration from Whig to Tory in 1834, Wellington, from 15 November until 9 December when he made way for Peel, was, in Elizabeth Longford's words, 'everybody from Prime Minister downwards, holding five major and three minor offices'. Elizabeth Longford, *Wellington: Pillar of State* (Weidenfeld and Nicolson, 1972), p. 303. It was Disraeli who recorded Wellington as saying 'in his curt husky manner . . . that he had to carry on the King's government'. Benjamin Disraeli, *Coningsby, Or the New Generation* (Colburn, 1844), pp. 199–200. Letter from Margaret Timblin, Secretary to the Librarian, The Royal Library, to the author, 23 June 1998.

30. 'The Back of the Envelope' as quoted in Hennessy, *Muddling Through*, p. 50.

31. Private information. Philip Ziegler originally spun the 'golden triangle' metaphor; conversation with Philip Ziegler, 13 June 1991, during the preparation of 'The Back of the Envelope'.

32. Private information.

33. PRO, PREM 13/878, 'General Election 1966: Arrangements for Prorogation and Dissolution of Parliament by Proclamation'. The document entitled 'Dissolution' is undated and there is no indication of its author, but it could either be by Mrs E. J. Cooper, No. 10's records officer in 1966, or by William Reid, then the Cabinet Office Under Secretary dealing with constitutional matters.

34. Ibid.

35. Ibid. 'Note for the Record. Election Timetable', DJM [Derek Mitchell], 27 February 1966.

36. Ibid.

37. Ibid.

38. Ibid. 'Spearhead', from 10 Downing Street to Royal Party on Tour, 27 February 1966.

39. 'Sword 52', from Royal Party on Tour to Prime Ministers [sic] Office, 28 February 1966.

40. Lord Armstrong speaking in 'The Back of the Envelope' and quoted in Hennessy, *Muddling Through*, p. 50.

41. PRO, PREM 13/878, 'Dissolution'.

42. *The Shorter Oxford Dictionary*, vol.2 (Clarendon Press, 1973), p. 1960.

43. PRO, PREM 13/878, 'Dissolution'.

44. Tom McNally speaking in 'The Back of the Envelope' and quoted in Hennessy, *Muddling Through*, p. 49.

45. Ibid., p. 41.

46. Letter from Amy Baker to Peter Hennessy, 28 January 1997.

47. House of Lords, *Official Report*, 18 July 1867, cols. 1960–61.

48. Letter from Amy Baker to Peter Hennessy, 28 January 1997.

49. Ibid.

50. D. R. Thorpe, *Alec Douglas-Home* (Sinclair-Stevenson, 1996), p. 313.

51. Private information.

52. Private information.

53. Private information.

54. Speaking in 'The Back of the Envelope' and quoted in Hennessy, *Muddling Through*, p. 45.

55. Ditto, ibid., p. 50.

56. Ditto, ibid., p. 38.

57. Ibid.

58. Sir Robin was speaking on the occasion of my Inaugural Lecture (which he kindly chaired) at Queen Mary and Westfield College, University of London on 1 February 1994.

59. PRO, PREM 13/878, 'Dissolution and the Queen's Absence Abroad', E. J. Cooper to Derek Mitchell, 18 January 1966.

60. PRO, PREM 11/4756.

61. PRO, PREM 5/232.

62. PRO, PREM 11/4756.

63. See Peter Hennessy, 'Searching for the "Great Ghost": The Palace, the Premiership, the Cabinet and the Constitution in the Post-War Period', *Journal of Contemporary History*, vol.30, no. 2 (April 1995), pp. 220–24.

64. Private information.

65. Neil Kinnock was delivering the annual GCHQ Lecture to the Association of First Division Civil Servants. It was reproduced as Neil Kinnock, 'Union ban: "Arrogant abuse of power"', *FDA News*, January 1995, pp. 6–7.

66. Private information.

67. Private information.

68. Speaking in 'The Back of the Envelope' and quoted in Hennessy, *Muddling Through*, p. 51.

51. The most famous handbag in world political history: Mrs Thatcher on *Nationwide* May 1981.

52. The most potent television image ever: Conservative Party Conference, 1983.

53. Mrs Thatcher on board the Polaris submarine *HMS Resolution*: She liked to play herself in war-games.

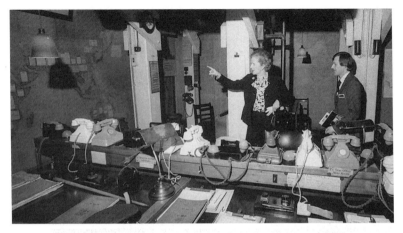

54. The Falklands War leader visits Churchill's War Rooms, April 1984.

55. A politicized Civil Service? Sir Robin Butler (left rear) tried to persuade Mrs Thatcher in 1987 that Charles Powell (right rear) had to move on.

56. 'The constitutional coup d'état': Mrs Thatcher leaves Downing Street for her final weekend at Chequers, 27 November 1990.

57. Sir John Hunt: Sustainer of the collective executive.

58. The Chancellor with the common touch: John Major with Treasury Press Secretary Gus O'Donnell, eight months before becoming prime minister.

59. The Dave Allen school of election-eering: John Major on high stool talks to his activists during the 1992 campaign.

60. John Major, doing what he likes best, watches Kent play Middlesex with the 'Voice of Summer', Brian Johnston (*right*) at Canterbury, August 1992.

61. Hague and chips: The Majors and William Hague dine at Harry Ramsden's in Cardiff, June 1996.

62. The Old and New Labour guards line-up behind Harold Wilson's coffin, Isles of Scilly, May 1995: Front row (*from left to right*) Tony Blair, Jim Callaghan, Barbara Castle and Gerald Kaufman (Robert Armstrong stands between Blair and Kaufman).

63. A few days away from power: The Blairs, watched by Richard Branson, prepare to ride to victory, 27 April 1997.

64. A step short of coalition: The first meeting of the Joint Consultative Committee with the Liberal Democratic Party in the Cabinet Room, September 1997. To the Prime Minister's right sits the Secretary of the Cabinet, Sir Robin Butler. Behind Sir Robin sits Jonathan Powell, Mr Blair's Chief-of-Staff. To his immediate left are Robin Cook, Donald Dewar and Peter Mandelson. Paddy Ashdown is in the foreground.

65. Tony Blair with his Cabinet Secretary, Sir Richard Wilson: Modernization as a cloak for creeping politicization?

66. Twin-stellar government in operation: Command Chancellor and Command Premier takes to the air-waves on *Talk Radio*, March 1998.

67. 'Call me Tony': The informal style in Downing Street, November 1999.

68. Tony-as-warrior: Mr Blair, flanked by
George Robertson, Secretary of State for
Defence, and Sir Charles Guthrie, Chief of
the Defence Staff, presides over the morning
meeting in PINDAR, the MOD's war-room,
on the last day of Gulf War II. In the foreground (left), Michael Pakenham, Chairman
of the Joint Intelligence Committee, and
(right), perhaps surprisingly, David
Miliband, Head of the Downing St
Policy Unit.

69. Joined-up communication? Sir Robin
Mountfield, Second Permanent Secretary
to the Cabinet Office (left), and Alastair
Campbell return to Whitehall after briefing
Parliament on the new Government
Information and Communication
Service, June 1998.

69. Bogdanor, *The Monarchy and the Constitution*, pp. 180–81.

70. Speaking in 'The Back of the Envelope' and quoted in Hennessy, *Muddling Through*, pp. 42–3.

71. *The Times*, 2 May 1950.

72. Private information.

73. Quoted in Hennessy, *Muddling Through*, p. 15. The Queen was attending a seminar in the Department of History at Queen Mary and Westfield College while opening the new Arts Faculty Building on 28 October 1992.

74. This was the title of the 1997 Johnian Society Lecture, delivered by the author at St John's College, Cambridge on 25 February that year, and on which this chapter is based.

4   Organized by History: The Premiership Before 1945

1. David Cannadine, *G. M. Trevelyan: A Life in History* (Fontana, 1992), p. 123.

2. PRO, CAB 21/4959, 'Sir Norman Brook: Miscellaneous engagements and personal correspondence'. 'Cabinet Government', delivered to the Home Office, 26 June 1959.

3. Anthony King, 'The British Prime Ministership in the Age of the Career Politician', in G. W. Jones (ed.), *West European Prime Ministers* (Frank Cass, 1991), p. 31.

4. Harold Wilson, *The Governance of Britain* (Weidenfeld and Nicolson/Michael Joseph, 1976), pp. 12–20.

5. Private information.

6. Wilson, *The Governance of Britain*, pp. 12–20.

7. Ibid., pp. 1–11. The book, he declared simply on page 1, 'is not concerned with theories'.

8. Ibid., pp. x–xi. Wilson wrote on p. x. of his 12–14 hour days and his reading of at least 500 documents or submissions on 'an average weekend'.

9. Ben Pimlott, *Harold Wilson* (HarperCollins, 1992), pp. 11–12. 'As Labour Leader', Pimlott wrote, Wilson 'liked to equate the Scouting Code with his brand of socialism . . .'

10. I remember sensing this when, as a young journalist on *The Times*, I called on Wilson in No. 10 a few weeks before his surprise resignation in 1976. I went to see him as part of preparing an article on the Cabinet Office. I almost couldn't get away. Each time I suggested he had been very kind to see me and that I knew how busy he was he would bid me to stay as the subject was so interesting to him. I've every reason to believe it was, as he quoted the resulting article in *The Governance of Britain*. Conversation with Harold Wilson, 1 March 1976: Peter Hennessy, 'A Magnificent Piece of Powerful Bureaucratic Machinery', *The Times*, 8 March 1976; Wilson, *The Governance of Britain*, p. 63fn; see also Harold Wilson, *A Prime Minister on Prime Ministers* (Weidenfeld and Nicolson, 1977).

11. Wilson, *The Governance of Britain*, p. x.

12. Winston S. Churchill, *The Second World War*, vol. 2, *The Twilight War* (Cassell, 1964), pp. 238–9.

13. See E. J. Hobsbawm, 'Obituary: E. P. Thompson', *Independent*, 30 August 1993.

14. Robert Blake, *The Office of Prime Minister* (British Academy/Oxford University Press, 1975), pp. 70–73.

15. B. W. Hill, *Sir Robert Walpole: 'Sole and Prime Minister'* (Hamish Hamilton, 1989), pp. 1–5, 206–7.

16. PRO, CAB 21/4548, 'UK Constitutional System, 1951–1959, Part 2'. The catalogue entry at the PRO describes the file as 'UK Constitutional System', but the Cabinet Office's own, original title for it was 'British Constitutional System'. It appears to have been compiled on their own initiative by the Treasury's machinery of government division under the leadership of the chess-master and wartime code breaker, Stuart Milner-Barry.

17. J. R. H. Weaver (ed.), *The Dictionary of National Biography 1922–1930* (Oxford University Press, 1937), p. 47.

18. J. H. Plumb, *England in the Eighteenth Century (1714–1815)* (Pelican, 1966), pp. 49–50.

19. Christopher Jones, *No. 10 Downing Street: The Story of a House* (BBC, 1985), p. 38.

20. William Rees-Mogg, 'When Parliament Becomes a Bore', *The Times*, 31 July 1995.

21. The term was already in common use in France. See Donald Shell and Richard Hodder-Williams (eds.), *Churchill to Major: The British Prime Ministership since 1945* (Hurst, 1995), p. 3; and Marcel Sibert, *Etude sur le Premier Ministre en Angleterre* (Rousseau, 1909), p. 37. Harold Wilson claimed that the epithet of 'prime minister' was first used in the 1670s against Danby in Charles II's time: Wilson, *A Prime Minister on Prime Ministers*, p. 8.

22. For the Bill of Rights 1689 see W. C. Costin and J. Steven Watson (eds.), *The Law and Working of the Constitution: Documents 1660–1914*, vol. 1, *1660–1783* (Adam and Charles Black, 1952), pp. 67–74.

23. Glyn Williams and John Ramsden, *Ruling Britannia: A Political History of Britain 1688–1988* (Longman, 1990), p. 20.

24. Ibid., pp. 29–30; Betty Kemp, *King and Commons, 1660–1832* (Macmillan, 1957), pp. 118–19; for the Act of Settlement see Costin and Watson, *The Law and Working of the Constitution*, vol. 2, pp. 92–6.

25. Walter Bagehot, *The English Constitution*, first published 1867 (Fontana, 1963), p. 65.

26. J. H. Plumb, *The Growth of Political Stability in England 1675–1725* (Macmillan, 1967), pp. 112–14.

27. Hill, *Sir Robert Walpole*, pp. 3–4.

28. For a display of Victoria's propensity to interfere see G. H. L. Le May, *The Victorian Constitution* (Duckworth, 1979), chapter 3, 'Victoria and Her Ministers'. For Le May's quote on Dilke see ibid., p. 93.

29. The former Secretary of the Cabinet, Lord Hunt of Tanworth, has been especially eloquent on the significance of the replacement of a single chief executive by a collective executive. See Edmund Dell and Lord Hunt of Tanworth, 'The Failings of Cabinet Government in Mid to Late 1970s', *Contemporary Record*, vol. 8, no. 3 (winter 1994), p. 466.

30. F. W. G. Benemy used this title for his 1965 study of prime ministerial power. F. W. G. Benemy, *The Elected Monarch: The Development of the Power of the Prime Minister* (Harrap, 1965).

31. Kemp, *King and Commons, 1660–1832*, p. 126.

32. Williams and Ramsden, *Ruling Britannia*, p. 106.

33. Kemp, *King and Commons, 1660–1832*, p. 126.

34. Wilson, *A Prime Minister on Prime Ministers*, p. 20.

35. Byrum E. Carter, *The Office of Prime Minister* (Faber and Faber, 1956), pp. 224–5.

36. The Carlingford case is the one usually cited to illustrate the inability of even Mr Gladstone's 'imperious vitality' (Sir Algernon West, *Recollections 1832 to 1886* (Nelson, 1899), p. 285) to remove unwanted ministers from the Cabinet. 'Early in 1884', writes Robert Blake, 'Gladstone wanted to remove Lord Carlingford, the Lord Privy Seal, in order to make a place for Lord Rosebery. There was nothing against Carlingford and he would not resign. Gladstone was most reluctant to dismiss him. "Mr Gladstone," wrote Harcourt to Morley, "entertains great doubts as to the right of a Prime Minister to require a Cabinet Minister to resign." In fact Carlingford stayed on till the end of the year when he did at last go of his own accord.' Blake, *The Office of Prime Minister*, p. 37.

37. W. E. Gladstone, *Gleanings of Past Years*, vol. 1 (John Murray, 1879), p. 243.

38. Lord Rosebery, *Miscellanies*, vol. 1 (Hodder, 1921), p. 197.

39. Peter Hennessy, *The Hidden Wiring: Unearthing the British Constitution* (Gollancz, 1995), pp. 78–9.

40. PRO, CAB 21/1638, 'Function of the Prime Minister and His Staff'. For the genesis of this see Peter Hennessy, 'Searching for the "Great Ghost": The Palace, the Premiership, the Cabinet and the Constitution in the Post-War Period', *Journal of Contemporary History*, vol. 30, no. 2 (April 1995), p. 220.

41. Le May, *The Victorian Constitution*, p. 125.

42. Roy Jenkins, *Gladstone* (Macmillan, 1995), p. 294.

43. Christopher Andrew, *Secret Service: The Making of the British Intelligence Community* (Heinemann, 1985), pp. 1–2.

44. PRO, CAB 21/4548.

45. For George III's last appearance see Blake, *The Office of Prime Minister*, p. 28. For the differences between the 'Nominal' and the 'Efficient Cabinets' see A. Aspinall, 'The Cabinet Council, 1783–1835', *Proceedings of the British Academy*, vol. 38 (1952), pp. 145–8.

46. Ibid., pp. 148–9; Kemp, *King and Commons, 1660–1832*, p. 128; Blake, *The Office of Prime Minister*, pp. 22–6.

47. Le May, *The Victorian Constitution*, p. 30.

48. She would remind Treasury officials of her position as First Lord on the rare occasions when signs of resistance came from that quarter. Private information.

49. Blake, *The Office of Prime Minister*, pp. 26, 32.

50. Olive Anderson, 'Cabinet Government and the Crimean War', *English Historical Review*, vol. 79 (1964), p. 549.

51. The historian was Kinglake. See John Mackintosh, *The British Cabinet* (University Paperback, 1968), pp. 166–7, 166 n.36. See A. W. Kinglake, *The Invasion of Crimea*, Students' edition (Blackwood, 1899).

52. Aspinall, 'The Cabinet Council, 1783–1835', pp. 181–93.

53. John Ehrman, *Cabinet Government and War, 1890–1940* (Archon Books, 1969), p. 6.

54. Ibid., p. 25.

55. Ibid., pp. 28–33.

56. Williams and Ramsden, *Ruling Britannia*, pp. 63, 129.

57. Blake, *The Office of Prime Minister*, pp. 30–31.

58. Aspinall, 'The Cabinet Council, 1783–1835', pp. 149–50.

59. Michael Brock, *The Great Reform Act* (Hutchinson University Library, 1973), p. 136.

60. Ibid.

61. Dr Peter Catterall to the Economic and Social Research Council, 11 June 1997: 'Cabinet Government: Progress Report'.

62. Aspinall, 'The Cabinet Council, 1783–1835', pp. 166–7. For the Wellington–Peel exchanges see Sir Robert Peel, *Memoirs* (John Murray, 1856), pp. 50–51.

63. PRO, PREM 5/211, 'Ministerial Appointments. Ministry of Winston Churchill (Coalition Government). Part 3', John Martin to Churchill, 19 March 1942.

64. A list of such appointments since 1924 (thirteen in all) was produced for Macmillan during his premiership. PRO, PREM 5/233, 'Ministerial Appointments. Ministry of Harold Macmillan (Conservative). Part 4'.

65. PRO, PREM 5/439, 'Ministerial Appointments. Harold Wilson (Labour). Part 2', Sorensen to Wilson, 4 January 1965; Wilson to Sorensen, 12 January 1965.

66. PRO, PREM 5/439, 'Note for the Record', DJM [Derek Mitchell, Wilson's Principal Private Secretary], 28 January 1965; Wilson to Gordon Walker, 22 January 1965.

67. PRO, PREM 5/430, 'Ministerial Appointments. Order of Procedure of Ministers, 1924–1940'. Curzon to Hankey, 16 December 1924. For Lord Hailsham's view see *A Sparrow's Flight* (Collins, 1990), p. 298.

68. PRO, LCO 2/3215, 'The Cabinet: Draft of a Broadcast by Lord Hankey'.

69. PRO, PREM 5/377, 'Ministerial Appointments. Ministry of Harold Macmillan (Conservative). Part 9', Sir Noel Hutton, Parliamentary Counsel, to T. J. Bligh, Principal Private Secretary to the Prime Minister, 10 April 1963 and 25 April 1963.

70. Sir William R. Anson, *Law and Custom of the Constitution*, vol. 1 (4th edn, Oxford University Press, 1935), pp. 90–95, and private information.

71. E. J. Feuchtwanger, *Gladstone* (Allen Lane, 1975), pp. 110–11.

72. W. Ivor Jennings, *Cabinet Government* (Cambridge University Press, 1936), pp. 182–3.

73. Feuchtwanger, *Gladstone*, p. 110; Henry Roseveare, *The Treasury: The Evolution of a British Institution* (Allen Lane, 1969), p. 140.

74. Mackintosh, *The British Cabinet*, p. 315.

75. Martin Gilbert, *Never Despair: Winston S. Churchill, 1945–65* (Heinemann, 1988), p. 510.

76. Robert Blake, *Disraeli* (Eyre and Spottiswoode, 1966), pp. 645–6.

77. Professor Philip Norton, 'Memorandum' to the Procedure Committee, 23 November 1994, House of Commons Select Committee on Procedure, *Prime Minister's Questions*, Seventh Report, Session 1994–95, HC 555 (HMSO, 1995), p. 1.

78. John Wilson, *CB: A Life of Sir Henry Campbell-Bannerman* (St Martin's Press, 1973), pp. 190–201; Le May, *The Victorian Constitution*, p. 80; Mackintosh, *The British Cabinet*, pp. 252–3.

79. Mackintosh, *The British Cabinet*, pp. 314–15; see also Ruddock F. Mackay, *Balfour: Intellectual Statesman* (Oxford University Press, 1985), pp. 144–55. Balfour, to be precise, engineered the resignation of the free traders rather than sacking them outright. I am grateful to Dr Graham Goodlad for this point.

80. I am grateful to Dr Peter Catterall for reminding me of the existence of this minute.

81. Anthony Eden, *Full Circle* (Cassell, 1960), p. 367.

82. Ehrman, *Cabinet Government and War, 1890–1940*, p. 29.

83. For the origins of this convention, see Geoffrey Marshall, *Constitutional Conventions: The Rules and Forms of Political Accountability* (Clarendon Press, 1984), pp. 48–51.

84. Jennings, *Cabinet Government*, pp. 311–13.

85. For example, Wilson took the 1970 decision with his 'Inner Cabinet' on 14 May 1970. See Barbara Castle, *The Castle Diaries 1964–70* (Weidenfeld and Nicolson, 1984), p. 799. Diary entry for 14 May 1970. In the autumn of 1994 John Major consulted his Chancellor, Kenneth Clarke and five other senior ministers over supper at No. 10 before deciding to threaten his Euro-rebels with a general election if the Government lost its vote on contributions to the EU budget. See Andrew Marr, *Ruling Britannia: The Failure and Future of British Democracy* (Michael Joseph, 1995), pp. 266–7. The government prevailed, so no dissolution request was placed before the Queen.

86. S. S. Wilson, *The Cabinet Office to 1945* (HMSO, 1975) p. 55.

87. Mackintosh, *The British Cabinet*, pp. 378–9.

88. Wilson, *CB*, picture caption facing p. 529.

89. See Sir Kenneth Berrill, 'Strength at the Centre – The Case for a Prime Minister's Department', in Anthony King (ed.), *The British Prime Minister*, 2nd edn. (Macmillan, 1985), pp. 242–57.

90. G. W. Jones, 'The Prime Minister's Secretaries', in J. A. G. Griffith (ed.), *From Policy to Administration: Essays in Honour of William A. Robson* (Allen and Unwin, 1976), pp. 29–30.

91. James Blitz and George Parker, 'Mandarins put the squeeze on Blair', *Financial Times*, 30 May 1997; Anthony Bevins, 'New sleaze row knocks at door of No. 10', *Independent*, 25 June 1997; Richard Norton-Taylor and Ewen MacAskill, 'Whitehall blocks Blair over favourite aide's role', *Guardian*, 3 June 1997.

92. Colin Brown, 'PM aide leaves for top Australia job', *Independent*, 15 August 1997.

93. For Midlothian see Philip Magnus, *Gladstone* (John Murray, 1954), pp. 259–67.

94. Michael Foley, *The Rise of the British Presidency* (Manchester University Press, 1993), chapter 5, pp. 120–47.

95. G. M. Young, *Stanley Baldwin* (Hart Davis, 1952), p. 83.

96. Ibid., pp. 117–18.

97. James Margach, *The Anatomy of Power* (W. H. Allen, 1979), p. 137.

98. Martin Gilbert, *Winston S. Churchill: Road to Victory 1941–1945* (Heinemann, 1986), p. 715.

99. PRO, PREM 11/565, 'Record of Events Leading to Dropping of Bombs on Hiroshima and Nagasaki', Cherwell to Churchill, 28 January 1953. Churchill asked Cherwell to prepare a note on, in Cherwell's words, 'the principal events leading up to the dropping of the atomic bombs at Hiroshima and Nagaski'.

100. For varying prime ministerial practice see Peter Hennessy, *Cabinet* (Blackwell, 1986), chapter 4, 'Cabinets and the Bomb', pp. 123–62 and Peter Hennessy, *Muddling Through: Power, Politics and the Quality of Government in Postwar Britain* (Gollancz, 1996), pp. 99–129.

101. David Butler, *British General Elections Since 1945* (Blackwell, 1989), p. 1.

102. The Prime Minister's Secret Service functions have to some extent been spelled out in the Security Service Act 1989 and the Intelligence Services Act 1994.

103. PRO, PREM 5/448, 'Ministerial Appointments. Ministerial changes. Personal correspondence . . .', Salisbury to Eden, September 1955; Eden to Salisbury, 19 September 1955.

104. 'Prime Minister' is always added in brackets after the First Lordship in the official notice of the new premier's swearing-in at a special meeting of the Privy Council called at Buckingham Palace for such purposes. See for example PRO, PREM 5/216 for Attlee in 1945, PREM 5/223 for Churchill in 1951, PREM 5/228 for Eden in 1955, PREM 5/230 for Macmillan in 1957, PREM 5/426 for Home in 1963 and PREM 5/438 for Wilson in 1964.

5 Beyond any Mortal? The Stretching of the Premiership Since 1945

1. *Daily Telegraph*, 31 March 1986, quoted in Antony Jay (ed.), *The Oxford Dictionary of Political Quotations* (Oxford University Press, 1996), p. 297.

2. Letter from Enoch Powell to Peter Hennessy, 17 March 1997.

3. *Observer*, 24 May 1925, quoted in Jay (ed.), *The Oxford Dictionary of Political Quotations*, p. 29.

4. PRO, PREM 5/233, 'Ministerial Appointments. Ministry of Harold Macmillan (Conservative). Part 4', Macmillan to Lloyd, 30 July 1960.

5. Michael Foley, *The Rise of the British Presidency* (Manchester University Press, 1993), p. 263.

6. PRO, PREM 5/233, Bligh to Macmillan, 22 July 1960. Churchill had delivered his remarks during a House of Commons debate on Halifax's appointment on 28 February 1938.

7. *Reflections*, Harold Macmillan talks to Ludovic Kennedy, BBC1, 20 October 1983.

8. John Grigg, *Lloyd George: From Peace to War 1912–1916* (Methuen, 1985), p. 474.

9. Personal knowledge.

10. ' "A Prime Minister governs by curiosity . . ." Harold Wilson talks about his job to Kenneth Harris', *Observer*, 24 October 1965. I am indebted to Professor M. R. D. Foot for finding this article in his collection and for kindly giving it to me on 27 October 1996.

11. See Edmund Dell and Lord Hunt of Tanworth, 'The Failings of Cabinet Government in Mid to Late 1970s', *Contemporary Record*, vol. 8, no. 3 (winter 1994), p. 466.

12. The phrase is John Morley's. See his *Walpole* (Macmillan, 1889), p. 157.

13. ' "A Prime Minister governs by curiosity . . ." '.

14. John P. Mackintosh, *The British Cabinet* (Stevens, 1962).

15. PRO, CAB 21/4324. 'Cabinet Government: Principle of Collective Responsibility, 1950–1960'; for Brook on Macmillan's thinking see PRO, CAB 21/4983, 'Function of Prime Minister and Staff, 1959–1964'. Brook to Bishop, 26 August 1959; Professor Max Beloff, 'British "President"; evolution of Prime Minister's Office', *Daily Telegraph*, 2 August 1960; Lord Boothby, 'Parliament in decline; way to bring back members' power,' *Daily Telegraph*, 4 August 1960; Earl Attlee, 'Premier and his team; advantages over presidential system', *Daily Telegraph*, 9 August 1960.

16. For an excellent collection encompassing the 1960s debate see Anthony King (ed.), *The British Prime Minister*, 2nd edn (Macmillan, 1985). For these extracts from the argument see Mackintosh, *The British Cabinet*, pp. 451–2; R. H. S. Crossman's 'Introduction' to the 1963 Fontana edition of Walter Bagehot, *The English Constitution*, p. 51; G. W. Jones, 'The Prime Minister's Power', *Parliamentary Affairs*, no. 28 (spring 1965), pp. 167–85. See also Patrick Weller, *First Among Equals: Prime Ministers in Westminster Systems* (Allen and Unwin, 1985), pp. 1–7.

17. Foley, *The Rise of the British Presidency*. 'Leadership stretch' is from the title of his chapter 5, pp. 120–47.

18. Anthony King, 'Executives', in Nelson Polsby and Fred Greenstein (eds.), *A Handbook of Political Science* (Addison-Wesley, 1975), pp. 232–3.

19. Private information.

20. PRO, CAB 21/1638, 'Function of the Prime Minister and His Staff'.

21. Ibid.

22. Private information. I have tried to have the position altered, but have been courteously refused.

23. For a detailed account of the very special relationship between No. 10 and Buckingham Palace see Peter Hennessy, *The Hidden Wiring: Unearthing the British Constitution* (Indigo edn, 1996), pp. 43–72.

24. PRO, PREM 5/377, 'Ministerial Appointments. Ministry of Harold Macmillan (Conservative). Part 9', Hutton to Bligh, 10 April 1963.

25. Private information.

26. PRO, PREM 11/1516, Lloyd to Eden, 11 April 1956, reporting his conversation that day with Hugh Gaitskell, the Leader of the Opposition.

27. PRO, PREM 11/3689, 'Situation in Cuba, Part 2', 'Record of a Meeting held at Admiralty House on Tuesday, October 23, 1962'.

28. PRO PREM 11/3859, 'Record of a Meeting Between Prime Minister and Mr Gaitskell, 20 November 1962'.

29. Ibid.

30. PRO, PREM 11/4892, 'Record of Meetings Between Prime Minister and Leader of HM Opposition. Note for the Record', 2 December 1963.

31. PRO, PREM 11/4733, 'Talk on Defence Policy with Members of HM Opposition'. See especially Thorneycroft to Douglas-Home, 3 February 1964, on his conversation that day with Denis Healey.

32. PRO, PREM 11/4892, 'Note for the Record', 25 February 1964; PRO, PREM 13/1447, 'Exchange Rate: Measures to Devalue the Pound Sterling; "Operation Patriarch". Provisional Timetable, Saturday 18th November – Sunday 9th November 1967'.

33. PRO, CAB 21/3719, 'Consultation with Leaders of the Parliamentary Opposition (Policy). Memorandum on Defence by Mr Churchill', 10 May 1949.

34. The minutes and memoranda of GEN 293 are preserved in PRO, CAB 130/47. The meetings were held on 13 and 20 July and 20 October 1949.

35. For a summary of this debate see Dennis Kavanagh and Peter Morris, *Consensus Politics from Attlee to Thatcher* (ICBH/Blackwell, 1989). See also Harriet Jones and Michael Kandiah (eds.), *The Myth of Consensus: New Views on British History 1945–64*, (ICBH/Macmillan, 1996).

36. Philip Goldenberg, 'How to co-operate without absorption', *Libdem News*. 1 August 1997; Philip Goldenberg, 'Lib–Lab liaison offers shift in political culture', *The Times*, 26 August 1997.

37. The precedents are cited in PRO, CAB 21/3718, 'Consultations With Leaders of the Parliamentary Opposition (Policy)'.

38. Lord Rosebery, *Sir Robert Peel* (Cassell, 1899), p. 33.

39. PRO, CAB 21/4548, 'UK Constitutional System, 1951–1959. Part 2'.

40. PRO, PREM 5/430, 'Ministerial Appointments. Order of Precedence of Ministers, 1924–1940'. Rupert Howarth to Bridges, 20 December 1939.

41. Ibid., O. S. Cleverly to Baldwin, 19 October 1936.

42. Ibid., E. B. Lloyd (Colonial Office) to Cleverly, 22 October 1936.

43. Ibid., Cleverly to Baldwin, 19 October 1936.

44. PRO, PREM 5/232, 'Ministerial Appointments. Ministry of Harold Macmillan (Conservative). Part 3', Sandys to Macmillan, 14 October 1959.

45. Ibid., Macmillan to Sandys, 14 October 1959.

46. PRO, PREM 5/228, 'Ministerial Appointments. Ministry of Sir Anthony Eden (Conservative). Part 1', Macmillan to Eden, 24 October 1955 from the Embassy in Paris.

47. House of Commons Debates, *Official Report*, 8 February 1960, col. 70.

48. *The Civil Service Code* (Cabinet Office, 1996).

49. For the genesis of the *Code* and the part played by select committees see Hennessy, *The Hidden Wiring* (Indigo edn), pp. 133–6.

50. *Ministerial Code: A Code of Conduct and Guidance on Procedures for Ministers* (Cabinet Office, 1997).

51. See Amy Baker, *Prime Ministers and the Rule Book* (Politico's, 2000), pp. 73–84.

52. Ibid., pp. 1–10.

53. Ibid., pp. 27–9.

54. PRO, CAB 21/5199, 'Question of Procedure for Ministers', Trend to Wilson, 16 October 1964.

55. Peter Clarke, 'The Edwardians and the Constitution', in Donald Read (ed.), *Edwardian England* (Croom Helm for the Historical Association, 1985), p. 46.

56. Lord Bancroft's last service to his country as a former Head of the Home Civil Service was to have recruitment examined as part of a wider House of Lords inquiry into the public service. See House of Lords session 1997–8, Select Committee on the Public Service, *Report*, HLP Paper 55 (HMSO, 1998).

57. *The Civil Service: Continuity and Change*, Cm2627 (HMSO, 1994), pp. 1, 8–9.

58. See Peter Hennessy, *Whitehall* (Fontana, 1990), p. 372 for an example of when the rubric of the Civil Service order in Council of 1982 was not followed.

59. See ibid., pp. 344–68.

60. Ibid., pp. 344–61.

61. Peter Hennessy, 'Central Government', in Peter Catterall (ed.), *Contemporary Britain: An Annual Review 1994* (ICBH, 1994), pp. 24–5; *Open Government*, Cm2290 (HMSO, 1993).

62. For the original 'Osmotherlys' see *Memorandum of Guidance for Officials Appearing Before Select Committees* (Cabinet Office, 1988). For the updated version which takes into account the 1993 *Open Government* White Paper see *Departmental Evidence and Response to Select Committees* (Cabinet Office, 1993).

63. *Ministerial Code: A Code of Conduct and Guidance on Procedures for Ministers*, 'Foreword by the Prime Minister', July 1997.

64. See Hennessy, *The Hidden Wiring* (Indigo edn), pp. 50–63.

65. Ibid., p. 82.

66. We were discussing the proofs of the second volume of Alistair Horne's biography of Macmillan (which I had carried with me to Lord Home's house in the Borders, the Hirsel) while lunching before undertaking a BBC radio interview. Conversation with Lord Home, 8 May 1989.

67. PRO, PREM 5/375, 'Ministerial Appointments. Ministry of Harold Macmillan (Conservative). Part 7', Macmillan to Hill, 15 July 1962.

68. PRO, PREM 5/218, 'Ministry of Clement Attlee (Labour). Part 3'.

69. PRO, PREM 5/439, 'Ministerial Appointments. Harold Wilson (Labour). Part 2', see Derek Mitchell's 2 August draft of Wilson's first thoughts.

70. PRO, PREM 5/374, 'Ministerial Appointments. Ministry of Harold Macmillan (Conservative). Part 6', Bligh to Macmillan, 19 April 1962.

71. Ibid.

72. Ibid. Bligh to Miss Summers, 4 July 1962.

73. Ibid. Bligh to Macmillan, 13 July 1962.

74. Percy Cradock, *In Pursuit of British Interests: Reflections on Foreign Policy Under Margaret Thatcher and John Major* (John Murray, 1997), p. 40.

75. Ibid., pp. 43–4.

76. Private information.

77. Lord Attlee, 'Lord Montgomery and his Memoirs', *The Listener*, 6 November 1958. I am grateful to my old History Master, Eric Pankhurst, for sending me this review.

78. Private information.

79. Private information.

80. G. W. Jones, 'The Prime Minister's Aides', in Anthony King (ed.), *The British Prime Minister*, 2nd edn (Macmillan, 1986), p. 85.

81. Hennessy, *Whitehall*, p. 385.

82. Conversation with Lord Hunt of Tanworth, 20 May 1998.

83. Private information.

84. Letter from John Holroyd, Downing Street Appointments Secretary, 2 July 1998.

85. See 10 Downing Street Press Notices of 4 March 1997, and for an example of an advertisement, *Church Times*, 19 July 1996.

86. John Campbell, *Edward Heath* (Cape, 1993), pp. 417–19.

87. The phrase is Simon Jenkins'. See his 'Smith wins the House', *The Times*, 1 July 1998.

88. Valerie Elliott, Philip Webster and Dalya Alberge, 'Angry arts establishment told of new Downing Street strategy', *The Times*, 30 June 1998.

89. Private information.

90. 'It is, I think, good evidence of life after death', he wrote in *The Listener* on 17 August 1978. Quoted in Jay (ed.), *The Oxford Dictionary of Political Quotations*, p. 346.

91. PRO, PREM 5/374, Bligh to Macmillan, 19 April 1962.

92. Ibid., Bligh to Macmillan, 13 July 1962.

93. Ibid.

94. Ibid.

95. His former Press Secretary, Joe Haines, has quoted Wilson on 'stardust' to me on more than one occasion.

96. Private information.

97. Conversation with Professor Oakeshott, Carlyle Club Dinner, London School of Economics, 14 February 1992.

98. This came from a usually reliable private source.

99. Private information.

100. Glyn Williams and John Ramsden, *Ruling Britannia: A Political History of Britain 1688–1988* (Longman, 1990), pp. 341–2.

101. Elliott, Webster and Alberge, 'Angry arts establishment told of new Downing Street strategy'.

102. For the workings of SASC see Hennessy, *Whitehall*, pp. 635–9. Since that book was written, a top businessman has joined the very senior civil servants engaged in this particular piece of peer-group review.

103. Private information.

104. Private information.

105. Lord Wakeham, 'Cabinet Government', paper delivered at Brunel University, 10 November 1993. Reproduced in *Contemporary Record*, vol. 8, no. 3 (winter 1994), pp. 473–83.

106. *Ministerial Code* (1997 edition), p. 3.

107. Ibid., p. 25.

108. I am grateful to Professor Robert Hazell of the Constitution Unit, University College, London, for this statistic; conversation with Robert Hazell, 8 April 1997.

109. I am grateful to a senior civil servant for bringing this factor to my attention in the mid 1990s, before the Blair changes.

110. David Wighton, 'Major attacks reform of PM question time', *Financial Times*, 10–11 May 1997.

111. Conversation with Sir Kenneth Berrill, 25 February 1997.

112. Lord Hunt of Tanworth, 'Cabinet Strategy and Management', CIPFA/RIPA Conference, Eastbourne, 9 June 1983.

113. Hennessy, *Whitehall*, p. 65.

114. Private information.

115. I devoted a chapter, at least, to it ('Overload: Stress and the Opposition of Events') in my *The Hidden Wiring* (Indigo edn), pp. 161–78.

116. PRO, PREM 127/274, 'Dissolution of the Wartime Coalition. Administration and Appointment of the "Caretaker" Government', J. A. C. Robertson to Sir Edward Bridges, 25 May 1945.

117. This fascinating information is contained in the confidential 'Table of Political Offices' prepared by the Parliamentary Counsel and preserved in PRO, PREM 5/436, 'Ministerial Appointments. Harold Wilson (Labour). Part 1'. For Derek Mitchell's warning to Wilson about an excessive number of appointments see ibid., Mitchell to Wilson, 18 October 1964.

118. For other examples of Prime Ministers wrestling with numbers see PRO, PREM 5/218, 'Ministerial Appointments. Ministry of Clement Attlee (Labour). Part 3', Helsby to Attlee, 12 September 1947; PRO, PREM 5/223, 'Ministerial Appointments. Ministry of Sir Winston Churchill (Conservative). Part 1. Composition of the Cabinet', Brook to Churchill, 26 October 1951; PRO, PREM 5/230, 'Ministerial Appointments. Ministry of Harold Macmillan (Conservative). Part 1', Bishop to Macmillan (undated but probably 10 January 1957); ibid., Macmillan to Brook, 12 January 1957; PRO, PREM 5/232, Ministerial Appointments. Ministry of Harold Macmillan (Conservative). Part 3', Bligh to Bishop, 17 September 1959; ibid., Bligh to Brook, 26 September 1959; ibid., Brook to Macmillan, 9 October 1959.

119. PRO, PREM 11/2351, 'The Burden on Ministers', Brook to Macmillan, 20 February 1957.

120. Private information.

121. PRO, PREM 11/2418, 'Middle East 1957–58', Brook to Macmillan, 6 December 1957.

122. PRO, PREM 13/1343, 'Correspondence with Cabinet Office on Joint Intelligence Committee Current Assessments'. Anonymous JIC figure to Michael Palliser, 31 October 1966; and private information.

123. Lord Armstrong of Ilminster, a former Principal Private Secretary to two Prime Ministers, described 'Old Stripey' in Michael Cockerell's documentary *How to Be Prime Minister*, BBC2, 22 September 1996.

124. Private information.

125. Private information.

126. I had not appreciated many of them until I came across the 1964 'Table of Political Offices' in the Public Record Office. PRO, PREM 5/436, 'Ministerial Appointments. Harold Wilson (Labour). Part 1'.

127. *New York Times*, 7 March 1991.

128. Private information.

129. PRO, PREM 11/1034, 'Prime Minister Designated Minister of Defence to Undertake Peacetime Co-ordination of Policies for Operational Use and Control of Radio in Time of War'; CAB 21/4548, 'British Constitutional System'.

130. Private information.

131. Private information.

132. For its history and its development see Keith Jeffery and Peter Hennessy, *States of Emergency: British Governments and Strikebreaking* (Routledge, 1982).

133. My knowledge of the post-Budd reorganization is based on private information.

134. Katherine Viner, 'The ministry of truth', *Guardian*, 9 August 1997; Peter Oborne, *Alastair Campbell: New Labour and the Rise of the Media Class* (Aurum, 1999).

135. William Waldegrave. 'The Future of Parliamentary Government', *Journal of Legislative Studies*, vol. 1, no. 2 (Summer 1995), p. 176.

136. Richard Eyre, 'Strut and fret up on the hustings', *Financial Times*, 12/13 April 1997.

137. Philip Stephens, 'The central line', *Financial Times*, 9 May 1997, and private information.

138. Larry Elliott and Michael White, 'The bold chancellor', *Guardian*, 7 May 1997; Robert Chote, 'Biggest upheaval in Bank's 300-year history', *Financial Times*, 7 May 1997.

139. Ibid.

140. Graham Serjeant, Caroline Merrell and Andrew Pierce, 'Bank of England announces fourth rate rise since election', *The Times*, 8 August 1997.

141. Private information. The texts of some of these agreements, such as the UKUSA agreement signed in June 1948, have 'never been officially acknowledged, let alone published'. See Christopher Andrew, *For the President's Eyes Only: Secret Intelligence and the American Presidency from Washington to Bush* (HarperCollins, 1995), p. 163.

142. PRO, CAB 21/4978, 'Nuclear Deterrent Policy: Polaris and European Medium Range Ballistic Missile,' Kennedy to Macmillan, 7 February 1961; Macmillan to Kennedy, 19 February 1961.

143. Sarah Hogg, head of Major's Policy Unit 1992–95, is especially eloquent on this both in seminars (such as the one she gave at the Institute of Historical Research on 19 June 1996) and in the book she co-authored with Jonathan Hill, *Too Close to Call: Power and Politics – John Major in No. 10* (Little Brown, 1995).

144. Raymond A. Jones, *Arthur Ponsonby: The Politics of Life* (Christopher Helm, 1989), pp. 143 and 151.

145. BBC Radio 3, *Premiership*. Interview with Lord Home broadcast on 4 October 1989.

146. BBC Radio 3, *Premiership*. Interview with Lord Callaghan broadcast on 18 October 1989.

147. PRO, DEFE 5/173. COS23/67. Annex. 'UK EYES ONLY TOP SECRET', 'Polaris – Command and Control of Firing Orders', discussed by the Chiefs of Staff on 15 March 1967.

148. Peter Hennessy, *Muddling Through: Power, Politics and the Quality of Government in Postwar Britain* (Gollancz, 1996), p. 10.

149. Private information.

150. Private information.

151. Sarah Helm, Mary Dejevsky and Christopher Bellamy, 'Peace in our children's time', *Independent*, 28 May 1997.

152. Conversation with Robert Hazell, 8 April 1997.

153. 'CX' derives, according to secret world legend, from its initial shorthand meaning denoting that it came from 'C' [i.e. Chief of the Secret Intelligence Service] exclusively. Private information.

154. Private information.

155. PRO, PREM 8/721A–920.

156. PRO, PREM 11/1–323.

157. F. W. S. Craig, *British General Election Manifestos* (Political Reference Publications, 1970), pp. 143–7.

158. Martin Gilbert, *Never Despair: Winston Churchill, 1945–1965* (Heinemann, 1988), pp. 748–9, 781–2, 797, 835–6.

159. Ibid., pp. 675–83, 707–11.

160. Alistair Horne, *Macmillan 1957–1986* (Macmillan, 1989), pp. 37–8.

161. PRO, PREM 11/2208–2581.

162. Salisbury's actual words (in 1877) were: 'No lesson seems so deeply inculcated by the experience of life as that you should never trust experts. If you believe the doctors, nothing is wholesome; if you believe the theologians, nothing is innocent; if you believe soldiers, nothing is safe. They all require to have their strong wine diluted by a very large admixture of insipid commonsense.' Lady Gwendolen Cecil, *The Life of Lord Salisbury*, vol. 2 (Hodder, 1921), p. 153.

163. PRO, PREM 13/112–703.

164. '"Centre Forward, Centre Half": Harold Wilson, 1964–70', 'Premiership' Lecture Four which I delivered at Gresham College on 6 February 1996.

165. Harold Wilson, 'A Prime Minister at Work', in King (ed.), *The British Prime Minister*, p. 12.

166. Conversation with Professor Richard Neustadt, 13 February 1996.

167. See Peter G. Moore, 'Obituary: James Harold Wilson, 1916–95', *Journal of the Royal Statistical Society*, A, 1996, 159, part I, pp. 165–75.

168. Harold Wilson, *The Governance of Britain* (Weidenfeld and Nicolson/ Michael Joseph, 1976), p. 85.

169. Ibid.

170. Margaret Thatcher, *The Downing Street Years* (HarperCollins, 1993), p. 20.

171. *Falkland Islands Review. Report of a Committee of Privy Councillors*, Cmnd 8787 (HMSO, 1983); see especially paragraph 291, p. 79.

172. *Report of the Inquiry into the Export of Defence Equipment and Dual-Use Goods to Iraq and Related Prosecutions*, House of Commons 115–1 to 5 (HMSO, 1996), D3.65, D3.102–5, D4.30, D1.82, D1.91, D3.23–5, D3.165, D6.11, D4.30, D6.260, D2.328–30.

173. Private information.

174. Anthony Howard, *RAB: The Life of R. A. Butler* (Cape, 1987), pp. 292–3.

175. See Hennessy, *The Hidden Wiring*, pp. 249–51.

176. Ferdinand Mount, *Umbrella* (Heinemann, 1994), p. 163.

177. R. A. W. Rhodes, 'Introducing the Core Executive', in R. A. W. Rhodes and Patrick Dunleavy (eds.), *Prime Minister, Cabinet and Core Executive* (Macmillan, 1995), p. 1.

178. R. A. W. Rhodes, 'From Prime Ministerial Power to Core Executive', ibid., p. 12.

179. Private information.

180. Private information.

181. Denning's actual words, delivered in 1975, were: 'The Treaty [of Rome] is like an incoming tide. It flows into the estuaries and up the rivers. It cannot be held back.' Quoted in Peter Riddell, *Parliament Under Blair* (Politico's, 2000), p. 24.

182. A. J. P. Taylor, *English History, 1914–1945* (Oxford University Press, 1965), p. 210.

183. House of Commons, *Official Report*, 9 June 1993, col. 283.

184. Winston S. Churchill, *The Second World War*, vol. 2, *Their Finest Hour* (Cassell, 1949), p. 15.

185. Private information.

186. George Orwell, *The Lion and the Unicorn: Socialism and the English Genius* (Secker and Warburg, 1941), pp. 11–12.

187. PRO, CAB 21/4959, 'Sir Norman Brook: Miscellaneous Engagements and Personal Correspondence, 1961–1964.' 'Cabinet Government', a private lecture to Home Office civil servants delivered by Brook on 26 June 1959.

6 Where the Bucks Stops: Premiers, 'War Cabinets' and Nuclear War Planning Since 1945

1. PRO, CAB 21/4959, 'Sir Norman Brook: Miscellaneous Engagements and Personal Correspondence, 1961–1964.' 'Cabinet Government', a private lecture to Home Office civil servants delivered by Brook on 26 June 1959.

2. Anthony Farrar-Hockley, *The British Part in the Korean War*, vol. 1, *A Distant Obligation* (HMSO, 1990), p. 33. Attlee was replying to the suggestion of his Cabinet Secretary that for Britain, Korea was 'a rather distant obligation'.

3. Eden used these words in the House of Commons on 1 November 1956. Antony Jay (ed.), *The Oxford Dictionary of Political Quotations* (Oxford University Press, 1996), p. 127.

4. Margaret Thatcher, *The Downing Street Years* (HarperCollins, 1993), p. 185.

5. Sir Dermot was speaking for the BBC Radio 3 documentary *A Canal Too Far*, shortly after the Suez papers were declassified. Peter Hennessy, *Muddling Through: Power, Politics and the Quality of Government in Postwar Britain* (Gollancz, 1996), p. 133.

6. Conversation with Lord Stockton, 30 April 1998.

7. Ibid.

8. Stephen Twigge and Len Scott, *Fail Deadly? Britain and the Command and Control of Nuclear Forces 1945–1964*, unpublished Nuclear History Program Project Report (Aberystwyth, 1997), p. 56.

9. PRO, AIR 20/10056, 'Coordination of nuclear strike forces 1960–1962'. Draft paper on initiation and control of nuclear strikes in overseas theatres. Assistant Chief of the Air Staff (Operations) to the Vice-Chief of the Air Staff, 21 December 1962.

10. Jay (ed.), *The Oxford Dictionary of Political Quotations*, p. 372.

11. Sir Frank Cooper in conversation with Tom Dibble and Peter Hennessy, Institute of Historical Research, 11 June 1998.

12. Thatcher, *The Downing Street Years*, pp. 181–3.

13. For Sir Frank Cooper's background see Peter Hennessy, *Whitehall* (Secker and Warburg, 1989), pp. 257–8.

14. Conversation with Sir Frank Cooper, 17 May 1996. Sir Frank gave me permission to attribute his recollections during a conversation on 29 December 1999.

15. Conversation with Sir Frank Cooper, 17 May 1996.

16. PRO, CAB 161/13, 'Cabinet Office: Committee Organisation Book, 1963'.

17. Conversation with Sir Frank Cooper, 17 May 1996.

18. Conversation with Sir Frank Cooper, 11 June 1998.

19. Ibid.

20. Private information.

21. *Reflections*, BBC1, 20 October 1983.

22. Private information.

23. Thatcher, *The Downing Street Years*, p. 188. In his memoirs, Howe concurs with his premier's line. 'It was no part of the Chancellor's duty at such time to argue against the use of the defence forces for the very purpose for which they had been provided . . .' Geoffrey Howe, *Conflict of Loyalty* (Macmillan 1994), p. 246.

24. Conversation with Harold Macmillan, 27 August 1975.

25. Private information.

26. Private information.

27. Private information.

28. Private information.

29. Private information.

30. Private information.

31. PRO, CAB 104/124, Committee of Imperial Defence, 'Supreme Control in War'. I am grateful to Dr Chris Brady of the Institute of Contemporary British History for bringing this document to my attention.

32. Conversation with Sir Frank Cooper, 17 May 1996.

33. Colin Seymour-Ure, 'British "War Cabinets" in Limited Wars: Korea, Suez, and the Falklands', *Public Administration*, vol. 62 (summer 1984), pp. 181–200.

34. The work of my own students is as follows: Roger Schindler, 'Cabinet Government and Conflict: An Assessment of the Attlee Administrations' "War" and Near War Cabinet Committees', unpublished undergraduate thesis, Department of History, Queen Mary and Westfield College (QMW), 1995; Mark Brown, 'The "Narrowest Possible Circle": Cabinet Government and the Suez Crisis', unpublished undergraduate thesis, Department of History, QMW, 1994; Tom Dibble, 'The Importance of Being Winston: A Study of the Churchill Government and the Korean War October 1951–July 1953', unpublished undergraduate thesis, Department of History, QMW, 1996; Matt Lyus, 'How Dark was the Thunder? The Intelligence Input into British Perceptions of the Berlin Crisis of 1948',

unpublished MA thesis, Department of History, QMW, 1997; Tom Dibble, 'The Missing Dimension? An Evaluation of the Intelligence Input into UK Policy Making During the Korean War in the Light of Recently Released Joint Intelligence Committee Files', unpublished MA research methods thesis, Department of History, QMW; Ian Matthews, 'Harold's Way: An Examination of Harold Wilson's Use of Cabinet Committees for Handling the Rhodesian Crisis Before and After the Unilateral Declaration of Independence in Relation to Limited Wars and Near Wars Since 1945', unpublished undergraduate thesis, Department of History, QMW, 1997; Tom Dibble, ' "Consequential Matters . . ." A Study of the Defence (Transition) Committee During the Suez Crisis of 1956', unpublished MA thesis, Department of History, QMW, 1997; Nicholas Unwin, 'An Assessment of the Accuracy of Denis Healey's Claim that the Falklands War Was a War that Need Never Have Happened', unpublished undergraduate thesis, Department of History, QMW, 1999.

35. PRO, CAB 104/124, 'Supreme Control in War'.

36. John Grigg, *Lloyd George from Peace to War 1912–1916* (Methuen, 1985), p. 488. See also Stephen Roskill, *Hankey Man of Secrets*, vol. 1, *1897–1910* (Collins, 1970).

37. See Robert Vansittart's description of Hankey's role as 'secretary of everything that mattered': Lord Vansittart, *The Mist Procession* (Hutchinson, 1958), p. 164.

38. PRO, CAB 104/124, 'Supreme Control in War'.

39. Ibid.

40. Ibid.

41. Franklyn A. Johnson, *Defence by Committee* (Oxford University Press, 1960), pp. 306–11.

42. PRO, CAB 21/1885, 'Situation in Berlin (June–July 1948)', Brook to Attlee, 29 June 1948.

43. PRO, CAB 21/1647, 'Structure of a War Cabinet, 1949–1951', Attlee to Shinwell, 12 March 1951.

44. Schindler, 'Cabinet Government and Conflict'; Peter Hennessy, *Never Again: Britain 1945–51* (Cape, 1992), p. 354.

45. Christopher Bellamy, 'Wind of change as US removes last nuclear bombs from Britain', *Independent*, 20 October 1996.

46. Schindler, 'Cabinet Government and Conflict'; Seymour-Ure, 'British "War Cabinets" in Limited Wars', pp. 185–6.

47. For details of the Malaya Committee's creation see PRO, CAB 21/2510, 'Malaya Committee: Composition and Terms of Reference', Shinwell to Attlee, 27 March 1950. I am very grateful to my former student, Roger Schindler, for illumination on the work of the Malaya Committee.

48. Seymour-Ure, 'British "War Cabinets" in Limited Wars', pp. 182–90.

49. Dibble, 'The Importance of Being Winston'.

50. Conversation with Dr Paul Addison, 20 May 1996.

51. See chapter 8.

52. PRO, AIR 8/2376, 'UK Command Organisation in War, 1950–1957';

'History of the Considerations of Military Command Structure', Appendix A to UK Commanders-in-Chief Committee, CIC(56)26, 6 June 1956.

53. Richard Rhodes, *The Making of the Atomic Bomb* (Simon and Schuster, 1986), pp. 776–8.

54. David Holloway, *Stalin and the Bomb: The Soviet Union and Atomic Energy 1939–1956* (Yale University Press, 1994), pp. 294–319.

55. PRO, DEFE 13/45, 'Thermonuclear Weapons Fall-Out: Report by a Group of Senior Officials Under Chairmanship of W. Strath', Brook to Macmillan, 8 December 1954.

56. Ibid.

57. Ibid., Macmillan to Churchill, 13 December 1954. Churchill wrote on Macmillan's submission the following day: 'Keep me informed please.'

58. Ibid., 'The Defence Implications of Fall-Out from a Hydrogen Bomb', Brook to Eden, 21 April 1955.

59. PRO, PREM 11/747, 'Letter to HM the Queen from Prime Minister concerning UK Manufacture of a Hydrogen Bomb', Churchill to HM Queen, 16 July 1954.

60. Ibid., Colville to Adeane, 16 December 1954. For Churchill's Cabinet paper see PRO, CAB 129/72. I suspect it is C(54)390 which has a 50-year closure upon it and will not be released until January 2005.

61. PRO, CAB 131/15, 'Defence Committee Papers 1–18, 7 January–2 March 1955'. The Strath material consists of two papers, D(55)17, and D(55)18, which are missing.

62. PRO, DEFE 13/45, 'The Defence Implications of Fall-Out from a Hydrogen Bomb', Brook to Eden, 21 April 1955.

63. Ibid.

64. Lord Allen of Abbeydale interviewed for the Channel 4/Wide Vision Productions programme *What Has Become of Us?*, 31 May 1994.

65. PRO, DEFE 7/731. 'Home Defence Committee: Working Party on Machinery of Government in War: Minutes of Meetings and Related Papers 1958–59'. 'Central Government in Global War: The Military Organisation', Annex to COS(59)91, 28 April 1959.

66. PRO, CAB 21/4704, 'Plan for Censorship in Event of Emergency', Padmore to Brook, 4 January 1957.

67. PRO, DEFE 7/731, 'Central Government in Global War: The Military Organisation'.

68. Ibid.

69. PRO, CAB 21/4959; Brook, 'Cabinet Government'.

70. Ibid.

71. PRO, AIR 8/2376, 'UK Command Structure in War'.

72. PRO, DEFE 7/737. 'Government War Book: Proposed Amendments to Chapter 1'. 'Revision of Ministry of Defence War Book: Note by the Secretary'. COS(59)1, 1 January 1959.

73. Twigge and Scott, *Fail Deadly?*, p. 139.

74. PRO, AIR 8/2400, 'Medium Bomber Force: Size and Composition'. 'Defence Board, The V-Bomber Force and the Powered Bomb. Memorandum by the Secretary of State for Air'. DB(58)10, 29 October 1958.

75. PRO, AIR 8/2201, 'UK/US Co-ordination: Offensive Bomber Operations 1957–1962'. 'Strategic Strike Planning by Bomber Command'. TOP SECRET; UK EYES ONLY, Assistant Chief of the Air Staff (Operations) to the Chief of the Air Staff, 5 October 1962.

76. Ibid.

77. PRO, AIR 8/2400, 'Russian Capacity to Absorb Damage'. Annex to DB(58)10.

78. PRO, AIR 8/2201, 'Strategic Strike Planning by Bomber Command'.

79. PRO, AIR 8/2400, 'Russian Capacity to Absorb Damage'.

80. PRO, DEFE 7/731, Day to Wright, 18 November 1959.

81. Twigge and Scott, *Fail Deadly?*, pp. 165–6.

82. PRO, DEFE 7/737, 'Supplement to Ministry of Defence War Book'. Annex to COS(59)1.

83. Ibid., 'Action to Be Taken by the Chiefs of Staff on a Strategic Warning'. Appendix 1 to Annex to COS(59)1.

84. Ibid.

85. Ibid., 'Supplement to Ministry of Defence War Book'.

86. Ibid., 'Action to Be Taken by the Chiefs of Staff on a Tactical Warning'. Appendix II to Annex to COS(59)12.

87. PRO, DEFE 13/45, Brook to Eden, 21 April 1955.

88. D. R. Thorpe, *Selwyn Lloyd* (Cape, 1989), p. 424.

89. PRO, DEFE 25/49, Nuclear Retaliation Procedures Report'. GEN 743/10c (Revise), 23 January 1962. I am very grateful to Len Scott and Stephen Twigge for bringing this file to my attention.

90. Ibid.

91. Conversation with Lord Allen of Abbeydale, 31 May 1994.

92. Ibid.

93. Ibid.

94. Private information.

95. PRO, AIR 8/2238, 'Operational Readiness of Bomber Command, 1958–1961', Hudleston to Cross, 11 August 1959.

96. Sir Frank Cooper interviewed for *What Has Become of Us?*, 28 March 1994.

97. PRO, CAB 21/4959; Brook, 'Cabinet Government'.

98. PRO, AIR 8/2201, Hooper to Orme, 22 January 1959.

99. PRO, AIR 8/2530, 'Command Directives 1961–1965', 'Bomber Command . . . Supplementary Directive', Pike to Cross, 25 September 1962.

100. Ibid.

101. Twigge and Scott, *Fail Deadly?*, p. 196.

102. Ibid., p. 197.

103. PRO, PREM 11/3689, 'Situation in Cuba. Part 2', Ormsby-Gore, tel. 2624, 20 October 1962.

104. Ibid., Ormsby-Gore to Macmillan, tel. 2636, 22 October 1962.

105. Harold Macmillan, *At the End of the Day, 1961–1963* (Macmillan, 1973), pp. 182–3.

106. He used the phrase as the heading for the Cuba chapter in his memoirs. Ibid., pp. 180–220.

107. Ibid., p. 184.

108. PRO, AIR 8/2400, DB(58)10.

109. *Guardian*, 26 October 1962.

110. House of Commons, *Official Report*, vol. 679, 16 June 1963, col. 68.

111. *The Listener*, 30 January 1969, p. 142.

112. Private information.

113. PRO, PREM 11/3689, 'Record of a Meeting held at Admiralty House at 5.00 p.m. on Tuesday October 23, 1962'.

114. PRO, PREM 11/3815, 'Emergency Arrangements in the Event of a Crisis in Berlin, 1961–1962'.

115. Macmillan Diary, Department of Western Manuscripts, Bodleian Library, Oxford. File d.42, entry for 25 June 1961.

116. PRO, PREM 11/3815, Brook to Macmillan, 28 July 1961, Macmillan to Brook, 29 July 1961.

117. Ibid., Brook to Lee, 25 August 1961.

118. Ibid., 'Organisation of Government to Deal with a Crisis in Berlin'. [Draft] 'Memorandum by the Secretary of the Cabinet', September 1961.

119. PRO, CAB 21/4959, 'Sir Norman Brook. Miscellaneous Engagements and Personal Correspondence', Bishop to Brook, 5 October 1961.

120. PRO, PREM 11/3815, 'Organisation of Government to Deal with a Crisis in Berlin'.

121. Ibid., Brook to Lee, 25 August 1961.

122. Ibid., 'Organisation of Government to Deal with a Crisis in Berlin'.

123. Ibid.

124. Ibid.

125. PRO, AIR 28/1657, 'Operation Record Book. RAF Waddington. January 1961–October 1962', Wing Commander O. E. Ness to RAF Waddington, 14 July 1961.

126. Ibid.

127. PRO, AIR 24/2689, 'HQ Bomber Command, November–December 1962', 'Operation Order 38/62. Measures to Exercise the Readiness of Bomber Command. Exercise Mick. 2 November 1962'.

128. PRO, AIR 25/1703, '1 Group, January 1962–September 1963'. 'Operations Record Book, HQ No. 1 Grp.'

129. PRO, AIR 28/1657, Ness to RAF Waddington, 14 July 1961.

130. Ibid. For the dispersal plan see PRO, AIR 8/2313, 'Medium Bomber Dispersal 1953–1957', 'Medium Bomber Dispersal Airfields, 8 August 1957'.

131. PRO, AIR 28/1657, Ness to RAF Waddington, 14 July 1961.

132. PRO, AIR 28/2530, Pike to Cross, 25 September 1962.

133. See L. V. Scott, *Macmillan, Kennedy and the Cuban Missile Crisis: Political, Military and Intelligence Aspects* (ICBH/Macmillan, 1999), pp. 48–50. Macmillan reproduced one of the photographs in his memoirs; Macmillan, *At The End of the Day*, between pages 198 and 199.

134. His absence is traceable through the Cabinet minutes. Brook missed all the Cuba Cabinets. PRO, CAB 128/36, CC(62)61, 23 October 1962; CC(62)62, 25 October 1962; CC(62)63, 29 October 1962. In fact, the Cabinet at its meeting on 23 October was informed of Sir Norman Brook's indisposition and asked that an expression of their sympathy and good wishes for a speedy recovery should be conveyed to him: CC(62)61, item 1.

135. Ibid., item 3.

136. PRO, CAB 128/36, CC(62)62, item 3.

137. Alistair Horne, *Macmillan 1957–1986* (Macmillan, 1989), p. 383.

138. Barbara Tuchman, *The Guns of August* (Macmillan, 1962).

139. Present were most of the ministers who were to be most closely involved in the crisis (Home, the Foreign Secretary; Butler, the Deputy Prime Minister; Thorneycroft, Minister of Defence) and the military too (Sir Richard Hull, Chief of the Imperial General Staff; Sir Thomas Pike, Chief of the Air Staff). Also present were the First Lord of the Admiralty, Lord Carrington, and the Secretary of State for War, John Profumo. Gaitskell was there too. PRO, PREM 11/3701, 'Meetings Between Prime Minister and General Norstad, Supreme Allied Commander, Europe, 1958–1962'. 'Draft Guest List for Prime Minister's Dinner on Monday October 22, 1962'.

140. Macmillan Diary, d.47, entry for 22 October 1962.

141. Macmillan, *At the End of the Day*, p. 190.

142. Macmillan Diary, d.47, entry for 4 November 1962.

143. Ernest R. May and Philip D. Zelicow, *The Kennedy Tapes: Inside the White House During the Cuban Missile Crisis* (Harvard University Press, 1997), p. 692.

144. Private information.

145. Conversation with Sir Philip Woodfield, 15 July 1998.

146. PRO, CAB 128/36.

147. PRO, CAB 129/111, C(62)66. 'Cuba: Threat Posed by Soviet Missiles'. 'Note by the Acting Secretary of the Cabinet', 26 October 1962.

148. Macmillan, *At the End of the Day*, p. 187.

149. Macmillan Diary, d.47, entry for 25 October 1962.

150. PRO, PREM 11/3689, Adeane to Macmillan, 31 October 1962.

151. Macmillan Diary, d.47, entry for 4 November 1962.

152. Harold Evans, *Downing Street Diary: The Macmillan Years 1957–1963* (Hodder, 1981), pp. 224–5. Diary entry for 28 October 1962.

153. Macmillan Diary, d.47, entry for 22 October 1962.

154. Ibid., entry for 23 October 1962.

155. Ibid., entry for 27 October 1962.

156. Conversation with Lady de Zulueta, 13 October 1997.

157. Conversation with Lord Stockton, 30 April 1998.

158. Evans, *Downing Street Diary*, p. 225, entry for 28 October 1962.

159. PRO, CAB 129/111, C(62)170, 'Cuba: Memorandum by the Lord Chancellor', 24 October 1962.

160. PRO, CAB 128/36, CC(62)61, item 3.

161. Macmillan Diary, d.47, entry for 22 October 1962.

162. Ibid. For Macmillan's relationship with Lady Waverley see Horne, *Macmillan 1957–1986*, p. 168.

163. PRO, CAB 131/27, 'Defence Committee Meetings, 16 January – 24 October 1962', D(62) 13th Meeting, 24 October 1962. The retained paper is D(62)47.

164. Sir Frank Cooper in conversation with Tom Dibble and Peter Hennessy, 4 August 1998.

165. PRO, DEFE 13/212 MM/COS(62)7, 'Record of a Meeting Between the Minister of Defence and the Chiefs of Staff on Sunday, 28 October, 1962'.

166. Ibid.

167. Macmillan Diary, d.47, entry for 28 October 1962.

168. PRO, DEFE 32/7, 'Chiefs of Staff Committee: Secretary's Standard Files. 1962'. Annex to COS1546/29/10/62, 'Record of a Conversation between the Chief of the Air Staff, First Sea Lord and the Chief of the Imperial General Staff held in the Ministry of Defence at 14.30, Saturday, 27 October, 1962'.

169. PRO, DEFE 13/212, MM/COS(62)7.

170. PRO, DEFE 7/737, 'Supplement to Ministry of Defence War Book'.

171. For a very balanced assessment of Penkovsky and his impact see Scott, *Macmillan, Kennedy and the Cuban Missile Crisis*, pp. 120–30.

172. Horne, *Macmillan 1957–1986*, pp. 369–70.

173. Scott, *Macmillan, Kennedy and the Cuban Missile Crisis*, p. 177.

174. Private information.

175. Horne, *Macmillan 1957–1986*, p. 381.

176. Stewart Menaul, *Countdown: Britain's Strategic Nuclear Forces* (Robert Hale, 1980), p. 115.

177. PRO, DEFE 32/7, annex to COS1546/29/10/62.

178. It was used in *What Has Become of Us?* programme 4, which was transmitted on Channel 4 television on 18 December 1994.

179. PRO, DEFE 32/7, annex to COS1546/29/10/62.

180. Ibid.

181. Ibid.

182. Ibid.

183. Ibid.

184. Ibid.

185. PRO, AIR 25/1703, 'Operational Record Book, Headquarters No. 1 Group, October 1962'.

186. PRO, DEFE 32/7, annex to COS1546/29/10/62.

187. Ibid.

188. Ibid.

189. PRO, AIR 24/2688. 'HQ Bomber Command October 1962'. 'Post-Exercise Report on Exercise Micky Finn II'.

190. Ibid.

191. PRO, AIR 24/2689, 'Commander-in-Chief's Conference of Group, Station and Squadron Commanders Held at Royal Air Force, North Luffenham, on 14 and 15 November 1962'.

192. Ibid., 'Appendix 71 to Form 540 for October 1962'.

193. PRO, AIR 20/11371, 'THOR IRBM: Deployment in UK', Cross to Kyle, 31 October 1962.

194. T. N. Hancock, *Bomber County: A History of the Royal Air Force in Lincolnshire* (Lincolnshire Library Service, 1978).

195. PRO, AIR 25/1703, 'Operations Record Book. Headquarters No. 1 Group. RAF Bawtry. October 1962'.

196. Ibid.

197. Scott, *Macmillan, Kennedy and the Cuban Missile Crisis*, p. 136.

198. Ibid., pp. 135–6. For the origins of QRA see PRO, DEFE 7/980, 'Medium Bomber Force: State of Readiness 1957–1961', 'Medium Bomber Readiness and Dispersal, 21 October 1960'.

199. Private information. In January 2001, the 'Ministry of Defence War Book 1963' was declassified (PRO, DEFE 2/225) which showed that 210 people were earmarked to go underground into TURNSTILE presided over the Prime Minister and up to five 'other Ministers of War Cabinet rank'.

200. Sir Frank Cooper in conversation with Tom Dibble and Peter Hennessy, 4 August 1998.

201. PRO, DEFE 5/136, 'Chiefs of Staff Committee Memoranda, 20 February – 28 May 1963', annex to COS96/63, 'United Kingdom Commanders-in-Chief Committee. Terms of Reference'.

202. Ibid.

203. PRO, DEFE 13/321, 'Government War Book 1963–1964', Trend to Thorneycroft, 21 May 1963.

204. PRO, DEFE 13/212, 'Minister's Meetings with Chiefs of Staff and Service Ministers 1960–1962'. 'Record of Meeting Between the Minister of Defence and the Chiefs of Staff on Sunday 28 October 1962'.

205. Ibid.

206. Conversation with Professor George Bain, 29 July 1998.

207. PRO, DEFE 13/321, Trend to Thorneycroft, 21 May 1963.

208. Ibid., 'Emergency Powers (Defence) Bill, Annex B'.

209. Ibid.,'Review of Government War Book Planning in the Light of the Cuba Crisis', Cabinet Office, 20 May 1963.

210. Ibid., 'Draft Emergency Powers (Defence) Bill'.

211. Ibid.,'Post-Cuba Review of War Book Planning', Trend to Macmillan, 1 August 1963.

212. Ibid., 'Review of Government War Book Planning in the Light of the Cuba Crisis'.

213. Ibid.

214. Ibid., 'Post-Cuba Review of War Book Planning', Trend to Macmillan, 1 August 1963.

215. Ibid.

216. PRO, CAB 131/27, 'Defence Committee Meetings, 16 January–24 October 1962', D(62)1, 'Evacuation Policy', 16 January 1962.

217. PRO, AIR 8/1940, 'Operation Musketeer General Papers 1956–1958', 'DH Message 41329, 6 November 1956'.

218. PRO, PREM 11/1163, 'The Queen. 1956'. *Bulletin No. 8 For H. M. the Queen* Covering the Period 24 hours Ending 7 a.m. 7 November, 1956'.

219. Ibid., *'Bulletin No. 10 For H. M. the Queen* Covering the Period 24 hours Ending 7 a.m. 9 November, 1956'.

220. PRO, CAB 159/25, 'Joint Intelligence Committee Minutes, October–December 1962', JIC (56) 101st Meeting, 8 November 1956, item 5, 'Daily Intelligence Estimates'.

221. PRO, PREM 11/1163, *'Bulletin No. 16 For H. M. the Queen* for the 24 hours Ending 7 a.m. 15 November, 1956'.

222. Twigge and Scott, *Fail Deadly?*, p. 56. They date the V force's operational readiness from 'the first live air drop of the Blue Danube weapon' over South Australia on 11 October 1956.

223. PRO, AIR 8/1940, 'DH Message 41329, 6 November 1956'.

224. Twigge and Scott, *Fail Deadly?*, p. 56.

225. PRO, DEFE 5/104,' Chiefs of Staff Committee Memoranda, 24 June–21 July 1960', COS(60)(75), 'Military Strategy for Circumstances Short of Global War – 1960–1970. A Joint Study. Part III, 24 June 1960'.

226. PRO DEFE 5/73, 'Chiefs of Staff Committee Memoranda, 1 January–19 February 1957', COS(57)17, 'Operational Requirements for Emergencies or Limited War in the Ministry of Defence. Note by Major-General W. G. Stirling, 11 January 1957'.

227. PRO, CAB 104/124, 'Supreme Control in War'.

228. Seymour-Ure, 'British "War Cabinets" in Limited Wars', pp. 194–5.

229. Conversation with Wing-Commander Teddy Haslam, 1978.

230. Private information.

231. *Nation at War* (Ministry of Information, 1945), p. 5. I am very grateful to Dr Keith Hamilton of the Foreign and Commonwealth Office Library and Records Department for bringing this publication to my attention.

232. Dr Hamilton cannot find traces of any declarations of war since January 1942. Letter from Keith Hamilton to Peter Hennessy, 3 November 1995.

233. Private information.

234. I am very grateful to Dr Nicholas Cox (then of the PRO) for finding it and for showing it to the QMW 'Cabinet and Premiership' course and to QMW's MA in Contemporary British History students on 2 December 1994: PRO, FO 371/24050, 'General and Miscellaneous: His Majesty's Government's Method of Declaring War', 23 August 1939, Fitzmaurice to Harvey.

235. Ibid.
236. Ibid.
237. Ibid.
238. Private information.
239. PRO, PREM 8/1562, 'International Status of Korean Conflict: Legal Status of Armed Conflicts in Which Armed Forces Are Involved', Brook to Attlee, 27 July 1951.
240. Ibid.
241. Ibid., Draft Cabinet Paper on 'Legal Status of Armed Conflicts in Which His Majesty's Forces Are Involved.'
242. Ibid.
243. Sir Frank Cooper was present at the meeting in the Air Ministry during which Sir Dermot Boyle delivered this verdict. See *RAF Historical Society Proceedings*, no. 3 (1987), p. 19.
244. In an interview with Tom Dibble and Peter Hennessy, 4 August 1998.
245. Conversation with Sir Frank Cooper, 17 August 1998.
246. Interview with Sir Frank Cooper, 4 August 1998.
247. Ibid.
248. Ibid.
249. Lord Home was speaking on 'A Bloody Union Jack on Top of It', BBC Radio 4, 1 May 1988. The text of the programme is reproduced in Hennessy, *Muddling Through*, pp. 99–129.
250. Ibid., p. 129.
251. Private information. That gripping last over can be relived by watching the BBC's *Cricket – The 60s Video* (BBC V 4407, BBC Enterprises, 1993).

7 A Sense of Architectonics: Clement Attlee, 1945–51

1. Francis Williams, *A Prime Minister Remembers* (Heinemann, 1961), p. 82.
2. 'Duty of ruthless sacking: "Stop Cabinet talking"', *The Times*, 15 June 1957. The paper's account of Attlee's unscripted address to the University of Oxford's Law Society. I am very grateful to Stanley Martin (who was present and had, indeed, invited Attlee down to Oxford) for bringing the occasion to my attention.
3. Quoted in Peter Hennessy, 'The Attlee Governments, 1945–1951', in Peter Hennessy and Anthony Seldon (eds.), *Ruling Performance: British Governments from Attlee to Thatcher* (Blackwell, 1987), p. 28.
4. Williams, *A Prime Minister Remembers*, p. 83.
5. Roy Jenkins, *Nine Men of Power* (Hamish Hamilton, 1974), p. 75.
6. Ben Pimlott, 'You're all invited this time', *Independent on Sunday*, 16 March 1997.
7. Williams, *A Prime Minister Remembers*, pp. 83–4.
8. Attlee confined this thought to an extraordinary 'Top Secret and Personal' letter to Nehru in the spring of 1949 in which he tried to persuade the Indian

Prime Minister that there might be benefits for India if it retained George VI as its head of state. PRO, CAB 127/344, Attlee to Nehru, 20 March 1949. I am grateful to Claire Cameron for bringing this letter to my attention.

9. Kenneth Harris, *Attlee* (Weidenfeld and Nicolson, 1982), p. 548. For his put-down of Laski see Williams, *A Prime Minister Remembers*, p. 169.

10. Ben Pimlott (ed.), *The Political Diary of Hugh Dalton 1918–40* (Cape, 1986). Diary entry for 26 November 1935, p. 196.

11. James Margach, *The Anatomy of Power: An Enquiry into the Personality of Leadership* (W. H. Allen, 1979), p. 52.

12. James Margach, *The Abuse of Power: The War Between Downing Street and the Media from Lloyd George to James Callaghan* (W. H. Allen, 1978), pp. 88–90.

13. Margach, *The Anatomy of Power*, p. 20.

14. Lord Jay made this judgement when delivering the 1983 Attlee Foundation Lecture.

15. Denis Healey, *The Time of My Life* (Michael Joseph, 1989), p. 153.

16. Peter Hennessy, *Never Again: Britain 1945–51* (Vintage, 1993), p. 56.

17. Lord Helsby, who became Attlee's Principal Private Secretary in 1947, gave this story to me. He had been given it by his predecessor, Sir Leslie Rowan. Conversation with Lord Helsby, 2 November 1976.

18. George Mallaby, *From My Level: Unwritten Minutes* (Hutchinson, 1965), pp. 60–61.

19. Douglas Jay, *Change and Fortune: A Political Record* (Hutchinson, 1980), p. 237.

20. Alistair Horne, *Macmillan, 1957–1986* (Macmillan, 1989), p. 160.

21. Alistair Horne, *Macmillan, 1894–1956* (Macmillan, 1988), p. 287.

22. Quoted unattributably in Peter Hennessy, *Cabinet* (Blackwell, 1986), p. 95. Since Lord Soames' death in 1987 I have felt free to attribute it.

23. *Premiership: Lord Callaghan*. BBC Radio 3, first broadcast on 24 August 1989.

24. James Callaghan, *Time and Chance* (Collins, 1987), p. 95.

25. Private information.

26. Conversation with Viscount Tonypandy, 21 September 1995.

27. Wilson's style was that of providing a running commentary on his colleagues' views (private information); and he expected all his colleagues to have views however remote the issue might be from their departmental responsibilities. Richard Marsh was especially funny about this. See Richard Marsh, *Off the Rails*, (Weidenfeld and Nicolson, 1978), pp. 91–2.

28. 'Duty of ruthless sacking', *The Times*, 15 June 1957.

29. Lord Grimond was speaking on *Attlee: The Reasonable Revolutionary*, a TV programme made for BBC2 by Roy Hattersley and Jeremy Bennett to mark the centenary of Attlee's birth in 1983.

30. Personal observation in both cases.

31. Nigel Lawson, '*The View from No. 11: Memoirs of a Tory Radical* (Bantam, 1992), p. 19.

32. Nigel Lawson, 'The New Britain: The Tide of Ideas from Attlee to Thatcher', Centre for Policy Studies, February 1988, quoted in Peter Hennessy, *Whitehall* (Fontana, 1990), p. 724.

33. Paul Gore-Booth, *With Great Truth and Respect* (Constable, 1974), p. 232.

34. Hennessy, *Never Again*, pp. 123–31.

35. Hennessy, *Whitehall*, p. 323.

36. Ibid., p. 322.

37. Hennessy, *Never Again*, pp. 216–44.

38. Peter Hennessy and Andrew Arends, *Mr Attlee's Engine Room: Cabinet Committee Structure and the Labour Government 1945–51*, Strathclyde Papers on Government and Politics, no. 26, Department of Politics, University of Strathclyde, 1983, p. 28.

39. Alec Cairncross, *The Wilson Years: A Treasury Diary 1964–1968* (Historians' Press, 1997), p. 78.

40. Private information.

41. Attlee was out of office by this time. The news was conveyed to him at Westminster by David Hunt, one of the No. 10 private secretaries: 'He was very deeply moved indeed, yes. He was crying. He was an outstanding example of the stiff upper lip – the upper-class Englishman. He wouldn't have liked to admit he'd wept. But he certainly did wipe his eyes several times. I got him out of a meeting of the Parliamentary Labour Party.' Interview with Sir David Hunt for the Wide Vision Productions/Channel 4 television series, *What Has Become of Us?*, 12 August 1993.

42. The origin of the 'Audience Notes' was explained to me by Lawrence Helsby. It had been explained to him by his predecessor as Principal Private Secretary in No. 10, Leslie Rowan, at one of their hand-over sessions. Conversation with Lord Helsby, 2 November 1976. A set of Attlee's 'Audience Notes' has been declassified at the Public Record Office. See PRO, CAB 21/2263, 'Prime Minister's Notes for Weekly Visits to the King, 1947–50'.

43. Conversation with Sir Edward Ford, 7 March 1994, for the Wide Vision Productions/Channel 4 television series, *What Has Become of Us?* See also Peter Hennessy, 'The Throne Behind the Power', *The Economist*, 24 December 1994–6 January 1995, p. 33.

44. For an acute account of the George VI/Attlee relationship see Robert Rhodes James, *A Spirit Undaunted: The Political Role of George VI* (Little, Brown, 1998), chapter 11, pp. 281–301.

45. Conversation with R. P. Fraser, 26 August 1993.

46. Mallaby, *From My Level*, p. 59.

47. Williams, *A Prime Minister Remembers*, p. 81.

48. He did it on one occasion to me. Conversation with Sir Harold Wilson, 19 October 1976.

49. Lord Wilson speaking on *Attlee: The Reasonable Revolutionary*.

50. Lord Strauss speaking on *Attlee: The Reasonable Revolutionary*.

51. Lord Wilson speaking on *Attlee: The Reasonable Revolutionary*.

52. 'Duty of ruthless sacking', *The Times*, 15 June 1957; conversation with Dr Marion Palmer, 6 August 1998.

53. Harold Wilson, *A Prime Minister on Prime Ministers* (Weidenfeld and Nicolson/Michael Joseph, 1977), p. 296.

54. Harry Hopkins, *The New Look: A Social History of the Forties and Fifties in Britain* (Secker and Warburg, 1963), pp. 100–103.

55. PRO, PREM 5/219, 'Ministerial Appointments. Ministry of Clement Attlee (Labour), Part 4', Belcher to Attlee, 13 December 1948.

56. Ibid., Attlee to Belcher, 14 December 1948.

57. Harris, *Attlee*, pp. 262–5; 347–50.

58. Alan Bullock, *Ernest Bevin: Foreign Secretary, 1945–51* (Heinemann, 1983), pp. 327–9.

59. Kenneth O. Morgan, *Labour in Power, 1945–51* (Oxford University Press, 1984), pp. 199–200.

60. Ibid., pp. 75–9.

61. Peter Hennessy, *Never Again*, p. 65; C. R. Attlee, *As It Happened* (Odhams, 1954), p. 171; Sir John W. Wheeler-Bennett, *King George VI, His Life and Reign* (Macmillan, 1958), p. 638.

62. The memorandum, 'written by me sometime in the 30s before I had had any actual experience of Cabinet', Attlee wrote in 1948 (Harris, *Attlee*, p. 589), is reprinted as appendix III, 'The Reorganization of Government', ibid., pp. 589–93.

63. This was contained in the 'Short Note' Attlee wrote in 1932 on much the same theme. Ibid., pp. 593–5.

64. C. R. Attlee, *The Labour Party in Perspective* (Gollancz, 1937), p. 175.

65. The paper is preserved in PRO, PREM 8/17, 'Civil Service (Organisation) 1945'. I am grateful to my former student, Chris Briggs, who brought this paper to my attention as part of the research for his MA in Contemporary British History at Queen Mary and Westfield College, University of London. Its full title is MG(42)6, 'War Cabinet, Committee on Machinery of Government. Note by the Deputy Prime Minister', 31 December 1942.

66. Ibid.

67. See John Turner, *Lloyd George's Secretariat* (Cambridge University Press, 1980).

68. 'Lord Normanbrook, 1902–67', *Obituaries from The Times 1961–1970* (Newspaper Archive Developments, 1975), p. 590.

69. Ibid.

70. Ibid.

71. Ibid.

72. Private information.

73. George Mallaby, *Each In His Office: Studies of Men in Power* (Leo Cooper, 1972), p. 55.

74. 'Lord Normanbrook, 1902–67'.

75. PRO, PREM 8/739, 'Criminal Justice Bill . . . Discussion of Possible Abolition of the Death Penalty', Brook to Attlee, 21 July 1948.

76. PRO, CAB 21/2248, 'Prime Minister's Briefs, July 1950–December 1950,' 'Overseas Operations (Security of Forces) Bill', Brook to Attlee, 15 November 1950.

77. Harris, *Attlee*, pp. 590–91.

78. PRO, PREM 8/17. 'Committee on Machinery of Government. Note by the Deputy Prime Minister', 31 December 1942.

79. Quoted in Peter Hennessy, *The Hidden Wiring: Unearthing the British Constitution* (Gollancz, 1995), p. 26.

80. Harris, *Attlee*, p. 591.

81. Peter Hennessy, *Never Again*, pp. 303–5, 370–76.

82. Sir David Hunt speaking on *What Has Became of Us?* Channel 4 Television, 27 November 1994.

83. Conversation with Professor George Jones, 12 August 1997.

84. Bernard Donoughue and G. W. Jones, *Herbert Morrison: Portrait of a Politician* (Weidenfeld and Nicolson, 1973), p. 36.

85. Ibid.

86. Ibid.

87. Hennessy, *Never Again*, pp. 230–34.

88. Jay, *Change and Fortune*, pp. 128–56.

89. Sir William Gorell Barnes, *Who's Who, 1981* (Adam and Charles Black, 1981), p. 1014.

90. G. W. Jones, 'The Prime Ministers' Secretaries', in J. A. G. Griffith (ed.), *From Policy to Administration: Essays in Honour of William A. Robson* (Allen and Unwin, 1976), p. 34.

91. Conversation with Douglas Jay, 4 March 1983.

92. Samuel Brittan, *Capitalism With a Human Face* (Fontana, 1996), p. 4.

93. Wilson, *A Prime Minister on Prime Ministers*, p. 297.

94. Hennessy, *Never Again*, pp. 299–305.

95. Ibid., pp. 367–76.

96. Trevor Burridge, *Clement Attlee: A Political Biography* (Cape, 1985), p. 187.

97. Hennessy, *Never Again*, p. 336.

98. Morgan, *Labour in Power*, p. 355.

99. C. R. Attlee, 'The Office of Prime Minister', *Municipal Review*, March 1965; conversation with Lord Jenkins of Hillhead, 5 May 1999; for the tea story see Douglas Jay, 'The quiet master at No. 10', *The Times*, 26 April 1980.

100. Burridge, *Clement Attlee*, p. 184.

101. Edwin Plowden, *An Industrialist in the Treasury: The Post-War Years* (André Deutsch, 1989), p. 109.

102. Dermot Englefield, Janet Seaton and Isobel White, *Facts About the British Prime Ministers* (Mansell, 1995), p. 288.

103. Hennessy, *Never Again*, pp. 416–18.

104. Harris, *Attlee*, p. 414.

105. Ibid., p. 564.

106. In Healey, *The Time of My Life*, p. 472.

107. Harris, *Attlee*, p. 412.

108. Ibid., p. 445.

109. Private information. See also Burridge, *Clement Attlee*, p. 38.

110. Conversation with Lord McNally, 17 November 1999.

111. PRO, CAB 21/1701, 'Organisation of Cabinet Committees, 1946–47', Bridges to Brook, 5 July 1946.

112. See Peter Hennessy, *Cabinet* (Blackwell, 1986), pp. 38–45.

113. PRO, CAB 21/1702, CP(46)357: 'Cabinet Committees, Note by the Prime Minister, 26 September 1946'.

114. Philip M. Williams (ed.), *The Diary of Hugh Gaitskell, 1945–1956* (Cape, 1983), p. 36.

115. Correlli Barnett, *The Lost Victory: British Dreams and British Realities 1945–1950* (Macmillan, 1995), p. 190.

116. Kenneth Wheare, *Government by Committee* (Oxford University Press, 1955).

117. S. S. Wilson, *The Cabinet Office to 1945* (HMSO, 1975), p. 121.

118. PRO, CAB 21/481, 'Cabinet, 'Composition of Cabinet Committees.' CP125(39), Composition of Cabinet Committees, Note by the Secretary'. For the wartime explosion of Cabinet committees, see Wilson, *The Cabinet Office to 1945*, pp. 95–109.

119. For the Anderson Report in full see PRO, PREM 4/6/9, 'Cabinet Organisation; Report of the Machinery of Government Committee', and Bridges to Martin, 23 May 1945 and Martin to Churchill, 25 May 1945.

120. Ibid.

121. Ibid.

122. Hennessy and Arends, *Mr Attlee's Engine Room*, appendix I.

123. Peter Hennessy, 'The Statecraft of Clement Attlee', The Thirteenth Annual Foundation Lecture delivered at Queen Mary and Westfield College, University of London, 14 February 1995.

124. Christopher Brady and Peter Catterall, *Assessing Cabinet Committees 1945–1966* (Macmillan, forthcoming).

125. Cairncross, *The Wilson Years*, p. 38. Diary entry for 12 February 1965.

126. Hennessy and Arends, *Mr Attlee's Engine Room*.

127. See Labour's manifesto, *Let Us Face the Future* (Labour Publications Department, 1945) for example, pp. 6–7.

128. PRO, T 229/208, 'Problems and methods of planning, 1947–1949', R. F. Bretherton to Robert Hall, 1 December 1949.

129. PRO, T 229/778, 'Central Economic Planning Staff Work, 1947–1952', Douglas Henley to D. A. V. Allen, 25 April 1951. I am grateful to my former student, Dr Keir Thorpe, for bringing this and related files to my attention.

130. Federation of British Industry Archive, MSS.200/F/3/51/14/31, 'The Work of the Economic Planning Board. Note for the Economic Policy Committee of the Federation of British Industry. 15 September 1950.'

131. I am very grateful to Dr Thorpe for his elucidation of the *Economic Surveys*. See Keir Thorpe, ' "The Missing Pillar": Economic Planning and the Machinery

of Government during the Labour Administrations of 1945–51', unpublished PhD thesis (University of London, 1999).

132. See Hennessy, *Cabinet*, pp. 123–34.

133. John P. Mackintosh, *The British Cabinet* (University Paperback, 1968), p. 469.

134. PRO, PREM 8/911, 'Proposals Agreed that Research and Development Work on Atomic Energy Be Undertaken.' 'Research on Atomic Weapons. Note for a Meeting of Ministers to be held at No. 10 Downing Street on Wednesday 8 January 1947 at 3 p.m.', Bridges to Attlee, 7 January 1947.

135. Ibid., J. G. Stewart to Attlee, undated. 'Atomic Energy Committee. Note for a Meeting to Be Held on Friday, 12 March 1948, at 3.15 p.m.'.

136. Harris, *Attlee*, pp. 34–40.

137. Hennessy, *Never Again*, pp. 271–2.

138. PRO, CAB 131/5, DO(48)14, Defence Committee meeting of 30 July 1948. I am grateful to my student Matt Lyus for bringing this to my attention. Matt Lyus, 'How Dark was the Thunder? The Intelligence Input into the British Perceptions of the Berlin Crisis of 1948', unpublished MA thesis, 1997, Department of History, QMW. For JIC threat assessments, see Alexander Craig, 'The Joint Intelligence Committee and British Intelligence Assessment, 1945–1956', unpublished University of Cambridge, Faculty of History PhD thesis, 1999.

139. PRO, CAB 131/5, DO(48)14.

140. Christopher Andrew, *For the President's Eyes Only: Secret Intelligence and the American Presidency from Washington to Bush* (HarperCollins, 1995), p. 163.

141. Ibid.

142. PRO, CAB 21/3426, 'Defence (Transition) Committee: War Planning in Minor Departments', Hewison to Chuter Ede, 22 April 1949.

143. PRO, AIR 20/11 367, 'Air Ministry. Notice to Directors and Heads of Division. Routine War Planning', 16 December 1948.

144. Ibid.

145. Ibid., 'Extract from the Minutes of the Defence Transition Committee Meeting, 5 January 1949'.

146. Ibid., 'Chiefs of Staff Committee, Transition from Peace to War . . . Report by the Joint Planning Staff', 4 May 1950.

147. PRO, CAB 134/2634, 'Cabinet Civil Defence Planning Committee. Home Defence Review. Note by the Home Office', 4 February 1966.

148. PRO, CAB 130/41, GEN 253, 1st Meeting, 1 October 1948. I am grateful to my former student Matthew Creevy for alerting me to this file.

149. PRO, PREM 8/1355, Chuter Ede to Attlee, 29 September 1948.

150. The funeral service was repeated in its entirety at the Service of Commemoration which I attended at Haileybury to celebrate the fiftieth anniversary of its famous old boy forming his government (Haileybury College, 21 September 1995).

151. PRO, PREM 8/1547. See especially Sir Norman Brook's 'Top Secret' brief for the Prime Minister on 'Clandestine Use of Atomic Weapons', 12 July 1951.

152. See Peter Hennessy and Gail Brownfeld, 'Britain's Cold War Security Purge:

The Origins of Positive Vetting', *Historical Journal*, vol. 25, no. 4 (1982), pp. 965–74. My former student, Paul Winter, uncovered a considerable swathe of new counter-intelligence material in 1998 during the preparation of his MA dissertation, 'An Examination and a Critique of the Security Service's Assessment of the Domestic Communist Threat, 1947–51'. For the relevant files in counter subversion see PRO, CAB 130/17, GEN 168, Cabinet Committee on Subversive Movements; CAB 130/20, GEN 183, Cabinet Committee on Subversive Activities; CAB 130/71, GEN 377, Attorney-General's Committee on Subversive Activities.

153. PRO, PREM 8/1365, 'Proposed Activities Behind the Iron Curtain', Brook to Attlee, 30 November 1950/54; for the Directorate of Forward Plans see PRO, PREM 11/257, Alexander to Churchill, 2 September 1952. See also PRO, DEFE 5/182, COS48/69, 'Chiefs of Staff Committee. Strategic and Tactical Deception', appendix 1, for a useful short history of UK deception capacity post-1945.

154. For the genesis and development of *Questions of Procedure for Ministers* in its modern form see Amy Baker, *Prime Ministers and the Rule Book* (Politico's, 2000). For the Anderson Report see PRO, PREM 4/619.

155. PRO, PREM 4/619.

156. In the 1980s I made an attempt to map one part of it – the increased use of royal commissions and committees of inquiry – in my *The Good and the Great: An Inquiry Into the British Establishment* (Policy Studies Institute, 1985).

157. House of Commons, *Official Report*, 24 October 1950, col. 2705.

158. The interview was re-run on *Attlee: The Reasonable Revolutionary*.

159. Margach, *The Abuse of Power*, pp. 90–91.

160. Personal knowledge.

161. Margach, *The Abuse of Power*, pp. 88–90.

162. Aneurin Bevan, 'Clem Attlee', *Tribune*, 16 December 1955.

163. PRO, T 222/21. I am grateful to my former student Chris Briggs for bringing this file to my attention.

164. Hennessy, *Whitehall*, pp. 121–7.

165. PRO, CAB 118/32, WP(43)199, 'The Application of Democratic Principles of Government: Memorandum by the Deputy Prime Minister', 11 May 1943.

166. *Clem Attlee: The Granada Historical Records Interview* (Granada, 1967), p. 29.

167. Lord Callaghan, Message to Haileybury College, on the occasion of its celebration of the fiftieth anniversary of Attlee's accession to the premiership, 21 September 1995. I am very grateful to Dan Hearn, President of the Haileybury Political Society, for sending me a copy.

168. Quoted in Englefield, Seaton and White, *Facts About the British Prime Ministers*, p. 288.

169. For the background to the Monnet visit and its aftermath see Hennessy, *Never Again*, pp. 390–404.

170. See Brady, Catterall and Kandiah, *Assessing Cabinet Committees, 1945–1960*, chapter 9.

171. Hennessy, *Never Again*, pp. 399–401.

172. Harris, *Attlee*, p. 551.

173. Jay, *Change and Fortune*, Chapter 13, pp. 339–408.

174. Conversation with Douglas Jay, 4 March 1983.

175. Minister of Education.

176. Francis Beckett, *Major Attlee* (Richard Cohen Books, 1997), pp. 289–90.

177. Jay (ed.), *The Oxford Dictionary of Political Quotations*, p. 231.

178. Burridge, *Clement Attlee*, p. 2.

179. Roy Jenkins, *Mr Attlee: An Interim Biography* (Heinemann, 1948), p. 257.

180. Sir John Wheeler-Bennett, *King George VI: His Life and Reign* (Macmillan, 1958), p. 796.

181. Williams, *A Prime Minister Remembers*, p. 83.

182. *Clem Attlee: The Granada Historical Records Interview*, p. 17.

183. Williams, *A Prime Minister Remembers*, p. 83.

184. *Clem Attlee: The Granada Historical Records Interview*, p. 55.

185. Stephen Brooke, 'The Labour Party and the 1945 General Election', *Contemporary Record*, vol. 9, no. 1 (summer 1995), p. 18.

186. Ibid. For Morrison's 1948 assessment see Ina Zweiniger-Bargielewska, 'Consensus and Consumption: Rationing, Austerity and Controls after the War', in Harriet Jones and Michael Kandiah (eds.), *The Myth of Consensus: New Views on British History, 1945–1964* (Macmillan, 1996), p. 91.

187. *Clem Attlee: The Granada Historical Records Interview*, p. 45.

188. C. R. Attlee, *As It Happened* (Heinemann, 1954), p. 208.

189. John Major, *The Autobiography* (HarperCollins, 1999), p. 307.

190. For my view see Peter Hennessy, *The Hidden Wiring: Unearthing the British Constitution* (Indigo, 1996), p. 64; for Sir Robert's see Rhodes James, *A Spirit Undaunted*, pp. 275–77.

191. PRO, PREM 8/1470, 'Personal Letters from HM the King to Prime Minister', George VI to Attlee, 1 September 1951.

192. Hennessy, *Never Again*, p. 422.

193. PRO, PREM 8/1470, the King to Attlee, 1 September 1951.

194. Ibid., the King to Attlee, 6 September 1951.

195. Attlee, *As It Happened*, p. 144. See also Harris, *Attlee*, p. 492.

196. Harris *Attlee*, pp. 491, 554–5.

197. Private information.

198. Harris, *Attlee*, pp. 490–91.

199. Edward du Cann, *Two Lives* (Images, 1995), p. 43.

200. Ibid., pp. 43–4.

8   In History Lie All the Secrets: Winston Churchill, 1951–55

1. John Ramsden, *The Age of Churchill and Eden, 1940–1957* (Longman, 1995), p. 93.

2. Lord Moran, *Winston Churchill: The Struggle for Survival 1940/1965* (Sphere,

1968), p. 366, diary entry for 20 September 1951. Moran's memoir was first published shortly after Churchill's death in 1965.

3. Ibid., p. 428. Diary entry for 28 April 1953.

4. Ibid., p. 401. Diary entry for 22 February 1953.

5. Quoted in Peter Hennessy, *Muddling Through: Power, Politics and the Quality of Government in Postwar Britain* (Gollancz, 1996), p. 194.

6. Quoted in John Ramsden, '"That Will Depend on Who Writes the History": Winston Churchill as His Own Historian', Inaugural Lecture delivered at Queen Mary and Westfield College, University of London, 22 October 1996.

7. Paul Addison, *Churchill on the Home Front, 1900–1955* (Cape, 1992), p. 439.

8. The phrase is Roy Jenkins'. See Roy Jenkins, 'Churchill: The Government of 1951–1955', in Robert Blake and Wm Roger Louis (eds.) *Churchill: A Major New Assessment of his Life in Peace and War* (Oxford University Press, 1993), p. 491.

9. See Anthony Seldon, *Churchill's Indian Summer: The Conservative Government, 1951–55* (Hodder, 1981).

10. Addison, *Churchill on the Home Front*, p. 412. 'In Churchill's view', Dr Addison wrote, 'they [the dominant elements in the TUC] formed a patriotic estate of the realm.'

11. PRO, PREM 11/385, 'Cuts in Expenditure on Adult Education. Requests by Prime Minister for Explanation from Minister of Education; Correspondence with TUC', Churchill to Horsbrugh, 9 February 1953; Churchill to Tewson, 11 March 1953.

12. Ibid.

13. Quoted in Henry Pelling, *Churchill's Peacetime Ministry, 1951–55* (Macmillan, 1996), p. 39. Churchill delivered these words as part of a warning about the fragility of the British economy on 11 June 1952.

14. Martin Gilbert, *Never Despair: Winston S. Churchill, 1945–1965* (Heinemann, 1988), p. 835.

15. Addison, *Churchill on the Home Front*, p. 434.

16. Jenkins, 'Churchill: The Government of 1951–1955', in Blake and Louis (eds.) *Churchill*, pp. 492–3.

17. Ibid., p. 493.

18. Though the book attracted severe criticism from those who worked with him, the account written by Churchill's doctor, Lord Moran, remains indispensable reading. See Moran, *Winston Churchill: The Struggle for Survival*. For Moran's critics see Sir John Wheeler Bennett, *Action This Day: Working With Churchill* (Macmillan, 1968). For the amphetamines see Andrew Pierce, 'Churchill "took amphetamines and barbiturates"', *The Times*, 9 June 1995.

19. Jenkins, 'Churchill: The Government of 1951–1955', in Blake and Louis (eds.) *Churchill*, p. 493.

20. Michael Cockerell, *Live From Number 10: The Inside Story of Prime Ministers and Television* (Faber, 1988), p. 56.

21. John Colville, *The Fringes of Power: Downing Street Diaries, 1939–1955* (Hodder, 1985), p. 632.

22. Ibid., p. 633.

23. PRO, PREM 5/224, 'Ministerial Appointments. Ministry of Sir Winston Churchill (Conservative). Part 2', Churchill to Alexander, 7 November 1951.

24. Lord Ismay, *The Memoirs of General the Lord Ismay* (Heinemann, 1960), pp. 452–3.

25. Gilbert, *Never Despair*, p. 656.

26. PRO, CAB 21/2804, 'Supervising Ministers', Brook to Churchill, date uncertain.

27. Mr Prescott's precise title was Deputy Prime Minister and Secretary of State for the Environment, Transport and the Regions. 'Complete List of Government', *The Times*, 14 May 1997.

28. Colville, *The Fringes of Power*, pp. 634–5.

29. John Colville, *The Churchillians* (Weidenfeld and Nicolson, 1981), p. 64.

30. Ibid.

31. Moran, *Winston Churchill: The Struggle for Survival*, p. 369, diary entry for 11 October 1951.

32. PRO, PREM 5/224, Churchill to Alexander, 7 November 1951.

33. Anthony Montague Browne, *Long Sunset: Memoirs of Winston Churchill's Last Private Secretary* (Cassell, 1995), p. 14.

34. Colville, *The Fringes of Power*, p. 634.

35. Harold Macmillan, *Tides of Fortune, 1945–55* (Macmillan, 1969), p. 491.

36. Peter Hennessy, *Muddling Through*, p. 188.

37. Montague Browne, *Long Sunset*, p. 14.

38. The Macmillan Diary, Department of Western Manuscripts, Bodleian Library, University of Oxford. File d.19, diary entry for 26 January 1955.

39. Ibid.

40. Monague Browne, *Long Sunset*, pp. 113–14.

41. Colville, *The Fringes of Power*, p. 635.

42. Hennessy, *Muddling Through*, pp. 105–6.

43. Montague Browne, *Long Sunset*, p. 116.

44. Ibid.

45. Ibid.

46. Mr Priestley, a former Cabinet Office civil servant, has used this phrase in conversation on more than one occasion.

47. Peter Hennessy, *Never Again: Britain 1945–51* (Cape, 1992), p. 81.

48. Gilbert, *Never Despair*, p. 655.

49. John Ramsden, *The Age of Churchill and Eden 1940–1957* (Longman, 1995), p. 244; Addison, *Churchill on the Home Front*, p. 408.

50. Ramsden, *The Age of Churchill and Eden 1940–1957*, p. 227.

51. John Stevenson, *Third Party Politics Since 1945* (Blackwell, 1993), p. 29.

52. Winston Churchill, 'The Dream', in John Gross (ed.), *The Oxford Book of Essays* (Oxford University Press, 1991), pp. 365–6.

53. Gilbert, *Never Despair*, p. 967.

54. PRO, PREM 4/6/9, 'Cabinet Organization. Report of the Machinery of Government Committee', May 1945.

55. PRO, PREM 11/174, 'Request by Prime Minister for List of all Committees in Whitehall . . .', Prime Minister's Personal Minute, M50c/51, Churchill to Brook, 16 November 1951.

56. Ibid.

57. Ibid., Prime Minister's Personal Minute, M32c/51, Churchill to Brook, 12 November 1951.

58. Ibid., 'Ministerial Committees', Brook to Churchill, 15 November 1951.

59. Ibid. The file contains the committees' compositions and terms of reference.

60. Ibid., Brook to Churchill, 15 November 1951.

61. Ibid., Churchill to Brook, 16 November 1951.

62. Ibid., Brook to Churchill, 20 November 1951.

63. Ibid.

64. Ibid. For reaction to the titling of the Mutual Aid Committee see Hugo Young, *This Blessed Plot: Britain and Europe from Churchill to Blair* (Macmillan, 1998), pp. 82–3, 90–92, 199.

65. PRO, PREM 11/174, Prime Minister's Personal Minute, M884c/51, Churchill to Brook, 23 November 1951.

66. Ibid., Brook to Churchill, 26 November 1951.

67. Ibid., Prime Minister's Personal Minute, M114c/51, Churchill to Brook, 30 November 1951.

68. Ibid., 'Cabinet Committees', Brook to Churchill, 6 December 1951.

69. Ibid.

70. PRO, CAB 161/7, 'Committee Organisation, January 1955'.

71. See chapter 7, pp. 163–4.

72. Amy Baker, *Prime Ministers and the Rule Book* (Politico's, 2000), pp. 11–16.

73. PRO, PREM 4/6/9, 'Cabinet Organisation', May 1945.

74. PRO, CAB 21/2654, 'Structure of Government. Notes of Papers to Be Prepared on the Hypothesis that Conservative Government is Formed After the General Election', undated.

75. John W. Wheeler-Bennett, *John Anderson, Viscount Waverley* (Macmillan, 1962), p. 352.

76. Ibid.

77. Ibid.

78. Hennessy, *Muddling Through*, p. 188.

79. C. R. Attlee, *As It Happened* (Odhams, 1954), p. 14.

80. PRO, CAB 21/2804, 'Supervising Ministers', Brook to Churchill.

81. House of Commons, *Official Report*, 3 November 1953, col. 15.

82. Ibid., col. 20.

83. R. S. Milne, 'The Experiment with "Co-ordinating Ministers" in the British Cabinet, 1951–3', *Canadian Journal of Economics and Political Science*, vol. 21, no. 3 (August 1955), p. 365.

84. As my research student, David Welsh, has pointed out in an early chapter of his PhD thesis, 'Second Among Equals: Deputy Prime Ministers from Attlee to Heseltine – A Study in Power and Personalities'.

85. PRO, CAB 21/2804, 'Co-ordinating Ministers', Brook to Churchill, 2 May 1952.

86. Churchill's full text, delivered in the Commons on 6 May 1952, is preserved in the big, widely spaced typescript he preferred, in PRO, CAB 21/2804.

87. Ibid.

88. PRO, PREM 5/225, 'Ministerial Appointments. Ministry of Sir Winston Churchill (Conservative). Part 3', Churchill to Bridges and Brook, 9 August 1953.

89. Ibid.

90. Ibid., Bridges to Colville, 20 August 1953.

91. Ibid., Brook to Churchill, 12 August 1953.

92. Ibid.

93. Ibid.

94. Michael Kandiah, 'Lord Woolton's Chairmanship of the Conservative Party Organization, 1946–51', unpublished PhD thesis, University of Exeter, 1993, p. 242.

95. Chas Loft, 'The Failure of the Overlord System: Lord Leathers, Secretary of State for the Co-ordination of Transport, Fuel and Power', memorandum for Peter Hennessy, August 1996.

96. PRO, PREM 11/28, Brook to Churchill, 30 April 1952.

97. Loft, 'The Failure of the Overlord System'.

98. Seldon, *Churchill's Indian Summer*, p. 105.

99. Moran, *Winston Churchill: The Struggle For Survival*, p. 492, diary entry for 2 September 1953.

100. PRO, PREM 5/225, Leathers to Churchill, 12 October 1952.

101. Ibid., Churchill to Leathers, 13 October 1952.

102. PRO, PREM 5/224, Churchill to Lady Woolton, 19 November 1952.

103. PRO, PREM 5/225, Churchill to Woolton, 2 September 1953.

104. Ibid., Churchill to Leathers, 31 August 1953.

105. Ibid., Churchill to Eden, 29 August 1953.

106. Ibid., Eden to Churchill, 3 September 1953.

107. PRO, PREM 5/215, 'Ministerial Appointments. Ministry of Winston Churchill (Conservative)'. Woolton to Churchill, 24 May 1945.

108. Gilbert, *Never Despair*, p. 905.

109. Ibid.

110. Hennessy, *Muddling Through*, p. 189.

111. Sir David Hunt, interviewed for the Wide Vision Productions/Channel 4 series *What Has Become of Us?*, 12 August 1993.

112. PRO, CAB 21/4551, 'Cabinet Meeting Arrangements', Brook to Churchill, 14 December 1951. It was the Cabinet meeting of 19 December which Churchill brought forward from 3 p.m. to 11 a.m.

113. Macmillan Diary, c.15/1, entry for 1 September 1953.

114. Ibid.

115. Ibid., entry for 30 December 1952.

116. Ibid., c.16/1, entry for 31 July 1954.

117. John Turner, 'Experts and Interests: David Lloyd George and the Dilemma as of the Expanding State', in Rory Macleod (ed.), *Government and Expertise in Nineteenth Century Britain: Essays in Honour of Oliver Macdonagh* (Cambridge University Press, 1988), p. 212.

118. Macmillan Diary, c.15/1, entry for 2 July 1953.

119. Ibid., c.14/1, entry for 30 December 1952.

120. PRO, CAB 21/4551, 'Cabinet Meeting Arrangements', Mallaby to Brook, 30 December 1953.

121. Ibid.

122. Ibid.

123. Macmillan Diary, c.15/1, entry for 29 December 1953.

124. For details of 'Robot' see Alec Cairncross, *Years of Recovery: British Economic Policy 1945–51* (Methuen, 1985), pp. 234–71.

125. Macmillan Diary, c.14/1, entry for 19 February 1952.

126. Hennessy, *Muddling Through*, pp. 106, 113.

127. PRO, CAB 130/100, GEN 464, Atomic Energy Development, 1st meeting, 13 April 1954. For the Defence Policy Committee, see PRO, CAB 134/808.

128. Martin Gilbert, *Winston S. Churchill: Road to Victory, 1941–1945* (Heinemann, 1986), p. 715.

129. Macmillan Diary, c.16/1 entry for 10 July 1954. The Cabinet minutes, of course, record Crookshank's dissent but reflect none of the disarray. PRO, CAB 128/27, Part 2, CC(54)47, 9 July 1954.

130. PRO, CAB 128/27, Part 2, CC(54)48, 10 July 1954; CC(54)53, 26 July 1954.

131. PRO, PREM 11/669. 'Meetings with the Soviet Union, 1954', Churchill to Eden, 16 July 1954.

132. Ibid.

133. PRO, PREM 11/565, 'Record of Events Leading to Dropping of Bombs on Hiroshima and Nagasaki', Pitblado to Searby, 29 January 1953.

134. Ibid., 'Events Leading Up to the Use of the Atomic Bomb, 1945', Cherwell to Churchill, 29 January 1953.

135. Ibid.

136. Ibid.

137. Ibid.

138. PRO, PREM 11/257, 'Request by Prime Minister for Report from Minister of Defence on Organisation which is Maintained for Misleading Enemy about Our Future Plans and Intentions', Prime Minister's Personal Minute, M439/52, Churchill to Brook, 16 August 1952.

139. Ibid.

140. John L. Garbutt, 'Tactical atom bomb exercise planned', *Sunday Express*, 17 August 1952. For details of the bomb's assembly in Australia see Brian Cathcart,

Test of Greatness: Britain's Struggle for the Atomic Bomb (John Murray, 1994), pp. 202–35.

141. PRO, PREM 11/257, Brook to Churchill, 18 August 1952.

142. Ibid.

143. Ibid., Prime Minister's Personal Minute, M.457/52, Churchill to Alexander, 26 August 1952.

144. Ibid., Alexander to Churchill, 7 September 1952.

145. Ibid., Churchill to Alexander, 26 August 1952.

146. Ibid., Alexander to Churchill, 7 September 1952.

147. Cathcart, *Test of Greatness*, p. 273.

148. Addison, *Churchill on the Home Front*, p. 9.

149. See chapter 6.

150. Hennessy, *Muddling Through*, p. 197.

151. Gilbert, *Never Despair*, pp. 1018–36.

152. PRO, PREM 11/669, draft Cabinet Paper on 'Two-Power Meeting with Soviet Government'.

153. Ibid.

154. Ibid.

155. Gilbert, *Never Despair*, p. 1036.

156. Hennessy, *Muddling Through*, p. 194.

157. Gilbert, *Never Despair*, p. 1111.

158. Ibid. p. 1112.

159. Edward Pearce, *The Lost Leaders* (Little, Brown, 1997), p. 80.

160. See Colville, *The Fringes of Power*, pp. 667–80, for the surrogate government. For Rab's fleeting opportunity to seize the prize see Ramsden, *The Age of Churchill and Eden*, p. 271 and Anthony Howard, *RAB: The Life of R. A. Butler* (Cape, 1987), pp. 197–200.

161. See Michael Cockerell, Peter Hennessy and David Walker, *Sources Close to the Prime Minister* (Macmillan, 1984), p. 120 and picture section.

162. Colville, *The Fringes of Power*, pp. 677–70; PRO, HO 290/96, 'Regency Acts. Powers of Counsellors of State in the Event of a Change of Administration'. See especially Maxwell Fyfe to the Queen, 10 November 1953. I am grateful to Claire Cameron for bringing this file to my attention.

163. Macmillan Diary, c.15/1, entry for 2 July 1953.

164. Gilbert, *Never Again*, pp. 647, 659.

165. Macmillan Diary. d.19, entry for 20 January 1955.

166. See his disquisition to the Cabinet on both the European Coal and Steel Community and the idea of a European army, PRO, CAB 129/48, C(51)32, 29 November 1951.

167. See Christopher Brady and Peter Catterall, *Assessing Cabinet Committees 1945–1966* (Macmillan, forthcoming), chapter 9, 'Britain and Europe.'

168. Hennessy, *Muddling Through*, p. 188.

169. Macmillan Diary, d.25, entry for 13 March 1956.

170. Tom Harrisson, *Living Through the Blitz* (Collins, 1976), p. 313.

171. Ben Pimlott, *The Queen: A Biography of Elizabeth II* (HarperCollins, 1996), p. 193.

172. Colville, *The Fringes of Power*, p. 708.

173. Hennessy, *Muddling Through*, p. 202.

9 The Colonel and the Drawing Room: Anthony Eden, 1955–57

1. Lord Thorneycroft, President of the Board of Trade 1951–57, interviewed for the Wide Vision Productions/Channel 4 television series *What Has Become of Us?*, 29 July 1993.

2. PRO, PREM 5/375, 'Ministerial Appointments. Ministry of Harold Macmillan (Conservative), Part 7', Macmillan to Lord Mills, 15 July 1962.

3. Lord Thorneycroft, interviewed for *What Has Become of Us?*, 29 July 1993.

4. It was. On 20 December 1956 Eden told Healey 'There were no plans got together [with Israel] to attack Egypt.' House of Commons *Official Report*, 20 December 1956, col. 1493.

5. Lord Healey, interviewed for *What Has Become of Us?*, 29 March 1994.

6. Sir Frank Roberts, a senior diplomat in 1956, interviewed for *What Has Become of Us?*, 7 March 1994.

7. PRO, PREM 5/229, 'Ministerial Appointments. Ministry of Sir Anthony Eden (Conservative). Part 2', bulletin issued by the Prime Minister's doctors, 8 January 1957.

8. Robert Rhodes James, *Anthony Eden* (Weidenfeld and Nicolson, 1986), p. 625.

9. David Dutton, *Anthony Eden: A Life and Reputation* (Arnold, 1996), pp. 1–2.

10. Quoted ibid., p. 2.

11. Ibid.

12. Rhodes James, *Anthony Eden*, p. 556.

13. D. E. Butler, *The British General Election of 1955* (Macmillan, 1956), pp. 67, 92, 157.

14. John Ramsden, *The Age of Churchill and Eden 1940–1957* (Longman, 1955), p. 281.

15. Ibid., p. 274.

16. Harold Macmillan Diary, Department of Western Manuscripts, Bodleian Library, University of Oxford, d.19, entry for 9 January 1955.

17. Ramsden, *The Age of Churchill and Eden*, p. 275.

18. Rhodes James, *Anthony Eden*, pp. 408–9.

19. Peter Hennessy, *Muddling Through: Power, Politics and the Quality of Government in Postwar Britain* (Gollancz, 1996), p. 201.

20. Ibid., p. 218.

21. Ibid., p. 205.

22. For the influence of Noel Skelton on Eden's thinking see Rhodes James, *Anthony Eden*, p. 101.

23. Lord Carr of Hadley quoted in Hennessy, *Muddling Through*, p. 208.

24. Ramsden, *The Age of Churchill and Eden*, pp. 278–9.

25. PRO, PREM 11/414, 'Cabinet, 1951–63', 'Economic Policy Committee', Brook to Eden, 29 May 1956.

26. Ibid.

27. Ibid., Brook to Eden, 30 May 1956.

28. Peter Hennessy, *Cabinet* (Blackwell, 1986), p. 53.

29. PRO, PREM 11/1238, 'Communist Influence in Industry and Trades Unions', Brook to Eden, 28 April 1956.

30. For defence and social spending see Hennessy, *Cabinet*, p. 53 and Rhodes James, *Anthony Eden*, p. 416; for Cabinet, Cabinet committees and Europe see Christopher Brady and Peter Catterall, *Assessing Cabinet Committees 1944–1966* (Macmillan, forthcoming).

31. I am grateful to Dr Chris Brady for alerting me to the discussions in the Middle East (Official) Committee in the spring of 1956. PRO, CAB 134/1297. See its meeting of 25 May 1956.

32. Graham Payn and Sheridan Morley (eds.), *The Noël Coward Diaries* (Macmillan, 1982), p. 308.

33. Ramsden, *The Age of Macmillan and Eden*, p. 293.

34. Jean Seaton (ed.), *Politics and the Media: Harlots and Prerogatives at the Turn of the Millennium* (Blackwell, 1998), p. 3.

35. PRO, PREM 11/669, 'Meetings with Soviet Union, 1954', Churchill to Salisbury, 21 August 1954.

36. P. M. Williams (ed.), *The Diary of Hugh Gaitskell, 1945–56* (Cape, 1983), p. 411.

37. Macmillan Diary, d.20.

38. Rhodes James, *Anthony Eden*, p. 407.

39. Ibid., p. 425–6.

40. Ibid.

41. Ibid. p. 426.

42. Ramsden, *The Age of Churchill and Eden*, pp. 294–303.

43. Amy Baker, *Prime Ministers and the Rule Book* (Politico's, 2000), p. 17.

44. Dutton, *Anthony Eden*, p. 463.

45. Evelyn Shuckburgh, *Descent to Suez 1951–56* (Weidenfeld and Nicolson, 1986), pp. 141–2.

46. James Callaghan, *Time and Chance* (Collins, 1987), p. 408.

47. Ramsden, *The Age of Churchill and Eden*, p. 285.

48. Rhodes James, *Anthony Eden*, p. 478.

49. Ibid.

50. Dutton, *Anthony Eden*, p. 478.

51. See the remarks of his Parliamentary Private Secretary, Robert Carr, in Hennessy, *Muddling Through*, p. 206.

52. Dutton, *Anthony Eden*, p. 479.

53. Robert Carr quoted in Hennessy, *Muddling Through*, p. 211.

54. Rhodes James, *Anthony Eden*, p. 597.

55. Hugh L'Etang, *Fit to Lead?* (Heinemann Medical, 1980), p. 7; Hugh L'Etang, *The Pathology of Leadership* (Heinemann Medical, 1969), p. 165.

56. Rhodes James, *Anthony Eden*, pp. 429–32.

57. Hennessy, *Muddling Through*, p. 131.

58. Rhodes James, *Anthony Eden*, p. 61.

59. Peter Wright, *Spycatcher* (Viking, 1987), pp. 82–5, 160–61.

60. Conversation with Sir Dick White, 23 July 1986.

61. Tom Bower, *The Perfect English Spy: Sir Dick White and the Secret War 1935–90* (Heinemann, 1995), p. 196.

62. Macmillan Diary, d.26, entry for 21 July 1956.

63. PRO, PREM 11/1152, 'Complaint by Cabinet Ministers that they were not sufficiently informed of decisions made by the Suez Committee [sic] on military operations and personal letters to the Prime Minister concerning discussions in Cabinet on Suez policy', Home to Eden, 24 August 1956.

64. Ibid., Lennox-Boyd to Eden, 24 August 1956.

65. Rhodes James, *Anthony Eden*, pp. 383, 410, 457.

66. Private information.

67. Anthony Montague Browne, *Long Sunset: Memoirs of Winston Churchill's Last Private Secretary* (Cassell, 1995), p. 210.

68. Ibid., p. 211.

69. Ibid., p. 213.

70. Lord Charteris, interviewed for *What Has Become of Us?*, 6 June 1994.

71. PRO, PREM 11/1163, '1956 The Queen'. The briefings, split into 'Allied Operations' and 'Intelligence', start on 1 November 1956 and finish on 22 November 1956.

72. Montague Brown, *Long Sunset*, p. 215.

73. Lord Charteris, interviewed for *What Has Become of Us?*, 6 June 1994.

74. Montague Browne, *Long Sunset*, p. 215.

75. Vernon Bogdanor, *The Monarchy and the Constitution* (Oxford University Press, 1995), p. 94.

76. House of Commons *Official Report*, 20 December 1956, col. 1493.

77. Lord Butler, *The Art of Memory: Friends in Perspective* (Hodder, 1982), p. 100.

78. Lord Bancroft, interviewed for the Brook Productions/Channel 4 television series, *All the Prime Minister's Men*, 10 April 1986.

79. Lord Hunt of Tanworth, interviewed for *What Has Become of Us?*, 14 March 1994.

80. Tom Dibble, ' "Consequential Matters . . ." A Study of the Defence (Transition) Committee during the Suez Crisis of 1956', unpublished MA thesis, Department of History, Queen Mary and Westfield College, London, 1997.

81. Lord Hunt of Tanworth, interviewed for *What Has Become of Us?*, 14 March 1994.

82. Sir Frank Cooper addressing the 'Hidden Wiring' seminar of the QMW MA in Contemporary British History programme, 10 February 1999.

83. For Smallwood's view see 'Air Chief Marshal Sir Denis Smallwood', Obituary, *The Times*, 30 July 1997.

84. Brook was replying to Eden's worries that Randolph Churchill might be seeking to talk to Whitehall officials about Suez. PRO, CAB 21/4943, 'The "Life of Anthony Eden" by Mr Randolph Churchill', Brook to Eden, 12 November 1958.

85. PRO, LCO 2/5760, 'Suez Canal Debate, 1956–1957', 31 October 1956. (I am grateful to Dr Brady for bringing this file to my attention.)

86. Hennessy, *Muddling Through*, p. 139.

87. D. R. Thorpe, 'Sir Anthony Nutting', Obituary, *Independent*, 3 March 1999.

88. PRO, CAB 128/30, CM(56)54, 27 July 1956.

89. PRO, PREM 11/1089B, 'Appointment of an Egypt Committee to Deal with the Suez Canal Negotiations', EC(56)1, 28 July 1956, 'Egypt Committee: Composition and Terms of Reference. Note by the Secretary of the Cabinet'.

90. Lord Hunt interviewed for *What Has Become of Us?*, 14 March 1994.

91. Sir Edward Heath, interviewed for *What Has Become of Us?*, 27 June 1994.

92. Dutton, *Anthony Eden*, pp. 413–15; Hennessy, *Muddling Through*, p. 140.

93. Avi Shlaim, 'The Protocol of Sèvres 1956: Anatomy of a War Plot', *International Affairs*, vol. 73, no. 3 (1997), p. 516.

94. Edward Heath, *The Course of My Life* (Hodder, 1998), p. 169.

95. Ibid.

96. Ibid., pp. 169–70.

97. PRO, CAB 128/30, CM(56)72, Confidential Annex, 23 October 1956.

98. For our use of it in the resultant BBC Radio 3 documentary, *A Canal Too Far*, see Hennessy, *Muddling Through*, pp. 130–49.

99. CAB 128/30, CM(56)74, 25 October 1956.

100. Alistair Horne, *Macmillan 1894–1956* (Macmillan, 1988), p. 440.

101. Robert Shepherd, *Iain Macleod: A Biography* (Hutchinson, 1994), p. 117.

102. PRO, CAB 21/4552, 'Cabinet Documents: Issue to and Return from the Head of State, 1937–1959', Brook to Adeane, 11 March 1958.

103. Shlaim, 'The Protocol of Sèvres 1956', p. 509.

104. Ibid.; Heath, *The Course of My Life*, p. 177. Heath dates the actual destruction of the British copy as 20 December 1956, the same afternoon that Eden had lied to Parliament about 'foreknowledge' of the Israeli invasion of Egypt. Brook emerged from the Cabinet Room to tell Heath and Freddie Bishop, Eden's Principal Private Secretary, that 'He's told me to destroy all the relevant documents. I must go and get it done.' In 1986, when the Cabinet Office was preparing its Suez archive for release, Brook's lineal successor, Sir Robert Armstrong, ordered a search to be made for the British copy of the Sèvres Protocol. Nothing could be found. Private information.

105. Shlaim, 'The Protocol of Sèvres 1956', p. 526. The first English translation of the Sèvres Protocol was published in Keith Kyle, *Suez* (Weidenfeld, 1991),

pp. 565–7. A copy of Ben Gurion's copy has now been deposited at the Public Record Office: PRO 22/88, 'The Sèvres Protocol'.

106. PRO, CAB 128/30, CM(56), 74th Conclusions. Item 1. 25 October 1956.

107. Ibid., CM (56), 75th Conclusions. Item 1. 30 October 1956.

108. PRO, PREM 11/4234, 'Former Prime Minister, 1958–1963', 'Record of a Conversation between the Foreign Secretary and Sir Anthony Eden at Broad Chalke on May 30, 1958'.

109. Ibid.

110. PRO, PREM 11/1163. See Her Majesty's 'Intelligence' reports for 7 and 8 November. The danger of such a move is discounted on the basis of further reports (including signals) intelligence from GCHQ, in further royal briefings on 9, 10 and 15 November.

111. John Lewis Gaddis, *We Now Know: Rethinking Cold War History* (Oxford University Press, 1997), p. 236.

112. Lady Park, interviewed for *What Has Become of Us?*, 31 May 1997.

113. 'Sino-Soviet Intentions in the Suez Crisis: The Estimate', 6 November 1956, reproduced in Scott A. Koch (ed.), *CIA Cold War Records: Selected Estimates on the Soviet Union, 1950–1959* (CIA, 1993), pp. 145–6.

114. Conversation with Sir Dick White, 23 July 1986; Bower, *The Perfect English Spy*, p. 200.

115. Ibid., p. 189.

116. W. Scott Lucas, *Divided We Stand: Britain, the US and the Suez Crisis* (John Curtis/Hodder, 1991), pp. 109, 116.

117. Ibid.

118. Ibid., pp. 193–4; PRO, FO 371/119306–7, 'Alleged British espionage ring in Egypt'. See also Bower, *The Perfect English Spy*, pp. 189–98.

119. Macmillan Diary, d.24, entry for 12 November 1955.

120. Ibid., entry for 26 November 1955.

121. Ibid., d. 25, entry for 16 March 1956.

122. Private information.

123. PRO, CAB 158/23, JIC(56)14/6, 'Weekly Summary of Current Intelligence as at 9 February 1956', item 2.

124. Ibid, JIC(56)14/15, 'Weekly Summary of Current Intelligence as at 12 April 1956', item 5.

125. PRO, CAB 158/24, JIC(56)33 (Final) (Revise), 28 February 1956, 'Egyptian Effectiveness in the Use of Soviet Aircraft.'

126. PRO, PREM 11/1079, 'US Analysis of Soviet Policy Completed by CIA', Makins to the Foreign Office, 14 October 1955, 'United States Analysis of Soviet Policy'. Makins adds that copies of the CIA estimate 'will go to JIC shortly' by diplomatic bag.

127. Ibid.

128. Ibid., Millard to Eden and Eden to Millard, 18 October 1955.

129. PRO, CAB 158/24, JIC(56)36 (Final), 21 March 1956, 'Probable Soviet Attitudes to an Arab/Israeli War'.

130. For the JIC Charter current in 1956 see PRO, CAB 158/25, JIC(56)71, 14 June 1956, 'Charter for the Joint Intelligence Committee'.

131. PRO, CAB 158/23, JIC(56)20 (Final), 4 April 1956, 'Factors Affecting Egypt's Policy in the Middle East and North Africa'.

132. Ibid.

133. For the JIC membership in 1956 see PRO, CAB 158/25, JIC(56)71, 'Charter for the Joint Intelligence Committee'.

134. PRO, CAB 158/25. JIC(56)73 (Final), 5 July 1956, 'The Likelihood of War Between Israel and the Arab States'.

135. Ibid., JIC(56)80 (Final) (Revise), 'Egyptian Nationalization of the Suez Canal Company'.

136. Ibid.

137. Ibid.

138. Ibid.

139. Ibid.

140. Ibid.

141. This was the reply Sir Maurice Oldfield gave, as Chief of the Secret Intelligence Service in March 1974, when the new Foreign Secretary, Jim Callaghan, asked 'C' what MI6 was for? See Peter Hennessy, 'The Itch After the Amputation? The Purposes of British Intelligence as the Century Turns: An Historical Perspective and Forward Look', in K. G. Robertson (ed.) *War, Resistance and Intelligence: Essays in Honour of M. R. D. Foot* (Leo Cooper, 1999), pp. 227–42.

142. Lord Hunt, interviewed for *What Has Become of Us?*, 14 March 1994.

143. PRO, CAB 158/25, JIC(56)82, 10 August 1956, 'Security of Planning for Action Egypt'; ibid., JIC(56)94, 24 August 1956, 'Operation Musketeer – Security'; ibid., JIC(59)96 (Final), 6 September 1956, 'Operation Musketeer – Security of Signal Traffic'.

144. PRO, PREM 11/1139, 'Circulation of UK Papers to French Chiefs of Staff and President' (I am very grateful to my student, David Frank, for discovering this on his first trip to the Public Record Office on 16 November 1998). See Dean's speaking notes, 'Security of Planning', for his meeting with the French Prime Minister, Guy Mollet, and his note of the meeting dated 14 August 1956 (the day they met).

145. Ibid., Laskey to Bishop, 29 August 1956.

146. Ibid.

147. PRO, PREM 11/1177, 'Exchange of Personal Messages Between the Prime Minister, Sir Anthony Eden, and President Eisenhower'. Eisenhower to Eden, 3 September 1956.

148. Ibid.

149. PRO, PREM 11/1152, Brook to Eden, 25 August 1956.

150. Ibid.

151. PRO, CAB 128/30, CM(56)62, 28 August 1956, item 2.

152. PRO, PREM 11/1152, Brook to Eden, 25 August 1956.

153. Ibid.

154. PRO, PREM 11/1123, 'Gallup Polls on HMG Action over Suez Crisis: Public Opinion Notes Provided by Conservative Central Office', 'Public Opinion', Poole to Eden, 6 November 1956.

155. PRO, T 236/4188, 'Measures Introduced to Protect Sterling During the Suez Crisis', Bridges to Macmillan, 8 August 1956.

156. Ibid., Bridges to Macmillan, 7 September 1956.

157. Ibid.

158. Quoted in Peter Hennessy and Mark Laity, 'Suez – What the Papers Say', *Contemporary Record*, vol. 1, no. 1 (spring 1987), p. 5.

159. Ibid., pp. 5–6.

160. I am virtually certain he bearded his old friend the Permanent Secretary to the Foreign Office, Sir Ivone Kirkpatrick (who was on the inner loop) and that Kirkpatrick told him the full story. Makins, though a good friend, would never quite admit this to me verbally, but his face gave it away when I put it to him. Interview with Lord Sherfield (as he had become) for *What Has Become of Us?* 12 August 1993.

161. Ibid.

162. Hennessy and Laity, 'Suez – What the Papers Say', p. 6.

163. Ibid.

164. Ibid.

165. PRO, CAB 158/25, 'Possible Soviet Assistance to Egypt's Military Effort in Certain Circumstances', Lee to the Chiefs of Staff, 30 October 1956.

166. Alexander Craig, 'The Joint Intelligence Committee and British Intelligence Assessment, 1945–1956', unpublished PhD thesis, University of Cambridge, Faculty of History, 1999.

167. PRO, PREM 11/1090, 'Lord Mountbatten, First Sea Lord, Writes to the Prime Minister Expressing His Doubts About the Operations in Egypt', Mountbatten to Eden, 2 November 1956; Mountbatten to Hailsham, 4 November 1956; Hailsham to Mountbatten, 5 November 1956; Hailsham to Eden, 5 November 1956; Eden to Hailsham, 5 November 1956.

168. Rhodes James, *Anthony Eden*, p. 574.

169. Keith Kyle is very interesting on the degree to which the position of sterling was or was not collapsing, though Macmillan certainly led the Cabinet to believe there was a severe run on the pound and a menacing depletion of the reserves. Kyle, *Suez*, p. 464.

170. Dutton, *Anthony Eden*, pp. 449–50.

171. Anthony Nutting, *No End of a Lesson: The Story of Suez* (Constable, 1967); for the Kipling original see 'The Lesson' (1899–1902), Rudyard Kipling, *The Complete Verse* (Kyle Cathie, 1996), pp. 242–3.

172. PRO, PREM 11/1152, Sandys to Eden, August 1956.

173. Ibid., Eden to Sandys, 22 August 1956.

174. Ibid.

175. Ibid., Brook's draft for Eden.

176. Ibid., Eden to Sandys.

177. Christopher Brady, 'Cabinet Government and the Management of the Suez Crisis of 1956', in Christopher Brady and Peter Catterall, *Assessing Cabinet Committees, 1945–66* (Macmillan, forthcoming). I am grateful to Dr Brady for letting me see his draft.

178. PRO, PREM 11/1089B, EC(56)1.

179. Hugh Thomas, *The Suez Affair* (Weidenfeld and Nicolson, 1967), pp. 49, 81; Butler took the chair, for example, on 8 October (EC(56)33) and 1 November (EC(56)36), PRO, CAB 134/121.

180. PRO, PREM 11/1089B, Brook to Eden, 13 September 1956.

181. Thomas, *The Suez Affair*, pp. 40–41, 75, 93–4.

182. Mark Brown, ' "The Narrowest Possible Circle", Cabinet Government and the Suez Crisis', unpublished undergraduate thesis, Department of History, Queen Mary and Westfield College, 1994.

183. Brady, 'Cabinet Government and the Management of the Suez Crisis of 1956'.

184. PRO, PREM 11/1069B, Brook to Eden, 13 September 1956.

185. Ibid., EC(56)1.

186. PRO, WO 32/16731. 'Lessons from Operation Musketeer', April 1957. Ward's analysis reflected the views of commanders in the field such as General Stockwell, see WO 288/79.

187. PRO, DEFE 4/91, Annex to JP(56)160 (Final), 'Military Implications of Mounting Operation Musketeer', 24 October 1956.

188. Ibid.

189. Hennessy, *Muddling Through*, p. 142.

190. Ibid.

191. PRO, DEFE 4/91, 'Military Implications of Mounting Operation Musketeer'.

192. PRO, WO 32/16731, 'Lessons from Operation Musketeer'.

193. PRO, CAB 134/1216, EC(56)36, 1 November 1956.

194. EC(56), 1 November 1956.

195. Ibid., EC(56)38, 3 November 1956.

196. Kyle, *Suez*, p. 304.

197. PRO, CAB 134/1216, EC(56)39, 4 November 1956.

198. Ibid., EC(56)40, 4 November 1956.

199. Hennessy, *Muddling Through*, p. 131.

200. Ibid., p. 132.

201. PRO, FO 800/728, 'Memorandum on Relations Between the United Kingdom, the United States and France in the Months Following Egyptian Nationalisation of the Suez Canal Company in 1956', 21 October 1957. I am grateful to Sir Guy for telling me about the 'small but significant alterations' to his original text – 'in particular a statement that the recall of Selwyn Lloyd from New York on October 14 . . . put paid to the last chance of a settlement by negotiation (in fact, I do not believe this was possible at least to the satisfaction of the British and French Governments), and a reference to the need for a pretext were omitted.' Sir Guy Millard to Peter Hennessy, 31 November 2000.

202. Denis Greenhill, *More by Accident* (WILTON 65, 1992), p. 85.

203. PRO, PREM 11/1105, 'Joint Communication (France-UK) to the Governments of Israel and Egypt', UK Del New York, telegram no. 1071 to Foreign Office, Sir P. Dixon, 5 November 1956.

204. PRO, AIR 8/1940, COS(57)220, 11 October 1957, 'Part II of General Sir Charles Keightley's Despatch on Operations in the Eastern Mediterranean November–December, 1956'.

205. Ibid.

206. Ibid.

207. Ibid.

208. PRO, CAB 158/25, JIC(56)82, 10 August 1956, 'Security of Planning for Action Against Egypt'.

209. Ibid. The JIC considered these issues again in late August. See ibid., JIC(56)94, 24 August 1956, 'Operation Musketeer – Security'.

210. House of Commons *Official Report*, V series, vol. 557, session 23 July–2 August 1956 (HMSO, 1956), p. 1613.

211. House of Commons *Official Report*, V series, vol.558, session 12 September –5 November (HMSO, 1956), p. 19.

212. For an overview of Eden, Parliament and the Suez crisis see Matt Lyus and Peter Hennessy, *Tony Blair, Past Prime Ministers, Parliament and the Use of Military Force*, Strathclyde Papers on Government and Politics no. 113, Department of Government, University of Strathclyde, 1999, pp. 5–11.

213. PRO, PREM 11/1123, 'Gallup Polls on HMG Action Over Suez Crisis; Public Opinion Notes Provided by Conservative Central Office.'

214. House of Commons *Official Report*, V series, vol. 558, 12 September–5 November 1956, p. 1625.

215. Kyle, *Suez*, p. 425.

216. PRO, AIR 8/1940, COS(57)220.

217. For the 'six principles' see Kyle, *Suez*, p. 286.

218. Hennessy, *Muddling Through*, p. 140.

219. Ibid.

220. Ibid.

221. CAB 158/26. JIC(56)117 (Final) (Prepared on 11 November and circulated on 15 November 1956), 'Soviet Designs in the Middle East'.

222. A point forcefully made by Sir Dudley Ward. See PRO, WO 32/16731, 'Lessons from Operation Musketeer'.

223. PRO, PREM 11/1138, 'Thoughts on the General Position after Suez', Bishop to Laskey, 28 December 1956.

224. Kyle, *Suez*, pp. 456–7.

225. PRO, AIR 8/1940, 'DH Message 41329', 6 November 1956.

226. It was used in the Channel 4/Brook Productions documentary, *All the Prime Minister's Men*, which I made with Phillip Whitehead in 1986.

227. Lord Hurd of Westwell, 'Can Peace and Justice Be Reconciled?' The First

Hinsley Memorial Lecture, St John's College, Cambridge, 4 March 1999. I am very grateful to Douglas Hurd for sending me his text.

228. Payn and Morley (eds.), *The Noël Coward Diaries*, p. 349.

10 Quiet, Calm Deliberation: Harold Macmillan, 1957–63

1. PRO, PREM 5/232, 'Ministerial Appointments. Ministry of Harold Macmillan (Conservative). Part 3', Macmillan to Lennox-Boyd, 23 June 1959.

2. PRO, PREM 5/375, ibid., Part 7, Macmillan to Kilmuir, 15 July 1962.

3. Harold Evans, *Downing Street Diary: The Macmillan Years 1957–1963* (Hodder, 1981), p. 248.

4. Macmillan Diary, Department of Western Manuscripts, Bodleian Library, University of Oxford, c.16/2.

5. Private information.

6. Anthony Sampson, *Macmillan: A Study in Ambiguity* (Allen Lane, 1967).

7. Ibid., picture caption between pp. 262 and 263.

8. Alistair Horne, *Macmillan 1957–1986* (Macmillan, 1989), pp. 540–41.

9. Harold Macmillan, diary entry for 8 October 1963 quoted in Horne, *Macmillan 1957–1986*, p. 541; see also Simon Heffer, *Like the Roman: The Life of Enoch Powell* (Weidenfeld and Nicolson, 1998), p. 320.

10. W. F. Deedes, *Dear Bill* (Macmillan, 1997), p. 180.

11. Horne, *Macmillan 1957–1986*, p. 541.

12. Lord Home interviewed for the Brook Productions/Channel 4 television series *All The Prime Minister's Men*, programme 1, July 1986.

13. Horne, *Macmillan 1957–1986*, p. 12.

14. Letter from the Revd Victor Stock (to whom Archbishop Ramsey had relayed the story, having heard it from Macmillan himself) to Peter Hennessy, 11 June 1997.

15. Conversation with Victor Stock, 10 June 1997.

16. Macmillan Diary, d.41, entry for 19 January 1961.

17. Ibid.

18. Ibid.

19. Lord Hailsham, interviewed for *All the Prime Minister's Men* and broadcast on programme 1.

20. Ibid.

21. Quoted in Harry Hopkins, *The New Look: A Social History of the Forties and Fifties in Britain* (Secker and Warburg, 1963), p. 375.

22. Sampson, *Macmillan*, p. 15.

23. 'Sir Edward Bridges', *Obituaries from The Times 1961–1970* (Newspaper Archive Developments, 1975), p. 99.

24. Macmillan Diary, c.16/1, entry for 1 August 1954.

25. Harold Macmillan, *Riding the Storm 1956–1959* (Macmillan, 1971), p. 197.

26. Ibid., p. 185.

27. Ibid., p. 197.

28. It appeared under the title 'Lord Hailsham: Memoirs of a Genuine Eccentric', Peter Hennessy, in *The Times* of 6 October 1975.

29. Conversation with Harold Macmillan, 27 August 1975.

30. Ibid.

31. Ibid.

32. Roy Jenkins, *Gladstone* (Macmillan, 1995), p. 463.

33. George Walden, *Lucky George: Memoirs of an Anti-Politician* (Penguin, 1999), p. 58.

34. Horne, *Macmillan 1957–1986*, p. 603.

35. Ibid., p. 610.

36. Lord Jenkins of Hillhead, 'Gladstone's Legacy', Twentieth Century British History Seminar, Institute of Historical Research, 11 October 1995.

37. Horne, *Macmillan 1957–1986*, p. 13.

38. It does – from *The Gondoliers*. A photograph of it is in Alan Thompson, *The Day Before Yesterday: An Illustrated History of Britain from Attlee to Macmillan* (Sidgwick and Jackson, 1971), p. 163.

39. Sir Frederick Bishop, speaking in *The Last Edwardian: Obituary Tribute to Lord Stockton*, broadcast on BBC Radio 4, 30 December 1986 and reproduced in Peter Hennessy, *Muddling Through; Power, Politics and the Quality of Government in Postwar Britain* (Gollancz, 1996), pp. 220–34.

40. Sir Frederick Bishop, speaking in *Living with Harold*, broadcast on BBC Radio 4, 26 September 1989.

41. He wrote a study called *The Past Masters: Politics and Politicians 1906–1939* (Macmillan, 1975).

42. Horne, *Macmillan 1957–1986*, p. 154.

43. Quoted in D. R. Thorpe, *Selwyn Lloyd* (Cape, 1989), pp. 272–3.

44. James Margach, *The Anatomy of Power* (W. H. Allen, 1979), p. 29.

45. James Margach, *The Abuse of Power* (W. H. Allen, 1978), p. 116.

46. Ibid., pp. 116–17.

47. For the 'paternal socialism' remark see Sampson, *Macmillan*, p. 33; for his Whiggery see Macmillan, *The Past Masters*, pp. 183–97.

48. Alistair Horne, speaking in *Living with Harold*.

49. Macmillan, *The Past Masters*, pp. 32–78.

50. Ibid., pp. 57–60.

51. J. M. Keynes, *The General Theory of Employment, Interest and Money* (Macmillan, 1936).

52. Private information.

53. Horne, *Macmillan 1957–1986*, p. 13.

54. Richard Lamb, *The Macmillan Years 1957–1963: The Emerging Truth* (John Murray, 1995), p. 1.

55. Lord Soames is quoted anonymously in Peter Hennessy, *Cabinet* (Blackwell, 1986), p. 95, but, since his death in 1987, I have felt able to attribute it.

56. Macmillan Diary, d.49, entry for 16 April 1963.

57. Horne, *Macmillan 1957–1986*, p. 242.

58. Macmillan Diary, d.42, entry for 21 June 1961.

59. Conversation with Sir Philip Woodfield, 10 July 1997.

60. PRO, PREM 11/1138, 'Lessons After Suez: Thoughts of Prime Minister'.

61. Lloyd was shown Eden's 'thoughts' 'on a personal basis', as were the Minister of Defence, Anthony Head, and the Lord President of the Council, Lord Salisbury. Ibid., F. A. Bishop to Denis Laskey, 28 December 1956.

62. He toyed with the idea of creating a separate Ministry of Science, as we shall see.

63. PRO, CAB 134/1555, 'The Balance Sheet of Empire', Macmillan to Salisbury, 28 January 1957.

64. PRO, PREM 11/2321, 'The Position of the United Kingdom in World Affairs'.

65. PRO, CAB 134/1935, 'Study of Future Policy 1960–1970'. See also PRO, FO 371/143702.

66. PRO, AIR 8/1940, COS(57)220, 11 October 1957. 'Part II of General Sir Charles Keightley's Despatch on Operations in the Eastern Mediterranean, November–December, 1956'.

67. Macmillan Diary, d.42, entry for 8 July 1961.

68. PRO, PREM 11/2351, 'The Burden on Ministers', Brook to Macmillan, 20 February 1957.

69. For the chief concerns of Attlee and his colleagues see the minutes of their first meeting on 26 June 1957. PRO, CAB 127/212. They are appended to a letter from the committee's secretary, Robert Marshall, to Hugh Dalton, the former Chancellor of the Exchequer, who was being invited to give evidence. Marshall to Dalton, 11 July 1957.

70. Douglas Hurd, *An End to Promises: Sketch of a Government 1970–74* (Collins, 1979), p. 39.

71. See Peter Hennessy, *The Hidden Wiring: Unearthing the British Constitution* (Gollancz, 1995), p. 165, and PRO, PREM 5/375, Macmillan to Kilmuir, 15 July 1962.

72. Michael Carver, *Out of Step: The Memoirs of Field Marshal Lord Carver* (Century Hutchinson, 1989), pp. 288–9.

73. Macmillan Diary, c.21/1, entry for 9 July 1960.

74. PRO, CAB 130/137, GEN 616, 'The Burden on Ministers', first meeting, 31 October 1957.

75. PRO, CAB 127/212. First meeting of the Committee of Privy Councillors on the Burden on Ministers.

76. PRO, PREM 5/374, 'Ministry of Harold Macmillan (Conservative). Part 6', 'Draft Minute to the Cabinet', undated but probably 20 or 21 October 1961.

77. PRO, PREM 5/232 contains a good deal of correspondence on the Ministry of Science question.

78. Ibid., Brook to Macmillan, 9 October 1959.

79. As his Parliamentary Private Secretary, Anthony Barber, later put it to me: 'The situation was entirely different in those days, and the whole atmosphere and people's attitude to the trade union movement and to trade union leaders.' Lord Barber speaking on *Living with Harold*, 1989.

80. Harold Macmillan, *At the End of the Day 1961–1963* (Macmillan, 1973), pp. 77–83. For the CCM group's composition and terms of reference see PRO, CAB 21/4586.

81. PRO, PREM 11/3311, 'Position of France in Western Alliance; "The Grand Design"; Discussions and Correspondence Between Prime Minister and President Kennedy'.

82. Macmillan Diary, c.21/1, entry for 11 November 1960.

83. Ibid., d.43, entry for 8 October 1961.

84. PRO, CAB 129/113, C(63)53, 'The Reshaping of British Railways. Memorandum by the Minister of Transport. 19 March 1963'.

85. PRO, CAB 129/87, C(57)137, 'The Roads Programme. Memorandum by the Minister of Transport and Civil Aviation. 5 June 1957'. This paper opens with the arresting claim that: 'There are votes in roads'.

86. PRO, CAB 129/115, CP(63)12, 'Traffic in Towns: Long Term Problems. Memorandum by the Minister of Transport. 19 November 1963'. This paper was presented to the Cabinet in Douglas-Home's time but it was based on the Buchanan Report, which had been commissioned in Macmillan's.

87. PRO, CAB 128/36, CC(62)63, 2 October 1962.

88. For the Cabinet Committee on Population and Employment see PRO, CAB 21/4811.

89. For Macmillan's attempts to link these factors see the unique (in Cabinet minute-taking terms) transcript of his opening remarks to the Cabinet meeting of 28 May 1962. PRO, PREM 11/3930, 'Remarks Made by Prime Minister at Cabinet on 28 May 1962'.

90. Ibid.

91. Ken Young, 'Orpington and the "Liberal Revival"', in Chris Cook and John Ramsden (eds.), *By-Elections in British Politics* (UCL Press, 1997), pp. 157–79.

92. PRO, PREM 11/3930.

93. Ibid.

94. PRO, PREM 11/4520, 'Town and Country Planning'. 'Cabinet, October 25th, Modernising Britain'. In fact, Macmillan used these notes at the Cabinet meeting of 29 October 1962, the day after the Cuban missile crisis ended. PRO, CAB 128/36, CC(62)63, item 4. I am grateful to Dr Chas Loft for discovering these files and showing them to me.

95. PRO, PREM 11/4520, 'Cabinet, October 25th, Modernising Britain'.

96. Ibid., 'Note for the Record', 27 November 1962, by Philip Woodfield.

97. Ibid., 'Note for the Record', 21 November 1962, by Philip Woodfield.

98. Ibid., Trend to Macmillan, 5 December 1962. CAB 128/36. CC(62)73, item 8.

99. PRO, CAB 129/111, C(62)201, 'Modernisation of Britain', 30 November 1962.

100. PRO, PREM 11/4521, meeting of 12 February 1963, item 1.

101. PRO, CAB 129/85, C(57)43, 'Nuclear Power Programme. Memorandum by the Minister of Power, 25 February 1957'.

102. PRO, CAB 128/36, CC(62), 76th Conclusions, 21 December 1962; PRO, CAB 128/37, CC(63) 2nd Conclusions, 3 January 1963.

103. PRO, PREM 11/4412, 'Polaris', Macmillan to Thorneycroft, 26 December 1962; PREM 11/4147, 'Record of a Meeting at Admiralty House, 31 December 1962'; PREM 11/4148, Amery to Thorneycroft, 15 January 1963.

104. Edward Heath, *The Course of My Life* (Hodder, 1998), p. 182.

105. Ibid., p. 381.

106. As captured on the cover of this book.

107. Sir Frederick Bishop, interviewed by Professor George Jones, 23 October 1974. I am grateful to Professor Jones for providing me with a copy.

108. Ibid.

109. Nicola Bliss, 'The Development of Downing Street Support Systems for the Prime Minister 1945–1979', unpublished undergraduate research project, Department of History, Queen Mary and Westfield College, 1999.

110. Horne, *Macmillan 1957–1986*, p. 12.

111. Bliss, 'The Development of Downing Street Support Systems for the Prime Minister 1945–1979'.

112. R. F. Harrod, *The Life of John Maynard Keynes* (Cambridge University Press, 1951).

113. Their correspondence, and the Treasury's comments on it, are preserved in PRO, PREM 11/2973, 'Correspondence Between Roy Harrod and the Prime Minister on Economic Policy and Growth'; PRO, PREM 11/4192, 'Correspondence Between Roy Harrod and the Prime Minister on Economic Matters'.

114. Macmillan, *Riding the Storm*, p. 728.

115. Sir Alec Cairncross, *Diaries: The Radcliffe Committee and the Treasury 1961–64* (ICBH, 2000), p. 53, entry for 29 August 1962.

116. Amy Baker, *Prime Ministers and the Rule Book* (Politico's, 2000), p. 23.

117. Ibid., pp. 23–4; PRO, CAB 21/5199, 'Questions of Procedure for Ministers', Robertson to Martin, 8 May 1962.

118. Horne, *Macmillan, 1957–1986*, pp. 335–7.

119. Ibid., pp. 339–45; Macmillan, *At the End of the Day*, pp. 93, 102; Lamb, *The Macmillan Years*, pp. 446–51.

120. Macmillan, *At the End of the Day*, pp. 365–8; Horne, *Macmillan, 1957–1986*, pp. 445–51; Lamb, *The Macmillan Years*, pp. 192–203.

121. Horne, *Macmillan, 1957–1986*, pp. 471–97; Matthew Parris, *Great Parliamentary Scandals: Four Centuries of Calumny, Smear and Innuendo* (Robson, 1995), pp. 138–63.

122. Horne, *Macmillan, 1957–1986*, pp. 546–7; Robert Shepherd, *Iain Macleod, A Biography* (Hutchinson, 1994), pp. 306–37; Heffer, *Like the Roman*, pp. 320–33.

123. He had not even implemented his plan to take time off from chairing Cabinet

(the idea was that the Lord Chancellor would stand in) to make extra time to think. Evans, *Downing Street Diary*, p. 264.

124. See especially Enoch Powell, 'How Macmillan Deceived The Queen', *The Spectator*, 13 October 1973. For Macmillan's punctilious attitude towards the remaining personal prerogatives of the Sovereign, see PRO, PREM 11/2654, 'Arrangements for Announcement of Date of General Election', Bligh to Adeane, 9 September 1959.

125. John Turner, *Macmillan* (Longman, 1994), pp. 274–5.

126. Macmillan Diary, c.20/1, entry for 26 July 1959.

127. Macmillan Diary, c.21/1, entry for 7 May 1960.

128. Edmund Dell, *Political Responsibility and Industry* (Allen and Unwin, 1973), p. 30.

129. Jock Bruce-Gardyne and Nigel Lawson, *The Power Game* (Macmillan, 1976), p. 28.

130. Private information.

131. Horne, *Macmillan 1957–1986*, p. 15.

132. PRO, PREM 11/262, 'Discussions on Budget, 1960', Heathcoate-Amory to Macmillan, 23 October 1958.

133. Dr Lowe was speaking at the Twentieth Century British History Seminar at the Institute of Historical Research, 25 October 1995.

134. PRO, CAB 128/31, part 2, CC(57)86, 31 December 1957, item 4; CAB 128/32, part 1, CC(58)1, 3 January 1958; ibid., CC(58)2, 3 January 1958; ibid., CC(58)3, 5 January 1958.

135. Horne, *Macmillan 1957–1986*, p. 74.

136. Nigel Lawson, *The View from No. 11: Memoirs of a Tory Radical* (Bantam, 1992), p. 33 and note.

137. Conversation with Lord Thorneycroft for *What Has Become of Us?*, 29 July 1993.

138. Antony Jay (ed.), *The Oxford Dictionary of Political Quotations* (Oxford University Press, 1996), p. 244.

139. Macmillan, *Riding the Storm*, pp. 350–51.

140. PRO, PREM 11/3883, 'Personal Minutes for Prime Minister to Mr Selwyn Lloyd During his Period as Chancellor of the Exchequer, 1960–1962', Macmillan to Lloyd, 28 February 1961.

141. Nicolson used this phrase when musing on the closure of the Festival of Britain in *The Listener*, 1 November 1951.

142. See Christopher Brady and Peter Catterall, *Assessing Cabinet Committees 1945–1966* (Macmillan, forthcoming), chapter 9.

143. For the 'Post-Brussels Committee' see PRO, CAB 21/4815, 'Post-Brussels Committee, Feb–Nov 1963; Composition and Terms of Reference'.

144. Macmillan Diary, d.48, entry for 28 January 1963; for the genesis of the 'steering group' (for whose meetings no minutes can be found) see PRO, PREM 11/4272, Trend to Bligh, 12 February 1963 and 'Note for the Record', Machinery of Government Post-Brussels Period – Admiralty House Meeting on 18 February 1963

attended by Macmillan, the Chief Whip (Martin Redmayne), Trend and Bligh.

145. PRO, T234/203, 'Initative in Europe (Plan G), Correspondence and General Papers', Prime Minister's Personal Minute, no. M 210/58, Macmillan to Lloyd and Amory, 24 June 1958. I am grateful to my colleague, Dr James Ellison, for bringing this minute to my attention.

146. Ibid.

147. Ibid.

148. Ibid., Makins to Amory and Amory to Makins, 26 June 1958.

149. Macmillan Diary, d.45, entry for 7 February 1962.

150. Private information.

151. Macmillan Diary, d.46, entry for 21 August 1962.

152. See plate section.

153. Horne, *Macmillan 1957–1986*, p. 449.

154. Hugo Young, *This Blessed Plot: Britain and Europe from Churchill to Blair* (Macmillan, 1998), p. 144.

155. Ibid., p. 142.

156. Heath, *The Course of My Life*, pp. 228–9.

157. Quoted in the *Observer*, 22 February 1981.

158. Alistair Horne speaking on *Living with Harold*.

159. Macmillan Diary, d.44, entry for 23 December 1961.

160. Sarah Curtis (ed.), *The Journals of Woodrow Wyatt*, vol. 1 (Macmillan, 1998), p. 263, entry for 2 January 1987.

161. Evans, *Downing Street Diary*, p. 248.

162. Nora Beloff, *The General Says No* (Penguin Special, 1963), p. 59.

163. PRO, CAB 134/1929, 'Study of Future Policy 1960–70', FP(60), 1st meeting, 23 March 1960. I am grateful to my former student, Nahdia Khan, who discovered this minute while preparing her undergraduate research project on 'Harold Macmillan and Foreign Policy Rethinks, 1957–60', for the Department of History at Queen Mary and Westfield College in 1996.

164. PRO, PREM 11/3930, 'Transcript of Prime Minister's Remarks to the Cabinet on May 28th 1962'.

165. John Grigg, *Lloyd George: From Peace to War 1912–1916* (Methuen, 1985), p. 474.

166. Anthony Sampson, *The New Anatomy of Britain* (Hodder, 1971), p. 655.

167. Harold Macmillan talking to Ludovic Kennedy, *Reflections*, BBC1, 20 October 1983.

168. Macmillan's grandson, Alexander, confirmed this particular one-liner for me. Conversation with Lord Stockton, 19 February 1997.

169. Margaret Thatcher, *The Downing Street Years* (HarperCollins, 1993), p. 37.

170. Ibid.

11   Country Values: Alec Douglas-Home, 1963–64

1. James Margach, *The Abuse of Power* (W. H. Allen, 1978), p. 129.

2. Cyril Connolly, *Enemies of Promise* (Routledge, 1938; André Deutsch paperback edition, 1988), p. 245.

3. David Cannadine, *The Decline and Fall of the British Aristocracy* (Yale University Press, 1990), pp. 666–7.

4. Quoted in Peter Hennessy, *Muddling Through: Power, Politics and the Quality of Government in Postwar Britain* (Gollancz, 1996), p. 241.

5. In conversation with Peter Hennessy, *The Quality of Cabinet Government*: 'The Unknown Premiership', broadcast on BBC Radio 3, 25 July 1985.

6. Conversation with Lord Peyton, 19 September 1997.

7. Conversation with Dominic Harrod, 5 March 1997. Mr Harrod was recalling the Prime Minister greeting him as he arrived at a party in No. 10 along with other Oxford friends of Douglas-Home's daughter and son-in-law.

8. Quintin Hogg, *The Case for Conservatism* (Penguin, 1947), p. 10.

9. John Boyd-Carpenter, *Way of Life* (Sidgwick and Jackson, 1980), p. 183.

10. Private information.

11. Robert Blake, *The Unknown Prime Minister: The Life and Times of Andrew Bonar Law 1858–1923* (Eyre and Spottiswoode, 1955). The remark which gave Robert Blake his title has been attributed to H. H. Asquith. He is supposed to have said at Bonar Law's funeral at Westminister Abbey: 'It is fitting that we should have buried the Unknown Prime Minister by the side of the Unknown Soldier,' ibid., p. 13.

12. Hennessy, *Muddling Through*, p. 235.

13. Lord Home, interviewed for the BBC Radio 3 *Premiership* series, broadcast on 4 October 1989.

14. Private information.

15. Information from Home's publisher, HarperCollins.

16. Margach, *The Abuse of Power*, p. 128.

17. Lord Home, *The Way the Wind Blows: An Autobiography* (Collins, 1976), p. 203.

18. Ibid.

19. Home, *Premiership* interview; see also D. R. Thorpe, *Alec Douglas-Home* (Sinclair-Stevenson, 1996), p. 257. Home's exact words were: 'When I have to read economic documents, I have to have a box of matches and start moving them into position to simplify and illustrate the points to myself', *Observer*, interview with Kenneth Harris, 16 September 1962.

20. For this fascinating and important story see Tony Benn, *Years of Hope: Diaries, Papers and Letters, 1940–1962* (Hutchinson, 1994), pp. 356–42; Tony Benn, *Out of the Wilderness, Diaries, 1963–67* (Hutchinson, 1987), pp. 1–59.

21. Thorpe, *Alec Douglas-Home*, pp. 260, 287, 289.

22. Home, *The Way the Wind Blows*, p. 215.

23. For Butler's lassitude see Thorpe, *Alec Douglas-Home*, p. 350.

24. Ibid., p. 365.

25. Hennessy, *Muddling Through*, p. 236.

26. Alan Watkins, in conversation with the author on more than one occasion.

27. Robert Shepherd, *Iain Macleod, A Biography* (Hutchinson, 1994), pp. 325–7.

28. For the distinction between 'advice' with a capital 'A' and a lower case 'a' (a distinction made for me by a long-serving court official) see Peter Hennessy, *The Hidden Wiring: Unearthing the British Constitution* (Indigo, 1996), pp. 58, 68; see also above, pp. 29–30.

29. Ben Pimlott, *The Queen: A Biography of Elizabeth II* (HarperCollins, 1996), p. 335; for an opposite view of the Queen's actions in October 1963 see Vernon Bogdanor, *The Monarchy and the Constitution* (Oxford University Press, 1995), pp. 97–8.

30. Thorpe, *Alec Douglas-Home*, p. 313.

31. Macmillan's memorandum to the Queen has never been published but Richard Thorpe's account contains all its essentials; ibid., pp. 313–14.

32. Reginald Maudling, *Memoirs* (Sidgwick and Jackson, 1978), pp. 129–30.

33. Thorpe, *Alec Douglas-Home*, p. 344.

34. Ibid., pp. 381–3.

35. For the remaining potency of the Queen's prerogative of appointment see Hennessy, *The Hidden Wiring*, pp. 48–63.

36. Quoted by Richard Thorpe while delivering his paper on 'Alec Douglas-Home: The Underrated Prime Minister' to the Twentieth Century British History Seminar, Institute of Historical Research, 9 October 1996.

37. Thorpe, *Alec Douglas-Home*, p. 289.

38. Anthony Howard, *RAB: The Life of R. A. Butler* (Cape, 1987), pp. 313–14.

39. Lord Butler, *The Art of Memory* (Hodder, 1982), p. 109.

40. Macmillan was graphic on this aspect of Hailsham's character in the early draft of the memorandum he prepared for the Queen. PRO, PREM 11/5008, 'Discussions on Future Leadership of Party and Prime Minister'.

41. Hennessy, *Muddling Through*, p. 238.

42. Maudling, *Memoirs*, p. 130.

43. Hennessy, *Muddling Through*, p. 237.

44. Pimlott, *The Queen*, p. 332.

45. Ibid., p. 333.

46. Conversation with Lord Home, 8 May 1989.

47. Thorpe, *Alec Douglas-Home*, p. 319.

48. BBC Radio 3, *The Quality of Cabinet Government*. Programme 5, 'The Unknown Premiership', broadcast on 25 July 1985.

49. BBC Radio 3, *Premiership* series.

50. BBC Radio 3, 'The Unknown Premiership'.

51. D. E. Butler and Anthony King, *The British General Election of 1964* (Macmillan, 1965), p. 23.

52. PRO, PREM 11/5008.

53. Lord Hailsham, *A Sparrow's Flight: Memoirs* (Collins, 1991), p. 358.

54. For a full assessment of the opposition to Heath on RPM see John Ramsden, *The Winds of Change: Macmillan to Heath, 1957–1975* (Longman, 1996), pp. 220–21.

55. Private information.

56. Margach, *The Abuse of Power*, p. 132.

57. Edward Heath, *The Course of My Life* (Hodder, 1998), p. 263.

58. BBC Radio 3, *Premiership* series.

59. Hailsham, *A Sparrow's Flight*, p. 359.

60. BBC Radio 3 'The Unknown Premiership'. As minister of state in the Scottish Office, Home was responsible for local government affairs north of the border.

61. Conversation with his son, David Home, the fifteenth Earl, 12 July 1999. 'My father and Attlee got on very well,' he said. 'In fact, my father liked all the Labour leaders he knew except Harold Wilson. He became very fond of Jim Callaghan.'

62. R. H. S. Crossman, *Diaries of a Cabinet Minister*, vol. 3 (Cape, 1976), p. 881, diary entry for 4 April 1970.

63. Conversation with Lord Hurd, 20 April 1999.

64. Kenneth Young, *Sir Alec Douglas-Home* (Dent, 1970).

65. He talked to me about this on one of my visits to the Hirsel for the BBC.

66. Hennessy, *Muddling Through*, p. 236.

67. Howard, *RAB*, p. 370.

68. Home, *The Way the Wind Blows*, p. 202.

69. Peter Hennessy, *Cabinet* (Blackwell, 1986), p. 168.

70. PRO, PREM 11/4113, 'Revised Committees', Trend to Home, 1 November 1963.

71. Private information.

72. PRO, PREM 11/4834, 'HM Opposition Proposals for Changes in Machinery of Government, 1963–1964'; Thorpe, *Alec Douglas-Home*, p. 376.

73. John Dickie, *The Uncommon Commoner: A Study of Sir Alec Douglas-Home* (Pall Mall, 1964), p. 214.

74. Peter Clarke, *Hope and Glory: Britain 1900–1990* (Allen Lane, 1996), p. 293.

75. Home, *The Way the Wind Blows*, p. 216.

76. Ramsden, *The Winds of Change*, p. 216.

77. Ibid.

78. PRO, PREM 11/4156, 'Top Secret and Personal. Deadlock. The Queen's Government must be carried on'. DJM [Derek Mitchell], 16 October 1964.

79. PRO, PREM 11/5006, 'My Philosophy', Home to Fraser, 30 December, 1963.

80. Ibid.

81. Ibid.

12   Centre Forward: Harold Wilson, 1964–70

1. Ben Pimlott, *Harold Wilson* (HarperCollins, 1992), p. 564.

2. Alec Cairncross, *The Wilson Years: Treasury Diary, 1964–1968* (Historians' Press, 1997), p. 52, entry for 22 May 1965.

3. Quoted in Pimlott, *Harold Wilson*, p. 521.

4. Cairncross, *The Wilson Years*, p. 156, entry for 30 July 1966.

5. Ibid., p. 193.

6. Harold Wilson, *The Governance of Britain* (Weidenfeld and Nicolson/Michael Joseph, 1976), pp. 8–9.

7. Winston S. Churchill, *The Second World War*, vol. 2, *The Twilight War* (Cassell, 1964), pp. 238–9.

8. For Wilson's early life and pre-prime ministerial career see Harold Wilson, *Memoirs 1916–64: The Making of a Prime Minster* (Weidenfeld and Nicolson/Michael Joseph, 1986); Philip Ziegler, *Wilson: The Authorised Life of Lord Wilson of Rievaulx* (Weidenfeld and Nicolson, 1993), pp. 1–38; Pimlott, *Harold Wilson*, pp. 3–322.

9. Pimlott, *Harold Wilson*, chapters 13 and 14, pp. 252–310.

10. See Labour's 1964 election manifesto, *Let's Go With Labour for the New Britain*, in F. W. S. Craig, *British General Election Manifestos, 1918–1966* (Political Reference Publications, 1970), pp. 229–46 (especially pp. 233–4).

11. Ziegler, *Wilson*, p. 157.

12. Ibid., p. 195. For his admiration of the 'vigour and freshness' Kennedy brought to government see the rather poignant letter Mrs Jacqueline Kennedy wrote to him on the evening of the day Wilson spoke at the unveiling of the Kennedy Memorial at Runnymede; PRO, PREM 13/685, 'Kennedy Memorial', Mrs Kennedy to Wilson, 14 May 1965.

13. Harold Wilson, *The Labour Government 1964–1970: A Personal Record* (Weidenfeld and Nicolson/Michael Joseph, 1971), p. 3.

14. Pimlott, *Harold Wilson*, p. 443.

15. He picked the vice-chancellors first with a view to improving relations between government and the universities. See PRO, PREM 13/513, 'Prime Minister Met University Vice-Chancellors, 11 January 1965', especially Mitchell to Reid, 16 December 1965 and Mitchell to Wilson, 10 January 1965.

16. PRO, PREM 13/353, 'Ministerial Responsibility for the Universities'. 'Confidential Note For the Record' prepared by Derek Mitchell on 16 December 1964 recording a meeting between Wilson and Sir Lawrence Helsby, Head of the Home Civil Service, on 14 December 1964.

17. Lord Wilson, 'Smoking Is Not Compulsory', *The Quality of Cabinet Government*, BBC Radio 3, 27 June 1985.

18. PRO, PREM 13/353.

19. Peter Hennessy, 'Summer views', *Independent*, 28 August 1997.

20. Quoted by John Ramsden in his Swinton Lecture delivered to the Conservative Political Centre on 4 July 1997.

21. Peter Hennessy, *Muddling Through: Power, Politics and the Quality of Government in Postwar Britain* (Gollancz, 1996), p. 259.

22. Conversation with Lord Glenamara, 10 September 1997.

23. Barbara Castle, *The Castle Diaries, 1964–70* (Weidenfeld and Nicolson, 1984), p. 17.

24. James Callaghan, *Time and Chance* (Collins, 1987), pp. 154–60; Wilson, *The Labour Government 1964–1970*, pp. 5–7; PRO, CAB 130/202, MISC 1, 1st Meeting, 17 October 1964. For the 'we have decided . . .' remark see Susan Crosland, *Tony Crosland* (Cape, 1982), p. 125. Her source, Sir William Armstrong, Permanent Secretary to the Treasury, was present at the first meeting of MISC 1.

25. Crosland, *Tony Crosland*, p. 136. For Brown's use of it see his 'Top Secret and Personal' note to Wilson, 22 December 1964 in PRO, EW 28/18, 'Minutes and Letters to Harold Wilson from George Brown . . . 1964–1965'.

26. Craig, *British General Election Manifestos, 1918–1966*, pp. 245–6.

27. Ibid.

28. Conversation with Professor Richard Neustadt, 16 January 1997.

29. PRO, PREM 11/4733, 'Talks on Defence Policy with Members of HM Opposition', Thorneycroft to Douglas-Home, 3 February 1964, on his talk that day with Denis Healey.

30. Conversation with Lord Home, April 1988.

31. PRO, CAB 130/212, MISC 16, 1st Meeting, 11 November 1964.

32. PRO, CAB 130/213, MISC 17, 4th Meeting, 22 November 1964.

33. PRO, CAB 128/39, CC(64), 11th conclusions.

34. PRO, CAB 148/19, ODP(65), 5th Meeting, 29 January 1965.

35. Peter Hennessy, 'How Bevin saved Britain's Bomb', *The Times*, 30 September 1982.

36. Peter Hennessy, *Cabinet* (Blackwell, 1986), p. 149.

37. Private information.

38. Private information.

39. For the majority Kings Norton Report see PRO, CAB 134/3121, part 2.

40. Ibid., 'Ministerial Committee on Nuclear Policy, PN, Meetings and Papers, 1968–1970', 'Letter from Lord Rothschild to the Chairman of the Working Party', 31 July 1968.

41. PRO, CAB 124/3031, 'PN, 1966–67'.

42. Hennessy, *Cabinet*, p. 150.

43. Private information.

44. Macmillan Diary, Department of Western Manuscripts, Bodleian Library, University of Oxford, d.49, entry for 11 July 1963.

45. PRO, PREM 13/08, 'Cabinet Committee', Trend to Wilson, 24 October 1964.

46. PRO, PREM 13/1343, 'Correspondence with Cabinet Office on Joint Intelligence Committee Current Assessments', anonymous JIC official to Michael Palliser, 31 October 1966.

47. Ibid., Palliser to anonymous JIC official, 4 November 1966.

48. PRO, PREM 13/2959, 'Soviet Foreign Policy, May 1968–January 1969', Palliser to Wilson, August 1968.

49. PRO, DEFE 5/173, 'Polaris – Command and Control of Firing Orders, Note and Annex A to Chiefs of Staff Committee', 15 March 1967; PRO, PREM 13/2571, 'Authorisation for Firing of Polaris Weapons, Installation of Closed-Circuit Television Link', 1967, Halls to Wilson, 21 March 1967, Trend to Wilson, 6 April 1967.

50. Churchill was thinking of Joe Chamberlain: Winston S. Churchill, *Great Contemporaries* (Readers' Union, 1939), p. 72.

51. Pimlott, *Harold Wilson*, pp. 303–4; Wilson, *The Making of a Prime Minister: Memoirs 1916–1964*, pp. 197–8; for the background to Wilson's Scarborough speech see Janet Morgan (ed.), *The Backbench Diaries of Richard Crossman* (Hamish Hamilton/Cape, 1981), pp. 1023–27, entry for 8 October 1963.

52. Craig, *British General Election Manifestos*, pp. 229–37.

53. Harold Wilson, 'A Prime Minister at Work', in Anthony King (ed.), *The British Prime Minister*, 2nd edn (Macmillan, 1985), p. 12.

54. Harold Wilson, *Purpose in Politics* (Weidenfeld and Nicolson, 1964).

55. For the Fulton inquiry see Peter Hennessy, *Whitehall* (Fontana, 1990), pp. 190–208.

56. Wilson, *The Governance of Britain*, p. 58.

57. Amy Baker, *Prime Ministers and the Rule Book* (Politico's, 2000), p. 27.

58. Hennessy, *Whitehall*, p. 302.

59. PRO, CAB 21/5199, 'Questions of Procedure for Ministers', note from Trend to Wilson, 16 October 1964.

60. Baker, *Prime Ministers and the Rule Book*, pp. 26–9; Wilson, *The Governance of Britain*, p. 48.

61. Paragraph 57 of the 1966 edition of *QPM*.

62. Ziegler, *Wilson*, p. 267.

63. Pimlott, *Harold Wilson*, p. 339.

64. Ibid., p. 341.

65. Ziegler, *Wilson*, p. 119.

66. Ibid., p. 339.

67. Ibid.

68. Private information. The 'feline' remark was made privately by George Wigg, Paymaster-General and Wilson's security sleuth inside No. 10. Private information.

69. 'Note of a Conversation with Mrs Marcia Williams on Nov. 6 1964', DJM, 8 November 1964. This note has yet to reach the Public Record Office and was acquired privately.

70. Ibid.

71. Ibid.

72. Ibid.

73. Ibid.

74. Ibid.

75. PRO, PREM 13/236, 'Prime Minister Requested his Personal and Political Secretary Should See Cabinet Papers: Arrangements Instituted', undated handwritten note from Harold Wilson to unnamed recipient.

76. Ibid., Mitchell to Wilson, 28 June 1965.

77. Ibid., Wilson to Mitchell, undated.

78. Ibid., indecipherable to Miss Hildreth et al. 30 June 1965.

79. Ziegler, *Wilson*, p. 213.

80. Private information.

81. Ziegler, *Wilson*, p. 213.

82. Wilson's minute to Helsby of 14 February 1966 is preserved in his private papers and quoted in Ziegler, *Wilson*, pp. 213–14.

83. Ibid., p. 214.

84. Ibid.

85. Hennessy, *Muddling Through*, p. 253.

86. PRO, EW 28/9, 'Cabinet Changes; December 1965. Correspondence Between Harold Wilson and George Brown', Brown to Wilson, 22 December 1965.

87. Ibid., Wilson to Brown, 22 December 1965.

88. PRO, PREM, 13/1647, 'Export of Arms to South Africa. Prime Minister Issued Directive to First Secretary of State Prior to His Departure to Australia', Wilson to Stewart, 20 December 1967.

89. Richard Crossman, *The Diaries of a Cabinet Minister*, vol. 2, *Lord President of the Council and Leader of the House of Commons 1966–68* (Hamish Hamilton/ Cape, 1976), p. 463, entry for 4 September 1967.

90. Cairncross, *The Wilson Years*, p. 229, diary entry for 14 September 1967.

91. PRO, PREM 13/1538. 'Prime Minister Assumed Responsibility for Department of Economic Affairs. . .', 'Note of the Meeting on August 27, 1967 at 10am at Chequers'. Among those present were Sir Burke Trend and Sir Lawrence Helsby.

92. Ibid., 'Note of Telephone Conversation Between the Prime Minister and the Secretary of State for Economic Affairs on Wednesday, August 30 1967 at 12.5 p.m.'

93. Peter Hennessy and Caroline Anstey, *From Clogs to Clogs? Britain's Relative Economic Decline Since 1851*, Strathclyde *Analysis* paper No. 3 (Department of Government, University of Strathclyde, 1991), p. 36.

94. For the early Wilson Cabinet committee structure see PRO, CAB 161/16, 'Committee Organisation Book, December 1964'.

95. For MISC 1 see PRO, CAB 130/202.

96. Castle, *The Castle Diaries, 1964–70*, p. 54, entry for 3 August 1965; see also PRO, CAB 128/39, Part 3, CC(65) 44th conclusions, minute 2, 3 August 1965.

97. PRO, PREM 13/274, 'The National Plan', Trend to Wilson, 2 August 1965.

98. Ibid., Seers to Castle (undated), left for Wilson after Seers had had a 'talk with the PM', probably on 5 August 1965.

99. Hennessy, *Whitehall*, pp. 189–90.

100. *The Times*, 29 September 1965.

101. Conversation with Lord Croham, 11 July 1997.

102. Alan Lord, 'A Strategy for Industry', Sir Ellis Hunter Memorial Lecture (University of York, 1979).

103. House of Commons *Official Report*, 27 July 1966, col. 1848.

104. Edmund Dell, *The Chancellors: A History of the Chancellors of the Exchequer, 1945–90* (HarperCollins, 1996), p. 339.

105. Alec Cairncross, *The British Economy Since 1945* (Blackwell, 1992), pp. 160–61.

106. Kenneth O. Morgan, *Callaghan, A Life* (Oxford University Press, 1997), p. 234.

107. Peter Clarke, *Hope and Glory: Britain 1900–1990* (Penguin, 1996), p. 311.

108. Balogh's May 1963 paper for Wilson, 'Civil Service Reform', developed the idea of, among other things, splitting economic responsibility between the Treasury and a new 'Ministry of Planning'. I am very grateful to Tony Benn and to his former research assistant Paul Fisher (who was also my student) for bringing this to my attention. Benn Archives, paper 54, 1963. Balogh had forwarded a copy to Benn (see Balogh to Benn, 12 June 1963).

109. PRO, PREM 13/360, 'Government Machinery'. 'Note on the Experience with the Government Machine', Balogh to Wilson, 25 February 1965. (Wilson's Principal Private Secretary, Derek Mitchell, sent a copy under a 'Personal' cover to the Cabinet Secretary, Sir Burke Trend, with the comment 'This may interest you!' Mitchell to Trend, 1 March 1965.)

110. Hennessy, *Whitehall*, pp. 171–2.

111. Crosland, *Tony Crosland*, p. 193.

112. Crossman, *Diaries of a Cabinet Minister*, vol. 2, p. 627, entry for 31 December 1967.

113. *Whitehall and Beyond* (BBC Publications, 1964), p. 27.

114. Lord Hunt of Tanworth, 'Cabinet Strategy and Management', CIPFA/RIPA Conference, Eastbourne, 9 June 1983.

115. Harold Macmillan, *Pointing the Way, 1959–61* (Macmillan, 1972), pp. 22–3.

116. PRO, PREM 13/530, 'Personal Minutes from Prime Minister to Ministers', Jan–Dec 1965', Wilson to Brown, 8 July 1965; Prime Minister's Personal Minute in M56/65.

117. With the change of government in October 1964, the Cabinet Office had decided to signal this in ad hoc Cabinet Committee terminology by replacing the GEN (or General) designation with MISC (or Miscellaneous). The practice of alternating one with another on the change of parties in power has continued to this day.

118. See PRO, PREM 13/271, 'Financial Policy Budget Discussion. Part 2'.

119. PRO, PREM 13/514, 'Budget Supper at No. 10 to Discuss Economic Affairs' (see Bancroft to Mitchell and Mitchell to Wilson, 11 May 1965). In fact, with Brown absent, this occasion ranged across the domestic economic scene as well.

120. I am grateful to Dr Chris Brady for this particular set of exchanges. Robert

Armstrong to William Reid, 10 August 1965 in a batch of CAB 21 papers that have still to reach the Public Record Office.

121. Ibid.

122. Conversation with Harold Wilson, 1 March 1976.

123. Trend to Philip Rogers, 11 August 1965.

124. PRO, CAB 130/255–58, MISC 100, The Rhodesia Steering Committee, was split into no fewer than six parts, MISC 100A–G.

125. PRO, PREM 13/854, 'July 1966 Economic Measures; "The Little Budget". UK Economic Situation: Outlook to End of 1966; Part 13', Trend to Wilson, 19 July 1966.

126. Ibid.

127. Ibid.

128. Ibid.

129. Castle, *The Castle Diaries, 1964–70*, p. 160, entry for 10 August 1966.

130. *Ministerial Committees of the Cabinet: Membership and Terms of Reference* (Cabinet Office, June 1997). Both Brown and the Deputy Prime Minister, John Prescott, sat on EA, as the Ministerial Committee on Economic Affairs was known – a repeat of Wilson's ED (though the PM's number 2 chaired ED rather than the Chancellor).

131. Castle, *The Castle Diaries, 1964–70*, pp. 160–6.

132. Cairncross, *The Wilson Years*, p. 171, diary entry for 12 November 1966.

133. Ibid., p. 229, diary entry for 14 September 1967.

134. Peter Riddell, 'Why Blair needs more time', *The Times*, 8 January 1996.

135. Wilson, *The Labour Government 1964–1970*, p. 711.

136. PRO, PREM 13/530, 'Co-ordination for the Social Services', Wilson to Houghton, 1 July 1965; Prime Minister's Personal Minute M55/65.

137. PRO, PREM 5/496, 'Ministerial Appointments. Harold Wilson. Part 9', Halls to Helsby, 2 April 1968.

138. Lord Jenkins of Hillhead. 'The 1992 Attlee Foundation Lecture,' Ironmongers' Hall, City of London, 18 February 1992.

139. Pimlott, *Harold Wilson*, pp. 340–41.

140. PRO, PREM 5/439, 'Ministerial Appointments. Harold Wilson. Part 2', Derek Mitchell's note of Wilson's 'provisional ideas for a re-shuffle given to me by the PM today', DJM, 2 August 1965.

141. Douglas Jay, *Change and Fortune* (Hutchinson, 1980), pp. 339–408.

142. I am grateful to my research student Helen Parr for the illumination she has brought to the first Wilson governments and Europe – not least the movement of the issue through the obscurer passages of Whitehall.

143. PRO, CAB 134/2705, 'Ministerial Committee on Europe, May–Oct 1966'.

144. PRO, CAB 130/298, MISC 126(66) 1st meeting, 'Europe', Chequers, 22 October 1966.

145. Pimlott, *Harold Wilson*, pp. 19–20.

146. Hugo Young, *This Blessed Plot: Britain and Europe from Churchill to Blair* (Macmillan, 1998), pp. 198–9.

147. For Wilson's European full Cabinets in the spring of 1967 see PRO, CAB 128/42 Part 1, CC(67) 21st Conclusions, 18 April 1967; PRO, CAB 128/42 Part 2, CC(67) 22nd Conclusions, 20 April 1967; ibid., CC(67) 23rd Conclusions, 27 April 1967; ibid., CC(67) 24th Conclusions, 29 April 1967; ibid., CC(67) 25th Conclusions, 30 April 1967 10.30 a.m.; ibid.; CC(67) 26th Conclusions, 30 April 1967 2.45 p.m.; ibid.; CC(67) 27th Conclusions, 2 May 1967.

148. *The Government's Response to the Radcliffe Report*, Cmnd 3312 (HMSO, 1967).

149. *Report of the Committee of Privy Counsellors on D-Notice Matters*, Cmnd 3309 (HMSO, 1967).

150. Crossman, *Diaries of a Cabinet Minister*, vol. 2, pp. 380–81, diary entry for 13 June 1967.

151. Matthew Creevy, 'A Critical Review of the Wilson Government's Handling of the D-Notice Affair 1967', *Intelligence and National Security*, vol. 14, no. 3 (autumn 1999), pp. 206–16.

152. Castle, *The Castle Diaries, 1964–70*, p. 268, entry for 20 June 1967.

153. Private information.

154. PRO, PREM 13/1818, 'Security: D-Notices'. Trend made his own record of the discussion for the files.

155. Hennessy, *Whitehall*, pp. 565–8.

156. Wilson's press officer, Henry James, told him of 'a pathological intensity of feeling' towards him that had manifested itself at a meeting of editors, '. . . the hatred of you had to be experienced to be believed'. PRO, PREM 13/1813, 'D-Notices: Reorganisation of Services, Press and Broadcasting Committee . . .', 'Note of a Meeting of 15 Editors at the Newspaper Proprietors' Association Offices in Fleet Street, 16 June 1967'.

157. Pimlott, *Harold Wilson*, p. 449.

158. Ziegler, *Wilson*, pp. 253–5.

159. PRO, CAB 128/46. 'Most Confidential Records, June 1966–February 1970', CC(67) 25th Conclusions. 'NO CIRCULATION RECORD', Sunday 30 April 1967, 10.30 a.m.

160. Ibid.

161. Ibid.

162. Ibid.

163. Morgan, *Callaghan*, p. 268.

164. Ibid., p. 269.

165. This is based on Callaghan's 'Note for the Record' of 14 November 1967 and reproduced in Morgan, *Callaghan*, p. 271.

166. PRO, CAB 128/42, CC(67) 66th Conclusions, 16 November 1967.

167. Morgan, *Callaghan*, p. 273.

168. Ibid.

169. Jon Davis and Peter Hennessy in conversation with Lord Jenkins of Hillhead, 5 May 1999.

170. Pimlott, *Harold Wilson*, p. 483.

171. Lord Jenkins in conversation with Davis and Hennessy.

172. Ibid.

173. Jenkins, *A Life at the Centre* (Macmillan, 1991), p. 227. For the minutes of the meetings see PRO, CAB 128/43, part 1, CC(68)1, 4 January 1968; CC(68)2, 5 January 1968; CC(68)3, 9 January 1968; CC(68)4, 11 January 1968; CC(68)5, 12 January 1968; CC(68)6, 12 January 1968; CC(68)7, 15 January 1968; CC(68)8, 15 January 1968.

174. Lord Jenkins in conversation with Davis and Hennessy.

175. Ibid.

176. Wilson, *The Labour Government 1964–1970*, p. 479.

177. Lord Jenkins in conversation with Davis and Hennessy.

178. Cairncross, *The Wilson Years*, p. 288, diary entry for 16 March 1968.

179. Lord Jenkins in conversation with Davis and Hennessy.

180. Jon Davis, ' "Staring Over the Precipice into the Abyss": An Anatomy and an Analysis of "Operation Brutus", November 1967–July 1968', unpublished MA in Contemporary British History thesis, Queen Mary and Westfield College, University of London, 1999.

181. Ibid.

182. PRO, PREM 13/2172, 'Visits to UK of Irish Prime Minister: Records of Talks with Prime Minister, 1967–1968'. 'Note of Meeting between the Prime Minister and the Prime Minister of the Irish Republic at No. 10 Downing Street . . . Friday, November 29, 1968'.

183. Pimlott, *Harold Wilson*, pp. 494–503.

184. George Brown, *In My Way: The Political Memoirs of Lord George-Brown* (Gollancz, 1971), p. 175; PRO, PREM 13/2051, 'Problem of Gold: Possibility of Separating Monetary and Industrial Gold Markets', Roger Dawe, 'Note for the Record', 15 March 1968.

185. Jenkins, *A Life At The Centre*, p. 235.

186. Ibid., pp. 236–7.

187. Alec Cairncross, *Managing the British Economy in the 1960s: A Treasury Perspective* (Macmillan, 1996), pp. 207–9.

188. Lord Jenkins in conversation with Davis and Hennessy.

189. Castle, *The Castle Diaries, 1964–70*, p. 462, entry for 13 June 1968.

190. PRO, CAB 130/497, MISC 205, 1st Meeting, 17 March 1968.

191. Private information.

192. PRO, PREM 13/2051, Note by the Treasury, 'Contingency Planning', annex II: 'Operation Brutus', 16 March 1968.

193. Lord Shore interviewed by Jon Davis on 27 July 1999.

194. PRO, PREM 13/2052, Treasury Paper, 'Brutus Framework for Decision', annex V: 'Brutus: Government Overseas Expenditure', 10 June 1968.

195. Ibid., 'Brutus: Framework for Decisions', annex VIII [Board of Trade: 'Brutus: Prohibition of Inessential Imports', 7 June 1968.

196. J. K. Galbraith, *The Culture of Contentment* (Hamish Hamilton, 1991).

197. PRO, PREM 13/2051, Michael Halls, 'Note for the Record', 17 March 1968.

198. Davis, ' "Staring Over the Precipice into the Abyss" '.

199. PRO, CAB 130/497, MISC 205, 2nd Meeting, 17 March 1968.

200. PRO, CAB 130/498, MISC 209, 1st [and only] Meeting, 13 June 1968.

201. Tony Benn, *Office Without Power: Diaries 1968–72* (Hutchinson, 1988), p. 295, entry for 19 June 1970.

202. Lord Armstrong was speaking at the Twentieth Century British History Seminar, Institute of Historical Research, 9 March 1994.

203. Letter from Lord Callaghan to Stephen Bailey, 21 April 1999.

204. Castle, *The Castle Diaries, 1964–70*, p. 426, entry for 9 April 1968.

205. Ibid., p. 430, entry for 23 April 1968.

206. Ibid., and ibid., p. 426, entry for 9 April 1968.

207. Ibid., p. 446, entry for 23 May 1968 for Lords reform and p. 597, entry for 31 January 1969, for prices and incomes.

208. Ibid., pp. 515–16, entry for 18 September 1968.

209. Ibid., pp. 553–5, entry for 22 November 1968.

210. PRO, CAB 134/3031–3032, 'Parliamentary Committee', 'Meetings, April 1968–April 1969'.

211. PRO, CAB 134/3031, Index of Meetings, 1968.

212. Ibid.

213. Ibid.

214. Ibid.

215. Stephen Bailey, 'The Use of Inner Cabinets "Formal" and "Informal" Since 1968', unpublished undergraduate thesis, Department of History, Queen Mary and Westfield College, University of London, 1999.

216. Castle, *The Castle Diaries, 1964–70*, p. 436, entry for 2 May 1968.

217. Ibid., p. 604, entry for 20 February 1969.

218. Crosland, *Tony Crosland*, p. 200.

219. Richard Crossman, *The Diaries of a Cabinet Minister*, vol. 3, *Secretary of State for Social Services, 1968–1970* (Hamish Hamilton/Cape, 1977), p. 243, entry for 29 October 1968.

220. Ibid., p. 433, entry for 8 April 1969. The actual words are Barbara Castle's: see Castle, *The Castle Diaries, 1964–70*, p. 633, entry for 8 April 1969.

221. Ibid., p. 640, entry for 29 April 1969.

222. PRO, PREM 13/2512, 'Parliamentary Committee', Dawe to Halls, 29 April 1969.

223. Crossman, *The Diaries of a Cabinet Minister*, vol. 3, p. 474, entry for 4 May 1969.

224. Peter Rose, *How The Troubles Came to Northern Ireland* (Macmillan, 2000).

225. The first of these reached Wilson as early as December 1965 via Roy Jenkins' predecessor at the Home Office, Sir Frank Soskice. PRO, PREM 13/980, Soskice to Wilson, 10 December 1965. Jenkins called upon Wilson on 4 March 1966 to

brief him on 'the possibility of renewed activity by the Irish Republican Army to mark the 50th anniversary of the Irish "Easter" rebellion', PRO, PREM 13/980, 'Note For the Record' by Peter le Cheminant, 4 March 1966.

226. PRO, DEFE 4/197, confidential annex to the minutes of the Chiefs of Staff Committee Meeting, 17 March 1966.

227. PRO, PREM 13/980, 'The IRA Threat Over Easter', Trend to Mitchell, 24 March 1966.

228. Ibid.

229. Ibid., Prime Minister's Personal Minute 13/66, Wilson to Jenkins, 28 March 1966.

230. Ibid., Trend to Wilson, 5 April 1966.

231. PRO, CAB 130/416, MISC 238 (69), 1st Meeting, 26 February 1969. Its members, apart from Wilson, were the Home Secretary, Callaghan; the Defence Secretary, Healey; the Foreign Secretary, Stewart; the Chancellor of the Exchequer, Jenkins; the Lord Chancellor, Gerald Gardiner; the Lord President, Fred Peart; and the Attorney-General, Sir Elwyn Jones.

232. For a particularly full account of the crisis meeting of the full Cabinet on 19 August 1969, see the confidential annex to the minutes of CC(69), 41st Conclusions. PRO, CAB 128/46, 'Extract'.

233. PRO, PREM 13/2843, 'Northern Ireland, Internal Situation, Contingency Planning for the Maintenance of Law and Order . . .' part 3, 'Intelligence in Northern Ireland', Callaghan to Wilson, 6 August 1969. See also PRO, PREM, DEFE 4/241, Chiefs of Staff Committee, 18 August 1969, Item 1.

234. PRO, PREM 13/2843, Report on 'Intelligence in Northern Ireland' attached to Callaghan's minute to Wilson.

235. PRO, CAB 130/416, MISC 238 (69)4, 'Northern Ireland and General Appreciation on Intervention. Memorandum by the Secretary of State for the Home Department', 1 May 1969; MISC 238 (69)5, Northern Ireland, 'Memorandum by the Secretary of State for Defence', 14 July 1969.

236. Castle, *The Castle Diaries, 1964–70*, p. 721, entry for 21 October 1969.

237. Benn, *Office Without Power*, p. 228, diary entry for 23 January 1970.

238. PRO, PREM 13/2512, Dawe to Halls, 29 April 1969.

239. PRO, CAB 134/3118. PM(69).

240. Castle, *The Castle Diaries, 1964–70*, p. 645.

241. Ibid.

242. Ibid.

243. Ibid.

244. Crosland, *Tony Crosland*, p. 208.

245. PRO, CAB 134/3118, PM(69), 3rd Meeting, 13 May 1969, Item 1.

246. Morgan, *Callaghan*, pp. 287, 293, 332–3, 339, 361, 369.

247. PRO, CAB 134/3118, PM(69), 8th Meeting, 17 June 1969.

248. Hennessy, *Muddling Through*, p. 256.

249. Castle, *The Castle Diaries, 1964–70*, p. 672, entry for 17 June 1969 ('The most traumatic day of my political life', she called it).

250. Ibid.

251. Ibid., pp. 676–9, entry for 18 June 1969. See also PRO, CAB 128/44, part 1, CC(69)29, 18 June 1969.

252. Morgan, *Callaghan*, pp. 341–2.

253. Immortalized as 'Mr Solomon Binding', see Peter Jenkins, *The Battle for Downing Street*.

254. Castle, *The Castle Diaries, 1964–70*, pp. 677–8, entry for 18 June 1969.

255. Pimlott, *Harold Wilson*, pp. 489, 504.

256. Castle, *The Castle Diaries, 1964–70*, p. 695, entry for 28 July 1969.

257. Ibid., p. 681, entry for 30 June 1969.

258. Ibid., p. 721, entry for 21 October 1969.

259. Ibid., pp. 749–50, entry for 14 January 1970; p. 758, entry for 2 February 1970; pp. 768–70, entry for 8 March 1970.

260. Morgan, Callaghan, p. 337.

261. Or, to be more accurate, echoing the words of MacDonald's No. 10 spokesman (probably George Steward), as the expression 'Doctor's Mandate' appeared non-attributably in *The Times* on the morning the Cabinet met to decide to go to the country. 'The Doctor's Mandate', *The Times*, 29 September 1931. I am grateful to Professor John Ramsden for discovering the precise origins of the phrase.

262. Castle, *The Castle Diaries, 1964–70*, p. 800, entry for 15 May 1970.

263. Ibid., pp. 705–7, entry for 5 September 1969; Crossman, *The Diaries of a Cabinet Minister*, vol. 3, pp. 627–31, entry for 5 September 1969.

264. In more than one conversation with the author.

265. *The Sunday Times*, 15 February 1970.

266. John Ramsden, *The Winds of Change: Macmillan to Heath 1957–75* (Longman, 1996), p. 317.

267. Wilson, *The Governance of Britain*, p. 70.

268. Ibid., p. 48.

269. Ibid., p. 46.

270. For their battles to secure access to Whitehall material and meetings see PRO, PREM 13/1955, 'Attendance of Economic Advisers at Meetings of Cabinet Committees . . . , Nov 1964–Nov 1968'.

271. Peter Riddell, *Parliament Under Blair* (Politico's, 2000), p. 18; PRO, PREM 13/2862, 'Attendance of Ministers Before Select Committees: Code of Practice; Part 2, March 1967–May 1969'.

272. See Hennessy, *Whitehall*, p. 198.

273. PRO, PREM 13/2528, 'Fulton Report; Government's Consideration of Recommendations; Enquiry Into Release of Official Information and Official Secrets Act; Part 2'.

274. Departmental Committee on Section 2 of the Official Secrets Act 1911, vol. 1, *Report of the Committee*, Cmnd 5104 (HMSO, 1972). See p. 1 for its terms of reference.

275. PRO, PREM 13/1077, 'Personal Minutes from Prime Minister to Ministers, 1966', Wilson to Crossman, 22 December 1966.

276. Michael Cockerell, Peter Hennessy and David Walker, *Sources Close to the Prime Minister* (Macmillan, 1984), p. 122.

277. Christopher Andrew and Vasili Mitrokhin, *The Mitrokhin Archive: The KGB in Europe and the West* (Allen Lane, 1999), pp. 528–9.

278. Ibid., p. 528.

279. Ibid.

280. Ibid.

281. PRO, PREM 13/2688, 'Reorganisation of Central Machinery for Politico-Military Planning Intelligence', Trend to Wilson, 13 March 1967, Trend to Wilson, 20 July 1967.

282. PRO, CAB 165/432, Official Committee on Communism (Home), 'Constitution and Terms of Reference of the Committee. Note by the Secretary of the Cabinet', 7 June 1951.

283. PRO, PREM 13/2688, Heaton to Trend, 2 January 1969.

284. For the latest version of this see Kenneth O. Morgan, 'The Wilson Years, 1964–1970', in Nick Tiratsoo (ed.), *From Blitz to Blair: A New History of Britain Since 1939* (Weidenfeld, 1997), pp. 149–50.

285. Quoted in Anthony Howard and Richard West, *The Making of the Prime Minister* (Cape, 1965), p. 198.

286. Private information. The 'stardust' point was made by Joe Haines in conversation with the author on 6 September 1976.

287. Louis Heren, *No Hail, No Farewell* (Hamish Hamilton, 1970), p. 231.

288. Paul Foot's spirited polemic, *The Politics of Harold Wilson* (Penguin, 1968), was an early version of this school.

289. Ziegler, *Wilson*, p. 201.

290. Phillip Whitehead, *The Writing On the Wall* (Michael Joseph/Channel 4 Television, 1985), p. 46.

13   The Somersaulting Modernizer: Edward Heath, 1970–74

1. Peter Hennessy, *Muddling Through: Power, Politics and the Quality of Government in Postwar Britain* (Gollancz, 1996), p. 273.

2. James Margach, *The Abuse of Power* (W. H. Allen, 1978), p. 160.

3. David Watt, 'The power of the Prime Minister', *Financial Times*, 5 May 1972.

4. Private information.

5. Margach, *The Abuse of Power*, pp. 164–5.

6. Jack Jones, *Union Man* (Collins, 1986), p. 70.

7. Ibid., p. 215.

8. Private information.

9. Dr David Owen interviewed for the BBC Radio 3 programme *Routine Punctuated by Orgies*, 10 November 1983.

10. John Campbell, *Edward Heath, A Biography*, (Cape, 1993), p. 282.

11. Ibid., p. 613.

12. Sir Edward Heath interviewed by Michael Cockerell in September 1996 for the BBC2 programme *How to Be Prime Minister*. I am very grateful to Mr Cockerell for the interview transcript.

13. Campbell, *Edward Heath*, p. xi.

14. Private information.

15. For the context, background and subliminal linkage of 'Selsdon Man' with 'Piltdown Man' see John Ramsden, *The Winds of Change: Macmillan to Heath 1957–75* (Longman, 1996), pp. 13, 249, 258, 300, 347, 351, 395.

16. Campbell, *Edward Heath*, pp. 266–7.

17. Ibid., p. 267.

18. Ibid.

19. Ramsden, *The Winds of Change*, pp. 282–3.

20. Sir Edward Heath, interviewed for the Channel 4 Television/Wide Vision Productions *What Has Become of Us?* series, 27 June 1994.

21. Lord Dahrendorf has done this in my presence.

22. David Watt, 'The twilight of the old tradition', *Financial Times*, 14 February 1975.

23. Ibid.

24. Ramsden, *The Winds of Change*, p. 252.

25. Watt, 'The power of the Prime Minister'.

26. For the impact of Lloyd George on several fronts see Peter Hennessy, *Whitehall* (Fontana, 1990), pp. 52–74.

27. Keynes' fears are quoted in G. M. Young, 'The Future of British Parliamentary Government', in Lord Campion et al., *Parliament: A Survey* (Allen and Unwin, 1952), p. 273.

28. See Hennessy, *Whitehall*, pp. 587–688.

29. Edward Heath, *The Course of My Life* (Hodder, 1998), p. 314.

30. Ibid., pp. 318–19.

31. For a full and detailed treatment of Heath's election planning on the machinery of government see Kevin Theakston, 'The Heath Government, Whitehall and the Civil Service', in Stuart Ball and Anthony Seldon (eds.), *The Heath Government 1970–74* (Longman, 1990), pp. 76–80 and Ramsden, *The Winds of Change*, pp. 251–3.

32. Hennessy, *Whitehall*, pp. 221–2.

33. Watt, 'The power of the Prime Minister'.

34. *The Reorganisation of Central Government*, Cmnd 4506 (HMSO, 1970).

35. *Report of the Machinery of Government Committee*, Cd 9230, 1918.

36. Hennessy, *Whitehall*, p. 292.

37. The Cabinet committee, GEN 616, met but once, in October 1957: PRO, CAB 130/137, GEN 616, 'The Burden on Ministers'. For the background to Attlee's inquiry which Macmillan himself commissioned, see Peter Hennessy, *The Hidden Wiring: Unearthing the British Constitution* (Gollancz, 1995), pp. 167–9.

38. PRO, CAB 128/36, CC(62)63, Cabinet conclusions for the meeting of 29 October 1962.

39. Ramsden, *The Winds of Change*, pp. 253–61; Douglas Hurd in conversation with Michael Cockerell for *How to Be Prime Minister*.

40. Edward Heath, *My Style of Government* (Evening Standard Publications, 1972), p. 5.

41. Ibid., p. 3.

42. *The Reorganisation of Central Government*, p. 3.

43. I have a copy of the undated *World in Action* interview transcript in my possession.

44. Hennessy, *Whitehall*, pp. 212, 227, 263, 592–4.

45. *The Reorganisation of Central Government*, p. 6.

46. Ibid., pp. 14–15.

47. David Howell in conversation with the author 21 February 1985. See Peter Hennessy, *Cabinet* (Blackwell, 1986), p. 76.

48. Private information quoted in Hennessy, *Whitehall*, p. 222.

49. Amy Baker, *Prime Ministers and the Rule Book* (Politico's, 2000), p. 34.

50. *How to Be Prime Minister*.

51. Heath, *The Course of My Life*, pp. 308–9.

52. Private information.

53. Lord Armstrong of Ilminster, interviewed by Michael Cockerell for *How to Be Prime Minister*.

54. David Howell, quoted in Hennessy, *Cabinet*, p. 77.

55. Lewis Baston and Anthony Seldon, 'Number 10 under Edward Heath', in Ball and Seldon (eds.), *The Heath Government 1970–74*, pp. 48–51, 56–61.

56. Douglas Hurd, *An End to Promises: Sketch of a Government 1970–74* (Collins, 1979), p. 32.

57. Heath, *The Course of My Life*, p. 313.

58. Private information.

59. Private information.

60. Lord Carrington, *Reflect On Things Past* (Collins, 1988), p. 252.

61. Anthony Barber, *Taking the Tide* (Michael Russell, 1996), p. 97.

62. Sarah Curtis (ed.), *The Journals of Woodrow Wyatt*, vol. 1 (Macmillan, 1998), p. 440.

63. Private information and, for the 'floating' episode, Barber, *Taking the Tide*, pp. 115–16.

64. Margach, *The Abuse of Power*, p. 162.

65. Douglas Hurd speaking on *How to Be Prime Minister*.

66. Lord Armstrong of Ilminster speaking at the Twentieth Century British History Seminar, Institute of Historical Research, 9 March 1994.

67. Carrington, *Reflect On Things Past*, p. 252.

68. Conversation with Lord Hurd, 20 April 1999.

69. Hurd, *An End to Promises*, p. 14.

70. William Waldegrave, 'Three Prime Ministers', Twentieth Century British History seminar, Institute of Historical Research, 10 December 1997.

71. Ibid.

72. Phillip Whitehead, *The Writing On the Wall* (Channel 4/Michael Joseph, 1985), p. 52.

73. Waldegrave, 'Three Prime Ministers'.

74. Whitehead, *The Writing On the Wall*, p. 52.

75. Private information.

76. Private information. Sir Edward gently alluded to this in a 1989 interview with the author. See Hennessy, *Muddling Through*, pp. 276–7.

77. Watt, 'The power of the Prime Minister'.

78. Ibid.

79. Heath, *The Course of My Life*, pp. 400–401.

80. John Ramsden, 'The Prime Minister and the Making of Policy', in Ball and Seldon (ed.), *The Heath Government 1970–74*, p. 40.

81. Campbell, *Edward Heath*, p. 485.

82. Simon James, *British Cabinet Government* (Routledge, 2nd edn, 1999), p. 76.

83. Barber, *Taking the Tide*, p. 77.

84. John Young, 'The Heath Government and the British Entry into the European Community', in Ball and Seldon (eds.), *The Heath Government 1970–74*, p. 276.

85. Ibid., pp. 266–78; Campbell, *Edward Heath*, pp. 396–405.

86. Heath, *The Course of My Life*, p. 372.

87. Ibid., p. 371.

88. Ibid., p. 372.

89. Ibid., p. 368.

90. Paul Arthur, 'The Heath Government and Northern Ireland', in Ball and Seldon (eds.), *The Heath Government 1970–74*, p. 235.

91. Campbell, *Edward Heath*, pp. 423, 487.

92. PRO, PREM 15/011, 'Committee Structure', Trend to Heath, 2 July 1970. See also the CAB 134 catalogue at the Public Record Office. We do not have a complete list of Heath's first ministerial committees at the PRO (the entries dealing with the Foreign and Defence policy ones are not there yet), but they included, as well as NI:

    Ministerial Committee on Economic Strategy (ES);

    Home Affairs Committee (HA);

    Legislation Committee (L);

    Management Project Committee (MPC);

    Ministerial Committee Regional Policy and Environment (RE);

    Sub-Committee on the Reorganisation of Local Government (RE(G));

    Ministerial Committee Rhodesia (RH);

    Ministerial Committee on Science and Technology (SCT).

93. Waldegrave, 'Three Prime Ministers'.

94. Heath, *The Course of My Life*, p. 436.

95. While peeing in adjacent pedestals at Glyndebourne, where we encountered each other during a break in Smetana's *The Bartered Bride* on 25 July 1999, Sir Edward and I agreed that the 'two great secrets' (my phrase not his) revealed in his memoirs were Eden telling him that the Suez collusion represented 'the highest

form of statesmanship' (Heath, *The Course of My Life*, p. 169) and Alec Home's views on the desirability of a united Ireland (Ibid., p. 436).

96. Hennessy, *Cabinet*, p. 78.

97. Ibid., p. 79. See also Keith Jeffery and Peter Hennessy, *States of Emergency: British Governments and Strikebreaking* (Routledge, 1982), pp. 236–7.

98. Private information.

99. Hennessy, *Muddling Through*, p. 271.

100. The occasion was the Institute of Contemporary British History's 1995 Summer School. Sir Edward delivered a lecture to it at Queen Mary and Westfield College on 11 July 1995.

101. Roy Jenkins, *A Life at the Centre* (Macmillan, 1991), p. 203.

102. Quoted in Margach, *The Abuse of Power*, p. 163.

103. See illustration.

104. Hennessy, *Muddling Through*, p. 272.

105. Heath, *The Course of My Life*, p. 380.

106. Ibid., p. 381.

107. Hennessy, *Muddling Through*, p. 275.

108. For the genesis of this celebrated remark of Bevan's see Michael Foot, *Aneurin Bevan, 1945–60* (Davis-Poynter, 1973), pp. 450–52.

109. Ramsden, *The Winds of Change*, p. 255.

110. Whitehead, *The Writing on the Wall*, p. 32.

111. For Heath and *Private Eye* see Campbell, *Edward Heath*, pp. 125n., 303–4, 373n., 385, 426, 501.

112. Hennessy, *Whitehall*, p. 210.

113. Hennessy, *Muddling Through*, p. 270.

114. Douglas Hurd in conversation with Michael Cockerell for *How to Be Prime Minister*.

115. Nigel Nicolson, *Long Life* (Weidenfeld and Nicolson, 1997), pp. 165–6.

116. Heath launched this phrase at his first Party Conference as Prime Minister. See Hennessy, *Muddling Through*, p. 311.

117. This was a view I often picked up during my years as a Whitehall correspondent in the late 1970s and early 1980s.

118. This was a theme reprised constantly to me by both politicians and civil servants during my time as a Whitehall correspondent, 1975–84.

119. Henry Kissinger, *Years of Upheaval* (Weidenfeld and Nicolson/Michael Joseph, 1985), pp. 191–2.

120. Peter Hennessy and Caroline Anstey, *Moneybags and Brains: The Anglo-American 'Special Relationship' Since 1945*, Strathclyde *Analysis* paper, No. 1 (Department of Government, University of Strathclyde, 1990), pp. 16–18.

121. Private information.

122. See chapter 3.

123. Campbell, *Edward Heath*, p. 576.

124. Heath, *The Course of My Life*, p. 512.

125. Private information.

126. Sir John Nott, speaking on 'Heath at the Helm', broadcast on Channel 4 Television, 1985.

127. Campbell, *Edward Heath*, p. 576.

128. Hurd, *An End to Promises*, p. 121.

129. Private information.

130. Margach, *The Abuse of Power*, p. 161.

131. Campbell, *Edward Heath*, pp. 307–8.

132. Margach, *The Abuse of Power*, p. 161.

133. Hennessy, *Muddling Through*, p. 274.

134. Douglas Hurd in conversation with Michael Cockerell for *How to Be Prime Minister*.

135. Private information.

136. Waldegrave, 'Three Prime Ministers'.

137. Dennis Kavanagh, 'The Fatal Choice: The Calling of the February 1974 Election', in Ball and Seldon (eds.), *The Heath Government 1970–74*, pp. 362–3.

138. For an elaborate chart on the calling and duration of general elections 1922–66, see PRO, PREM 13/878, 'General Election 1966: Arrangements for Prorogation and Dissolution of Parliament by Proclamation', undated.

139. Whitehead, *The Writing on the Wall*, p. 112.

140. Hennessy, *Muddling Through*, p. 36.

141. Ibid., pp. 35–7; Heath, *The Course of My Life*, pp. 518–20; Jeremy Thorpe, *In My Own Time* (Politico's, 1999), pp. 113–17.

142. Vernon Bogdanor, *The Monarchy and the Constitution* (Clarendon Press, 1995), p. 149; Ramsden, *The Winds of Change*, pp. 387–9.

143. Lord Charteris who, as Sir Martin Charteris, was the Queen's Private Secretary in 1974, interviewed for the Wide Vision Productions/Channel 4 Television series *What Has Become of Us?*, 6 June 1994.

144. Campbell, *Edward Heath*, p. 579.

145. Hennessy, *Whitehall*, p. 243; Hennessy, *Cabinet*, p. 237.

146. Hennessy, *Whitehall*, p. 596; Hennessy, *Cabinet*, p. 88.

147. Hennessy, *Whitehall*, pp. 27–8, 312, 653, 655–7.

148. Gavin Drewry (ed.), *The New Select Committees* (Oxford University Press, 1987), pp. 6–7.

149. Private information.

150. Vernon Bogdanor, 'The Fall of Heath and the End of the Postwar Settlement', in Ball and Seldon (eds.), *The Heath Government 1970–74*, pp. 371–90.

151. See Lord Donoughue's testimony in Hennessy, *Muddling Through*, p. 259.

152. See S. E. Finer (ed.), *Adversary Politics and Electoral Reform* (Macmillan, 1975).

153. Anthony King, 'Overload: Problems of Governing In the 1970s', *Political Studies*, vol. 22, nos. 2–3 (June–September 1975).

154. Ramsden, *The Winds of Change*, pp. 316–17.

155. See Jeremy Thorpe's account of his meetings with Heath on 1 and 2 March

1974 in Hennessy, *Muddling Through*, pp. 36–7 and Thorpe, *In My Own Time*, pp. 114–17.

156. Bogdanor, 'The Fall of Heath', p. 373.

157. Hurd, *An End to Promises*, p. 142.

158. Pre-conference message to Conservative Party workers, 30 September 1973, quoted in Martin Wiener, *English Culture and the Decline of the Industrial Spirit 1850–1980* (Cambridge University Press, 1981), p. 162.

14   Centre Half: Harold Wilson, 1974–76

1. Conversation with Lord Hunt of Tanworth, 7 January 1993.

2. Tony Benn, *Against the Tide: Diaries 1973–76* (Arrow, 1990), p. 305, entry for 21 January 1975.

3. Conversation with Joe Haines, 4 January 1993.

4. Private information.

5. Private information.

6. Private information.

7. Donald Sassoon, *Reuniting the Centre-Left: The Case for a Labour–Liberal Partnership* (LINC, 1997), p. 10.

8. Peter Hennessy, *Muddling Through: Power, Politics and the Quality of Government in Postwar Britain* (Gollancz, 1996), p. 259; Bernard Donoughue, *Prime Minister: The Conduct of Policy Under Harold Wilson and James Callaghan 1974–7* (Cape, 1987), p. 47.

9. Hennessy, *Muddling Through*, p. 259.

10. Kenneth O. Morgan, *Callaghan, A Life* (Oxford University Press, 1997), p. 406.

11. Hennessy, *Muddling Through*, p. 260.

12. Donoughue, *Prime Minister*, p. 47.

13. Harold Wilson, *The Governance of Britain* (Weidenfeld and Nicolson/ Michael Joseph, 1976), p. 91.

14. For the Fulton recommendation see Peter Hennessy, *Whitehall* (Secker and Warburg, 1989), p. 197; Wilson's guidance on the appointment of special advisers was incorporated in the 1976 edition of *Questions of Procedure for Ministers*. See Amy Baker, *Prime Ministers and the Rule Book* (Politico's 2000), pp. 24–44.

15. Wilson, *The Governance of Britain*, p. 204; for the decision to keep the CPRS see Hennessy, *Whitehall*, pp. 245–6.

16. Nicholas Henderson, *Mandarin: The Diaries of an Ambassador, 1969–1982* (Weidenfeld and Nicolson, 1994), p. 72, entry for 11 June 1974.

17. Ibid., p. 71.

18. Ibid., p. 69.

19. Hennessy, *Muddling Through*, p. 260.

20. Private information.

21. Peter Hennessy, *Whitehall* (Fontana, 1990), pp. 254–6.

22. Hennessy, *Muddling Through*, p. 250.

23. PRO, PREM 13/854, Trend to Wilson, 19 July 1966.

24. Hennessy, *Muddling Through*, p. 260.

25. Harold Wilson, *Final Term: The Labour Government, 1974–1976* (Weidenfeld and Nicolson/Michael Joseph, 1979), p. 22.

26. Conversation with Lord Lever, 18 September 1992.

27. Harold Lever, 'The Cabinets of 1964–70 had highly gifted individuals. Why then was so little achieved?' the *Listener*, 22 November 1984, pp. 24–5.

28. Hennessy, *Whitehall*, p. 187.

29. Peter Hennessy, *Cabinet* (Blackwell, 1986), p. 70.

30. Wilson, *Final Term*, pp. 22–3.

31. Conversation with Sir Kenneth Stowe, 26 August 1998.

32. Sir Douglas Wass, former Permanent Secretary to the Treasury, quoted in Hennessy, *Whitehall*, p. 244.

33. Denis Healey, *The Time of My Life* (Michael Joseph, 1989), p. 389.

34. Ibid., pp. 389–90.

35. Hennessy, *Muddling Through*, p. 255.

36. Healey, *The Time of My Life*, p. 388.

37. He was speaking on Michael Cockerell's documentary, *How to Be Chancellor*, broadcast on BBC2, 2 June 1997.

38. Ibid.

39. Ibid.

40. Private information.

41. She was speaking on Michael Cockerell's documentary, *The Red Queen: A Film Portrait of Barbara Castle*, broadcast on BBC2, 29 January 1995.

42. Hennessy, *Muddling Through*, p. 255.

43. Ibid.

44. Sonia Orwell and Ian Angus (eds.), *The Collected Essays, Journalism and Letters of George Orwell*, vol. II, *My Country Right or Left 1940–1943* (Penguin, 1970), p. 77.

45. Roy Jenkins, *A Life at the Centre* (Macmillan, 1991), p. 371.

46. Ibid.

47. House of Commons, *Eleventh Report from the Expenditure Committee, Session 1976–77*, 'The Civil Service', vol. 2, part 2 (HMSO, 1977), pp. 782–3.

48. Hennessy, *Muddling Through*, pp. 281–2.

49. Morgan, *Callaghan*, p. 409.

50. Ibid.

51. Hennessy, *Cabinet*, p. 86.

52. Barbara Castle, *The Castle Diaries, 1974–76* (Weidenfeld and Nicolson, 1980), pp. 219–24, entry for 17 November 1974.

53. Private information.

54. Conversation with Baroness Williams, 5 January 1993.

55. Ben Pimlott, *Harold Wilson* (HarperCollins, 1992), p. 597.

56. Morgan, *Callaghan*, p. 427.

57. Pimlott, *Wilson*, p. 659.

58. Bernard Donoughue, 'Harold Wilson and the Renegotiation of the EEC Terms of Membership, 1974–5: A Witness Account', in Brain Brivat and Harriet Jones (eds.), *From Reconstruction to Integration: Britain and Europe since 1945* (Leicester University Press, 1993), p. 204.

59. Philip Ziegler, *Wilson* (Weidenfeld and Nicolson, 1993), p. 470.

60. Pimlott, *Harold Wilson*, p. 675.

61. Hennessy, *Muddling Through*, p. 264.

62. Pimlott, *Harold Wilson*, p. 674.

63. Hennessy, *Muddling Through*, p. 264.

64. Pimlott, *Harold Wilson*, p. 675.

65. Quoted ibid., p. 659.

66. Donoughue, 'Harold Wilson and the Renegotiation of the EEC Terms of Membership', p. 194.

67. Barbara Castle records this as an unnamed Cabinet minister's verdict. *The Castle Diaries, 1974–76*, p. 287, entry for 21 January 1975.

68. Wilson, *The Governance of Britain*, pp. 194–7.

69. Castle, *The Castle Diaries, 1974–76*, p. 287, entry for 21 January 1975.

70. Donoughue, 'Harold Wilson and the Renegotiation of the EEC Terms of Membership', p. 194.

71. Castle, *The Castle Diaries, 1974–76*, p. 345, entry for 19 March 1975.

72. Wilson, *Final Term*, p. 103.

73. Castle, *The Castle Diaries, 1974–76*, pp. 345–6, entry for 19 March 1975.

74. Benn, *Against the Tide*, p. 351, entry for 20 March 1975.

75. Pimlott, *Harold Wilson*, p. 657.

76. Donoughue, 'Harold Wilson and the Renegotiation of the EEC Terms of Membership', p. 202.

77. Conversation with Tony Benn, 7 January 1993.

78. Donoughue, 'Harold Wilson and the Renegotiation of the EEC Terms of Membership', p. 202.

79. Pimlott, *Harold Wilson*, p. 656.

80. Ibid., p. 658.

81. Ibid.

82. Ibid.

83. Wilson, *Final Term*, pp. 143–4.

84. Ibid., pp. 195–200; Healey, *The Time of My Life*, pp. 407–8; Hennessy, *Muddling Through*, pp. 263–4.

85. Donoughue, *Prime Minister*, pp. 712–22.

86. Conversation with Lord Shore, 8 January 1993.

87. Hennessy, *Muddling Through*, p. 262.

88. Ibid., pp. 261–2.

89. Donoughue, *Prime Minister*, pp. 52–5.

90. Hennessy, *Cabinet*, p. 86.

91. Ibid.

92. Baker, *Prime Ministers and the Rule Book*, p. 37.

93. Wilson, *The Governance of Britain*, p. 44.

94. Baker, *Prime Ministers and the Rule Book*, p. 37.

95. Benn, *Against the Tide*, p. 177, entry for 17 June 1974.

96. Ibid.

97. He has shown them to me and my students on more than one occasion.

98. Castle, *The Castle Diaries, 1974–76*, pp. 671–2, entry for 4 March 1976.

99. Hennessy, *Muddling Through*, p. 265.

100. Wilson, *Final Term*, pp. 228–32.

101. Pimlott, *Harold Wilson*, pp. 625–30.

102. Personal knowledge.

103. Conversation with Lord Armstrong of Ilminster, 9 December 1999, quoted with his permission.

104. See Lord Hunt of Tanworth's remarks on this in Hennessy, *Muddling Through*, p. 261.

105. Private information.

106. Private information.

107. Private information.

108. Peter Wright, *Spycatcher* (Viking, 1987), p. 364.

109. Private information.

110. Morgan, *Callaghan*, p. 625, n.54.

111. Ibid., p. 610.

112. Hennessy, *Muddling Through*, pp. 264–5.

113. Ziegler, *Wilson*, pp. 494–9.

114. Antony Jay (ed.), *The Oxford Dictionary of Political Quotations* (Oxford University Press, 1996), p. 390.

115. Ferdinand Mount (ed.), *The Inquiring Eye: A Selection of the Writings of David Watt* (Penguin, 1988), p. 17.

116. Paul Kennedy, *The Rise and Fall of the Great Powers: Economic Change and Military Conflict from 1500 to 2000* (Fontana, 1989), p. 698.

117. Strachey's line on Gladstone was: 'Speech was the fibre of his being.' Quoted in Robert Blake, *Disraeli and Gladstone: The Leslie Stephen Lecture 1969* (Cambridge University Press, 1969), p. 14.

15   The Sea-Changer: James Callaghan, 1976–79

1. Denis Healey, *The Time of My Life* (Michael Joseph, 1989), p. 448.

2. Lord Callaghan in conversation with Michael Cockerell for the 1996 BBC2 programme *How to Be Prime Minister*. I am grateful to Mr Cockerell for showing me the transcript of the interview.

3. Roy Jenkins, *A Life at the Centre* (Macmillan, 1991), pp. 441–3.

4. Peter Hennessy and Caroline Anstey, *Moneybags and Brains: The Anglo American 'Special Relationship' Since 1945*, Strathclyde *Analysis* papers No. 1 (Department of Government, University of Strathclyde, 1990), p. 21.

5. Tony Benn talking at the House of Commons to the 'Cabinet and Premiership' course and students from the MA in Contemporary British History programme, Queen Mary and Westfield College, 27 January 1999.

6. Peter Hennessy, *Muddling Through: Power, Politics and the Quality of Government in Postwar Britain* (Gollancz, 1996), p. 126.

7. Lord Callaghan in conversation with Michael Cockerell, 1996.

8. Sir Kenneth Stowe's recollection quoted in Kenneth O. Morgan, *Callaghan, A Life* (Oxford University Press, 1997), p. 665.

9. Lord Callaghan in conversation with Michael Cockerell, 1996.

10. Morgan, *Callaghan*, p. 482.

11. Ibid.

12. Steve Richards, 'Interview: Callaghan', *New Statesman*, 20 December 1996.

13. Private information.

14. Morgan, *Callaghan*, p. 473.

15. Ibid., p. 474.

16. Private information.

17. Private information.

18. Bernard Donoughue, *Prime Minister: The Conduct of Policy Under Harold Wilson and James Callaghan* (Cape, 1987), p. 191.

19. Prime Ministerial Broadcast BBC1, 5 April 1976.

20. Private information.

21. John Turner, *Lloyd George's Secretariat* (Cambridge University Press, 1980), pp. 2–3.

22. Private information.

23. Bernard Donoughue to the Prime Minister, 'Themes and Initiatives', 15 April 1976. Acquired privately.

24. Ibid.

25. Ibid.

26. James Callaghan, *Time and Chance* (Collins, 1987), pp. 409–11.

27. Kenneth Baker, *The Turbulent Years: My Life in Politics* (Faber and Faber, 1993), pp. 164, 168.

28. Donoughue, 'Themes and Initiatives'.

29. Ibid.

30. Ibid.

31. Lord Callaghan in conversation with Michael Cockerell, 1996.

32. Ibid.

33. Donoughue, 'Themes and Initiatives'.

34. For the best studies of the political economy of the IMF crisis see Edmund Dell, *A Hard Pounding: Politics and Economic Crisis 1974–76* (Oxford University Press, 1991); Kathleen Burk and Alec Cairncross, *'Goodbye Great Britain': The 1976 IMF Crisis* (Yale University Press, 1992). For the best encapsulation of the Callaghan-and-Cabinet government debate see Edmund Dell and Lord Hunt of Tanworth, 'The Failings of Cabinet Government in Mid to Late 1970s', *Contemporary Record*, vol. 8, no. 3 (winter 1994), pp. 453–72.

35. Morgan, *Callaghan*, p. 535.

36. Callaghan, *Time and Chance*, pp. 425–7.

37. Morgan, *Callaghan*, p. 537.

38. Brian Brivati, *Hugh Gaitskell* (Richard Cohen Books, 1996), pp. 373–5.

39. Ben Pimlott, *Harold Wilson* (HarperCollins, 1992), pp. 303–5.

40. Michael Leapman, *Kinnock* (Unwin Hyman, 1987), pp. 102–5.

41. Pimlott, *Harold Wilson*, p. 531; Callaghan, *Time and Chance*, pp. 272–7; Jenkins, *A Life at the Centre*, p. 287; Barbara Castle, *The Castle Diaries 1964–70* (Weidenfeld and Nicolson, 1984), pp. 650–51, entries for 12 and 13 May 1969.

42. Edmund Dell, *The Chancellors: A History of the Chancellors of the Exchequer, 1945–90* (HarperCollins, 1996), p. 423.

43. Sir James Callaghan, interviewed for the Brook Productions/Channel 4 Television series *All the Prime Minister's Men*, May 1986.

44. Hennessy, *Muddling Through*, p. 280.

45. Private information.

46. Conversation with Dr Jack Cunningham, 18 May 1999.

47. Private information.

48. Sir James Callaghan, *All the Prime Minister's Men* interview.

49. Private information.

50. Denis Healey speaking on 'The Party's Over', Channel 4 Television, 1985.

51. Phillip Whitehead, *The Writing on the Wall: Britain in the Seventies* (Michael Joseph/Channel 4 Television, 1985), p. 187.

52. Dell, *The Chancellors*, pp. 426–7.

53. Hennessy, *Muddling Through*, p. 285.

54. David Marquand, *Ramsay MacDonald* (Cape 1977), pp. 638–70.

55. Callaghan, *Time and Chance*, p. 47; see also his reference to 1931 in Tony Benn's *Against the Tide: Diaries 1973–76* (Hutchinson, 1989), p. 677.

56. Hennessy, *Muddling Through*, p. 285.

57. In Peter Hennessy, *Cabinet* (Blackwell, 1986), p. 91, I stated erroneously, that 'It took twenty-six separate Cabinet meetings to resolve the issue.' This was based on private information from an insider who had totted up the *ministerial* meetings required. When Tony Benn's diaries were published, it became plain that only nine of these had been full meetings of the Cabinet. Benn, *Against the Tide*, pp. 620–90.

58. Healey, *The Time of My Life*, p. 430.

59. Burk and Cairncross, 'Goodbye Great Britain', pp. 64–7, 77–80, 91–4, 111–18.

60. Ibid., pp. 77–82.

61. Lord Armstrong of Sanderstead, former Permanent Secretary to the Treasury, used this metaphor in a conversation with me.

62. Private information.

63. Dell, *The Chancellors*, p. 436.

64. Mr Benn has made this point to me in several conversations and recorded it on 'The Party's Over'.

65. Susan Crosland, *Tony Crosland* (Cape, 1982), p. 381. For Tony Benn's account see Benn, *Against The Tide*, pp. 670–79.

66. Dell, *The Chancellors*, pp. 437–8.

67. Roy Hattersley, *Fifty Years On: A Prejudiced History of Britain Since the War* (Little, Brown, 1997), p. 252.

68. Lord Healey was speaking on 'The Party's Over'.

69. Morgan, *Callaghan*, pp. 427–8.

70. Hattersley, *Fifty Years On*, p. 252.

71. Hennessy, *Muddling Through*, p. 282.

72. Ibid., p. 285.

73. Healey, *The Time of My Life*, p. 431.

74. Private information.

75. Dell and Hunt, 'The Failings of Cabinet Government in Mid to Late 1970s', p. 461.

76. Ibid.

77. Ibid., pp. 467–70.

78. Dell, *The Chancellors*, p. 436.

79. Private information.

80. For details of Callaghan's 'Economic Seminar' see Hennessy, *Cabinet*, p. 92.

81. Letter from Lord Callaghan to Amy Baker quoted in Amy Baker, *Prime Ministers and the Rule Book* (Politico's, 2000), p. 42.

82. Ibid.

83. See p. 166 above.

84. Ibid.

85. See p. 290 above.

86. Morgan, *Callaghan*, p. 604.

87. Hennessy, *Muddling Through*, p. 286.

88. Hennessy, *Cabinet*, pp. 134–42.

89. Healey, *The Time of My Life*, p. 449.

90. Private information.

91. Callaghan, *Time and Chance*, p. 375; For the Franks Report see *The Franks Report: Falkland Islands Review* (1992 Pimlico edition of the 1983 report), p. 18; private information from a former member of the Secret Intelligence Service. The naval vessels involved were the submarine HMS *Dreadnought* and the frigates HMS *Phoebe* and HMS *Alacrity*; see Dan van der Vat, 'Hugh Balfour' obituary in *Guardian*, 2 August 1999.

92. He did so in his interview for *All the Prime Minister's Men*.

93. Ibid.

94. Quoted in Peter Hennessy, 'The Itch After the Amputation? The Purpose of British Intelligence as the Century Turns', in K. G. Robertson (ed.), *War, Resistance and Intelligence: Essays in Honour of M. R. D. Foot* (Leo Cooper, 1999), p. 239.

95. Went on to be Permanent Secretary at both the Northern Ireland Office and the Department of Heath and Social Security.

96. Went on to become a Second Permanent Secretary at the Treasury.

97. Went on to become Permanent Secretary of the Overseas Development Administration and the Department of Education and Science.

98. Finished his career as Head of the Diplomatic Service.

99. *All The Prime Minister's Men* interview.

100. Hennessy, *Cabinet*, p. 92; Donoughue, *Prime Minister*, pp. 79–102.

101. Callaghan, *Time and Chance*, p. 408.

102. Ibid., p. 409.

103. Private information.

104. House of Commons, *Seventh Report from the Treasury and Civil Service Committee: Session 1985–86*, 'Civil Servants and Ministers: Duties and Responsibilities', vol. 2 (HMSO, 1986), p. 225.

105. Callaghan, *Time and Chance*, pp. 502–3.

106. Hennessy, *Muddling Through*, p. 44.

107. Healey, *The Time of My Life*, p. 403.

108. Private information.

109. Hennessy, *Muddling Through*, p. 44.

110. Private information.

111. Callaghan, *Time and Chance*, pp. 275–6.

112. Letter to Stephen Bailey, 21 April 1999, cited in Stephen Bailey, 'The Use of Inner Cabinets "Formal" and "Informal" Since 1968', unpublished undergraduate thesis, Department of History, Queen Mary and Westfield College, University of London, 1999.

113. Joel Barnett, *Inside the Treasury* (André Deutsch, 1982), p. 175.

114. Private information.

115. Mr Powell has used this phrase in my presence.

116. Kenneth O. Morgan, *Labour People: Leaders and Lieutenants – Hardie to Kinnock* (Oxford University Press, 1987), p. 266.

117. Richards, 'Interview: Lord Callaghan'.

118. Private information.

119. Lord Callaghan in conversation with Michael Cockerell, 1996.

120. Morgan, *Callaghan*, p. 649.

121. Michael Foot interviewed by Michael Cockerell, 1996.

122. Lord Callaghan in conversation with Michael Cockerell, 1996.

123. Conversation with Lord Hurd, 20 April 1999.

124. Lord Callaghan in conversation with Michael Cockerell, 1996.

125. Private information.

126. Peter Hennessy, *The Importance of Being Tony: Two Years of the Blair Style* (Guy's and St Thomas' Hospital Trust, 1999), p. 1.

127. Tim Hulse, 'Sunny Jim keeps mum on Tony', *Independent on Sunday*, 21 September 1997.

16 A Tigress Surrounded by Hamsters:
Margaret Thatcher, 1979–90

1. *The Thatcher Years*, part 2, BBC1, 13 October 1993.

2. Douglas Hurd, interviewed by Michael Cockerell for the BBC2 documentary, *How to Be Prime Minister*, 1996. I am very grateful to Mr Cockerell for providing me with the transcript.

3. Percy Cradock, *In Pursuit of British Interests: Reflections on Foreign Policy Under Margaret Thatcher and John Major* (John Murray, 1997), pp. 20–21.

4. Sir Charles Powell, interviewed by Michael Cockerell for the BBC2 documentary, *How to Be Prime Minister*, 1996. I am very grateful to Mr Cockerell for providing me with the transcript.

5. Tony Benn, interviewed by Michael Cockerell for the BBC2 documentary, *How to Be Prime Minister*, 1996. I am very grateful to him for providing me with the transcript.

6. A. J. P. Taylor, 'Preface' in A. J. P. Taylor (ed.), *Lloyd George: A Diary by Frances Stevenson* (Hutchinson, 1971), p. ix.

7. Ibid.

8. 'My first five years – John Major', *Daily Telegraph*, 27 November 1995.

9. Douglas Hurd, 'Chairing from the front', *Spectator*, 6 November 1993.

10. G. M. Young, *Stanley Baldwin* (Hart-Davis, 1952), p. 41.

11. 'The fall of Thatcher', *The Economist*, 9 March 1991.

12. Peter Hennessy, 'The Last Retreat of Fame: Mrs Thatcher as History', *Modern Law Review*, vol. 54, no. 4 (July 1991), p. 492.

13. Ibid.

14. Alan Watkins, 'Political Diary', 'Our Prime Ministers have been a funny lot,' *Observer*, 7 April 1991.

15. Hugo Young, 'The lady's for earning – and the legend is dead', *Guardian*, 23 November 1995.

16. Andrew Marr, 'The ghost in the Tory machine', *Independent*, 23 November 1995.

17. Quoted in Jonathan Steinberg, *All or Nothing* (Routledge, 1990), p. xv.

18. 'Lloyd George: Rise and Fall' is reproduced in A. J. P. Taylor, *Politics in Wartime* (Hamish Hamilton, 1964), pp. 123–49.

19. Margaret Thatcher, *The Downing Street Years* (HarperCollins, 1993); Margaret Thatcher, *The Path to Power* (HarperCollins, 1995).

20. These range from the sympathetic (Nicholas Ridley, *My Style of Government: The Thatcher Years* (Hutchinson, 1991)) through the restrained and gentlemanly (William Whitelaw, *The Whitelaw Memoirs* (Aurum, 1989)) and the sycophantic (Lord Young, *The Enterprise Years: A Businessman in the Cabinet* (Headline, 1990)) to the acidly critical (Ian Gilmour, *Dancing with Dogma: Britain Under Thatcherism* (Simon and Schuster, 1992)) and the detailed and revealing (Nigel Lawson, *The View From No. 11: Memoirs of a Tory Radical* (Bantam, 1992)) and

the understated, but revealing (Geoffrey Howe, *Conflict of Loyalty* (Macmillan, 1994)).

21. Conversation with Alistair Parker, 1 April 1997.

22. Ridley, *My Style of Government*, pp. 29–30.

23. Norman St John-Stevas, 'Prime Ministers rise and fall but the Cabinet abides', *Daily Telegraph*, 7 August 1986.

24. Conversation with Lord Soames, 1984.

25. Jim Prior speaking on *The Thatcher Years*, part 1, BBC1, 6 October 1993.

26. 'Friday's People', *Guardian*, 22 November 1985.

27. Gilmour, *Dancing with Dogma*, p. 4.

28. Lawson, *The View from No. 11*, p. 127.

29. Ibid., p. 125.

30. Interview with Kenneth Harris, *Observer*, 25 February 1979.

31. John Cole, *As It Seemed to Me: Political Memoirs* (Weidenfeld and Nicolson, 1995), p. 78.

32. John Campbell, *Edward Heath, A Biography* (Cape, 1993), pp. 315–16.

33. Conversation with David Howell, 21 February 1985.

34. Private information.

35. *The Times*, 21 June 1982.

36. Sir Charles Powell, interviewed by Michael Cockerell for *How to Be Prime Minister*.

37. This choice episode was recalled by Malcolm Rifkind on *Maggie's Ministers*, BBC2, 11 September 1993.

38. Private information.

39. Nigel Lawson speaking on *The Thatcher Years*, part 4, BBC1, 27 October 1993.

40. Geoffrey Howe, 'The triumph and tragedy of the Thatcher years', *Weekend Financial Times*, 24 October 1993.

41. *The Thatcher Years*, part 2.

42. *The Thatcher Years*, part 3, BBC1, 20 October 1993.

43. Private information.

44. *The Thatcher Years*, part 4.

45. For superb accounts of her last days in power see Robert Shepherd, *The Power Brokers: The Tory Party and Its Leaders* (Hutchinson, 1991), and Alan Watkins, *A Conservative Coup; The Fall of Margaret Thatcher* (Duckworth, 1991).

46. *The Thatcher Years*, part 4.

47. Anthony Seldon, *Major, A Political Life* (Weidenfeld and Nicolson, 1997), p. 739.

48. *The Thatcher Years*, part 1.

49. Ibid.

50. 'Thatcher pours scorn on federalist creed of "No Nation Tories",' *The Times*, 12 January 1996.

51. *The Thatcher Years*, part 1.

52. Anthony Bevins, 'Decision to quit followed loss of faith among friends', *Independent*, 29 June 1991.

53. Peter Hennessy, *Cabinet* (Blackwell, 1986), p. 94.

54. John Biffen, 'The revenge of the unburied dead', *Observer*, 9 December 1990.

55. Peter Riddell, 'Thatcher's role as prophet is true to tradition', *The Times*, 11 January 1996.

56. Biffen, 'The revenge of the unburied dead'.

57. See his 'R. A. Butler' in Roy Jenkins, *Gallery of 20th Century Portraits* (David and Charles, 1988), p. 51.

58. The phrase is Lord John Russell's; quoted in Olive Anderson, 'Cabinet Government and the Crimean War', *English Historical Review*, vol. 79 (1964), p. 549.

59. PRO, PREM 13/353, 'Ministerial Responsibility for the Universities'.

60. Percy Cradock, *Experiences of China* (John Murray, 1994), p. 549.

61. For the circumstances of his resignation on health grounds see Whitelaw, *The Whitelaw Memoirs*, pp. 268–70.

62. *The Thatcher Years*, part 4.

63. Ibid.

64. Whitelaw, *The Whitelaw Memoirs*, pp. 264–5.

65. Sir Charles Powell, interviewed for *How to Be Prime Minister*.

66. Private information.

67. Private information.

68. Cradock, *In Pursuit of British Interests*, p. 14.

69. Ibid.

70. Ibid., p. 15.

71. Ibid.

72. Ibid.

73. Ibid., p. 130.

74. George R. Urban, *Diplomacy and Disillusion at the Court of Margaret Thatcher* (I. B. Tauris, 1996), pp. 118–59.

75. Ibid., p. 153.

76. Lawson, *The View from No. 11*, p. 680.

77. Several of them have expressed it to me in this fashion.

78. John Vincent, 'The Thatcher Government, 1979–1987', in Peter Hennessy and Anthony Seldon (eds.), *Ruling Performance: British Governments from Attlee to Thatcher* (Blackwell, 1987), p. 288.

79. Jean Seaton (ed.), *Politics and the Media: Harlots and Prerogatives at the Turn of the Millennium* (Blackwell, 1998), p. 3.

80. Phillip Whitehead, *The Writing On the Wall: Britain in the Seventies* (Channel 4/Michael Joseph, 1985), p. 330.

81. William Waldegrave, 'Three Prime Ministers', Paper delivered to the Twentieth Century British History Seminar at the Institute of Historical Research, University of London, 10 December 1997.

82. J. M. Keynes, *Essays in Persuasion* (Macmillan, 1931), p. 328.

83. Waldegrave, 'Three Prime Ministers'.

84. See John Keegan, *Six Armies in Normandy: From D-Day to the Liberation of Paris* (Pimlico, 1992).

85. Richard Cockett, *Thinking the Unthinkable: Think-Tanks and the Economic Counter-Revolution, 1931–1983* (HarperCollins, 1994), pp. 234, 236–42, 259–66.

86. Thatcher, *The Downing Street Years*, p. 42.

87. Whitehead, *The Writing On the Wall*, p. 367.

88. Ibid., p. 368.

89. Howe, 'The triumph and tragedy of the Thatcher years'.

90. Prior, *A Balance of Power*, p. 133.

91. Whitehead, *The Writing On the Wall*, p. 367.

92. Hennessy, *Cabinet*, pp. 154–5.

93. Thatcher, *The Downing Street Years*, pp. 246–7.

94. Hennessy, *Cabinet*, p. 155.

95. Private information.

96. Private information.

97. Thatcher, *The Downing Street Years*, p. 247.

98. Michael Quinlan, *Thinking About Nuclear Weapons* (RUSI, 1997), p. 76.

99. Lady Thatcher speaking on *The Thatcher Years*, part 1.

100. Howe said: 'The 1981 budget was crucial to the continued success, the strengthened credibility and effectiveness of the Thatcher government.' Quoted in Whitehead, *The Writing On the Wall*, p. 383.

101. Industry was especially worried by the high sterling exchange rate. The pound was rapidly becoming a petro-currency thanks to the inflow of North Sea oil. See Michael Edwardes (then of British Leyland) quoted in ibid., p. 377.

102. Thatcher, *The Downing Street Years*, p. 138.

103. Whitehead, *The Writing On the Wall*, p. 382.

104. Ibid., p. 383.

105. Thatcher, *The Downing Street Years*, p. 138.

106. Ibid., p. 152.

107. Ibid., p. 122.

108. Speaking on *A New Style of Politics*, Channel 4 Television, 1985.

109. Thatcher, *The Downing Street Years*, p. 153.

110. See ibid., pp. 143–7 for her own assessment of them.

111. See ibid., pp. 154–5.

112. Quoted in Peter Hennessy, *The Blair Centre: A Question of Command and Control?* (Public Management Foundation, 1999), p. 17.

113. Quoted in Peter Riddell, *Parliament Under Blair* (Politico's, 2000), p. 24.

114. Robert Rhodes James, *Churchill. A Study in Failure* (Weidenfeld and Nicolson, 1970).

115. Thatcher, *The Downing Street Years*, p. 173.

116. Ibid., p. 208.

117. Sir Frank Cooper in conversation with Tom Dibble and Peter Hennessy, 4 August 1998.

118. Lord Franks et al., *The Franks Report: Falkland Islands Review* (HMSO, 1983).

119. Thatcher, *The Downing Street Years*, p. 173.

120. Franks et al., *Falkland Islands Review*, p. 45.

121. Ibid., p. 82.

122. Sir Colin McColl, 'Risks and Forecasts in World Affairs', The Roskill Memorial Lecture, Churchill College, Cambridge, 16 February 1999, p. 6.

123. Thatcher, *The Downing Street Years*, p. 179.

124. Sir Frank Cooper in conversation with Tom Dibble and Peter Hennessy, 11 June 1998.

125. Thatcher, *The Downing Street Years*, p. 179.

126. Private information.

127. Thatcher, *The Downing Street Years*, p. 179.

128. Ibid.

129. Ibid.

130. Quoted in Hennessy, *Cabinet*, p. 118.

131. Thatcher, *The Downing Street Years*, p. 180.

132. Ibid., p. 181.

133. Matt Lyus and Peter Hennessy, *Tony Blair, Past Prime Ministers, Parliament and the Use of Military Force*, Strathclyde Papers on Government and Politics, no. 113 (1999), p. 12.

134. Simon Heffer, *Like the Roman: The Life of Enoch Powell* (Weidenfeld and Nicolson, 1999), p. 856; for Tass on the 'Iron Lady' see Thatcher, *The Downing Street Years*, p. 65. For her account of the debate see ibid., pp. 183–5.

135. Ibid., p. 184.

136. Ibid.

137. Lyus and Hennessy, *Tony Blair, Past Prime Ministers, Parliament and the Use of Military Force*, p. 12.

138. Thatcher, *The Downing Street Years*, p. 184.

139. Ibid., pp. 185–6.

140. Howe, *Conflict of Loyalty*, p. 246.

141. Thatcher, *The Downing Street Years*, p. 188.

142. Ibid., pp. 188–9.

143. Hennessy, *Cabinet*, pp. 118–19.

144. Thatcher, *The Downing Street Years*, p. 189.

145. Private information.

146. Sir Frank Cooper in conversation with Tom Dibble and Peter Hennessy, 11 June 1998.

147. Private information.

148. Private information.

149. *The Thatcher Years*, part 1.

150. *The Thatcher Years*, part 2.

151. Private information.

152. Private information.

153. Private information.

154. Private information.

155. Lawson, *The View from No. 11*, p. 126.

156. Thatcher, *The Downing Street Years*, p. 181.

157. Lawson, *The View from No. 11*, pp. 126–7

158. Thatcher, *The Downing Street Years*, p. 205.

159. Ibid., p. 207.

160. Ibid.

161. Ibid., p. 208.

162. Ibid., p. 211.

163. Ibid., p. 212.

164. Michael Charlton, *The Little Platoon: Diplomacy and the Falklands Dispute* (Blackwell, 1989), p. 158.

165. Private information.

166. Private information.

167. Private information.

168. Private information.

169. Private information.

170. Private information.

171. Private information.

172. Private information.

173. Private information.

174. Private information.

175. Private information.

176. Hennessy, *Cabinet*, p. 120; Peter Hennessy, *Whitehall* (Secker and Warburg, 1989), pp. 645–6.

177. Thatcher, *The Downing Street Years*, p. 235.

178. Private information.

179. Hennessy, *Whitehall*, p. 643; Thatcher, *The Downing Street Years*, p. 341.

180. Conversation with Dr John Ashworth, 6 May 1998.

181. Sarah Curtis (ed.), *The Journals of Woodrow Wyatt*, vol. 1 (Macmillan, 1998), p. 585, entry for 18 June 1988.

182. Whitehead, *The Writing On the Wall*, p. 333.

183. Thatcher, *The Downing Street Years*, p. 306.

184. Hugo Young, *One of Us* (Pan, 1993), p. 332.

185. Thatcher, *The Downing Street Years*, p. 308.

186. See Hennessy, *Whitehall*, pp. 649–50.

187. Thatcher, *The Downing Street Years*, p. 30.

188. Ibid.

189. Hennessy, *Whitehall*, pp. 638–43.

190. Ibid., pp. 592–605.

191. Ibid., p. 652.

192. David Willetts, 'The Role of the Prime Minister's Policy Unit', *Public Administration*, vol. 65, no. 4 (winter 1987), pp. 443–55.

193. Private information.

194. Hennessy, *Cabinet*, pp. 102–3.

195. Sir Charles Powell, interviewed by Michael Cockerell for *How to Be Prime Minister*.

196. Thatcher, *The Downing Street Years*, p. 305.

197. Ibid., p. 306.

198. Ibid.

199. For a comparative chart see Hennessy, *Whitehall*, p. 501.

200. Waldegrave, 'Three Prime Ministers'.

201. Conversation with Lord Hurd, 20 April 1999.

202. Ibid.

203. Lawson, *The View from No. 11*, p. 467.

204. Ibid.

205. Curtis (ed.), *The Journals of Woodrow Wyatt*, vol. 1, p. 174.

206. Andrew Neill, *Full Disclosure* (Macmillan, 1996), pp. 195–8.

207. Curtis (ed.), *The Journals of Woodrow Wyatt*, vol. 1, p. 174, diary entry for 23 July 1986.

208. Peter Hennessy, 'The Blair Style of Government: An Historical Perspective and an Interim Audit', *Government and Opposition*, vol. 33, no. 1 (winter 1998), pp. 11–12.

209. 'Howe: I was right and I won't resign', interview by Robin Oakley, *Daily Mail*, 6 February 1984.

210. Peter Hennessy, *The Importance of Being Tony: Two Years of the Blair Style* (Guy's and St Thomas's Hospital Trust, 1999), p. 4.

211. Hennessy, *Whitehall*, pp. 313–14.

212. Thatcher, *The Downing Street Years*, pp. 694–8; Lawson, *The View from No. 11*, pp. 928–35, 494–500.

213. Thatcher, *The Downing Street Years*, pp. 709–13; Lawson, *The View from No. 11*, pp. 928–35; Howe, *Conflict of Loyalty*, pp. 578–80.

214. Lord Lawson, 'Cabinet Government in the Thatcher Years: Some Reflections and Wider Lessons', paper delivered to the Twentieth Century British History Seminar, Institute of Historical Research, 9 March 1994. An edited transcript of the proceedings was published as Lord Lawson and Lord Armstrong of Ilminster, 'Cabinet Government in the Thatcher Years', *Contemporary Record*, vol. 8, no. 3 (winter 1994), pp. 473–83.

215. Thatcher, *The Downing Street Years*, p. 698.

216. Lawson, *The View from No. 11*, p. 499.

217. Lord Lawson speaking at the IHR on 9 March 1994. See also his *The View from No. 11*, pp. 561–2.

218. Thatcher, *The Downing Street Years*, p. 536.

219. Ibid.

220. Margaret Thatcher, 'Changing the Face of Britain, But at What Cost?', *Saga*, September 1998, pp. 73–7.

221. Thatcher, *The Downing Street Years*, p. 536.

222. Hugo Young, *This Blessed Plot: Britain and Europe from Churchill to Blair* (Macmillan, 1998), pp. 333–7.

223. Ibid.

224. Thatcher, *The Downing Street Years*, p. 536.

225. Michael Heseltine, 'When I knew I had to go', *Observer*, 12 January 1986.

226. Mrs Thatcher speaking on Tyne Tees TV, *Face the Press*, 26 January 1986.

227. Ibid.

228. Amy Baker, *Prime Ministers and the Rule Book* (Politico's, 2000) pp. 49, 50–51.

229. Ibid., pp. 49–50.

230. Curtis (ed.), *The Journals of Woodrow Wyatt*, vol. 1, p. 59, entry for Saturday, 18 January 1986.

231. R. H. S. Crossman, *Inside View* (Cape, 1972).

232. Curtis (ed.), *The Journals of Woodrow Wyatt*, vol. 1, p. 59, entry for Saturday, 18 January 1986.

233. Private information.

234. Lawson, *The View from No. 11*, p. 500.

235. Private information.

236. Howe, *Conflict of Loyalty*, pp. 603–5.

237. Lawson, *The View from No. 11*, p. 129.

238. Lawson, 'Cabinet Government in the Thatcher Years'.

239. Lawson, *The View from No. 11*, p. 799.

240. Thatcher, *The Downing Street Years*, p. 757.

241. Ibid., p. 755.

242. Private information.

243. Private information.

244. Howe, *Conflict of Loyalty*, pp. 648–50.

245. Thatcher, *The Downing Street Years*, pp. 850–55.

246. Lord Wakeham, 'Cabinet Government', delivered at Brunel University, 10 November 1992.

247. Howe, 'The triumph and the tragedy of the Thatcher years'.

248. Thatcher, *The Downing Street Years*, p. 851.

249. Thatcher, *The Path to Power*, p. 165.

250. The phrase belongs to the former Cabinet Secretary, Lord Hunt of Tanworth. Lord Hunt delivered it as a discussant on 'The Failings of Cabinet Government in the Mid to Late 1970s', a paper delivered by Edmund Dell to the Twentieth Century British History Seminar, Institute of Historical Research, 20 October 1993.

251. It was reproduced, with amendments, as 'The Last Retreat of Fame: Mrs Thatcher as History', in Peter Hennessy, *Muddling Through: Power Politics and the Quality of Government in Postwar Britain* (Gollancz, 1996), pp. 290–97.

252. Ibid., p. 296.

253. Peter Riddell, *The Thatcher Decade: How Britain Has Changed During the 1980s* (Blackwell, 1989), pp. 13–26.

254. Alan Murrie, 'Housing and the Environment', in Dennis Kavanagh and

Anthony Seldon (eds.), *The Thatcher Effect: A Decade of Change* (Clarendon Press, 1989), pp. 218–21.

255. The phrase is Anthony Verrier's. See his *Through the Looking Glass: British Foreign Policy in the Age of Illusions* (Cape, 1983), p. 4.

256. Hennessy, *Muddling Through*, p. 297.

257. Hennessy, *Cabinet*, p. 122.

17 The Solo-Coalitionist: John Major, 1990–97

1. Chris Patten speaking on *The Major Years*, part 1, BBC1, 11 October 1999.

2. Private information.

3. John Major, *The Autobiography* (HarperCollins, 1999), p. 209.

4. Lord Waldegrave speaking on *The Major Years*, part 2, BBC1, 18 October 1999.

5. John Major speaking on *The Major Years*, part 2, BBC1, 18 October 1999.

6. Gillian Shephard, 'Cabinet and Premiership Under John Major', lecture delivered at Queen Mary and Westfield College, University of London, 4 November 1999.

7. Conversation with Lord Hurd, 20 April 1999.

8. Viscount Cranborne speaking on *The Major Years*, part 3, BBC1, 25 October 1999.

9. Conversation with Gillian Shephard, 11 May 1999.

10. Private information.

11. 'Bagehot', 'Selling a new spirit', *The Economist*, 8 December 1990. It only emerged later that this was Chris Patten's evocation; private information. This metaphor has also been attributed to Major's Cabinet Secretary, Sir Robin Butler; see Dennis Kavanagh and Anthony Seldon, *The Powers Behind The Prime Minister: The Hidden Influence of Number Ten* (HarperCollins, 1999) p. 224.

12. Private information.

13. Private information quoted in Peter Hennessy, 'Whitehall Watch: War gives Major a new gravitas', *Independent*, 21 January 1991.

14. Private information.

15. Major, *The Autobiography*, p. 188.

16. Ibid., p. 190.

17. Quoted in Anthony Seldon, *Major: A Political Life* (Weidenfeld and Nicolson, 1997), p. 130.

18. John Major speaking on *The Major Years*, part 1.

19. Douglas Hurd, ibid.

20. Major, *The Autobiography*, p. 135.

21. Private information.

22. Major, *The Autobiography*, p. 190.

23. Shephard, 'Cabinet and Premiership Under John Major'.

24. Major, *The Autobiography*, p. 291.

25. Ibid., p. 210.

26. Private information.

27. Private information.

28. See a senior intelligence figure quoted in Peter Hennessy, 'The Itch After the Amputation? The Purposes of British Intelligence as the Century Turns: An Historical Perspective and a Forward Look', in K. G. Robertson (ed.), *War, Resistance and Intelligence: Essays in Honour of M. R. D. Foot* (Leo Cooper, 1999), p. 233.

29. Private information.

30. Major, *The Autobiography*, p. 221.

31. Private information.

32. Private information.

33. Peter Hennessy, *A Question of Control: UK War Cabinets and Limited Conflicts Since 1945* (CESER, University of the West of England, 1996), p. 9.

34. Private information.

35. *Ministerial Committees of the Cabinet* (Cabinet Office, May 1992).

36. Major, *The Autobiography*, p. 221.

37. It is reproduced in Percy Cradock, *In Pursuit of British Interests: Reflections On Foreign Policy Under Margaret Thatcher and John Major* (John Murray, 1997), opposite p. 117.

38. Major, *The Autobiography*, pp. 237–8.

39. Private information.

40. Private information.

41. Major, *The Autobiography*, p. 536.

42. Private information.

43. Shephard, 'Cabinet and Premiership Under John Major'.

44. Sarah Hogg and Jonathan Hill, *Too Close to Call: Power and Politics – John Major In No. 10* (Little, Brown, 1995), opposite p. 148.

45. Ibid., pp. 14–15.

46. Major, *The Autobiography*, p. 214.

47. Private information.

48. Norman Lamont, *In Office* (Little, Brown, 1999).

49. Kenneth Clarke speaking on *The Major Years*, part 3.

50. Lord Butler of Brockwell, 'Cabinet Government', the 1999 Attlee Foundation Lecture, the Mansion House, 18 March 1999.

51. Private information.

52. Private information.

53. The resignation speech is reproduced in full in Lamont, *In Office*, pp. 518–24.

54. Ibid., p. 35.

55. Lobby correspondents were eloquent in praise of O'Donnell. I remember a former journalist colleague of mine saying 'Gus is almost honest to a fault. He cannot deceive us. His face would give it away. Perhaps it has to do with his Catholic background.'

56. Private information.

57. Major, *The Autobiography*, pp. 319–20.

58. Hogg and Hill, *Too Close To Call*, p. 28.

59. Rodric Braithwaite, 'Secret Sensations', *Prospect*, November 1999, pp. 26–9.

60. Private information.

61. Cradock, *In Pursuit of British Interests*, pp. 46–7.

62. We were colleagues on *The Times* (where we got on just fine).

63. Seldon, *Major*, p. 145. Mrs Chaplin died suddenly and tragically after winning Newbury for the Conservatives at the 1992 general election.

64. Private information.

65. Private information.

66. Major, *The Autobiography*, p. xvii.

67. Ibid., p. 251.

68. Hogg and Hill, *Too Close To Call*, p. 104n.

69. Gyles Brandreth, *Breaking the Code: Westminster Diaries, May 1990–May 1997* (Weidenfeld and Nicolson, 1999), p. 120, entry for 28 September 1992.

70. Hogg and Hill, *Too Close To Call*, pp. 93–4.

71. Major, *The Autobiography*, p. 247.

72. Ibid., p. xviii.

73. Ibid., p. 246.

74. Ibid., p. 245.

75. Ibid., pp. 252–3.

76. *The Citizen's Charter: Raising The Standard*, Cm 1599 (HMSO, 1991).

77. William Waldegrave, 'Three Prime Ministers', paper delivered to the Twentieth Century British History Seminar, Institute of Historical Research, 10 December 1997.

78. Peter Hennessy, *The Hidden Wiring: Unearthing The British Constitution* (Gollancz, 1995), p. 21.

79. Waldegrave, 'Three Prime Ministers'.

80. Ibid.

81. Figures supplied by the Cabinet Office in May 1997.

82. *Competing for Quality: Buying Better Public Services*, Cm 1730 (HMSO, 1991).

83. Peter Hennessy, 'The Civil Service: Mr Gladstone's Legacy as the Century Turns', *The Stakeholder*, July 1999.

84. Sarah Hogg, 'Policy Making in Government', *Sunday Times* Lecture, 7 March 1995.

85. Ibid.

86. Sir Robin Butler, 'The Themes of Public Service Reform In Britain and Overseas', *Policy Studies*, vol. 16, no. 3 (autumn 1995), p. 4.

87. Amy Baker, *Prime Ministers and the Rule Book* (Politico's, 2000), p. xii.

88. *The Best Future for Britain* (Conservative Central Office, 1992).

89. Private information.

90. *Questions of Procedure for Ministers* (Cabinet Office, 1992); *Ministerial Committees of the Cabinet* (Cabinet Office, 1992).

NOTES

91. Peter Hennessy, *The Importance of Being Tony: Two Years of the Blair Style* (Guy's and St Thomas's Hospital Trust, 1999), p. 8.

92. Peter Hennessy and Chris Westcott, *The Last Right? Open Government, Freedom of Information and the Right to Know*, Strathclyde *Analysis* papers, no. 12 (Department of Government, University of Strathclyde, 1992).

93. Andrew McDonald, head of Records Management Department, Public Record Office, to Peter Hennessy, 22 November 1999.

94. As witnessed by Chris Westcott and myself on 17 June 1992.

95. *Open Government*, Cm 2290 (HMSO, 1993).

96. Private information.

97. Private information.

98. Seldon, *Major*, pp. 399–400.

99. *Code of Practice On Access to Government Information* (Cabinet Office/OPSS, April 1994).

100. See *Open Government . . . 1994 Report* (Cabinet Office/OPSS, 1995).

101. *The Civil Service Code* (Cabinet Office, 1996); *The Civil Service: Taking Forward Continuity and Change*, Cm 2748 (HMSO, 1995).

102. *Standards in Public Life: First Report of the Committee On Standards in Public Life*, vol. 1, *Report*, Cm 2850-1 (HMSO, 1995); *Report of the Inquiry Into the Export of Defence Equipment and Dual-Use Goods to Iraq and Related Prosecutions*, House of Commons 113–14 (HMSO, 1996).

103. Peter Hennessy, 'Whitehall Watch: Thatcher declines to disclose rules of the ministerial game', *Independent*, 1 May 1989; Peter Hennessy, 'Whitehall Watch: Major considers revealing hidden Cabinet workings', *Independent*, 25 November 1991.

104. Shephard, 'Cabinet and Premiership Under John Major'.

105. Chris Patten speaking on *The Major Years*, part 1.

106. Seldon, *Major*, p. 203.

107. Chris Patten speaking on *The Major Years*, part 1.

108. Major, *The Autobiography*, p. 208.

109. Quoted in Seldon, *Major*, p. 202.

110. Private information.

111. Shephard, 'Cabinet and Premiership Under John Major'.

112. Major, *The Autobiography*, pp. 225–6.

113. President George Bush speaking on *The Major Years*, part 1.

114. John Major speaking on *The Major Years*, part 1.

115. Sarah Hogg, 'Prime Minister and Cabinet In the 1990s: A View from the Policy Unit', Twentieth Century British History Seminar, Institute of Historical Research, 19 June 1996.

116. John Major speaking on *The Major Years*, part 1.

117. Major, *The Autobiography*, p. 217.

118. Ibid., pp. xxi–xxiii.

119. Ibid., pp. xxi–xii.

120. Ibid., p. 269.

121. Private information.
122. Major, *The Autobiography*, p. 265.
123. Ibid., p. 266.
124. Shephard, 'Cabinet and Premiership Under John Major.'
125. Ibid.
126. Major, *The Autobiography*, p. xxi.
127. Kenneth Clarke speaking on *The Major Years*, part 1.
128. Major, *The Autobiography*, p. 307.
129. Peter Hennessy, *Cabinet* (Blackwell, 1988), pp. 100–101.
130. Major, *The Autobiography*, p. 431.
131. *Ministerial Committees of the Cabinet: Membership and Terms of Reference* (Cabinet Office, October 1995).
132. Private information.
133. Private information.
134. *Ministerial Committees of the Cabinet* (Cabinet Office, October 1995).
135. Private information.
136. Lord Wakeham, 'Cabinet Government', delivered at Brunel University, 10 November 1993.
137. Private information.
138. Private information.
139. Valerie Elliot, 'Civil Service chief steered yacht plan through Cabinet', *The Times*, 14 January 1997; Alan Hamilton, 'Rushed decision gave Queen no time for advice', *The Times*, 28 January 1997.
140. Elliot, 'Civil Service chief steered yacht plan through Cabinet', and private information.
141. Private information.
142. Private information.
143. *Ministerial Committees of the Cabinet: Membership and Terms of Reference, May 1992* (Cabinet Office, 1992).
144. *Ministerial Committees of the Cabinet: Membership and Terms of Reference, 25 October 1995* (Cabinet Office, 1995).
145. Ibid.
146. Private information.
147. Private information.
148. Lamont, *In Office*, pp. 220–45.
149. Private information.
150. Samuel Brittan, 'ERM: The True Stories', *Prospect*, December 1999, p. 60.
151. Major, *The Autobiography*, p. 155.
152. Ibid., p. 160.
153. Ibid., p. 163.
154. Brittan, 'ERM: The True Stories', p. 61.
155. John Major speaking on *The Major Years*, part 2.
156. Lamont, *In Office*, pp. 208–19.
157. Ibid., p. 217.

158. John Major speaking on *The Major Years*, part 2.
159. The best account of the story is in Philip Stephens, *Politics and the Pound: The Conservatives' Struggle with Sterling* (Macmillan, 1996).
160. Brittan, 'ERM: The True Stories', p. 60.
161. Sarah Hogg speaking on *The Major Years*, part 2.
162. Major, *The Autobiography*, p. 326.
163. Private information.
164. Stephens, *Politics and the Pound*, pp. 244–55.
165. Ibid., p. 255.
166. This was the figure cited in *The Major Years*, part 2.
167. John Major, ibid.
168. Stephens, *Politics and the Pound*, p. 246.
169. John Major speaking on *The Major Years*, part 2.
170. Sarah Hogg quoted in Stephens, *Politics and the Pound*, p. 246.
171. John Major speaking on *The Major Years*, part 2.
172. Major, *The Autobiography*, p. 329.
173. Ibid., p. 330.
174. Private information.
175. Major, *The Autobiography*, p. 330.
176. Lamont, *In Office*, p. 249.
177. Ibid.
178. Ibid.
179. John Major speaking on *The Major Years*, part 2.
180. Lamont, *In Office*, p. 249.
181. Stephens, *Politics and the Pound*, p. 247.
182. Brandreth, *Breaking the Code*, pp. 115–16, diary entry for 17 September 1992.
183. Lamont, *In Office*, p. 250.
184. Major, *The Autobiography*, p. 331.
185. Lamont, *In Office*, p. 250.
186. Major, *The Autobiography*, p. 680.
187. *The Major Years*, part 2.
188. Major, *The Autobiography*, p. 332.
189. Kenneth Clarke speaking on *The Major Years*, part 2.
190. Major, *The Autobiography*, pp. 333–4.
191. Conversation with Lord Hurd, 20 April 1999.
192. Kenneth Clarke speaking on *The Major Years*, part 2.
193. Private information.
194. Major, *The Autobiography*, p. 334.
195. Lord Hurd speaking on *The Major Years*, part 1.
196. Robert Worcester and Roger Mortimer, *Explaining Labour's Landslide* (Politico's, 1999), pp. 62–7.
197. John Major and Norman Tebbitt speaking on *The Major Years*, part 2.
198. Major, *The Autobiography*, p. 361.
199. Professor Stuart Ball, 'Conservative Defeats and Recoveries', paper presented

to the Twentieth Century British History Seminar, Institute of Historical Research, 1 December 1999.

200. Norman Fowler, 'When Major asked me: "Should I resign?"', *Sunday Telegraph*, 26 September 1999.

201. Lamont, *In Office*, p. 269.

202. Major, *The Autobiography*, pp. 307–8.

203. Lamont, *In Office*, p. 269.

204. Private information.

205. Lamont, *In Office*, pp. 304–5.

206. Private information.

207. Worcester and Mortimer, *Explaining Labour's Landslide*, p. 71.

208. Baker, *Prime Ministers and the Rule Book*, p. 74.

209. Ibid., p. 73.

210. Zai Bennett, one of my students, quoted in Hennessy, *The Hidden Wiring*, p. 187.

211. *Questions of Procedure for Ministers*, May 1992 edition, paragraph 1.

212. Nicholas Timmins and Patricia Wynn Davies, 'Private gain, public interest', *Independent*, 10 December 1994.

213. *First Report of the Committee on Standards in Public Life*, Cm 2850–1 (HMSO, May 1995), paragraph 3.13.

214. Gillian Shephard, 'Ministers and Departments in the 1990s', Queen Mary and Westfield College, 2 December 1999.

215. Seldon, *Major*, pp. 403–4.

216. John Major speaking on *The Major Years*, part 3.

217. Kavanagh and Seldon, *The Powers Behind the Prime Minister*, p. 233.

218. Peter Riddell, 'Oh, for a modest speech', *The Times*, 29 August 1994.

219. Shephard, 'Cabinet and Premiership Under John Major'.

220. Michael Portillo speaking on *The Major Years*, part 3.

221. Worcester and Mortimer, *Explaining Labour's Landslide*, p. 4.

222. Major, *The Autobiography*, p. 304.

223. Ibid., pp. 599–600. The colleagues he bound into this decision were Hurd, Rifkind, Clarke and Heseltine.

224. See Hennessy, *The Hidden Wiring*, pp. 10–13.

225. Lord Cranborne used this phrase while being filmed for *The Major Years*, but it was not used on screen. Private information.

226. Conversation with John Major, 5 July 1993.

227. Private information.

228. Shephard, 'Cabinet and Premiership Under John Major'.

229. Major, *The Autobiography*, p. 343.

230. Ibid.

231. Ibid., p. 343–4.

232. Ibid., p. 336.

233. Peter Oborne, *Alastair Campbell: New Labour and the Rise of the Media Class* (Aurum, 1999), p. 119.

234. Ibid.
235. Ibid., p. 120.
236. Major, *The Autobiography*, pp. 606–7.
237. John Major speaking on *The Major Years*, part 3.
238. Sir Teddy Taylor, ibid.
239. John Major, ibid.
240. Ibid.
241. Major, *The Autobiography*, p. 617.
242. Ibid., pp. 617–18.
243. Shephard, 'Cabinet and Premiership Under John Major'.
244. Kenneth Clarke speaking on *The Major Years*, part 3.
245. Seldon, *Major*, p. 584.
246. Major, *The Autobiography*, pp. 688–9.
247. Hennessy, *The Hidden Wiring*, pp. 17–19.
248. Private information.
249. Private information.
250. Private information.
251. Private information.
252. Private information.
253. Peter Hennessy, 'Cabinet Government', in Peter Catterall (ed.), *Contemporary Britain: An Annual Review* 1994 (ICBH, 1994), pp. 25–6.
254. Major, *The Autobiography*, p. xxi.
255. Mr Hurd (as he still was) speaking on BBC Radio 4 on 24 June 1996.
256. Private information.
257. Sir Charles Powell, interviewed by Michael Cockerell for *How to Be Prime Minister*, 1996.
258. John Major speaking on *The Major Years*, part 3.
259. Ibid.
260. Private information.
261. Private information.

18   Command and Control: Tony Blair, 1997–

1. 'Address by the Rt. Hon. Tony Blair MP, Leader of the Labour Party, to the Newspaper Society, London, March 10th 1997' (Labour Party Media Office, 10 March 1997).
2. Tony Benn, interviewed by Fraser O'Brien and Susan Higgins, students on the MA in Contemporary British History Programme, Department of History, Queen Mary and Westfield College, 3 March 1997.
3. Peter Riddell, 'Tories should focus on what really matters', *The Times*, 1 August 1997.
4. Private information.
5. Tony Blair, interviewed by Michael Cockerell on *Blair's Thousand Days: What*

Makes Tony Tick?, BBC2, 30 January 2000. I am very grateful to Mr Cockerell for supplying me with a transcript of the programme.

6. Private information.

7. Private information.

8. The Prime Minister was speaking to Sir David Frost during *Breakfast with Frost*, BBC1, 16 January 2000. Tom Baldwin, 'Blair takes cautious tone on the euro', *The Times*, 17 January 2000.

9. House of Commons *Official Report*, 28 July 1998. Mr Blair made these remarks during the course of answering a parliamentary question from Mrs Gwynneth Dunwoody about the report from the recently appointed Cabinet Secretary, Sir Richard Wilson, about the future of the Cabinet Office.

10. The distilled essence of the advice given to the Labour shadows by seasoned former Whitehall figures was published as Peter Hennessy, Rosaleen Hughes and Jean Seaton, *Ready, Steady, Go! New Labour and Whitehall* (Fabian Society, April 1997).

11. Private information.

12. 'Address by the Rt. Hon. Tony Blair MP, Leader of the Labour Party, to the Newspaper Society, London, March 10, 1997'.

13. Interview with Kenneth Harris, *Observer*, 25 February 1979.

14. Peter Hennessy, 'Capacity at the centre', *Financial Times*, 26 March 1997.

15. 'How Britain is Governed', BBC Radio 4 *Analysis*, 24 April 1997.

16. Private information.

17. The overflights, in the order in which they were mounted, were as follows: Peter Hennessy, 'The Blair Style of Government: An Historical Perspective and an Interim Audit', the Leonard Schapiro Lecture delivered at the London School of Economics on 2 December 1997 and published in *Government and Opposition*, vol. 33, no. 1 (winter 1998), pp. 3–20; Peter Hennessy, *Re-engineering the State in Flight: A Year in the Life of the British Constitution*, Lloyds TSB Forum Lecture delivered in Glasgow on 28 April 1998 and published by Lloyds TSB; Peter Hennessy, *The Blair Centre: A Question of Command and Control?*, delivered to a seminar organized by the Public Management Foundation in London on 20 October 1998 and published by the PMF in February 1999; Peter Hennessy, 'The British Civil Service: The Condition of Mr Gladstone's Legacy as the Century Turns', Founder's Day Address delivered in honour of W. E. Gladstone at St Deiniol's Library, Hawarden on 8 July 1999 and published as a special supplement to *The Stakeholder*, July 1999 edition; Peter Hennessy, *The Importance of Being Tony: Two Years of the Blair Style*, the Lord Mayor's Lecture 1999 delivered at St Thomas' Hospital on 12 July 1999 and published by the Guy's and St Thomas' Hospital Trust the same day; Peter Hennessy, *The Blair Revolution In Government?*, delivered to the Centre for British Government at Leeds University on 14 February 2000 and published by Leeds University's Institute for Politics and International Studies in April 2000.

18. Private information.

19. David Lipsey, *The Secret Treasury: How Britain's Economy is Really Run* (Viking, 2000), pp. 6–8.

20. Private information.

21. Private information.

22. Private information.

23. Lipsey, *The Secret Treasury*, p. 7.

24. Ibid.

25. Private information.

26. Private information.

27. Lipsey, *The Secret Treasury*, p. 7.

28. Sir Alan Budd, 'The Role of the Treasury: Whose Money Is It Anyway?', lecture delivered at the Royal Society of Arts, 16 February 2000.

29. Philip Stephens, 'The Central Line', *Financial Times*, 9 May 1997.

30. Ibid.

31. Hennessy, 'The Blair Style of Government', p. 7.

32. Ibid., pp. 7–8.

33. Hennessy, *The Blair Centre*, p. 8.

34. Hennessy, *The Importance of Being Tony*, p. 4.

35. Private information.

36. Private information. Quoted in Hennessy, 'The Blair Style of Government', p. 12.

37. Ibid., p. 11.

38. Hennessy, *The Blair Revolution in Government?*, p. 8, and private information.

39. Private information.

40. Hennessy, 'The Blair Style of Government', p. 11.

41. Ibid.

42. Private information. Quoted in Hennessy. *The Importance of Being Tony*, p. 5.

43. See, for example, *Cabinet Committee Business: A Guide for Departments* (Cabinet Office, January 2000), p. 3.

44. Ibid., pp. 5–8.

45. Ibid., pp. 9–10.

46. The formal minutes had yet to be published in report form as this book went to press.

47. PRO, PREM 4/6/9, 'Cabinet Organisation. Report of the Machinery of Government Committee', May 1945. See pp. 163–4 above.

48. Peter Riddell, 'Advising the Prime Minister', speech for their ESRC 'Advising Whitehall' Conference, Cabinet Office, 24 September 1997. I am very grateful to Mr Riddell for providing me with a copy.

49. Sonia Purnell, 'Cabinet big guns gagged by Blair', *Daily Mail*, 2 June 1997.

50. Riddell, 'Tories should focus on what really matters'.

51. *Ministerial Code: A Code of Conduct and Guidance on Procedures for Ministers* (Cabinet Office, July 1997), p. 30.

52. Peter Preston, 'Not without a note from the PM, Minister,' *Guardian*, 18 August 1997.

53. Riddell, 'Tories should focus on what really matters'.

54. Sir Bernard was speaking on the BBC Radio 4 programme *The Matrix of Power*, 10 September 1998.

55. Quoted in Hennessy, *The Importance of Being Tony*, pp. 9–10.

56. Philip Gould, *The Unfinished Revolution: How the Modernisers Saved the Labour Party* (Abacus, 1999), p. xxiii.

57. Ibid.

58. Quoted in Hennessy, *The Blair Centre*, p. 17.

59. Quoted in Hennessy, *The Importance of Being Tony*, p. 9.

60. *Reinforcing Standards: Review of the First Report of the Committee on Standards in Public Life*, Sixth Report of the Committee on Standards in Public Life, vol. 1, Cm 4557–1 (Stationery Office, January 2000).

61. House of Commons Select Committee on Public Administration, Press Notice: Making Government Work, 1999/2000/07, 20 January 2000.

62. Peter Riddell, 'A few words of advice on reining in special advisers', *The Times*, 8 February 2000.

63. Private information.

64. Private information.

65. Quoted in Hennessy, *The Importance of Being Tony*, p. 2.

66. Private information.

67. The minutes of this session had yet to appear in a formal report as this book went to press.

68. Ibid.

69. Ibid.

70. Lipsey, *The Secret Treasury*, p. 27; Philip Webster, 'Brown puts "crony" in top Treasury job', *The Times* 23 October 1999.

71. An organogram of the expanded No. 10 was presented to the Public Administration Committee by Sir Richard Wilson early in 2000, but it had still to be published as this book went to press.

72. Private information.

73. Private information.

74. Quoted in Nicholas Jones, *Sultans of Spin; The Media and The True New Labour Government* (Gollancz, 1999), p. 290.

75. *Guidance On the Work of the Government Information Service* (Cabinet Office, July 1997), p. 1.

76. *Report of the Working Group On the Government Information Service* (Cabinet Office, November 1997), Annex A, p. 32.

77. Ibid., p. 26.

78. Jones, *Sultans of Spin*, p. 102.

79. For the Mountfield recommendations see *Report of the Working Group on the Government Information Service*, pp. 26–31.

80. House of Commons Select Committee on Public Administration, 6th Report, evidence for 23 June 1998.

81. *Reinforcing Standards: Review of the First Report of the Committee on Standards in Public Life*, vol. 1, pp. 68–83.

82. House of Commons Select Committee on Public Administration, *Press Notice: Making Government Work*, 1999/2000/07, 20 January 2000.

83. Sir Robin Mountfield, 'Reflections on Retirement', *Scoops*, April 1999, p. 5.

84. Private information.

85. Private information.

86. Peter Mandelson and Roger Liddle, *The Blair Revolution: Can New Labour Deliver?* (Faber and Faber, 1996), pp. 232–46.

87. Private information.

88. Sir Richard Wilson, 'Modernising Central Government: The Role of the Senior Civil Service', speech to senior civil servants, London, 13 October 1998.

89. Quoted in Hennessy, *The Blair Centre*, p. 13.

90. Ibid.

91. Private information.

92. Private information.

93. Hennessy, *The Blair Centre*, pp. 13–15.

94. House of Commons *Official Report*, 28 July 1998, cols. 132–3.

95. Ibid.

96. Ibid.

97. See Peter Hennessy, 'Government and Risk', *The Stakeholder*, supplement, March/April 2000.

98. *Modernising Government*, Cm 4310 (Stationery Office, 1999).

99. Hennessy, *The Blair Centre*, p. 15.

100. House of Commons *Official Report*, 14 July 1998, cols. 187–8; *Ministerial Committees of the Cabinet* (Cabinet Office, October 1998).

101. Hennessy, *The Blair Centre*, p. 15.

102. Quoted in Hennessy, 'The British Civil Service: The Condition of Mr Gladstone's Legacy as the Century Turns', p. 5.

103. Ibid.

104. Ibid.

105. Ibid.

106. *Professional Policy-Making for the Twenty-First Century. A Report by the Strategic Policy Making Team* (Cabinet Office, September 1999).

107. House of Commons *Official Report*, 28 July 1998, col. 134.

108. Ibid.

109. Hennessy, *The Blair Centre*, p. 16.

110. Ibid., p. 10.

111. Hennessy, *The Importance of Being Tony*, p. 8.

112. Ibid.

113. Ibid.

114. Ibid.

115. Ibid.

116. Hennessy, *The Blair Revolution in Government?*, p. 17.

117. Ibid.

118. Private information.

119. Hennessy, *The Blair Revolution in Government?*, p. 17.

120. Private information.

121. Private information.

122. Private information.

123. Private information.

124. The Cabinet committee list has no specific nuclear weapons entry; *Ministerial Committees of the Cabinet* (Cabinet Office, October 1998).

125. Private information.

126. *The Strategic Defence Review*, Cm 3999 (Stationery Office, 1998), p. 17.

127. Ibid., p. 18.

128. Ibid., p. 19. Current stocks were listed as 7.6 tonnes of plutonium, 21.9 tonnes of highly enriched uranium and 15,000 tonnes of 'other forms of uranium'.

129. Ibid.

130. Ibid.

131. Private information. See also Blair's praise of the 'unsung work' of British Intelligence officers; Richard Norton-Taylor, ' "Your spies are the best", says Russia', *Guardian*, 27 April 2000.

132. *Ministerial Committees of the Cabinet* (October 1998); *Cabinet Committee Business* (January 2000), pp. 7–8.

133. Private information.

134. Private information.

135. *Ministerial Committees of the Cabinet* (October 1998); *Cabinet Committee Business* (January 2000), pp. 7–8.

136. Private information.

137. Private information.

138. Hennessy, *The Importance of Being Tony*, p. 13.

139. Private information.

140. See Matt Lyus and Peter Hennessy, *Tony Blair, Past Prime Ministers, Parliament and the Use of Military Force*, Strathclyde Papers on Government and Politics, no. 113 (Department of Government, University of Strathclyde 1999); and House of Commons *Official Report*, vol. 306, no. 121, Session 16th February–20th February 1998 (Stationery Office, 1998), p. 927.

141. Lyus and Hennessy, *Tony Blair, Past Prime Ministers, Parliament and the Use of Military Force*, pp. 16–17.

142. Private information.

143. Private information.

144. Private information.

145. Private information.

146. Hennessy, *The Importance of Being Tony*, p. 13.

147. Ibid.

148. Ibid.

149. Ibid.

150. Peter Riddell, 'A hawk's eye view from No. 10', *The Times*, 31 May 1999.

151. Private information.

152. Private information.

153. Private information.

154. Private information.

155. Private information.

156. Private information.

157. Private information.

158. Private information.

159. Private information.

160. Private information.

161. Hennessy, *The Importance of Being Tony*, p. 15.

162. Private information.

163. Hennessy, *The Importance of Being Tony*, p. 16.

164. Ibid.

165. Private information.

166. John Hibbs, ' "Napoleon" Blair fends off attacks on his ruling style', *Daily Telegraph*, 24 June 1999.

167. Paul McCann, 'Political broadcast by the Best Friends Party', *Independent*, 12 March 1999.

168. John F. Harris, 'Clinton at war, hears history calling', *International Herald Tribune*, 21 April 1999.

169. Roy Jenkins, *Gladstone* (Macmillan, 1995), p. 177.

170. Mr Mandelson was speaking on 'New Labour plc', BBC Radio 4 *Analysis*, 1 March 1999.

171. Janet Jones, *Labour of Love: The Partly-Political Diary of a Cabinet Minister's Wife* (Politico's, 1999), p. 246, entry for 16 June 1998.

172. Private information.

173. 'Warning for Blair', *The Times*, 3 January 2000.

174. Hennessy, *Re-engineering the State in Flight*, p. 4.

175. A leak from the unpublished diary of the former leader of the Liberal Democrats, Paddy Ashdown, in November 1999 confirmed that in the autumn of 1997 Mr Blair had floated the idea of offering Cabinet seats to two Liberal Democrats, Alan Beith and Menzies Campbell. Joe Murphy, 'Revealed: Blair's secret plan to form coalition', *Sunday Telegraph*, 28 November 1999.

176. This eventually appeared as *Standards in Public Life, The Funding of Political Parties in the United Kingdom*, Fifth Report of the Committee on Standards in Public Life, vol. 1, Cm 4057–1 (Stationery Office, October 1998).

177. A. J. P. Taylor, *English History, 1914–1945* (Oxford University Press, 1965), p. 513.

178. 'Man In the Middle', *Public Service Magazine*, April 1998.

179. *Ministerial Committees of the Cabinet* (Cabinet Office, June 1997).

180. Private information.

181. Private information.

182. Private information.

183. Quoted in Hennessy, *Re-engineering the State in Flight*, p. 10.

184. Ibid.

185. Ibid.

186. *Concordats* (Cabinet Office, 1998).

187. Ibid.

188. *Devolution: Memorandum of Understanding and Supplementary Agreements between the United Kingdom Government, Scottish Ministers and the Cabinets of the National Assembly for Wales*, Cm 4444 (Stationery Office, 1999), p. 9.

189. Andrew Grice, 'Blair to delay electoral reform', *Independent*, 11 September 1998.

190. Hennessy, *The Blair Revolution in Government?*, p. 7.

191. Ibid.

192. This can best be traced by following the trail that led from the original White Paper of December 1997, *Your Right To Know: Freedom of Information*, Cm 3818, through the draft bill Jack Straw submitted for consideration by a Commons and a Lords select committee in the spring and summer of 1999, *Freedom of Information: Consultation Draft Legislation* (Home Office, May 1999), Cm 4355; the highly critical reports which emanated from those select committees, House of Commons Select Committee on Public Administration, Session 1998–99, Third Report, *Freedom of Information Draft Bill*, vol. 1 (Stationery Office, July 1999) and House of Lords, Session 1998–99, *Report From the Select Committee Appointed to Consider the Draft Freedom of Information Bill*, HL Paper 97 (Stationery Office, July 1999); to the Home Office's Bill, *Freedom of Information*, published in November 1999 (Stationery Office, November 1999).

193. Select Committee on Public Administration, *Freedom of Information Draft Bill*, vol. 1, p. xxxv.

194. Private information.

195. Private information.

196. Conversation with Sir John Browne, 15 November 1999.

197. Peter Riddell, 'Blair wrong to ignore constitution', *The Times*, 3 March 2000.

198. Hennessy, *The Importance of Being Tony*, p. 3.

199. Gordon Brown, 'Modernising the British Economy – The New Mission For The Treasury', speech to mark the thirtieth Anniversary of the IFS, HM Treasury Press Release, 86/99, 27 May 1999.

200. *Modern Public Services for Britain: Investing in Reform*, Cm 4011 (HM Treasury, July 1998).

201. Hennessy, *The Blair Centre*, p. 12.

202. Private information. For EA's brief see *Cabinet Committee Business*, January 2000, pp. 5–6.

203. Lipsey, *The Secret Treasury*, p. 165.

204. See *Review of the Social Exclusion Unit* (Cabinet Office, December 1999) and Blair's statement on its continuation at least until 2003, ibid., pp. 17–18.

205. Delivered at the Old Vic Theatre in London, 27 February 2000. I am grateful to Dr Brian Brivati for providing me with a text.

206. Cm 4310.

207. Hennessy, 'The British Civil Service: The Condition of Mr Gladstone's Legacy as the Century Turns', pp. 2–3.

208. *Civil Service Reform: Report to the Prime Minister from Sir Richard Wilson, Head of the Home Civil Service* (Cabinet Office, December 1999).

209. *Wiring It Up: Whitehall's Management of Cross-Cutting Policies and Services* (Performance and Innovation Unit, Cabinet Office, January 2000).

210. Its terms of reference were: 'To identify reforms to existing accountability arrangements and incentive structures which will encourage better cross-departmental policy-making and implementation without weakening financial discipline or formal accountability to Parliament'. Quoted ibid., p. 10.

211. *Reinforcing Standards: Review of the First Report of the Committee on Standards in Public Life*, vols. 1 and 2, Cm 4557 (Stationery Office, January 2000).

212. Mr Blair interviewed by Michael Cockerell on *Blair's Thousand Days: What Makes Tony Tick?*; Peter Riddell, 'No bugs can spoil Blair's millennium', *The Times*, 26 January 2000.

213. Anthony Bevins, 'Why Tony Blair is the greatest', *New Statesman*, 17 January 2000.

214. Michael White, 'Blair turns on his critics', *Guardian*, 22 January 2000; Colin Brown, '"Forces of reaction" will not defeat us, says Blair', *Independent*, 22 January 2000.

215. Hennessy, *The Blair Revolution in Government?*, p. 7.

216. *The Civil Service*, vol. 1, *Report of the Committee 1966–68* (HMSO, 1968).

217. *The Re-organisation of Central Government*, Cmnd 4506 (HMSO, 1970).

218. Peter Hennessy, *Whitehall* (Secker and Warburg, 1989), pp. 589–622.

219. *The Citizen's Charter: Raising the Standard*, Cm 1599 (HMSO, 1991).

220. Wilson, 'Modernising Central Government'.

221. Quoted in Hennessy, *The Blair Revolution in Government?*, p. 8.

222. Ibid.

223. *Reinforcing Standards*, vol. 2, *Evidence*.

224. *Reinforcing Standards*, vol. 1, p. 56.

225. *Civil Service Reform*, pp. 6, 14.

226. Quoted in Hennessy, *The Blair Revolution in Government?*, p. 9.

227. Sir Richard Wilson speaking on *Blair's Thousand Days*.

228. Quoted in Hennessy, *The Blair Revolution in Government?*, p. 9.

229. Ibid.

230. For the full list of the Board see *Civil Service Reform*, p. 27.

231. Hennessy, *The Importance of Being Tony*, p. 2.

232. Quoted in Hennessy, *The Blair Revolution in Government?*, p. 2.

233. *Professional Policy Making for the Twenty First Century* (Modernising Government Secretariat, Cabinet Office, September 1999).

234. *Wiring It Up*, pp. 47–51; see also the new range of cross-departmental studies announced by the Treasury at the end of 1999: 'Public Services Reform . . . More Cross Departmental Studies in 2000 Spending Review', Treasury Press Release 199/99, 24 November 1999.

235. Perhaps the most eye-catching and stimulating of the SEU's productions to date has been *Sharing the Nation's Prosperity* (Social Exclusion Unit, Cabinet Office, December 1999). See Peter Riddell, 'Even exclusion units can be done on the outside', *The Times*, 7 December 1999.

236. *Reinforcing Standards*, vol. 1, pp. 123–7.

237. Quoted in Hennessy, *The Blair Revolution in Government?*, p. 10.

238. Ibid.

239. Patrick Wintour, 'Tony – spend the money', *Observer*, 23 November 1997; Michael Prescott, 'Thatcher calls Blair "bossy" ', *Sunday Times*, 31 January 1999; ' "I'm not bossy, just firm", says Blair', *Evening Standard*, 1 February 1999; Roland Watson, ' "Blair Unedited" comes unstuck', *The Times*, 2 February 1999; Jon Hibbs, ' "Napoleon" Blair fends off attacks on his ruling style', *Daily Telegraph*, 24 June 1999.

240. For two important but different studies of Blair, Blair's people and the media see Nicholas Jones, *Sultans of Spin* and Peter Oborne, *Alastair Campbell: New Labour and the Rise of the Media Class* (Aurum, 1999). For Campbell's view that journalists are as much 'spinners' of stories as spinned against, see Alastair Campbell, 'A man more spinned against than spinning', *The Times*, 31 January 2000.

241. Mr Blair speaking on *Blair's Thousand Days*.

242. Ibid.

243. Ibid.

244. Nigel Lawson, *The View From No. 11: Memoirs of a Tory Radical* (Bantam, 1992). For the most revealing passage in this 'Consent of the Victims' chapter, see p. 129. For 'creeping bilateralism' see Lord Lawson and Lord Armstrong of Ilminster, 'Cabinet Government in the Thatcher Years', *Contemporary Record*, vol. 8, no. 3 (winter 1994), pp. 473–83.

245. Private information.

246. Private information.

247. Private information.

248. See above p. 465.

249. Private information.

250. Robert Harris, 'The Testing of Tony Blair', *talk*, May 2000, p. 74.

251. Ibid., p. 76.

252. Ibid., p. 77.

253. Peter Riddell, 'Will history remember him as Tony the Timid?', *The Times*, 17 April 2000.

254. Ibid.

255. Roy Jenkins, 'It is unwise to tip the waiter until the meal is over. Blair has shown himself a competent Prime Minister. Whether he will be a great one remains to be seen. But I am not unhopeful', *Evening Standard*, 27 April 2000.

256. Matthew Taylor, 'Blairite Blues', *Prospect*, May 2000, p. 41.

257. For a vivid account of the chaotic Cabinet Meeting of 19 June 1997, which Blair left Prescott to chair as ministers shambled across the issue leaving the Cabinet Secretariat aghast, see Janet Jones, *Labour of Love*, pp. 86–7.

258. Private information.

259. Jack Straw, Briefing for the 'Cabinet and Premiership' course, Department of History, Queen Mary and Westfield College, University of London at the House of Commons, 19 April 2000.

260. Harris, 'The Testing of Tony Blair', p. 77.

261. John Rentoul, *Tony Blair: Prime Minister* (Little Brown, 2001), pp. 570–71.

262. 'Fuel Crisis' COBR [Cabinet Office Briefing Room] Sitrep No. 1: 0600, 12 September 2000.

263. Private information.

264. Private information.

265. Between 14 and 23 September 2000, the four main opinion polls gave the Conservatives a lead ranging from two to eight points in a year in which, till then, Labour had rested atop an average lead of fifteen points. Rentoul, *Tony Blair*, p. 572 & fn 2 on p. 578.

266. Quoted in Peter Hennessy, 'When Tony wants and Gordon requires', 'The NS Essay', *New Statesman*, 18 December 2000, pp. 25–7. This was an abridged version of my late-2000 'overflight' – 'The First Blair Premiership' – delivered to the Public Management Foundation on 12 December 2000.

267. Rentoul, *Tony Blair*, p. 570.

268. Private information.

269. Magnus Linklater, 'Wrong, wrong, wrong, wrong', *Times* 2, 24 May 2001; Peter Riddell, 'Blair finally takes charge of farming emergency', *The Times*, 26 March 2001; Peter Riddell, 'The last days of the court of King Tony', *The Times*, 30 April 2001.

270. Quoted in Hennessy, 'When Tony wants and Gordon requires.'

271. Private information.

272. Private information.

273. Private information.

274. Private information.

275. Private information.

276. Private information.

277. Private information.

278. Private information.

279. Anne Applebaum, 'I am still normal', *The Sunday Telegraph*, 18 March 2001.

280. Private information.

281. Andrew Rawnsley, *Servants of the People: The Inside Story of New Labour* (Hamish Hamilton, 2001).

282. Private information.

283. Peter Riddell, 'Blair As Prime Minister' in Anthony Seldon (ed.), *The Blair Effect: The Blair Government 1997–2001*, (Little, Brown, 2001), p. 36.

284. Private information.

285. Quoted in Hennessy, 'When Tony wants and Gordon requires.'

286. Rentoul, *Tony Blair*, pp. 557–8.

287. Private information.

288. Quoted in Hennessy, 'When Tony wants and Gordon requires.'

289. Private information.

290. Quoted in Hennessy, 'When Tony wants and Gordon requires.'

291. Private information.

292. Lord Haskins was speaking on *The Top Job 2: The King of the Beasts*, BBC Radio 4, 16 October 2000.

293. *Public Services Productivity: Meeting the challenge* (HM Treasury, 2000), p. 10.

294. Ibid.

295. Lord Haskins interviewed for *The Top Job*, 4 September 2000.

296. *Public Services Productivity: Meeting the challenge*, p. 10.

297. Private information.

298. Private information.

299. Sixth Report of the Committee on Standards in Public Life, *Reinforcing Standards: Review of the First Report of the Committee in Public Life*, Cm 4557–1, (Stationery Office, 2000), chapter 6, pp. 68–83.

300. House of Commons, Session 2000–2001, Public Administration Committee, Fourth Report, *Special Advisers: Boon or Bane?* HC 293 (Stationery Office, 2001), p.xxv.

301. House of Commons, *Official Report*, 13 July 2000. Pt 16 on the Stationery Office's Parliamentary website.

302. House of Commons, Session 2000–2001, Select Committee on Public Administration, Third Report, *The Ministerial Code: Improving the Rule Book*, HC 235 (Stationery Office, 2001), p. xvi.

303. Ibid, p. xvii.

304. Ibid. Appendices, pp. 2–3.

305. Ibid, p. 2. Wright to Blair, 10 May 2000.

306. Ibid, p. 3. Blair to Wright, 26 May 2000.

307. Private information.

308. Peter Hennessy, *Whitehall* (Secker and Warburg, 1989), pp. 305–6, 335, 667.

309. *The Ministerial Code: Improving the Rule Book*, Appendices, p. 3. Wright to Blair, 8 June 2000.

310. Ibid. Blair to Wright, 17 June 2000.

311. House of Commons, Sessions 2000–2001, Liaison Committee, First Report, *Shifting the Balance: Unfinished Business*, Vol. 1, HC 321–1 (Stationery Office, 2001), p. xliii, Sheldon to Blair, 14 December 2000.

312. Ibid, p. xliv, Blair to Sheldon, 29 January 2001.

313. Applebaum, 'I am still normal.'

314. House of Commons, Session 2000–2001, Public Administration Select Committee, Seventh Report, *Making Government Work: The Emerging Issues*, HC 94 (Stationery Office, 2001), p. xviii.

315. Colin Brown and Jo Dillon, 'Blair plots revenge on Civil Service,' *The Independent on Sunday*, 29 April 2001.

316. Private information.

317. Peter Riddell, 'Blair looks to business for Whitehall fix', *The Times*, 1 June 2001.

318. I am very grateful to Peter Riddell for sending me a copy of the transcript.

319. Private information.

320. Private information.

321. Private information.

322. Private information.

323. Private information.

324. Jill Sherman, 'Brown protects powerbase from No. 10', *The Times*, 15 June 2001.

325. Ibid.

326. 'Improving Public Services', 10 Downing Street Press Notice, 22 June 2001.

327. Private information.

328. Private information.

329. Private information.

330. Sherman, 'Brown protects power base from No. 10.'

331. Roy Jenkins, 'Gladstone and Books', in Peter Francis (ed.), *The Grand Old Man: Sermons and Speeches in Honour of W. E. Gladstone* (Monad Press, 2000), p. 25.

332. Private information.

333. Roy Jenkins, 'It is unwise to tip the waiter until the meal is over . . .' *Evening Standard*, 27 April 2000.

334. Ibid.

335. Private source and it is confirmed in Paddy Ashdown, *The Ashdown Diaries, Volume One, 1988–1997* (Penguin, 2000), p. 440. Diary entry for 20 June 1996.

336. Conversation with Lord Young of Dartington, 24 March 1994.

337. Lord McNally has used this phrase in my hearing on several occasions.

338. Michael Cockerell, 'An Inside View on Blair's Number 10', in Seldon (ed.), *The Blair Effect*, p. 573.

339. 'Tony Blair's first keynote speech of the campaign', Labour Party, 13 May 2001.

340. Michael Young, *The Rise of the Meritocracy, 1870–2033* (first published in 1958), (Penguin edn, 1961).

341. See Anthony Wright, *R. H. Tawney* (Manchester University Press, 1987), Chapter 5, 'Choosing Equality', pp. 105–29.

342. Ibid, pp. 19–22. At the moment that this edition of this book went to press, Lord Young of Dartington reached an identical conclusion: Michael Young 'Down with meritocracy', *Guardian*, 29 June 2001.

19 The Premier League: The Inevitability of Disappointment

1. J. Enoch Powell, *Joseph Chamberlain* (Thames and Hudson, 1977), p. 151.

2. David Marquand, *Ramsay MacDonald* (Cape, 1977), p. 791.

3. Edward Thomas, 'Parting', in *Edward Thomas: Collected Poems* (Faber and Faber, 1991), p. 125.

4. Conversation with Lord Jenkins of Hillhead, 5 May 1999.

5. Lord Hailsham was speaking *In the Psychiatrist's Chair*, BBC Radio 4, 16 August 1989.

6. Simon Heffer, *Like The Roman: The Life of Enoch Powell* (Weidenfeld and Nicolson, 1998), chapter 3, pp. 56–98; Lord Hailsham, *A Sparrow's Flight* (Collins, 1990), pp. 65–8, 83–8.

7. Margaret Thatcher, *The Downing Street Years* (HarperCollins, 1993), p. 831.

8. John Major, *The Autobiography* (HarperCollins, 1999), p. xxi.

9. Peter Hennessy, *Muddling Through: Power, Politics and the Quality of Government in Postwar Britain* (Gollancz, 1996), p. 283.

10. Ibid., p. 282.

11. Alistair Horne, *Macmillan, 1957–1986* (Macmillan, 1989), p. 153.

12. 'On the Trail of the First Eleven: Writing About Britain's Postwar Prime Ministers', Historical Association Dining Club, London, 22 April 1998.

13. The most elaborate version of this I have encountered is Elizabeth J. Ballard and Peter Suedfeld, 'Performance Ratings of Canadian Prime Ministers: Individual and Situational Factors', *Political Psychology*, vol. 9, no. 2 (1988), pp. 291–302.

14. Conversation with Lord Jenkins of Hillhead, 5 May 1999.

15. I sensed this more than once in my own conversations with them.

16. Thatcher, *The Downing Street Years*, p. 860.

17. Winston S. Churchill, *Great Contemporaries* (Readers Union edition, 1939), p. 72.

18. Nigel Lawson, 'The New Britain: The Tide of Ideas from Attlee to Thatcher', Centre for Policy Studies, February 1988.

19. Paul Addison, *The Road to 1945: British Politics and the Second World War* (Pimlico, 1994), p. 14.

20. Horne, *Macmillan, 1957–1986*, p. 155.

20 Towards a New Specification: Premiership for the Twenty-First Century

1. John Lloyd, 'Interview: Roy Jenkins', *New Statesman*, 30 May 1997.
2. Tom Jones' Papers, National Library of Wales, Aberystwyth, class A, vol. 1, document 45, Bridges to Jones, 7 January 1948. I am grateful to Dr Peter Catterall for bringing this letter to my attention.
3. 'The lighter touch', *The Times*, 30 September 1998.
4. Letter from Andrew Adonis to Peter Hennessy, 5 February 1999.
5. Michael Foley, *The Rise of the British Presidency* (Manchester University Press, 1993), pp. 120–47.
6. He did so at my request in April 1997.
7. Sir Patrick Nairne to Peter Hennessy, 15 April 1997.
8. Baroness Williams of Crosby speaking at a dinner in Gresham College after delivering her Gresham Special Lecture on 'Snakes and Ladders: A Reflection on a Post-War Political Life' at the Mansion House on 17 November 1999.
9. John Morley, *The Life of William Ewart Gladstone*, vol. 1 (Macmillan, 1903), p. 297.
10. Adonis to Hennessy, 5 February 1999.
11. Ibid.
12. Nairne to Hennessy, 15 April 1997.
13. Ibid.
14. Ibid.
15. Harold Wilson, *The Governance of Britain* (Weidenfeld and Nicolson/ Michael Joseph, 1976), p. x.
16. Conversation with Lord Hurd, 20 April 1999.
17. Ibid.
18. PRO, PREM 13/854, 'July 1966 Economic Measures; "The Little Budget". UK Economic Situation: Outlook to End of 1966; Part 13', Trend to Wilson, 19 July 1966.
19. PRO, CAB 164/395, 'Government Organisation to Deal with Disasters and Emergencies Involving the UK, 1967–1968', Trend to Rogers, 25 April 1967; see also Trend to Wilson, 2 December 1968.
20. PRO, PREM 13/2688, 'Reorganisation of Central Machinery for Politico-military Planning and Intelligence, 1967–1968', Trend to Wilson, 13 March 1967.
21. Ibid., Prime Minister's Meeting of 31 July 1967, 'Note for the Record', 2 August 1967; see also Peter Hennessy, 'The Itch After the Amputation. The Purposes of British Intelligence as the Century Turns: An Historical Perspective and a Forward Look', in K. G. Robertson (ed.), *War, Resistance and Intelligence: Essays in Honour of M. R. D. Foot* (Pen and Sword, 1999), p. 238.
22. Robert Taylor, *Lord Salisbury* (Allen Lane, 1975), p. 191.

Index